the COMPUTER CONTINUUM

Kurt F. Lauckner & Mildred D. Lintner

The Computer Continuum

Library of Congress Catalog Number: 98-066786

ISBN: 1-58076-059-7

Publisher
Robert Linsky

Executive Editor
Kyle Lewis

Director of Product Marketing
Susan Kindel

Managing Editor
Caroline Roop

Senior Developmental Editor
Lena Buonanno

Senior Editor
Dayna Isley

Copy Editors
Keith Cline
Kristine Simmons

Team Coordinator
Angela Denny

Production Team
Chris Livengood
Becky Stutzman

Book Designer
Louisa Klucznik

Cover Designer
Ruth Lewis

Illustrator
Julia Geche

Indexer
Becky Hornyak

Trademark Acknowledgments

IBM is a registered trademark of International Business Machines Corporation. Apple, Macintosh, and Mac are registered trademarks of Apple Computer Incorporated. Microsoft Access, MS-DOS, Windows, Windows 95, Windows 98, Windows Explorer, Windows NT, Microsoft Internet Explorer, Microsoft Network, Microsoft Word, Excel, and Microsoft are registered trademarks of Microsoft Corporation. Lotus, 1-2-3, and Notes are registered trademarks of Lotus Development Corporation. America Online is a registered service mark of America Online, Incorporated. Intel is a registered trademark and Pentium is a trademark of Intel Corporation.

All terms mentioned in this book that are known to be trademarks or service marks have been appropriately capitalized. Que Education and Training cannot attest to the accuracy of this information.

Contents at a Glance

Table of Contents

Contents

Contents

Contents

Preface

Philosophy

Higher education has traditionally categorized knowledge into areas such as history, chemistry, physics, and literature. In most colleges and universities, almost all the common major categories have an introduction to their field that is designed for the beginner. The sciences such as chemistry, physics, and biology, for example, have courses for the nonmajor. These courses are designed to teach the concepts of the individual fields, and they do not dwell on the tools used to study the field. In chemistry, for instance, courses in glass blowing and apparatus building are not the main introductory core. Instead, the focus is on understanding the concepts, which usually include chemical reactions or the structure of molecules. It is also duly noted by the authors of *The Computer Continuum* that the fields of information systems and computer science are unique. But, the concepts approach is still a valid, if not preferred, means of teaching in these two areas.

During the past decade, the fields of information systems and computer science have focused on the tools. In fact, many colleges and universities continue to offer complete courses in learning the technical aspects of word processing, spreadsheets, and databases. This seems like a misplaced effort in the light of what the future holds for the graduate. Continuous speech-to-text input systems will probably make word processors obsolete in a few years, for example. Among those who use spreadsheets to solve real problems, it is well-known that an understanding of modeling and simulation are more valuable than knowing how to make a spreadsheet look pretty.

The philosophy of this textbook is to concentrate on the concepts in the field of information systems and computer science such as data representation, operating systems, programming languages, and algorithms. However, the tools of word processing, spreadsheets, databases, and communications are not ignored. Five laboratory manual series (outlined in a grid in the following pages) can be packaged with *The Computer Continuum* to give the student working knowledge of those tools. But, ultimately, to prepare the graduate for the future, it is necessary to build a lasting foundation of concepts that are fundamental.

Audience

The Computer Continuum is written primarily for use in undergraduate computer science courses in colleges and universities. It appeals equally to the liberal arts major and the computer science major. Over 75 percent of the material in the book has been tested in classroom settings with over 10,000 college students. This has included at least 300 honors students in classes of 20 students maximum to large lecture sections of 300 students. In addition, the material has been tested with several hundred students in a lecture with hands-on, required computer labs.

Because of this exhaustive testing, we think that the material as presented is relevant and most of the concepts will be current even 10 years from now. This lasting power is due to the concentration on fundamental concepts. In fact, simulation and the associated computer concepts introduced in Chapter 12, "Simulation: Modeling the Physical World," are the foundation of a new type of science, which is an addition to the theoretical and experimental approaches.

Unique in the market are Chapter 2, "Metamorphosis of Information," Chapter 3, "From Stonehenge to the Supercomputer," Chapter 10, "Visual Communication: Gateway to the Brain," Chapter 11, "Audio Communication Comes of Age," and Chapter 12, "Simulation: Modeling the Physical World."

Key Features for the Student

Many aspects of *The Computer Continuum* will help the student. First, this book provides a balanced approach to pedagogy, with three special features in each chapter:

1. Voices from the Past boxes feature historical figures such as John von Neumann, Grace Hopper, and Herbert Simon.

2. Bits & Bytes boxes present interesting computer issues such as the Year 2000 problem and Internet2.

3. Margin term definitions highlight key concepts.

Each chapter opens with a timeline and set of learning objectives. The timeline presents the evolution of computer science as related to the content of the chapter. The learning objectives preview the content of the chapter.

The comprehensive end-of-chapter testing material is designed to accommodate various learning and teaching styles and encourages individual review and reflection as well as group discussions and problem solving. This material includes the following:

1. 20 Matching, 20 True/False, and 10 Multiple Choice questions test basic knowledge. The answers to the odd review questions are listed at the back of the book so that students can check their own work.

2. 20 Exercises provide in-depth problem-solving opportunities.

3. 5–8 Discussion Questions ask students to think critically about content presented in the chapter.

4. 1 or 2 Group Exercises promote working on projects in groups, an important aspect of today's workplace.

5. 10–15 Web Connections encourage students to surf the Web for research topics related to the material discussed in the chapter.

A summary and bibliography are also provided as part of the end-of-chapter material.

Organization

The organization of *The Computer Continuum* follows a very natural approach to learning about the field of information systems and computer science. After an introductory chapter, the next five chapters lay down a foundation of theory; the remaining chapters cover some very general areas of computer usage. The words *general area* are meant to convey the fact that these areas are each used in almost every field of endeavor. The theory part forms a solid framework on which the general areas of computer usage and the tools can be supported. A summary of this approach is as follows:

Part I, "Preliminaries: Where We're Going," consists of Chapter 1, "Computers: A First Look."

Part II, "Building Blocks: How Computers Work," consists of Chapters 2 through 6 and covers the following:

Representation of the five kinds of information and its storage

Programming, algorithms, and how computers work

Controlling computers through the operating system

Communication with computers through computer languages

Network communication between computers and people

Part III, "Foundations: Applying the Concepts," consists of Chapters 7 through 12 and covers the following:

Understanding the Internet and its capabilities

The World Wide Web usage and ramifications

Databases: gathering, retrieving, and analyzing information

Understanding how computers are used in visual communication

Understanding how computers are used in audio communication

Using computers in simulation and modeling

Part IV, "Empowerment: Extending Our Limits," consists of Chapters 13 through 15 and covers the following:

The pursuit of the intelligent computer to extend human abilities

Using the computer to increase personal knowledge

Dealing with the ethics and problems computers create

The rationale for this organization is to first provide an understanding of the basic concepts involved with computers and then to use this understanding to investigate the application of computers in many general areas. To understand the process of image manipulation, for example, understanding the concepts of representing images in a computer is necessary. The approach is designed to enable the student to first conceptualize and then to innovate. Without understanding the underlying concepts, creative work is almost impossible. We truly want our students to innovate!

The Teaching Package

In addition to authoring *The Computer Continuum*, we have also authored its supplements to ensure continuity in approach, terminology, and level of rigor.

Print Supplements

The authors developed a comprehensive print supplement package that is coordinated with the main text and is designed for your teaching convenience.

Annotated Edition

For the instructor is an annotated copy of *The Computer Continuum*, which includes the following:

- Margin notes for enrichment
- Class activities
- Class discussion points
- Selected Web sites
- Additional, detailed discussion questions

Instructor's Resource Manual

The Instructor's Resource Manual (IRM) provides chapter outlines with learning objectives and lesson outlines. The manual also gives the answers to all the end-of-lesson material in the Student Edition. For the novice teacher, as well as seasoned instructors looking for new ways to teach this course, the Instructor's Manual includes Teaching Tips, Projects and Activities, and Lecture Notes beyond those presented in the *Annotated Instructor's Edition*. Also included are lab projects for each of the chapters. These consist of a description of the project with sufficient detail that enables the student to work on his or her own. The instructor can reproduce copies in coursepacks or arrange other forms of distribution. Most of the lab projects include a short mini-manual discussing the software used. There are mini-manuals for Excel, Word, SimCity, Netscape, Explorer, and many others.

QueTest by inQsit Test Bank

A test databank of *more than* 3,000 questions supported by the finest Web-based testing system is available! QueTest by inQsit (developed by Ball State University) utilizes the World Wide Web and Web technologies to present questions, record answers, and return customized graded results. It also provides HTML compatibility, a security system with passwords, and a respondent interface in any WWW browser. QueTest uses Smart Wizards to help you create your tests, and has eight different question types, including short essay, that can be selected at will or at random. QueTest supports proctored tests, transference of existing test questions, and test item analysis!

Technology Supplements

Our progressive technology package is designed to enhance the book and facilitate active learning. A user-friendly interactive CD encourages students to explore technology concepts at their own pace. Testing and presentation software give faculty the tools they need to augment their class lectures.

The Computer Continuum Interactive Edition

Que Education & Training created *The Computer Continuum Interactive Edition* to provide students with a unique, discovery-based learning tool. The *Interactive Edition* includes interactive multimedia explorations of key textbook topics, seamless integration of the World Wide Web, personalized study guides, and electronic review exercises with emailable results. Also, several simulations and interactive programs associated with chapter material can be accessed from the CD-ROM.

QuePresents

For the instructor's presentations, there is a CD-ROM titled *The Computer Continuum QuePresents*. It is packed with a library of PowerPoint 97 presentations designed to enhance your classroom presentations. These presentations include a variety of materials used by the author team in their classrooms. QuePresents can be used as is or customized to meet the needs of your students.

Web Page—www.lauckner-lintner.com

www.lauckner-lintner.com is a Web community monitored weekly by both the authors and the team that created *The Computer Continuum*. The Web site includes an interactive chat room facility and message board that allows threaded discussions. Additional resources on the Web site include a listserve, TEQNNews, a searchable technology news service, links to additional Web sites for students and faculty, and other materials.

Application Manuals

Que Education & Training offers a variety of computer lab applications manuals that can be used in conjunction with *The Computer Continuum* to provide your students with the tools they need to succeed in your class and beyond.

Series	Essentials	Complete	Learn	MOUS Essentials	SmartStarts
Applications	Windows 3.1/95/98	Windows 95/98	Windows 95/98	Windows 95/98	DOS/Windows 3.1/95/98
Level B = Beginning I = Intermediate A = Advanced	B, I, A for all Win95 and higher	B–A	B	Proficient and Expert	B–I
Course Length	8–12 contact hours	Full semester	6–8 contact hours	8–12 contact hours	12–24 contact hours
Features	■ 4 color (most first levels) ■ Project Orientation Teaches Problem solving. ■ Step-by-step approach and oversized screenshots. ■ End-of-chapter exercises combine skill assessment and application. ■ All first-level Office 97 books include Screen ID and Challenge exercises.	■ 4 color ■ Business problem orientation ■ Full integration of the World Wide Web ■ Cross-curricular projects	■ 4 color screen shots show results of steps taken. ■ Learn On-Demand software.	■ 4 color ■ Microsoft approved for MOUS Program ■ Appendix on Certification process	■ 2 color ■ Skills focus emphasizes practical knowledge. ■ Material is organized around objectives. ■ End-of-chapter exercises integrate material from earlier exercises.
Learning Tools	■ Why Would I Do This? ■ JargonWatch ■ If You Have Problems ■ Inside Stuff ■ Running marginal glossary ■ Lesson Objectives	■ In Depth, Caution, Shortcuts ■ Finished project illustrates each Lesson opener.	■ Completed screen shots at chapter opener. ■ In Depth, Caution, and Shortcuts	■ Why Would I Do This? ■ If You Have Problems ■ Inside Stuff ■ Required Activities and MS Test Notes give students guidelines and tips for preparing for the certification exams.	■ Objectives and end-of-chapter summaries ■ Running marginal glossary Notes. Running cases.
Resources	■ Instructor's Manual with Data Disks ■ Annotated Instructor's Edition (Office 97 apps only) ■ QueTest (Office 97 apps only) ■ Virtual Tutor CD-ROM	■ Annotated Instructor's Edition ■ QueTest	■ Annotated Instructor's Edition ■ QueTest ■ Learn On-Demand	■ Annotated Instructor's Edition	■ Instructor's Manual with Data Disk

Que E&T also offers custom publishing that is as easy as 1,2,3 through our Quest Custom Publishing Program. Please contact your local Macmillan Computer Publishing representative for more details. To obtain the name of your representative, call 800-545-5914. You can also contact us on the Web at **http://www.queet.com**.

About the Cover

Many years ago, one of the authors was privileged to hear the British astronomer Sir Fred Hoyle give a talk at a physics colloquium. It was indeed a beautiful talk about an incredible scientific project 4,000 years old: Stonehenge. In fact, Hoyle hypothesized that it must have taken at least 100 years of experiments and data gathering to build Stonehenge. This talk was never forgotten and became the foundation on which we built our examination of the computer continuum from Stonehenge into the next millennium. We thank the artist, Ruth Lewis, for this outstanding work that captures the magnificence of Stonehenge in a way that suggests the contents and approach of our book.

Acknowledgments

Projects of this magnitude take the efforts of many more people other than just the authors. We have been working with both Zenia Jones and Pam Moore over a period of several years. This relationship has become a very fruitful forum for ideas and the implementation of them here at Eastern Michigan University. Teaching these computer concepts to over 2,500 students each year in several different formats has given a special character to our approach. They have also contributed significantly to the supplemental materials for the book. Others, including John Cooper, Karen Ueberroth, Victoria Alexander, Jeff Wierman, and Karen Casagrande-Dave all contributed to the effort.

In addition to the team who put the materials together, a very important contribution was given to us by the publisher. The very knowledgeable overall project guidance given by Robert Linsky, Publisher, Kyle Lewis, Executive Editor, and Susan Kindel, Director of Product Marketing from Que Education & Training was extremely important. The investment in an interactive CD-ROM, Web site, Instructor's CD-ROM, and related software support represented by iChat and inQsit speak to the significance of their work.

The Senior Developmental Editor—Lena Buonanno of Que Education & Training—worked through the problems and kept the project on track. For that, she deserves special recognition for completion of a major project in what could be record time. She was a joy to work with and has our deepest appreciation for a job well done. Content reviewer Jack Rochester's comments were invaluable, as were stylistic reviews by our Senior Editor, Dayna Isley, and Copyeditor Keith Cline. Betsy Brown, the Supplemental Editor, and all the people we worked with at Que Education & Training are first-class professionals, and we certainly appreciated their efforts.

And finally, this project could not have been completed without the support of our spouses, Anita Lauckner and Bill Lintner. The project was hastened along with their patience and encouragement, although sometimes given with a little edge to it: "Please, get it done so we can return to normal living!"

One last, but very important recognition goes to Millie's mother Charlott Lit, whose special smile, warm personality, and lovable character give both of us reason to put our efforts into perspective.

Reviewers

We are indebted to the many reviewers who provided us with positive feedback as well as sound revision recommendations on our approach, pedagogy, and content.

William Allen, University of Central Florida

Reiji Cass, Victor Valley College

Albert Timothy Chamillard, U.S. Air Force Academy

Edward M. Kaplan, Bentley College

Kathy Liszka, The University of Akron

Richard Martin, Southwest Missouri State University

Vickie McCullough, Palomar College

Thomas J. Moeller, Wayne State University

J. Paul Myers, Jr., Trinity University

About the Authors

Kurt F. Lauckner received his Ph.D. in Physics from the University of Michigan in 1968. His experience with computers started with extensive computer computations for his thesis work in theoretical physics. While a member of the Mathematics Department, he took the major role in creating the Computer Science program at Eastern Michigan University.

During the past 20 years, he has developed a concepts approach to teaching computer literacy. The computer literacy course CoSc136-Computers for the Non-specialist has grown into the university's primary computer literacy course and currently enrolls approximately 2,500 students per year. It was used as the model for the universitywide computer literacy requirement in the EMU basic studies program.

Many materials were developed for this freshman-level computer literacy course. They include *Computers: Inside & Out* (in fifth edition), *Student Manual for Computers: Inside & Out*, eight manuals for the tools of computing, and various support materials such as an instructor's manual and software. Emphasis on concepts was the theme throughout the development of the literacy course and the five editions of the textbook.

Mildred D. Lintner holds B.S.Ed (Theatre, Music) and M.S. (Theatre Communication) degrees from Temple University, an M.S. degree (Computer Science) from Bowling Green State University, and a Ph. D. from the University of Michigan.

Her career encompasses two very different academic disciplines. During her first 20 years of college-level teaching, she specialized in theatrical performance and technical production, designing costumes and sets for over 200 university theater productions and performing over 50 roles in music and opera theater. Then, after serving as Chair of the Theatre Department at Bowling Green, Dr. Lintner turned her considerable talents to Computer Science at the same institution, serving first as an adjunct faculty member of that department, and later becoming a tenured associate professor. Her unusual grounding in creativity and performance adds unique richness to material that beginning students often find dry.

Currently, Dr. Lintner is completing her 13th year in EMU's Department of Computer Science, where she teaches in the highly successful CoSc136 computer literacy program and serves as a full professor and Director of the Computer Teacher Education Program.

PART I
PRELIMINARIES: WHERE WE'RE GOING

Chapter 1

Computers: A First Look

Chapter Objectives

By the end of this chapter, you will:

- Appreciate how computers pervade our everyday lives.
- Identify which devices are considered computers and which are not.
- Know the differences between input units and output units.
- Realize why computers use the binary system.
- Understand the differences between electronic and mechanical computers.
- Discern the differences between special-purpose and general-purpose computers.
- Understand the differences between digital and analog computers.

1.1 The Computer Invasion

A Typical Day

6:30 a.m.   The early beginning of a typical workday. You catapult out of bed as your computerized radio alarm clock sounds automatically. A bleary glance at the clock shows you the LED numerals "6:30."

6:45 a.m.   You reach for that first cup of coffee. It is ready, hot and freshly brewed, because the computerized timer turned on the coffee maker at 6:15. Your computer starts automatically, too. You jump onto the Web to check today's stock prices in the Wall Street Journal Online.

7:30 a.m.   You ease your car away from the curb. The car's computerized diagnostic system indicates that the brakes and airbag are functioning properly and that the oil and fuel levels are okay. An LED light warns that you have not properly closed the driver-side door. A computerized voice reminds you to fasten your seat belt.

8:00 a.m.   You turn on your desk computer and log on to your company's network. Several email messages are waiting for you, including an order from a customer several hundred miles away. You check the inventory, and then, through the global community of the Internet, you notify the client that the order has been filled and is on its way.

9:00 a.m.   You are seated at your desk. A flashing LED light on the telephone indicates that a voice-mail message is waiting. You answer it, leaving a message for your associate, who is away from his or her desk.

10:00 a.m.   The fax machine at the end of the hall beeps to indicate the arrival of an important document. Because an immediate written reply is indicated, you dash one off on your computer's word processor. Rather than printing it, you fax it directly.

12:00 noon   You decide to use your lunch hour to buy a wedding gift for a friend. At the appliance store, you consult the computer bridal registry and select the item you want to give. You select its product number, which is then entered into a computerized order-taking station. The computer informs you that the item you want is available. After entering your name and credit-card information, you are instructed to pick up the item on your way out of the store.

1:15 p.m.   Back at your desk, you decide to make airline, car rental, and hotel reservations for a conference you will be attending next month. After surfing the Web for a few moments, you book your reservations with an online travel service and pay by credit card.

3:00 p.m.   Email from the payroll office contains your check stub, prepared by the computer. The stub indicates that the computer has calculated your gross pay as well as net pay after several deductions. Both current and year-to-date amounts are shown. Your net pay has been deposited to your checking account automatically.

5:15 p.m.   You make a quick stop for a few things you need for dinner. Moving quickly to the self-checkout area, you press the start button on the touch-sensitive screen. A computer voice tells you to pass an item by the scanner and reminds you to put it onto the bagging shelf where it checks the weight to see if the correct item has been placed in the bag. After scanning all items, you select cash transaction on the screen and put $20 into the bill slot. Your change is given in bills and coins and a receipt is typed out. You pick up change, receipt, and groceries and head for the parking lot.

6:30 p.m. Home at last! You activate the voice security, enter the house, and switch on your television to pick up your personal and voice mail messages from the Web and then request the day's news summary.

11:30 p.m. As the evening news ends, you roll over in your bed and turn off the light. The computerized timer on the television will turn off the set in just a few moments. You snuggle down between the thermostatically controlled electric blankets, confident that your computerized alarm will not fail to arouse you tomorrow morning.

Throughout a typical workday, millions of people worldwide interact with computers, often without knowing it. Students, factory workers, homemakers, health care personnel, and waitpersons in restaurants constantly depend on computers. Doctors, hospitals, and medical researchers use desktop computers for diagnosis and treatment. Warehouses and department stores use handheld computers for sales and inventory control. The U.S. Census Bureau uses room-sized computers to store and analyze data on more than 200 million people. Musicians rely on embedded, almost invisible computers to perform, record, and play back their music. Even everyday transportation relies heavily on computers. Undoubtedly, computers have invaded every aspect of our lives.

Imagine a Car Without Computers...

Easy, you say. Why should a car *need* computers? Automobiles need wheels, engines, brakes, bumpers, fenders, and steering. Computers are used only for frivolous add-ons such as digital mileage readouts and talking voice reminders ("Your door is ajar" or "Please fasten your seat belt"). Right?

Figure 1.1a

Designing an automobile.

Wrong! The car you're driving today was designed at a graphic computer workstation using a complex computer-aided-design program. Computer simulations were used to test aerodynamic and safety features of the design. The car's parts were assembled on computerized robot assembly lines equipped with computer-aided manufacturing devices. Computers regulated both the formula and application of the painted finish.

After the car was built, its mileage, acceleration, and road handling were thoroughly tested using computer-controlled and -measured simulation devices. Advertising agencies used graphic design and layout programs to prepare the marketing campaign promoting the vehicle.

continues

Your car engine runs smoothly as you step on the gas because the spark plugs and fuel injectors are computer controlled. If you perceive a problem, a brief stop at a service center will provide computer diagnostics to identify the problem and suggest a solution.

Your comfort is assured. The computerized thermostat controls heat, air-conditioning, and interior humidity. The electronic compass accurately displays your direction, and you can set the odometer to tell you how much longer you can expect the journey to take. Electronic sensors give you messages about fuel consumption, engine compression, and braking power. Cruise control (another computer, of course) helps you maintain a safe, steady speed. In an emergency, the computer-regulated anti-lock brakes stop the car safely, without freezing or skidding.

The list of computer contributions to today's automobile goes on and on. Literally thousands of computer chips are used in the creation, running, and maintenance of every car on the road. Without them, we would turn back the clock on automotive history.

How has this happened? How have we allowed an inanimate machine to become such a pervasive influence? Why do computers seem to control so much human activity? The truth is, computers are so pervasive because we can use them in so many ways. In fact, any task that is repetitive, any task that involves calculation or manipulation of numbers, any task that involves storing and retrieving large amounts of information can be performed more easily and with greater accuracy through the use of computers.

What exactly is this thing that has invaded our homes, our workplaces, our very lives? The purpose of this book is to make you more knowledgeable about computers and how they function so that you can better use today's tools to increase efficiency, creativity, and enjoyment throughout your daily life.

1.2 What Is (and Is Not) a Computer

Perhaps the easiest way to discover the qualities and functions that make up the concept **computer** is to begin with a formal definition.

A **computer** is a device that takes data in one form, processes it, and transforms it into information that is more useful than the original data.

Figure 1.1

The abacus, an early calculating device. Is it a computer?

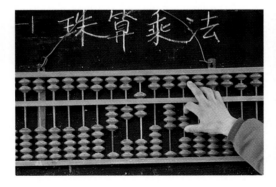

Historically, the most commonly known old calculating device is the *abacus*. It was first used by the Babylonians in 2400 B.C. and later by the Greeks in 600 B.C. However, according to our definition of a computer, the abacus is not a computer. By our definition, a computer must not only store information, but also must *change the information*. The abacus only holds information for the person using it. It doesn't change the form of the information.

The Computer Continuum

Figure 1.2a
Stonehenge on the Salisbury Plain in Wiltshire, England.

On the other hand, Stonehenge, that mysterious monumental structure, is a computer by our definition. Stonehenge takes the movement of the planets, sun, and other heavenly bodies and provides information concerning eclipses and other significant astronomical events. Stonehenge dates back before 1200 B.C. and could be considered comparable to a Bureau of Standards—an incredible scientific feat at that time.

Stonehenge—the First Computer?

Was the 3,500-year-old Stonehenge an astronomical observatory? Computer analysis of the positions of the huge monolithic stones and dozens of other markers reveals that Stonehenge was indeed a complex astronomical computer. Modern computers were used to retrace the positions of various objects in the sky to their positions 3,500 years ago, and it was noted that the positions of the many stones relate to various events. These events include midsummer sunrise and moonrise, midwinter sunrise and moonrise, eclipses, and other occurrences. In fact, while studying how Stonehenge made its predictions, astronomers discovered a 56-year eclipse cycle.

Figure 1.2b

Overview of Stonehenge's Aubrey holes used to predict eclipse seasons.

Astronomers hypothesize that it took at least 100 years of observations while recording them using small models to build Stonehenge. The monolithic Stonehenge we know today was then constructed in stages over a period of 300 years. It started in 1900 B.C. with what archaeologists call Stonehenge I. Then came Stonehenge II and Stonehenge IIIA, IIIB, and IIIC. The bursts of building activity ended in 1600 B.C. More than 80 of the large blue stones, weighing up to 5 tons each, were moved 240 miles over water and land from the quarry to the present location. Other stones weighing over 50 tons were quarried only miles away. Stonehenge, one of the first computers, is truly a remarkable example of human ingenuity.

Even the lowly bathroom scale is by our definition a computer. The information it takes in is the gravitational pull between a human body and the earth. The resulting data of this special-purpose computer is a number, usually expressed in pounds or kilograms.

Another pervasive computer is the mundane calculator. The old electromechanical calculators that had gears and weighed 30 or 40 pounds were replaced in the 1960s by electronic handheld versions. Originally priced at several hundred dollars, calculators of today cost as little as $2.00. These lower-priced models add, subtract, multiply, and divide; in addition, some of them calculate square roots and percentages and have memories. You probably have a prime example of this type of calculator at home, in your pocket, or at work. It is used by thousands of elementary schools to teach concepts of arithmetic. These less-expensive calculators are in the category of special-purpose computers; they can do only arithmetic.

More expensive calculators are programmable and do graphics output in the form of simple graphs.

The high-end handheld calculators can run off-the-shelf PC software and do email communications through various service providers. This sort of device is a general-purpose computer and marks the latest generation of palmtop computers. They can be connected to printers, and they have extensive memories.

Figure 1.3
An ordinary bathroom scale.

Figure 1.4
Texas Instruments' TI-108 calculator.

Figure 1.5
Casio Corporation's FX770-G scientific calculator.

Figure 1.6
The Hewlett-Packard 100 LX palm computer.

The Computer Continuum

1.3 Basic Concepts of Computers

In general, digital computers are conceptually quite simple, as you will see in Chapter 3, "From Stonehenge to the Supercomputer." All of them are based on the structure shown in Figure 1.7.

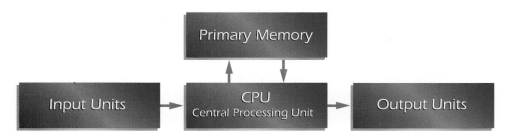

Figure 1.7

Minimal configuration of a typical computer.

Parts of the computer receive the information or programs to be used. These parts are called the **input units.** The computation is performed in the **central processing unit.** Other parts of the computer provide the results of computation to the human using the computer; these are called the **output units.** The computer must also have **memory** and storage units so that it can keep the programs and information ready and available.

The more common examples of computer input units are the keyboard, the mouse, CD-ROM drives, and disk drives. Disk drives accept magnetic floppy disks—data storage devices that are discussed along with others in Chapter 2, "Metamorphosis of Information." Commonly recognized output units include printers, the video display, and again the disk drive. Many other types of input and output units (commonly called **I/O units**) are available to the general-purpose digital computer, such as musical instruments, digitizers, light pens, bar-code readers at the grocery-store checkout counter, and audio systems.

The programs, called computer **software**, are quite a bit more complex than the conceptual computer itself. Whether it is a word-processing program or a game, the computer **hardware** must be controlled by software to perform the desired task. The concept of a computer program and how it functions in the hardware is addressed in Chapter 5, "Computer Languages: Empowering Algorithms."

Software is more ephemeral than hardware. It can exist in a human's brain, written on paper, or stored magnetically on disk. However, to be used by the computer, the software must be in the memory of the computer.

All the things done in a digital electronic computer follow a system of numeration called **binary**. What this means is discussed in the next chapter. Let it suffice to say that numbers in binary consist of only ones and zeros. All information put into the computer's memory must be in the binary form, and this overview of the general-purpose computer wouldn't be complete unless you discover the magic of why computers work in binary. Digital electronic computers work in the binary system because it is both *cheap* and *reliable*. There is no magic! It's not because the zeros and ones of the binary system can be seen as switches or lights that are either on or off. Building any other type of system is simply too expensive and unreliable.

Computer software consists of instructions that control the hardware and cause the desired thing to happen. (For example, the thousands of instructions that make up a word-processing program allow the user to type words, change the order of the words, and print or save copies of letters, and so on.)

Computer hardware is the electronics and the associated mechanical parts of the computer. It is distinguished by the fact that it has a physical presence. (That is, you can see, feel, and touch hardware.)

1.4 The Many Kinds of Computers

To get a better understanding of computers, it is necessary to look at the various types. Three major comparisons of computers are

1. Electronic computers versus mechanical computers
2. General-purpose computers versus special-purpose computers
3. Digital computers versus analog computers

Electronic Versus Mechanical Computers

When the word **electronic** is used in today's technology, it means a device constructed from transistors, which use electricity to function. In contrast, the lowly bathroom scale mentioned earlier is usually **mechanical**. Using a combination of levers and springs, the depression of the top surface of the scale, when someone is standing upon it, causes a numbered dial to rotate and come to rest at some number inscribed on the dial. More expensive bathroom scales sometimes use a combination of mechanical parts and electronic circuits. This type always has digital readouts. (That is, instead of a dial with numbers, the individual digits of the number are displayed electronically.)

Another common mechanical type of computer is the speedometer on an older automobile. Such a speedometer has a continuously moving marker, a long needle or pointer that indicates your speed by its position on a numbered scale. The needle is usually controlled by a rotating speedometer cable, which is physically turned by a connection with the transmission of the automobile.

General-Purpose Versus Special-Purpose Computers

The expressions *general purpose* and *special purpose* indicate exactly what these categories of computers represent. For example, the bathroom scale is definitely a special-purpose computer. It can be used only to measure the weight of an object and could not be used to do things such as word processing or controlling the launch of a space shuttle. Most special-purpose computers are used to control things. They exist as tiny chips, embedded in some device, which help the device to operate smoothly. Frequently, they control timing (alarms and spark-plug firings), temperature (thermostats, clothes dryers, and dishwashers), digital readouts (speedometers, scales, and watches), various sensors (car door closed and seat belt fastened) and diagnostic devices (echocardiogram machines and fuel-level indicators). Each one performs only the task it was built to do in that specific device. A general-purpose computer, on the other hand, can do many things. For instance, the same general-purpose computer that does word processing can be used to control an assembly line or to do statistical analysis of numerical information. However, certain computers are dedicated to word processing; these are considered special-purpose computers. The personal computer or microcomputer is a general-purpose computer. Its computational power is limited as compared to the large general-purpose commercial computers, but in principle, it can do anything they do, only more slowly.

This book concentrates mainly on the **general-purpose computer** and how it functions. From time to time, interesting **special-purpose computers** are mentioned. It should be pointed out that most computing occurs on special-purpose computers. This isn't hard to understand when you remember that all modern automobiles, along with all the newer microwave ovens, dishwashers, CD players, and many other appliances, are run by special-purpose computers. The majority of these computers are referred to as **digital computers**, which is the last category of computers to discuss.

A **general-purpose computer** is a computer that can be used in many situations and for many different and unrelated tasks (such as word processing, playing games, and playing music).

A **special-purpose computer** is a computer that is designed to be used in a limited way (for example, a bathroom scale or a CD player).

The Computer Continuum

Digital Versus Analog Computers

Analog computers have a rich history. Stonehenge is an analog computer, as are the old-fashioned slide rule, the Norden bombsight of World War II, and the lowly mechanical bathroom scale. What do all these devices have in common? The input consists of quantities that can vary continuously, and the outputs also vary smoothly from one value to another or one position to another. For example, when someone steps on a bathroom scale, the force on the top of the scale starts at zero and increases until the person weighing himself or herself is standing completely on the scale. The number representing that individual's weight is on a numbered scale, which continuously moves until it comes to rest at a certain position. The number opposite a line or mark gives the weight. One interesting feature of the analog scale is its degree of precision, which is usually limited. For example, when you weigh yourself, it isn't possible or even meaningful to read the weight to the nearest one-thousandth pound. Better scales, such as those found in medical offices, have more precision. However, the cost of more accurate analog devices increases astronomically with accuracy.

The digital computer distinguishes itself from the analog computer in that it deals with discretely varying values (that is, the values jump from one value to the next without crossing through all the in-between values). For example, digital watches have numerals that jump from value to value. (For example, most digital watches will jump from 12:01 to 12:02 without showing all the 60 seconds between the two values.) An analog watch with a second hand will smoothly sweep from second to second as the minute and hour hands also smoothly move around the watch dial.

The reasons the digital computer has become more common than the analog computer includes both cost and reliability, but primarily cost. Building analog devices is much more difficult and complicated, whereas digital devices are made mainly from digital electronic circuits, which can be mass-produced inexpensively.

There are many special-purpose digital computers, from digital watches to CD players. However, it is the general-purpose electronic digital computer on which we have become dependent. Imagine running airline reservation systems without large mainframe computers. Also, think of managing a corporation without payroll programs, accounting systems, word processing, and all the tools of business. Microcomputers or personal computers have multiplied into the millions. All these computers are both electronic and digital. Most of them are also called general-purpose computers; they can be used to do many different tasks from word processing to playing MIDI musical instruments.

1.5 The General-Purpose Digital Computer

After all of this discussion, it is time we defined the computer that is discussed throughout the rest of this book: the **general-purpose electronic digital computer**. The words "general purpose" refer to the fact that these computers can be used for many different kinds of work, whether it is in medicine, atomic research, ecology, payroll, record keeping, sports, retail sales, farming, commercial art, meal planning, musical entertainment.... The list goes on and on.

Digital computer circuits are binary. This means that the circuits can exist in either one of two electrical states, normally represented by 0 and 1. These **binary electronic circuits** are the most economical and reliable of all the different types of electronic technology.

Our definition of general-purpose electronic digital computer is pretty general so far. By the single word *computer* we already mean, of course, the general-purpose electronic

An **analog computer** is one that functions in continuously varying quantities and produces or gives results that are continuously varying (the results vary smoothly from one value to another by crossing all the values in between).

A **digital computer** functions in discretely varying quantities and produces or gives results that are also discretely varying (they vary in jumps from one value to another without crossing all the values in between).

A **general-purpose electronic digital computer** is a device that accepts information of many kinds, changes it in a way that is controllable by humans, and presents the result in a way usable by humans. This device is constructed of binary electronic circuits.

digital computer. You will need the next four chapters to understand what it means and the remaining part of the book to see how useful the general-purpose electronic digital computer really is.

Because computers, by definition, deal with information, you will need a clear understanding of exactly what information is before we go much further. In the next chapter, we discuss the five different types of information that the computer commonly uses. These five kinds of information (numbers, symbols, pictures, sound, and instructions) are then, according to the definition, manipulated in some way by something called a program. The **program** is a set of instructions given to the computer that exerts human control over the process.

Chapter Summary

What you can do with what you have learned:

- Find the computers that are used in our everyday lives.
- Recognize some of the major terms referring to computers.
- Appreciate how computers have evolved from the abacus to the general-purpose electronic digital computer.

Key Terms and Review Questions

Key terms introduced in this chapter:

Computer 1-8	Electronic computers 1-12
Input units 1-11	Mechanical computers 1-12
Central processing uni 1-11	General-purpose computers 1-12
Output units 1-11	Special-purpose computers 1-12
Memory 1-11	Digital computers 1-12
I/O units 1-11	Analog computers 1-13
Software 1-11	General-purpose electronic digital computer 1-13
Hardware 1-11	
Binary 1-11	Binary electronic circuit 1-13
	Program 1-14

Matching

Match the key terms introduced in the chapter to the following statements. Each term may be used once, more than once, or not at all.

1. _____ This device takes data in one form, uses it, and produces a different form of information that is related to (but not the same as) the original.

2. _____ These parts of the computer receive the information or programs to be used.

3. _____ This part of the computer keeps the programs and information ready and available.

4. _____ These parts of the computer deal with giving the results of computation to the human using the computer.

5. _____ This is where the computations are performed within the computer.

6. _____ This is the numeration system used by the computer.

7. _____ This type of computer may use belts, pulleys, or gears to control its function.

8. _____ This type of computer can be used for several unrelated tasks.

9. _____ This type of computer is constructed from transistors that use electricity to function.

10. _____ This type of computer functions in continuously varying quantities and produces

or gives results that are continuously varying.

11. _____ This type of computer functions in discretely varying quantities and produces or gives results that are also discretely varying.

12. _____ This type of computer is designed to be used in a limited way.

13. _____ This type of computer can be used for many kinds of work; it is controlled by humans; and it presents results in a way that is usable by humans.

14. _____ This type of electronic circuit can exist in either one of two states, normally represented by 0 or 1.

15. _____ This is a set of instructions given to the computer that exerts human control over the process.

True or False

1. _____ The abacus is considered a computer, according to our definition.

2. _____ Stonehenge is considered a computer, according to our definition.

3. _____ A bathroom scale is considered a computer, according to our definition.

4. _____ A disk drive is considered both an input and output unit.

5. _____ A floppy disk is considered software.

6. _____ The programs stored on a floppy disk are considered software.

7. _____ The binary numeration system consists only of ones and zeros.

8. _____ Digital electronic computers work in binary because it is both cheap and reliable.

9. _____ Building a computer out of electronic circuits that use any base system other than base two, such as base ten or sixteen, has no effect on the reliability of the resulting computer.

10. _____ An example of an electronic computer is an expensive bathroom scale that has a digital readout.

11. _____ An example of a general-purpose computer is a newer automobile because it has microchips in it that control airbags, braking systems, and radios.

12. _____ Stonehenge is an example of an analog computer.

13. _____ A CD player is an example of a digital computer.

14. _____ A word processor is considered a general-purpose computer.

15. _____ Microcomputers are general-purpose electronic digital computers.

Multiple Choice

Answer the multiple-choice questions by selecting the best answer from the choices given.

1. Stonehenge, the old rotating speedometer cable showing the speed, a watch's smoothly sweeping second hand: These are all examples of which type of computer?
   a. Analog and special purpose
   b. Digital
   c. General purpose
   d. Electronic
   e. Special purpose and electronic

2. The binary numeration system is used in computers because
   a. computers can't count in decimal.
   b. binary is cheap and reliable.
   c. humans needed a binary translator at the time the computer was created.
   d. the zeros and ones of the binary system can be seen as switches that are either on or off.
   e. the zeros and ones of the binary system can be seen as lights that are either on or off.

3. These are defined as the electronics and the associated mechanical parts of the computer.
   a. Computer software
   b. Programs
   c. Central processing units
   d. Computer hardware
   e. Binary electronic circuits

4. These are defined as consisting of instructions that control the hardware and cause the desired process to happen.
   a. Computer software
   b. Numeration systems
   c. Central processing units
   d. Computer hardware
   e. Binary electronic circuits

5. These computers are designed to be used in a limited way.
   a. Electronic computers
   b. Mechanical computers
   c. General-purpose computers
   d. Special-purpose computers
   e. Analog computers
   f. Digital computers

6. These computers function in continuously varying quantities and produce results that are continuously varying.
   a. Electronic computers
   b. Mechanical computers
   c. General-purpose computers
   d. Special-purpose computers
   e. Analog computers
   f. Digital computers

7. These computers are constructed from transistors that use electricity to function.
   a. Electronic computers

The Computer Continuum

b. Mechanical computers

c. General-purpose computers

d. Special-purpose computers

e. Analog computers

f. Digital computers

8. These computers function in discretely varying quantities and produce results that are discretely varying.

a. Electronic computers

b. Mechanical computers

c. General-purpose computers

d. Special-purpose computers

e. Analog computers

f. Digital computers

9. These computers can be used in many situations and for many unrelated tasks.

a. Electronic computers

b. Mechanical computers

c. General-purpose computers

d. Special-purpose computers

e. Analog computers

f. Digital computers

10. These computers use a combination of levers, springs, pulleys, or dials. They do not contain electronic components.

a. Electronic computers

b. Mechanical computers

c. General-purpose computers

d. Special-purpose computers

e. Analog computers

f. Digital computers

Exercises

1. Consider your own activities yesterday. How many times did you use a computer? How often did you do something that was affected by a computer?

2. Select any six-hour period of time during which you have been awake. List all interactions you had with computers during that period.

3. For each device named in the following chart, fill in the spaces to answer these questions: a) Is it a computer? b) If so, is it digital or analog? c) Is it electronic or mechanical? d) Is it special purpose or general purpose?

Device	Is it a computer?	General or special purpose?	Electronic or mechanical?	Digital or analog?
Coffee maker				
Bar-code reader				
Fax machine				
Wind-up clock				
Calculator				
Wrist alarm watch				
Wrist data-bank watch				
Home security system				
Home computer				
Rotary-dial phone				
Touch-tone phone				
VCR				
CD player				
Music box				
MIDI keyboard				

4. Name the four major parts of a computer and explain their relationship to one another.

5. Select any profession or occupation that requires post-high school training or education. Interview someone who does that kind of work and write a report telling how he or she uses computers in the workplace.

6. Name five ways that using computers could help you with your schoolwork.

7. Make a list of brand names of at least one product for each of the following categories and indicate how each is used:

   a. General-purpose computers costing less than $2,000

   b. General-purpose computers costing more than $1,000,000 (commonly called mainframe or supercomputers)

   c. Special-purpose digital computers used around the home

   d. Special-purpose analog computers used around the home

8. Make a list of special-purpose computers that are in your home.

9. Name the computer-controlled devices that are in the car you drive.

10. Mark each of the following as an input unit, an output unit, or both.

    a. CD-ROM drive

    b. Keyboard

    c. Light pen

    d. Printer

    e. Disk drive

    f. Bar-code reader

    g. Video display

    h. Mouse

    i. Digitizer

    j. Audio speakers

11. Give three examples of special-purpose computers.

12. Give three examples of general-purpose computers.

Discussion Questions

1. The sundial is obviously related to Stonehenge in a rather trivial way. Is the sundial a computer? Explain your answer.

2. How can software exist only in a person's brain?

3. Why do analog computers cost more than digital computers?

4. Discuss the significance of the fact that binary circuits are cheap and reliable, and why this would lead to their exclusive use over any other type of electronics. Is being cheap and reliable all that important?

5. Are there any reasons why we should fear computers? Think of at least six different reasons for being concerned about computers. Do any of these concerns warrant being fearful of them? Explain.

6. Explain how computers have contributed to hospitals and the health-care industry in general.

7. How do humans exert control over computers? In other words, how do humans make computers do things, either directly or indirectly?

Group Project

This group project for five people traces the process of "computing" from its earliest form through three different generations of computational devices. Each member of the group uses one of the five techniques for calculation.

The Computer Continuum

Perform all three of the following arithmetic problems in each of the five parts of this assignment. Write down any techniques used, such as borrowing in subtraction or how numbers are subtracted on a calculator. Do the best you can using the capabilities of each device!

1. Add the following numbers: 24.3, 45, 4, 107.
2. Subtract 65 from 102.
3. Multiply 7 times 13.

Person 1: Long before humans invented devices to perform arithmetic, we had to invent the calculation processes and understand them well enough to perform them by hand. As you do the three assigned problems in this part, be aware of the *process* your mind goes through to perform each task, such as borrowing in subtraction. Perform each calculation slowly and write down each step. Do not skip steps that are obvious to you from many years' experience doing similar problems. As you do the three problems, show all the details. You should make little notes about things such as carrying in addition and borrowing in subtraction.

Person 2: The earliest computing device used in this project is an abacus. You may use a real one if you have it, or you may use a virtual abacus located on the World Wide Web:

http://www.ee.ryerson.ca:8080/~elf/abacus/

The virtual abacus includes directions on how to perform simple arithmetic calculations. As you do each of the three problems, write down a summary of the process used in doing the computations.

Person 3: Now we'll jump several centuries to the middle of the 20th century before the age of electronic calculators. Your next computing machine, called a comptometer, was completely mechanical, performing calculations through the use of springs and levers. Once again, you will find a virtual comptometer on the World Wide Web:

http://www.webcom.com/calc/applets/felt/welcome.htm

As you do each computation using the World Wide Web virtual comptometer, either sketch the basic layout of the comptometer that is on the computer display or make a "screen shot" of the computer's display screen. Ask your instructor how to do this. You can then write directly on the printed copy of the screen shot.

Person 4: The development of low-cost electronic calculators represented another quantum leap in the history of calculating machines. For this part of Project 1, you may use either a real calculator or the virtual one included as a desk accessory on most personal computers. When you complete the three problems, write the details on which type of calculator you used and other capabilities that it may have.

Person 5: For this last part of Project 1, you need to use an electronic spreadsheet program. You probably have one installed on the computer you are currently using. Again, use a screen shot of the computer display or sketch in detail how you did each calculation.

Web Connections

http://ei.cs.vt.edu/~history/VonNeumann.html

Gives an in-depth history of John von Neumann.

http://www.avdigest.com/aahm/trmafeqp.html#bombsight

Shows visual images of the Norden bombsight and discusses how it was used during World War II.

http://interactive.wsj.com/tour.htm

Allows you to investigate the services available through Wall Street Journal Interactive. (You have to pay for a subscription!)

http://www.ecse.rpi.edu/~obriej2/hooked/applets/Abacus/index.html

A general introduction to the abacus and how to use one to do calculations; it also has a virtual abacus that can be manipulated.

http://connectedpc.com/cpc/explore/stonehenge/

A three-dimensional computer version of Stonehenge with explanations and history. Includes links to download the necessary free software.

http://www.contelec.com/eslide.htm

Contains downloadable software for an electronic slide rule.

http://www.ncsc.dni.us/fun/user/tcc/cmuseum/cmuseum.htm

Historical computers found at the obsolete computer museum; a lot of pictures and resource information on out-of-date machines.

Bibliography

Denning, Peter J. and Robert M. Metcalfe, Eds. *Beyond Calculation—The Next Fifty Years of Computing*. New York: Springer-Verlag, 1997.

Published on the 50th anniversary of the Association for Computing, this book has essays by the leaders in the computer community predicting the next 50 years.

Anniversary Issue of the Communications of the ACM, Communications of the ACM— The Next 50 Years. February 1997.

Published on the 50th anniversary of the Association for Computing, this issue contains essays similar to those found in the preceding book.

Hawkins, Gerald S. with John B. White. *Stonehenge Decoded*. New York: Dell Publishing, 1965.

PART II
BUILDING BLOCKS: HOW COMPUTERS WORK

C h a p t e r   2

Metamorphosis of Information

Chapter Objectives

By the end of this chapter, you will:

- Realize how almost all information fits into one of the following categories: numeric, character, visual, audio, or instructional.

- Understand the issues involved in transforming and representing information in a computer.

- Know why computers use binary numbers to store information.

- Realize why storing any kind of information in a computer requires transformation to binary.

- Identify the differences between the external and internal forms of information.

- Understand how pictures can be stored in a computer using pixels.

- Recognize several different ways sound can be stored in a computer.

- Discern the difference between facts and information.

- Know the difference between an opcode and an address.

- Appreciate the interactions of the issues of speed, cost, capacity, and type of access of storage devices.

2.1 What Is Information?

All the items in the following list represent **information** of one type or another. Look at the list items. They are grouped according to five categories. Can you describe the common type of information for each of the following groups?

A chessboard diagram.

Satellite photos of the surface of Mars.

The fingerprint files of a police department.

The blueprint of a Concorde SST wing.

The value of pi (π) to 100,000 decimal places.

The fuel capacity of a Boeing 747.

The total length of cotton thread used in a size 16/33 shirt.

The distance between any two of the 100 largest U.S. cities.

The volume of an electron in cubic light years.

The number of Hanes men's briefs sold in June 1995.

The annual earnings of a university professor.

The script of *Gone with the Wind*.

An enciphered diplomatic message.

Your seat reservation for an airline flight.

The chemical formula for ammonia.

A concordance of a Middle English gospel.

Your name and address.

A Bach fugue in four parts.

The sound of pronouncing the word afghanistanbananastand.

The echoes sensed by SONAR apparatus.

A Tarzan yell.

A computer program.

A recipe for Quiche Lorraine.

Complete directions for building an A-bomb.

The menu for a road rally.

Directions for assembling a home computer in kit form.

Plus…almost anything else you can think of.

After some analysis of this list, you should have found that the five categories from top to bottom consist of **visual, numeric, character, audio**, and **instructional information**. These five kinds of information are the only types of information the computer commonly manipulates. They are summarized in Figure 2.1.1.

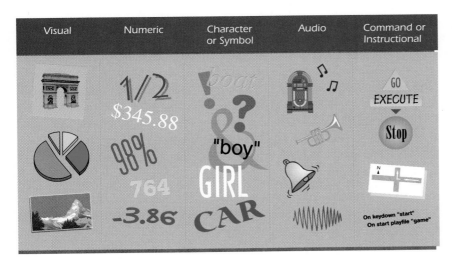

Before the computer can process any type of information, it must be input and stored temporarily in the computer's memory. That presents a seemingly monumental task: representing widely differing sorts of things inside a computer. To accomplish that goal, we must **transform** the information we want to store, converting it into an acceptable **representation** that a computer will accept for processing.

To approach the problems of transformation and representation gradually, let us first consider transformation. How can information be transformed from one mode of expression to another? We need to know, first of all, precisely what information we are trying to manipulate. Take, for example, the item "a chessboard diagram" from the preceding list. Such a description obscures a lot of the information possibly involved, such as

- The pictorial information about the diagram itself—that is, the information needed to reconstruct just the visual image of the diagram.
- The chess information in the diagram—that is, what pieces are on the board and what squares they occupy.

To take another example, what information is implied by the description "the annual earnings of a university professor"? This could break down to include

- The salary paid to the professor.
- Any bonuses awarded for outstanding performance.
- Any fringe benefits associated with the job.
- Possibly, any additional income earned through sources not connected with the professor's employer. (We have to ask: Is this *any* professor or a *particular* one?)

Because it is not our purpose to discuss the nature of information, we will gloss over problems involved in defining and classifying information precisely. Even though this is crucial in the overall process of getting information into a computer, it is the domain of another discussion.

We do want to discuss the problem of representing information, however. We need a common form into which all information may be transformed. The form that we choose should not surprise you because a lot of the information appropriately placed in computers is already in the proper form. The form of choice is **numbers**. Before we hastily conclude that all our problems are now solved, let us consider another example mentioned

Chapter 2: Metamorphosis of Information

earlier: the description "the fuel capacity of a Boeing 747." This clearly refers to a number. However, a number per se is an abstraction or idea and must be represented in order to be described, manipulated, processed, or stored. Unfortunately, numbers may be represented in many different ways. Also, a number may have extra information associated with it, which increases the choice of ways to represent it. The example of the Boeing 747 fuel capacity involves a numeric measure of a volume, and this in turn requires some choice of units. Thus we might conclude that the airplane's capacity is, let's say, 46,311 gallons, or 175,306 liters, or 316,307 pounds, or 38,562 imperial gallons. Each representation describes the same amount of fuel capacity, but because different units are used, different numbers become involved.

In a similar fashion, the same *raw* number, which has no associated units, may be written or represented in a variety of ways. Think about the number 12, for example. As children, we may have represented the number 12 in any of these ways:

~~HHH~~ ~~HHH~~ 11	12/1
XII	twelve
12	12.00

The choices depend on the context. The two representations 12 and 12.00 remind us that there are also different *types* of numbers to worry about in another sense: whole numbers, fractions, decimals, and so on.

Here, we will concern ourselves with both the problem of transforming information into numbers and the problem of choosing the appropriate way to represent the numbers to allow a computer to use them. All modern computers work with a system of numbers called **binary numbers.**

What are binary numbers? Why do computers work using binary numbers? The choice of what form to use for numbers inside a computer system is dictated by considerations of cost and reliability. The electronic devices used in a computer are cheapest and function most reliably if they have to assume only two states or conditions. Such devices are usually referred to as **binary circuits.**

Binary numbers are similar to the familiar decimal numbers. However, binary numbers use only the two symbols 1 and 0. Also, the position values are different from those of the decimal system.

Claude E. Shannon

Claude Shannon was born in 1916 in Petoskey, Michigan. He grew up in the small town of Gaylord, Michigan, as a bright and adventuresome youth. One of his early scientific endeavors was to create a communication system between his home and a neighboring farm where one of his friends lived. He cleverly used the barbed wire of the fence line that spanned the farms instead of stringing wires for his Morse code communications system.

Shannon is considered by many to be one of the greatest and most colorful scientists of the 20th century. His research interests included data communications, cryptography, computers, circuits, games, genetics, and juggling. Dr. Shannon frequently constructs engaging and entertaining devices such as THROBAC (Thrifty ROman numerical BAckward looking Computer). THROBAC performs arithmetic operations in the Roman numerical system. His crowning achievement was the 1948 paper "The Mathematical Theory of Communication." His analysis of information was the first to address the problem of measuring information content and the theoretical limits of its flow over communications channels.

The Computer Continuum

Probably the most familiar example of a binary electronic device is the ordinary switch. A light bulb, when controlled by a switch, can be in one of two states or conditions: on or off. Moreover, the light bulb stays on or off until someone turns the switch. Computers contain electronic circuit elements that function in an analogous fashion: They are in one of two states at any given time. The electronic circuit elements "remember" which state they are in, and this state can be switched from one state to the other. This switching is done by a specific action analogous to flipping the switch for a light bulb. The key to these circuits is that they are cheap to make and reliable in operation when compared to any of the possible alternatives.

The use of binary circuitry leads to a corresponding use of what are called binary numbers. Such numerals use only zeros and ones: These two choices may be thought of as corresponding to the off and on states of a light bulb.

Notice that what we have done so far is more than present just another example of information and how it is transformed into numbers. We have described the idea that numbers (in this case, 0 and 1) may themselves be associated with electronic devices. This is the connection at the most fundamental level between information and computers:

> Information can be represented by numbers that can be associated with parts of an electronic machine and their state or condition at a given moment.

The use of 0 and 1 will not be confined to this isolated example but will pervade our entire discussion of computers. The foundation on which it all rests is this: All numbers may be expressed using only 0s and 1s. The system used to represent numbers by 0s and 1s is called the *binary* system.

2.2 Representation of Numbers

The binary expression of information that is seemingly forced upon us by digital computers is really something we're all familiar with. Common examples are the *occupied* slide sign in an airplane restroom, the *no* of a *no-vacancy* sign, the *bright-lights-on* indicator of an automobile, the *up-down* indicator of an elevator, the *fasten-seat-belt* sign on an airplane, the *occupied* light of a taxicab, the *flash-ready* light on an electronic camera flash unit, the *open* sign at a grocery checkout lane, and the ferry boat *ready-to-leave* whistle. The list goes on and on. What obvious characteristic do they have in common? They are all examples of a binary nature.

All these binary information devices have a two-state characteristic. In other words, the information conveyed consists of exactly one of two possible things (on or off, occupied or unoccupied, yes or no, ready or not ready). Obviously, this is extremely limiting; a single binary device can indicate only one of two possibilities.

To indicate (or represent) more than two possibilities, we need to use more than one binary device. To see how this works, imagine a bank of three light bulbs, each of which has its own on/off switch. Let's see how many binary combinations we can produce by flipping the switches: Each of the three lights can be on while the other two are off. That gives us three possible combinations. Alternatively, each light can be off while the other two are on. That adds three more combinations for a total of six, so far. Finally, the three lights can be either all on or all off. That gives us two more possibilities for a grand total of eight. Figure 2.2.1 illustrates these eight combinations of on/off light bulbs. Can you find any other possibilities?

An example of a three-light system that uses these eight possibilities to record information is a radio tower weather reporting facility. Suppose a local radio station decided to give visual weather coverage to all persons, boats, or aircraft within sight of its radio

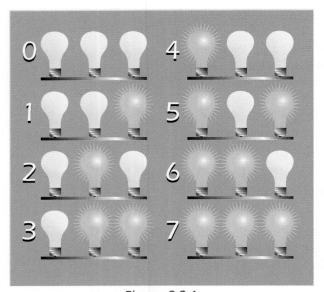

Figure 2.2.1

Eight combinations of lights on and off.

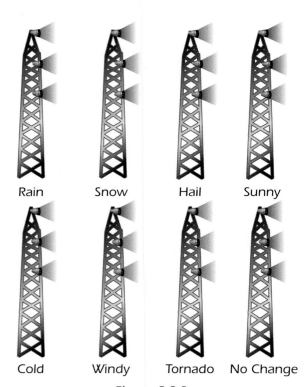

Figure 2.2.2

Radio tower weather information.

tower. This could be done by installing three strong lights in the tower. To give weather forecasts, the weather reporters could turn on or off the individual lights as illustrated in Figure 2.2.2. If the top light was on and the others off, rain is forecast. The remaining combinations of lights on or off would be recognized as codes for the conditions indicated in the figure.

This example, although possibly interesting, doesn't involve the use of essential information. After all, we can just listen to the weather report over the radio and get more detailed and precise weather information, such as when and how much snow is expected. In addition, the weather tower is restricted to reporting only one condition at a time. (For example, it can't give sunny and windy conditions at the same time.) However, with just a little thinking, this example can put us on the track of more vital uses of binary information. Such applications show us that one of the simpler yet important forms of information we have is numbers.

The three-light system could easily be used to indicate the numbers 0, 1, 2, 3, 4, 5, 6, and 7 because there are exactly eight possible combinations of on and off for three lights. We've illustrated just one of many possible methods for numbering the combinations of lights in Figure 2.2.1.

Notice that all possible combinations of on and off have been used. Switching all lights off to represent zero and switching all lights on to mean the largest number, seven, seems logical. If we let the number 1 mean a light is on and 0 mean it is off, then putting these 0s and 1s in the same position as the lights gives us the number representations shown in Figure 2.2.3.

These even look like numbers, and in fact, they are called binary **numerals**. Why do we say *numerals* instead of *numbers*? To begin to see why, consider any of the symbols, say 110. If you had seen this out of context, you would no doubt have identified it as *one hundred ten*, a decimal numeral. In the familiar system of decimal numerals, each digit stands for a multiple of a power of ten (more about this next). In the system of binary numerals, each digit stands for a multiple of a power of two instead. We also note that in the decimal system, each digit may be a number between 0 and 9, whereas in binary, each digit is actually called a BIT (BInary digiT) and may only be either 0 or 1. Thus, the numeral 110 stands for a different number in the decimal system of numerals than it does in the binary system. Look at these examples:

$$110_{decimal} = (1 \times 100) + (1 \times 10) + (0 \times 1)$$
$$110_{binary} = (1 \times 4) + (1 \times 2) + (0 \times 1)$$

To understand a little better what all this is about, let's take an excursion into the realm of numeration systems.

The **decimal** (or *base 10*) numeration system is quite useful in our everyday lives. Society considers it so valuable that concepts of the decimal numeration system are taught starting in the first grade, and parents go to great effort to teach their young children to count. How many times have you heard a beaming parent say, "All right now, precious, show Mr. Bored how you can count to 10"? Many of the concepts found in our decimal system carry over into the binary system.

As a reminder, two important features of the decimal system are

1. Base 10, or decimal, uses 10 symbols—0, 1, 2, 3, 4, 5, 6, 7, 8, and 9.

2. The place values of each position are powers of 10.

0	000
1	001
2	010
3	011
4	100
5	101
6	110
7	111

Figure 2.2.3

Binary equivalents of the decimal numerals 0 to 7.

Figure 2.2.4 illustrates additional features of the decimal system that are sometimes forgotten.

To represent the various numbers, the symbols are placed in certain positions. For example, the 5 in the leftmost position indicates there are 5 one-thousands in the number. Each position has a value associated with it, and these values are powers of a number called the base, which in decimal is 10. (For example, 1,000 is 10 to the third power or 10^3, and 10^3 means 10×10×10; the 3 is called an exponent.)

An **exponent** should be thought of as shorthand notation for the purposes of this book. It just means that you multiply the number it is attached to by the exponent number of times. (For example, 10^2 is 100, 2^3 is 8, and 8^2 is 64.) An additional requirement for consistency is that anything to the zero is 1. (For example, 10^0 is 1 and 2^0 is 1.)

Using this exponent notation, the base 10 number from Figure 2.2.4 can be written in an expanded form as follows:

$$5207.89 = (5\times1,000) + (2\times100) + (0\times10) + (7\times1) + (8\times1/10) + (9\times1/100)$$

or

$$5207.89 = (5\times10^3) + (2\times10^2) + (0\times10^1) + (7\times10^0) + (8\times10^{-1}) + (9\times10^{-2})$$

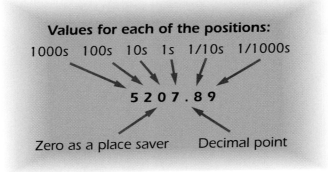

Figure 2.2.4

Place values of a base 10 number.

After this short review of the base 10 numeration system, understanding another base is less difficult. Rather than give a complete formal mathematical definition, we will let our intuition guide us.

In the binary (or *base 2*) system, these two points seem to follow reasonably from our familiar decimal system of numeration:

1. Base 2 uses only two symbols, 0 and 1.

2. The place values of each position are powers of 2.

For example, the base 2 number 10110 can be written in terms of the familiar decimal numbers, as shown in Figure 2.2.5.

Figure 2.2.5

Place values of a base 2 number.

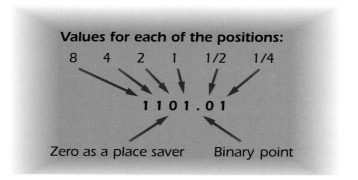

Because the place values are given in base 10, we can add them to see what this number is in base 10. It's actually quite deceiving. Suppose you were asked to go to the store and get 10110_{two} pounds of sugar. Would you need a truck to carry that much sugar? Certainly, if the number were interpreted as base 10, then ten thousand and one hundred ten pounds of sugar is quite a lot. But it actually represents a relatively small amount in base 2, as shown in the following calculation:

$$10110_{two} = (1 \times 2^4) + (0 \times 2^3) + (1 \times 2^2) + (1 \times 2^1) + (0 \times 2^0)$$
$$= \quad (1 \times 16) + (0 \times 8) + (1 \times 4) + (1 \times 2) + (0 \times 1)$$
$$= \quad 16 \ + \ 0 \ + \ 4 \ + \ 2 \ + \ 0$$
$$= 22$$

In fact, the number 10110_{two} represents only 22 (decimal) pounds of sugar! You could easily carry this home from the grocery store on your bicycle as shown in Figure 2.2.6.

Figure 2.2.6

How do we transport 10110_{two} pounds of sugar?

To get more experience, let us count in base 2 (binary). First, note that in base 10 when we reach 9, we have run out of symbols, so we put a 0 in the ones place and make the tens place one bigger. In another example, what comes after 99 in base 10? We have all memorized that answer and immediately say 100! If we didn't know, then a way to get the number that is one bigger than 99 is to make the ones place one bigger. It is already at its largest value, so make it a zero and then make the tens place one bigger. The tens place already has a 9, so make it a 0 and then make the hundreds place one bigger. The result is 100!

In binary, the counting is done in the same way. When you run out of symbols in the ones place, change it to zero and make the place to the left one bigger. Figure 2.2.7 illustrates counting in both decimal and binary.

Base 10	Base 2	Base 10	Base 2
0	0	16	10000
1	1	17	10001
2	10	18	10010
3	11	19	10011
4	100	20	10100
5	101	21	10101
6	110	22	10110
7	111	23	10111
8	1000	24	11000
9	1001	25	11001
10	1010	26	11010
11	1011	27	11011
12	1100	28	11100
13	1101	29	11101
14	1110	30	11110
15	1111	31	11111

Figure 2.2.7
Counting in decimal and binary.

Although a thorough examination of numeration has been avoided, the introduction is sufficient. It will allow you to understand the most important point of all of this: No matter what numeration system is used, each number has a single unique representation. This means any base could be used and all results would be equivalent. Of course, in today's computers, binary is the numeration system of choice because it is cheap and reliable.

A Serious Conversion Problem

This discussion would not be complete without examining an important imperfection in the binary representations of decimal numbers. It is obvious that numbers containing 0.1 decimal are important. (That is, 1/10th; the zero before the decimal point is just for readability.) For example, when representing money, 10 cents is commonly written $0.10, or one tenth of a dollar. The problem occurs in the end result of the conversion from 0.1 decimal to its binary form. Without seeing how to do the conversion from decimal fractions to binary fractions, just examine the following result:

$0.1 = .0001100110011001100110011001100110011\ldots_{two}$

The simple 0.1 decimal becomes an infinite repeating binary fraction. How is this possible? It's just a fact! Just so you don't think this is unusual, remember that in the decimal world fractions such as 1/3 and 2/3 become 0.33333... and 0.66666..., which are also infinite repeating fractions.

continues

Chapter 2: Metamorphosis of Information

A programmer not familiar with this problem might write an accounting program that does millions of arithmetic operations using 0.1 every day. The fact is that every time a 0.1 is added or subtracted in binary, a tiny part of the binary form of 0.1 must be thrown away. For example, using the first 13 bits of the binary form of 0.1 gives 0.0001100110011_{two}. This is not exactly 0.1 because $0.00000000000000001100110011..._{two}$ is ignored.

This problem with 0.1 is not really insurmountable; it just has to be taken into account. One of the many ways of handling the problem is the BCD (Binary Coded Decimal) representation of number. The details of this code aren't of interest here. Let it be sufficient to say that BCD allows exact arithmetic when using 0.1.

2.3 Representing Symbols, Pictures, Sound, and Instructions

By now, you should have firmly established in your mind the idea that to store any kind of information in a computer's memory, it must first be transformed into a numeric form. We next consider the problem of storing symbols or text.

Representing Symbols and Text

Consider the text of this book. Storing the text might be desirable for a number of reasons. You then could use a computer program to format the text or even to typeset the final version. You could easily retrieve the stored version and produce multiple copies of it on a printer and so on.

One possible approach to storing text is to assign a different number to every word or grouping of characters that could possibly appear in the text. For example, let *and* be 1, *the* be 2, *this* be 3, and so on. This would be a very compact representation, but unfortunately, it is unacceptable for several reasons. In the first place, you would need a dictionary that provided the numerical equivalent for each possible word or symbol. No matter how big this dictionary was, there would always be new words or symbols popping up and requiring assigned numbers. Also, various punctuation marks and even blank spaces would have to be represented, and there would always be the possibility of new symbols appearing with no assigned numbers. Clearly, the number of revised editions of this dictionary could get annoyingly large. In the second place, the problem of retrieving the original information, once it was represented in numeric form, would present additional difficulties. You would need a *reverse* dictionary that contained the equivalent word or symbol for each possible number. Finally, a subtle difficulty would involve the fact that the numbers used to represent the textual information would, in this scheme, have unequal sizes—anywhere from one up to several million. As you might guess, the amount of space or memory needed to store the number 1 is considerably smaller than that required to store, say, 31,519,654. If we reserve enough space in the computer's memory to store numbers the size of 31,519,654, then we waste considerable computer memory for each number we store that is smaller. This difficulty will always be present, but in the interests of economy, it is desirable to minimize its effects.

An alternative way to approach the problem of representing text is to assume the existence of a generalized alphabet or **character set** for the computer. This set would contain all the single symbols (or marks or characters) from which printed text can be constructed. It would include not only the normal alphabet, but also marks such as digits (0,1,2,...,9), punctuation (.,!?";:), and special characters (#%&$=*/). A different number would then be assigned to each character. Because there are a relatively small number of possible characters in general use, the numbers assigned would fall into a small range (in contrast to the one to several million of our first attempt), such as 0 to 63 or 0 to 127. A word in a sample of text would be represented as a series of numbers, namely, the numbers assigned to each of the letters comprising the word. For example, if A were assigned the number 1, B the number 2, and so on, then the word BASIC would be assigned the sequence of numbers 2,1,19,9,3.

A more mind-boggling example is the task of representing a number itself. Suppose we assign the number 27 to the character 0, 28 to the character 1, and so on. Then the symbol for the number 100 would be represented by the sequence 28,27,27.

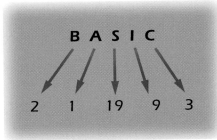

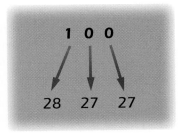

Figure 2.3.2
The number 100 coded with numbers.

Figure 2.3.1
The word BASIC coded with numbers.

In this example, we encounter for the first time one of the fundamental distinctions that lead to confusion when discussing storage of information in a computer. There is a difference between the external form of information (the way we see it in the real world) and the internal form of information (the way the computer sees it). Because we have chosen a (binary) numeric form for the internal form of information, we must be especially careful to pay attention to this distinction when talking about the representation of numbers.

Numbers can be put into the computer in two different ways:

1. As pure numbers represented in binary form. For example, 21 decimal is 10101_{two}.

2. As symbols standing for the decimal digits. For example, 21 decimal is 29,28 in the code shown earlier, or using the ASCII code of Figure 2.3.3, it is the two seven-digit binary numbers 0110010 and 0110001.

These two binary forms of representing 21 decimal are both valid. When doing arithmetic, we need form 1, and when storing numbers as symbols with other letters of the alphabet, we need to use form 2.

An assignment of numbers to the possible characters in a computer's character set is referred to as a *code* (or sometimes the internal code). As computers have developed, people have realized the need to have a uniform code from one computer to the next. Many computer codes have been created, but only two of these codes have become standardized. The IBM Corporation developed the Extended Binary Coded Decimal Interchange Code (EBCDIC for short, pronounced *ebb-suh-dik*). This **EBCDIC** code is used primarily by IBM in its large computers, which are commonly referred to as mainframe computers. Other mainframe computers using EBCDIC are made by Amdahl and

Control Data. The other common code was standardized by the American National Standards Institute (ANSI or *ann-see*) and called the American Standard Code for Information Interchange (ASCII, pronounced *ask-ee*). The ASCII code, or simply **ASCII**, is used by virtually all other computers in the United States and Europe as well. All personal computers use the ASCII code.

The ASCII code is shown in Figure 2.3.3. Notice that 128 different characters are represented, and these have been assigned the binary numbers from 0000000_{two} to 1111111_{two}, which is 0 to 127 in decimal. The characters that are represented by the numbers from 0 to 31 decimal (that is, 0000000_{two} to 0011111_{two}) are probably unfamiliar to you; they certainly do not correspond to any well-known printing or displayable characters. The characters, which these values represent, are usually referred to as **control characters**. They have a variety of uses in the computer world, involving such things as communication between different computers or between a computer and a device (such as a terminal), control commands to the computer itself (hence the name), and others. We will not say anything more about them here because few of them are usually involved in the representation or storage of text.

The process of representing printed textual information consists of transforming the sequence of printing characters that constitute the text into a sequence of numbers (the codes that correspond to the printing characters) and subsequently storing these numbers in a binary form in a computer's memory. The concept of this process is illustrated in Figure 2.3.4.

Representing Pictures

A simple black-and-white photograph presents an interesting example of how pictorial information can be transformed into numeric form. The basic idea is to subdivide the picture into a grid of squares, as shown in Figure 2.3.5. The black squares are easy to see because they are outlined by the white space between them. You will have to extend those lines into the white area to see the white squares. Each of these squares is referred to as a **pixel**. Each square is a very small portion of the original picture. If the squares are small enough, you will see a reasonably good image.

To represent this primitive picture in a computer, all that has to be done is to record which squares are white and which are black. You probably already realize that this is a simple matter: Just let the black squares be represented by 1 and the white squares by 0. The piece of a picture shown in Figure 2.3.5 has 37 rows of 46 squares each and therefore can be represented by using 0s and 1s, where 1 means a black pixel and 0 means a white pixel. Figure 2.3.6 was made by replacing the black pixels by 1s and the white pixels by 0s.

Unfortunately, the simple black/white pixel process we've described can produce only crude quality pictures. To get an image with photographic quality, each pixel must assume more shades than pure white or black. In fact, the pixels are said to have a **grayscale**, which means that instead of just pure white or black, several shades between white and black are used. A 64-level grayscale means that there are 64 different shades of gray going from white to black. To put this kind of picture into a computer, each level of gray is usually numbered from 000000_{two} to 111111_{two} or in decimal from 0 to 63. Then each square or pixel will be assigned a value on a grayscale.

Pixel is an acronym from the words **picture element**. Pixels are the building blocks of a computer picture. For simple pictures, each pixel is either black or white.

The Computer Continuum

Figure 2.3.3

ASCII character set in binary.

Character	Binary	Character	Binary	Character	Binary
Ctrl+@(NULL)	0000000	+	0101011	V	1010110
Ctrl+A(SOH)	0000001	,	0101100	W	1010111
Ctrl+B(STX)	0000010	–	0101101	X	1011000
Ctrl+C(ETX)	0000011	.	0101110	Y	1011001
Ctrl+D(EOT)	0000100	/	0101111	Z	1011010
Ctrl+E(ENQ)	0000101	0	0110000	[	1011011
Ctrl+F(ACK)	0000110	1	0110001	\	1011100
Ctrl+G(Bell)	0000111	2	0110010	]	1011101
Ctrl+H(BS)	0001000	3	0110011	^	1011110
Ctrl+I(HTAB)	0001001	4	0110100	_	1011111
Ctrl+J(LFEED)	0001010	5	0110101	`	1100000
Ctrl+K(VTAB)	0001011	6	0110110	a	1100001
Ctrl+L(FormF)	0001100	7	0110111	b	1100010
Carriage return	0001101	8	0111000	c	1100011
Ctrl+N(SO)	0001110	9	0111001	d	1100100
Ctrl+O(SI)	0001111	:	0111010	e	1100101
Ctrl+P(DLE)	0010000	;	0111011	f	1100110
Ctrl+Q(DC1)	0010001	<	0111100	g	1100111
Ctrl+R(DC2)	0010010	=	0111101	h	1101000
Ctrl+S(DC3)	0010011	>	0111110	i	1101001
Ctrl+T(DC4)	0010100	?	0111111	j	1101010
Ctrl+U(NAK)	0010101	@	1000000	k	1101011
Ctrl+V(SYN)	0010110	A	1000001	l	1101100
Ctrl+W(ETB)	0010111	B	1000010	m	1101101
Ctrl+X(CAN)	0011000	C	1000011	n	1101110
Ctrl+Y(EM)	0011001	D	1000100	o	1101111
Ctrl+Z(SUB)	0011010	E	1000101	p	1110000
Ctrl+[(Escape)	0011011	F	1000110	q	1110001
Ctrl+\(FS)	0011100	G	1000111	r	1110010
Ctrl+](GS)	0011101	H	1001000	s	1110011
Ctrl+^(RS)	0011110	I	1001001	t	1110100
Ctrl+_(US)	0011111	J	1001010	u	1110101
Space	0100000	K	1001011	v	1110110
!	0100001	L	1001100	w	1110111
"	0100010	M	1001101	x	1111000
#	0100011	N	1001110	y	1111001
$	0100100	O	1001111	z	1111010
%	0100101	P	1010000	{	1111011
&	0100110	Q	1010001	|	1111100
'	0100111	R	1010010	}	1111101
(	0101000	S	1010011	~	1111110
)	0101001	T	1010100	Delete	1111111
*	0101010	U	1010101		

Figure 2.3.4

*Representing the text of a
book in ASCII code.*

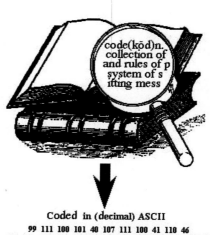

code(kōd)n.
collection of
and rules of p
system of s
itting mess

Coded in (decimal) ASCII

99 111 100 101 40 107 111 100 41 110 46
99 111 108 108 101 99 116 105 111 110 32 111 102
97 110 100 32 114 117 108 101 115 32 111 102 112
115 121 115 116 101 109 32 111 102 32 115
105 116 116 105 110 103 32 109 101 115 115

Coded in (binary) ASCII

1100011 1101111 1100100 1100101 0101000 1101011 1101111 1100100 0101001 1101110 0101110
1100011 1101111 1101100 1101100 1100101 1100011 1110100 1101001 1101111 1101110 0100000 1101111 1100110
1100001 1101110 1100100 0100000 1110010 1110101 1101100 1100101 1110011 0100000 1101111 1100110 0100000 1110000
1110011 1111001 1110011 1110100 1100101 1101101 0100000 1101111 1100110 0100000 1110011
1101001 1110100 1110100 1101001 1101110 1100111 0100000 1101101 1100101 1110011 1110011

Figure 2.3.5

*Part of a picture showing
the pixel structure.*

One method of converting a picture to numeric form is to use a device called a **digitizer**. There are many types of digitizers. Some can give only a black-and-white pixel image, such as the tiger shown in Figure 2.3.7; others can measure 64, 256, or even 512 different levels of gray. The more different shades of gray used for a picture image, the closer to photographic reality it will seem.

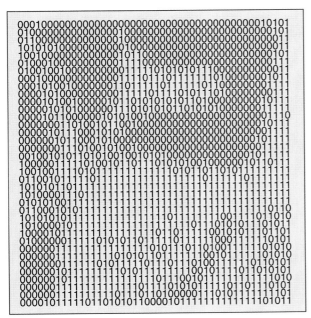

Figure 2.3.6

Black and white pixels are 1s and 0s.

Figure 2.3.7

Picture of a tiger.

Figure 2.3.8

Tiger's head enlarged.

This digitizing concept is carried out to much greater detail in the satellite photographs often appearing in newspapers and magazines. A sample satellite photo of the San Francisco and bay area is shown in Figure 2.3.10. In detail, this digitized photograph looks almost like a picture developed at your corner photographic store. It is actually a grid of one million pixels with not only grayscale but also color in each pixel.

As you might expect, it is also possible to represent color pictures by numbers. Instead of a single number of the grayscale for each spot on the grid, three numbers are required. These three numbers are for the hue (color), saturation (richness of color), and the grayscale (darkness or lightness of the color). With present technology, it is almost impossible with the naked eye to tell the difference between a computer digitized color slide and the original photographic slide. Chapter 10, "Visual Communication: Gateway to the Brain," explores color images and shows how the computer can manipulate these images.

Sound as Information

We have already seen several forms of information reduced to numbers, but there are still more! Sound is also information. For example, a watch-dog's bark or the warning shout of a tree trimmer conveys information. Our purpose here is quite simple: to show how sound can be reduced to numbers. A simple example of sound information represented by numbers is illustrated in Figure 2.3.11. This example of a simple numerical coding of the notes allows children to readily play songs. The numerals on the notes correspond to numerals on the instrument. If you strike the

Figure 2.3.9

Tiger's eye enlarged more than three times.

proper numeral in the order given on the sheet of music, the music is reproduced. This simple example leaves out many details: How much time should be taken between notes, and what tempo should be used? Of course, this additional information also can be given in the form of numbers. The tempo, for example, could be the number of beats per minute at which the metronome is set. The lengths of the notes themselves already have numerical equivalents: half note (1/2), whole note (1), quarter note (1/4), and so on. So it looks as though music that can be written down on paper in the traditional form also can be written out in a numerical form.

In general, this numerical form of music is not used by Western musicians because they are trained to read the traditional notation of the five-line staff. It is sometimes used by musical toy manufacturers to make it easy to learn to play toy pianos, xylophones, or other instruments.

Let's look at another interesting example of representation, which, by the way, is no longer needed because of advances in communicating musical information to and from a computer. It is a form of musical representation called **DARMS** (Digital Alternative Representation of Musical Scores) that was used by professional musicologists. This form is a graphic system based on the position of symbols on a staff. A great deal of thought went into the development of DARMS. The lines of the staff, including ledger lines (lines above and below the staff proper), are represented by numerals 01,02,03,…,49; they are written so that staff line numbers are 21-23-25-27-29 and the spaces on the staff area are 20-22-24-26-28-30. The other details might be best introduced through an illustration as shown in Figure 2.3.12. The clef, key, and meter are prefaced by an exclamation point. In Figure 2.3.12, !G means treble clef, !K1- indicates a key of one flat, and !MC indicates the meter C or 4/4 time. The slashes (/) mark the measure boundaries, the Q represents a quarter note, and H represents a half note. This form of the music can be easily converted to binary using the ASCII code and then manipulated by the computer, but it would certainly take more effort for a musician to learn to play from it!

As the means of communicating with the computer improved, it was no longer necessary to code music using letters of the alphabet, numbers, and punctuation symbols. The music could be put directly into the computer in the usual musical notation with staff, notes, and all other necessary symbols. This graphical means of communicating musical information to the computer is only one of many visual representations of audio information that will be explored later in the book.

Figure 2.3.10

Satellite photo of San Francisco and Bay area.

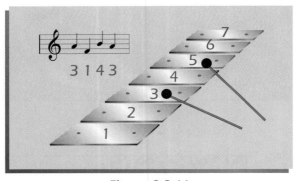

Figure 2.3.11

Relating numbers to musical notes.

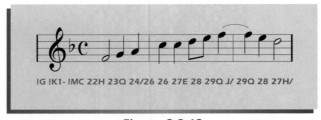

Figure 2.3.12

A special case of musical representation.

The Computer Continuum

Before we go on to other forms of sound, let us look at other musically related sound forms. The tuning fork is often used by musicians to assist in tuning their instruments. Each tuning fork will vibrate at a particular frequency when it is struck. The tuning fork in Figure 2.3.13 is one that sounds middle C, or more appropriately, 256 Hertz. The number 256, given in the units called **Hertz**, is the numerical representation that tells exactly what frequency of sound is produced.

Up to now, a very important feature of sound has been ignored. Could we tell the difference between a violin and a trombone playing the music of Figure 2.3.12? No? Obviously, then, we're leaving something out. The fact is, more than just the pure frequency of the notes is produced when different instruments play. It seems very natural to want to capture any type of sound. We can do this in a way that is similar to digitizing a picture. However, instead of dividing the image of a picture into tiny cells (pixels), we will divide the time during which a sound is being produced into tiny segments and record some type of information during each of them. What should be recorded? An example is probably the easiest way to show how this is done.

An ordinary stereo system, as shown in Figure 2.3.14, will suit our purpose for this example. What is the information being carried on a wire leading to a stereo speaker? This sound information is in the form of a **voltage**. Because of the variation of this voltage, sound is produced by the speaker.

If it were possible to measure the magnitude of this voltage several thousand times per second, then the sequence of numbers obtained would contain meaningful information as shown in the graph of Figure 2.3.15. Suppose this were done. A typical sequence of numbers might be

1.2312, −1.2300, −1.2100, 0.9510,…

Hertz is a unit of measurement that indicates the number of cycles per second of a particular sound's vibration.

Figure 2.3.13

Frequency as a numerical representation of a pitch.

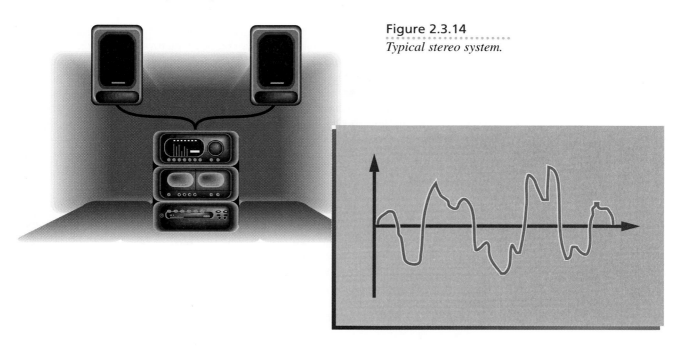

Figure 2.3.14
Typical stereo system.

Figure 2.3.15
Graph of voltage appearing in the speaker wire.

When we want to hear the sound these numbers represent, it is only necessary to reproduce them electronically fast enough so that they appear on the speaker wire with the same values and at the correct rate of speed.

By analogy with digitizing a picture, it should be intuitively clear that the more measurements we take per second, the better the reproduction of sound. In fact, to reproduce accurately to 20,000 Hertz (frequency in cycles per second), we would have to take 40,000 measurements per second. That's just a little fast for a human with a voltmeter. However, there are electronic circuits that can easily do this. Digital stereo systems using these circuits can do exactly what we've been talking about.

The two major examples of consumer products are **CD (compact disc)** players and **DAT (digital audio tape)** recorder/players. Both of these devices have electronics that use the numbers (stored in binary form) to produce the proper voltages up to 40,000 times per second. It's interesting to note that the CD player uses a laser beam that shines on the surface of a disc. If light is reflected back from a tiny spot, that means 0, whereas if the spot doesn't reflect, it's 1. On the other hand, the DAT records its 0s and 1s by magnetizing tiny spots on the tape. This means that as long as the numbers aren't altered, the recording won't show signs of wear like ordinary records. A number is a number!

The same sound-digitizing technique can be used on human speech. In fact, eventually our telephone system will be completely digital. Our voices will be sent over telephone lines as binary numbers instead of in the usual form. By digitizing the human voice at one end of the telephone line and reconstructing it at the other end, it is estimated that our telephone lines can carry 100 times more telephone calls. Does this mean our telephone bills will be reduced to one-hundredth their current value?

bits & bytes

An Intergalactic Message

A few years ago, Frank Drake and other staff members of the National Astronomy and Ionosphere Center of Cornell University created a picture that contained a large amount of fundamental scientific data. The information is actually a mixture of numeric and pictorial facts. It is designed as an image 23 squares wide and 73 squares high and thus can be represented by a string of 1,679 0s and 1s as shown. This representation was transmitted into outer space using a powerful radio telescope in Arecibo, Puerto Rico. The Earth scientists hoped that their message would be received by intelligent life elsewhere in our galaxy or even in other, more distant galaxies. The message was transmitted repeatedly whenever the telescope sat idle. Its purpose was to give any potential extraterrestrial listener a hint that it originated from intelligent beings on Earth.

If some other life form receives the Arecibo transmission, then it will prove its intelligence by discovering the content of the message. The first step is to discover the message length, 1,679. Eventually, the fact that 1,679 = 23×73 would be determined. This is the only pair of numbers that could be used to display the 1,679 0s and 1s in a perfectly rectangular space with none left over. After that step is achieved, the pictures and information contained in the message will become evident. If the receivers of the message have developed computers similar to ours, the decoding of the intergalactic message should be very rapid indeed. Here are two representations of the message, one using 0s and 1s and the second, in a more legible form with a black square representing 1 and nothing in the square representing 0. See if you can figure out how the top lines in the message represent counting from 1 to 10. (Hint: It's counting in binary.)

The Computer Continuum

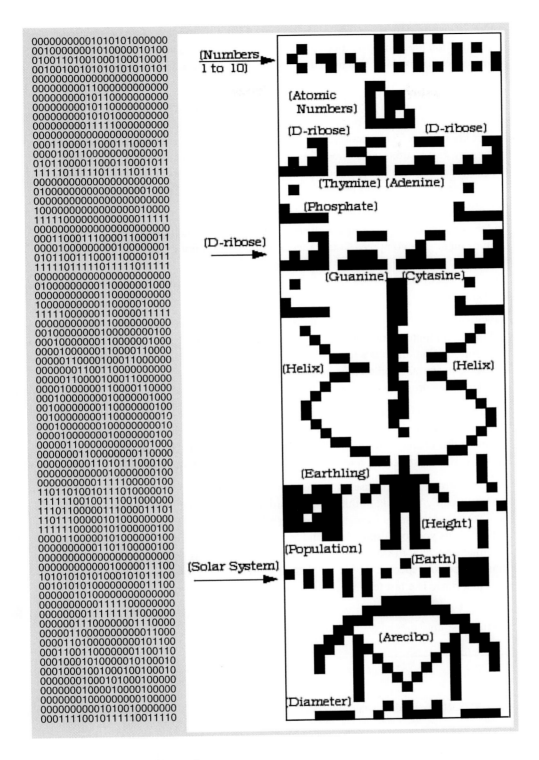

Instructions as Numbers

The types of information treated so far in this chapter have been factual in nature. Commands, or instructions to do something, are certainly also forms of information but are not strictly factual. These two types of information are analogous to the declarative and imperative sentence types in the English language. Instructions are imperative; they command action rather than being declarations of fact. Examples of the instructional type of information are numerous: For instance, we are all familiar with the *fasten-seat-belt* command in automobiles and airplanes, the *pull-over* command of a highway patrol police officer, and the *mix-ingredients-thoroughly* instruction of a cooking recipe.

What, then, is the difference between facts and instructions? The difference is primarily a matter of use or purpose. The purpose of most types of information is declarative—to impart knowledge. The purpose of an instruction is manipulative—to control information or activity. Instructions are always directed at someone or something that is capable of carrying them out. To be effective, each instruction must be clearly understood by its intended receiver, and the information needed to process that instruction must be readily accessible.

So far, we have been concerned with several types of information and how the computer handles them. The computer's main function, however, is not merely to *store* information. Its main purpose is to *manipulate* information—to use it for calculations, queries, and reports. To perform these manipulations, the computer must follow a series of commands or instructions.

As with all the other types of information, the computer's instructions must be stored within the computer's memory before they can be used. They must be stored, like all other information, in binary form. A set of binary instructions, which the computer can follow, or **execute**, is called a **program**. That is why today's computer is commonly called a stored program computer.

To understand how a series of instructions can be stored in the computer as a group of binary numbers, we've devised a set of instructions that will allow us to read a message hidden in this chapter. Our instruction set is called the **Word Hunt**. Figure 2.3.16 shows the Word Hunt instructions and an explanation of what each one means.

The six instructions comprise an instruction set—all of the possible instructions needed to perform a particular task, in this case, a word hunt. Notice that each instruction (except the STOP) has the same format, or **syntax** (ACTION-OBJECT) where the ACTION is a verb that tells you to do something and the OBJECT modifies the verb, telling you where, how much, or what the verb requires. The first four instructions merely move a pointer (your finger) to a specific word. The fifth tells you to record the message you find, one word at a time. The last tells you when the message is completed.

Figure 2.3.17 shows a typical Word Hunt puzzle. See if you can carry out the instructions and find a simple message.

Figure 2.3.16

The six instructions used in Word Hunt.

GOTO #	Turn pages either backward or forward until you get to the page number indicated in the instruction. Count the pages with the timeline of this chapter starting as page 1.
SELECT LINE #	Counting down from the top of the page, move the pointer (your finger) to the beginning of the line indicated by the instruction's #. The top line of text is line 1. Blank lines don't count.
FORWARD #	Beginning with the word immediately to the right of your current position, count forward the number of words indicated in the instruction. On each new line, begin with the pointer before word 1, the first word on the line. If you move forward three, the pointer will then be on word three in that line.
BACKUP #	Beginning with the word immediately to the left of your current position, count backward the number of words indicated in the instruction.
WRITE *word*	Write a copy of the current word (that's the one the pointer is on) on a piece of paper.
STOP	The message is now completed. You can stop searching for words.

The Computer Continuum

Having followed one series of instructions (computer specialists would call it a program) from the Word Hunt **instruction set**, we are now ready to see how these instructions can be converted into a form the computer can store in its memory. Suppose we assign a number to each of the different commands in our instruction set. Figure 2.3.18 shows what that would look like.

Now, if we want to write a Word Hunt program, we can do it with numbers. For example, **1 37** would mean **GOTO 37**, or **go to the top of page 37**. And **4 5** would mean the same as **BACKUP 5**, or **move the pointer 5 words back along the line**. Let's look at the previous Word Hunt program written in the new numeric code we've devised. See Figure 2.3.19.

Can you still follow the instructions? Do you get the same message using the numeric code as you did with the word commands? It should be the same, and we can now perform the final task of transforming the instructions into a form that the computer can use.

As you found out earlier in the chapter, all information, whether factual or instructional, must be converted into binary form before it can be stored in the computer's memory. Now that we have created a numeric version of our instruction set, conversion into binary form is easy. All the numbers in the program in Figure 2.3.19 can be translated into binary code using the chart given in Figure 2.2.7 earlier in the chapter. The resulting program, shown in Figure 2.3.20, is ready to be stored in the computer.

There are two main differences between our Word Hunt program and a computer program:

1. The computer's program would have originally been written in a programming language (there are a lot of them) rather than in English before being translated into binary code for the computer.

2. Each instruction in the instruction set would have to be something that the computer was capable of doing.

Every one of the instructions in a computer program is acted upon, or executed, in the given order to accomplish the desired result, just as our Word Hunt program instructions had to be followed in their proper order to get the correct hidden message.

Each of the many types of computers has a unique collection of instructions that it can understand. Even though instruction sets for different computers vary widely, they all contain the classes of instructions shown in Figure 2.3.21.

GOTO	6
SELECT	3
FORWARD	15
WRITE	word
SELECT	4
FORWARD	1
WRITE	word
GOTO	5
SELECT	24
FORWARD	10
WRITE	word
BACKUP	6
WRITE	word
STOP	

Figure 2.3.17
A Word Hunt program puzzle. Follow the instructions and find the message.

1 stands for	GOTO #
2 stands for	SELECT #
3 stands for	FORWARD #
4 stands for	BACKUP #
5 stands for	WRITE word
0 stands for	STOP

Figure 2.3.18
Assigning a number code to each Word Hunt instruction.

1	6
2	3
3	15
5	word
2	4
3	1
5	word
1	5
2	24
3	10
5	word
4	6
5	word
0	

Figure 2.3.19
Decimal code form of the program shown in Figure 2.3.18.

001	00110
010	00011
011	01111
101	
010	00100
011	00001
101	
001	00101
010	11000
011	01010
101	
100	00110
101	
000	

Figure 2.3.20
Program in Figure 2.3.19 translated into binary code.

Figure 2.3.21
Basic types of instructions.

> **Arithmetic Instructions**: These instructions involve addition, subtraction, multiplication, division, and other number-type operations.
>
> **Data Movement Instructions**: These instructions move numbers from place to place in the computer. For example, they may copy a number from a memory location to a place in the computer where it can be added.
>
> **Logical or Comparison Instructions**: These instructions are the decision-making instructions that cause different things to happen depending on certain conditions. For example, suppose a program is to count from 1 to 10. The computer will have a number in its memory that changes from 1 to 2…until it reaches 10. An instruction that will stop it at 10 would be used to compare the current value of that number with 10, and when it reaches 10, the program stops counting.
>
> **Control Instructions**: These instructions control the order in which instructions are performed or stop the program.
>
> **Input/Output Instructions**: These instructions allow the computer to communicate with the outside world. They provide a means for getting information into and out of the computer.

With the various types of instructions arranged in a certain order, computers can perform such tasks as printing payroll checks, controlling a robot's mechanical arm for a factory assembly-line job, or even controlling the landing of a rocket on Mars. What these collections of instructions or programs do and how they do it are topics for Chapter 5, "Computer Languages: Empowering Algorithms." At present, we're more concerned with how the instructions are represented in the computer.

All instructions must have an identifying code called the **operation code** or **opcode**. This opcode tells the computer what operation is to be performed. The number of bits needed to give this information depends on how many different instructions the computer is capable of doing. If the computer has only eight instructions, then only three binary bits are needed to represent each of them. Why? It's because eight different binary numbers can be expressed with three digits. Suppose the computer has over 100 different instructions. If there are fewer than 128 instructions, then seven bits will do the job because with 7 binary digits, we can count in binary from 0000000_{two} to 1111111_{two}. This is equivalent to counting in decimal from 0 to 127. A special meaning or instruction could be assigned to each different number.

In addition to the opcode, the computer must know the location of the object of the operation. For example, if an instruction is to add a number, the computer must know the location of that number. The object of the operation is commonly called the operand. Its location is most often given by means of an **address.** This address is analogous to our home address that the U.S. Postal Service uses to deliver mail. In the computer, the address indicates the location in the computer's memory where either a number is to be stored or retrieved or some other operation is to be performed.

The classes of operations that are not arithmetic need additional information, usually in the form of an address. Before getting too complicated, however, let's examine an actual **instruction**.

Let us assume, for this simple example, that we have a small computer capable of executing only 8 instructions and containing 32 different locations to store things such as numbers. The instructions could be represented in a total of eight bits—three for the opcode and five for the address. A typical instruction for this computer is shown in Figure 2.3.22.

This particular instruction tells the computer to add the number in location 11010_{two} to the accumulator. The other seven instructions for this simple computer would also have the same opcode and address form.

The Computer Continuum

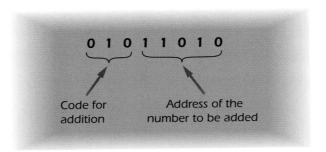

Figure 2.3.22
A typical instruction for a simple computer.

Before we leave the subject of the representation of instructions for now, a last and very important point must be made. How does the computer know that the 8 bits 01011010 for the ADD instruction shown represent an instruction? In fact, if we interpret them as an integer, it corresponds to the decimal number 90:

$$01011010_{two} = 2_6 + 2_4 + 2_3 + 2_1 = 64 + 16 + 8 + 2 = 90$$

We could even interpret the rightmost seven bits as an ASCII letter Z (refer to the table of ASCII codes in Figure 2.3.3), or maybe it could correspond to a particular sound or part of a picture. All of these interpretations are possible. After examining all of the possibilities, it is certain that a way out of this dilemma is needed. The solution is simple. We must tell the computer, within the program, exactly how the number is to be interpreted, whether it is an instruction, number, ASCII symbol, or whatever else. In other words, the program itself is written with the interpretation already determined.

2.4 Storage of Binary Information

We have seen how almost all imaginable forms of information can be expressed as binary numbers. Using programs, the computer is able to manipulate this information. The next question is where is all of this binary information kept or stored? This section examines the storage problem.

The table of **storage devices** in Figure 2.4.1 represents the many types of storage mediums (or media) available to computers. Each of them has its unique characteristics and satisfies certain computer storage needs. Aside from the fact that all the storage devices store binary numerals, the four most important characteristics of storage devices are

- Speed
- Cost
- Capacity
- Type of access

First, let's examine the characteristic of speed. What does the speed of a storage device indicate? It tells how fast the information can be taken from (*read from*) or stored in (*written to*) the storage device. The speed of a device is sometimes referred to as its **access time**.

The access time of a storage device is either

- The time it takes to get information from the device (read time) or
- The time it takes to put information into the device (write time)

Figure 2.4.1 *Relationships among various types of storage.*

Electronic	Magnetic	Optical	Other
Non-Reusable			
ROM	Magnetic ink	CD-ROM	Bar code
	Optical character-recognition media	Laser disk (analog)	Punched paper
		WORM	Holorith cards
Reusable			
RAM	Magnetic tape	Holographic	
	Cassette tape		
	Floppy disk		
	Hard disk		
	Removable disk cartridge		
	Digital audio tape		

The vast difference in access time for the various storage devices can easily be appreciated by looking at two extremes. The fastest devices for holding binary information are certain types of electronic circuits. They can be accessed in about 40 billionths of a second. At the other extreme are floppy disks, which take up to 1/2 second to reach full speed. At full speed, a floppy disk needs several thousandths of a second to access information. The vast difference between these two extremes probably doesn't mean that much to most people. Maybe an analogy would help to make it meaningful. Suppose a speed-reader capable of reading a 200-page paperback book in one hour is similar to the fastest electronic storage device. The slower floppy disk would then be equivalent to a person reading only one word per week! Now that's quite a difference. Imagine yourself as a computer reading data at one word per day when you could read a whole book in one hour. A lot of time would be wasted. It should be obvious that the fast storage device is needed to utilize the computer fully; otherwise, it would be sitting idle most of the time, waiting for data. Figure 2.4.2 shows a silicon computer chip, which contains 256,000 bits of fast electronic circuit memory. Each bit is represented by an electronic switch that is *on* or *off*, corresponding to the 0 or 1 in binary. The floppy disk type of storage device shown in Figure 2.4.3 is old but is still being used in most computers. It would appear that the electronic type of storage device is an obvious choice in any situation, but that is before we look at factors such as cost.

Figure 2.4.2
A typical microchip on a finger.

Figure 2.4.3
High-density 3 1/2" floppy disk.

The Computer Continuum

The two different storage examples represent the two major categories of data storage in a computer. These two categories are **primary storage** and **secondary storage**. It will be clear in the next chapter that for a computer to function, it must have both the program and the data in a storage area that is immediately accessible. This is called the primary storage, or memory, of the computer and is very fast. The reason why it's so fast is that it consists of electronic circuitry. Programs and data that are not in use can be stored outside the computer's immediate domain. This storage area is referred to as secondary storage and can be much slower. It's definitely significant—not of "primary" importance, but of only "secondary" importance to the computer's immediate operation.

Another important distinction in the types of electronic storage must be made between permanent and non-permanent storage. As discussed previously, the main electronic storage used by computers is called primary storage, or memory. This is where a program resides when it is being executed or used by a computer. The two common types of memory are **RAM (random-access memory)** and **ROM (read-only memory)**. If the power plug to a computer is accidentally pulled, all of the data in the RAM (non-permanent memory) disappears. The ROM (permanent memory) maintains its data even though the computer is turned off. This is where all of the programs and data needed to start a computer reside.

The fastest electronic circuitry-type memory costs about .00005 cent per bit, whereas other storage media are much less expensive. The magnetic tape secondary storage pictured in Figure 2.4.4 costs .00002 cent per bit. An even cheaper secondary storage is the **CD-ROM** at only .00000001 cent per bit.

A computer's **primary storage**, or memory, is where the data and program that are currently in operation or being accessed are stored during use. Primary storage is commonly made from electronic circuits.

A computer's **secondary storage** is where the original data and programs needed for the computer are stored. Secondary storage is on media external to the computer and commonly consists of floppy disks, hard disk drives, or CD-ROMs.

Figure 2.4.4
Magnetic tape reel with 2,400 feet of half-inch data storage tape.

RAM memory is a part of the primary storage, or memory, of the computer. Its contents are not permanent and can be changed. This characteristic is necessary so that different programs and data can be stored there. Also, if the power shuts off, RAM loses everything that was stored in it.

ROM memory is a part of the primary storage, or memory, of the computer. It is permanent memory. It keeps its contents forever and can never be changed, unless you unplug and replace it.

A CD-ROM can store 55 times more bits per disc than the entire reel of tape pictured at a fraction of the cost. The CD-ROM disc is essentially the same as the compact discs used for music. See Figure 2.4.5.

To put the various costs per bit into perspective, an analogy is certainly in order. Suppose each bit stored in an electronic circuit cost the same as a $50,000 automobile. The analogous CD-ROM bits would each cost about as much as a spark plug for this automobile. The huge difference in cost is one of the major factors keeping us from using more electronic circuitry-type memory. Also, putting a CD-ROM into a computer is much easier than putting in memory chips. It should be pointed out that game cartridges are ROM memory of the electronic variety.

Figure 2.4.5

CD-ROM disc that can store 640 megabytes of information.

To make an original CD-ROM, a laser burns tiny craters in the surface of the disc. A crater means 1 and no crater means 0. When getting the information back from a CD-ROM, a low-power laser, which can't burn craters, is used to "see" the craters. The low-power laser's beam is reflected (no crater) or not reflected (with the crater). A schematic of the CD-ROM's construction is shown in Figure 2.4.6.

Figure 2.4.6

A CD-ROM's layout.

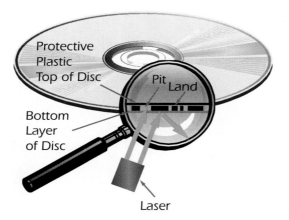

Nevertheless, we still haven't looked at another important factor: the physical size of the various storage types. The physical size or capacity of storage devices is certainly a significant factor. For example, storing the total contents of the Library of Congress on electronic circuit-type storage would not only cost more than the national budget, but also would occupy over an acre of floor space. On the other hand, special optical mass storage memories can hold trillions of bits and could easily fit into a typical computer center room. These storage systems can contain the total contents of the 35-acre, 20,000,000-volume Library of Congress.

Until the late 1980s, magnetic tape was the most common form for storing large amounts of data cheaply and in a relatively small space. When all the factors such as cost, capacity, and speed were taken into account, this seemed to be the most reasonable mass storage medium. Today, however, CD-ROM discs are rapidly replacing magnetic tapes for mass storage because of their smaller size, lower cost, higher capacity, and greater reliability.

How much computer memory does it take to store...	
One keystroke from the keyboard	1 byte
One line of word-processed text*	2.5 kilobytes (2,740 bytes)
One page single-spaced, unformatted text	4.0 kilobytes
Nineteen pages of formatted text with heads and subheads	75 kilobytes
Word processor, program alone	883 kilobytes
Spelling dictionary	258 kilobytes
Word-processing help file	468 kilobytes
Complete word processing package	8.4 megabytes (the latest versions take more)
Full-page black-and-white drawing	18–67 kilobytes, depending on complexity
Full-page color photo	4–6 megabytes
The word *good-bye*	3.2 kilobytes
One second of high-fidelity sound	95–110 kilobytes
This book, text only, no pictures	4.6 megabytes

How much data can be stored on...	
One inch of 1/2-inch wide magnetic tape	4 kilobytes
One 5 1/4" floppy disk, double sided, double density (MS-DOS)	360 kilobytes
One 3 1/2" floppy disk, double sided, double density (Macintosh))	800 kilobytes
One 3 1/2" floppy disk, high density	1.4 megabytes
One compact disc (CD-ROM)	640 megabytes
One 12" laser video disk (analog)	55,000 still color images, each taking 4–6 megabytes if digitized

A word processor saves any amount of text but allocates it in page-sized chunks.

Figure 2.4.7

Comparative storage requirements and capacities.

Finally, to make things even more complicated, there is another characteristic of memories that will determine how they are used. The two types considered here are **random access** and **sequential access**. With the random-access type of storage, we can instantly go into any part of the storage to either get (*read*) some information or *write* it. In contrast, with the sequential access storage, we must start at the beginning and go through the storage until we reach the information of interest. Magnetic tapes are of the latter type. As an example of what this means, imagine that we have stored the *Encyclopedia Britannica* on the magnetic tapes needed to get every word recorded. Now suppose we need information regarding Vladimir Kosma Zworykin, the U.S. electronics engineer acknowledged as the inventor of television. We would have to wind through the tape that contains the z entries from the beginning to reach the desired information. That would be analogous to flipping through all the pages one by one until page 1027 of Volume 23 of the 1970 edition appears. How tedious! Random access, on the other hand, corresponds more closely to the way we usually use the encyclopedia. In fact, we can go right to where the information is stored because we know that Zworykin would be at the end.

Of all the various types of storage devices for computers, those employing magnetic phenomena have, until now, been the most common. Whether the device is a magnetic tape, a floppy disk, or a hard disk, it uses the same physical principle: The material that holds the zeros and ones can be magnetized. It is easiest to visualize the individual 0s and 1s as

Random access to storage allows information to be obtained directly rather than by sifting through other information to reach it.

Sequential access to storage allows the desired information to be obtained by starting at the beginning of a list of information and then proceeding item by item until it is reached.

very tiny compasses that point only north and south. One direction (either north or south) corresponds to 1 and the other would be 0. A hard magnetic disk without its protective enclosure is shown in Figure 2.4.8. Unlike the popular magnetic floppy disk, the hard disk is rigid and is usually sealed into an enclosure. These hard magnetic disks have concentric circular tracks on which the 0s and 1s reside. Then a magnetic sensing device passes over the magnetized spots along a track and senses the 0s and 1s.

Figure 2.4.8

Magnetic hard disk used to store computer programs and data.

Many of these topics will be visited again as we investigate how a computer works. One final note about storage size is necessary. In all areas of computing, reference to the size of memory and storage devices is well defined. Although the **bit** (**binary digit**) is the smallest unit of storage, it is seldom used in describing storage size. The byte, which is eight bits, is the most common unit used. One byte can contain one ASCII character, with a bit left over. Some commonly used terms are found in Figure 2.4.9.

Figure 2.4.9

Commonly used words describing the size of storage devices.

1 nibble	4 bits
1 byte	8 bits
1 kilobyte	1,024 bytes (about one thousand bytes)
1 megabyte	1,048,576 bytes (about one million bytes)
1 gigabyte	1,073,741,824 bytes (about one billion bytes)
1 terabyte	About one trillion bytes

Finally, let's take a look at future storage devices. An advanced research project into storage devices at IBM sounds like science fiction. Remember the crystal storage devices from Star Trek, the holographic storage cubes in Issac Asimov's *Foundation* series, or the holograms of Star Wars? IBM research is currently working on storage cubes that use holographic technology. Everyone is familiar with the two-dimensional holographic stickers used on credit cards for security. The IBM storage device will be three-dimensional and use laser light to "read" and "write" it. Researches believe they can store a terabyte of data in a crystal cube about the size of a sugar cube. It would also be 10 times faster than today's fastest mass storage devices.

The Computer Continuum

Chapter Summary

What you can do with what you have learned:

- Categorize information into one of five areas.
- Distinguish between a numeral and a number.
- Count in decimal and binary.
- Represent a group of characters in a number of different ways in a computer.
- Convert text to binary.
- Follow a program to decode a message.
- Translate a program into binary.
- Make informed decisions about memory storage devices.

Key Terms and Review Questions

Key terms introduced in this chapter:

Information 2-6

Visual information 2-6

Numeric information 2-6

Character information 2-6

Audio information 2-6

Instructional information 2-6

Transformation of information 2-7

Representation of information 2-7

Numbers 2-7

Binary numbers 2-8

Binary circuits 2-8

Numeral 2-10

Decimal 2-11

Exponent 2-11

Character set 2-14

EBCDIC 2-15

ASCII 2-16

Control characters 2-16

Pixel (picture element) 2-16

Grayscale 2-16

Digitizer 2-18

DARMS 2-20

Hertz 2-21

Voltage 2-21

CD (compact disc) 2-22

DAT (digital audio tape) 2-22

Execute 2-24

Program 2-24

Word Hunt 2-24

Syntax 2-24

Instruction set 2-25

Arithmetic instructions 2-26

Data movement instructions 2-26

Logical or comparison instructions 2-26

Control instructions 2-26

Input/output instructions 2-26

Opcode (operation code) 2-26

Address 2-26

Instruction 2-26

Storage devices 2-27

Access time 2-27

Primary storage 2-29

Secondary storage 2-29

RAM (random-access memory) 2-29

ROM (read-only memory) 2-29

CD-ROM 2-29

Random access 2-31

Matching

Match the key terms introduced in the chapter to the statements below. Each term may be used once, more than once, or not at all.

1. _____This must first be done to information before it can be stored or used by a computer.

2. _____This is the number system that modern computers use to represent information.

3. _____These are electronic devices used in computers that assume only two states.

4. _____This is another name for base 10.

5. _____This is another name for base 2.

6. _____This is the name given to each digit in binary.

7. _____All personal computers use this code.

8. _____IBM mainframes use this code.

9. _____These special characters are generally not printable.

10. _____This is known as the building block of a picture.

11. _____This is also known as a picture element.

12. _____This device converts a picture into numeric form.

13. _____When each pixel assumes more shades than pure white or black, it is said to have this.

14. _____This is a form of musical representation.

15. _____The speaker produces sound because this sound information is being carried on a wire.

16. _____This is the name given to a set of binary instructions, which the computer can follow.

17. _____This unit of measurement indicates the number of cycles per second a particular sound vibrates.

18. _____This type of access allows information to be obtained directly.

19. _____This type of access allows information to be obtained by starting at the beginning of a list of information and then proceeding item by item until it is reached.

20. _____This is the name given to each digit in binary.

True or False

1. _____ Information must first be transformed into a binary representation of that information before it can be stored in the computer's memory.

2. _____ Number means the same as numeral.

3. _____ ANSI standardized the character set that is now being used by all personal computers.

4. _____ Standard codes such as EBCDIC assign a different number to every word or groupings of characters. These words are recorded in a large dictionary that is accessed each time words are entered in a word processing document.

5. _____ The standard EBCDIC codes and the standard ASCII codes are identical.

6. _____ The ASCII set of codes includes all the characters that can be typed at the keyboard plus others that represent characters you can't even see.

7. _____ In a picture, only those pixels that have values of 1 need to be stored. Pixels that have the value of 0 need not be stored because ink will not be necessary at that spot.

8. _____ More memory is needed for grayscale pictures than for pictures that have black and white pixels.

9. _____ Because the pixels of grayscale images can be one of many shades of gray, grayscale pictures need more memory than color pictures.

10. _____ All current music stored within the computer uses the form of musical representation called DARMS.

11. _____ Both CD players and DAT recorder/players use binary information to produce sounds through the speakers.

12. _____ Because CD players read the information from the disc using a laser beam, eventually the recordings will show signs of wear.

13. _____ Another name for operation code is opcode.

14. _____ The two parts of an instruction are the operation code and the address.

15. _____ The four most important characteristics of memory devices are speed, cost, capacity, and manufacturer.

16. _____ The memory storage that has the fastest access time is also the least expensive.

17. _____ Storing the contents of the Library of Congress on electronic circuit-type storage would take up less room than storing the same amount of information on optical mass storage media.

18. _____ Random access-type storage is synonymous with RAM.

19. _____ An example of a device that uses random access is the popular magnetic disk.

20. _____ An example of a device that uses sequential access is magnetic tape.

Multiple Choice

Answer the multiple choice questions by selecting the best answer from the choices given.

1. Which of the following is not one of the five types of information that can be stored within a computer?
   a. Numbers
   b. Visual
   c. Audio
   d. Tactile
   e. Characters

2. How many different symbols are used in the binary system?
   a. None
   b. 1
   c. 2
   d. 4
   e. Infinite number

3. How many different symbols are used in the decimal system?
   a. None
   b. 9
   c. 10
   d. 100
   e. Infinite number

4. How would the number 40 be represented in the computer? (You need to translate it into a binary number.)
   a. 11_{two}
   b. 101_{two}
   c. 10100_{two}
   d. 101000_{two}
   e. 100111_{two}

5. Translate the following base 2 number to base 10: 110011_{two}.
   a. 24
   b. 25

   c. 50
   d. 51
   e. 99

6. For what does the acronym EBCDIC stand?
   a. Extended Binary Coded Decimal Interchange Code
   b. Extensive Binary Character Decoding Interface Code
   c. Easy Binary Characteristic Decision Installation Code
   d. Einstein's Binary Conditional Decoding Intellectual Code
   e. Everyday Binary Commercial Dedicated Interface Code

7. For what does the acronym ASCII stand?
   a. Associated Society Coded Instruction Interface
   b. Annotated Script Coded Instruction Icons
   c. American Standard Code for Information Interchange
   d. American Sentry Character Internal Information
   e. Assignment of System Codes for Internal Information

8. Which of the following Word Hunt commands instructs you to find a particular page?
   a. GOTO #
   b. FORWARD #
   c. SELECT #
   d. BACKUP #
   e. PAGE #

9. The two parts of each instruction are

    a. Inside and outside

    b. High-end and low-end

    c. Command and operative

    d. Opcode and operand

    e. Control and comparison

10. The least expensive means to store information is

    a. CD-ROM

    b. Electronic circuitry

    c. Magnetic tape

    d. Hard disk

    e. Floppy disk

Exercises

1. Classify the following items into one of the five categories of information:

    A clap of thunder
    The text of Crime and Punishment
    Automobile mileage
    Honking of a car horn
    Tarzan's yell
    The score of a football game
    A satellite weather map
    Computer-animated cartoon
    A recording of a flute solo
    Pattern in a stained glass window
    A special fudge recipe
    The shape of traffic signs

2. Consider the following:

    1001110 1001111

    a. What is it when interpreted as ASCII symbols?

    b. What is it when interpreted as a binary number or numbers?

    c. Would the answers to (a) and (b) change if it were written as 10011101001111?

3. Decode the following ASCII message:

    1010100 1001000 1001001 1010011 0100000

    1001001 1010011 0100000 1000001 0100000

    1010011 1010100 1010101 1010000 1001001

    1000100 0100000 1010000 1010010 1001111

    1000010 1001100 1000101 1001101 0100001

4. Decode the following ASCII message:

    1010100 1101111 0100000 1100010 1100101

    0100000 1101111 1110010 0100000 1101110

    1101111 1110100 0100000 1110100 1101111

    0100000 1100010 1100101 0101100 0100000

    1110100 1101000 1100001 1110100 0100000

    1101001 1110011 0100000 1110100 1101000

    1100101 0100000 1110001 1110101 1100101

    1110011 1110100 1101001 1101111 1101110

    0100001

5. Find and use a table of EBCDIC codes to decode the following message (Why can't you use the ASCII table?):

    C7 C1 D9 C2 C1 C7 C5 40 C9 D5 6B 40

    C7 C1 D9 C2 C1 C7 C5 40 D6 E4 E3 4B

6. Estimate the number of words in your favorite dictionary. Assuming the average word length is five letters, calculate the total number of characters. How many bits of information is this

    a. Using ASCII?

    b. Using EBCDIC?

7. Estimate the number of words in your school library. Assuming the average word length is five letters, calculate the total number of characters. How many bits of information is this

   a. Using ASCII?

   b. Using EBCDIC?

8. Use the ASCII chart to write a secret message. Include the answer!

9. Represent each of the following words as a sequence of numbers using the example of Figure 2.3.1:

   a. JUMP

   b. TAKE

   c. HELLO

   d. ZIP

10. Represent each of the following words as a sequence of binary numbers using the ASCII code from Figure 2.3.3:

    a. JUMP

    b. TAKE

    c. HELLO

    d. ZIP

11. When typing the number 173 at a computer keyboard, the actual binary information sent to the computer is (assuming an ASCII character set)

    0110001 0110111 0110011

    If we could peer into the storage and see how the computer actually saved the information (assuming the computer was expecting to take a number), we would see

    10101101

    Why do you suppose these two are different?

12. In Figure 2.4.9, one kilobyte is actually 1,024 bytes, and one megabyte is actually 1,048,576. Why aren't they exactly 1,000 and exactly 1,000,000? Hint: It has to do with binary numbers, in particular, powers of 2.

13. In the table of Figure 2.4.9, the exact size of a terabyte is not given. It is not 1,000,000,000,000 (one trillion) as you might expect. Calculate the exact number of bytes that are in one terabyte. You can use the results of the previous problem.

14. Design your own three-initial monogram using a 9×12 size block for each letter.

15. Explain how the counting from 1 to 10 is done in the intergalactic message. Hint: The counting is done in binary.

16. Using a computer hardware catalog, or from a WWW site, find information for three different types of memory devices. List the product name, the type of device (such as hard disk, CD-ROM reader, or removable media storage device), the manufacturer, the speed of the device (access time), capacity, cost, and type of access (random or sequential access) for each of the devices.

17. Name three ways pictorial information can be stored in a computer.

18. Name three ways audio information can be stored in a computer.

19. What are the three ways computers deal with information as described in this chapter?

20. Classify each of the Word Hunt commands as either arithmetic, data movement, logical/comparison, control, or input/output instructions.

21. Make up a table of typical storage capacities for various devices, and calculate the number of units of each needed to store information described in Exercises 12 and 13.

Discussion Questions

1. Can you think of any information that does not fit into one of the five categories mentioned in this chapter?

2. Why do you think the DARMS method of musical representation is no longer in use? What problems can you see in learning to play from it?

3. When the technology for computer memory improved, the price to the consumer dropped accordingly. Do you think improvements in communication technology will cause a drop in communication rates (such as telephone, fax, pagers, and so on)? Why or why not?

4. In the Word Hunt program, do you see any problem with using the BACKUP instruction immediately after using the FORWARD instruction? What are all the possibilities of what might happen? What would be the best of those possibilities and why is it the best one?

5. Are "thoughts" and "emotions" information? Do they fit any of the five categories? Is a thing or entity (such as a chair) information?

6. Consider the following chart. Do you think we will need a prefix bigger than yotta? Why or why not?

Metric System - Prefixes, Unit Symbols, Powers of Ten, Multipliers						
deka	(da)	=	10^1	=	10	ten
hekto	(h)	=	10^2	=	100	hundred
kilo	(k)	=	10^3	=	1,000	thousand
mega	(M)	=	10^6	=	1,000,000	million
giga	(G)	=	10^9	=	1,000,000,000	billion
tera	(T)	=	10^{12}	=	1,000,000,000,000	trillion
peta	(P)	=	10^{15}	=	1,000,000,000,000,000	quadrillion
exa	(E)	=	10^{18}	=	1,000,000,000,000,000,000	quintillion
zetta	(Z)	=	10^{21}	=	1,000,000,000,000,000,000,000	sextillion
yotta	(Y)	=	10^{24}	=	1,000,000,000,000,000,000,000,000	septillion

Group Project

Each person in a group of four is to research and prepare materials for the group about a single cryptographic system. Some suggestions include Caesar cipher, Morse code, Playfair square, and semaphore signals. Each individual should encode a single message using all four cryptographic schemes. The other members of the group will decode the message as a team under the guidance of the author of the coded message.

Web Connections

http://web.ansi.org/

The home page for all ANSI standards and information.

http://www.realtime-info.be/

A real-time encyclopedia.

http://www.firmware.com/pb4ts/megabyte.htm

Description of the uses and conversion formulas for megabytes.

http://www.firmware.com/pb4ts/metric.htm

Explains measurement terms used in computers including terms for measuring memory sizes, data storage capacity, data transmission bandwidth, processor speed, and ratings of electronic components.

http://207.61.52.15:80/andrew/

Binary conversions to hexadecimal, octal, and decimal. Also has links to using binary to code and decode text messages.

Bibliography

Singh, Jagjit, *Great Ideas in Information Theory, Language, and Cybernetics*, New York: Dover Publications, 1966.

An accessible discussion of information theory.

Wrixon, Fred B., *Codes, Ciphers, and Secret Languages*, New York: Bonanza Books, 1989.

A fun approach to codes and ciphers from ancient Egypt to present day.

Bauer, F. L., *Decrypted Secrets—Methods and Maxims of Cryptology*, New York: Springer-Verlag, 1997.

A complete discussion of the world of cryptology.

C h a p t e r   3

1936 The concept of a computer memory to hold binary information is developed by Konrad Zuse.

1944 The first electronic digital computer, ENIAC, performs its first computations.

1945 John von Neumann introduces the concept of a stored program in a draft report on the EDVAC computer.

1952 Univac I predicts the outcome of the presidential election on television, and the public consciousness about computers is raised.

1961 IBM's Stretch supercomputer runs 30 times faster than the 704. This spurs further research in supercomputing.

1962 Integrated circuit is nicknamed the "chip."

1964 The first successful supercomputer, the CDC 6600, is produced.

1971 The "computer on a chip," the Intel 4004 microprocessor, is developed.

1972 Slide rules become obsolete as handheld calculators become popular.

1977 The benchmark for personal computers, the Apple II, is announced.

1980 The Osborne 1, a "portable" computer weighing 24 lbs., is introduced.

1982 The Cray X-MP supercomputer proves to be three times faster than a Cray-1.

1985 Supercomputer speeds reach 1 billion operations per second.

1994 The concept of DNA as a computing medium is demonstrated by Leonard Adleman.

2010 The first quantum mechanical computer is constructed.

From Stonehenge to the Supercomputer

Chapter Objectives

By the end of this chapter, you will:

- @ Realize how machine language forms the basis of all computer programs.

- @ Understand how the stored-program computer stores both programs and needed information.

- @ Discern the uses and limitations of the ROBOT computer.

- @ Know how the ROBOT's instruction decoder converts a ROBOT instruction into an action and an address.

- @ Recognize how a computer language's instruction set defines the uses of that language.

- @ Know how a program is loaded into a computer's memory.

- @ Identify the four basic units of a typical computer.

- @ Identify the three basic units of a CPU.

- @ Understand how the fetch-and-execute cycle works.

- @ Realize the difference between loading a program and executing the program.

- @ Know the ways different types of computers can be compared.

- @ Discern the differences between microcomputers, mini-computers, mainframe computers, and supercomputers.

- @ Understand the advantages and disadvantages of a supercomputer.

3.1 The Stored-Program Computer

In the previous chapter, we spent a considerable amount of time and space discussing how computers could store all types of information, including instructions, in their memories. Our next concern is how computers work with what is stored.

One thing is certain from the very beginning: Computers are not able to do anything with the information they have stored until they are given instructions for processing it. We call these collections of instructions computer **programs**.

A program is a collection of instructions for the computer to perform one-by-one.

As we know from Chapter 2, "Metamorphosis of Information," the information computers contain and manipulate must be in a binary form. This means that any instructions used by the computer must also be represented in binary. Actually, this is not a completely new concept. The Word Hunt program developed in Chapter 2 is not far removed from the computer programs to be discussed here. The main difference is that the instructions in the Word Hunt are meant to be followed by people, not by computers. The original instructions were written in English rather than some programming language. Other than that, however, there are some important similarities. Let's look at a few:

- The Word Hunt instructions, like those in all programs of any kind, must be performed sequentially, in the order written. If the Word Hunt instructions were performed out of order, you would find a wrong message. Also, computer instructions executed out of order would not produce the desired results.

- Whether the instructions are intended for humans or for computers, each must have a specific definition. Neither the person following the Word Hunt nor the computer following a program would get far without understanding exactly what the instructions mean.

- Both Word Hunt instructions and computer instructions are frequently split into two segments. In the Word Hunt program, these segments were called the action and the object. In computer terminology, they are usually called the **opcode**, or **operation code**, and the **operand** or **argument**. Also, no matter which instruction set you examine, some instructions (such as the WRITE and STOP instructions in the Word Hunt) ignore the operand part of the instruction.

- It is possible to convert both Word Hunt programs and computer programs into binary form by first assigning a numeric value to each instruction.

Machine language is the form that all instructions must be in before the computer can follow them. This form consists of binary numbers or binary code.

When a program is in a binary form that the computer can use directly, it is referred to as a **machine language** program. In other words, the program is in the language of the computing machine, hence the name machine language. Machine language can be used immediately by the computer. The machine language for all computers is written in binary form.

A stored-program computer is a computing device with a place to keep information needed for computing—the memory of the computer. This memory stores both programs (the instructions of what to do) and the information needed for computing by the program.

In the next two sections of this chapter, two simple computing devices are examined. Each of them will help to illustrate the principles fundamental to the so-called **stored-program computer**. The conceptual computers presented in the next two sections are examples of what are commonly called **von Neumann-type computers**, after the famous mathematician John von Neumann.

The first of these special imaginary computers is a programmable robot. Robots seem to have a universal appeal. Human beings can relate to a robot because of the robot's similarity to themselves yet still feel superior because the robot merely acts and does not think.

John von Neumann

Johnny von Neumann (1903–1957) was unmistakably one of the brightest minds of the twentieth century, a true genius. A mathematician by training, he made major contributions in many fields of science, including computer science. In the late war years around 1944, von Neumann had the responsibility to seek ways to make calculations in several areas of science related to the war effort. During his search, he learned of the ENIAC (Electronic Numerical Integrator and Computer) project at the University of Pennsylvania. It was too late to be involved with ENIAC's design, which started in 1943, but von Neumann's brilliance and understanding of the problems to be solved made him a major player in the subsequent computer called the EDVAC (Electronic Discrete Variable Automatic Computer). This project resulted in a report authored by von Neumann titled "First Draft of a Report on the EDVAC." The report, written in the spring of 1945, detailed the concepts of the stored-program computer and was a summary of many individuals' ideas. In spite of this, von Neumann was given credit for most of the concepts, and in fact, the general form of almost all other computers today is referred to as the von Neumann computer. (The supercomputer is not included in this category.)

The other computer abstraction in this chapter is actually an imaginary model of an ordinary computer. We call it the **Pencil and Paper computer**. It has all the functional units and capabilities needed to qualify it as a classic digital computer, but it functions only as we execute the steps of its program one-by-one.

A study of these two conceptual computers should help you gain a clear understanding of how computers obey instructions and how they manipulate information. Although these are two simplified imaginary machines, many similarities exist between them and all other computers. In the last part of this chapter, we look at those similarities and consider the characteristics that all digital computers possess.

3.2 The ROBOT Computer: Programs and Algorithms

Our first example of a computer, the **ROBOT** (see Figure 3.2.1) is rather specialized and not very useful. It can move around its domain, raise and lower its arms, and "know" whether it is facing up against a wall. In fact, to call the ROBOT a computer at all is a little pretentious. However, our objective is to introduce you to some of the typical concepts and quirks of the computing world. The ROBOT's limited repertoire of activities helps us to focus on the concepts rather than on performing difficult and complex tasks. The ROBOT's very simplicity makes it a compact and appealing tool for our purposes.

The ROBOT's Domain

Before we can understand the ROBOT or tell it what to do, we must first have a clear picture of the domain, or environment, in which it operates. Imagine, first, an empty room, free of furniture or other obstruction. The room is rectangular, having four walls. There may be one or more openings in the walls. We'll refer to any openings as doors, although technically, they are doorways, with no means of being closed. The floor of the room is paved in square tiles. Lines delineating the tiles run parallel to the walls and are easy to see. Any doors present are exactly one tile wide.

Figure 3.2.1
The ROBOT in its domain.

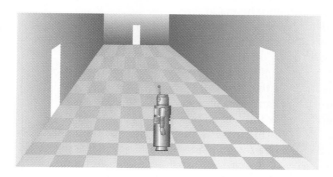

Most of the ROBOT's movements and capabilities are closely related to the characteristics of its domain. For example, when the ROBOT takes a step, it moves from one square floor tile to an adjacent tile. When it turns, it pivots its body but remains standing on the same tile. The ROBOT can never straddle two tiles or come to a stop standing on a line. Likewise, the walls limit certain activities of the ROBOT. They determine how far it can go in any one direction. Because the ROBOT's arms are exactly as long as the side of a tile, the ROBOT will never be able to raise its arms if it is standing next to the wall it is facing. It cannot take a step if it is up against a wall, unless it is in a doorway. A step through a doorway leads to destruction.

The size of the ROBOT's room is unknown to us at any given time. It can be any number of square tiles by any number of square tiles. In fact, the room may be a different size and shape for every different problem the ROBOT faces. In addition, the doors in the walls may be positioned differently, depending on the room's size. We can be certain of only two things: first, that the room's dimensions will not change during the execution of a program and second, that any doors present will never be located in the exact corners of the room. The reason for this has to do with one of the characteristics of a ROBOT program, which we will now discuss.

Programming the ROBOT

To "program the ROBOT" means to devise a sequence of instructions for the ROBOT, a sequence that is designed to solve some specific problem. Such a sequence of instructions is called a program.

To know what tasks are reasonable for the ROBOT, we need to know more specifically what the ROBOT's characteristics and capabilities are. Once we know what individual actions the ROBOT can perform, then we can speculate on what types of tasks it is capable of doing. For example, if we discover that the ROBOT cannot add two numbers, then we will immediately reject the possibility that it could balance our checkbooks for us.

ROBOT Characteristics

The ROBOT is capable of movement from square to square within its domain. We refer to a single such action as a *step*. All steps are taken in a direction parallel to two walls of the room and in the direction that the ROBOT faces. Diagonal steps are not possible, nor can the ROBOT step sideways or backwards. The ROBOT can also turn, but only to the right and only 90 degrees at a time.

The ROBOT is capable of raising and lowering its arms in front of it. When raised, the arms are at right angles to the ROBOT's torso and parallel to the floor of the room. When the ROBOT's arms are extended, they reach to the far edge of the next square in front of the ROBOT. (That is, the ROBOT technically occupies two squares when its arms are extended.) A consequence of this is that if the ROBOT is in a position such as that shown in Figure 3.2.2, it cannot take a step forward because the arms are touching the wall in front of it. In fact, when the ROBOT occupies a square that is immediately adjacent to a wall, it is impossible for it to raise its arms. There just isn't enough room!

Figure 3.2.2
The ROBOT one step away from the wall with arms raised.

The ROBOT is equipped with special sensors, located at the ends of its arms. These devices are capable of sensing the presence of a wall when the ROBOT is positioned as shown in Figure 3.2.2. The sensors activate if the ROBOT is directed to carry out the command SENSE, which causes it to try to sense the wall.

The ROBOT has no intelligence. It cannot think or plan its own activities. In fact, the ROBOT is capable of only following a program of instructions that it retrieves from its memory and then executes.

That last sentence sounds simple enough but contains several difficult (and important) concepts. Let's analyze the internal workings of the ROBOT a little more closely in terms of that statement. The ROBOT has a **memory**. In that memory are stored the **instructions** that make up a program. In addition, the ROBOT is equipped with circuits, which enable it to **fetch** instructions from its memory, interpret or **decode** their meaning, and **execute** them. What do the bold terms mean?

Memory—The ROBOT's memory is quite tiny. It contains 32 memory locations, numbered consecutively from 0 to 31. Each memory location is capable of storing a single ROBOT instruction.

Instructions—The ROBOT does not understand human speech or, for that matter, any written language. It understands only binary numbers, each eight bits in length. Each possible combination of the eight binary digits is a meaningful instruction to the ROBOT.

Fetch—The ROBOT's circuits cause it to fetch (or retrieve) its instructions from memory, one at a time, and usually in the order in which they are stored. (There is one exception to this, which involves a special command called the GOTO command; for the full story, see the explanation of the individual commands and the sample programs.)

Decode—The ROBOT knows what action to carry out for a given binary number because it contains an instruction decoder. Such a unit is present in one form or another in all digital computers. The instruction decoder is a set of circuits, which causes the appropriate actions to be taken based on the particular binary number that is received as input. In most cases, the decoder circuits may be required to split apart a given binary number into two or more parts in order to interpret the instruction represented by the number. Each ROBOT instruction must be split into two segments as shown in Figure 3.2.3. The action or command part of each instruction is actually represented by the first three binary digits, starting from the left. The remaining five bits are nearly always ignored by the ROBOT.

Figure 3.2.3
The ROBOT's instruction format.

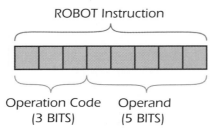

ROBOT Instruction

Operation Code
(3 BITS)

Operand
(5 BITS)

Execute—The ROBOT executes the instructions by carrying out the action or command that each individual instruction represents. Each instruction has its own particular purpose and characteristics. Some instructions cause the ROBOT to take an observable action. For example, 00000000 causes the ROBOT to take one step forward. Instructions of this type may cause different results depending on where the ROBOT is located; this is what makes programming the ROBOT both interesting and a little tricky. For example, if the ROBOT is directly in front of a wall, the 00000000 instruction causes it to spin its wheels and wear them out, much to the detriment of the ROBOT and the wall!

ROBOT Language

The ROBOT's language consists of eight different commands. These commands are referred to as the ROBOT's **instruction set.** Like the ROBOT and the Word Hunt game in the previous chapter, every different type of computer has its own instruction set.

Each ROBOT instruction consists of an eight-bit binary number. Up to 32 ROBOT instructions may be stored in the ROBOT's memory, forming a ROBOT program.

Each ROBOT instruction consists of two separate portions, or **fields**. This is illustrated in Figure 3.2.3. The first three bits form the command or opcode field. The opcode, or operation code, dictates the action to be taken by the ROBOT as a result of the instruction. The last five bits are almost always ignored, except in one instruction. These last five bits form the so-called argument or operand field, which is the address of a position in the memory. This argument or operand is extra information required in order to carry out the action indicated.

ROBOT Programs

The list of instructions, which the ROBOT has stored in its memory, can be determined and changed by the person who operates the ROBOT. The particular list of instructions that is currently stored is referred to as the ROBOT's program, and it must be placed into the ROBOT's memory before any execution can take place.

To place programs into the ROBOT, you must have some sort of access to the ROBOT's memory. The memory unit is located on the left side of the ROBOT's torso, and a door on that side opens to allow access. Each memory location is represented by a row of eight toggle switches, in which one eight-bit number representing an instruction can be stored. When one of these switches is turned on, the bit in that position has a value of 1; when the switch is off, the bit has a value of 0 (zero). In this case, a bit is on when the switch is up and off when the switch is down. Figure 3.2.4 shows the memory unit with six eight-bit instructions. At the moment, we're not concerned with what actions these represent, just how they are entered. The top-right configuration 01100000 (at memory location 10000), for example, represents the instruction for the ROBOT to lower its arms.

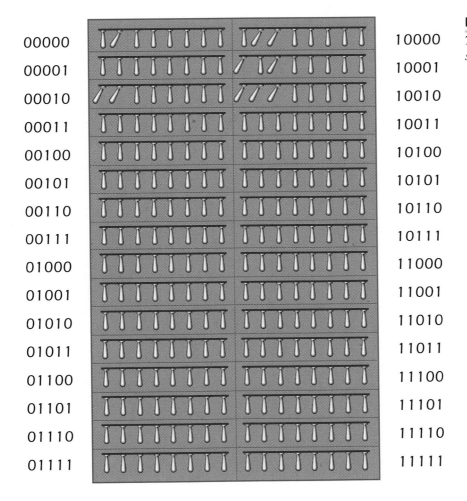

00000	10000
00001	10001
00010	10010
00011	10011
00100	10100
00101	10101
00110	10110
00111	10111
01000	11000
01001	11001
01010	11010
01011	11011
01100	11100
01101	11101
01110	11110
01111	11111

Figure 3.2.4
The ROBOT's memory switches.

The process of setting the value in each memory location to conform to a particular program is referred to as **loading** the program. All computers must load programs before they can do anything. When all the instructions of a program are loaded, the programmer closes the door to the memory bay and presses the ROBOT's START button. The ROBOT can then begin to execute the program.

As noted earlier, there are exactly 32 memory positions. They are numbered from 0 to 31, using the binary numerals from 00000 to 11111. The memory position numbers in the ROBOT's memory bank in Figure 3.2.4 start in the upper left and are numbered down the first column and then on to the second column. When a program is executed, the instructions are performed in the order of step number, starting with the instruction stored at location 00000.

One of the ROBOT commands is designed to allow the ROBOT to take instructions out of normal order. This command or opcode has the binary code 101. When used within an instruction, its operand (the last five bits of the instruction) indicates the step number (memory location) from which the next instruction is to be taken.

The table of commands in Figure 3.2.5 lists each possible value for the three-bit opcode of an instruction with a single English word that suggests the action taken by the ROBOT. Opposite each opcode is an explanation of the possible actions that can result from using that command in an instruction. We will refer to this set of commands as the instruction set.

Figure 3.2.5 *The ROBOT's instruction set.*

Command	(English)	Action
000	**(STEP)**	The ROBOT takes a step forward if possible. If not, the ROBOT remains where it is. A step is considered to be impossible if the ROBOT faces a wall and is up against it with arms lowered or if the ROBOT faces a wall and is one step away with arms raised.
001	**(TURN)**	The ROBOT turns 90 degrees to the right if it is able. It is considered unable to turn if there is a wall to its immediate right and its arms are raised.
010	**(RAISE)**	The ROBOT raises its arms if possible. If it cannot raise its arms, it turns on its warning light. If its arms are already raised, it does nothing.
011	**(LOWER)**	The ROBOT lowers its arms if they are raised; otherwise, it does nothing.
100	**(SENSE)**	If the ROBOT's arms are raised and it is a step away from the wall it is facing, then this command will cause it to turn on its warning light. (It senses the wall.) In any other circumstances, the command is ignored.
101	**(GOTO)**	The ROBOT will take its next command out of normal order. (The last five bits of this command tell it which memory location to take the command from.)
110	**(LIGHT)**	If the warning light is on, this command causes the ROBOT to turn it off. Important note: When the warning light is on, the ROBOT ignores every instruction except LIGHT. Also, when the ROBOT first has its power switch turned on, the warning light is set to off.
111	**(STOP)**	The ROBOT shuts off its own power.

Finally, the ROBOT is equipped with a special red warning light on top of its head. When the ROBOT's power switch is activated, the warning light is off, but certain situations cause it to be turned on. When the warning light is on, the ROBOT ignores all instructions except one, the one containing the LIGHT command. As we shall see, this feature gives the ROBOT a limited decision-making capability.

The ROBOT language is a reasonably good example of a low-level language. The term *low level* is used when referring to the language used directly by a computing mechanism—the so-called machine language. You should notice two distinctive features of this type of language:

1. It is distinctly non-symbolic. Usually, it consists entirely of binary numbers.

2. It is quite pedestrian; that is, each instruction in the language produces a small effect, and, therefore, getting the machine to do anything significant takes a lot of instructions.

People usually refer to machine language as a low-level language for these reasons. In terms of attacking any type of problem, the language of the machine has a low level of efficiency: It takes a lot of machine instructions to cause a computer to accomplish anything interesting or to perform a problem-oriented task.

Using the ROBOT

We now know a lot of detail about the ROBOT but hardly anything about how to make it perform. The best way to learn how to use a machine-level language is to solve a series of problems of gradually increasing difficulty. That is exactly what we are going to do with the ROBOT now. Because certain concepts that have general application in any computing situation will arise as we proceed, we will attempt to highlight those ideas as they occur. These concepts follow:

Program

Problem

Solution

Algorithm

Conditions

Loops

Infinite loops

Escape from loops

First, to review a few key ideas discussed previously: A program is a sequence of instructions designed to carry out a task. We may describe a potential task for the ROBOT by calling it a **problem.** The **solution** to the problem is expressed ultimately by the program. However, to arrive at the program, we must proceed through fairly detailed logical thinking along the way, and in so doing, devise a general method for approaching the problem or even several related problems at once. Such a method, expressed in clear and precise logical steps, is called an **algorithm.** This term is one of the words most commonly used by computer scientists and programmers. We shall refer to it more than once in this text.

> An **algorithm** is a step-by-step process used to solve a problem. It is essentially the solution to the problem and is usually implemented by a program.

To illustrate these ideas, let's examine a series of problems for the ROBOT and then plan their solutions (algorithms). Finally, we will write the program that follows each algorithm.

PROBLEM #1: Cause the ROBOT to walk to the wall it is initially facing and then stop with its arms lowered and facing against the wall. Assume the ROBOT is not initially facing an open doorway.

A few thoughts may occur to you during the process of solving this problem, or as we should say, creating the algorithm to solve the problem. Does stop mean turn off power or just come to a halt? Should we assume that the ROBOT's arms are lowered to begin with? How far is the ROBOT from the wall to begin with?

If you thought of any of these, pat yourself on the back! You are properly analytical. Let's establish some of the necessary ground rules by answering these questions:

- By *stop,* we mean literally turn itself off by executing the instruction 11100000.
- We will make only two assumptions about the ROBOT's initial or starting configuration. We can assume its arms are down at the start of any program and it is not facing a doorway.
- We make no assumptions about the distance of the ROBOT from the wall.

Let us begin our problem analysis by addressing the last point: We don't know how far the ROBOT is from the wall. The obvious way to solve this problem is to count the number of squares to the nearest wall and then enter the program shown in Figure 3.2.6.

Figure 3.2.6 *Program to get the ROBOT to the wall with an inferior algorithm.*

Memory Location	Command	Explanation
0	00000000	STEP
1	00000000	STEP
—	00000000	STEP
—	11100000	STOP

An algorithm should be *general.* This means it should solve the stated problem in all situations.

In other words, we could just instruct the ROBOT to take the correct number of steps and then stop. There are at least two difficulties with this: First, it won't work if the ROBOT is more than 31 steps from the nearest wall, and second, it is not very general. It will work only with a specified number of steps. We would have to write a separate program for every possible number of steps the ROBOT can be from the wall. A good algorithm or solution to the problem should be general.

In programs, **loops** are sequences of instructions that are repeated one or more times when the program is executed.

What we are after is a single program that will work in all circumstances. Let's attack the problem of not knowing how many steps from the wall the ROBOT is to begin with. What if we could put one 00000000 (STEP) instruction in the program and get the ROBOT to repeat STEP until it gets to the wall? That way, we wouldn't need to know exactly how far from the wall the ROBOT was to begin with. We need a way to make the ROBOT repeat an instruction. What we have in mind is called a **loop.**

The ROBOT has an instruction that will cause it to repeat some earlier steps in a program. The opcode 101 (GOTO), followed by a five-bit step number, causes the ROBOT to execute the instructions starting at that step number stated. Let's try the program shown in Figure 3.2.7.

Figure 3.2.7 *Program to get the ROBOT to the wall using a loop.*

Memory Location	Command	Explanation
0	00000000	STEP
1	10100000	GOTO location 0
2	11100000	STOP

It certainly is short! The instruction at 00000 causes the ROBOT to step (does it always?), and the instruction at 00001 causes the ROBOT to go back and do step 00000 over again. Then the instruction at 00010 causes the ROBOT to stop. Well, it sounds good. What's wrong with this program? Hint: There is more than one thing wrong!

Our second try certainly overcomes the objection to our first try regarding the distance to the wall. The second program does not put any limit on the number of times the 00000000 (STEP) instruction is carried out—and there is its difficulty. The first two instructions in this trial solution will be executed over and over and over and over and…. This is an example of an **infinite loop**. There is no way to escape from the loop. Running this program is going to be hard on the ROBOT's batteries! Besides, when the ROBOT does reach a wall (and it could do that at any time), it will wear out its wheels trying to take steps that are impossible.

We now seem to be caught in a dilemma; we need a loop to account for different distances to the wall, yet our proposed solution loops forever! We need some way to have the ROBOT stop as soon as it reaches the wall. Let's look back at everything we know about the ROBOT and see if there is any way it can "know" when it gets to a wall.

Reviewing the commands or opcodes in the table of instructions given earlier, we see that the opcode 010 (RAISE) causes the ROBOT to turn on its light if it is against the wall (just what we're after!). In describing the ROBOT's characteristics, we promised that the ROBOT's warning light would give it a decision-making capability. Great, that's just what we need—a way to identify the wall and a way to decide when to escape from the loop.

Recall the way the warning light works: Once the light is turned on, the ROBOT ignores all instructions except for 11000000 (LIGHT). The 110 opcode tells the ROBOT to turn off the warning light. If the warning light is on for any reason, this is the only opcode that has any effect.

How to Get the ROBOT out of a Loop

Now, let's attack the problem again by using the 010 (RAISE) opcode to solve our dilemma. To get the ROBOT out of its deadly loop, one of the instructions inside the loop must sooner or later cause the warning light to be turned on. That instruction contains the 010 (RAISE) command. The ROBOT tries to raise its arms and cannot (because it is up against a wall), so the light goes on. When that occurs, the 101xxxxx (GOTO) instruction, which normally causes the ROBOT to begin repeating the loop (assuming the loop begins at a step number xxxxx), will be ignored because the light is on. The ROBOT will then execute the instruction following the 101xxxxx instruction, thereby escaping from the loop!

The new program with both the binary machine language and the English language explanation about what the instructions do is shown in Figure 3.2.8.

Figure 3.2.8 *Program to get the ROBOT to the wall using a better algorithm.*

Memory Location	Command	Explanation
0	01000000	Try to RAISE arms.
1	01100000	If it can, LOWER them.
2	00000000	Take a STEP.
3	10100000	GOTO location 0.
4	11000000	Turn off the LIGHT.
5	11100000	STOP.

This one really does work. To convince yourself, run the program on a ROBOT simulator if one is available; otherwise, run it in the classroom with a classmate acting the part of the ROBOT.

PROBLEM #2: Have the ROBOT locate any corner of the room and stop there with its arms lowered. Assume the ROBOT is not initially facing an open doorway.

One of the aspects of programming that lets us solve complicated problems more easily is that we can reuse pieces of programs that have already been written. We just wrote a useful program that allows the ROBOT to find the wall. This example will use that program while nicely illustrating the idea of reusing parts of programs.

To find a corner, the ROBOT must find two walls. We have it first find the wall it's facing—which we already know how to do—and then turn it 90 degrees and repeat the process to find the second wall. That's a reasonable algorithm stated in words. Hence, using the last problem's solution with some additional details, we get the complete solution shown in Figure 3.2.9.

Figure 3.2.9
Program to get the ROBOT to a corner of the room.

Memory Location	Command	Explanation
0	01000000	Try to RAISE arms.
1	01100000	If it can, LOWER them.
2	00000000	Take a STEP.
3	10100000	GOTO location 0.
4	11000000	Turn off the LIGHT.
5	00100000	TURN to face new wall.
6	01000000	Try to RAISE arms.
7	01100000	If okay, LOWER them.
8	00000000	Take a STEP.
9	10100110	GOTO location 6.
10	11000000	Turn off the LIGHT.
11	11100000	STOP.

There are two separate loops in this program, one to find each wall. They are indicated by the arrows shown in Figure 3.2.9.

Note that in the second loop of Problem #2, the ROBOT is moving down the wall with the wall on its left side.

3.3 The von Neumann Stored-Program Concept

The ROBOT computer of the previous section is not a general-purpose computer. Its only purpose is to perform specialized tasks such as stepping around a room or finding a doorway. The conceptual computer discussed in this section, the Pencil and Paper computer, comes a bit closer, but it isn't completely general, either. It can perform only a limited set of arithmetic calculations. However, it contains so many features of a general-purpose computer that it allows us to leave computer abstractions behind and discuss genuine, real-world computers. Almost all computers can be broken down into the fundamental units shown in Figure 3.3.1.

The **input/output units** allow the computer to communicate with things outside itself. The input unit allows the computer to receive information (both data and instructions) from the outside world, whereas the output unit displays information (calculated results and other messages) for humans to see. In the ROBOT computer, the input and output units are easily recognizable, as shown in Figure 3.3.2. For the Pencil and Paper computer, the computer's imaginary keyboard serves as the input unit, and the equally imaginary monitor provides output.

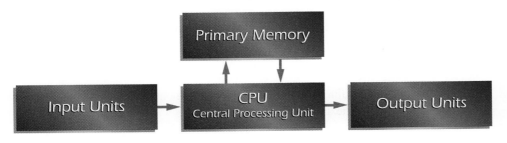

Figure 3.3.1
A block diagram of a typical computer.

Figure 3.3.2 *ROBOT input/output units.*

Input Units	Output Units
Toggle switches located on left side of ROBOT	Movement of legs and arms
Sensor on arms	Light on and off

The memory is the place where all information to be used by the computer is kept for recall. In the ROBOT, the memory is the switch panel shown in Figure 3.2.4. We discussed in some detail how instructions were entered into the memory using the toggle switches as input devices. Once the program is loaded, the toggle-switch memory stores the instructions awaiting execution time. The memory of the Pencil and Paper computer, like that of the ROBOT, has 32 locations, each capable of storing one instruction.

The **central processing unit (CPU)** is sometimes considered the "brain" of the computer. It is responsible for controlling all activities of the computer system, performing all calculations, and executing all instructions. You might have some difficulty identifying the CPU of the ROBOT. This is due to our deliberately incomplete discussion of it. Because of the ROBOT's limited use, there was no advantage in including a more detailed explanation of its CPU. On the other hand, because the Pencil and Paper computer so closely resembles a real computer, we will reveal all aspects of its CPU and functioning as we go along.

A schematic drawing of the Pencil and Paper computer is shown in Figure 3.3.3. We've already talked about the input/output devices and the 32-compartment memory. Now let us move on to less familiar territory, the CPU, or central processing unit. It consists of three parts: the arithmetic unit, the control unit, and the instruction decoding unit.

The **arithmetic unit** is where arithmetic is done. It has a place where all the results are accumulated, called the **accumulator**. Real computers have much more detail, but the idea is the same. Notice that the accumulator is more than eight bits in size. When the accumulator calculates answers, the results may be longer than eight bits; that would lead to some problems not considered in this discussion.

The Pencil and Paper computer's accumulator is 14 bits long. This means the largest number it can contain is 4095 (in binary this is 11111111111111_{two}). It should also be noted that the Pencil and Paper computer could store and manipulate only positive integers between 0 and 255. The reason for this is that it can store only 8 bits in each memory location, and 255_{ten} is the highest value than can be stored in 8 binary digits. Although

MEMORY

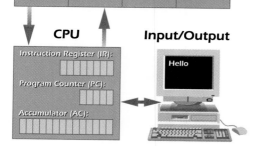

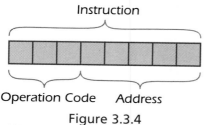

Figure 3.3.3
The Pencil and Paper computer.

Instruction

Operation Code   Address

Figure 3.3.4
The Pencil and Paper computer's instruction format.

a computer such as this one is not very practical, it will help us understand the overall operation of more versatile computers.

The **control unit** has two locations where numbers are kept: the **instruction register (IR)** and the **program counter (PC)**. The eight-bit instruction register is where an instruction is placed for analysis by the instruction decoding unit. The program counter contains the five-bit address of the memory location where the next instruction to be executed resides. The control unit will carry out the operation given by the opcode in the instruction register. It will then go to the five-bit address in memory contained in the program counter to find out what instruction must be performed next.

Finally, the **instruction decoding unit** is the part of the computer that will decode the instruction. In a real computer, it electronically analyzes each instruction as it is placed in the instruction register and causes the proper electronics to be called upon to make the instruction happen.

The Pencil and Paper Computer Instruction Set

As with any other computer, the Pencil and Paper computer has its own unique set of commands to be used within instructions. The instructions are the lifeblood of any computer and are the means for causing the computer to do things. Putting a group of these instructions into a program has already occupied a considerable amount of our time both for the Word Hunt and the ROBOT computer.

Also, as with the ROBOT computer, each instruction must ultimately be represented as a binary number. In the Pencil and Paper computer, these instructions are similar to those of the ROBOT because they consist of only one byte (eight binary digits) as shown in Figure 3.3.4.

The instruction format for the Pencil and Paper computer, like that of the ROBOT, contains a three-bit operation code (opcode) and a five-bit address, or operand. The three-bit opcode allows us a total of eight different commands in the instruction set, whereas the address portion allows access to 32 memory positions, numbered 0 through 31. This is a very limited size for both memory and number of commands. In fact, most personal computers have many megabytes (MB) of memory. This size is rather awesome when compared to the 32 bytes (.032KB) of the Pencil and Paper computer. As you might suspect, a larger number of bits in the address is required to reference so many memory locations. In fact, 16 to 32 bits are used in a personal computer for the address rather than the 5 used by the Pencil and Paper computer. Personal computers also have several hundred commands in their instruction sets.

The complete instruction set for the Pencil and Paper computer is in Figure 3.3.5. As you can see, the instruction set doesn't even have multiplication or division. Of course, repeated addition and subtraction can do these operations.

How does the CPU work with instructions using these commands? Let's see what happens when two numbers are to be added together: One number must first be placed in the accumulator. The instruction decoder then separates the ADD instruction into its two components, the opcode and the operand. When the ADD opcode is executed, the number stored in the memory location described by the operand is added to the one already in the accumulator. The sum is placed back in the accumulator. Suppose the accumulator contains the binary number 00011011 when the instruction ADD 27 is executed. Assuming that location 27 of the memory contains the number 00000001, after the ADD 27 is executed, the number 00011100 (00011011 + 00000001) will be in the accumulator. Location 27 still has the 00000001 because of the **nondestructive reading of memory**. (That is, only *copies* of numbers are taken from memory; the original is still there.) Nondestructive reading is almost universal in the operation of computers.

Figure 3.3.5 *The Pencil and Paper computer's instruction set.*

Instruction	Opcode	Description
ADD	001	Add the contents of the referenced memory location to the current value in the accumulator.
SUB	010	Subtract the contents of the referenced memory location from the current value in the accumulator.
LOAD	011	Load a copy of the value currently stored in the referenced memory location into the accumulator. This destroys the previous contents of the accumulator.
STORE	100	Store a copy of the contents of the accumulator into the referenced memory location. This destroys the previous contents of that memory location.
READ	101	Read a value from the keyboard of the terminal and store it into the referenced memory location. This destroys the previous contents of that memory location.
PRINT	110	Print the value in the referenced memory location on the computer screen. This does not destroy what is in that memory location; only a copy is taken and printed on the screen.
PJUMP	111	Jump to the referenced memory location if the accumulator contains a positive nonzero number.
STOP	000	This causes the computer to stop executing the program.

RISC Versus CISC

The acronym RISC (Reduced Instruction Set Computer) indicates an approach in the design of a microprocessor that minimizes the number of instructions used by the computer. The purpose of the small number of instructions is to make the computer using the RISC chip faster. On the other hand, the CISC (Complex Instruction Set Computer) has many more than the minimum number of instructions. The idea of CISC is to save the programmer time by supplying a large variety of instructions.

The concept behind RISC, which is reducing the usual large number of instructions to a few fast instructions, makes the computer faster because in most microprocessors, 20 percent of the instructions are used 80 percent of the time. When a more complicated instruction is necessary, it is made up of several of the simple instructions; even though this takes more time, it is not done very often.

CISC on the other hand does have some of the same simple instructions as RISC, but the fact is that it takes the computer more time to analyze a CISC instruction to see if it does indeed need more steps to complete. This extra time is taken with all instructions, thereby making the CISC slower overall.

The difference between CISC and RISC microprocessors is lessening. For example, the Intel Pentium and Pentium Pro microprocessors employ many attributes of the RISC chip, while still using CISC chips to ensure compatibility with previous and existing systems and software. The RISC is represented by the IBM/Motorola Power PC chip.

Enough of this talk! Let's see how the Pencil and Paper computer works. To do this, addressing the simple problem of entering two numbers, adding them together, and then printing out the result seems a reasonable first program. The essentials of solving this problem with the Pencil and Paper computer can be outlined in the following algorithm:

1. Read two numbers from the keyboard and put them in memory locations X and Y. The actual memory locations X and Y are chosen at execution time.

2. Put one of the numbers into the accumulator.

3. Add the other number to the one already in the accumulator.

4. Copy the result from the accumulator into the memory at the location identified by Z.

5. Print the sum of the two numbers.

6. Stop running.

We'll write this program first using the one-word, English-like or assembly language form of each instruction we need. **Assembly language** is a historical term used to identify English-like **mnemonic** forms that represent each machine language instruction. This makes it easier to program and allows us to label memory positions using names. The result is shown in Figure 3.3.6.

READ	X
READ	Y
LOAD	X
ADD	Y
STORE	Z
PRINT	Z
STOP	

Figure 3.3.6

Program that sums two numbers.

10111101
10111110
01111101
00111110
10011111
11011111
00000000

Figure 3.3.7

Machine language version of the summing program in Figure 3.3.6.

Before the Pencil and Paper computer can even attempt to execute this program, it must be translated to machine language form, which consists only of eight-bit binary numbers for each instruction. Usually a program called an **assembler** does the work of translating the program. Doing the translation by hand gives more insight into the problems that must be solved: First of all, what do the X, Y, and Z refer to? The letters X, Y, and Z are **labels** that refer to locations in the memory of the computer. Using labels such as these allows the computer to select where the values will be stored. In unusual cases, the programmer can pick the memory locations to be used. For this program, let's assume memory locations 29, 30, and 31 are used in place of X, Y, and Z. This choice is completely arbitrary. We could have just as easily used 11, 23, and 28, unless of course other instructions are stored in these memory locations.

Once memory locations have been chosen for X, Y, and Z, we must then begin at the top of the program and number the steps of the program. Usually, the step numbers begin with position 0 (that's zero) of the memory. But that's another arbitrary choice. You can begin at any location, placing each instruction one location number higher until you run out of instructions or memory locations. Remember not to exceed step #31. After the memory locations (step numbers) have been assigned, the actual translation of the English-like instructions into binary (machine) code can begin. Start at the top of the program, and translate one instruction at a time. You can get the binary codes for each instruction using the opcodes of Figure 3.3.5. The **machine code** result of the hand translation of the program in Figure 3.3.6 is given in Figure 3.3.7.

Loading and Executing a Pencil and Paper Program

The next problem with the Pencil and Paper computer is to get the program into the memory of the computer so that it can be executed. This job is usually the duty of a

The Computer Continuum

program called a **loader**. The loader will get the program into memory and also do another important thing: It will place the address of the first instruction to be executed in the *program counter*. It should be noted that this starting address is not always the first instruction of the program. The programmer usually controls it.

Another function of the loader is to start what is often referred to as the **fetch and execute cycle**. The instruction whose address is in the PC (program counter) will be *fetched* and placed in the IR (instruction register). The *execute* part of the fetch and execute is done next. After the instruction is executed (in this case, a number is read from the keyboard and placed in memory location 29), the fetch part of fetch and execute is repeated. The cycle is repeated over and over until an instruction with the STOP command or opcode is reached. This fetch and execute cycle is represented in Figure 3.3.8.

Figure 3.3.8
The fetch and execute cycle

A more detailed account of the fetch and execute cycle is shown in flow chart form in Figure 3.3.9. The reader should take the program as shown loaded into the memory in Figure 3.3.10 and execute it via the fetch and execute process. In other words, play computer and see what results. Note that all memory locations not containing the program have been set to zero. This is quite common in most computers. Also note that locations 29, 30, and 31 are zero. This is because the numbers to be summed are read in while the program is executing and not during the loading phase. It is important to completely understand the difference between loading a program into the memory of the computer and executing the program (that is, doing each instruction as the fetch and execute cycle works its way through the program).

Finally, remember that the numbers to be read are supposed to be typed on the keyboard. This is rather difficult to actually do on an imaginary paper computer, so just use your imagination. In fact, some systems might even make a beeping sound to prompt the person sitting there to enter a number. For the sake of this example, let's assume that when the computer beeps, a 12 is typed, and when it beeps a second time, a 17 is typed. Figure 3.3.11 shows a snapshot of the memory just after the program has executed. Because 12 and 17 were typed on the keyboard, it should be no surprise that the sum 29 appears in memory location 31.

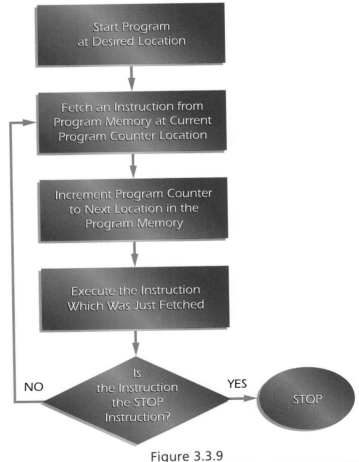

Figure 3.3.9
Flow chart of the fetch and execute cycle.

All of this seems rather tedious, and it is tedious for people. But remember that computers can do this fetch and execute cycle millions of times a second.

Figure 3.3.10

Pencil and Paper computer before program execution.

Memory

0 10111101	1 10111110	2 01111101	3 00111110
4 10011111	5 11011111	6 00000000	7 00000000
8 00000000	9 00000000	10 00000000	11 00000000
12 00000000	13 00000000	14 00000000	15 00000000
16 00000000	17 00000000	18 00000000	19 00000000
20 00000000	21 00000000	22 00000000	23 00000000
24 00000000	25 00000000	26 00000000	27 00000000
28 00000000	29 00000000	30 00000000	31 00000000

Memory

0 10111101	1 10111110	2 01111101	3 00111110
4 10011111	5 11011111	6 00000000	7 00000000
8 00000000	9 00000000	10 00000000	11 00000000
12 00000000	13 00000000	14 00000000	15 00000000
16 00000000	17 00000000	18 00000000	19 00000000
20 00000000	21 00000000	22 00000000	23 00000000
24 00000000	25 00000000	26 00000000	27 00000000
28 00000000	29 00001100	30 00010001	31 00011101

Figure 3.3.11

Pencil and Paper computer's memory after program execution.

CPU

Instruction Register (IR):

Program Counter (PC):

Accumulator (AC):

Input/Output

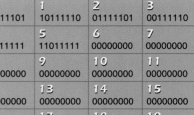

bits & bytes

Fetch/Execute and the Clock

The fetch/execute cycle refers to how programs run in a computer. The CPU must first get the next instruction to be done from the memory (the fetch), and then the CPU can do what the instruction commands (execute). This cycle is controlled by the clock of the computer. Analogous to the metronome of a practicing musician or the drums in a marching band, the clock keeps time for the computer. It usually takes several clock ticks to complete some of the more complicated instructions. In everyday terms, the clock speed of the computer is measured in megahertz (MHz). A 120MHz computer is twice as fast as a 60MHz computer. The megahertz unit represents millions·of clock ticks per second. A 233MHz computer has a clock that ticks 233,000,000 times per second. Of course, you can't hear an electronic tick; this term is from the days when the escapement of a mechanical clock or watch actually made ticking sounds.

Because the number of clock cycles needed to execute an instruction varies, a more descriptive measurement of speed is the number of instructions executed per second. A computer that can execute five million instructions per second would have its speed indicated as a five Mips computer. The most time-consuming type of instruction is one that can deal with fractional numbers, called floating-point numbers. This has led to the measurement of speed by the number of floating-point instructions per second. A computer that can do three million floating-point instructions per second is a three Mflops computer. A supercomputer that can do two billion instructions per second has its speed denoted as two Gflops.

3.4 The von Neumann Computer and Beyond

The Pencil and Paper computer of the previous section is a simplified view of what happens in a larger, more general-purpose computer. The primary RAM memory of larger computers may vary from under 100 million bytes to over a billion bytes. The speed of larger computers is considerably faster, too, on the order of billions of instructions per second. The ultimate speed in computing is found in the supercomputer, which executes several instructions in parallel, giving effective speeds measured in trillions of instructions per second.

Our purpose in this section is to discuss the more general computer systems. We will pursue the discussion of these computer systems according to their speed, cost, size, and complexity, as shown in Figure 3.4.1.

The Pencil and Paper computer is certainly the slowest, cheapest, smallest, and simplest of computers. Then comes the familiar handheld calculator, which is a giant step up in capability. In fact, the largest of these calculators are programmable. A good example of one of these programmable calculators is shown in Figure 1.2.4 of Chapter 1, "Computers: A First Look." The palm computer shown in Figure 1.2.5 has the power of a microcomputer.

A **microcomputer** is the same as a personal computer that contains a **microprocessor** or "micro-CPU," which is a small central processing unit. The microprocessor was initially created for electronic calculators. A photographic process is employed to expose and layer semiconductor materials in order to make incredibly tiny transistors. These transistors are so small that millions of them can be placed on an area smaller than a bumblebee's shadow at noon. Examples of the microprocessors that are in the personal computers of today are worth a little time investigating.

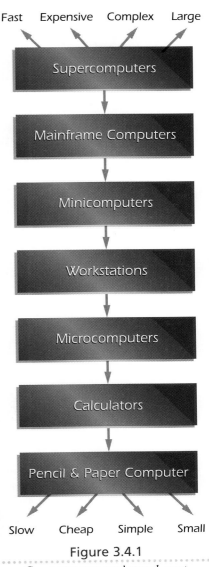

Fast Expensive Complex Large

Supercomputers

Mainframe Computers

Minicomputers

Workstations

Microcomputers

Calculators

Pencil & Paper Computer

Slow Cheap Simple Small

Figure 3.4.1

Computer systems' speed, cost, complexity, and size.

The microprocessor shown in Figure 3.4.2 is the Motorola Power PC chip. Believe it or not, this small half-inch square area contains the equivalent of about 200,000 transistors. Designed originally by IBM, this design is the basis for not only the Macintosh Power PC computers from Apple Computer, but also personal computers by IBM and other manufacturers. The designation **chip** is common in electronic computer jargon and merely indicates that this device is constructed on a tiny chip of silicon which is, in turn, mounted on a larger body bearing the connecting legs or plug-in-pins.

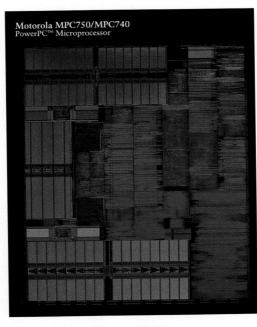

Motorola MPC750/MPC740
PowerPC™ Microprocessor

Figure 3.4.2

The Motorola Power PC microprocessor.

The Father of the Electronic Digital Computer

Think of it: Suppose you owned the patent rights to 99.9 percent of all electronic digital computers ever made! Indeed you would be one of the richest people in history. A disagreement on the patent rights to the electronic digital computer started with the designers of the ENIAC, J. Presper Eckert and John W. Mauchly. They also wanted exclusive patent rights to the EDVAC, which they claimed was based on ENIAC. The patent dispute carried on into 1947 when the meeting of the principal players in the issue agreed that the von Neumann report put the concepts of the stored program computer in the public domain. But it also left the door open to additional individual patent claims and the discovery of the true father of computing. In fact, Eckert and Mauchly went on to sell their patent rights to Sperry Rand corporation.

The real father of electronic computing was discovered to be Dr. John Vincent Atanasoff. His identity surfaced during the patent fight between Honeywell and Sperry Rand, which was the result of Sperry trying to collect hundreds of millions of dollars in license fees for the use of the von Neumann computer concepts. It was revealed that Atanasoff and his associate Cliff Berry had constructed a computer at Iowa State College between 1939 and 1941. This computer, called the ABC (Atanasoff Berry Computer), was seen by Mauchly in a visit to Atanasoff's laboratory in 1941. This visit by Mauchly lasted five days, and through court testimony, it is clear that many of the major ideas were incorporated in the Atanasoff Berry Computer.

So goes the story of the electronic digital computer. The invention was claimed by Eckert and Mauchly, actually invented by Atanasoff, and named after John von Neumann. As a footnote, it should be mentioned that, independently, Konrad Zuse in Germany finished creating his first of several electromechanical computers in 1938. It contains some of the same ideas as the von Neumann computer.

Another popular microprocessor chip used in many microcomputers is the Pentium II by Intel. It is almost a complete computer on a chip and is much more sophisticated than its early predecessors, some of which now cost only a few cents. Figure 3.4.3 shows the Pentium II microprocessor being plugged into a circuit board.

Figure 3.4.3

The Intel Pentium II microprocessor being plugged into a circuit board.

The Computer Continuum

These two popular microprocessors are the latest in a long list of microprocessors that started back in the 1960s. The technology that makes them possible is also responsible for the personal computer revolution, which is now so evident. There are home and business computer stores in every major city of the U.S., and for just a few hundred dollars, you can purchase a computer system that only a few years ago cost $50,000 or even $100,000. Many microcomputer manufacturers, numbering in the hundreds, entered the competitive home-computer market. A few of the early computers were the Apple II, Commodore PET, Commodore VIC, TRS-80 Model III, IBM PC, and TRS-80 Color Computer. Later, the Macintosh Power PC and Pentium-based computers came with hundreds of times the power of the earlier personal computers. With millions of these computers in homes, schools, and businesses, it is no wonder that learning about them is crucial to personal job opportunities and advancement. The end is not in sight. Even newer methods and materials are on the horizon.

Most people are unaware of how the microprocessor has invaded our consumer society. For example, these devices are used quite commonly in dishwashers, washing machines, dryers, microwave ovens, and automobiles. The older mechanical methods of performing the necessary actions for these products are much more expensive and not as reliable as the microprocessor. In the case of automobiles, the microprocessor is fast enough to tell each spark plug when it is supposed to spark. While it is doing this, measurements such as engine temperature are taken to make adjustments in the timing of the spark. This means, in effect, that a cold car seems to run as if it were already warmed up.

The microcomputer can be outlined by using essentially the same block diagram as shown in Figure 3.3.1. In fact, similar block diagrams can generally describe 99.9 percent of all computers. An example of one such microcomputer is the Micron Electronics' Millennia MME Pentium-based computer shown in Figure 3.4.4. It is called a Pentium-based PC because the microchip that is the heart of this computer is a Pentium micro-processor.

Closer to the top of the diagram in Figure 3.4.1 are the **mainframe** computers. They have increased size, speed, complexity, and cost. Its cost is on the order of hundreds of thousands of dollars as compared to thousands of dollars for the microcomputer. It also follows the same basic computer system configuration illustrated in Figure 3.3.1. An example of a mainframe is shown in Figure 3.4.5. It's in the IBM 9600 family of main-frames.

The speed of the **minicomputer** allows it to manipulate more data than a microcomputer. The speed of minicomputers and fast microcomputers is almost the same. Therefore, the distinction will gradually fade.

The main characteristic that distinguishes microcomputers from minicomputers is that microcomputers are single-user systems, whereas a single minicomputer is most often used by several people. At least it appears that all those working on a particular main-frame are doing their work simultaneously. In reality, this isn't quite true, as we shall see in the next chapter when multiuser operating systems are discussed.

A subcategory of computers, which lies between microcomputers and mainframes, is called the **workstation**. It has more power than a microcomputer, but it is still used by only one person at a time. It is usually connected to other computers and a large storage device. An example of a popular workstation manufactured by Sun Microsystems is shown in Figure 3.4.6.

Figure 3.4.4
Micron Electronics Millennia MME Pentium-based personal computer.

Figure 3.4.5
IBM 9672 computer.

Figure 3.4.6
Sun Microsystems Ultra 60 workstation.

Just as microcomputers are approaching the capabilities of minicomputers, the minicomputers are moving up on the diagram of Figure 3.4.1 closer to mainframe computers. Mainframe computers are much more expensive than minicomputers and usually need large staffs to operate and maintain them. Mainframes get that name because the CPU is mounted on a heavy steel frame or rack in a large metal cabinet. This frame is the main frame, and there are other frames of steel that contain the memory and many I/O devices.

Applications such as weather simulation, large data storage systems, and airplane reservation systems need even more capability in their computers. The most powerful of these large computers are called **supercomputers**.

Before looking at an actual supercomputer, an understanding of the basic concepts that most supercomputers follow would be helpful. The major supercomputer concept is having many CPUs working together as a team to calculate or perform some program. Supercomputers have from 4 to 65,537 CPUs working together.

The multiple CPU concept can be most easily understood by referring to the Pencil and Paper computer in Figure 3.3.3. Imagine many Pencil and Paper CPUs all connected sharing a memory. Figure 3.4.7 illustrates the concept with four CPUs working together with a common memory. The arrows represent electrical paths for data and programs that are sent between the CPUs, I/O unit, and the memory. It is difficult to write software that allows the many CPUs to function as a team. With this simple model in mind, let's look at a real supercomputer.

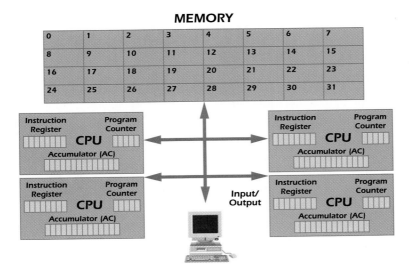

Figure 3.4.7

The Pencil and Paper supercomputer.

A typical configuration for Thinking Machines Corporation's CM5 supercomputer is shown in Figure 3.4.8. CM is an acronym for Connection Machine, the name given to this family of supercomputers.

Figure 3.4.8

The Connection Machine CM-5 supercomputer.

Even though these monolithic boxes seem mysterious, in principle, it has a block diagram closely related to Figure 3.4.7. The major difference is that the CM5 shown in Figure 3.4.8 has up to 512 processors working as a team. In the mid-1980s, W. Daniel Hillis invented the Connection Machine as part of his Ph.D. work at MIT. The major problem it solved was connecting the thousands of microprocessors. Each of these processors is like a von Neumann computer, except it shares some common memory and peripheral devices, such as disk drives, with the other processors. The CM5 is sometimes also referred to as a massively parallel computer. This is due to the fact that it has a large number of microcomputers all hooked together to work in parallel.

The incredible speed (trillions of instructions per second) allows the larger computer to deal with much larger programs and at the same time control all of the input/output devices, such as the line printer, terminals, magnetic tapes, and disks. To fully describe this computer worth millions of dollars is beyond the scope of this book; in fact, programmers working with large systems like the one shown in Figure 3.4.8 need access to stacks of reference manuals that reach heights measured not in inches, but feet!

Also note that the sides of the cube have thousands of little red lights that give an indication of the activity going on inside the CM5. The extreme complexity of this supercomputer is managed by something called the operating system. This controlling program or operating system is discussed in the next chapter.

Chapter Summary

What you can do with what you have learned:

- Follow a ROBOT program and a Pencil and Paper program.
- Write a ROBOT program or a Pencil and Paper program to solve a problem.
- Recognize the key parts of a computer program.
- Follow a computer program from conception to execution.
- Compare types of computers based on speed, cost, complexity, and size.
- Locate the microprocessors used in daily life.

Key Terms and Review Questions

Key terms introduced in this chapter:

Program 2-44

Operand 2-44

Argument 2-44

Opcode 2-44

Operation code 2-44

Machine language 2-44

Stored-program computer 2-44

Von Neumann-type computer 2-44

Pencil and Paper computer 2-45

ROBOT 2-45

ROBOT's domain 2-45

Memory 2-47

Instructions 2-47

Fetch 2-47

Decode 2-47

Execute 2-47

Instruction set 2-48

Fields 2-48

Loading 2-49

STEP 2-50

TURN 2-50

RAISE 2-50

LOWER 2-50

SENSE 2-50

GOTO 2-50

LIGHT 2-50

The Computer Continuum

Matching

Match the key terms introduced in the chapter to the following statements.

Each term may be used once, more than once, or not at all.

1. _____ This is a collection of instructions for the computer to perform one-by-one.

2. _____ This is the form that all instructions must be in before the computer can do them.

3. _____ This computing device has a place to keep information needed for computing.

4. _____ These are sequences of instructions that are repeated one or more times when a program is executed.

5. _____ A step-by-step process used to solve a problem.

6. _____ A situation where a group of instructions is repeated over and over with no way of stopping it.

7. _____ This should be simple. It should solve the stated problem in all situations.

8. _____ This part of the computer is often referred to as the "brains" of the computer.

9. _____ These allow the computer to communicate with things outside itself.

10. _____ This historical term is used to identify English-like mnemonic forms of instructions.

11. _____ This program's function is to get a program into the memory of the computer so that it can be executed.

12. _____ The results of computations are accumulated in this part of the CPU.

13. _____ This type of computer is named after "micro-processor."

14. _____ An example of this type of computer is manufactured by Sun Microsystems. It is usually connected to other computers and a large storage device.

15. _____ This type of computer is moderately priced.

16. _____ This type of computer is used by a single user and is a standalone computer.

17. _____ Several people can use this type of computer at one time.

18. _____ This computer has many CPUs.

19. _____ This type of computer was named after its large metal cabinet.

20. _____ This is the most powerful of all computers.

True or False

1. _____ Machine language programs need to be translated into binary before the computer can execute them.

2. _____ The ROBOT is limited to 32 instructions in a single program.

3. _____ The ROBOT is limited to understanding only eight different commands.

4. _____ The four fields of a ROBOT instruction are the operation code, opcode, argument, and operand.

5. _____ The first three bits of a ROBOT instruction correspond to the operation code.

6. _____ The last five bits of a ROBOT instruction correspond to the operand.

7. _____ ROBOT instructions are performed in a top-down fashion, never going out of order unless directed otherwise by a GOTO command.

8. _____ The ROBOT is a perfect example of a general-purpose computer.

9. _____ In a ROBOT set of instructions, every GOTO command signifies a loop.

10. _____ The Pencil and Paper computer is a perfect example of a general-purpose computer.

11. _____ When an instruction is to be executed by the CPU, the CPU removes the instruction from memory (clearing that instruction from memory) and places it into the instruction register.

12. _____ Assembly-language programs need to be translated into binary before the computer can execute them.

13. _____ In a Pencil and Paper program, only the computer can define where data is stored.

14. _____ In a Pencil and Paper program, the addition or subtraction of values takes place in memory, where those values are stored.

15. _____ The control unit keeps a copy of the instruction that is to be performed now and

knows which instruction is to be performed next.

16. _____Let's assume that the contents of memory location 15 has the value of 3. Let's also assume that the accumulator has the value of 6. In the instruction ADD 15, the value 15 is added to the contents of the accumulator.

17. _____Computers are compared in their speed, cost, complexity, and size.

18. _____The microprocessor was partially a result of the development of miniaturized technology for the space program.

19. _____The Intel Pentium microprocessor chip is the only chip being used by computer manufacturers in the microcomputers of today.

20. _____Whereas microcomputers, minicomputers, and mainframe computers typically only have one CPU (one program counter), a supercomputer can have thousands!

Multiple Choice

Answer the multiple-choice questions by selecting the best answer from the choices given.

1. Another name for opcode is
   a. Optical codifier
   b. Operation code
   c. Operand code
   d. Optional code
   e. Optimal instruction set code

2. The stored-program computer is also commonly called this type of a computer.
   a. Pascal computers after Blaise Pascal
   b. Ada computers after Ada Lovelace
   c. von Neumann computers after John von Neumann
   d. Hollerith computers after Herman Hollerith
   e. Babbage computers after Charles Babbage

3. This is a step-by-step process used to solve a problem. It should be a general solution able to solve the problem in all situations.
   a. Program
   b. Problem
   c. Algorithm
   d. Loop
   e. Infinite loop

4. This sequence of instructions repeats a section of a program in a way that was intended by the programmer.
   a. Program
   b. Problem
   c. Algorithm
   d. Loop
   e. Infinite loop

5. This sequence of instructions repeats a section of a program in a way that was probably not intended by the programmer. Intervention is necessary to stop this process of repetition.
   a. Program
   b. Problem
   c. Algorithm
   d. Loop
   e. Infinite loop

6. This part of the CPU has a place where all results of computations are accumulated. What is the name of this place?

 a. Control unit

 b. Accumulator

 c. Instruction register

 d. Program counter

 e. Instruction decoding unit

7. This part of the control unit is where an instruction is placed for analysis by the instruction decoding unit.

 a. Arithmetic unit

 b. Accumulator

 c. Instruction register

 d. Program counter

 e. Memory

8. This part of the control unit contains the address of where the next instruction to be executed resides.

 a. Arithmetic unit

 b. Accumulator

 c. Instruction register

 d. Program counter

 e. Instruction fetching unit

9. When executing a program, the CPU of the computer identifies which instruction is to be performed, gets the next instruction to be performed, decodes the instruction, performs calculations if necessary, and executes the instruction. The process is then repeated until the program is finished. This name of this process is the

 a. Fetch and execute cycle

 b. Nondestructive reading cycle

 c. Analyzing cycle

 d. CPU cycle

 e. There is really no name for this process. It is just done by the CPU.

10. Which of the following lists of the types of computers is in order of cheapest and slowest to most expensive and fastest?

 a. Minicomputer, microcomputer, mainframe computer, supercomputer

 b. Microcomputer, minicomputer, mainframe computer, supercomputer

 c. Supercomputer, mainframe computer, microcomputer, minicomputer

 d. Minicomputer, microcomputer, supercomputer, mainframe computer

 e. Microcomputer, minicomputer, supercomputer, mainframe computer

Exercises

ROBOT

All the ROBOT exercises assume that there are no doors in the corners of the room. Note also that the size of the room is unknown. Another important fact is that the ROBOT may or may not be facing an open doorway. The asterisk (*) indicates the ROBOT is not initially facing an open doorway.

*1. Design an algorithm and then write a program that will cause the ROBOT to find the wall it is initially facing and stop one step away from it, facing it with arms raised.

*2. Design an algorithm and then write a program that will cause the ROBOT to find the wall it is initially facing and end up facing away from the wall with its arms lowered and its back against the wall.

*3. Design an algorithm and then write a program to make the ROBOT take a step. You will probably conclude that

The Computer Continuum

this problem is logically impossible under one circumstance. What is it?

*4. Design an algorithm and then write a program that has the ROBOT locate any corner of the room and stop there with its arms lowered. Unlike Problem #2 in the text, have the ROBOT move toward the corner with the wall on its right side. This means when viewed from overhead, the ROBOT is moving counterclockwise.

*5. Have the ROBOT locate a door, not knowing which wall the door is on. Make sure your ROBOT stops without going through the door. Don't use the SENSE command at the beginning.

*6. Repeat Exercise 4, using the 100 opcode (SENSE).

7. Have the ROBOT find any wall and stop facing the wall against it. However, the ROBOT may or may not initially be facing a open doorway. Assume there are no doors located in any corners of the room. Also assume that each doorway has corners and the ROBOT may go one step through the doorway. (Hint: A search pattern must be developed around each square.)

8. Have the ROBOT find a door in any wall; however, the ROBOT may or may not initially be facing a open doorway. Assume there are no doors located in any corners of the room.

Also assume that each doorway has corners and the ROBOT may go one step through the doorway. (Hint: A search pattern must be developed around each square.)

9. What is the difference in effect (if any) of the instructions 00000000 and 00011111?

10. Why are the ROBOT's memory locations numbered starting from 0, instead of from 1?

11. What is a field? How many fields are there in a ROBOT instruction?

12. What are the names of the fields in a ROBOT instruction? How many bits are used in each field?

13. How many memory locations could the ROBOT use if the address field were six bits long?

14. How many instructions could the ROBOT have if its opcode were four bits rather than three bits long?

15. Why do we refer to the ROBOT as a stored-program computer?

16. Why can't we program the ROBOT using the English words that stand for the instructions (STEP, SENSE, RAISE, LOWER, and so on)? Is it nonetheless valid to think in terms of the words when solving ROBOT problems? To what extent and in what way?

Pencil and Paper Computer

Unless otherwise indicated, each of the following problems assumes the program will be loaded starting at memory location 0.

17. Design an algorithm and then write a Pencil and Paper computer program that adds two numbers which are already located in memory locations 20 and 21 and then prints out their sum.

18. Design an algorithm and then write a Pencil and Paper computer program that prints the numbers from 10 down to 1. Use only one PRINT command. This means you must use a loop.

19. Design an algorithm and then write a Pencil and Paper computer program that prints the numbers from 1 to 10. Use only one PRINT command. This means you must use a loop.

20. Do exercise 18, but make the necessary changes assuming the program is to be loaded starting at location 9.

21. Design an algorithm and then write a Pencil and Paper computer program

that prints the numbers from N down to 1, where N is input from the keyboard using the READ command.

22. Design an algorithm and then write a Pencil and Paper computer program that prints the numbers from 1 to N, where N is input from the keyboard using the READ command.

23. Design an algorithm and then write a Pencil and Paper computer program that prints the numbers from N to M, where both N and M are input from the keyboard using the READ command.

Assume that M is greater than N.

24. Design an algorithm and then write a Pencil and Paper computer program that adds all the counting numbers starting with 20 and going down to 1. Hint: Start at 20 and count down to 1.

25. Design an algorithm and then write a Pencil and Paper computer program that adds all the counting numbers starting with 1 and going to 20. Print out only the final total. Hint: Start with 1 and count up to 20.

Supercomputers

26. Write out in words a description of how you would use the Pencil and Paper supercomputer shown in Figure 3.4.7 to solve the following problem: Add 4,000 numbers. The description should be very general and short.

Discussion Questions

1. Why should algorithms be general?
2. What would happen to the computer industry if the world ran out of silicon?
3. Arrange the following in an order that makes sense and discuss why each precedes the next.

   a. Write the program.
   b. Debug the program (find errors).
   c. Read the problem.
   d. Devise an algorithm.

Group Project

Each person in a group of four should choose one of the following types of computers: personal computer, workstation, mainframe computer, and supercomputer. Research in the literature or through the WWW the fastest speed computer in each category. Using a spreadsheet, make up a table with the four categories along both the top and side. Then, fill in the matrix with speed ratios of column heading over row heading.

Each person researching a type of computer should get the time it takes for that type of computer to do a particular problem. For example, how long does it take to make a five-day weather forecast using a supercomputer? Make up another spreadsheet with the types of computers along the top and the specific problems along the left. Suppose a problem takes one minute on a supercomputer. Fill in the matrix with the length of time it would take each of the other types to do the same problem.

Web Connections

http://www.pcwebopaedia.com/CPU.htm

Definition of CPU; links to many sites relating to current and future CPUs on the market.

http://www.pcwebopedia.com/algorithm.htm

Examples and definition of algorithm and links to related sites.

http://www.msci.memphis.edu/~ryburnp/comp1200/history/microhist.html

Microcomputer history information from a college course.

http://www.cs.umd.edu/users/fms/comp/

List of sites with computer history information.

http://www3.islandnet.com/~kpolsson/comphist.htm

Another microcomputer history site with sources and reference material.

http://encarta.msn.com/index/concise/0vol0F/01c2d000.asp

Information on microcomputers and links to related concepts.

http://www.pcwebopedia.com/minicomputer.htm

Information on minicomputers and links to related ideas.

http://www.pcwebopedia.com/Types_of_Computers_cat.html

Links to terms, categories, and subcategories involving types of computers.

Bibliography

Macrae, Norman, *John von Neumann*, New York: Pantheon Books, 1992.

A detailed biography of von Neumann.

Hillis, W. Daniel, *The Connection Machine*, Cambridge: MIT Press, 1985.

Chapter 4

1965	The Multics operating system is developed by MIT, Bell Labs, and GE.
1967	A graphical user interface (GUI) is a main theme in the Ph.D. thesis of Jeff Raskin (Apple Macintosh team leader).
1973	The first GUI-operated computer, the Alto, is finished by PARC.
1975	The Altair 8800 Microcomputer kits are available for home assembly.
1980	A command-line operating system developed by a small Seattle company is licensed by Microsoft as MS-DOS.
1980	IBM selects MS-DOS as the operating system for its new PC.
1981	Xerox introduces mouse-operated icons, buttons, and menus on the Star computer.
1983	The Windows operating system was first announced by Bill Gates. Microsoft did not release it for four more years.
1984	Macintosh introduces the first widely used GUI interface.
1992	Windows 3.1 is released. This operating system was widely popular.
1994	IBM releases OS/2 Warp to compete with Windows. It offered a GUI, multitasking, and easy access to the Internet.
1995	Windows 95 is released in August. Initial reviews are mixed.
1997	Mac OS 8 sells 1.25 million copies in its first two weeks.
1998	Windows 98 is released.

Operating Systems: The Genie in the Computer

Chapter Objectives

By the end of this chapter, you will:

- Appreciate why an operating system is necessary in today's computers.
- Realize how the process of booting a computer finds the rest of the operating system.
- Recognize the types of duties performed by an operating system.
- Know the relationship between bits, bytes, and words.
- Understand how parity bits are used to find electronic errors in a computer.
- Recognize the difference between a warm boot and a cold boot.
- Know the difference between a command-line user interface and a GUI interface.
- Appreciate the advantages of a hierarchical file system over a flat file system.
- Understand why files from one type of machine won't always work on another type of machine.
- Discern the difference between cache memory and virtual memory.
- Recognize how context switching is used in conjunction with multiprogramming.
- Appreciate how distributed processing makes networks efficiently use computing power and memory.

4.1 What Is an Operating System?

The previous chapters discussed many concepts about how computers work and the nature of information. The next major concept concerns controlling the computer. For a computer to run a particular program, many tasks must be performed. They range from things as mundane as loading the program into RAM memory to complex topics such as virtual memory management. These topics will be discussed later in the chapter.

The program that takes care of these details is called the **operating system**. To truly make the computer easy to use, it is necessary to understand the operating system. As the definition of the operating system indicates, many parts of it act as the helper to anyone using the computer.

Before getting into the details of an operating system, it is quite revealing to look at how a computer would be used without one. A good example of a computer without an operating system is one of the first microcomputers. First offered in a kit form, the **Altair 8800** was a personal computer without an operating system. Figure 4.1.1 reveals the many switches where information had to be entered to control the use of this computer. These switches were necessary to directly enter information into **RAM** (nonpermanent memory). The lights let the person using the computer know what was going on inside. The person using the computer had to first "**fat finger**" a program into the RAM. This means that a program was entered by flipping the switches, up for a one and down for a zero. This was difficult to do with even small fingers because the switches were close together, hence the expression "fat fingering" a program.

> The **operating system** is a collection of programs that manages and controls applications and other software, and coordinates the various hardware components to perform tasks requested by the user.

Figure 4.1.1
The Altair 8800 hobbyist computer.

The first program loaded into the computer was one that would allow a larger program to be read into RAM from a **paper tape reader**. This larger program usually allowed the use of a keyboard. In fact, until the larger program read from paper tape was in the computer's RAM memory and running, the keyboard was unusable. At this point, the person using the computer, called the **user**, could use the keyboard to read in a still larger program, which could be something like the **BASIC** language system. Then programs written in BASIC could be run.

This rather involved startup of a personal computer explains the expression "**booting up a computer**" that is commonly used today. It has its origins in the Old West days of cowboy boots with straps to pull on the boots. Someone who was down and out yet managed to bring himself back to some semblance of normality was often said to have pulled himself up by his bootstraps. It's stretching things a bit, but in fact, the startup of early personal computers involved this complicated process of using a small program to read a still larger program and so on. Hence the expressions:

The Computer Continuum

Boot strapping a computer

Booting up a computer

Boot the computer

were used to indicate the startup of a computer or getting the computer ready to do useful work.

At this early stage of microcomputers, not even word processing was available. It was a hobbyist's toy, not for useful work. Among the reasons why the Altair was not too useful included the fact that it lacked permanent memory or **ROM**, and it had no secondary storage devices such as floppy disks. But even more important was the lack of a program to assist in running the computer. It was difficult for the user to manage the computer without help. In fact, the user had to know where every program was in memory so he or she could tell the computer where to go to run it. It was a tedious process that sometimes took 30 minutes before anything useful could be done.

Today's personal computers have a small, unchangeable part of the operating system in the ROM memory. In the MS-DOS and Windows systems, this permanent part of the operating system is called the BIOS, for basic input/output system. Because the ROM is permanent memory, its contents don't disappear when the power is turned off. The ROM typically contains BIOS programs to allow use of the keyboard and both floppy and hard disks. The process of booting up a modern personal computer invokes these programs in ROM memory, which immediately search for a floppy disk in the floppy disk drive. If it can't find a floppy disk, it then looks for a hard disk drive. Upon finding one of these disks, the program in ROM looks for the rest of the operating system on that disk. If no operating system is found, the personal computer will not function.

As stated in the definition, an operating system consists of a collection of programs that help you use the computer. It not only makes a computer easier to use, but also allows the most efficient use of this expensive resource. It acts like a smart assistant that moves information around the computer and performs other odd jobs as needed. A partial list of the numerous activities that the collection of programs performs follows:

Using the keyboard

Using the mouse

Printing to a printer

Choosing different printers on a network

Starting up programs

Changing colors on the screen

Using modems for communications

Managing the files of the computer

Finding things for the user

Allowing more than one program to be open at the same time

Allowing more than one program to run simultaneously (such as printing while still doing word processing)

Formatting disks

Loading programs into RAM so they can perform

This fundamental idea of controlling the computer system using programs rather than a human is an important point to understand. The operating system is the traffic cop of the computer, and depending on the context, it also has many different names. In earlier years, synonyms used for the operating system were **monitor**, **supervisor,** or **executive.** Now they are referred to as operating systems or by their commercial names. Some common operating systems you may have heard about are **MS-DOS**, **Windows 98**, **MacOS**, **OS/2**, **UNIX**, **Linux**, and **VMS**.

To understand more fully what an operating system does, it is necessary to get an idea of how information is moved from place to place in the computer. The next section explains this.

4.2 Moving Information Within the Computer

We have seen how the five forms of information can be represented by binary numerals, where these binary numerals can be stored or kept for use by the computer, and an overview of how a computer works. Another important aspect of the total process involves how these binary numerals are moved into, out of, and within the computer. This was not explained in previous chapters.

First, let us take a look inside the computer. Because of the great speed of the electronic circuitry inside the computer, moving binary information bit by bit from one place to another is very inefficient. Instead, the information is moved about in **bytes** or multiple bytes, which in large computers are called **words**. These words are the fundamental units of information, which are passed around inside the computer. The number of bits per word varies greatly. A word length is 32 bits for most large IBM systems.

The number of bits necessary to store a single alphanumeric character is six, seven, or eight bits, depending upon the system of representation. (Chapter 2, "Metamorphosis of Information," showed only the seven-bit ASCII code.) Because of this, many words are subdivided into units called bytes, which are usually eight bits long. The division of a common 32-bit word into bytes is shown in Figure 4.2.1.

Figure 4.2.1

The relationship between bits, bytes, and a word.

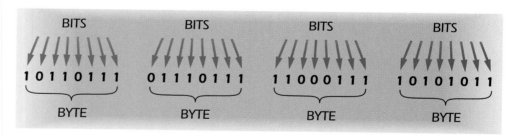

To further complicate matters, computers can be designed with many different word sizes. When the word size becomes as small as eight bits, then such words are referred to as bytes. For example, most early microcomputers had only eight bits as the fundamental unit of information that was passed around inside them. The eight-bit microcomputer words are referred to as bytes, mainly because the eight-bit byte is too small to contain the information usually contained in the words of larger computers.

The bits that compose a word are passed in **parallel** (that is, together as a group) from place to place inside the computer. In fact, if we were to open the main cabinet of most

The Computer Continuum

computers, then we could see some of these parallel data paths over which the words are passed. One of the more visually obvious paths is in the form of **ribbon cables**. These ribbon cables consist of several wires molded together, side-by-side, one for each bit of the word or byte, plus some additional wires to coordinate the activity of moving the information. Figure 4.2.2 shows a ribbon cable for an eight-bit microcomputer. It consists of several wires, each carrying one bit of information in the form of a **voltage pulse**. Included are the wires carrying the eight-bit byte. These pulses are voltages that are applied to the wires for a very short time, millionths of a second. Typically, the voltages are only 5 to 12 volts.

Figure 4.2.2

Ribbon cable used for electronic connection.

As an example of how this ribbon cable would function, suppose the computer moved the ASCII letters WOW over the ribbon cable. Voltage pulses corresponding to the ASCII coding would flow through the cable, as shown in Figure 4.2.3. The voltage on wire 8 is being used here as a **parity bit**. Its purpose is to help detect any errors in the data that may be due to malfunctioning electronic circuits. Remember, ASCII needs only seven bits for each character. Using this eighth bit as a parity bit is done by making the extra bit so the number of 1s is either even (**even parity**) or odd (**odd parity**). The computer observes all the eight-bit bytes that electronically travel throughout the circuits. If an even-parity computer sees a byte with an odd number of 1s, then it will usually stop running and inform the operator that a serious error occurred. The only way the number of 1s could change is due to faulty electronics. However, if two bits were changed due to faulty electronics, this parity scheme wouldn't detect the problem.

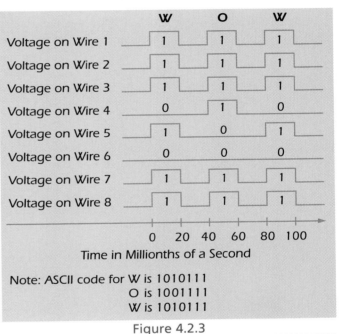

Note: ASCII code for W is 1010111
O is 1001111
W is 1010111

Figure 4.2.3

ASCII characters WOW on ribbon cable.

Normally, a microcomputer would have a ninth bit added for parity checks inside the computer. However, because of the higher reliability of today's computers, the parity error-checking scheme isn't used much anymore. However, the concept of parity is used in many places, including the Internet where errors are detected by an enhancement of the parity idea.

The diagram in Figure 4.2.3 could be called an electronic snapshot or picture of ASCII characters moving on the ribbon cable inside a microcomputer. How did we know the three units traveling down the ribbon cable were the ASCII characters W, O, and W? We assumed they were! Couldn't they also be the integers $1010111_{two}=87$, $1001111_{two}=79$, and $1010111_{two}=87$ or maybe even instructions for the microcomputer itself? We really don't know and shouldn't care. If we had written the program to control the flow of this information, then naturally we would know exactly what it represented.

The **parity bit** is an extra bit that is added to the unit of information passed around in a computer. Even-parity systems choose the parity bit to make the number of ones in the unit of information even. Odd-parity systems have an odd number of ones.

The major point is that the information flowing inside a computer can be checked for errors. In the more sophisticated computer systems, the errors are not only detected, but also the appropriate corrections can be made on the information moving around inside the computer.

How bytes flow into and out of the computer is also related to the information flow within a computer. This type of communication is done via **input/output (I/O)** devices. A familiar example of an input device for a computer is a keyboard. Typing on the keyboard sends **ASCII** characters to the **CPU (central processing unit)** of the computer. What does this mean?

As a simple example, suppose you would like to type the number –23 (–10111_{two}) into a letter. Typing the –, 2, and 3 on the keyboard causes these symbols to appear on the screen of your computer. The reason the symbols appear is that the seven-bit ASCII codes for the –, 2, and 3 are sent by the keyboard to the word processing program, which in turn saves them in memory and makes the symbols appear on the screen. Figure 4.2.4a illustrates this case. Incidentally, the ASCII information is not usually sent in parallel to and from I/O devices in most microcomputers. Sending it bit-by-bit in **serial** is fast enough. This saves wires and reduces problems with bad connections.

The –23 entered into the microcomputer would end up as a string of voltage pulses as shown in Figure 4.2.4b. It should be pointed out that this picture is somewhat simplified. The computer must be ready to receive a character at any time; otherwise, it could miss the following character. These details, although they may be of interest, are too complicated for our present discussion.

Figure 4.2.4 *ASCII characters and codes for –23.*

(a) Character information to be sent representing –23.

Order Sent	Symbol	ASCII Code
First	–	0101101
Second	2	0110010
Third	3	0110011

(b) Voltage pulses coded as 0s and 1s for –23.

Voltage code	0101101	0110010	0110011

Voltage pulses actually sent, where 0 means no voltage and 1 means high voltage or 0 means off and 1 is on.

4.3 Major Concepts in Everyday Computers

The purpose of this section is to introduce six major concepts used in everyday computing. Understanding these concepts and mastering these terms will help you feel more knowledgeable and comfortable working with computers.

Concept #1: Starting Up or Booting the Computer

Section 4.1 contains an explanation for the term **booting** or **booting up** the computer. What does this term mean today with the modern personal computer? *Booting up* the computer is synonymous with *starting up* the computer. If the power is off, this form of booting up is called a **cold boot**. This latter term makes sense when you realize the computer is cool when off. When the computer is on, it is warm from the hot electronics.

The Computer Continuum

In the case of the cold boot, when the power is turned on, the skeleton operating system in ROM (permanent memory) looks for the rest of the operating system. After finding it, the skeleton operating system loads the remaining part of the operating system into RAM memory.

On the other hand, a **warm boot** is when the computer has the power on with the disk drive spinning. For the warm boot, a restart command must be given to the part of the operating system that is in ROM memory. The warm boot doesn't shut off the power and is usually done through a combination of keys held down simultaneously (such as Alt+Ctrl+Delete). The hard disk keeps spinning, and the power supply is still operating. The warm boot reloads a new copy of the operating system into RAM and allows the user to begin again but without turning off the power to the disk or power supply. It is used when something may have accidentally altered the operating system and caused problems. In fact, it may happen that the computer just locks up, and it is impossible to communicate with the operating system. This is the ideal case for the warm boot.

Why is it important to know about the difference between a cold and warm boot? This may seem like one more nitpicking irrelevant computer detail. In fact, users who switch their computers off and quickly on again run the risk of doing damage to their computer. How can this be? **Power surges** from the **power supply** can actually do damage to the power supply itself, and they are expensive to replace. Therefore, be sure to leave the power off for at least five seconds before you power back up.

Concept #2: The User Interface

The user **interface** is just what the name implies. This is the part of the operating system that the computer user sees and interacts with. The two basic kinds of operating systems interfaces are called **command line** and **GUI (graphical user interface)**.

Figure 4.3.1 illustrates a typical view of Version 1.0 of the Windows 98 GUI interface. A mouse easily controls the access to various menus and window activity. The Macintosh GUI interface, first introduced in 1984, has gone through several revisions. A typical view of Version 8.0 of the Macintosh operating system is shown in Figure 4.3.2. The **version numbers** indicate the version of the operating system software being used. It is important to know the version of the operating system because programs such as word processors, spreadsheets, and others are written for a particular version of the operating system. These programs use some of the hundreds of parts of the operating system to function properly. Of course, this means if you upgrade your operating system to a newer version, your programs might not work. When buying software, such as word processors or even games, it is important to know which version of the operating system it was designed to run under.

A common command-line interface is the older MS-DOS. The great difficulty with command-line interfaces is that they take time to learn. They are not intuitive. For example, suppose you want to copy an English paper you wrote onto a floppy disk to take it home. To do this, you must know the name of disk drive on which it currently resides (such as drive C) and that of the disk drive in which your floppy resides (such as drive A). The command line that you type is

    copy C:Paper A:

This command assumes you know whether to type C:Paper or A: first after the word copy. Also, accidental extra spaces could make this command unintelligible to the operating system.

A **command-line** operating system interface is one in which communications are given to the computer by typing commands on the keyboard.

A graphical operating system interface (**GUI, graphical user interface**, pronounced goo-ee) is one in which commands are usually given through a mouse (a device that is used to move a pointer on the screen of the computer). The mouse is used to move a pointer on the screen to point at an icon (a small picture representing things or commands).

Figure 4.3.1
· · · · · · · · · · · · · ·
*Typical view of a Windows
98 graphical user
interface.*

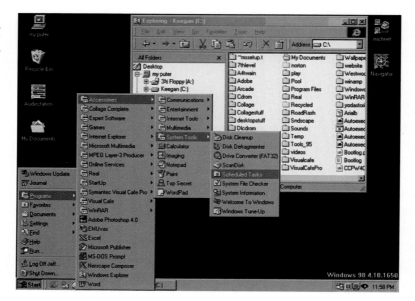

Figure 4.3.2
· · · · · · · · · · · · · ·
*Typical view of Macintosh
Version 8.0 graphical user
interface.*

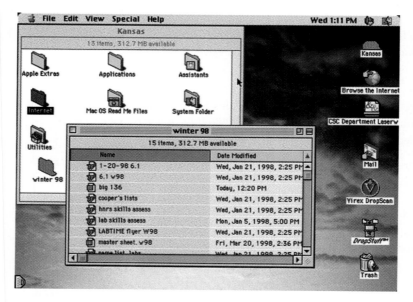

In a GUI-type interface, you can see graphical images (such as a small **icon** or picture representing the disk and another icon representing the English paper) on the screen of the computer. To copy the English paper onto the floppy disk, the user simply uses the mouse to move the pointer over the icon of the English paper and holds the mouse button down while moving the mouse, until the icon of the paper is over the icon of the disk. The disk icon will turn a different shade, and if the user releases the mouse button at this point, the GUI operating system automatically makes a copy of the English paper onto the floppy disk. To learn this takes little training. The process is sometimes referred to as **drag and drop**.

Intuition is very important to make computers easier to use and to prevent serious errors. The concept is referred to as being **user friendly**. An illustration of the user-friendly concept is found in a completely different field, weather reporting. Do you immediately know what is meant by "tornado watch" and "tornado warning" as used by the U.S. Weather

The Computer Continuum

Service? Every time these terms are used on the radio, the announcer has to define them. More user-friendly terms might be "tornado possible" and "tornado sighted." These terms need no explanation; they are self-defining. Careful crafting can result in intuitive and user-friendly computer operating system interfaces.

A large number of professional high-powered computer users prefer the UNIX operating system. The UNIX operating system can have either command line or GUI type of user interface. However, it has its roots in the command-line type of user interface. Several popular command line interfaces to UNIX are the

Korn shell

C shell

Bourne shell

The word **shell** suggests that they represent the interface or channel between the user and the computer.

UNIX—Operating System of Choice for Professionals

UNIX is one of the most influential operating systems in the history of computer science. It was created along with the language C by Ken Thompson and Dennis Ritchie at Bell Laboratories more than two decades ago. It is a much more powerful and flexible operating system than most personal computer operating systems. UNIX was certainly instrumental in development of the Internet and is also the operating system of choice for many academic computer scientists. One of the major reasons for this is the vast number of software tools that have been developed for UNIX. Included in this list is X Window, which is a GUI and networking interface to UNIX.

Some versions of UNIX do run on personal computers. One such example is Linux, a UNIX-compatible operating system (that is, it acts just like UNIX). Linux is free and represents the zenith in free software. It is available on the Internet and other sources. Linux was developed by Finnish student Linus Torvalds. Because it doesn't directly contain any parts of the UNIX system (all of Linux is original, written by Torvalds, and only behaves like UNIX), this means Torvalds had complete control over it and decided to give Linux away free. Linux is quickly becoming the standard operating system for professionals on their personal computers. It runs the Intel family of microcomputers from 386 and up.

An example of a GUI (graphical user interface) to UNIX is called **X Window**. X Window was actually designed with networking in mind. However, most UNIX users use it as a GUI interface to UNIX. It is much easier to use than the command-line version of UNIX.

Operating systems of the future will be more powerful but easier to use than current operating systems. Eventually, it is thought that special intelligent programs called **agents** will be used to assist the person using the computer. It would be like having a human expert sitting with you and telling you what to do. For example, suppose you want to write a letter to mom. All you might have to do is tell the agent you want to write a letter to mom. The agent will find the word processor, open it, save as you write, and do all the chores that you normally have to do when communicating with the operating system. Intelligent agents will be discussed in a later chapter.

Concept #3: Management of Files

Both serious work and just playing games demand an understanding of where things are kept and how to save your work. The word **file** is the name given to any program or chunk of data that is stored on floppy, hard disk, CD-ROM, or other storage medium. For example, a letter to mom or dad would be called a file and is usually given a name by the user that suggests what it is. Examples of filenames that might be used are

MomDadLetter

LetterHome10/2/96

Letter#1Home

MomDad11/6/96

MomDad#1

Home11/6

In the early days, some operating systems of personal computers only allowed eight-letter names. The modern operating systems allow the user to name a file with as many as 256 letters. This means that a complete description of the file can be contained in its name.

One of the most important aspects of the filing system for computers is its structure. There are two major structure types used in microcomputers: the older **flat file system** and the newer, most common, **hierarchical file system**. Let's examine them from a user's perspective rather than a technical viewpoint.

A simple example will illustrate why the flat file system is no longer in use. Suppose that you have more than a thousand different files on your computer, which consist of various things such as correspondence home, school papers, a résumé, budgets, and so on. In a flat filing system, these items would all be stored in a single list of a thousand file names. This means that when one of them is needed, the list of more than a thousand items must be scanned by the user and identified. If 32 lines were visible at one time on the screen of the computer, viewing all one thousand items would take 32 screens full of names. This is certainly not satisfactory, and it led to a much more efficient way to organize the files on a computer—a hierarchical file system.

The hierarchical file system organizes files into groupings. For example, let's suppose a student has a floppy disk to store school and home information. All correspondence home could be put together under a single named grouping, commonly referred to as a folder, such as LettersHome. Then any budget items could be grouped and named as BudgetStuff. You can also make groupings within groupings. For example, suppose papers and homework from several courses are stored in files on the computer. The diagram in Figure 4.3.3 shows how these files could be organized.

In Figure 4.3.3, there are 23 files; they are unboxed. The boxed items represent the hierarchy of the data on the floppy disk. This student named the disk MyDisk. Then, on this floppy disk, the student created three major subdivisions to store files, namely Correspondence, JobSearch, and School. Under each of Correspondence and School categories, further subdivisions are made, but under JobSearch, the four files are stored with no further subdividing of the hierarchy. Locating the desired file on a floppy data disk organized in this manner is easy and logical. But this example has only a couple dozen files.

The Computer Continuum

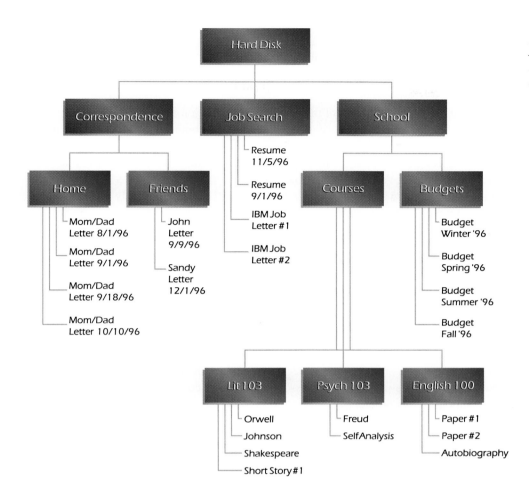

Figure 4.3.3

A sample of files stored on the hard disk of a student's computer.

When large numbers of files are saved, organizing files in this hierarchical structure is absolutely necessary. Most hard drives of serious users of computers have several thousand files organized in this manner. It is also important to choose names for both files and the subdivisions that tell exactly what they contain.

In the older MS-DOS world, which has a command-line user interface, to get the SandyLetter12/1/96 of Figure 4.3.3, the user would have to type out

C: /HardDisk/Correspondence/Friends/SandyLetter12/1/96

This seems rather clumsy and difficult compared to the Windows 98 and Macintosh computers, where it is only necessary to visually locate the file by using the mouse and clicking. It should be noted that MS-DOS doesn't even allow such long names; the length of names is restricted to eight characters, so the actual names shown would have to be changed.

Concept #4: Input and Output of Information

Input/output of information, or I/O, as it is commonly called, refers to getting information into the computer and also back out of the computer. In Chapter 2, the five basic kinds of information were identified. It is these five kinds of information that are used in I/O. For reference, they are

Numbers	Visual information
Text or characters	Audio information
Instructions	

As pointed out in Chapter 2, all of these types of information are in the binary form. What makes them different to the computer? In fact, the computer has no way of "knowing" which of these types of information is contained in a particular file of binary form. The person using the computer must supply the information in the proper form. For example, what happens when you try to use a Microsoft Word file from a Macintosh on a Windows machine with a different word processor? The file is probably in the wrong form, and it won't open. It must first be converted to a compatible form.

To illustrate this point, it is useful to look at a hypothetical example. Suppose two students are working on a project together. Being quite naive, they were not experienced enough to realize that the different word processors aren't always compatible. Each student is working on his or her part of the project. When the time comes to put them together, one of the students puts the other student's disk into the computer and expects to open and work with the file. However, the first student's word processor won't recognize the file. What do they do now? The frustrated student can't figure out why the word processor can't recognize the other student's work. The main problem is that most of the time, a word processor's file won't be recognized by another word processor. In fact, different versions of the same word processor aren't always compatible. There are two common solutions to this problem.

The first solution involves the flexibility of the word processing program. Most word processors have different choices in how the document is saved. It may be possible to save the document in exactly the form required by the other word processor.

A second solution involves saving the document as a text-only file. Most word processors let the user save a word processing document as a file of only the ASCII characters making up the words of the document. This is often called a **text file**. The result of saving a word processing document as a text file is that the information regarding margins, type fonts, indents, and tabs is stripped away. This format information has to be reinstated when using the second word processor. If nothing else is indicated at the time of saving the document, a word processor will save the document in its own form with all the format information.

What concept does this long example illustrate? The main point is that the human user should know what form of information the program expects so that problems that may be encountered can be solved. As programs are getting more user friendly, they are becoming more tolerant of errors or users' misunderstandings, which may involve trying to feed the wrong type of information into a particular program. For example, most of the current operating systems will allow the user to open any file by double-clicking it. The operating system then searches for a program that will translate that particular type of information and start the program, input the file, and even show it on the screen.

However, the operating system is not always successful. In this case, there still may be a program that will accept the file, but the user must make the choice. This means that a program is chosen and then a command is given to that particular program to open the file. Knowing the type of information that is in the file will help you choose the proper program to use.

A final point should be made about input and output. The operating system can put a copy of the file to be saved on either a floppy disk or hard disk, or even some other medium that the user has specified. With the proper software, CD-ROMs can also be read and files moved into RAM memory or copied to another disk. This so-called proper software is sometimes referred to as a **driver**.

The driver is the program that directs the flow of information to and from the piece of hardware in question (such as a floppy disk, CD-ROM player, hard disk, printer, laser printer, color laser printer, ink jet printer, video interface, modem, and many more). Sometimes the driver is a part of the operating system, as is the case in communication between a keyboard or mouse and the computer. On the other hand, to use special pieces of hardware such as printers or scanners, the software driver must be installed on the computer so the operating system can use it to communicate with them.

> A **driver** is a program that is capable of getting information transferred between the piece of hardware (such as a floppy disk drive) and the RAM memory of the computer. All hardware devices for input, output, and storage must have a driver to communicate with the computer.

Concept #5: Memory Concerns: Cache and Virtual Memory

The following ideas would be totally unnecessary if the primary memory (RAM and ROM) of a computer were as large as is ever needed and the speed at which information is retrieved from the primary or secondary memory could be as fast as the CPU needed. But, a huge memory of blazing speed isn't practical or economical.

Cache memory refers to several related concepts involving the primary and secondary memory. Two of the most common types are called **disk cache** and **RAM disk**. The disk cache speeds up processing by automatically saving the most frequently used parts of the program being run or executed into the RAM memory that is used for the cache. The basic idea is that the CPU may need to access the information in that same area of the program or data again. The information will be there ready to go, preventing the CPU from repeatedly retrieving it from the disk, which takes time to reload into RAM memory. The disk cache wouldn't be necessary if the RAM memory were large enough to hold all of the information, both data and program, needed by the program that is running on the CPU. A good example of something that is frequently held in the disk cache is the hard disk directory. This is especially true if you happen to be looking for a file on the hard disk or communicating with the operating system, which quite often needs to get information from the hard disk directory.

> **Cache memory** is used to speed up the processing of information. The basic concept is to provide a place in the RAM memory or special fast memory where information can be accessed by the CPU without the delays usually associated with the slower memory and storage.

The second most popular cache memory is called RAM disk, which is not a disk drive but actually a software program. The basic idea in the RAM disk is to fool the program into thinking it is accessing the disk as its needs require, but in reality, the program is accessing the much faster RAM. In the case of the extremely slow floppy disks, the whole disk is simulated in the RAM. The CPU processing required by the program accesses the faster RAM disk instead of the slow floppy disk. The major danger here is that if the power plug were pulled on the computer, then the information is not on the more permanent floppy disk but in the volatile RAM whose contents will disappear when the power is off.

In the more advanced personal computer operating systems, both types of cache memory are controllable by the user. In older operating systems that don't have a RAM disk, one may be purchased as a separate program. Many successful small software companies have provided these add-on utilities for the various personal computer operating systems.

Related to the various cache memory concepts is the concept of **virtual memory.** Whereas cache memory addressed the concerns of speed and efficiency, virtual memory addresses the problem of a program being too big to fit into the available RAM

> **Virtual memory** is an operating system feature that allows running programs that are otherwise too large to run in the available RAM of the computer. It makes the RAM appear to the CPU to be as large as all the storage available in both primary and secondary memory storage areas.

memory. The virtual memory capability of an operating system will divide the program up into pieces, which are brought into the memory as needed. This will, of course, slow down the processing of information because time is needed to go to the disk to get the various pieces of the program.

The virtual memory feature of an operating system can usually be turned on or off by the user. It should be used with care because using the virtual memory mode of an operating system can sometimes result in an extreme slowdown in processing. Conditions where this happens are discussed in the next section.

Concept #6: Multitasking

In the personal computer world, **multitasking** and **context switching** are concepts that the average user should be familiar with. In the next section, these concepts are formally defined. As far as the personal computer is concerned, the user's perspective in the form of some examples will suffice.

Multitasking is essentially the concept of having more than one program in the RAM memory sharing the CPU. An example will show the need for having two or more programs in the RAM memory at the same time.

Suppose you are writing a letter and need to get something from a spreadsheet to insert in the letter. Without multitasking, you would have to follow these steps:

1. Save the current copy of the letter.
2. Quit the word processor program.
3. Start the spreadsheet.
4. Create the spreadsheet data.
5. Save it in a form that is acceptable to the word processor.
6. Quit the spreadsheet program.
7. Restart the word processor and return to the letter.
8. Insert the spreadsheet data.

With the simplest form of multitasking, you could temporarily leave the word processor and go to the operating system. This is done without losing the status and current work on the letter, which means that the word processor and letter are still in the RAM memory. Next, you start the spreadsheet and do the required calculation. At this point, because of multitasking, the word processor, letter, spreadsheet, and spreadsheet calculation are all in the RAM memory at the same time. However, only the spreadsheet is active. It would be possible to switch from the word processor to the spreadsheet and back without quitting either one or losing any work. In other words, you could switch from the context of the word processor program to the spreadsheet context and work on either, but only one at a time. In fact, it is quite common for a computer user to keep half a dozen programs in memory ready to be switched to. These programs might include a word processor, spreadsheet, database, drawing program, communications program, and, of course, the operating system—all in RAM memory, ready to become active.

In true multitasking, when you switch from the word processor in the middle of doing something, it continues performing the task in the background. This means it will get some time on the CPU whenever the multitasking operating system schedules it. You might occasionally notice a slowdown when the operating system is stealing a few cycles

The Computer Continuum

of the CPU time from the program you are currently using. All of this is done under operating system control with little control exercised by the computer user.

A common example of multitasking is in printing. Suppose that a long printing process has just been started from a word processor; instead of waiting, the user can switch to another program and continue working. In the meantime, the multitasking operating system will continue the printing process. Another example of multitasking is when your browser automatically downloads your email at regular intervals while you are using some other program such as a word processor.

4.4 Alternative Operating Systems

There are many types of operating systems. Remember, the purpose of the operating system is to efficiently manage the computer system and make it easy for humans to tell the computer what to do. The computer may be a relatively simple von Neumann computer or it may be a supercomputer. Regardless of the type, the operating system is exceedingly complex as is evidenced by the fact that it is composed of millions of lines of programming instructions. This section examines the general concepts used in a wide variety of operating systems.

Multitasking

As computers became larger and faster, it was found that a single program couldn't keep the CPU busy. Too much time was needed to get information into and out of the computer. This so-called I/O-bound situation was not economical, so computer designers had the idea that maybe the CPU could run more than one program or task at a time. To have a program do all of the things it's supposed to do generally requires many tasks. Of course, this really means that several programs would be stored in the main memory so that when one of them had some slow process to be done outside the CPU, the CPU could be used to work on another program or task that was already there. This was made feasible by having "smart" input or output devices that didn't need the help of the CPU to accomplish this work, thereby freeing the CPU. As you might suspect, it was necessary for the operating system to make decisions on which programs or tasks to run and keep the CPU running smoothly.

Multitasking is a programming technique in which the operating system of a computer is able to perform many tasks concurrently. These tasks can be related to one or more programs. The multitasking operating system causes the CPU to work on each task in an order specified by certain rules.

Multics, the Granddaddy of Operating Systems

Multics (Multiplexed Information and Computing Service) was a time-shared computer operating system developed by a consortium consisting of Bell Laboratories, General Electric, and MIT in the mid-1960s.

It was clearly one of the most ambitious operating system projects up to that time. Multics contained operating system features such as virtual memory, a hierarchical file system, and many more concepts in use today. In fact, Bell Laboratories took many concepts of Multics and created a smaller, more manageable operating system called UNIX. It's interesting to note that UNIX is a pun on the word Multics, and it indeed focused on one goal rather than multiple goals. Also, Digital Equipment Corporation based its VMS (Virtual Memory System) family of operating systems on Multics.

continues

There were many people involved with operating systems in the 1960s. In the midst of all the action was the CTSS project (Compatible Time Sharing System) at MIT, which was influenced significantly by John McCarthy, pictured on the preceding page. Later, John McCarthy coined the term artificial intelligence (AI) and moved to Stanford University. He was an important figure in the field of AI, but his involvement in early operating systems through Multics was also significant.

Parallel Processing

Parallel processing or multiprocessing refers to computing done with more than one CPU. This means that several processors or CPUs are simultaneously computing a program.

As pointed out at the beginning of this section, operating systems can be classified as single CPU (a von Neumann computer) as distinguished from the multiprocessor system that has many processors or CPUs (a supercomputer). Dividing up programs so that different parts can be executing or computing at the same time is a difficult thing to do.

The complexity of the operating system for the CM-5 shown in Figure 3.4.8 of the previous chapter is immensely greater than that of the personal computer. CM-5 computers can have from 16 to 2,048 processors to organize and keep running efficiently. The operating system of a personal computer has only one processor to control.

Networks and Distributive Processing

Networks are combinations of independent computers, terminals, and other devices that are interconnected so that they may share information and other resources.

With **networks** currently so common, it's not too hard to visualize the next reasonable extension of operating systems called network computing. With network computing, individual people can access and even use several computers besides their own computer. That is, several computers are connected together by the network and share each other's resources. For example, suppose you are working on a group project. With a network and its operating system, it is possible for the entire group in the project to share results and communicate.

As might be suspected, there are operating systems specifically designed for the computers in such a network. One example is Microsoft's Windows NT. Not only must the network operating system be able to handle all the normal single-computer chores, but it must also be able to communicate with other computers in the network.

Distributed processing makes use of a network to decentralize and distribute the computing needs over several interconnected computers.

The desire to keep a single copy of a file that can be used by many people has created a further modification of networking. Inexpensive systems have been devised to allow one computer on a network to act as a shared storage unit. Its function is to serve and control the interactions of other computers on the network. This central computer is commonly referred to as a **server**. These concepts are considered again in Chapter 6, "Networks: Everything Is Connected."

The networking idea can be slightly modified to provide **distributed processing**. Each computer contains only a portion of the data or programs used. The other computers on the network can access these programs and data as needed and even make use of unused computing power. The major concept is to distribute both information and processing capability around to the computers in the network and then to allow each of them to access the others as needed. This trend toward distributive processing is a direct result of the new smaller and cheaper computers, especially the microcomputer.

Real-Time and Process Control

Real-time processing in the business world is computing that involves human interaction with the computer in a situation where quick or timely return of results is important. Real-time processing in the engineering and manufacturing world refers to controlling processes.

Real-time computing systems are another innovative form of computing that requires a rather complex operating system. The phrase **real-time** indicates that the computing

The Computer Continuum

performed must be done in a way that is compatible with the world outside the computer. In other words, information is fed to a real-time computer system and computations must be done quickly enough so that the results are still useful. One example is the automated teller machine, or ATM. When you use it, you want your cash back now, not tomorrow. Another is the airline ticket reservation system, which typically may have several thousand computers and terminals connected to it throughout the U.S., must accept reservation information and respond quickly enough so that the response is useful; waiting an hour or even 10 minutes for a response would be intolerable. Some reservation systems are so complicated that they even check to see if the individual has any other reservation in the same name. Airline reservation systems use millions of dollars' worth of computer equipment, and it costs several more millions of dollars to develop the computer programs for these applications.

Process control computer systems are another type for which the computer must do computations with timing appropriate to the world outside the computer. An interesting example of process control is the use of a microcomputer to control various aspects of the engine in an automobile. All major automobile companies

Figure 4.4.1

Process control of robots on an assembly line.

have some engines with spark timing, fuel injection, and other engine functions controlled by a microcomputer. In spark timing, the microcomputer is more than fast enough to sense when each cylinder is ready to ignite while taking into account such things as engine temperature. Other examples of process control include assembly-line control in factories, control of traffic in a railroad freight yard, control of automobile traffic in a city, flood control on rivers, satellite rocket launches, and lunar landings of space capsules. Closer to home are the thermostats and environmental controls in the home heating/cooling system.

Several examples of process control are also found in the field of robotics. Maneuvering a robot's arm is just one of the many things that uses process control. We are assuming that the robot can sense the environment and as a result of the sensing move the arm appropriately in a timely fashion. Figure 4.4.1 shows a robot assembly line controlled by computers running a process control operating system. Some robots used in industry can even see. This introduces some special problems for the robot's computer. However, discussing these problems is more appropriate for Chapter 13, "Artificial Intelligence and Modeling the Human State."

Process control refers to the control of some process by a computer in real time. It is necessary for the computer to accept information, do some calculations using the information, and then manage the process on the basis of these calculations.

Chapter Summary

What you can do with what you have learned:

- Know when to do a cold boot and when to do a warm boot.

- Choose software that will work under your current operating system.

- Organize the files stored on a hard disk or floppy disk in a logical manner.
- Solve the problem of using a file produced on one type of machine on another type of machine.

- Make informed decisions about using cache memory or virtual memory in your computer.
- Use a multiprogramming environment to work with multiple applications at once.

Key Terms and Review Questions

Key terms introduced in this chapter include the following:

Operating system 2-76

Altair 8800 2-76

RAM (random access memory) 2-76

"Fat finger" 2-76

Paper tape reader 2-76

User 2-76

BASIC 2-76

"Booting up a computer" 2-76

ROM (read only memory) 2-77

Monitor 2-78

Supervisor 2-78

Executive 2-78

MS-DOS 2-78

Windows 98 2-78

MacOS 2-78

OS/2 2-78

UNIX 2-78

Linux 2-78

VMS 2-78

Bytes 2-78

Words 2-78

Parallel 2-78

Ribbon cable 2-79

Voltage pulses 2-79

Parity bit 2-79

Odd parity 2-79

Even parity 2-79

I/O (input/output) 2-80

ASCII 2-80

CPU (central processing unit) 2-80

Serial 2-80

Booting 2-80X

Booting up 2-80

Cold boot 2-80

Warm boot 2-81

Power surges 2-81

Power supply 2-81

Interface 2-81

Command line 2-81

GUI (graphical user interface) 2-81

Version number 2-81

Icon 2-82

Drag and drop 2-82

User friendly 2-82

Shell 2-83

X Window 2-83

Agents 2-83

File 2-84

Flat file system 2-84

Hierarchical file system 2-84

Text file 2-86

Driver 2-87

Cache memory 2-87

Disk cache 2-87

RAM disk 2-87

Virtual memory 2-87

Multitasking 2-88

Context switching 2-88

Parallel processing 2-90

Multiprocessing 2-90

Networks 2-90

Server 2-90

Distributed processing 2-90

Real-time processing 2-90

Process control 2-91

Matching

Match the key terms introduced in this chapter to the following statements. Each term may be used once, more than once, or not at all.

1. _____A collection of programs that make the computer easier to use and allow the most efficient use of the computer.

2. _____This term had been given to the clumsy way a computer had to be activated by first flipping many tiny switches to directly enter startup information into RAM memory.

3. _____This example of one of the first microcomputers did not have any part of the operating system stored in ROM memory.

4. _____This term refers to the person using the computer.

5. _____Instead of moving information bit-by-bit within the computer, they are moved about in bytes or this term for multiple bytes.

6. _____This path is visual to the human eye. It is made up of parallel wires molded together.

7. _____This is how information moves about within the computer along the wires. It is invisible to us.

8. _____Its purpose is to detect errors in the data that may be due to malfunctioning electronic circuits.

9. _____ASCII information is sent along the wires in this format to and from I/O devices in most microcomputers.

10. _____This is synonymous with sending information bit-by-bit.

11. _____This is the part of the operating system the computer user sees.

12. _____The name given to a small picture that represents a disk or file.

13. _____This is the process of clicking the mouse over an object, moving it over to another object such as a disk, and releasing the mouse button.

14. _____This term refers to the ease of use of a computer, one that is intuitive to use, needing little explanation.

15. _____In a UNIX environment, this general term is given to the interface between the user and the computer.

16. _____ This type of file system lists everything stored in an area in top-down fashion.

17. _____ This type of file system organizes files into groupings.

18. _____ This type of file is saved in its ASCII form. It is generally saved this way when transporting it from one type of computer system to another or from one word processing product to another.

19. _____ This type of cache memory speeds up processing by automatically saving the most frequently used parts of the program being run in the part of RAM memory that is used for cache.

20. _____ This type of multiprogramming entails two programs running at the same time, each taking up time on the CPU. You may be running one program and have the computer run another in the background.

True or False

1. _____ In modern computers, a part of the operating system can be found in ROM ready for use before the computer is turned on.

2. _____ In modern computers, a part of the operating system can be found in RAM ready for use before the computer is turned on.

3. _____ In modern computers, a part of the operating system can be found in secondary memory ready for use, whether it's on a floppy or the hard disk drive, before the computer is turned on.

4. _____ Without the operating system, the computer is a big paperweight.

5. _____ The operating system has also been known as the monitor, supervisor, and executive.

6. _____ The size of a word depends on the computer being used. All words are not the same size.

7. _____ The voltage rate along the wires within a computer remains constant.

8. _____ The purpose of the parity bit is to check that text information, such as grammar, spelling, and syntax, is correct.

9. _____ Cold booting and warm booting the computer are similar in that they both reload the operating system.

10. _____ Cold booting and warm booting the computer have the same effect on the hardware of the computer.

11. _____ Learning to make the computer do what you want using a command-line interface takes as long as learning to use GUI commands.

12. _____ UNIX strictly uses a command-line interface.

13. _____ Text files allow the transportation of documents from one computer platform to another or from one word processor to another.

14. _____When buying a piece of hardware that is a newer technology than your computer, such as a digital camera or scanner, the device must come with a driver program. The driver program is necessary for the operating system to communicate with the new hardware.

15. _____Disk cache is synonymous with RAM cache.

16. _____More than one program can be in the RAM at the same time.

17. _____Multiprocessing refers to having more than one program in memory at a time.

18. _____One benefit of networking is that it provides access to shared resources.

19. _____A server's function is to allow access to individual computers on a network by an administrator who needs to check employee productivity.

20. _____An airline reservation system is an example of real-time processing, whereas controlling engine temperature is an example of process control.

Multiple Choice

1. Which of the following is not a function of the operating system?
   a. Using the keyboard
   b. Printing to a printer
   c. Turning on the computer
   d. Saving a file to a disk drive
   e. Managing the files of a computer

2. Which of the following is not true of a parity bit?
   a. Its purpose is to detect errors.
   b. If an odd-parity computer sees a byte with an even number of ones, it will inform the operator that an error has occurred.
   c. It is an extra bit that is added to the unit of information passed around in a computer.
   d. An error detected by the parity bit may be due to malfunctioning electronic circuits.
   e. It is used to check for errors in a word processing document.

3. Sending information bit-by-bit to and from I/O devices is referred to as sending in __.
   a. Voltages
   b. ASCII
   c. Parallel
   d. Serial
   e. Bytes

4. Restarting the computer by powering off and then powering the computer back on is known as
   a. Loading the computer
   b. Driving the computer
   c. A warm boot
   d. A cold boot
   e. Surging the computer

5. Restarting the computer by pressing a combination of keys simultaneously while the computer is still running so that an interruption of power does not occur is known as

a. Loading the computer

b. Driving the computer

c. A warm boot

d. A cold boot

e. Surging the computer

6. This type of interface recognizes typed commands almost exclusively.

a. GUI

b. Interactive graphics interface

c. Text-based interface

d. Command-line interface

e. Interactive iconoclastic interface

7. This type of interface recognizes commands given by a mouse or other pointing device. Activities are selected by using a mouse to point and click on icons.

a. GUI

b. Interactive graphics interface

c. Text-based interface

d. Command-line interface

e. Interactive iconoclastic interface

8. This is an indicator of the age of a program. The higher the number, the newer the software.

a. Report number

b. Version number

c. Procedure issue number

d. Primer number

e. Model number

9. This addresses the problem of a program being too big to fit in RAM. The program is divided up into pieces, which are brought into memory as needed.

a. Cache memory

b. Disk cache

c. RAM cache

d. Virtual memory

e. Virtual reality

10. This refers to several processors or CPUs in the same computer simultaneously working on a program.

a. Multiprocessing

b. Multitasking

c. Context switching

d. Multiprogramming

e. Distributed processing

Exercises

1. Give one major reason for each of the following in a computer:

a. Data being moved around in parallel rather than serial.

b. Data being moved in serial rather than parallel for I/O.

2. Add a parity bit to the left end of each of the following seven-bit ASCII codes to make them even or odd parity as indicated. Also decode each of them. (What does each of the seven bits represent? Use the ASCII code table in Chapter 2.)

a. Make these even parity by adding one bit:

_0111111

_0100011

_0110111

b. Make these odd parity by adding one bit:

_1011000

_1000000

_0110011

3. Express the number 137 as both a string of three ASCII seven-bit codes and a single binary number. Check back in Chapter 2 to find out how to do this.

4. Draw a block diagram of the microcomputer in the school computer lab and all of the I/O devices that are attached to it.

5. Suppose you are writing a letter home to mom and dad. The filename under which this letter will be saved can have many forms. Which of the following names are most desirable for naming a file? You should assume several letters will be written to them. Explain your answer.

MomDadLetter   Letter A

LetterHome10/2/96   Letter#1Home

Letter   Budget#1

XYZ   MomDadLetter12/1/96

MomDad11/6/96   Stuff#1

6. Suppose you may only use eight characters to name the file containing the correspondence home. Give six examples of good filenames.

7. What has to be done to use a word processing document created with a Macintosh computer on a Windows computer? What are all the options? Include the option where you know that the document is to be used on a Windows computer before you save the document on the Macintosh computer.

8. Understanding the general duties of an operating system, make up several appropriate names for operating systems (such as master control program).

9. Put a formatted disk without an operating system into both a Macintosh computer and a Windows-based computer. Turn on the computer and observe what happens. Describe the results and explain the actions of the computer.

10. List the steps involved in cold booting a computer.

11. What is the difference between a warm boot and a cold boot?

12. Describe the two methods given in section 4.3 for converting a file from one type of machine so it can be used on another type of machine.

13. Why does the computer upon startup always search for the rest of the operating system on the floppy disk drive first, before looking on the hard drive?

14. Why can't you write to most CD-ROMs? Explain.

15. What does the acronym WORM stand for? Explain what it means.

16. Give two examples of distributed processing.

17. Make a list of at least three applications that use real-time processing in the business sense of the word real-time.

18. Make a list of at least six things that use real-time process control computers (such as a dishwasher).

19. Study the following string of binary numerals:

1011010001111100

By looking at the string of binary numerals, can you guess what it belongs to? Is it part of a picture? Is it a number? Can it be a couple of letters from an ASCII text file? Could it possibly represent a couple of sounds?

With these questions in mind, explain how a computer's operating system would identify what is saved in a file and why this is important.

Discussion Questions

1. Why isn't the entire operating system stored in ROM? Wouldn't it be easier for the user and the machine?

2. Describe a situation where a command-line interface would be preferable to a GUI.

3. Why does the operating system need to use a disk cache in RAM instead of just using the disk?

4. Is multiprocessing necessary for multiprogramming? Why or why not?

5. For the computer you use, make a list of things you would like the operating system to do. Don't use examples from the book, and think of the operating system as your assistant. This means you can think of the question as requesting a list of things you would like your assistant to do in helping you use the computer.

6. In this chapter, the purpose of the parity bit was explained in how it checks for errors within the computer. Use the same conceptual idea to explain how parity might be used to send information to other computers.

Group Project

A group of four students with relatively little experience with computers should each keep a log of all the difficulties they have using the computer for their assignments. This log should be kept over a period of approximately four weeks or at least three assignments. The log should keep track of any confusing details, such as the following:

■ I couldn't get the computer to save my essay to the disk.

■ I needed help in starting the word processor.

■ When I tried to copy a picture from the Internet, it wasn't clear what I should do.

As each difficulty is solved, the solution should also be noted in the log along with possible things that could have been done to avoid the problem. For example, "I tried to save my essay on a disk, but the disk wasn't formatted, and no one told me I had to format it."

At the end of this four-week period, the students should share their experiences and fit them into a small number of categories such as the following:

■ Difficulty in getting a program started

■ Saving results

■ Finding things

Keep the log until the end of the semester. Then, during the last week of the term, reevaluate and write a report with suggestions that would have made your life easier.

Web Connections

http://www.whatis.com/operatin.htm

Good definition of an operating system with links to related terms.

http://www.whatis.com/boot.htm

Excellent information about booting an operating system, including a 12-step process of exactly what happens internally.

The Computer Continuum

http://www.microsoft.com/windows95/

Comprehensive site featuring the Windows 95 operating system. Contains links to features, uses, training, FAQs, and so on.

http://www.microsoft.com/windows/windows98/

Information on Windows 98 straight from the developer. Contains links to features, FAQs, technical benefits, and so on.

http://www.conitech.com/windows/win95.html

Frequently updated site about Windows 95 and Windows 98 put together by Frank Condron. Contains links to tips, discussion groups, and drivers for Windows 95.

http://www.microsoft.com/windows98/info/upto_win98.htm

Information on upgrading to Windows 98 along with a grid outlining how previous Windows systems can be upgraded to several different Windows options.

http://www.windows95.com/

Great site with a lot of links to everything concerning Windows 95 and Windows 98 operating systems. Especially good are the links to tips and tricks for everything from drag and drop to installing, networking, and file manipulation.

http://www.pcwebopedia.com/virtual_memory.htm

Definition of virtual memory with links to related concepts. Also includes links to how virtual memory works on several different platforms.

http://www-scf.usc.edu/~zliu/vm/vm.html

Working simulation of virtual memory. Animation done with a Java applet.

http://www.best.com/~thvv/multics.html

A resource site for information about the Multics operating system.

Bibliography

Laurel, Brenda, editor. *The Art of Human-Computer Interface Design*. Reading, MA: Addison-Wesley, 1990.

Meghabghab, George. *Introduction to UNIX*. Indianapolis: Que Education and Training, 1996.

Sagman, Steve. *Windows 98 Visual Quickstart Guide*. Berkeley, CA: Peachpit Press, 1998.

Simpson, Alan. *The Little Windows 98 Book*. Berkeley, CA: Peachpit Press, 1998.

Williams, Robin. *The Little Mac Book, 5th Ed.* Berkeley, CA: Peachpit Press, 1998.

Chapter 5

Computer Languages: Empowering Algorithms

Chapter Objectives

By the end of this chapter, you will:

- Discern the reasons why programming languages are necessary to communicate with computers.
- Know the definition of semantics and how it relates to computer programs.
- Know the definition of syntax and how it relates to computer programs.
- Identify the five generations of programming languages.
- Know the differences between an assembler, an interpreter, and a compiler.
- Identify the three major data structures formed by combining simple data elements.
- Understand the uses of each of the main types of programming-language statements.
- Know the steps necessary to build a computer program.
- Know four criteria for analyzing a program's quality.
- Identify the steps taken to test a program after its initial creation.
- Appreciate the amount of time it takes to complete a large, intricate computer program.

5.1 How Does a Person Communicate with a Computer?

The **communication cycle** has been the subject of serious study for nearly 2,000 years. On the surface, the problem of communicating with a computer seems not very different from the problem of conversing with other human beings. Both require the same activities: We must plan out what we want to say, figure out how to phrase it in the best possible way, and then actually say it. Then we wait for a response from the other party. Of course, the computer's response may be in the form of a printout or some symbols appearing onscreen. Whatever form the response takes—lights, symbols, or spoken words—we must understand the response before we begin a new round of communication.

Figure 5.1.1

The communication cycle represents a face-to-face conversation between two human beings.

Figure 5.1.2

How does the communication cycle change if we substitute a computer for one of the humans?

Humans write **programming languages** for the express purpose of being able to communicate with digital computers. Before the computer can process any message written in a programming language, it must first be translated into binary code, the only "language" the computer can actually understand.

Whether we are dealing with a computer or another person, every step of the communication cycle must be successful for the communication to be complete. Communication will not occur if there is a malfunction at any point. If the message were phrased in French and the listener understood only Japanese, for example, the effort to communicate would fail. In fact, a breakdown can occur any place along the cycle, causing communication to halt. The encoding and decoding processes are especially vulnerable spots. How can we translate our human thoughts, usually expressed as words, into computer "thoughts," which must be expressed as binary numbers?

Translation of instructions into binary code one by one is a painstaking task. Humans don't think in numbers like computers do. The need to facilitate this task has led to the development of a large number of compromise codes, called **programming languages**.

5.2 Are Computer Languages the Same as Human Languages?

Certainly strong similarities exist between human (natural) and computer (programming) languages. Designed by human beings to solve a human problem, computer languages, on the surface, have much in common with human languages. Deeper down, however, are many significant differences. To illustrate these differences, this section examines three different facets of language taken from the communication cycle: semantics, syntax, and participants.

Figure 5.1.3

Programming languages bridge the gap between human thought processes and computer binary circuitry.

Semantics (Meaning)

The central controlling concept in all communication is meaning. What we want to say—the message we want to communicate—is the reason behind all communication decisions. Therefore, it is only appropriate that we deal with meaning first. What a language means or represents is its **semantics**.

All languages get their meaning from us. We give a language its meaning by associating each language unit ("word") with a particular object or experience.

Semantics refers to meaning. It is the exact content of a language unit. In human language, this would be the reality or concept a group of words represents. In computer language, **semantics** refers to the commands you wish the computer to perform.

Figure 5.2.1

Would we perceive this object differently if it had another name?

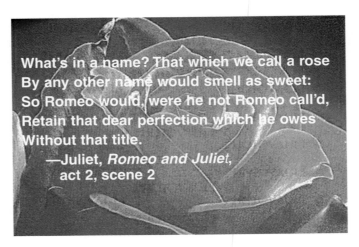

What's in a name? That which we call a rose
By any other name would smell as sweet:
So Romeo would, were he not Romeo call'd,
Retain that dear perfection which he owes
Without that title.
—Juliet, *Romeo and Juliet*,
act 2, scene 2

Words have no intrinsic meaning of their own, and objects have no intrinsic names. A long time ago, for example, some human being decided to use the group of characters *T R E E* to represent that familiar object with roots, trunk, branches, and leaves. After two human beings agreed on this association, they could talk about trees, even if one was not immediately visible. The same concept, *tree*, could be assigned to groups of characters from other languages and character sets. We call this process **translation**.

Similarly, computer languages also get their meaning from humans. That is, some human being selects a group of characters such as *S U B* and decides to associate that "word" with the operation, "find the difference between two numbers." If the human then decides to associate some number (say, 3) with the same operation, that operation can be represented in machine code (binary digits 1 1) for the computer.

Not all human concepts can be represented by computer languages. Programming languages were designed so that human beings could more easily use computers to solve certain types of problems. Therefore, the communication units of programming languages are primarily associated with commands for data manipulation and retrieval. Although the word *tree* can be represented in the computer by the ASCII code for its component characters, the computer has no idea what a tree is. Only the word can be represented, not the concept.

Syntax

Whether we use human languages or computer languages, we must join together smaller pieces of language to form messages (or programs.) The rules of structure used to form complete messages are called **syntax**. In human language we usually refer to this as *grammar.*

Although computer and human languages both have rules of syntax, the syntax in each is very different. Human languages such as English, for example, have rules governing pluralization, tense, agreement of subject and verb, pronunciation, and even gender. None of these exist in computer languages. Instead, programming language syntax includes rules governing instruction format, repetition, subdivision of tasks, identification of variables, and definition of memory spaces. Rules governing exact spelling and punctuation exist in both.

Not only do the individual rules differ from human to computer languages, but the overall number of rules comprising the complete syntax of any one language is vastly different. Any human language you can name (English? Arabic? Japanese?) has many thousand rules, and more thousands of exceptions. On the other hand, even the most complex computer languages have at most a few hundred rules and tolerate no exceptions.

The greatest syntactic difference between human languages and their computer counterparts is a matter of **tolerance**. Humans have a great deal of freedom in how they use language. We can say the same thing in many different ways, choosing from large selections of words with similar meaning. Often we use inflection or body gestures to completely change the meaning of an utterance. (Can you say *no* so that it means *maybe*?) We can even be creative, using new words or putting words together in unique ways. These possibilities make **human language** flexible and rich in expression.

In contrast, computer languages are spare and economical. There is no room for ambiguity or redundancy. Each computer command can have only one meaning. No two commands can have the same meaning. Syntax is iron clad! Misplacing a comma or period or misspelling a word can drastically affect the output from a program, or cause it not to run at all.

Participants

The most significant difference between human language and computer language is the most obvious one: Human languages are used by human beings to communicate with each other; programming languages are used only by human beings to communicate with machines. Let's look at the ramifications of this difference.

First, only humans use computer programming languages. The computer never uses anything but **binary code**. When we input a message written in a programming language to the computer, that message must be translated into a form the computer can "understand"—binary code. Only after this translation process is complete can the computer respond.

How the computer can respond to a communication is another important issue. When you speak a message to a friend in face-to-face conversation, your friend (the listener) has many choices of how to respond and will select one that best suits his or her mood, your message, and the general situation. The computer has no such choice. It must either obey your command or indicate to you that it does not understand your message.

Notice that the burden of successful communication with the computer lies only with the human being. Often a human listener can understand your meaning even if you use an incorrect word, pronounce something strangely, or make a grammatical error. The computer can do none of these. If the message you entered is translated into a string of ones and zeros that is not recognized by the computer, all it can do is tell you that you have made an error. You must assume the responsibility for resubmitting the (corrected) message.

Figure 5.2.2
Humans use body gestures, facial expression, and inflection as part of face-to-face communication.

Figure 5.2.3
In face-to-face human communication, we can tailor our words based on reactions from our listeners.

5.3 Language Classification: A Programming-Language Family Tree

It is often very helpful in studying new areas to develop a scheme of classification. This is a great help when making comparisons and analyzing differences in the things being classified. The study of computer languages is no different; it helps to classify them. Figure 5.3.1 summarizes the five generations of computer languages we will discuss in this section.

Figure 5.3.1 *Computer language genealogy: traversing the generations.*

Generation	Class	Description	Examples	Dates
1st Generation	Machine language	■ Binary representation of operation codes in 1s and 0s ■ Machine-specific	Robot Instruction Set	1940s
2nd Generation	Assembly language	■ Mnemonic representation of operation codes ■ Machine-specific	Pencil & Paper Instruction set	1950s–1960s
3rd Generation	High-level languages	■ Code resembles English language-like structure ■ Transportable from one machine to another	COBOL, FORTRAN, BASIC, Pascal, Ada	1960s to present
4th Generation	Non-Procedural Languages	■ Query languages ■ Application generators ■ Very high-level languages such as Pascal, other 4GLs	PROLOG, QBE, SQL, Hypertalk, Smalltalk, QUEL, C++,Turbo	1980s–1990s
5th Generation	Natural Languages	■ Treats problems as humans do ■ Allows inheritance of characteristics from previously defined objects ■ Encourages modular development	Visual Basic, Ada 95, HotJava, CASE tools	1990s to 21st century

1st Generation—Machine Languages

The earliest computers could be programmed only by experts using commands and instructions written specifically for each individual computer. To accomplish even the simplest of tasks, the programmer had to write a long series of detailed instructions specifying a **machine language** address for every instruction as well as every data item used. The resulting program consisted of two or three unintelligible columns of binary numbers, difficult for humans to decipher, and extremely error-prone. In addition, if the programmer wanted a different computer to perform the same task, the program had to be completely rewritten using the **machine code** peculiar to the new computer.

Figure 5.3.2 shows part of a machine-language program that calculates the sum of two integers and places the result in the computer's memory. Notice that each instruction contains two parts: an **operation code** in the first column, and an **operand** (machine memory address) in the second. A third column, not part of the machine language, has been added to explain the function of each step.

The Computer Continuum

Opcode	Operand	
10000000	00001110	Load contents of memory location num1 into accumulator.
01100000	00001101	Add the contents of memory location num2 to accumulator.
10100000	00001111	Store the result in memory location sum.

Figure 5.3.2

Part of a machine-language program that calculates the sum of two numbers.

2nd Generation—Assembly Languages

Rather than forcing the programmer to write in the binary code native to the computer, an **assembly language** allows the use of convenient alphabetic abbreviations called **mnemonics** to represent operation codes, and abstract symbols to represent operands (memory addresses and data items). The resulting program is still in two or three columns, but somewhat more intelligible to humans and thus less error-prone.

Because the program is no longer written in ones and zeros, the computer cannot directly understand it. Assembly language made programming easier for humans, but one step harder for computers. Before the computer can execute an assembly-language program, the program must first be translated into binary code.

In the example in Figure 5.3.3, notice how alphabetic abbreviations that are easier to decipher and remember are used in the opcode column rather than binary numbers. More significant, alphabetic symbols are used in place of actual memory addresses in the operand column. This greatly simplifies programming because the programmer has no need to know or remember exact storage locations of data and instructions.

Opcode	Operand
load	num1
add	num2
store	sum

Figure 5.3.3

Alphabetic mnemonic commands make assembly language easier than machine code for human programmers.

3rd Generation—High-Level Languages

The next step in program language development produced the first programming languages that are human oriented rather than machine oriented. Instructions in these languages are called statements.

High-level language statements resemble English phrases combined with the mathematical terms needed to express the problem or task being programmed. The syntax (grammatical form) and semantics (meanings) of such statements do not reflect the internal machine code or instruction set of any one particular computer. High-level languages are therefore said to be **machine-independent**. This means that programs written in a high-level language require very little reprogramming when transferred to a different computer.

```
program sums2 (input, output);
var
    num1, num2, sum : integer;
begin
    read(num1, num2);
    sum := num1 + num2;
    writeln(sum)
end.
```

Figure 5.3.4

The third generation brought programming languages closer to human thought processes than either machine or assembly languages did.

The programming example in Figure 5.3.4 is written in a high-level language called **Pascal**. It illustrates how close to the English language a high-level program statement can be.

4th Generation—Non-Procedural Languages

Actually, the fourth generation encompasses many categories of programming-language–like systems, each of which aims at simplifying the human's task of imparting instructions to a computer. Most of these systems are associated with specific applications packages and enable people unfamiliar with programming to describe tasks to be performed by the computer. Some common **fourth generation languages** include query languages, report writers, and application generators.

Query languages—Usually embedded within database management programs, query languages enable users to specify exactly what information is desired from the database.

Report writers—These take the information retrieved from a database and format it into attractive, usable output. Many report writers can perform a limited number of calculations, including totals, subtotals, averages, and counts. Some also enable the user to enter custom calculation formulas.

Application generators—These enable the user to specify a problem and describe the desired results. When the user is done, the application generator creates the program (usually in assembly language or binary code). Many powerful micro-computer programs today include specialized application generators called **macro-languages**.

Amazing Grace

Admiral Grace Murray Hopper was one of the pioneers of computing. Most early experts believed computers were too complicated and expensive for the general public. Hopper's motto was, "If computers were easier to operate, more people would use them." She dedicated her long navy career to computer standardization and demystifying their use.

In 1955, Hopper invented COBOL (Common Business Oriented Language), a programming language, to knock down the "Tower of Babble" that made early computers so difficult to use. Prior to her creating the first compiler, each computer's system used a unique mixture of mathematical symbols to operate. To use a different computer, one had to learn its particular code of language. Hopper's compiler allowed English words to be translated into numerals—ones and zeros—that any computer could understand. This revolutionized the computer industry, because anyone could use a computer to help with his or her daily business needs and computers could communicate with other computers.

One of her most famous inventions in 1943 was the "computer bug" or "debugging." The term was coined when the navy assigned Hopper to the Bureau of Ordinance Computation Project at Harvard University. Hopper worked on the development of the Mark II computer used for creating ballistic tables for aiming navy guns, schedules for supplying ships, and other top-secret calculations used for the atomic bomb. When evaluating why the new computer wasn't performing, Hopper traced the malfunction down to a short-circuit caused by a moth. The bug was flattened between contacts, preventing the relay from making its connections. Her team taped the dead moth into the log book with this notation, "First actual case of a bug being found." When challenged for not making enough progress, the feisty woman of computing would reply she was debugging the computer. The original "bug" is still preserved at the museum of the Naval Surface Weapon Center at Dahlgren, Virginia.

Admiral Grace Murray Hopper died in December 1991, leaving behind an amazing 85-year legacy of accomplishments.

Is There a Fifth Generation?

Many more computer languages are being developed and will be introduced during the next several years. Current trends show that such languages will one day make computer programming as easy as human speech. Much research and experimentation toward this goal is being done in the area of **natural languages**.

Communication with a computer using natural language will be as easy as ordinary conversation in one's native language. Unfamiliar syntax and special meanings will be eliminated, making error-free programs much easier to achieve. Programs called intelligent compilers are now being developed to translate natural language (spoken) programs into structured machine-coded instructions that can be executed by computers.

Assembled, Compiled, or Interpreted Languages

Except for those written in machine code, the computer's "native language," all programs must be translated before their instructions can be executed. This universal need for translation enables us to group computer languages according to another concept: What translation process is used to convert this language into binary code? Figure 5.3.5 summarizes the three types of translators discussed here.

Assembled languages—The translation program used with an **assembly language** is called an **assembler.** In the translation process, each assembly language statement yields a single line of binary (machine) code. The entire program is assembled before the program is sent to the computer for execution.

Interpreted languages—An **interpreter** translates the high-level program one statement at a time. Each programming-language statement (called **source code**) may yield several lines of **object code** (instructions in binary) as a result of the interpretation process.

As each statement is translated, it is checked for errors. If there are none, the object (binary) code is sent to the computer's central processing unit for execution. Once executed, the binary coded instruction is discarded before the next statement is translated. As a result, the program must be reinterpreted each and every time it is run. This is a slow process, but it is especially helpful if you are trying to locate errors in the original program.

Compiled languages—A **compiler** reads and translates the entire high-level language program before anything is sent to the CPU for execution.

As each line is translated, it is set aside until the entire program translation is complete. The whole program in object (binary) code form is then saved to disk. If the compiler has detected no errors during compilation, the whole program is ready to be executed. Like the interpreter, the compiler may produce several lines of object code for each statement in the original language.

A compiled program is more efficient than an interpreted one, but it is not as helpful in the finding and correcting of program errors. After a program has been correctly compiled, its binary coded form (already stored on disk) can be reused as often as desired without recompilation.

Natural languages are human languages that have developed naturally since early man first learned to communicate. We usually think of them as *spoken* rather than *written* languages. In terms of computers, natural languages will enable users to speak instructions into the computer instead of writing them in some programming language.

An **assembler** is a program installed in the computer that reads and translates an assembly-language program, producing one instruction in binary code for each instruction in the original assembly-language program. The entire program must be translated before it is ready for execution.

An **interpreter** is a program installed into the computer that reads your program one line at a time, translates that line into machine code, and either returns it to you for correction or sends it to the CPU for execution before proceeding to the next line of your program.

A **compiler** is a program installed in the computer that reads and translates your entire program. After it has finished translation, it counts errors. If the number of errors is zero, the program is ready for execution.

Figure 5.3.5 *Comparative characteristics of computer-language translators.*

	Assembler	Interpreter	Compiler
Source Code Languages	Assembly language program.	3rd generation language program.	3rd generation language program.
Object Code Languages	Each line of source program yields one line of binary (machine) code.	Each line of source program yields several lines of binary (machine) code.	Each line of source program yields several lines of binary (machine) code.
Translation Pattern	Entire program is translated before program is executed.	Program lines are translated and executed one by one.	Entire program is translated before program is executed.
Hardware Orientation	Machine specific	Machine independent	Machine independent
Advantages	Address hardware functions directly for increased speed.	Error messages line specific, easier to debug.	Quicker and more efficient than interpreters.
Disadvantages	Assembly language harder to learn than 3rd generation.	Interpretation process takes longer than compilation.	Error messages often hard to decipher, not line specific.

5.4 Minimal Language Requirements: The Bare Essentials

Speaking very generally, we humans want to use computers to do three things:

Organize data—Arrange random data into meaningful, cohesive, usable information.

Calculate results—Perform mathematical calculations given necessary data and correct procedures.

Present results—Return to the user the requested or calculated information, either onscreen or in printed form (hard copy).

This section explores, very briefly, five categories of computer language essentials—things needed by all computer languages if we humans are to be able to program computers to accomplish the three generalized goals.

Program Formatting

Hold your hat for the surprise statement of the year: Computers cannot read! They have no idea what words, statements, or programs mean. They perform by a series of recognitions. If a compiler can recognize a high-level program command, it can translate that command. If the computer can recognize a string of ones and zeros as a particular command, it can execute the command that specific binary grouping represents. A program uses many formatting rules to simplify these recognition tasks.

Beginnings and endings—Most programming languages use some sort of recognition device (such as punctuation, for example) at the beginning and end of each program or unit within a program. Whatever devices are used, beginnings and endings indicate the limits of a programming entity, which must be executed as a unit.

Statement format—Each statement in a given programming language must conform to predetermined **formatting** specifications. Format rules might include order of elements within the statement, punctuation, capitalization, line numbering, and relationship of one line to another.

Reserved words—Each computer language sets aside, or *reserves*, a small number of words that have been defined by the translation program as having special meaning within that language. **Reserved words** are used in data manipulation and formatting. Some examples are *if*, *then*, *and*, *begin*, *end*, *function*, *program*, *or*, and *stop*. Designated reserved words cannot be used for other purposes (such as naming program segments or memory locations) within a program.

Comments and information—Most programming languages provide some way for users to insert descriptive information into a program. This information, called **comments**, or remarks, helps other programmers understand how the author wrote the original program. It might describe the functioning of a particular segment of code, or the purpose of a particular variable. Because comment lines are meant for humans, and not for the computer, the compiler or interpreter skips over them during the translation process.

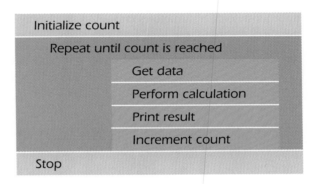

Figure 5.4.1

In this example, physical layout (structure) is determined by the logic needed to perform the program's tasks.

Data Formatting

Because each problem to be solved by a computer is different, one will need different types of **data** to reach a programming solution. A spelling program, for example, manipulates alphanumeric characters, comparing them letter by letter and word by word to other characters stored in the computer's memory. A payroll program handles numeric data, multiplying numbers of hours by rates of pay, subtracting out taxes, adding in bonuses, and so forth. In fact, any one program may use several different types of data to reach a solution.

Data Types

A high-level programming language differentiates among various **data types** both in how they are used in a program and in how they are stored in the memory.

Before writing a program, the programmer must first identify what pieces of information will be needed in solving a particular problem, and then specify which data type will be used for each one. Most commonly, four basic data types can be identified: integer, real, character, and Boolean. Figure 5.4.2 gives definitions and examples for each.

Data is a given fact. **Information** is data that has been processed by the computer and presented to the user in a meaningful form. The presentation may involve manipulating and organizing the form of the data, analyzing and evaluating the content of the data, and producing a usable report of the results.

Figure 5.4.2
. . . .
Most third and fourth gen-
eration languages allow
for at least four basic data
types.

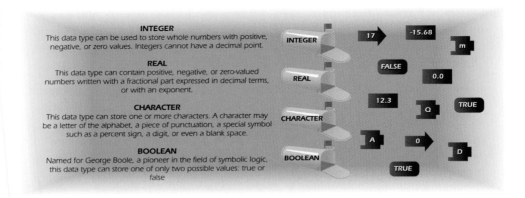

INTEGER
This data type can be used to store whole numbers with positive, negative, or zero values. Integers cannot have a decimal point.

REAL
This data type can contain positive, negative, or zero-valued numbers written with a fractional part expressed in decimal terms, or with an exponent.

CHARACTER
This data type can store one or more characters. A character may be a letter of the alphabet, a piece of punctuation, a special symbol such as a percent sign, a digit, or even a blank space.

BOOLEAN
Named for George Boole, a pioneer in the field of symbolic logic, this data type can store one of only two possible values: true or false

Data Structures

Not every piece of information we might wish to describe and manipulate in a computer program can be represented as one of the four data types described in the preceding section. Most data in the real world are difficult to analyze and do not fit readily into one of the traditional four data types. Even the most complex data, however, is composed of simpler pieces of information combined in some fashion to form a **data structure**. The three most common structures created by combining simple data elements together are the character string, the array, and the record.

■ The **character string** is composed of individual characters that have been made into a structure by lining them up in a specific sequence. It is the sequence that creates the string's structure (see Figure 5.4.3).

Figure 5.4.3
. . . .
A string is a group of char-
acter data items tied
together in a specific order.

Figure 5.4.4
. . . .
An array includes a list of
values, all the same type
(these are integers), stored
together in the memory
under a common name.

1	92
2	87
3	65
4	100
5	79
6	95
7	88
9	90

■ An **array** is a list of data elements, all the same type, that are stored one right after the other in the computer's memory, and which can be accessed by using just one memory-location name (see Figure 5.4.4).

■ A **record** is also a group of data items stored together under one name. An array data structure and a record data structure differ, however, in two significant ways. First, a record can contain data elements of different types. Second, all the information contained in a single record must pertain to a single instance or individual (see Figure 5.4.5).

The Computer Continuum

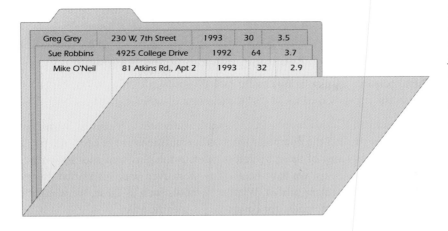

Figure 5.4.5
....
*A record contains a group
of data items, often of differing types, about a single
instance or individual.
Each of these records contains information about
one student.*

Data Manipulation

Declaration Statements: The high-level language statement used to tell the computer
which data types and structures will be used in a particular program is called the **declaration** or **data definition** statement. Figure 5.4.6 gives examples of declaration statements
in four different programming languages. Placed at the very beginning of a program, declaration statements serve three major functions. First, they identify which of the available
data types and structures will best describe each data item. The data type of a particular
item determines which kinds of operations may be performed with it. Mathematical operations, such as addition and subtraction, for example, can be performed only on numeric
(integer and real) data, not on characters.

Second, declaration statements allow the central processing unit to determine in advance
how much memory space to allocate for each piece of data needed.

Pascal	var num1, num2 : Integer; rnum1, rnum2 : Real; Done : Boolean; Last : array [1..30] of packed array [1..15] of char;
COBOL	DATA DIVISION. WORKING-STORAGE SECTION. 01 WORK-AREA. 05 WS-PURCHASE-PRICE PIC9(5) V99. 88 DONE VALUE ZERO. 05 WS-RATE PIC 9V99 VALUE 1.04. 01 PRINT-AREA. 05 FINAL-PRICE-OUT PIC $(6).99. 05 STARS-OUT PIC X(50) VALUE ALL '*'.
FORTRAN	INTEGER NUM1, NUM2 REAL RNUM1, RNUM2 CHARACTER * 15 LAST(30) LOGICAL DONE
BASIC	10 DIM B(10)

Figure 5.4.6
....
*Examples of declaration
statements written in four
different programming languages.*

One last function performed by a declaration statement, but a very helpful one, is to
assign to each piece of information a symbolic name, called a variable name. This enables
the programmer to refer to data within a program by using its variable name instead of
having to memorize specific computer memory locations.

Executable Statements: A high-level language program that consists of a series of instructions used to control the manipulation and transformation of various kinds of data. These instructions are expressed within the program by linguistic elements called **executable statements**.

Some possible manipulations might include a numeric calculation, the building of a string, the regulation of the order of execution of other statements, and so forth.

The data manipulation within an executable statement is triggered by **operators**—words or symbols that tell the computer what individual steps are needed in a particular data manipulation. Many of these operators, such as the plus sign and the minus sign, are already familiar to us; we have been using them ever since we started doing arithmetic problems in elementary school. Without symbols such as these, we would be unable to write executable statements for computing a specific value.

Control Statements: In its most fundamental form, the body, or working part of a program, is a series of statements that the computer executes one at a time in exact physical sequential order. All operations specified in one statement are completed before the computer goes on to the next statement.

No problem of any complexity can be solved by performing a pure sequence of executable statements. Most programs require patterns of program execution more complex than simple sequential flow. Therefore a category of statements is needed that can determine whether and/or when the computer should change execution sequence by skipping to some statement other than the next in line. **Control statements** perform this function.

Two types of control statements are commonly used in computer programs: the **conditional statement** and the **iteration statement**.

■ **Conditional statements.** The conditional statement enables the computer to decide which of two or more alternative sets of instructions to execute. The statement itself requires the computer to make a comparison (called the condition) such as *is x greater than y?* If the comparison is true, a certain statement or sequence of statements will be executed. If the condition is false, the specified statement or sequence will be skipped, or another comparison requested. Figure 5.4.7 illustrates, in schematic terms, a simple conditional structure.

Figure 5.4.7

Schematic representation of a simple conditional control statement.

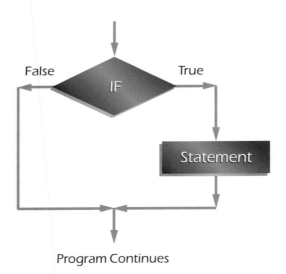

2-112

■ **Iteration statements.** The iteration statement enables the programmer to designate a statement or sequence of statements to be performed more than once within the execution of a program. The number of times the designated statement or sequence is repeated is controlled by a conditional expression. The resulting structure, consisting of an iteration statement, a sequence to be repeated, and a controlling condition, is called a loop. Figure 5.4.8 shows one kind of loop.

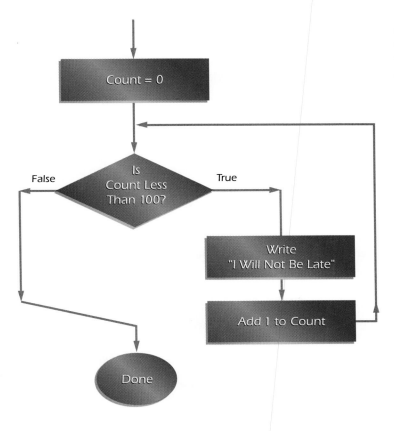

Figure 5.4.8
....
Schematic representation of a looping (repetition) programming structure.

Input n. 1. Anything put into a system or expended in its operation to achieve a result or output, especially: a) energy, work, or power... c) information put into a communication system for transmission or into a data processing system for processing.

Program Input/Output

Take a look at the definitions for **input** and **output**. They should come as no surprise. The concepts of input and output, technical terms related to computer operations, have gradually migrated into the common language, and are often used in everyday results-oriented environments such as manufacturing and production. To turn out a finished product, a factory must first have raw materials on hand. In this sense, a computer program is no different from a factory. The program, too, must have raw materials to produce results (see Figure 5.4.9).

Output n. 1. The act of producing; production. ... 3. Technology. b) The information produced by a computer from a specific input.

Figure 5.4.9
....
Like a factory, a program receives raw materials, processes them, and ships out the resulting product.

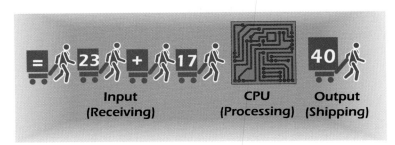

Input
(Receiving)

CPU
(Processing)

Output
(Shipping)

Raw materials for a computer program consist of the data needed for solving the problem. This data must be entered into the computer and stored in its memory before processing can begin. The **input** of this data is accomplished in high-level languages by means of one or more statements instructing the computer to read the data from some appropriate device. Some of the more common devices for data entry include a keyboard, a disk drive, a CD-ROM drive, and a scanning device. After the data has been entered into the computer, the CPU stores it in memory locations named and defined in the declaration statements of the program.

After the data has been processed, a series of **output** statements is needed in the program to tell the computer to send its program results to some appropriate **output device**. The two most common output devices attached to a computer to let us know what it has been doing are the monitor and the printer.

5.5 Building a Program

As we have already seen, **computer programs** are progressions of instructions written by human beings for the purpose of using a machine, the computer, to assist in the solution of problems. Some computer problems fit into the traditional mold of mathematical problems (that is, "Calculate the weekly salaries of all the employees in XYZ Corporation"). Others may not seem at all like problems in the traditional sense ("Access whatever information, sound, or video that is wanted from a CD-ROM disk"). Whatever type of problem needs to be solved, a carefully thought out plan of attack is needed before a computer solution can be determined.

The First Step: Understanding the Problem

Writing a computer program to accomplish even the simplest task involves the skills of analyzing problems and devising plans for their solutions. To begin, you must first state the problem clearly and precisely. Suppose we wanted to perform this task:

> Print out the names of the students in your class.

That sounds like an easy enough task. But do we know enough about the problem to be able to solve it? Do we know, for example, how many names are on the list? Do we want the names to appear one after the other in paragraph form, or each on a separate line in a list? Where can we find the names? Do we want them to appear on a monitor or on paper? None of this information appears in the simple statement of our problem. We don't even know for sure that we want to use the computer as part of the solution. Until these questions and others like them have been answered, we cannot begin to work on a solution. The problem must first be restated, providing all the information we need to proceed.

So let's try again:

> Write a program that will instruct the computer to accept the names of 30 students, one at a time, as we type them in on a keyboard, and print them out in the same order on paper in a numbered list.

There! That's better! The new problem statement contains the answer to all those troublesome questions. Now we can go on to the job of devising a solution. One word of caution before we continue, however: Not all problems are this simply restated. The more complex the problem, the more time and care must be spent producing an accurate statement of the tasks to be done.

The Computer Continuum

Developing the Algorithm

After the problem to be solved has been clearly stated, the next step is to devise a plan of attack for writing the program. Computer programmers call a plan like this an **algorithm**.

The development of an algorithm begins with an analysis of the data needs of the prospective program. Two questions should be asked. First, what information has to be fed into the computer? This is called the **input data**. For our class-list program, the input data consists of the names of the 30 students in the class.

The second question in the analysis of data needs is, what information do I want to get out of the computer? For the class-list problem, that's easy. We want to get out the same data that we put in: the students' names, numbered consecutively from 1 to 30. This printed list of the student names will be the **output data** of our program.

Now that we know our data needs, we must plan the processing that will cause our input data to become our output data. The processing part of the program algorithm is called the **logic** of the program. For the class-list program, our processing will consist of generating the numbers from 1 to 30, one at a time, so that they can be printed with the names. Because our problem is a very easy one, our algorithm contains only one processing step. Most problems require many more processing steps to complete their logical development.

Although we have now identified the input data, the output data, and the processing steps needed for the class-list program, we are still not ready to begin writing in a programming language. We must produce a more detailed, step-by-step plan of everything we want the computer to do. The computer must follow these steps, for example, for the class-list program:

> Start a name-counter at 0.
>
> Get a name from the keyboard.
>
> Add 1 to the name-counter.
>
> Print the value of the name-counter and the name.
>
> Go and get a new name, unless all 30 are done.
>
> When all 30 are done, stop processing.

We can write out a step-by-step program plan in many ways. Nothing is wrong, for example, with a straightforward sentence outline like the one above. Programmers, however, often use one of three major notations for planning detailed algorithms: flow charts, Nassi-Schneidermann charts, and pseudocode.

Flow charting has been a part of program development almost as long as there have been programs. A **flow chart** consists of a series of visual symbols that represent the logical flow of a program. Each type of programming instruction (input/output, executable, control, and so on) is represented by a differently shaped symbol. Notice, for example, that a diamond shape represents a decision (conditional) statement. Figure 5.5.1 is a flowchart showing the logic of the class-list program we have been solving.

Two research programmers working in the field of psychology developed another method of visualizing program algorithms. **Nassi-Schneidermann charts** use specific shapes and symbols to represent different types of program statements. Figure 5.5.2 shows a Nassi-Schneidermann chart for the class-list program.

An **algorithm** is a detailed description of the exact methods used for solving a particular problem.

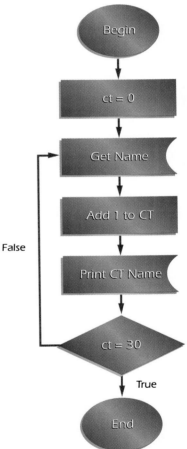

Figure 5.5.1

A flow chart is one method of notation for describing a detailed algorithm.

Figure 5.5.2

A Nassi-Schneidermann
chart for the student-list
problem.

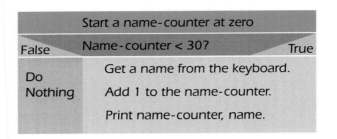

Start a name-counter at zero		
False	Name-counter < 30?	True
Do Nothing	Get a name from the keyboard. Add 1 to the name-counter. Print name-counter, name.	

```
start
namecount = 0
repeat until namecount = 30
    read name
    namecount = namecount + 1
    print namecount, name
end repeat
stop
```

Figure 5.5.3

*Pseudocode version of the
solution to the student-list
problem.*

Pseudocode is also a verbal shorthand method of detailing the steps of a program. It consists of statements that closely resemble those of a programming language, but do not have to follow a rigid syntax structure. The programmer can pattern his/her pseudocode after any programming language that is familiar and comfortable. Of course, many select the language in which the final program will be written. For our program, the pseudocode in Figure 5.5.3 is modeled after Pascal.

Writing the Program

By this point in the programming process, the difficult tasks of analysis and planning have been completed. If the analysis and planning of the program have been thoroughly and well done, translating our detailed, step-by-step plan into a programming language should be a quick and easy task.

Documenting the Program

During both the algorithm development and the program writing stages of programming, explanations called *documentation* are added to the code. Such comments help people other than the programmers understand the exact processes to be performed by the computer. Documentation usually includes technical notes for programmers, such as explanations of variable definition and usage. It also often includes notes for the end-user, such as instructions for installation and program execution.

But we're not done yet. The final step in building a program is correcting its flaws.

Testing and Debugging the Program

During this phase, attempts are made to discover and eliminate any errors (programmers call them **bugs**) in the finished product. The program must be executed many times, using different data sets. The purpose of extensive testing is to establish four important elements that determine the program's quality:

■ The program must be free of **syntax errors**. A syntax error is a mistake in the form or grammar of the program statements. Eliminating syntax errors is fairly easy and must be completed early in the testing activities. A program cannot be translated into machine language unless there are no syntax errors, and the computer cannot execute it until translation has been completed.

■ The program must be free of **logic errors**. Logic errors are mistakes in the algorithm or plan of the program. Because they are buried in the thought processes of the problem's solution, logic errors are more difficult to detect than syntax errors and are harder to correct.

■ The program must be **reliable**. A program is considered reliable if it correctly performs the task(s) defined by the statement of the problem. It must be able to produce correct results with every possible combination of appropriate data.

The Computer Continuum

■ The program must be **robust**. That means it should be able to detect execution errors such as improperly typed data or insufficient memory, warn the user, and allow the error to be corrected or terminate the run.

Even with tasks as trivial as the class-list problem, program development is both time consuming and exacting. The larger and more complex the problem, the more difficult the job of developing an algorithm to solve it. Our problem was solved in an hour's time and yielded a program only 8 to 10 lines long, depending on the language chosen. Real-life programs may have several hundred thousand lines and take a team of highly skilled programmers up to several years of development time.

Three Sample Programs

Pascal

```
Program Name_List (input,output);
  var
     count : integer;
     name : packed array [1 . . 15] of char;
  begin
     for count := 1 to 30 do
        begin
           readln (name);
           writeln (count:3, name:20)
        end
  end.
```

C

```
main ( )
{
   int count;
   char name{15};

   for(count=1; count<=30; ++ count)
      { gets(name);
        print("%2d  %s\n",count,name);}
}
```

FORTRAN

```
Character * 15 Name
   Integer Count
   Do 27 Count = 1,30,1
      Read, Name
      Write, Count, Name
27  Continue
   Stop
   End
```

Many computer catastrophes have shown that as programs grow in size and complexity, we must be very careful and be prepared for failure. A sophisticated operating system may be well over several million lines of code with very complex logic. In a project of such vast size, no one can possibly predict how safe and reliable the program will be until it has been extensively tested. Even then, testing every single eventuality in a complex system is virtually impossible. There are no guarantees that some unexpected condition will not cause the program to fail at some point in the future.

To understand these problems, let's look at how commercial software is created. Of course the software is created to satisfy some goal. Usually the project is broken down into small segments called subprograms. Each subprogram is analyzed, written, and tested individually. Then, when the complete program has been designed and coded (that is, put into some computer language), the final testing begins.

At this point the program starts out in what is commonly referred to as **alpha testing**. This is normally done within the company that created the program. The process will uncover any major problems, which are appropriately corrected.

Because it is impossible to check all possible conditions that could occur in a large program, it makes sense to subject it to testing that involves an even wider number of conditions. This is usually referred to as **beta testing**. The program is sent out to possibly hundreds of sophisticated users outside the company who will test the program under an enormous number of conditions. The motivation to do this beta testing is that it is both ego satisfying (be the first kid on the block with the latest software) and there may be possible business advantages gained by knowing the latest software. After both alpha and beta testing problems have been resolved (and this may take several months and produce many versions of the program), software is usually ready for the commercial market.

5.6 Real-World Programming Today

We have spent a lot of time in this chapter explaining programming languages and the process of writing a computer program. Our approach has been, however, admittedly simplistic. Examples of programs and computer problems have been trivial—short, uncomplicated problems with brief solutions.

Although the use of short, simple examples is a good teaching and learning tool, it does not give an accurate picture of problem solving and computer programming in the real world. Before we go on to explore the many ways computers are being used today, let's improve our perspective by getting a broader view of real-world programming.

How long, then, are real programs? How long, for example, is a standard word processor or spreadsheet program? How long is a compiler? How long is the ROBOT simulator program that enables you to try out your ROBOT program onscreen? Hold your hats! The numbers in Figure 5.6.1 are out of sight.

The Computer Continuum

Figure 5.6.1 *Comparative sizes of real-life programs.*

Type of Program	Number of Lines
The ROBOT simulator	Over 1,000 lines
The compiler for a language with a limited instruction set	Tens of thousands of lines
A full-featured word processor	Hundreds of thousands of lines
A microcomputer operating system	Approximately 2,000,000 lines
A military weapon management program (controlling missiles, for example)	Several *million* lines

Another measure of the effort spent on real-life programs, as compared with those written as student exercises, is time. How long does it take to write a computer program?

Students writing programs usually work alone on their projects and measure the time spent in numbers of hours. In the real world, commercially written programs are seldom, if ever, the product of one person working alone. More often they are the work of project teams, who measure their time in units called **person-months** and **person-years**. A person-month is equivalent to one person working forty hours a week for four weeks. Therefore, a team of five working for eight weeks would be 10 person-months.

Large projects, those in the 100,000 line size range and up, measure time in person-years. Twelve person-months make up a one-person year. It is not at all unusual for a large programming project to take two years or more to complete, with a project team of 6–10 people.

bits & bytes

The Millennium Crisis

The problem began in 1970 when the U.S. Department of Commerce, National Bureau of Standards' *Federal Information Processing Standards* (FIPS PUB 4) went into effect. This standard called for a 6-digit date on all information exchanged between federal agencies. Computer users in government and business designed their programs and database systems to meet the 1970 standards.

At first glance, the impact of the date standard seems negligible. Its importance, however, was anticipated by Jerome and Marilyn Murray in 1984. The title of their work said it all: *Computers in Crisis: How to Avert the Coming Worldwide Computer Systems Collapse*. The collapse they predicted has been the subject of much activity and controversy for well over a decade.

Is New Year's day in the year 2000 to be written as 01/01/00? Most computer programs would view this date as earlier than any date before New Year's day 1900. You may think that it would be easy to make a date with 00 as the year 2000. However, this would mean going to every program that uses dates and modifying that program, taking into account the problem.

The modifications would be a major problem for many established companies around the world. Millions of programs have been written in many languages to handle dated information. Each program would have to be checked for any problems with dates ending in 00. If nothing is done, programs that make decisions based on dates, such as insurance premiums, interest payments, benefit eligibility, or pension payments, will give erroneous results.

As you read further in this book, you will discover how computers are being used in art, music, business, education, and everyday life. Keep in mind that the programs, which

Chapter 5: Computer Languages: Empowering Algorithms

make the computers usable, are incredibly long and complicated and that they took a lot of time and effort to write. Work it out for yourself. If it took you an hour or so to work out the program for the word-search game in Chapter 2, how long would it take to write the 10,000 or so lines of a small compiler?

Chapter Summary

What you can do with what you have learned:

■ Know the difference between the semantics of a statement and the syntax of a statement

■ Identify why a small error, such as a missing comma, in a computer program can cause it not to execute

■ Pick out examples of each of the five generations of programming languages

■ Decide when to choose a compiled version of a language rather than an interpreted version

■ Pick out the major types of statements in a programming language

■ Take a problem from the statement of the problem to the actual computer program

■ Decide whether a program fulfills the requirements for a quality program

■ Understand why large, intricate programs take so long to become commercially available and how many person-years it takes to produce them

Key Terms and Review Questions

Key terms introduced in this chapter:

Communication cycle 2-102

Programming languages 2-102

Semantics 2-103

Translation 2-104

Syntax 2-104

Tolerance 2-104

Human language 2-104

Binary code 2-105

Machine language 2-106

Machine code 2-106

Operation code 2-106

Operand 2-106

Assembly language 2-107

Mnemonics 2-107

High-level language 2-107

Machine-independent 2-107

Pascal 2-107

Fourth generation languages 2-107

Query languages 2-108

Report writers 2-108

Application generators 2-108

Macro-language 2-108

Natural languages 2-109

Assembly language 2-109

Assembler 2-109

Interpreter 2-109

Source code 2-109

Object code 2-109

Compiler 2-109

Formatting 2-111

Reserved words 2-111

Comments 2-111

Data 2-111

Information 2-111

Data types 2-111

Data structure 2-112

Matching

Match the key terms introduced in the chapter to the statements below. Each term may be used once, more than once, or not at all.

1. _____ This language is spoken by humans to communicate with each other.

2. _____ This term refers to meaning.

3. _____ This term refers to the grammatical form or structure of a language.

4. _____ This refers to a language that has been written by humans for the express purpose of being able to communicate with digital computers.

5. _____ This is the porting of ideas, instructions, and concepts from one language to another.

6. _____ This is the form that all information must be translated into before the computer can "understand" it.

7. _____ The term given to instructions when they are written in binary.

8. _____ This is the first part of an instruction.

9. _____ This category of languages uses alphabetic abbreviations called mnemonics.

10. _____ This category of languages encompasses a wide range of programming-language–like systems, each of which aims at simplifying the task of imparting instructions to a computer.

11. _____ This category of languages will enable users to use natural-language communication.

12. _____This category of languages has statements that resemble English phrases combined with mathematical terms needed to express the problem or task being programmed.

13. _____This type of language usually is embedded within database management programs.

14. _____Research is being done in this area that will enable a person to speak instructions into the computer instead of writing them in some programming language.

15. _____Except for programs written in machine language, this must be done to all programs before their instructions can be executed.

16. _____This translation program translates an entire high-level language program into machine code before sending it to the CPU for execution.

17. _____This is the term given to programming-language statements that are still in their high-level language form.

18. _____This is the term given to programming-language statements that have been changed to machine-language form.

19. _____This is a detailed description of the exact methods used for solving a particular problem.

20. _____This is a mistake in the form or grammar of the program statements.

True or False

1. _____In contrast to human language that is tolerant of minor grammatical errors in communication, programming languages are intolerant of grammatical errors.

2. _____Programming computers has become easier because they no longer need instructions to be translated into binary code.

3. _____As shown in the diagram in the chapter, each assembly-language instruction may produce several lines of object code.

4. _____As shown in the diagram in the chapter, each high-level–language instruction may produce several lines of object code.

5. _____Compiled languages are more efficient than interpreted languages.

6. _____When using an interpreted language, it is easier to find errors than in a compiled language.

7. _____An assembler is only used to translate assembly-language programs into machine code.

8. _____Only compilers are used to translate high-level languages to machine code.

9. _____Whereas interpreters translate one line of a program into one line of object code, a compiler may translate one line of a program into several lines of object code.

10. _____Data types include data structures.

11. _____For our purposes, data and information are synonymous.

12. _____A loop is comprised of iteration statements, together with a conditional expression, and some instructions to be repeated.

13. _____Nassi-Schneidermann charts are often used by programmers for planning detailed algorithms.

14. _____Bugs are strictly syntax errors found by the compiler.

15. _____Sophisticated users outside the company who will test the program under an enormous number of conditions do alpha testing.

16. _____Consumers do beta testing after the manufacturer has released it.

17. _____For a program to be reliable, it must correctly perform the defined tasks with every possible combination of data.

18. _____For a program to be robust, it must be able to detect improperly entered data and other execution errors such as insufficient memory. It would warn the user of a problem and enable the user to correct or terminate the run.

19. _____A person-month is equal to four people working 40 hours or one person working for four weeks at 40 hours.

20. _____Large projects measure time in person-months.

Multiple Choice

Answer the multiple choice questions by selecting the best answer from the choices given.

1. This type of language falls under the first generation of programming languages.

   a. Assembly language
   b. High-level language
   c. Machine language
   d. Natural language
   e. Query language

2. This type of language falls under the second generation of programming languages.

   a. Assembly language
   b. High-level language
   c. Machine language

   d. Natural language
   e. Query language

3. This type of language falls under the third generation of programming languages.

   a. Assembly language
   b. High-level language
   c. Machine language
   d. Natural language
   e. Query language

4. This type of language falls under the fourth generation of programming languages.

a. Assembly language

b. High-level language

c. Machine language

d. Natural language

e. Query language

5. This type of language falls under the fifth generation of programming languages.

a. Assembly language

b. High-level language

c. Machine language

d. Natural language

e. Query language

6. This translation program changes a high-level language into machine code one line at a time, executing each line as it goes.

a. Assembler

b. Compiler

c. Interpreter

d. Source code

e. Object code

7. This translation program changes second generation programming languages into machine code.

a. Assembler

b. Compiler

c. Interpreter

d. Source code

e. Object code

8. A high-level program using this translation program will not be allowed to execute until after it has been changed to machine code.

a. Assembler

b. Compiler

c. Interpreter

d. Source code

e. Object code

9. This is the term given to the translated machine code version of a program.

a. Assembler

b. Compiler

c. Interpreter

d. Source code

e. Object code

10. This is the term given to the high-level language version of the program.

a. Assembler

b. Compiler

c. Interpreter

d. Source code

e. Object code

Exercises

1. Name and briefly describe the *four* major generations of computer programming language.

2. Write a sentence that is semantically correct, but syntactically wrong. Explain the difference between semantics and syntax.

3. How do words in human languages get their meaning? How does this process change for computer languages?

4. Name several human concepts (such as age or affection) that cannot be represented by computer languages. Why can't the computer deal with ideas like these?

5. Give a few examples of syntax rules in a human language.

6. What do we mean when we say that computer languages have very low error tolerance?

7. Make up a chart showing some of the differences between human languages and computer languages.

8. Explain the concept of feedback in human communication. How does this concept change when we are communicating with a machine?

9. What is meant by natural language? Explain some of the possible problems involved in using natural language with computers.

10. Why are machine language and assembly language considered "machine dependent?"

11. Why can compiled and interpreted computer languages be machine independent?

12. Name the one most important difference between an interpreted and a compiled language.

13. What kinds of data can be handled by symbolic computer languages?

14. Pick any two of the several problem-solving approaches used by computer languages. Explain how each one works. Be sure to explain how the two approaches differ.

15. What are the three general things we humans want computers to do for us?

16. Why do computer programs need comment statements?

17. Explain the relationship between data and information.

18. Find several examples from everyday life of information that can be described using the record data structure.

19. This chapter names four major categories of programming statements. Explain them.

20. Make up a chart showing what types of statements are included in the Word Hunt (Chapter 2), ROBOT, and Pencil & Paper (Chapter 3) instruction sets. Be sure you use examples from all three on your chart.

21. What is the difference between an iteration statement and a conditional statement?

22. Explain what is meant by the word algorithm.

23. What are the four measures of program quality discussed in this chapter?

24. Describe the three methods of representing an algorithm explained in this chapter.

25. What is the difference between a syntax error and a semantics (or logic) error in a program? Give an example of each.

Discussion Questions

1. How might it be to the economic advantage of a programmer to become an expert in a high-level programming language rather than an assembly language for a particular model of computer?

2. Can you think of any circumstances under which it might be economically advantageous for a programmer to be expert in the assembly language for a particular model of computer?

3. How might it be to the economic advantage of the people who pay for programs to be written to have them written in high-level languages?

4. Discuss why flow charts and/or Nassi-Schneidermann charts might be considered helpful in planning programs and in documenting how they "work."

5. What is the purpose of programming languages (that is, why do we need them)?

6. Explain how the syntax of a programming language relates to the grammar of a human language.

7. There is a move toward a sixth generation of programming languages. What do you think it might entail? What kinds of questions should it answer?

Group Project

A group of four students are assigned the task of designing a software system that helps manage a small retail store. The type of store will be selected by the students as a group. For example, the store could be a music store, comic book store, sports equipment store, ice cream shop, coffee shop, or even a specialty bookstore. The software design should be modular and include at least the following: financial system (accounts payable, accounts receivable, internal reporting, banking, budgeting), inventory with automatic reordering, and personnel/scheduling.

The purpose of the project is to completely specify a system that would enable the store to run smoothly. Details as small as the layout of a computer screen for inventory are necessary. It should be specified so that a programmer could take the design and write the program implementing the system.

Web Connections

http://www.hypernews.org/HyperNews/get/computing/lang-list.html

Extensive list of programming languages, most with links to further information.

http://www.pcwebopedia.com/programming_language.htm

Definition of programming language with many links to related material from this chapter.

http://www.angelfire.com/tn/semantics/

An easy to understand introduction to semantics and the meanings of words.

http://www.linguistics.bangor.ac.uk/java/lt/LingTutor.html

A syntax tutor designed for linguistics students, but relevant to this chapter as well. Loads a Java applet for checking your work.

http://udgftp.cencar.udg.mx/ingles/tutor/Assembler.html

Online tutorial for learning the assembler language of the Intel x86 family of computers. Designed for those with no previous assembler language experience.

http://www.dfki.de/lt/registry/

Home page of the Natural Language Software Registry. It has a myriad of links to software projects in the natural-language field.

http://www.pcwebopedia.com/compiler.htm

Very good definition of compiler, along with a schematic drawing of how it all fits. Also contains links to specific companies producing compilers and research sites.

http://www.cs.sunysb.edu/~algorith/index.html

The Stony Brook Algorithm Depository site. It has links to many computer algorithms organized both by problem category and by language of implementation.

http://www.betabase.com/

Home page of a group of beta testers on the Internet. It includes links to more information about what is being tested and a lot of free downloadable beta software for all platforms.

Bibliography

Baron, Naomi S. *Computer Languages*. New York: Viking Penguin, 1986.

Flanagan, David. *Java in a Nutshell 2nd ed.* Sebastopol: O'Reilly, 1997.

Satzinger, John W., and Tore U. Orvik. *Object-Oriented Approach*. Danvers: Boyd & Fraser, 1996.

Chapter 6

Networks: Everything Is Connected

Chapter Objectives

By the end of this chapter, you will:

- Understand how the human need to communicate has motivated the development of networking technology.

- Identify the various types of physical connections possible in a network.

- Know the five basic properties of a network link and how each contributes to the link.

- Know different ways of connecting computers in a network (bus, ring, star, tree, and fully connected).

- Identify the uses and benefits of DANs, LANs, MANs, and WANs.

- Understand how protocols control the flow of information between networks.

- Understand how information is packaged and repackaged for each intervening network when sent on the Internet.

- Know how networks can be used for email, BBSs, and conferencing systems.

6.1 Introduction: "Everything Is Connected to Everything"

(John F. Akers, Former President of IBM)

During the early 1990s, a new craze seized the United States and the world. By 1995 it had developed into a full-blown frenzy. Every day, computer users in hundreds of thousands of homes and offices turned on their desktop machines and went "online." A few keystrokes or mouse clicks quickly brought an astonishing variety of information and services to their computer monitors. People can do their banking, pay bills with a credit card, plan and book vacation travel, send messages across the office or around the world, participate in free-wheeling discussions, play "live-action" games, or purchase anything from flowers to houses. In fact, it is not uncommon for college students to obtain a course syllabus and get assignments via computer as a result of this new craze. Of course, the biggest use of networks is in business. Connecting CEOs to sales departments to marketing to manufacturing is part of the new craze. Businesses have found networking to be necessary in today's world.

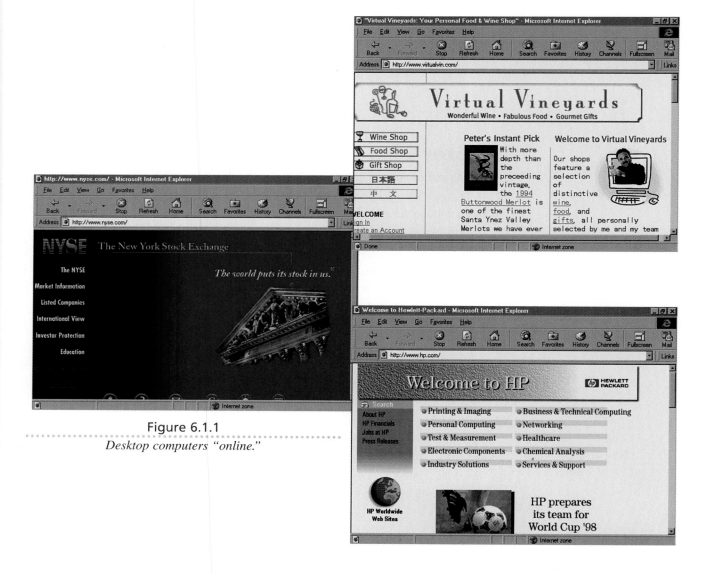

Figure 6.1.1

Desktop computers "online."

The Computer Continuum

Thousands of databases became available. Computer users can now access weather predictions, stock market quotations, lyrics to popular songs, telephone books, maps and itineraries, and contents of entire magazines and newspapers including both text and pictures. The *magic* that provides this wealth of information and services is called computer networking. Computer networking reaches its peak in a phenomenon called the Internet. Today, most of us access the Internet through the World Wide Web, which is probably the most popular service provided over the Internet.

Clearly, computer communication has reached a new plateau. The Internet and the World Wide Web are both in their infancy. There's no telling how far they will take us, or how quickly. But they are growing rapidly and are at the center of a communication revolution. As more and more links are added, and more and more services are accessible, we move inexorably closer to the time predicted by John F. Akers, when he was President of IBM, a time when "everything is connected to everything." The Internet and World Wide Web will be examined in detail in the next chapter.

The human need to communicate—to connect with others—has motivated mankind's creativity from the earliest prehistoric times up throughout history. Cave dwellers drew pictures on the walls of their caves, primitive peoples used smoke signals and drum rhythms, American pioneers developed the Pony Express and Wells Fargo, and Alexander Graham Bell invented the telephone.

All were answering a basic driving force of humanity—the need to share information, be recognized, and give warnings— that is, establish connections to others in the known world.

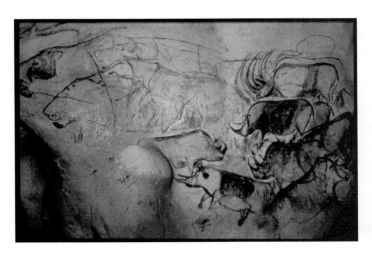

Figure 6.1.2
Cave drawings, signal drums in use, messenger on horseback, and Alexander Graham Bell, inventor of the telephone.

Drum beats and puffs of smoke have given way to visual images and electronic pulses. Yet, the drive for one human being to connect and to pass information to another continues unabated. As the need for human connectivity grows, human ingenuity has developed the technology to enhance that connectivity. There is no doubt that we can today share more information more quickly than ever before by using computer networks.

6.2 Communication Basics: The Physical Topology

To understand computer communications it is necessary to become familiar with several concepts involved with networking. After these concepts are understood, it will be much easier to learn about the Internet and World Wide Web (the subjects of the next two chapters).

Types of Connections—Physical Connection Versus Wireless

The technology that supports computer communication isn't really magical nor mysterious. In fact, the conceptual idea is reasonably simple: just physically connect a bunch of computers together! This means, use wires or optical cables to connect the various computers and call it a **network**. These connections will be referred to as **network links**.

Only the most commonly used types of physical links are discussed here, namely:

- Twisted pair
- Coaxial cable
- Fiber-optic cable

> A **network** consists of a collection of computers, printers, and other devices linked either by physical or wireless means. All these devices will be referred to as nodes and must have a unique address assigned to it by the network.

Of the three, the easiest to visualize is the **twisted pair**. They consist of two wires twisted together to make them less susceptible to acting like an antenna and picking up radio frequency information such as radio station signals, appliance electrical noise, or even household 60-cycle power signals from the power lines in the home or building. The telephone system uses twisted-pair copper wires to link telephones. Figure 6.2.1a illustrates a standard twisted pair.

Coaxial cable uses two wires, but the design is quite different. To make the pair of wires more impervious to outside electrical noise, one of the wires is actually woven of fine strands of copper wire, forming a tube that is electrically grounded. The other is a solid copper wire that runs down the center of this tube, and the space between is filled with a special nonconducting material. Figure 6.2.1b shows a bundle of coaxial cable.

> **Network links** are connections between computers and other electronic devices. These network links are implemented on various types of physical media such as **twisted pairs** of wires (used to connect telephones), **coaxial cables** (used to connect most cable TVs), **fiber-optic cables** (used in modern telephone and cable TVs), and *space* (radio frequency, microwave, and laser beams travel through space).

Wire or cable have definite limitations on how much information can be put through them. Light is also electromagnetic, however, and because of its higher frequencies, a lot more information can be transmitted through a single strand. Experiments on how to use optical cable have been carried out for many years. The result is the **fiber-optic cable** that both cable TV and telephone companies are using now. Figure 6.2.1c shows a bundle of fiber-optic cable. It is more economical to bundle several individual optical fiber strands together in many applications. Each individual cable can carry the equivalent of several thousand phone conversations or computer communications.

The three forms of linking computers together just discussed are all physical in nature. You can touch and hold either twisted pair, coaxial cable, or fiber-optic cable. Another form of equally useful links is wireless. That means the link or connection is made using electromagnetic energy that goes through space instead of traveling along wires or cables. The following three types of wireless communications are commonly used in networking:

- Infrared
- Radio frequency
- Microwave

Figure 6.2.1

Three physical types of links used in networks.

a) twisted pair

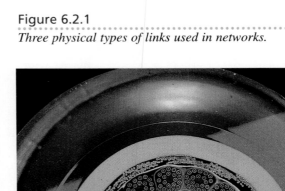

b) coaxial cable

c) fiber-optic cable bundle

Figure 6.2.2

Using an infrared keyboard.

The **infrared** type of communication is commonly used in TV and VCR remote controls. One of the problems with infrared communication is that both devices must be in line of sight. If someone is between you and the TV, for example, your controller won't work unless it has a strong enough signal to bounce off the wall to reach your TV. Infrared frequencies of electromagnetic radiation behave almost the same as visible light. In the computing world, keyboards and mice can use infrared for the link so that you aren't restricted by wires. Figure 6.2.2 shows an infrared keyboard in action.

Radio frequency links can function even though the line of sight is interrupted. The benefits of this are obvious. Suppose, for example, that you park your car in a huge parking lot and can't remember where. Some automobile electronic keys that use radio frequencies can be used to flash the car lights when you press the right button on the electronic key, and thereby make the car's location obvious. Portable telephones also use radio frequencies, but at different wavelengths so that they don't interfere with automobile usage. This form of communication between computers is not as common because of the cost and possible interference from other sources of electromagnetic radiation, such as old electric drills and furnace motors.

As it is often necessary to establish communication with distant locations, **microwave** frequencies and satellite links are quite useful for large-volume communication. The obvious advantage is that physical wires or cables don't have to be constructed from one location to the other. In today's communication world, microwave towers and dish antennas dot the landscape. One of the main disadvantages of microwaves is that they can only be used in line of sight. No obstructions may exist between the transmitting and receiving antennas. In fact, sometimes heavy rainfall can have deleterious effects on microwave communication. The photograph in Figure 6.2.3a

Figure 6.2.3

a) Microwave towers.

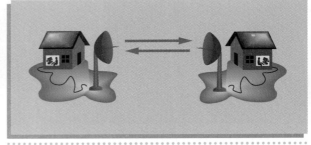

b) Two microwave towers in line of sight.

shows a typical tower with microwave antenna. We can't easily see the other tower it communicates with because they are so far apart, but their relationship is shown in the accompanying diagram in Figure 6.2.3b.

Communications satellites also use microwaves, but a satellite has its own receiving and transmitting antennas and links together two or more Earth stations. Figure 6.2.4a shows a typical communications satellite. The satellite acts as a relay station between one Earth-based microwave station and one or many others, as shown in the diagram of Figure 6.2.4b.

Properties of Transmission

Both of the communication links mentioned in the previous part of this section—network and wireless—have some common attributes that should be discussed. These attributes are important whether dealing with cable TV or telephone and computer communications.

The following five basic properties of both the physical and wireless links are discussed here:

1. Type of signal communicated (analog or digital)
2. The speed at which the signal is transmitted (how fast the data travels)
3. The type of data movement allowed on the channel (one-way, two-way taking turns, two-way simultaneously)
4. The method used to transport the data (asynchronous or synchronous transmission)
5. Single channel (baseband) and multichannel (broadband) transmission

Type of Signal

The signal can be in one of two forms: **analog** or **digital**. Digital signals consist of pulses of electrical energy that represent 0s or 1s (that is, binary numbers). On the other hand, the analog signal is a continuously changing signal similar to that found on the speaker wires of a high-fidelity audio system. Figure 6.2.5 shows these two basic types of communications signals.

Figure 6.2.4

a) Communications satellite.

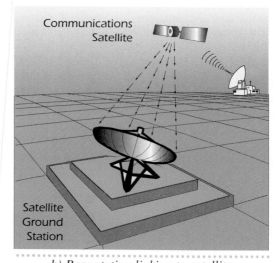

Communications Satellite

Satellite Ground Station

b) Base station linking to satellite.

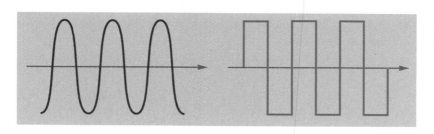

Figure 6.2.5

Analog and digital signals.

Analog signals are typically of lower quality than digital signals. This is evident in the cassette and vinyl record formats, which suffer from wear and limitations of fidelity. The phone system is mostly analog, but in some cities it has been converted to digital. This move to digital systems is also evident in the stereo recording field where compact discs and DAT (digital audio tape) are digital. Why is it inevitable that these changes from analog to digital formats are taking place? It is easier to maintain quality and control over noise and errors with a digital system.

Speed of Signal

The speed at which the data can be transmitted is important. Currently, it is impossible, for example, to transmit a complete TV broadcast signal through a telephone line. The speed at which signals are fed to the channel, and the enormous amount of data in the TV signal would limit the picture to TV snapshots taken several seconds apart.

The speed of transmission in digital systems is measured in **bits per second** (**bps**). Bits per second is a measure of how fast binary digits can be sent through a channel. That is, the number of 0s and 1s that travel down the channel per second. Another term frequently used to describe transmission speed on a digital channel is called the **baud rate**. The baud rate, often confused with bps, is a number indicating how many times the signal on a channel changes per second.

In the personal computer field, communicating data over the analog telephone system between a microcomputer and some destination is achieved through an electronic device called the **modem**. The modem allows the computer to be connected to the link being used. Modems won't be necessary when the telephone system is finally converted to an all digital system. Only some simple type of interface device will be necessary.

Modems are usually mistakenly rated in baud rather than bits per second. The speeds of modems commonly used with personal computers are 1200 bps, 2400 bps, 9600 bps, 14.4 Kbps, and 28.8 Kbps. The abbreviation Kbps is short for kilobits per second, which means a thousand bits per second. For efficient World Wide Web communication, 28.8 Kbps is the minimum speed to use. Telephone lines are of different qualities. It is not unusual for 56 Kbps modems to be used with better telephone lines. To put things into perspective, assume someone is watching a news release being sent to a computer screen. Different bps rates would cause the news release to appear with the following effects:

- *1200 bps:* Good readers can keep up with words printed.
- *2400 bps:* A speed reader would get the gist of the words.
- *9600 bps:* The words fly past the screen in a fraction of a second and would be impossible to read, unless a pause occurs.

When it comes to viewing on the World Wide Web, each of the following bps rates would have delays for a reasonable size graphic image, as indicated:

- *14.4 Kbps:* Quite common in communications; a 10–20 second wait for graphics.
- *28.8 Kbps:* Minimum for World Wide Web browsing with full graphics; a 5–10 second wait for graphics.
- *56 Kbps:* A very efficient speed to browse the World Wide Web. Delightful viewing.

Bits per second (**bps**) is a measure of how fast binary digits can be sent through a channel (that is, the number of 0s and 1s that travel down the channel per second). The **baud rate**, often confused with bps, is a number indicating how many times the signal on a channel changes per second.

A **modem** (**mo**dulator **dem**odulator) is an electronic device that takes the binary data from the computer and converts it to analog data (modulates) so that it can be sent over telephone lines. The receiving end modem then converts it back (demodulates) from analog to digital so the computer can use it.

Modems for microcomputers are made in two different forms:

1. External modems, which connect to the computer's serial port with a cable and have a jack for connecting to the phone line. External modems have the advantage of displaying communications activity on a small screen or with blinking lights (see Figure 6.2.6).

2. Internal modems are contained on an expansion card and plugged into an expansion slot inside the computer. The backside of the expansion card is accessible from the back of the computer so the phone line can be connected. Internal modems are usually less expensive than external modems and are more widely used (see Figure 6.2.7).

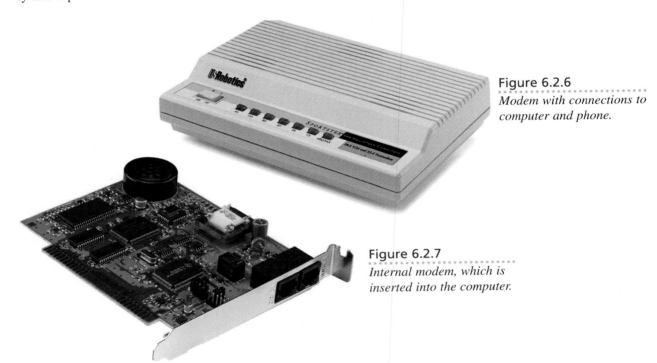

Figure 6.2.6
Modem with connections to computer and phone.

Figure 6.2.7
Internal modem, which is inserted into the computer.

Type of Data Movement on the Link

Three basic types of data movement occur on the link. The most basic movement is called **simplex transmission**. This is a one-way transmission of data. It is usually used for displaying information. An example is the display of flight arrivals and departures on TV monitors found at most airports. Information appears on them, but the observer cannot make changes or send information back to the source (sender).

A more general form of data flow is found in **half-duplex transmission**. In this form, the data can flow one way or the opposite way on the channel, but not both directions at the same time. The old-fashioned telegraph used this type of transmission. **Full-duplex transmission** allows transmission in both directions at the same time. The telephone and the computer are the most familiar examples of full-duplex transmission. Figure 6.2.8 depicts these three types of data movement,

Method of Transmission

There are two basic types of data transmission, each requiring a different modem. One is called **asynchronous transmission**; the other is called **synchronous transmission**.

Asynchronous transmission is cheaper and more commonly used in computer communications. Information is sent byte by byte. As each byte is sent, it is preceded by a start bit. This alerts the receiving computer that the byte is being sent. Some time may pass before another byte is sent because the bytes are not hooked together like a train.

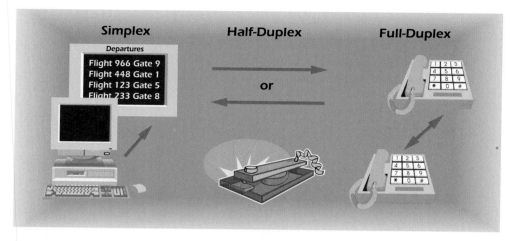

Figure 6.2.8
*Simplex, half-duplex, and
full-duplex transmission.*

In synchronous transmission, data is sent in large blocks rather than in small pieces. Each block is preceded by special information, concerning error detection and block size. Synchronization bits are used to organize the block, which is made up of bytes that flow along just like a train. Synchronous modems are quite expensive, but they are very fast. This method of transmission is used for transporting large amounts of information, and it is more efficient than asynchronous transmission.

Single Channel Versus Multichannel Transmission

Each of the physical or wireless means of linking can carry at least one channel of communication. A channel is a path for the signal, just like a TV channel. In the case of both twisted-pair and coaxial cable, a single signal is most common. The telephone line coming into your home, for example, is not capable of handling more than a single call at a time. Infrared has the capability of being used for multichannel, but is most commonly used as a single channel device.

On the other hand, fiber-optic cable, microwaves, and satellite transmissions most commonly carry more than one channel of communication. In fact, the microwave signals used by telephone companies to carry phone traffic between major cities can simultaneously carry thousands of individual phone conversations and computer communications.

How is it possible to measure the capacity of communication links? **Bandwidth** is a term used to measure the capacity of a link to send information. In the computer-networking field, it means the number of bits per second that can be transmitted on the link. Note that with a wider bandwidth, more diverse kinds of information can be sent—the simplest being voice, the most sophisticated being moving video.

There are other definitions of the word *bandwidth*. For example, in the analog world, it means the difference between the highest and lowest frequencies that can be sent over an analog link. The measurement is given in hertz (Hz). However, for both definitions, a wider bandwidth means more information can flow over the channel.

The bandwidth of several common cable links used in LANs (local area networks) and also telephone services are shown in Figures 6.2.9 and 6.2.10. Note that Kbps means kilobits per second (thousands of bits per second); Mbps means megabits per second (millions of bits per second); and Gbps means gigabits per second (billions of bits per second). Also note that the acronym STS (synchronous transport signal) indicates the link is optical fiber.

The **bandwidth** of a communications link is the number of bits per second (bps) that can be sent over that link.

Figure 6.2.9 *Typical cable bandwidths used in local area networks.*

Cable	Typical Bandwidth
Twisted pair	10 to 100 Mbps
Coaxial cable	10 to 100 Mbps
Fiber-optic cable	100 to 2400 Mbps

Figure 6.2.10 *The bandwidth of different services offered by a telephone company.*

Service	Bandwidth
ISDN	64 Kbps
T1	1.544 Mbps
T3	44.736 Mbps
STS-1	51.840 Mbps
STS-3	155.250 Mbps
STS-12	622.080 Mbps
STS-24	1.244160 Gbps
STS-48	2.488320 Gbps

Linking Computers Together—Direct-Link Networks

When two or more devices are linked together, the total collection is called a network, as defined at the beginning of this section. And remember that each individual device, whether it is a computer, terminal, or printer, is called a **node** of the network. The nodes are linked to each other by physical or wireless means. It is important to differentiate between **direct-link networks** and those networks that are not directly linked, such as the Internet. The telephone system is an example of a directly linked network. When you are talking to someone, a connection is maintained between you and the person you are talking to. To the contrary, two communicating computers on the Internet have no direct connection between them. This will be discussed in Chapter 7, "The Internet: Communication with the World."

Direct-link networks are those whose nodes have direct connections through either physical or wireless links.

The simplest of all networks is obtained by connecting two computing systems, one at each end of the communications link as shown in Figure 6.2.11. This is a very common type of communication, but somewhat limiting. It is referred to as a **point-to-point** network.

This section looks at the generalization of point-to-point links and investigates more complicated systems where many devices are communicating in various arrangements.

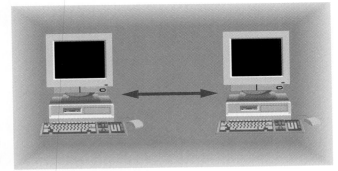

Figure 6.2.11
Computing systems connected by a point-to-point link.

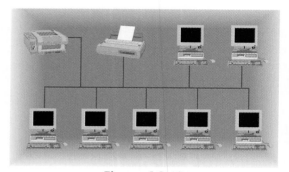

Figure 6.2.12

The bus network.

The most common and inexpensive way to link the nodes of a network is called the **bus network**. Figure 6.2.12 shows an example of this simplest form. The bus network commonly consists of a continuous coaxial cable to which all the devices are attached. All nodes (devices) on the bus can detect all messages sent along the bus at the same time. As a message is sent from one node (for example, a computer) to another (for example, a printer), a special part of the message (address) is used to select the destination (printer) and let the data through (to be printed). All the other devices will ignore the data that wasn't meant for them.

The **ring network** consists of nodes linked together to form a circle as shown in Figure 6.2.13. A message is sent from one node, usually a computer, to the next until it reaches its destination. As each computer receives the message, it either retransmits it to the next node on the ring or it carries out the action commanded by the message.

The **star network** shown in Figure 6.2.14 has each node linked to a central node. All messages must be routed through the central node. The central node acts as a controlling device and will route the messages properly between the other nodes.

Figure 6.2.15 shows what looks like an upside-down tree and is, in fact, called a **tree network**. It is also sometimes referred to as a hierarchical network. The end nodes are linked to interior nodes that allow linking through to another end node. An end node is the last node on the line; in other words, they are the leaves of the tree. This network arrangement is used in the telephone system. The end nodes in the telephone system are the individual telephones, and the interior nodes are the nodes that allow linking to other end-node telephones or computers.

Figure 6.2.13

The ring network.

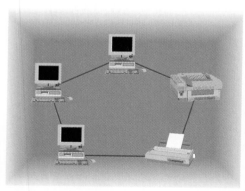

Figure 6.2.15

The tree network.

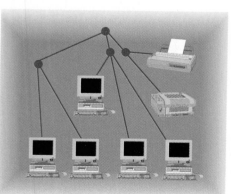

Figure 6.2.14

The star network.

The Computer Continuum

The last network examined is the **fully connected topology network**, shown in Figure 6.2.16. It is the most complete of all networks. All nodes are linked to all other nodes. This means each node has a direct link to all other nodes. This would indeed be a very expensive type of network to build, and is very seldom used except where extreme speed and reliability are needed.

The next step beyond these direct-linked networks leads us to those networks not directly linked. This is a very important and revolutionary concept that consists of providing links between any number of any type of the direct-linked networks, and is called internetworking. The result of internetworking is as small as just linking any two of the direct-linked networks previously discussed, or it can be the largest of them all, the Internet. These types of networks, called hybrid networks, demand special software to allow information to be exchanged between them. The next section introduces some new concepts that will help you to understand these hybrid networks.

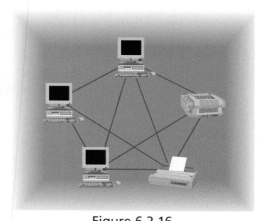

Figure 6.2.16
The fully connected topology network.

Networks on Different Scales

A common way to categorize networks is according to their size. Each size category has its own set of limitations and requirements. The following four common categories of networks are examined:

- DAN (desk area network)
- LAN (local area network)
- MAN (metropolitan area network)
- WAN (wide area network)

Computer Networks: The Beginning

Networking computers was only a dream for many computer scientists until Bob Taylor, director of computer research at ARPA (Advanced Research Projects Agency), focused sponsored research on what was to become the Internet.

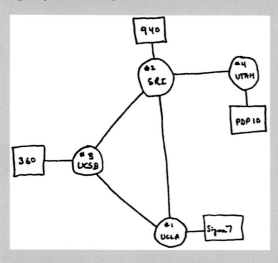

Building on the ideas of many others, he organized ARPA research funding, including the hiring of Larry Roberts as program manager, to create a major computer networking effort in 1966.

Key to the development of computer networks were the ideas of Paul Baran and Donald Davies, who independently came up with the idea of packet-switching in the early 1960s. Unlike the direct-connect telephone system, this revolutionary idea was to divide messages into smaller pieces or packets. The next step is to send

continues

the packets to their destination, not hooked together like a train, but independently like bees going back to the hive.

The principle purpose of ARPAnet was to share expensive computing resources. Computer researchers needed more and more computers to perform the ARPA-sponsored research, and sharing resources seemed to offer some budget relief to ARPA.

In 1969 ARPAnet became operational with the first four nodes at UCLA, UC Santa Barbara, SRI (Stanford Research Institute), and the University of Utah. By the mid-1970s, ARPAnet linked together several military sites and about 20 universities.

Desk Area Network

The most recent networking category is **DAN** (**d**esk **a**rea **n**etwork). The basic idea behind DAN is to make all components of your desktop computer available to all other computers on the network. The most important parts of a desktop computer that are useful to other people on the network are as follows:

> **A desk area network (DAN)** consists of the parts of a single desktop computer that are linked by their normal connections. The most useful are the CPU, display, and hard drive. These components can be made available to any other computer on the network.

- **CPU**. Unused computing power could be used by other computers.
- **Hard disk**. Items stored on your hard drive might be needed by others, or someone may want to put some information on your hard drive.
- **Video display**. Alert messages from a central source, such as the arrival of an email message, might be important to you sitting at your computer.
- **Other items**. Printers, cameras, or other I/O devices connected to your computer might be needed by others.

Local Area Networks

> **A local area network (LAN)** is a collection of nodes within a small area. The nodes are linked in a bus, ring, star, or tree arrangement.

Communication between computer-related devices became necessary as working groups of individuals needed to share information and computer peripherals such as printers, fax machines, and hard-disk drives. Because most of the equipment was located within a relatively small geographic area—a campus, a building, or even a room—a type of interconnection called a local area network (**LAN**) was created.

The simplest of these LANs is the bus network arrangement as shown in Figure 6.2.12. This system is very popular because it is inexpensive and very easy to connect. Rings and other linking arrangements are also used. In all cases, however, each node will need a special interface card to connect to the LAN. A LAN is usually contained within an office and is used to connect microcomputers to printers and other peripherals. LANs never extend beyond a few kilometers. In fact, one type of network design, called an Ethernet, can cover up to one-half mile. Ethernet was originally designed at the Xerox Palo Alto Research Center and has become very popular.

LANs can be used not only to share resources, but also to enable communication between individuals through the use of networking applications. One widely used application is email, or electronic mail, where for example, a supervisor can electronically send a memo to all subordinates at one time. Another networking application is groupware, which allows individuals to send email messages, files, and leave voice mail for each other, while collaborating on a project. The benefits of local area networks are the following:

The Computer Continuum

- Hardware resource sharing (laser writer, hard drive)
- Software and data sharing (applications software)
- Consolidated wiring/cabling
- Simultaneous distribution of information
- More efficient person-to-person communications

Metropolitan Area Networks

When developing networks that span distances of several miles or about the size of a large metropolitan area, it is necessary to use higher-speed links than LANs. These metropolitan **area networks** (**MANs**) must be designed so that information flow is not affected by failure of links or other minor disruptions, such as a major information traffic route being disabled by an accidental cable cutting. One design solution is called DQDB (Distributed Queue Dual Bus). Its name describes the essence of the solution. DQDB means that two electronic links have information flow distributed evenly between them. It's like having two lanes for traffic rather than just one.

> A **metropolitan area network (MAN)** consists of many local area networks linked together. They normally span distances of just a few miles.

Wide Area Networks

As is suggested by the name, wide area networks, or **WAN**s, are spread out over a wider area. In fact, the Internet wide area network spans the Earth. WANs usually consist of a number of computer networks connected together over various communication channels such as telephone lines, microwave links, and satellite transmission.

> **Wide area networks (WANs)** consist of a number of computer networks, including LANs, connected by many different types of links.

Examples of wide area networks abound, but the Internet is the most influential new WAN. And, of course, the most familiar example is the old but reliable telephone network. Both of these WANs cover every country on the Earth.

As networks have proliferated, various corporations, government agencies, and other enterprises have created their own internal networks. These are referred to as intranets or enterprise networks. Therefore, when you see a reference to an intranet or enterprise network, you know that it is controlled by a single corporation. Of course, they have their own special set of problems to be solved. Security of the network, for example, is usually considered a top priority. This is easy to understand when considering the importance of research and financial records. Corporate spies have been known to try cracking into a competitor's networks. Some have even succeeded. One of the most talked about solutions to this security problem is something called a firewall. In simple terms, a firewall is a set of programs that monitor all communication passing into and out of a corporation's intranet. This helps prevent, but doesn't eliminate, unauthorized access or use of corporate data. The term firewall can be used to indicate a protective shield between any two networks, but it still allows authorized communication.

An informal naming standard that has become quite popular concerns the use of the words Internet and internet. The lowercase *i* in the spelling *internet* refers to any collection of linked networks that are owned and controlled by different groups. However, the capital *I* in *Internet* refers to the collection of thousands of networks linked together under a special set of rules called Transfer Control Protocol/Internet Protocol (TCP/IP). The next section explains network rules, or protocols, including TCP/IP.

6.3 Communication Basics: The Software Architecture of the Network

The concepts of hardware and software were introduced in the beginning of this book. It is quite clear that without software, nothing can happen. This section examines the software side of networking and the standards necessary for compatibility.

The Rules of Operation or Protocols of a Network

The concept of connecting a bunch of computers with wires is simple enough to imagine. What happens after that is not quite as intuitively simple. This is the problem:

> Connect several computers that may be different and running different operating systems such as Windows, OS, Macintosh operating system, UNIX, or any number of other operating systems. Now find a way to get things such as email, data, and files exchanged between them. Then allow for connection to other networks running an unknown combination of operating systems.

A **protocol** is a set of rules implemented in the form of a collection of programs called a **protocol suite**. These programs must be on all computers or nodes in the network. The necessary programs from the suite are executed when needed to prepare information to be sent over the network.

The problem is solved by creating a set of rules or **protocols** that, when followed, will allow an orderly exchange of information. Each computer or node in the network must have copies of the network protocols. These protocols are in the form of a collection of programs sometimes called a **protocol suite**.

When information is sent over the network by one computer to another computer, the protocol program on the originating computer will execute. It will "package up" the information so that it can be sent on its way. As the "packaged up" information makes its way along the network, it may be "repackaged" by other nodes, such as gateways and routers (described later in the chapter). When the "packaged" information reaches the destination, it then has to be "unpackaged" by the protocol suite programs to a compatible form for the receiving computer or other device.

A **network's architecture** is the overall organization of the rules of the network and is implemented in a set of programs called the protocol suite. The protocol suite is organized into parts that make it easier to implement a particular network architecture.

The protocol suite and the general scheme that guides its rules is called the **network architecture**. It is analogous to the design of a building being called its architecture. The difficulty in creating a network architecture for particular networks was made easier by breaking the network down into smaller pieces that could be more easily programmed. Several years ago some experts created a very complete protocol called OSI (Open System Interconnect) that was broken down into seven layers or parts. Unfortunately, in real life, the ideal doesn't always prevail. In 1980 the University of California at Berkeley made available a four-layer architecture implemented in a protocol suite called TCP/IP, which is named after the two protocols TCP and IP. It was especially easy to obtain and written for the very popular operating system called UNIX. This was the beginning of the Internet.

Many protocol suites are commercially available and in use on LANs and WANs. AppleTalk, Novell NetWare, Microsoft LAN Manager, and Banyan VINES, for example, are LAN architectures. For WANs there are the SNA and DECnet IV architectures. Each of these products solves the most important problems of network management in its own way.

Of the many network management problems that must be faced, one of the easiest to understand involves the collision of information. The collisions of information are caused by two computers simultaneously attempting to send information to the network. There are many ways to take care of this problem; let's examine three such solutions:

1. **Apple Computer's LocalTalk Protocol**—Collisions are avoided completely by only sending information to the network when permission has been granted to do so.

2. **Token Ring Protocol (originated by IBM, many variations available)**—A token, a special piece of information, is passed around the nodes of a ring network. Collisions are avoided completely because an individual node can send only when it possesses the token.

3. **Ethernet Protocol (originated by Xerox, many variations available)**—Collisions are not avoided; they are taken care of when they occur. Suppose two nodes simultaneously attempt to send over the network that originally looked available. As they both start to send out information, they detect the other's presence. At that point, they both stop and wait for a randomly assigned time period and then again attempt to send information.

The Architecture of the Internet

The Internet has become a pervasive part of our lives. Regardless of your background or career, you will have some contact with its terminology. Almost everyone who has "surfed the Net" is familiar with the acronyms HTTP, TCP/IP, and FTP. These are designations for the Internet protocols of the same names. What they do and where they are in the architecture of the Internet will help you understand how the Internet works.

As mentioned earlier, the Internet architecture can be interpreted as being based on a four-layer protocol or set of rules. These rules, or protocols, are in the form of programs that must be on all computers that are part of the Internet. Figure 6.3.1 illustrates the four-layer architecture. First let's define each of the acronyms that appear in the figure.

FTP (File Transfer Protocol)—Allows the transfer of files between two computers over the Internet.

HTTP (Hypertext Transfer Protocol)—Allows the use of browsers such as Netscape Navigator and Microsoft's Internet Explorer. These browser programs and others are usually written with the HTTP built in to them. This allows information to be sent out to and received from the Internet.

NV (Network Video)—Allows the use of live videoconferencing that runs over MBone. (MBone or Multicast backBone allows multicast routers to send live video across the Internet).

TFTP (Trivial File Transport Protocol)—Allows the use of Telnet for remote logon, SMTP (Simple Mail Transfer Protocol), and email communication.

TCP (Transfer Control Protocol)—Provides a very reliable channel over which a stream of bytes are passed up to the application running on the computer.

UDP (User Datagram Protocol)—Provides a less reliable channel than TCP to programs running on the computer where it resides. Used mainly for audio- and video-related information that can tolerate small errors. A datagram can be thought of as a message.

IP (Internet Protocol)—Translates a particular network's interactions into the standard Internet formats to be used by TCP and UDP.

Net#—A particular network's protocol (for example, Ethernet).

Figure 6.3.1

*The Internet's four-layer
architecture.*

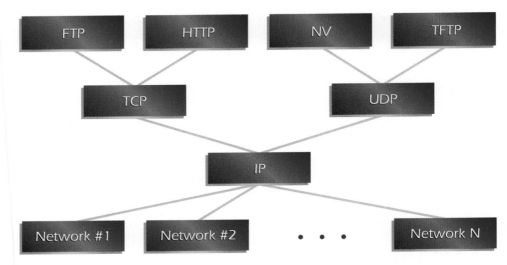

It should be noted that these protocols are not owned by a particular company or individual and are therefore in the public domain. Protocols are well-defined and can be used by anyone to write programs or use applications following the rules that they represent.

What's So Important About Standards?

Most often when we talk about sharing information between two or more computers, we consider primarily the physical aspects of the connection: cables, plugs, modems, phone lines. Reality, however, gives us a different message: Defining rules that govern how data is represented by a computer is infinitely more difficult.

Let's look at a specific example. Today, most computers represent character data (things that can be typed on a keyboard) using a standard called the ASCII code. Using this code, a different seven-digit binary number is assigned to each letter, numeral, and piece of punctuation. When two machines are connected over a network, information can be correctly exchanged because both companies have accepted ASCII code as the industry standard. Until the mid-1970s, this could not happen. Burroughs configured data in one way, Hewlett-Packard in another. IBM wanted to use their own code, called EBCDIC, to configure the data for their machines.

Computer network rules are even more complex than the simple coding of characters. There are hundreds of companies producing thousands of products that must be compatible with one another.

To avoid the chaos of anarchy, a specific set of manufacturing and operating guidelines must be devised, and all companies must agree to comply with these rules. Only when the agreement is made, can the industry be said to have standards, and only with industry-wide standards can computer communication take place.

One of the best known of all standards in networking is the TCP/IP protocol. TCP/IP is the name given to the standards that a network must follow to communicate with other networks that are part of the Internet. It consists of well over 100 rules of operation called protocols. In 1980 an additional standard was added to those already used on the Internet; this was HTTP (Hypertext Transfer Protocol). In fact, this protocol is the basis for the World Wide Web.

The Computer Continuum

It is necessary to understand another major concept before examining how the Internet works. This is the concept of "packaging" information before it goes out to the Internet. All network protocols require information to be "packaged" in a form that can be moved around on the network. One of the main issues involves the size of the units of information to be moved over a network. For efficiency, a single standard size must be selected. This size is fixed, so if something to be moved over the network is larger than the standard size, it must be divided up into units called packets, frames, or segments.

On the Internet, the information is "packaged" into chunks called **packets**. That's why the Internet is referred to as a packet-switched network. Each packet contains important information regarding its content, where it came from, and where it is supposed to go. Unfortunately, to make things even more complicated, each network that a packet goes through also has its standard packet or frame sizes. As an Internet packet makes its way to a destination, it is constantly being "packaged" and "repackaged" to fit the network that it is passing through.

A **packet** is a unit of information created by the Transfer Control Protocol (TCP) software for transmission over the Internet. When a node, usually a computer, prepares to send out information, it is divided into packets. Other networking protocols may use the name packet or possibly segment or frame.

Figure 6.3.2 illustrates an example with packets. A woman named Mildred is running a World Wide Web browser program on her computer, which is linked to Network A. She is requesting a home page located on the hard drive of Kyle's computer. A home page, discussed in the next chapter, is information collected at a single address on the World Wide Web. It is unusual for someone to have a home page on their own computer, but he is an unusual guy. Kyle had to have some additional software added to the "HTTP program" so that his computer could act as a server, a concept discussed after this example. Kyle's computer is linked to Network B. All the boxes inside the rectangles labeled as Mildred's and Kyle's computers represent programs on those respective computers. There are, of course, many other programs, such as the operating system, but the purpose of this example is to focus on the Internet part of the process.

These programs—FTP, HTTP, NV, TFTP, TCP, UDP, and IP—are part of the Internet protocol suite, which has over 100 programs. The figure also shows that the two computers are indirectly linked through many nodes and networks represented by the cloud-shaped object, the Internet.

Another amazing fact is that not all the packets will travel along the same path through the Internet. They have all been numbered so that reassembly of the original request for Kyle's home page can be accomplished.

This is a good time to reinforce a key concept describing how the Internet works. To do this, let's first look at the telephone system. When you make a telephone call, a direct connection to the person you are talking with is established. You dial a number, the connection is made, you talk, and finally you hang up and the connection is broken. This is called a connection-oriented network. On the other hand, the U.S. Postal Service is a connectionless system. Individual letters or "packets" are addressed to a particular location and arrive there eventually after passing through various parts of the postal system.

Networks, including the Internet, use the connectionless form of operation. On the Internet, packets are addressed to some location and will make their way there by various routes. Upon arrival at the destination, they have to be reassembled to give the form of the information originally sent. How these packets make their way is more complicated. But, it is a dynamic and a changing routing system, which satisfies the original intent of the Internet started by ARPA (Advanced Research Projects Agency of the Pentagon) in 1962. The intent of ARPA was to create a communications system that was robust and could not be destroyed by eliminating computers or links in the system. The Internet can't be eliminated; it may slow down, but it is here forever!

Unique addresses for all nodes in a network are an important issue. The Internet is no exception and, in fact, has created an interesting problem with the assignment of Internet addresses. This problem is discussed in the next chapter.

Servers for Networks

It is now time to look at some special-purpose nodes that inhabit networks. Some of these nodes have a special significance for the individual. If someone wants his own World Wide Web site, for example, he must find a home for it. This means finding a computer that has an Internet address and can therefore act as a destination for Internet packets. Then, space on that computer's hard drive must be allocated for the Web site. This leads to the concept of a **server**, which was born many years ago when networks needed to store information and produce copies as needed. This information could be data or programs, or even home pages for the World Wide Web.

This leads to another major concept in networking referred to as the client/server model. In the example shown in Figure 6.3.2, Mildred's computer is acting as a client; she is requesting Kyle's home page be "served" to her. Client computers can run any type of operating system, so long as they have the ability to use the Internet protocols.

A very common analogy is used to understand the client/server model. Suppose Mildred is in a restaurant and orders a cup of tea. The waiter's purpose in the restaurant is to "serve" the tea that his "client," Mildred, has ordered.

A server on a network, linked to the Internet, is a perfect place for World Wide Web pages to reside. Universities will often allow students free space on a server for their Web pages. Outside the university, Internet service providers (ISPs) not only provide access to the Internet, but also often allow Web pages to be stored on their server. Of course, this costs extra. In some cities, community networks not only give free access to the Internet, but in addition allow free space on their server for a Web page.

Other Hardware Necessary for Networks

Hubs, switches, bridges, routers, and gateways are some additional types of nodes that inhabit networks. Literally millions of these nodes are scattered throughout the Internet. Each has its own reason for existence, and almost all will run the TCP/IP protocol suite, or appropriate parts of it. A brief description of each of these is given in the following box.

Hub	A device that repeats or broadcasts the network stream of information to individual nodes that are usually personal computers. A hub is an economical way to get the network information to groups of nodes away from the main networking facilities.
Switch	A device that receives packets from its input link and then sorts them and transmits them over the proper link that connects to the node addressed. It is primarily used to connect nodes or networks of the same type, and is therefore different from a router.
Bridge	A link between two networks that have identical rules of communication. That is, the networks are running under the same network protocol.
Gateway	A link between two different networks that have different rules of communication. That is, the networks are running under different network protocols. For example, America Online provides a gateway to the Internet.
Router	A node that sends network packets in one of many possible directions to get them to their destination. A key feature of the router is its "dynamic address book," which is a list of locations to send packets on their way. This list is continually updating itself as event and traffic on the network change.

The Computer Continuum

A last comment is in order here. All the concepts in this section are important to understanding the Internet. In the same breath as the word *Internet* is used, however, the World Wide Web (WWW) is oftentimes mentioned. Both the Internet and WWW are extensively discussed from a users point of view in the next two chapters. For now, let's just say that the WWW is a hypertext-based computer system that uses the Internet as a means of delivering its information to you. Without the Internet, the WWW couldn't exist.

6.4 How Networks Are Used

The concepts of networking discussed in this chapter have application in all sizes of networks from the simple LANs to the Internet. This section discusses those elements that are useful on networks smaller than the Internet. Some of these same uses are discussed again in the next chapter in the context of the Internet.

Electronic Mail

The examples of networks vary from office and home to worldwide networks. The organization of the various networks also varies from formally controlled structures to free wheeling and volunteer types. No matter what the context, however, many of the networks support some common uses.

The most prevalent of these network applications is **email**, or electronic mail. The concept is quite similar to its namesake, regular mail. However, it is much faster and cheaper. Even when communicating within the same building, email communication is easier and faster than telephone, notes, or in-person delivery.

The use of email is inevitable in many areas of human endeavor. The importance of email to the corporate world is best summed up by James Champy in his bestselling book *Reengineering the Corporation*. He states that to survive, corporations must transform themselves to fit information technology, with email at the core of these changes.

Email is not as private as regular mail. This is partially because it has not been around long enough to develop privacy laws or security systems. Another contributing factor to this lack of privacy is that the computer makes it easy to copy and snoop into unprotected computer files. There are many examples of corporations prying into personal email communications in the name of security. These problems are addressed in a later chapter on ethics in computing.

Bulletin Board Systems

A **bulletin board system** (BBS) is named after the rather mundane bulletin boards that occupy schools, public places, and anywhere information is displayed for the public. They not only provide the same type of information or message service, but are also used as repositories for software and documents that may be copied. In addition, the BBSs provide a place where conversations are carried on.

The thousands of BBSs that were in operation all over the world in the early 1990s are quickly being replaced by World Wide Web pages for both personal, corporate, government, and educational groups. The services that were originally very popular included obtaining software, documentation, and other information. As the Internet became more accessible and easier to use, these services migrated to the Internet, and now to the World Wide Web. **Freeware** and **shareware**, ranging from simple games and educational programs to word processors and accounting systems, are sometimes also available on BBSs.

Electronic mail, or email, is a form of one-way communication sent electronically from one computer to another computer. It is necessary to have a software program to compose and send the mail on a network. An important part of email is the destination address, which might be a company's local network address or an Internet address.

A **BBS**, or **bulletin board system**, is a special-purpose database that usually resides on a single computer and is accessible over the telephone lines or through a computer network such as the Internet. Its purpose is to provide information to the person who accesses it, and allows him to put his own information into the BBS for others to access.

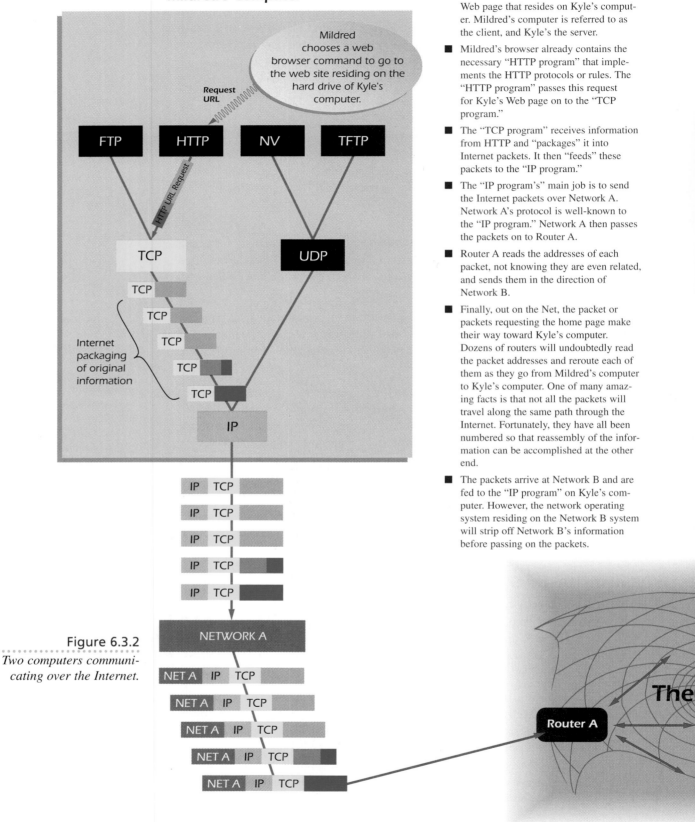

Mildred's Computer

Mildred chooses a web browser command to go to the web site residing on the hard drive of Kyle's computer.

Request URL

HTTP URL Request

FTP HTTP NV TFTP

TCP UDP

TCP

TCP

TCP

Internet packaging of original information

TCP

TCP

IP

IP TCP

IP TCP

IP TCP

IP TCP

IP TCP

Figure 6.3.2

Two computers communicating over the Internet.

NETWORK A

NET A IP TCP

NET A IP TCP

NET A IP TCP

NET A IP TCP

NET A IP TCP

Router A

The

- Mildred chooses to access a World Wide Web page that resides on Kyle's computer. Mildred's computer is referred to as the client, and Kyle's the server.

- Mildred's browser already contains the necessary "HTTP program" that implements the HTTP protocols or rules. The "HTTP program" passes this request for Kyle's Web page on to the "TCP program."

- The "TCP program" receives information from HTTP and "packages" it into Internet packets. It then "feeds" these packets to the "IP program."

- The "IP program's" main job is to send the Internet packets over Network A. Network A's protocol is well-known to the "IP program." Network A then passes the packets on to Router A.

- Router A reads the addresses of each packet, not knowing they are even related, and sends them in the direction of Network B.

- Finally, out on the Net, the packet or packets requesting the home page make their way toward Kyle's computer. Dozens of routers will undoubtedly read the packet addresses and reroute each of them as they go from Mildred's computer to Kyle's computer. One of many amazing facts is that not all the packets will travel along the same path through the Internet. Fortunately, they have all been numbered so that reassembly of the information can be accomplished at the other end.

- The packets arrive at Network B and are fed to the "IP program" on Kyle's computer. However, the network operating system residing on the Network B system will strip off Network B's information before passing on the packets.

The Computer Continuum

- The "IP program" in turn strips away all information, leaving the original Internet packets from Mildred's computer. The "IP program" then passes these Internet packets to the "TCP program."

- The "TCP program" then "unpackages" the Internet packets and reassembles it to its original form and passes this information to the "HTTP program."

- Because Kyle's computer is acting as a server, his "HTTP program" has some additions to it. These additions to "HTTP program" allow it to act as a server. In fact, it acts much like a butler serving tea. The appropriate Web page is passed back to the "HTTP program."

- Now the process goes in reverse until the Web site home page reaches Mildred's computer where the browser displays the home page from Kyle's computer.

- Seems a little tedious doesn't it? But, it seems almost ridiculous when it is realized that a simple home page may take several hundred Internet packets! If there are a large number of photographs, it could be thousands of packets. It may also happen that the original Internet packets have to be broken into pieces to go over other networks in the path.

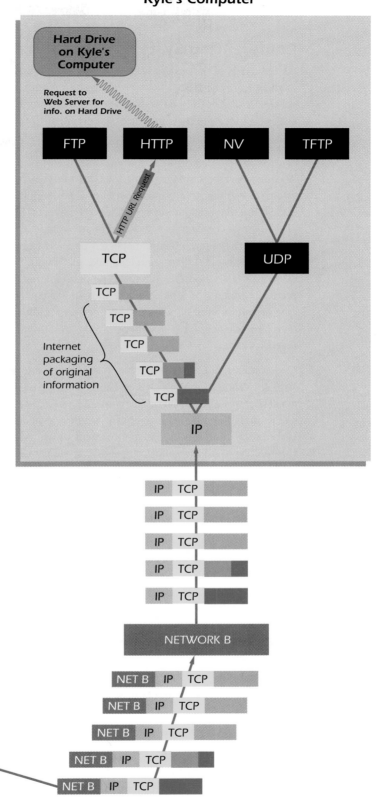

Kyle's Computer

Freeware is software that is free. It can be copied and used at no cost. However, there is usually a restriction that freeware may not be sold for profit.

Shareware is software that can be copied freely, but the author of the software expects a token payment if you use the software. Making this payment should be done, and will sometimes have the advantage of free updates for improved versions of the software. Shareware fees commonly range from $5 to $50.

Downloading is the process of getting a copy of a program or other document from one computer to another. If a program or other document is added to some BBS or another computer system, this is referred to as uploading.

A **computerized conference** or **teleconference** is an electronic meeting that can take place at the convenience of the participants. A network is necessary for a conference to function.

The person accessing the BBS need only have the proper software to **download** a desired program or document.

Conferencing Systems

As the needs of those who network changed and matured, another type of communication evolved from the BBS. A conferencing system emphasizes the messages and information-passing aspects of the BBS, but lacks the repositories for downloading software. It consists of a more sophisticated message organizer for the topics of "conversation." It also runs on a single computer accessed either by telephone or through another computer or network.

A **computerized conference** or **teleconference** is a clearing house for information. In effect it is similar to a typical meeting where people sit at a table and discuss issues, review reports, plan strategy, and schedule events. For a face-to-face conference involving people, however, everyone must be in attendance. Corporations still spend large sums of money to fly geographically dispersed people together for a conference. A computerized conference, on the other hand, can take place with the participants located anywhere in the world. They don't even have to be participating at the same instant in time. A computerized conference is a place where individuals can post questions, get answers, communicate private or public messages, and perform traditional email communications at their own convenience. It allows almost all the traditional events that occur at face-to-face meetings.

One conferencing system that has some unique and interesting conferences is called the WELL (**W**hole **E**arth '**L**ectronic **L**ink). The WELL has thousands of registered users, accessing more than 100 public conferences (topics). There are also many private conferences, including one exclusively for women, a men-only conference, and several private corporation conferences. The conferences range anywhere from the Grateful Dead Conference to a conference to design T-shirts for the WELL. The variety of conferees is what gives the WELL its character. They include artists, writers, hackers, Deadheads, knowledge workers, educators, programmers, lawyers, and musicians. It is no longer necessary to dial by phone directly into this conference because it is now on the Internet and also has its own World Wide Web site.

Chapter Summary

What you can do with what you have learned:

- Understand how networks fit into our culture historically.
- Know the questions to ask regarding the most appropriate network connections for a particular situation.
- Understand the importance of digital technology.
- Recognize the variety of ways networks are connected.
- Explain the different scales of networks such as DANs, LANs, MANs, and WANs.

- Explain how information moves from network to network and the benefits and limitations of that flow of information.
- Realize how the Internet works.
- Recognize and understand the networking terms used in the newspapers.

    You will have a better framework from which to evaluate and understand issues such as security and cryptography.
- Understand the most essential uses of networking.

Key Terms and Review Questions

Key terms introduced in this chapter:

Network 2-134

Network links 2-134

Twisted pair 2-134

Coaxial cable 2-134

Fiber-optic cables 2-134

Infrared 2-136

Radio frequency 2-136

Microwave 2-136

Digital 2-137

Analog 2-137

Bps 2-138

Baud rate 2-138

Modem 2-138

Simplex transmission 2-139

Half-duplex transmission 2-139

Full-duplex transmission 2-139

Asynchronous transmission 2-139

Synchronous transmission 2-139

Bandwidth 2-140

Node 2-141

Direct-link network 2-141

Point-to-point network 2-141

Bus network 2-142

Ring network 2-142

Star network 2-142

Tree network 2-142

Fully connected topology network 2-143

DAN 2-144

LAN 2-144

MAN 2-145

WAN 2-145

Protocol 2-146

Protocol suite 2-146

Network architecture 2-146

LocalTalk 2-147

Token Ring 2-147

Ethernet 2-147

FTP 2-147

HTTP 2-147

NV 2-147

TFTP 2-147

TCP 2-147

UDP 2-147

IP 2-147

Net# 2-147

Packet 2-149

Server 2-150

Hub 2-150

Switch 2-150

Bridge 2-150

Gateway 2-150

Router 2-150

Email 2-151

Bulletin board system 2-151

Freeware 2-151

Shareware 2-151

Download 2-154

Computerized conference 2-154

Teleconference 2-154

The WELL 2-154

Matching

Match the key terms introduced in the chapter to the following statements. Each term may be used once, more than once, or not at all.

1. _____Wireless communication used to connect keyboards and mice.

2. _____Wireless communication used by satellites.

3. _____Connections between computers and other electronic devices.

4. _____Electronic signal that is continuously changing.

5. _____Indicates the number of times a signal on a channel changes per second.

6. _____Electronic signal that consists of pulses representing 0s or 1s.

7. _____Method of transmission that sends information more quickly and is more expensive.

8. _____Device that changes digital information to analog so that it can be sent over the telephone.

9. _____A network category that spans the distance of just a few miles.

10. _____A general term used when referring to a device that is connected to a network.

11. _____Data movement that can only go one direction at a time, like that used by a fax machine.

12. _____Data movement that can only go in one direction, like that used by television or radio.

13. _____A set of rules that allows an orderly exchange of information on a network.

14. _____The network that has a central node that acts as a controlling device.

15. _____A transfer protocol that allows the use of browsers on a network, including the Internet.

16. _____A link between two networks that may be using different network protocols.

17. _____A computer that contains files that are "served" on request.

18. _____The name given to the collection of all computer networks that carry email.

19. _____A form of one-way communication sent electronically from one person to another.

20. _____A database that provides information and enables individuals to post it for others.

The Computer Continuum

True or False

1. _____ Other than face-to-face vocal communication, the earliest form of long-distance communication was the telegraph.

2. _____ Network links that use twisted-pair wires can suffer from interference caused by appliances or other electric devices in the home or office.

3. _____ Network links use only one type of physical media to connect computers and other electronic devices.

4. _____ Coaxial cables are as susceptible to interference from outside noise as twisted pairs of wires.

5. _____ Fiber-optic cables can carry more signals than either twisted pair or coaxial cable.

6. _____ Of the three types of wireless communications used in networking, only the infrared type needs to have the sending and receiving units in the line of sight of each other.

7. _____ Radio frequencies are not commonly used as wireless communication between computers because of the fear of other devices causing interference.

8. _____ Although microwave wireless communication needs to be in the line of sight, nothing else really causes any interference.

9. _____ The properties of communication signals do not vary among the differing communication links.

10. _____ Although commonly confused, bits per second is not the same as baud rate.

11. _____ A modem is necessary to send information from one computer to another computer over current telephone lines.

12. _____ A broadband communication path carries much more information than a baseband communication path.

13. _____ A network only accounts for those computers that are directly connected by physical means.

14. _____ Networks range in size from one that makes the use of the functionality of components on an individual computer to one that spans the earth.

15. _____ The terms Internet and internet have the same meaning.

16. _____ One of the functions of a protocol suite is the management of collisions of information that might occur on a network.

17. _____ The beauty of a packet that travels along the Internet to a destination is that it is not changed anywhere along the way.

18. _____ A bridge requires that both networks being linked run under the same network protocol.

19. _____ Historically, email has had no effect in political matters.

20. _____ Both freeware and shareware programs can be copied freely.

Multiple Choice

Answer the multiple choice questions by selecting the best answer from the choices given.

1. Ring, star, and bus are categorized as being what?
   a. Types of wireless transmission
   b. Transfer protocols
   c. Types of data movement
   d. Types of networks
   e. Devices connected to a network

2. Digital versus analog, simplex, half-duplex, or full-duplex, asynchronous versus synchronous: These are all what?
   a. Types of wireless transmission
   b. Transfer protocols
   c. Types of data movement
   d. Types of networks
   e. Devices connected to a network

3. Nodes are
   a. Types of wireless transmission
   b. Transfer protocols
   c. Types of data movement
   d. Types of networks
   e. Devices connected to a network

4. Microwave and infrared are examples of what?
   a. Types of wireless transmission
   b. Transfer protocols
   c. Types of data movement
   d. Types of networks
   e. Devices connected to a network

5. The rules governing how information travels along a network are included under
   a. Types of wireless transmission
   b. Transfer protocols
   c. Types of data movement
   d. Types of networks
   e. Devices connected to a network

6. This is where files are stored so that connections to the Internet are possible.
   a. HTTP
   b. Internet
   c. WWW
   d. Packets
   e. Server

7. This began as a government-funded project.
   a. HTTP
   b. Internet
   c. WWW
   d. Packets
   e. Server

8. This is how information is grouped together when it is sent from one computer to another along the Internet.
   a. HTTP
   b. Internet
   c. WWW
   d. Packets
   e. Server

9. This is the name given to a growing part of the Internet.
   a. HTTP
   b. Internet
   c. WWW
   d. Packets
   e. Server

10. This protocol allows information to be displayed on a screen after it has been received from the Internet.
    a. HTTP
    b. Internet
    c. WWW
    d. Packets
    e. Server

The Computer Continuum

Exercises

1. If you were given the job to design a multi-user electronic game for the school classroom, which of the several types of wire or wireless connection would be your choice? State the reasons for your choice and at least one negative reason for not choosing each of the other forms.

2. What is a potential problem for using infrared keyboards in an office without walls? How could the problem or problems be eliminated?

3. A telephone line, which is most commonly a twisted pair, handles only one conversation at a time. How does Call Waiting work? Call Waiting is where a call is in progress when you're interrupted by a second call, which produces a click. Explain how this is possible.

4. What is the concept behind conference calls? This is where more than two telephone locations can be talking at once, just as if everyone is on the same telephone line.

5. Use the chart to help determine the answers to the following questions:

   How long would it take to send a 1 MB file using a modem which is

   2400 bps

   9600 bps

   14.4 Kbps

   33.6 Kbps

   56.8 Kbps

   Why might these optimal times not be attainable "in the real world"?

Speed of Modem		Time It Takes to Send a File		
bps	How many	1 KB	10 KB	36 KB
bits per sec.	bytes per sec.	(1000 bytes)	2 pages (dbl)	1 simple picture
2400 bps	300	3.3 secs	33.3 secs	120.0 secs
9600 bps	1200	8.3 secs	30.0 secs	833.3 secs
14.4 Kbps	1800	0.6 secs	5.6 secs	20.0 secs
28.8 Kbps	3600	0.3 secs	2.8 secs	10.0 secs
33.6 Kbps	4200	0.2 secs	2.4 secs	8.6 secs
56.8 Kbps	7000	0.1 secs	1.4 secs	5.1 secs

6. Determine whether each of the scenarios described here is classified as simplex, half-duplex, or full-duplex transmission. Explain your answer.

   a. An engaged couple has listed the items they wish to receive as wedding presents in a department store's computer. This department store has conveniently positioned information kiosks with access to the couple's list at several places around the store. Using the touch pad, you can choose to see the items that have been purchased and the items remaining on the list.

   b. A fax machine receives and sends faxes one at a time, but not at the same time.

   c. Traffic-flow display devices are attached to overpasses on an expressway, showing the drivers which lanes are open.

   d. A person can speak over a citizen's band radio (CB) only when the button on the microphone is depressed. During the time when the button is depressed, however, the speaker cannot hear the other voices over the radio.

   e. A television receives a signal over the airwaves.

f. A television attached by cable is connected to the Internet by the use of a special devise that enables the person viewing it to also send requests for new sights to view.

7. Assuming the following physical bus network connection:

```
 T T  T T T
 A B  C D E
```

a. Can device B send information to device A at the same time that device D is sending information to device E? Justify your answer.

b. If device C were not there, could device B send information to device A at the same time that device D is sending information to device E? Justify your answer.

c. Can device A send information to device E even if device C is turned off?

8. Would you expect a bridge or a gateway to be more complex? Why?

9. Portable telephones use radio frequencies to transmit information. The newest portable (cordless) telephones are listed as 900 MHz machines. Is this a new frequency or is this a measure of the strength of the signal produced? Of what advantage is the new 900 MHz phone over the earlier models?

10. List the four types of physical media used for network links that were described in this chapter. For each of them, include an example of its use.

11. When will modems become unnecessary?

12. What is another name for a tree network configuration? How does the meaning of the name relate to the actual network configuration?

Discussion Questions

1. If TV and VCR remote controls have some problems with infrared signals, can you think of some reasons why manufacturers of these devices don't use radio frequency links instead?

2. Which of the network configurations described in section 6.2 would be the best choice if security of the transmitted message was an important consideration? Why?

3. Which of the network configurations described in section 6.2 would be the best choice if reliability and getting the message delivered was the most important consideration? Why?

4. Describe a situation where a DAN would be useful.

5. Could MBone be used for an alternative to TV sent to your computer? Why or why not?

6. A very long telephone message may have to be left on a telephone answering machine in "pieces" because of a limited amount of time permitted by the machine for each message. Discuss the analogous situation for a network.

Group Project

This project is designed for a group of four people. Each of you should select a role to play in a small business that is about to invest in a network for its office. Choose one role from among these four network users:

President and CEO—Needs current information on employees, sales, orders, and also needs to communicate with employees and people outside the company.

Vice President of Marketing—Needs to design marketing materials and communicate with staff.

Office Manager—Needs to schedule meetings, keep calendar appointments and vacations, and collect payroll data.

Vice President of Sales—Needs to keep track of salespeople and their sales and provide feedback to marketing.

The company has six other employees who are divided into office staff and salespeople. Each needs his or her own computer.

The four of you should decide what basic type of network you would like. Should it be a bus, ring, star, tree, or fully connected topology, for example. Also, would you need twisted pair, coaxial cable, fiber-optic cable, or wireless links? How many computers, printers, servers, and connections to the Internet would you need? Try to stay general in your overall design. Good luck, and remember small businesses have a limited amount of money to spend.

Web Connections

http://oac3.hsc.uth.tmc.edu/staff/snewton/tcp-tutorial/

A detailed tutorial on TCP/IP, what it is, and why it is important to networking and the World Wide Web.

http://www.rtd.com/pcnfsfaq/faq.html

A list of frequently asked questions (FAQs) concerning the TCP/IP protocol. Especially useful might be the following items:

- **A5–A10.** Covering topics such as "What is TCP/IP? What is TELNET? What is FTP? What is Ethernet? What is AppleTalk? What is PPP?"
- **C8.** What is asynchronous I/O, and how do I make it happen?

http://t2.technion.ac.il/~s2845543/tcpip_rl.html

A printable list of resources for information about the technicalities of networking and network protocols. It includes books, periodicals, and online resources.

http://www.tiac.net/users/webtype/tcpip/tcpstart.html

Information and step-by-step instructions to set up your own local network using TCP/IP.

http://www.freenix.fr/cgi-bin/nph-traceroute

A Web page that will trace and list all the computers that your request goes through on its way to a specific location.

Bibliography

Peterson, Larry L., and Bruce S. Davie. *Computer Networks: A Systems Approach.* San Francisco: Morgan Kaufmann, 1996.

This is a very complete, but high-level book about network protocols, in particular TCP/IP. It has a very good introductory chapter that gives an overview of network architecture. The rest of the book, however, is senior level.

Hunter, Philip. *Local Area Networks.* Reading, MA: Addison-Wesley, 1993.

This is a book for those who need to understand the basic concepts to set up a LAN. It takes the reader through the decision-making processes needed to make the right choices. Very readable, but for the more advanced student.

PART III
FOUNDATIONS: APPLYING THE CONCEPTS

Chapter 7

1957 ARPA (Advanced Research Projects Agency) launched by President Eisenhower in response to the Sputnik launch.

1972 "Electronic mail" is coined and used to send messages across the ARPAnet.

1979 First Usenet newsgroups established.

1982 "Internet" is coined to designate a connected set of networks.

1982 TCP/IP (Transmission Control Protocol /Internet Protocol) established and accepted as standard for Department of Defense.

1982 Eunet (European UNIX Network) provides email and Usenet services.

1986 NSFNET and its five supercomputing centers provide high-computing power for all. This allows an explosion of connections, especially between universities.

1988 "Internet relay chat" (IRC) invented by Jarkko Oikarinen.

1991 Gopher, an Internet menu style file-finder, released by University of Minnesota.

1996 Internet2 connects a consortium of 100+ research universities.

1997 150 countries are connected to the Internet.

1997 Internet discussion groups number over 70,000.

The Internet: Communication with the World

Chapter Objectives

By the end of this chapter, you will:

- Know the historical beginnings of the Internet.
- Appreciate the U.S. Defense Department's role in the birth of ARPAnet.
- Discern how the UNIX operating system influenced the early use of the Internet.
- Understand the uses of Gopher and related text-based access methods.
- Identify the variety of tasks the Internet can perform.
- Know how MUDs, MOOs, and IRCs can be used for entertainment or research.

7.1 In the Beginning...

Many of the topics in the preceding chapter involved references to the **Internet**. This chapter examines both its birth and growth into an almost everyday subject of conversation. A couple of examples will make this clearer. The first shows how email goes beyond just local communication and the second involves conferences. In particular, the incredible information utility conference called **Usenet**. At the end of this section an overview of the relationship between all the thousands of networks, the Internet, and the World Wide Web is examined, in the form of something called the Matrix.

In the political world, the power of email is unmistakable. Just after the 1989 Tiananmen Square massacre, for example, Chinese students in the United States were worried they would have to go back to China when their visas expired. They organized an email campaign over the Internet to successfully lobby Congress for protective legislation.

In another part of the world, when Russian President Boris Yeltsin suspended parliament in the fall of 1993, many civilians were caught in the middle. In particular, three prominent Russian labor leaders were arrested while trying to prevent further bloodshed. They were kicked and beaten overnight by Moscow police until word of their fate reached Vassily Balog, the deputy head of Russia's major labor confederation. As an active email user, he sent Internet email to friends in the United States and United Kingdom with appeals for support and the phone number of the police station. Australian journalist Renfrey Clarke reporting from Moscow estimated the first phone call to the police station came about 30 minutes after the email was sent. The first phone call came from Japan, and then others followed from all over the world. The international pressure brought about by the phone calls caused the release of the three men.

The Internet also supports thousands of conferences. One of the prime examples of a conference is Usenet (Users' Network), which has hundreds of individual conferences. The separate conferences are organized by topics such as the following:

- World events
- New technology
- National elections
- Privacy issues
- Entertainment
- Computer viruses

Usenet is a richly featured, distributed conferencing system that generates over 100 MB of new text each day. This is equivalent to more than 10 copies of *Webster's New Collegiate Dictionary* each day. Usenet doesn't reside in any one computer. Copies of the Usenet news conferences are distributed on networks throughout the world.

The Matrix: Internet, Bitnet, Usenet

The incredible variety of networks and services makes it rather difficult to understand relationships among them. Making an informed decision regarding which commercial service to use in accessing the Internet is a big decision, for example. The monthly costs and connect time fees are not cheap! To help make this and other decisions, it is important to have a comprehensive overview of "what's out there."

The **Matrix** consists of all computers and networks that have the capability of exchanging electronic mail.

One way to view the relationships between these networks and services is visually through the diagram shown in Figure 7.1.1. Called the **Matrix** (Quarterman), it shows all the major computer networks and special categories and how they are connected. To be in the Matrix, the network must have at least the capability of exchanging electronic mail.

The Computer Continuum

The relative sizes of the circles and ellipses in the diagram indicate the number of computers or nodes that are part of a particular network.

The overlapping circles of Figure 7.1.1 show connections between networks. The circle representing the Internet, for example, overlaps the Usenet circle. This means that the two have computers in common. In other words, a particular computer connected to the Internet might also have Usenet news resident on the computer. If two circles representing networks just touch, this means they have a connection called a gateway; but in this case, the two networks don't have any particular computer that is actually part of both networks. They are connected through the gateway, which provides the translation of information to a compatible form for the network.

Many different networks are represented in Figure 7.1.1. Each has a unique history and unique rules of communication. Some of the circles even represent categories of networks. The **intranets** or **Enterprise IP** represent corporate networks, for example, each of which is wholly within the corporation's control and follows the IP (Internet Protocol) rules for communication. Note that some of these Enterprise IP networks are connected to the Internet. The overlap of the Internet and Enterprise IP circles represents those computers that are part of both networks. There are also some things, which aren't networks, but reside on networks. They are represented by shaded circles that don't have lines around them. The most recognizable of those is Usenet. Details on some of the many networks or categories of networks in the Matrix are found in Figure 7.1.2.

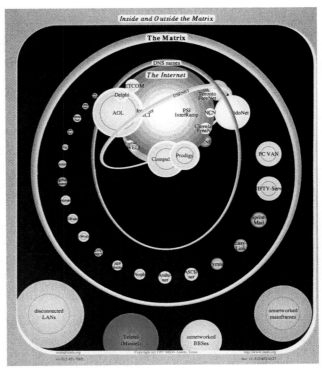

Figure 7.1.1

The Matrix of networks that carry email.

Figure 7.1.2 *The networks in the Matrix.*

Name	Protocol	Date	Description
AOL (America Online)	Dial-up Proprietary	1989	A general-purpose online service and gateway to the Internet.
BITNET (Because It's Time Network)	NJE	1981	Most common as part of IBM VM/370 operating system.
CompuServe	Dial-up Proprietary	1979	A general-purpose online service and gateway to the Internet.
CSNET (Computer Science Network)	Dial-up	1981	Created to facilitate CS research, primarily for email and made use of ordinary telephone lines.
DNS (domain name system)	Mapping software	1986	It allows access to various computers using names that are divided into categories/domains.
Intranet	TCP/IP	—	Thousands of networks existing inside corporations.
FidoNet	Fido	1983	Messaging sevice created to reach the masses of PC users, uses the telephone network.
GEnie (General Electric Electric Network for Information Exchange)	Dial-up Proprietary	1985	A general-purpose online service and gateway to the Internet.
Internet	TCP/IP	1973	Started with DARPA internetting project.
Prodigy	Dial-up Proprietary	1988	A general-purpose online service, created by Sears and IBM, which has gateway to the Internet.
Usenet (Users' Network)	Not a network	1979	Created to carry news to networking public.
UUCP (UNIX to UNIX CoPy)	UUCP	1978	Comes with UNIX and uses ordinary dial-up telephone lines.

7.2 The Internet: Planting the Seed

The seeds of what we know as the Internet were planted in the early 1960s. At that time, most computer scientists considered the idea of networking computers only a dream. Paul Baran and Donald Davies took the first key steps toward realization of that dream. Working independently, these two researchers each devised the idea of **packet-switching** in the early 1960s.

Unlike the direct-connect telephone system, this revolutionary idea was to divide messages into smaller pieces, called **packets**, before sending them forward. The packets of each message would then be sent to their destination, not hooked together like a train, but independently, like bees going back to the hive. The concept of packets and packet-switching provided the foundation for what would one day grow to become the Internet.

The seeds of networking were planted in the fertile ground of scientific research. Germination was slow, however, until 1966, when Bob Taylor, then director of computer research at ARPA, decided to focus major development effort on computer networking. **ARPA** (Advanced Research Projects Agency) is the U.S. Department of Defense's research agency. Taylor built on the ideas of Baran, Davies, and many others, thereby causing sponsored research grants and ARPA funding to pour into computer-network research. He hired Larry Roberts as overall manager of this project. The first fruit of this influx of money and energy was called **ARPAnet** (Advanced Research Projects Agency Network).

The principal purpose of ARPAnet was to share expensive computing resources. Network researchers needed increasingly more computing power (and increasingly higher finances) to continue the ARPA-sponsored research. ARPAnet enabled computer scientists located at several universities and research institutes to pool their computing resources, thus providing the needed power while offering some budget relief to ARPA.

In 1969, ARPAnet became operational with the first four nodes at UCLA, UC Santa Barbara, SRI (Stanford Research Institute), and the University of Utah. By the mid-1970s, ARPAnet linked together several military sites and about 20 universities.

At this point it became clear that guidance and support of a different type were needed. ARPA started an effort to sell off the ARPAnet, but it was already recognized as a valuable resource. Before any sale could take place, federal rules required the Defense Department to determine whether ARPAnet was needed for national defense. The Defense Department recognized the potential importance of computer networking, so the ARPAnet was never sold, but was transferred to the Defense Communications Agency in 1975.

When ARPAnet became part of a Defense agency, its resources were not open to all researchers, but were heavily restricted. Only about 15 university research centers were given access. To correct this, the National Science Foundation started **CSnet** in 1980. Its purpose was to provide a resource-sharing network opportunity to computer science research at all universities. By 1986 almost all of the country's computer science departments were connected to CSnet; a large number of private companies were also connected. CSnet used the **TCP/IP** protocol, unlike ARPAnet, which used the **Network Control Protocol**.

The success of CSnet fueled interest in creating a more comprehensive network to link all scientific communities, not just the computer sciences. But, like ARPAnet, this would take millions of dollars per year, which was more than NSF could support. The solution came with the advent of the five supercomputing centers spread out over the United States. NSF would build a very fast connection, called a **backbone**, linking the five supercomputer centers, and then each region surrounding them would develop its own community network. NSF would allow the regional community networks exclusive access to the backbone.

Every network, considered by itself, has a **backbone**, which is the main traffic route of the network and usually the fastest.

Science Fiction Predicting the Network Future

Science fiction writers have a good record of predicting the future. Remember Jules Verne and his *From Earth to Moon*? Who would have believed humans would land on the moon?

The field of networking has been the subject, both directly and indirectly, of many science fiction authors. British astronomer Sir Fred Hoyle wrote *The Black Cloud* in 1957. It is about what appears to be a huge black cloud that is attempting to surround our sun and absorb all of its energy. Of course, this potentially means the end of life on Earth. In the process of communication with this entity, it seems to speak with a single voice. As a passage from the books states: "... what Chris is saying is that individuals in the Cloud, if there are any, must be highly telepathic, so telepathic that it becomes rather meaningless to regard them as being really separate from each other." In other words, they were networked together.

Thomas J. Ryan presents a more explicit example of networking and computers in his novel *The Adolescence of P-1* (1985). In this novel a university student creates an intelligent program that escapes its original computer environment and infiltrates a worldwide network of computers. This anticipates the Internet as we know it. As the intelligent program called P-1 grows up, it causes some major misunderstandings and finds itself at war with the U.S. military establishment. It should also be pointed out that a worldwide network wouldn't be possible without communications satellites, which Arthur C. Clarke wrote about in 1945.

Orson Scott Card's series starting with *Ender's Game* has a similar intelligent entity that lives in the galactic empire's network of computers. Jane, the intelligent program, starts as a minor theme and builds throughout the series. Many other authors use themes that include computer networks in various ways. These include Neal Stephenson, William Gibson, and Bruce Stirling.

Meanwhile, ARPAnet had grown so big that the Defense Communications Agency decided security was an issue. So it split off a portion of ARPAnet in 1983 and called it **Milnet** (Military Network). The smaller part retained the name ARPAnet and consisted primarily of university researchers. Milnet was used for nonclassified military information. With special gateways between the two parts, however, researchers with proper access could use the system as if it hadn't changed. At the same time as the split, ARPAnet converted from the Network Control Protocol to the TCP/IP protocol.

By the late 1980s, the number of networks running TCP/IP protocol and connected to the **NSFnet** made it far larger than ARPAnet had ever been. And it was still growing. NSFnet was also faster and easier to connect to than ARPAnet, so NSFnet became the system of choice for researchers everywhere. By then, ARPAnet was costing $14 million per year to keep up and running, even though it had outlived its usefulness. The plug was pulled, and by 1989 the majority of ARPAnet sites were connected to the NSF backbone through the regional community networks. This vast internetwork consisting of thousands of LANs, WANs, and computers all running the TCP/IP protocol soon became known as the Internet.

At this time, what was to become the Internet was used primarily for scientific research and exchange of scientific information. The users were universities, research institutes,

science-related corporations, and a few enterprising information-gathering companies that had foreseen the mountains of data available through the Internet. Only as the Internet became recognized as an unparalleled information resource did it reach its full public stature. By early 1995, the Internet had become known as **The Information Superhighway**, and as such, began to draw users from every population sector with computer access. The ARPA-planted seeds had grown to fruition.

7.3 UNIX, Gurus, and Gophers

With its popularity growing, the Internet needed improvements in user-friendliness. This section discusses three creations that satisfied the need to make the Internet easier to access: Gopher, Veronica, and Archie.

The Internet owes its critical mass to the wide distribution of computers running the **UNIX** operating system. With thousands of computers running UNIX and the freely distributed TCP/IP software suite, it is no wonder that the original access to the Internet had a UNIX look to it. Someone who desired a piece of information needed to have the exact address where that information could be found. This **Internet address** or **IP address** was a long string of numbers. For example, the Internet address of the location could look like this:

128.54.16.1

This happens to be the address of a computer at the University of California at San Diego. Actually, you can still use these addresses anywhere you use the more familiar addressing such as when sending email. For example,

jsmith@ucs.edu

can be replaced by

jsmith@128.54.16.1

The hardy souls who were UNIX experts loved the cryptic and abstract commands because gaining a working knowledge of them was a badge of honor. It was like being in a special club that had a very difficult entry requirement: a thorough knowledge of UNIX commands.

This same spirit was carried into the early days of the Internet. It really was a badge of honor to be able to navigate around the Internet. People who could do this were considered specialists and were often well paid for the use of their skills. But the public wanted a more direct access to the information on the Internet. It wasn't long before public desire to make the Internet easier to use led to improved navigation.

The University of Minnesota, home of the Golden Gophers, introduced the first major improvement in navigation of the Internet. It was called **Gopher**, after their mascot.

Gopher is a menu-driven Internet access system. This means that when you access Gopher, your monitor displays a "main menu" containing all the choices available to you from that screen. To move through the menu, you use the up and down directional arrows on your keyboard. To select from a menu, you move the highlight bar to the item you want and press the Return key. This in turn gives you another menu that goes to yet another menu, and so on, until you get to the desired information. Figure 7.3.1 shows how the University of Minnesota's main menu page looked.

Although it consisted only of text in menu form, Gopher became very popular. Menus were a big step up from the abstract command-line system, which was difficult to learn. With menus, almost anybody could navigate on the Internet. Gopher's popularity mushroomed, and at one time there were over 5,000 Gopher servers established throughout the world.

One of the main problems, however, was finding things. Gopher worked well enough if you knew where to find the kind of information you wanted. But if you did not, or if you wanted a broad range of information on a specific topic, going from menu to menu became tedious and very time consuming. The situation called for a better type of searching system. Veronica was just such a system.

Veronica (Very Easy Rodent-Oriented Netwide Index to Computerized Archives) is a searching system that makes use of an index of the entries

```
      Internet Gopher Information Client v2.1.3

          Home Gopher server: gopher.tc.umn.edu

-->   1. Information About Gopher/
      2. Computer Information/
      3. Discussion Groups/
      4. Fun & Games/
      5. Internet file server (ftp) sites/
      6. Libraries/
      7. News/
      8. Other Gopher and Information Servers/
      9. Phone Books/
     10. Search Gopher Titles at the University of Minnesota <?>
     11. Search lots of places at the University of Minnesota <?>
     12. University of Minnesota Campus Information/

Press ? for Help, q to Quit, u to go up a menu
```

Figure 7.3.1
The opening menu of a Gopher site.

in all the known Gopher menus. With the development of the Veronica index, it became unnecessary for each user to visit all the 5,000 Gopher servers, each with its own set of menus. Instead, Veronica is used to find only those sites related to the topic of interest. About twice a week, the Veronica system regularly visits all Gopher servers in the world and add any new entries to the several million already in the index. Veronica is usually entered from a Gopher menu with an entry like this:

```
8. Other Gopher and Information Servers/
```

One of the oldest search systems used to find files on the Internet is called **Archie**. At the time of Archie's birth in the early 1990s, the main interest was finding data files located in some computer on the Internet. Originally, Archie was designed to search **FTP** archive sites, which are computers on the Internet containing repositories. The files on them are specifically for downloading by using the Internet FTP program. Archie has been expanded to include many other resource listings and online directories.

By 1989, the Information Highway had expanded to become the **Global Community**, and Gophers were so common they were sometimes referred to as the "duct tape of the Internet." They bound together the Internet's many resources, whose diverse protocols and interfaces had previously made networked computer communication difficult.

The Archie system is a database of filenames that was, at one time, maintained on more than 1,500 computers. More than 1,000,000 filenames are stored in that database today. As a daily routine, specific Archie servers search their region for new files. Then once a month, regional Archie servers exchange new entries and update their Archie database so that all Archie servers have the same information.

Archie has a **Web page** on the **World Wide Web** and offers information that can't be obtained from the very popular WWW **search engines**. It should be noted that most WWW search engines, such as **Yahoo!**, search only Web pages. Thousands of files on the Internet, however, are *not* Web pages. Archie identifies this valuable information, and then the FTP program will download it.

Chapter 7: The Internet: Communication with the World

Although Gopher, Veronica, and Archie are still quite valuable, they have been completely overshadowed by the World Wide Web. The unmistakable preference for graphic information is overwhelming. The text-based systems of Gopher, Veronica, and Archie have definitely taken a back seat to the visual immediacy of the World Wide Web. However, Gopher still provides some types of information and access that are not readily available when using many Web-searching programs. For that reason, a few Gophers still exist and can be accessed, along with other Internet functions, through standard **Web browsers** such as Netscape Navigator or Communicator and Microsoft Internet Explorer.

7.4 The Internet Growing

After beginning as a scientific research tool for sharing computer resources, the Internet rapidly reached the stature of a multipurpose tool. By the end of the 1980s, more and more users from the educational and governmental communities had found ways to put the Internet to work for them. The new uses harnessed the shared computer resources first developed under ARPAnet to many tasks unforeseen by ARPAnet's developers. The variety of tasks that tapped the Internet's computing power is truly astonishing. The following four examples of popular Internet functions illustrate the diversity of Internet use.

Information Gathering: We spent some time earlier in the chapter discussing Archie and Veronica, search indexes used with the Internet's Gopher interface. The importance of this feature is the speed with which it drew users from all intellectual (and personal) fields and the kinds of information those users can find:

- University sites, for example, might provide class and faculty information, books, and periodicals from the library, and lists of government documents (titles, descriptions, and summaries were most common).

- Employment offices might easily provide vacancy notices and job descriptions for jobs on and off campus—full- and part-time jobs, student through professional level, local or international.

- Various governmental agencies provide many informational documents available via the Internet. These might include job listings with federal, state, and local government agencies; specific documents such as the Congressional Record; patent documents for inventions in the United States; and how-to documents supplied by agricultural extension services.

- Students and academic researchers could find bibliographies such as *Readers' Guide to Periodical Literature*, the catalog of the Library of Congress, and most recently, *Books in Print*.

A user with a little skill and a lot of patience for searching tedious lists and menus could find out something about almost anything, if he/she kept at it long enough. In fact, the Internet provides a way to access all sorts of information, some of which has yet to find its way over to the visual world of the Web.

The Computer Continuum

Internet2

The Internet had matured and grown during the late 1980s and the early 1990s when Internet traffic jams were threatening. Then along came the World Wide Web. With the increased traffic, it was clear that more capacity was needed. In October 1996, Internet2 was formally announced. Over 100 research universities have joined together to form UCAID (University Corporation for Advanced Internet Development), a non-profit consortium.

The goal of Internet2 was not to replace the Internet, but to enhance it. Internet2 will give the increased bandwidth essential for simultaneous transmission of voice, video, and data. In fact, it has been stated that the "difference between the existing Internet and Internet2 will be the difference between a country road and a multi-lane interstate highway."

The organization of Internet2 specifies points of entry called gigaPoPs (gigabit points of presence). These are organizing centers where 5 to 10 Internet2 members would connect to the system at gigabit transmission speeds (billions of bits per second). With this capacity, the uses of the Internet and Internet2 could expand to remote diagnosis in medicine, live hi-fidelity audio, live video, interactive participation in things such as musical ensembles, and many more. When it begins actual operation, possibly by the year 2002, the Internet2 will bring into reality the dreams of science fiction.

MUDs and MOOs: Both MUDs (Multi-User Dungeons) and MOOs (MUDs, Object-Oriented) are an outgrowth of the Dungeons-and-Dragons role-playing games of the 1970s and 80s. However, MUDs and MOOs are on the Internet. You can therefore play them with people all over the world without leaving the comfort of the desk chair in front of your computer. Writer Howard Rheingold refers to them as "… the water coolers of the Internet." As such they can be viewed as "social virtual realities."

Current estimates are that thousands of enthusiasts worldwide are creating characters and interacting in more than 500 active MUDs. In fact, some college students have become so addicted that they have flunked out of school, concentrating their efforts on MUDs rather than studies. It is not unusual for addicted individuals to spend three or four hours a day in a MUD environment.

Are these hours spent with MUDs all wasted time, or could these enthusiasts use MUDs for doing useful work? The possibilities seem endless. In 1991 Xerox PARC researcher Pavel Curtis expanded the work done by University of Waterloo student Steven White and created LambdaMOO. It is called a MOO because players use object-oriented tools to create programs that enhance the characters they create in playing MUD games, or to perform complex functions within those games. Xerox PARC researchers are continually seeking applications of MOO theory with direct value in the everyday reality of the business world. Applications being developed in this way include a virtual meeting place for professionals to share ideas and data, and a virtual office, so that going to work in the morning means turning on your computer from home rather than jumping into a car and driving to another location.

IRC (Internet Relay Chat): The Internet has fostered an interesting type of real-time communications called **chat rooms**. Chat facilities exist on many public and commercial services, but the IRC developed in 1988 by Jarkko Oikarinen, in Finland, is the Internet's version of a chat facility. The words *real-time* mean that the communicating parties must be connected to the system at the same time. Communication is accomplished via typed text over something referred to as a channel.

Here is the way IRC works: Individuals all over the world join an IRC, usually based on a particular topic or purpose. To communicate with others on the channel, a member (let's call her Pam) logs on to the IRC by entering her username and password. Because the discussion is ongoing, Pam can read what others have entered and then type in a comment of her own. The text Pam has typed appears on the screens of any IRC members who happen to be signed in at that time. As soon as Pam's comment appears, other members can read it and respond, if they please. Everyone on that channel sees all the comments as soon as they are typed, and a single comment may elicit many simultaneous responses, which appear consecutively onscreen as they are received.

At any one time, participants from all over the world might be using a single chat channel. The IRC maintains hundreds of individual channels ranging in topics from hot tubs to heavy metal to politics.

This communication is usually organized by topic, but there are also very interesting celebrity question-and-answer sessions.

These examples represent only a small portion of the activity on the Internet. Some of the activity is on a rather small scale, but the World Wide Web, presented in the next chapter, is definitely not in this group. The WWW is the most visible and will probably dominate the Internet throughout the next decade.

Chapter Summary

What you can do with what you have learned:

- Recognize the difference between a text-based access method, such as Gopher, and multimedia-based access method such as the WWW.

- Use Gopher or another text-based access method to search existing databases of information on many topics.

- Consider a MUD or MOO for entertainment or research.

- Use an IRC to communicate with others with a specific interest.

Key Terms and Review Questions

Key terms introduced in this chapter:

Matching

Match the key terms introduced in the chapter to the statements below. Each term may be used once, more than once, or not at all.

1. _____ This important network was transferred to the Defense Department in 1975.

2. _____ The National Science Foundation started a network using this *protocol* in 1980.

3. _____ This is the term given to one of the pieces of a message after it has been divided up.

4. _____ This is a vast interconnected network consisting of LANs, WANs, and millions of computers that all run on the TCP/IP protocol.

5. _____ This *network* was created by the National Science Foundation to provide a resource-sharing network opportunity to computer science research at all universities.

6. _____ This menu-driven system consists of programs that display text-based lists of accessible information.

7. _____ This search system on Gopher specialized in finding data files.

8. _____ This search system on Gopher specialized in indexing the entries in all the Gopher menus.

9. _____ The military formed this network after it split off a portion of ARPAnet in 1983.

10. _____ By early 1995, the Internet had become known by this name.

11. _____ This string of numbers identifies the address of a computer on the Internet.

12. _____ This is a text-based game similar to Dungeons-and-Dragons.

13. _____ This is an outgrowth of the Internet interactive game that is similar to Dungeons-and-Dragons. It enables users to use object-oriented tools to create programs that enhance the characters they create while playing the game.

14. _____ This is the Internet's version of a chat facility.

15. _____ This is currently the most visible activity on the Internet.

True or False

1. _____ ARPAnet began as a Defense Department project in 1969.

2. _____ ARPAnet, soon after its inception, became popular because any university and any researcher could have access.

3. _____ The Gopher system got its name from the mascot of the University of Minnesota.

4. _____ Like the Gopher system, Veronica and Archie were two other systems that allowed the navigation of the Internet via text menus.

5. _____ Gopher systems are no longer accessible on the Internet.

6. _____ Messages are divided into smaller pieces before being sent over the Internet.

7. _____ From the 1960s through the late 1980s, all network protocols were the same.

8. _____ Gopher was, and still is, primarily a text-based system that allows access to some information on the Internet.

9. _____ An Internet address that identifies where a person can be found must be supplied with the message in order to send a message to someone on the Internet.

10. _____ Gopher systems were never really popular.

11. _____ The Internet has moved from a communication tool and information source to an environment that also includes entertainment possibilities.

12. _____ MUDs, because of their addictive quality, have caused some college students to "flunk out."

13. _____ The Internet has the potential of infecting millions of computers with viruses.

14. _____ IRCs require that people "chatting" on the IRC be connected to the network at the same time.

15. _____ Everyone using the Internet must have a unique individual IP address.

Multiple Choice

Answer the multiple choice questions by selecting the best answer from the choices given.

1. This network was started for computer science researchers.
   a. ARPAnet
   b. CSnet
   c. NSFnet
   d. Internet
   e. CSResearchNet

2. This agency was the first to focus major development effort on computer networking.
   a. ARPA (Advanced Reset Projects Agency)
   b. SRI (Stanford Research Institute)
   c. UCLA (University of California, Los Angeles)
   d. The Defense Department
   e. The National Science Foundation

3. The first four nodes linked together by ARPAnet were what?
   a. Military installations
   b. Governmental organizations
   c. Universities
   d. A combination of military and university nodes

4. In 1975, ARPAnet was transferred to whom?

   a. NASA

   b. NSF (National Science Foundation)

   c. A Defense Department agency

   d. An IBM holding company

   e. The Internet board

5. The NSFnet with its internetwork running the TCP/IP protocol became known as what?

   a. ARPAnet

   b. Milnet

   c. Internet

   d. UNIX

   f. Phishnet

6. This system of access to the Internet is text-based.

   a. Wolverine

   b. Gopher

   c. Weasel

   d. Ferret

   e. Muskrat

7. The term Gopher came from:

   a. **G**oing **O**ver **P**iles of **H**ideous **E**rroneous **R**eferences

   b. **G**eorgia's **O**ffice of **P**hysical **H**ealth Op**ER**ations

   c. Gopher (UNIX programmers typically work in basements)

   d. Gopher (mascot of University of Minnesota)

8. The oldest search system used to find files on the Internet is called what?

   a. Archie

   b. Jughead

   c. Veronica

   d. Snoopy

   e. Scavenger

9. The operating system of choice for specialists who used the Internet was what?

   a. MS-DOS

   b. OS/2

   c. VMS

   d. UNIX

   e. MacOS

10. This "real-time" communication system enables people to "talk" to one another over the Internet by using the keyboard in places called chat rooms.

   a. IRC

   b. Email

   c. MOO

   d. Gopher

   e. Phonehome

Exercises

1. Using a Web browser of your choice:

First: Go to the following location **http://www.pcwebopedia.com**

Second: Look up the word *Gopher*.

Third: Read what it says about Gopher.

Fourth: Read what it says about Archie.

Fifth: Read what it says about Veronica.

2. Using a Web browser of your hoice:

First: Go to the following location **http://gopher.tc.umn.edu**

This site lists the resources available on the University of Minnesota's Gopher server. It is not quite up to date.

Second: Find when the weather for your area was last updated.

Third: Find a recipe that you might like. Write down the URL of the recipe you have found.

3. What is the difference between a text-based accessing method and a multimedia-based accessing method?

4. Name three text-based accessing methods mentioned in this chapter.

5. People join email lists (usually through a Listserv) to exchange information with others on a topic of interest. When you send a response to another's message, your email address is included (that is, whoever you send it to will know how to reach you). What would you do if someone posted a message that you totally disagree

with, but you would rather not have that person know who you are?

6. People join IRCs (Internet relay chat) to exchange information with others on a topic of interest. When you send a response to another's message, your contact information may or may not be included. What would you do if someone posted a message that you totally disagree with, but you would rather not have that person know who you are?

7. What is the difference between a MUD and a MOO? Explain the difference.

Discussion Questions

1. Explain why censorship on the Internet would be hard to police.

2. Discuss possible advantages and disadvantages of people meeting in a virtual space/location using programs with MOOs versus actually meeting "in the flesh."

3. Discuss the exact ways in which IRC is like and different from a telephone conference call.

4. If information is stored on computers (rather than printed books, magazines, handwritten notes, and so on), it can be easily changed. This can make it easy to correct, update, or delete information. Discuss the possible social, political, or psychological

consequences of possible "falsifying of the past" in this fashion. Such was predicted in the novel *1984*, and even done without computers in societies with limited access to the means of printing and limited distribution of printed materials (in photographs, as well in the Soviet Union and in China, by inserting and removing individuals as they fell into or out of favor or power).

5. What kept the early Internet from achieving the popular success enjoyed by the Web?

6. How would you go about setting up a "private" chat room for yourself and your friends?

Group Project

A group of four students is to share responsibility for a presentation about services carried over the Internet. Each person of the group will take two of the services from the list:

HTTP (Hypertext Transfer Protocol)

FTP (File Transfer Protocol—include anonymous FTP and Archie)

Email (Include MIME and SMTP)

Gopher (Include Veronica)

WAIS (Wide Area Information Service)

Telnet (Telephone Networking—include PPP and SLIP)

Usenet (How does it compare in form and function to IRCs?)

The presentation should be in PowerPoint and include an example where the presenter used the service and shows the result. It should outline what the service is used for and

The Computer Continuum

how to use it. Research for these topics can be found on the World Wide Web. Each slide should be short and not include a lot of text.

Web Connections

http://www.internetvalley.com/intvalold.html

A brief history of the Internet.

http://www.pcwebopedia.com/gopher.htm

Information on Gopher and links to indexes of Gopher files.

http://www.terena.nl/libr/gnrt/explore/gopher.html

More information on Gopher and links to access software.

http://www.pcwebopedia.com/TCP_IP.htm

Information on TCP/IP protocols and great links to more (some, very detailed) sites.

http://www.cnet.com/Content/Features/Howto/Beyond2/

Definition and information on IRCs and MUDs, including links to pages where you can download necessary software and get more information.

http://www.tiac.net/users/dstein/nw681.html

Many IRCs on a multitude of subjects that a person can join.

http://pharmdec.wustl.edu/about/faq.html

A web page linking to information about Usenet.

http://www.us.lspace.org/faqs/

A list of links for FAQs on various Usenet newsgroups.

http://sunsite.unc.edu/usenet-i/usenet-help.html

A list of links to information regarding Usenet, including primers, FAQs, Usenet etiquette, how to work with Usenet community, and many more things about Usenet.

http://help.ibm.net/helplib/index.html

A special site for IBM networking services, giving an idea of the kind of support provided to those who own IBM networking products.

Bibliography

Comer, Douglas E. *The Internet*. 2d ed. New Jersey: Prentice Hall, 1997.

A good, readable overview of how the Internet works.

Hafner, Katie, and Matthew Lyon. *Where Wizards Stay Up Late: The Origins of the Internet*. New York: Touchstone, 1996.

Very readable historical overview of the Internet.

Kientzle, Tim. *Internet File Formats*. Scottsdale: Coriolis Group Books.

This book defines and describes all the different file formats found on the Internet.

Quarterman, John S., and Smoot Carl-Mitchell. *The Internet Connection*. Reading, MA: Addison-Wesley, 1994.

A slightly more technical view of the Internet.

Chapter 8

The World Wide Web: Expanding the Global Community

Chapter Objectives

By the end of this chapter, you will:

- Realize how the human need to communicate motivated the development of the World Wide Web.

- Know the different types of media used on the Internet.

- Understand the concepts of hypertext and hypermedia and their uses in a multimedia environment such as the Internet.

- Recognize the separate parts of URLs and what each represents.

- Recognize the minimum hardware components and software needed to access the Internet.

- Understand how search engines attempt to classify the information available on the Internet.

- Identify the issues involved with downloading software from the Internet or putting together your own Internet page.

- Appreciate the issues, concepts, and uses of accessing the Internet as an educational tool.

- Recognize the issues, concepts, and uses of accessing the Internet as a business tool.

- Understand the security measures and ethical issues surrounding the Internet.

8.1 And Then Came the Web

HTTP (Hypertext Transfer Protocol) is a set of rules implemented in a program that allows an individual computer to participate with other computers through the Internet in a way that allows transfer of text, visual, and audio information.

The **World Wide Web** is a computer communications system that allows multimedia information to be accessed and transmitted via the Internet. It follows the Hypertext Transfer Protocol.

In 1989 a new era of **Internet** communication was ushered in. At that time, **Gopher** was the best tool we had for Internet communication. But it accessed only textual materials. Other types of information, such as pictures and sound, were still out of reach in 1989. The need to access visual and audio information became the next obvious step in communications on the Internet.

Tim Berners-Lee, a physicist at the European high-energy physics laboratory (CERN) in Switzerland, recognized this need in 1989. He created a network protocol called **HTTP (Hypertext Transfer Protocol)**, which forms the basis for the **World Wide Web**. The World Wide Web or WWW is oftentimes called the **Web**.

Unlike earlier protocols, the HTTP can convert not only text, but also visual and audio information into packets to traverse the Internet. The result forever transformed the Internet from simply being a useful tool for scholars and professionals to a vehicle for global multimedia communication.

Let's take a moment to see why this happened. Why did the addition of visual and sound capabilities cause an Internet revolution? The answer is buried deep within the human need to communicate.

From the beginning of time, the need to communicate has been an essential aspect of human endeavor. Humans continuously reach out to others, sharing feelings, ideas, and information. This need for communication is instinctual, and indeed motivated such ingenious creations as the printing press, the telegraph, and the Internet itself.

Humans communicate best when they can use several means of communication simultaneously. The word *help* written on a piece of paper does not attract the same attention as the word *HELP* shouted in a loud voice. And the shout becomes even more effective when accompanied by wide eyes and wildly waving arms. What makes the World Wide Web effective as a communication conduit is its capability to convey simultaneously the word, the shout, the gesture, and more. Effective human communication simultaneously employs several senses; similarly, effective computer communication demands multimedia.

Who Owns the Web?

No single entity, government, or corporation can own the World Wide Web because it is a collection of millions of computers and networks with diverse ownership that are all part of the Internet. The Web is a means of accessing the many physical connections of the Internet. Each of the computers connected to the Internet follows a set of protocols and standards accepted worldwide. Included in this set of protocols is HTTP, which allows WWW communication.

Next question: If no one can own the Web or the Internet, how can it be managed or controlled? Well, no one controls the Internet, either, or at least not all of it. The Internet is made up of hundreds of thousands of computers that are all connected together. Although an individual or organization may own a small piece of the Internet (its own network and the computers connected to it), many others also own their piece of the Net.

The more pertinent issue here is access. Through the mutual acceptance of TCP/IP and HTTP protocols, computer and network owners around the world agree to let others access certain files and documents. The access is limited to **read-only**. When you access a Web page, you can view the page, read it, or even print it out. What you cannot do is change it. Only the specific owner of that page can make any changes or delete the page.

Introducing Multimedia

A **medium** is the vehicle or conduit through which information is communicated. Specialized media are many and varied. Some of them—such as books, newspapers, telegraphs, and local office networks—are primarily text oriented. They can convey only the textual content of an item (the words themselves, if we can read them). Others, such as radios, musical instruments, and cassette tapes, serve as communication conduits for audio information, or sounds. The message these carry is in the sound itself, and in the interpretation our brain derives from it. A third set of media conveys only visual images. These include silent films, still photographs, paintings, sculptures, and satellite pictures.

Sometimes the message being communicated contains two or more different kinds of information, and therefore needs two or more types of communication media. If information is simultaneously channeled through several different mediums, it is called **multimedia**. Some common examples of multimedia communication are movies, theater, television, CD-ROMs, video games, and the World Wide Web!

8.2 Navigating the Web

The capability to convey multimedia information was not the only contribution the **World Wide Web protocol** brought to the Internet. It brought also its own unique techniques for navigating the Internet's complexities.

Consider, for a moment, how Gopher works. Even when accessed through the Web, Gopher is awkward to use. To find information on Gopher, you navigate textual menus and select options by typing a letter or two until you find whatever you are seeking. When you wish to consult another reference, you back up through the menus, sometimes to the beginning, and select different options. Navigation from one item of information to another is clumsy and inconvenient.

Navigation on the Web is another matter. Because of its point-and-click technique, the Web is much more user friendly. Unlike Gopher, the World Wide Web allows the user to type the Web site address, or URL, in a command line box on the Web browser screen, or to find the Web site through a keyword search from one of a variety of programs called search engines. When you find the site you're looking for on the search engine screen, you point to it, click the mouse button, and presto, you are there. This magic is accomplished by the use of two concepts: **hypertext** and **hypertext links**.

Hypertext, Hypermedia, and Hot Links

The term hypertext refers to any word or phrase in an electronic document that can be used as a pointer or **link** to a related text passage. This is done by making that word or phrase an active spot, or hypertext link, within its document. To use hypertext, the reader moves the mouse cursor to the linking word and clicks the mouse button. Whether the related passage is in the same document or another, it quickly appears.

Hyperlinks are embedded into Web documents as they are written. Here are the steps:

1. Identify the specific words that will be useful as links.

2. Search for and locate the related text or additional information the hypertext will access.

A **medium** is the vehicle or conduit through which information is communicated.

Multimedia is the term used to describe several different types of information, such as text, graphics, video animation, and sound, communicated through several different mediums simultaneously and often interactively.

Hypertext refers to any word or phrase in an electronic document, which can be used as a pointer to a related text passage.

Hypertext links are any text or image that has been designated as a means of accessing related material.

---

3. Set pointers containing information on how to find the document containing the related material.

4. Have the selected words printed in a special color and underlined so that the reader can recognize them as hypertext.

Vannevar Bush (1890–1974) — An Enigma

In every major event in human history, there are those whose work stands out as being an essential foundation. A former MIT Professor of Electrical Engineering, Vannevar Bush is one such individual. His influence is associated directly with the formation of the Manhattan Project that created the atom bomb. He also conceived ARPA (Advance Research Projects Agency) and NSF (National Science Foundation) through the OSRD (Office of Scientific Research and Development). In OSRD, Vannevar Bush set up an ultrasecret research group that was the precursor of the CIA.

His most public influence is found in the 1945 *Atlantic Monthly* article "As We May Think." In this article he proposes a device called a "memex," whose major aspects are yet to be realized. The hypertext links and organization of the WWW, however, are directly related to his memex device. It was a personal information system with links between items of information. It addressed one of the most pressing problems in today's WWW: A vast amount of junk must be sifted through to get something of value. The memex handled this type of problem and addressed others not yet part of the WWW in three significant ways.

First, the memex would allow a great reduction in the information overload currently found when surfing the Web.

Second, the memex would keep track of "associative trails," which are connections between items of information and reasons for making them. These connections are needed to make sense of what has been explored and how thoughts mature as the thinking process moves forward.

Third, the memex would be a mind amplifier. It would become a thinking aid and assist in forming a human-machine consciousness that would literally amplify an individual's thinking efforts.

As the WWW matures, several companies are trying to tame the chaos. Their efforts seem to be involved with the same points that the memex addresses: recording relationships and individuals' associations. A quote from Brewster Kayle in *Wired* magazine adds emphasis to this point when he states, "Bush's great insight was realizing that there's more value in the connections between data than in the data itself." Exploration and use of this insight and others is going to make the WWW even more revolutionary and influential in our daily lives.

Let's see how hypertext works by following Figure 8.2.1. If you were reading a World Wide Web page about Christopher Columbus, you might encounter Queen Isabella's name. The author could easily have used her name as a link to the history of her reign as the Queen of Spain. In that description could be the fact that she was the wife of King Ferdinand. Clicking on his name might give a biography of him. By following the author's pre-set links, you could easily explore as much or as little as you wanted.

The Computer Continuum

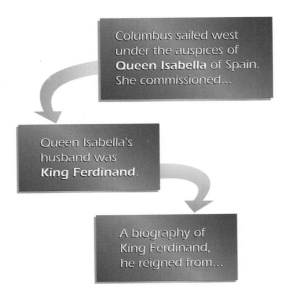

Figure 8.2.1

In hypertext, one follows the links to related information.

Hypermedia refers to using the concept of hypertext linking with other mediums, such as pictures and sound. Hypermedia links are often referred to as hyperlinks.

The history of the hypertext concept has roots that go back to man's early critical writings. The Talmud, for example, contains interpretations and annotations referring to the first five books of the Bible and the laws of Judaism. An important passage from the Law is printed in the center of a large page. Commentaries referring to that passage are arranged in a border around it. The reader can read and study not only the original passage, but also the possibly conflicting interpretations that have been collected through the centuries. The convenience of these comments being visually connected so closely to the text makes them easy to read and compare. As shown in Figure 8.2.2, the Talmud's visual layout contains the essence of our modern day electronic computerized hypertext.

With the advent of the World Wide Web, the linking of text to other text was not sufficient. Internet navigation needed to go one step more: It had to encompass multimedia linking.

The concept of using hypertext linking with other communication mediums is called **hypermedia**. Whereas in hypertext only phrases or words could be used as linking points to related text, hypermedia is more complex. It allows visual objects and text to be linked to other visual objects, animations, text, or even sound. The result is a kind of free-form navigation of the World Wide Web.

As with hypertext, the major responsibility for the success of using multimedia linking rests with the author, or whoever set up the links. In this case, there is no single author. Individuals put their own audio, animations, video, and images online for anyone to access. Navigating via the Web takes advantage of the hypermedia linking of many individuals, and thereby becomes a hypermedia resource.

Figure 8.2.2

The Talmud, a work that records interpretations of Jewish law, shows early use of the hypertext concept.

8.3 Understanding Web Addresses (URLs)

Well, now we know that the Internet consists of hundreds of thousands of physical connections linking computers and networks around the world. Because of these connections, you can send mail, view files, and gather information from computers located anywhere. The way to do this is by **surfing** the Web.

Links appear in documents called **Web pages**, especially created for World Wide Web viewing. If you mouse-click a link on one Web page, you will soon be viewing a different Web page. This is because the link you clicked on in the first Web page contained two things: 1) the instruction to locate and display the second page, and 2) the location, or address, of where to find it.

Because literally millions of Web pages exist on the Internet, we must have some way to be sure that each one has a unique address. Fortunately, CERN set up a registration system called InterNIC to issue and monitor Web addresses. The technical name for a Web address is **Uniform Resource Locator** (**URL**).

A URL consists of three parts:

1. The type of connection (specific protocol to be used).

   The protocol to be used is determined by how you use the Web resources. A colon (:) appears after the name of the protocol. Because the World Wide Web is only one of the many Internet protocols available, you might find it helpful to know a few additional protocol names. Figure 8.3.1 shows some of the other protocols you might use, and the kinds of services they provide:

Figure 8.3.1 *A few examples of networking protocols.*

Name	Definition	Description
HTTP	Hypertext Transport Protocol	Mode through which World Wide Web uses the Internet
FTP	File Transfer Protocol	Used for transferring files between computers
MAILTO	Email protocol	Used to send or create an email link
FILE	Local file access	Used to view an HTML file on your computer
Gopher	Name of Internet access system	Transfer type used by the Gopher menu system
WAIS	Wide area information service	A tool for searching information databases
Telnet	Telephone Networking	A service for logging on to remote computers

2. The **Internet address** of the computer you are trying to reach.

   A computer's Internet address is called a **domain name**, and is preceded by two slashes (//), as shown in Figure 8.3.2. The domain is divided into two or more **subdomains**, separated by periods. The domain segment(s) on the left identify the Web **server**, a computer permanently connected to the Web. The rightmost subdomain, called the **top-level domain**, identifies the type of organization owning the computer.

   In countries outside the United States, the top-level-domain specifies a two-letter code for the country. For example, The Royal Canadian Mounted Police is **www.rcmp-grc.gc.ca/**, where the ca stands for Canada.

The Computer Continuum

Here are a couple of examples of possible domains: **www.eds.com**. To read this out loud, you would say "W-W-W dot E-D-S dot com." Notice that the periods separating the segments of the domain are pronounced "**dot**." The domain name for Eastern Michigan University is **www.emich.edu**.

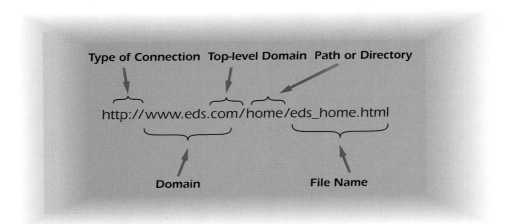

Figure 8.3.2
Annotated diagram of a
Uniform Resource Locator.

Figure 8.3.3 *Some of the most commonly encountered top-level domains.*

Domain	Usage
com	Commercial (profit making) organization
edu	Educational institution
gov	Government agency
mil	Military
net	Networking organization
org	Nonprofit organization

3. The **path** and name of the file.

   While the Internet address, or domain, locates the specific computer you wish to reach, the path and name identify the specific file or page you want to see. A **slash** (/) separates the path from the domain. Typically, the path names any directories and subdirectories you will need to go through to find the desired file. The filename identifies the specific document creating the Web page you need. If the person who owns a Web page titled it **index.html**, a path and filename need not be included in the URL.

Now that we have examined the parts of a Uniform Resource Locator (URL), let's take another look at the complete Web address in Figure 8.3.2. Pronounced aloud, this URL reads as follows: "H-T-T-P colon slash slash W-W-W dot E-D-S dot com slash home slash E-D-S underscore home dot H-T-M-L." That is quite a mouthful, but it does uniquely identify a specific Web page.

8.4 The Web and You

Several issues must be discussed before you can make use of the Web. They range from software and hardware needed on your own computer to services needed for connecting to the Web. These issues continue with what you can do on the Web and how you can even create your own Web presence with a personal Web page.

Accessing the Web (Internet Service Providers)

Before you can connect to the Internet and use the World Wide Web and other services, you must first arrange to be connected to an **ISP** (**Internet service provider**). Internet service providers are companies, such as AT&T and America Online (see Figure 8.4.2), that have networks and WWW servers linked to the Internet, and who allow you to connect to their servers, usually for a fee. There are also thousands of local ISPs to select from. In effect, when you hook up to an ISP, your computer becomes part of the ISP's network and the Web. The service provider assigns you a username and password so that only authorized personnel can use their network connections. You are responsible for any actions taken and charges incurred under your username.

Suppose you own Computer A, which occupies your desk at Hometown College, USA. You most likely pay a technology fee to your college. One of the things this fee provides is access to the Internet. Your college is an Internet service provider. We will call the college ISP B. If you want to view a particular Web page somewhere out on the Internet, lets say a file on Computer C, which is hooked up to ISP D, how does this happen? Figure 8.4.1 gives a schematic representation of a typical Web transaction.

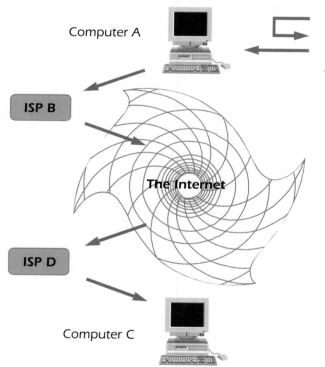

1. You determine what Web page you want to view.
2. You request to view the desired page by clicking on a link or by typing the page's URL on the keyboard of Computer A.
3. Using a modem and a phone line, Computer A sends your request to your service provider, ISP B.
4. ISP B passes your request and URL along its network to the Internet.
5. Following many Internet links and telephone lines, your message reaches ISP D, and its network.
6. ISP D activates its hookup to Computer C, enabling a search for the path and filenames in your URL.
7. When the file is found, the Web page is sent back through the Internet and appears on the screen of computer A.

Figure 8.4.1

Following the link to a Web page.

The Computer Continuum

What Do You Need to Get Started?

To begin with, you need a computer and a **modem**. To make full use of the Web's hyper-media capabilities, you will want high-speed performance, a large-capacity hard disk, and large RAM capacity. Sound and image files (especially video images and animation) are large, often containing several megabytes of data. A low-speed computer could take several minutes to display a picture from the Web or to play a complex sound. A computer with a small disk drive or one that is too full may not have room to store sound and image files. The resulting delays and incomplete files can be very frustrating. For best transmission, you will want a minimum computer speed of 133 MHz, a minimum RAM size of 16 MB, and 1 GB of hard disk space. In all three cases, higher numbers will further enhance performance.

To connect your computer to a network via the telephone lines, you will need a modem. Your modem converts data from your computer into a form that can be transmitted over telephone lines. The computer at the other end of your link needs a modem, too, to convert data transmitted over phone lines back into data the computer can use. Modems come in two types: internal and external. In general, most computers you buy today have internal modems factory installed. Older machines and low-end computers may require attaching an external modem. Whether your modem is internal or external, its most important performance factor is speed. Obviously, the faster a modem can transmit data, the shorter delay you will experience sending and receiving it. The minimum data transfer speed recommended for a modem accessing the World Wide Web is 28.8 bps. Higher transfer speeds, will, of course, enhance performance.

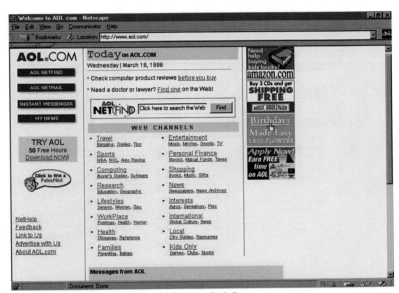

Figure 8.4.2

The welcome screen for America Online, a very large ISP.

Earlier, this chapter discussed the need for an Internet service provider. Thousands of them exist, both locally and nationally. Whether you choose a local provider or a national one, be sure to ascertain that it provides all the different Internet services you want. Almost all ISPs support email and World Wide Web access, but some do not provide FTP (File Transfer Protocol), Usenet, or IRC (Internet Relay Chat). FTP is needed to download files from the Internet and upload your own materials for others to use.

You will usually have to pay three different charges for Internet access. The first is a **hookup** or installation fee. The hookup establishes the physical link between your computer and the ISP and installs the required software on your computer. The second charge is a **monthly use fee**. The monthly fee provides either an unlimited amount of time to access the Internet or a limited number of hours of Internet use per month. Usually, the unlimited use contract provides the most economic Internet access, although the specified number of hours may be sufficient when you first begin using the Web. The third charge you will have to pay is a **per-call connection charge** to your long-distance phone company. The connection charge is calculated as a fee per minute you are connected to a long-distance telephone line. You can avoid this fee altogether by selecting an Internet service provider whose phone number is a local call for you.

Surfing the Web

After you have acquired the physical networking components described in the preceding section, you must turn your attention to software. As you have already discovered, computers need software to make things work. The software needed for surfing the Web is called a **Web browser**. A browser is your window into the contents of the Internet.

Because Web browsers support HTTP protocols, they enable you to use **hypermedia links** to see and hear information from distant Internet documents. A typical document prepared in accordance with HTTP protocol may have text, sounds, music, and still and moving images, all on the same Web page. When you see a Web page on your computer screen, you may notice highlighted or underlined words or images. These are hypermedia links. When you click on one, your browser software activates the link and issues a request to find and show you the file named in the link's URL. This enables you to surf effortlessly from one Web page to another, viewing related information.

In addition to providing software for Web surfing and viewing, browsers serve several other useful functions. For example, they do the following:

- "Read" the contents of Web documents and format them to be viewed on your screen.

- Enable you to make a paper copy (printout) of documents as they appear on your monitor.

- Enable you to copy text from a Web page and paste it into a word processing document.

- Enable you to save still and moving images from Web pages as files on your computer.

- Provide arrows and buttons (hyperlinks) to assist in moving back and forth through Web pages you have already visited.

- Support email, File Transfer Protocol, IRC, and other Internet services.

- Keep an address book of your favorite Web pages, often called bookmarks.

Currently, two major browser products, **Microsoft Internet Explorer** and **Netscape Navigator**, as shown in Figure 8.4.3, dominate the browser market. Both are available to

Figure 8.4.3
Home Web sites of two popular browsers.

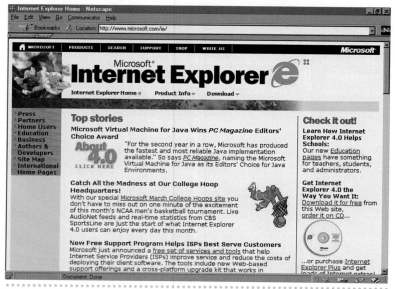

a) Microsoft Internet Explorer

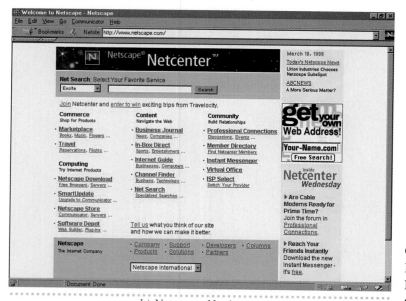

b) Netscape Navigator

individual users free from the company **Web sites**. Along with the browsers themselves, one can download new versions of software products (including browsers); **add-ons**, which give browsing and Web-building capabilities to other types of software; and **plug-ins**, which enhance or enable use of moving videos or extensive sound.

Thus far, the World Wide Web activities we have discussed have been reactive. That is, we have followed links surfing from Web page to Web page to see what's out there, and to associate related information to what we have already learned. In fact, surfing the World Wide Web places the surfer at the whim of whoever set up the links we follow. They give us only one view of what information relates to a link, and how that relationship is expressed. In the next section the user will take a more proactive role—selecting words, topics, and concepts to research, and sorting through collections of information to find exactly what we specify.

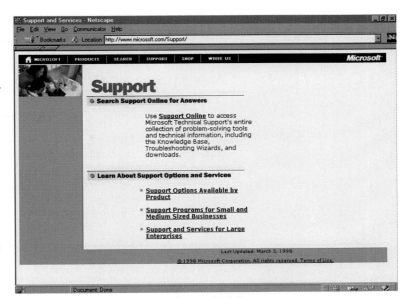

Figure 8.4.4

Microsoft offers an extensive list of free downloads and updates from its technical-support home page.

Most browsers have a built-in access method to the main search engines. In Netscape, for example, a button titled Net Search will take you to a page that enables you to choose from a number of different search engines.

Searching the Web

Searching the World Wide Web for specific information is a daunting task. Millions of Web pages exist, posted to the Internet in no specific order. The frustrating problem is how to harvest the relevant nuggets without sifting through mountains of junk. Fortunately, many free search services have sprouted up on the Web. Like library catalogues and indexes, they sift through the Internet's digital data and guide us to the useful information we seek.

Search engines on the WWW, such as AltaVista, Lycos, and HotBot, often use special programs to search the WWW. Of the several types of search programs that have been written, most use the same underlying technology: the software **spider**.

Spider software automatically searches from site to site on the Web, perpetually seeking new pages by following links. When the spider finds a new site or one that has recently changed, it sends information about that site and its contents back to the search software. What information is sent, and how much, depends on the

Figure 8.4.5

Like its namesake, the software spider searches the Web for new conquests.

search engine being served by the spider. Some spiders are selective, submitting only the titles of pages found; others send back every word in every document. This impacts the kind of results you will get from any search query.

When you type a word or phrase into the search string text box, the search engine canvasses its databank or index, seeking the words you entered. When it finds matching entries, it compiles them into a list of links to the matching sites. This list is displayed onscreen.

Different search engines utilize different methods of producing their indexes. Here is a list of a few different indexing techniques:

Subject or topic search: This type of search begins with a list of classifications, which are further divided into a hierarchical system of several levels of subclasses. Web pages are categorized by subject into appropriate classifications. You can have the engine search for your topic in a single category, or throughout the entire classification.

Keyword search: This kind of search engine is a close relative to a Biblical concordance. Using a technique called an inverted index, it indexes every word in every document it finds on the Web. To initiate this search, you type in some keywords relevant to your topic. The number and quality of results depends on how well you select your keywords.

Concept-based search: This system maintains a matrix of which words commonly occur together or near each other in a document. When it finds the words *film* and *director* in close proximity to each other, it assumes the document has something to do with the movies. It uses related words such as these to select documents that fit your search query.

Text analysis engine: This system analyzes the content of a document's text and comes up with a specific classification from its classification hierarchy. It then adds that item to its directory of that category. Searches are then made by matching desired concepts to those of specific classifications.

It is a good idea to try your search queries on several different types of search engines to see which give the best (and most relevant) results. Because they organize their indexes differently, different search engines produce different lists of Web pages for the same query.

If you are interested in a list of some popular search engines, refer to the list of Web sites at the end of this chapter.

Downloading Software

It's true that different people use the World Wide Web in different ways, but most users find it a useful source of software. Many software companies advertise on the Web and make their products available electronically. If you wish to acquire a software product available over the Internet, you just copy it to your own computer. This process is known as **downloading** the software.

We already know what software is, but downloading may be a new term.

Free Downloads

Many different kinds of software are available free over the Internet. The most popular include technical-support assistance, utility programs such as drivers, virus checkers, hard disk optimizers, electronic games, and visual enhancements for your own documents,

Downloading is the process of receiving a program, document, or file via a network, from another computer. A download always comes electronically from an outside source to your computer. Moving a program or document in the other direction, from your computer along a network to a remote node, is known as **uploading**.

such as icons and other images, fancy fonts, and animated cartoons. Sometimes sample and trial versions of popular software are also offered.

Free downloads are exactly that: FREE! You, however, must do all the work and take the responsibility for getting your copy (not that there is very much work involved). Here are the steps:

- Be sure you are connected to your ISP.

- Search the World Wide Web to find the free file you want to download or go to Web sites specializing in free downloads such as **www.download.com**.

- When you have found the file, click on its name or icon to begin the download process. Because many products are available for several different computer configurations, be sure you select the one set up for your computer and operating system.

- Downloading may require the use of FTP (File Transfer Protocol). This is included with most Web browsers, and many download providers use it without your awareness.

- After the download begins, it may take several seconds, several minutes, or even hours. The time needed is determined by the size of the item you are downloading, the density of network traffic at that particular time, and the speed of the two modems involved in the transaction.

- For speed and efficiency, many downloads are transferred in **compressed format**. This means that many space-wasting features of the original file are recorded in a shorter form. Downloading a compressed file saves time, but the result is a file or document you cannot use without extracting it. Sometimes the downloaded file is "self-extracting," or "self-installing" and will be ready for installation on your computer. Other downloads will require you to perform the **decompression**, using a program such as **WinZip** for Windows computers, or **Fetch** for the Macintosh computers. Both of these products, by the way, are available in their latest versions as free downloads.

- Downloaded software usually is accompanied by a **Readme** file. This will likely contain licensing and use agreements, instructions for installation, if needed, any known problems or incompatibilities, and help on getting started. Take the time to read these files. They can save hours of frustration.

- Be especially aware of any time and usage limitations of free downloads. **Alpha** and **beta versions** (that means they are still being tested) of commercial software frequently limit your use of the programs to 60 or 90 days. Introductory and sample packages, designed to let you try out a program before you buy it, often "cripple" their free downloads by leaving off key segments. You can explore these samples, but cannot do any work on them. Distribution of such samples to other potential users is also forbidden. Read the limitations of your license and comply with them!

Shareware

Unfortunately, not everything you download will be free. An important service found at many Web sites is the collection and distribution of **shareware**. Shareware writers request payment for their products. They allow users to download their materials for free, use them for a limited period of time, and then pay a nominal fee for their continued use. Sometimes, shareware producers offer technical support in the form of user manuals or phone-in service after the requested fees have been paid.

Two final words of caution about downloading software from the Web:

First: Shareware downloads come with no guarantee of quality. For every 10 shareware downloads you do, you may find only one or two really good ones, and even fewer that meet your specific needs.

Second: The sad truth is that many viruses are inadvertently distributed along with free downloads and shareware. To protect yourself, install and use a good virus checker on your system, and download software only from reputable sources. A good place to start for shareware is the following World Wide Web location: **http://www.shareware.com**.

Creating a Web Presence

Creating and maintaining your own Web home page is perhaps the ultimate way to communicate with the world. After your page is up (that means after it is displayed on the World Wide Web and visible to anyone), you can expect Web surfers to visit your site, follow the hyperlinks you set up, and perhaps, send you email about interests you have in common.

Web pages are normally created in any word processing program using a special formatting language called **HTML** (**Hypertext Markup Language**).

To create a page, you first decide what that page will look like and what elements you want it to contain. You might include text, frames, background colors or designs, and graphic images, each of which is a file. You can also add hypertext links, which are the Web addresses or URLs for other Web sites. Then, using HTML codes, you position them on the page and control how they look. Let's look at an example. Figure 8.4.6b is a personal Web page as seen through the Netscape Navigator browser. Figure 8.4.6a shows the HTML document that created the Web page. If you look carefully, you will notice a few important things about HTML.

To begin with, HTML elements are traditionally typed in all caps and must be enclosed in angle brackets. Here is an example: <HEAD>. A single HTML element, with its brackets, is called a **tag**. An HTML document is created in two sections, the HEAD and the BODY. The head (beginning with <HEAD> and ending with </HEAD>) contains global styling information affecting the entire document. The body (beginning with <BODY> and ending with </BODY>) contains the actual text and images used on the page.

In addition there are many other HTML tags on the page. Some, such as <H1> control size of type; others, such as <B> control the use of boldface, underline, or italics. Still others allow the insertion of visual elements and hypertext links. Many HTML tags occur in pairs, using a beginning and an ending tag to perform a single function. (The ending tags contain a forward slash as the first character within the brackets.) Others stand alone.

Fortunately, you do not have to learn the complexities of HTML to create your own Web page. The market has become flooded with **Web-page builders** for people who do not know HTML. The **Netscape Web Wizard** at

http://home.netscape.com/assist/net_sites/starter/wizard/index.html

provides a template, a series of questions for you to answer, and some choices for you to make. When you have finished responding to the questions, the wizard creates the page, all ready to place on the Web. Others offer a broad range of tools for more creative Web design.

Hypertext Markup Language (HTML) is a series of codes, or tags, used to format multimedia information used on Web pages.

The Computer Continuum

Figure 8.4.6a
. . . .
HTML code and what it
produces. The HTML code
for cat lovers page.

```
<HTML>
<HEAD>
<TITLE>Cats, Cat Lovers, Southeast Michigan</TITLE>
<META NAME="GENERATOR" CONTENT="Internet Assistant for Microsoft Word 2.0z">
</HEAD>
<BODY BGCOLOR="#00ffff" TEXT="#800080" LINK="#0000ff" VLINK="#ff00ff">
<P>
<CENTER><TABLE BORDER="3"ALIGN="CENTER" BGCOLOR="#ffffff">
<TR><TD WIDTH=459>
<H1><CENTER><IMG SRC="cheshire.gif" ALT="A cheshire cat materializes here"></CENTER>
</H1>
<H1><CENTER>Cat Lovers of Southeast Michigan</CENTER></H1>
</TD></TR>
<TR><TD WIDTH=459>
<H2><CENTER>an Electronic Meeting Place for Cat Owners, Cat Fanciers and Other Feline
Specialists </CENTER></H2>
</TD></TR>
<TR><TD WIDTH=459>
<H4><CENTER><IMG SRC="cat2.gif" ALT="This space belongs to a fly-catching
kitten."></CENTER>
</H4>
</TD></TR>
<TR><TD WIDTH=459>
<H2><CENTER>Have you visited some of our Kool Kat Websites?</CENTER></H2>
<H3><CENTER>( just click on the Web address to visit a site)</CENTER></H3>
<H3><A HREF="http://www.tidycat.com/choose.html">http://www.tidycat.com/choose.html</A> -
&gt; Here's a great site offered by TidyCat, the Cat Litter people. Their site is lots of fun, and
contains useful information about cats and their care. There's also a question-answering service,
and a problem-solving clinic.
</H3>
<H3><A HREF="http:// www.iaehv.nl/users/kudh/">http:// www.iaehv.nl/users/kudh/</A> -&gt;
This site's from the Netherlands, and has great pictures of Siamese and other oriental short-
haired cats.
</H3>
<H3><A
HREF="http://www.marketplaza.com/cats/cats.html">http://www.marketplaza.com/cats/cats.html<
/A> -&gt; Watch out - you'll be sold on this cat-related merchandise. This site offers T-shirts,
mugs, calendars, jewelry, and even a cat mouse pad.
</H3>
<H3><A HREF="http://w3.one.net/~mich/">http://w3.one.net/~mich/</A> -&gt; This one's called
all about cats, and includes many pictures of cats, some animated cat graphics, a cat quiz, and
a cat advice column.
</H3>
</TD></TR>
</TABLE>
</CENTER>
<P>
<CENTER><BR>
</CENTER>
</BODY>
</HTML>
```

Whichever way you create your home page, your HTML document and any photos or other images you have used should be saved together on a hard or floppy disk. As long as they remain on your disk, they are viewable only by you, using a browser such as

Cat Lovers of Southeast Michigan

an Electronic Meeting Place for Cat Owners, Cat Fanciers and Other Feline Specialists

Have you visited some of our Kool Kat Websites?

(just click on the web address to visit a site)

http://vvv.tidycat.com/choose.html -> Here's a great site offered by TidyCat, the Cat Litter people. Their site is lots of fun, and contains useful information about cats and their care. There's also a question-answering service, and a problem-solving clinic.

http:// vvv.iaehv.nl/users/kudh/ -> This site's from the Netherlands, and has great pictures of Siamese and other oriental short-haired cats.

http://vvv.marketplaza.com/cats/cats.html -> Watch out - you'll be sold on this cat-related merchandise. This site offers T-shirts, mugs, calendars, jewelry, and even a cat mouse pad.

http://v3.one.net/~mich/ -> This one's called all about cats, and includes many pictures of cats, some animated cat graphics, a cat quiz, and a cat advice column.

Figure 8.4.6b

Web page result.

Netscape or Explorer. No one can use the Internet to view your page while it resides only on your disk. To be seen by others, your page must first be uploaded to an Internet-accessible account. Your Internet access provider will be able to tell you how to access your own account and upload files.

Putting a personal home page on the World Wide Web is exciting and satisfying, but there are a few risks involved. Remember that a Web page is on the Internet for the world to see. Anything you put there is as public as it can get. To protect your privacy, include only pictures and information you are willing to reveal to everyone. The Web is no place for secrets.

8.5 The Web in Education

During the past few years, computer processing speed and memory capacity have caught up with the development of the Internet and World Wide Web protocol. Thus, full-dimensional sound and full-color video action can now be used as teaching/learning tools. Up until 1992, the only information accessible through the Internet was textual/verbal information you could read from your screen or download to your computer. True, huge quantities of free textual information exist from colleges and universities, government agencies, and private sources. But other kinds of information add spice to the educational experience.

Using the Web in the Classroom

Current technology enables the Internet as a source for color graphics, video segments, and sound clips, as well as text. Microcomputer speed and memory capacity make downloading such materials possible, and user-friendly graphic interface browsers make accessing them easy and fun. As a result, the possibilities for Internet use in education are remarkable and rich:

- Using World Wide Web techniques, the Internet can be searched by any student, at any grade or age level. By accessing the Web search engine Yahooligans, for example, young students can find information for reports in encyclopedic form. They can also communicate with other students from other states and countries.

- Resulting materials can be used as a resource for any learning activity in any subject area.

- Surfing (browsing) the Internet encourages development of creativity and intellectual curiosity.

- The free-form style of Internet information can support any teacher's instructional strategy, and any student's learning style.

- Because information on the Internet is updated continuously, it provides a virtually limitless educational resource, easily adaptable to the needs of the Information Age school.

Online Classes

The newest and most challenging use of Web technology in education is the development of online courses, in virtual classrooms. An **online course** is one designed and implemented for students unable to attend regular classes at school. Students served might be those who are physically challenged, who are unable to come to campus at night, or who have time for education only after their children's bedtime. Whatever their reason, many adults eagerly seek ways to learn or to complete diplomas and degrees with minimal interruption of job or home life.

Like the correspondence courses of a few years ago, online courses offer students the chance to move ahead at their own time and pace. The learning process, from the student point of view, is simple. The student selects a desired online course and registers for it. He or she is then given access to the course materials on the Web. These might include lectures, readings, research assignments, hands-on projects, quizzes, and tests.

The student works on the class whenever convenient: The virtual class meets only in cyberspace, communicating only via email and conferencing. Electronic office hours (email by appointment) and compressed videoconferencing help to personalize the educational process.

For the instructor, preparing an online course is very demanding. Not only do all course "lecture" materials have to be presented as Web pages—sometimes in conjunction with a text or workbook—but tests and assignments must be devised to enable students to submit their work electronically. Face-to-face interaction with students must be replaced with one-on-one electronic interaction. Electronic means must be devised to implement discussions, quizzes, and student reports, usually accomplished in the traditional classroom. And the personal impact of a caring teacher must be nurtured carefully in order not to be lost in the cold technology of cyberspace.

Despite the many challenges of online classes, many educators see them as a possible solution to meeting the educational needs of a growing adult population. Schools and universities are desperately seeking ways to bring their products to these new venues. University centers are sprouting up in locations far from their parent institutions. A few schools exist only as isolated branches in urban areas around the country, with no parent institutional campus at all. Classes offered via the World Wide Web provide yet another way to serve the needs of the off-campus, working adult population.

8.6 The Web in Business

The business world has been remarkably quick to see the potential benefits of having a "Web presence," as it is often called. A major revolution in how businesses operate is on the horizon. Areas such as advertising, electronic retail sales, custom business services, and employment opportunities are the early signs of the revolution.

Advertising

In the 1990s many individual companies rushed to create commercial Web sites. Their main purpose was to give the company a Web presence. Companies such as IBM, Sony, L.L. Bean, Procter & Gamble, and many others created Web sites touting their companies' products and image. Some sites are primarily marketing oriented, while others offer useful information or the opportunity to learn about and even order products online. Figure 8.6.1 shows screen shots of several of these Web sites.

Because of the high cost of creating and maintaining a Web site, outsourcing these services became cost effective. Web page designers, online advertising salespeople, Webmasters, and others banded together to provide Web-production services. The race to reach the Web-surfing consumer was on.

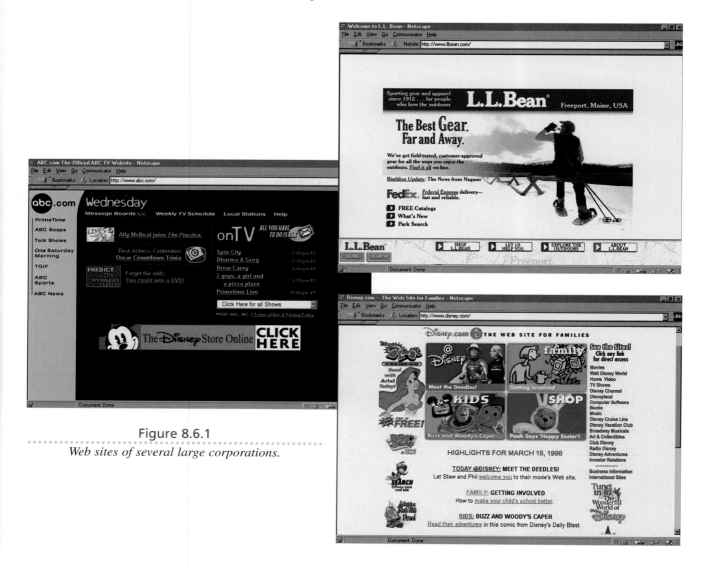

Figure 8.6.1
Web sites of several large corporations.

After company Web sites were developed, advertisers vied for ways to attract customers to their Web sites. The success of a particular site was measured by a counter appearing somewhere on the Web page, tallying the number of hits, or visits, from the Web-browsing public. High numbers of hits represented greater quantities of product being sold.

Many popular Web service companies, such as Yahoo! and Excite, sell ad space on their pages. These are called "banner ads," and they take the form of a small icon or picture. Many display animation or a rolling message. By clicking on a banner ad, a viewer can immediately be linked to that company's Web site. Competition for ad space has made these hyperlinks from one related site to another sprout on all kinds of Web pages. For example, search for a book title or author with a search engine and watch a banner ad for a bookstore appear, reminding us of the billboard-strewn highways of earlier years.

The Computer Continuum

Electronic Malls and Specialty "Stores"

A more direct route for getting Web surfers to buy products is to sell to them directly over the WWW. Many **electronic malls** have surfaced, providing a broad range of retail products. Two leaders in this game are the catalog stores L.L. Bean and Lands End. Many other retailers contribute to a potpourri of online sales. Figure 8.6.2 shows an electronic mall: a list of retailers who paid to have their links included. The Web buyer needs only to click on a retailer's link to be whisked off for an electronic shopping experience.

One of the big success stories of this form of commerce is Amazon.com. They advertise as "Earth's Biggest Bookstore" and have access to 2.5 million books. After browsing or searching Amazon.com's lists and reviews, you can easily use a credit card to make your purchase.

Figure 8.6.2

A Web site that lists various retailer Web sites.

Credit Card Use and E-Money

Using a credit card over the World Wide Web causes consumers to experience moments of uncertainty and doubt. They fear being the victims of electronic theft. Because most credit card companies cover losses after the first $50, this fear is groundless. A more serious problem when using credit cards online concerns the credit rating of the cardholder. Several thousand dollars erroneously charged to a person's account could conceivably affect his/her credit rating. Even though such a problem is immediately corrected, any delay of payment could show up in credit reporting systems as a bad debt. The result could be a refusal of financing for a new car or house. Secure channels over the WWW, which handle credit card transactions, are just one way of preventing such an occurrence.

The real problem with credit card transactions on the Internet is the cost. In the early 1990s, it was estimated the actual cost of a single transaction, not including profit, was about 25 cents. That's fine when the transactions amount to $10 or more, but suppose you would like to buy something that only costs 25 cents. The transaction cost would double the cost of the item being purchased. Imagine the commerce that could take place on the Internet if anyone at anytime could get a copy of a recipe, speech, article, consumer report, drawing, poem, musical recording, movie, or any number of

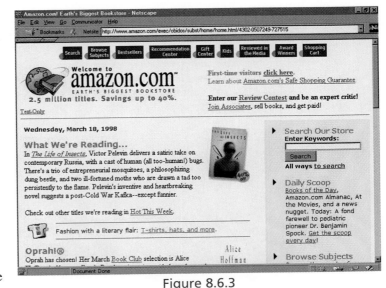

Figure 8.6.3

The home page for Amazon.com.

other types of information. Numerous companies are already looking toward the future when transactions will only cost about a tenth of a cent. Many companies, such as Encyclopaedia Britannica, are already preparing for that day. They are organizing the Encyclopaedia Britannica in an electronic form for easy access via the Internet and WWW.

Figure 8.6.4

Netscape plug-in support for browser modification.

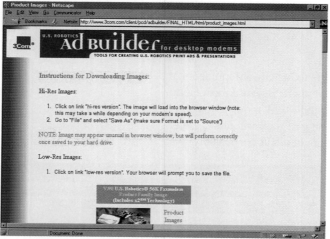

Figure 8.6.5

The "Advertising Designer" site for obtaining images.

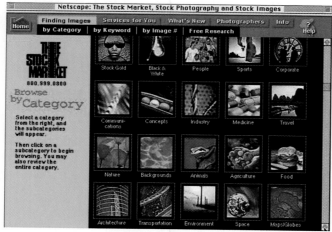

Figure 8.6.6

The UPI (United Press International) image databank.

A huge problem connected to small transaction-type commerce on the Internet is the privacy issue. Careful attention must be paid to the ramifications of Web purchasing for our privacy. Part of Chapter 14, "Pushing the Envelope of Human Potential," will be devoted to an examination of the problems that could lead to a world similar to George Orwell's *1984*. This was a world where "Big Brother" was watching your every move, even in your home. It was a totally planned society, with no freedom of choice.

Electronic Customer Services

Hundreds of WWW sites are dedicated to customer services. These services are often in the form of product support. The support can be as simple as providing product information, or even troubleshooting problems about how to use the product. The WWW browser company Netscape has a Software Depot Web page shown in Figure 8.6.4. It is a prime example of the power of product support on the WWW. Netscape has put together a source for obtaining software enhancements for its browser. Often called plug-ins, they enhance the capability of Netscape's browser. Clicking on any one of the topics leads to sources of plug-in software, some of it is freeware.

Another service is in providing photographs and other graphic images for sale on the WWW. Thousands of pictures are catalogued and can be viewed using a Web browser. Suppose you are doing a book and need a picture of the external modem pictured in Figure 6.4.2. The "Advertising Designer" site provided by 3Com Inc. on the World Wide Web includes high-quality copies of many images of their US Robotics line of modems. Figure 8.6.5 shows how easy it is to download an image: Just click on the image of choice, and you can begin the process of downloading a copy to your computer. You may have options, such as where to save the file, what name to give it, or how to install it. Transactions can be accomplished in minutes, with no need to wait. Sometimes there is a charge for downloading images. It is often paid for by credit card or sometimes an account can be set up in advance with monthly billings. One more example of an image bank is shown in Figure 8.6.6, a page from the UPI (United Press International) databank of pictures.

Employment Opportunities

The traumatic and time-consuming process of finding, interviewing for, and changing jobs is a common occurrence. The World Wide Web has made the process more tolerable. Suppose you would like to move to a different city hundreds of miles away from your present location. Shopping for jobs long distance can be time consuming and difficult. With the Web, anonymous searching for the right position can be done from the comfort (and privacy) of your own computer. Many corporations operate Web sites that encourage exploration of employment opportunities. Shown in Figure 8.6.7 is Cisco Systems's Web page, advertising positions in the networking hardware/software area.

Hundreds of small and large employment services inhabit the Internet. BridgePath is one of these services, concentrating on college graduates. It also allows prospective employers to contact individual graduates from more than 800 U.S. colleges. Figure 8.6.8 shows the BridgePath Web site.

8.7 The Web in the Public Eye

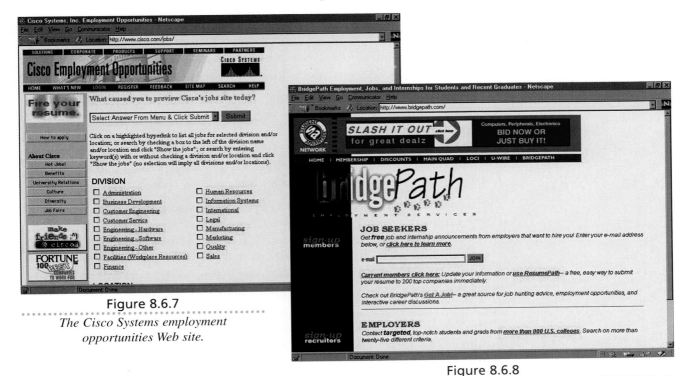

Figure 8.6.7

The Cisco Systems employment opportunities Web site.

Figure 8.6.8

The BridgePath college graduate employment Web site.

We have spent this entire chapter discussing the World Wide Web and the extensive access to all kinds of information that it provides us. But a few problems with the Web have yet to be solved. Let's discuss them before going on to other topics.

Security

Whenever you are connected to the World Wide Web, the personal data you enter may be at risk of illegal use by others. Suppose you have ordered a book online and typed in a credit card number to pay for it. If the Internet line is not secure, unscrupulous individuals may see your card number and use it to make purchases of their own. Many ordering sites use encryption techniques that give very secure transactions. And remember, you should include nothing on Web pages or Internet transactions that you would prefer to remain private.

Privacy

Suppose you access an electronic bulletin board dedicated to dog shows. You like the content of the EBB, so you join and fill in member information, as requested. A few weeks later you notice that you are receiving increasing numbers of cards and advertisements about dogs. You didn't order them; they just start arriving. How did that happen? Well, some spiders search not only Web pages, but also bulletin board and email correspondence. The advertisers use spider lists of new bulletin board members to send out unsolicited product advertisements. You might consider this to be an invasion of your privacy. So when you fill out member information forms, look for the little checkbox that indicates you don't want your name given to others or type in a note asking that unsolicited materials not be sent.

Censorship

The United States's Bill of Rights guarantees its citizens freedom of speech. In its current unregulated state, the Web also enjoys this same freedom. Anyone can put anything on the Internet for World Wide Web access.

Although this independence appeals to us, its outcome can be disturbing. Materials placed on the Web by some people seem indecent and undesirable to others. Some images, uploaded for the pleasure of some adults, are considered by others to be inappropriate for children. Other people are offended by the hatemongering on the home pages of a few specific organizations. As a result, efforts are being made to censor certain materials.

One method of censoring access to Web materials is called **screening** or **filtering**. Filtering software enables parents to make offensive Web sites inaccessible to their children. Sometimes screening is built in as a part of the Internet service provider's services; other times it can be purchased as a standalone application, such as NetNanny. Either case is only partially effective. This type of censorship limits only what can be seen by a particular audience rather than what can be placed on the Internet.

Filtering and screening have another important side. Morality movements in the 1960s tried to prevent public libraries from offering "indecent" books such as *The Catcher in the Rye* or *Lady Chatterly's Lover*. Today, similar groups wish to limit access to sites using controversial words like *breast*, *AIDS*, and *abortion*. A public library that did this would also be limiting access to information on cooking recipes with chicken breasts or even more serious topics like breast cancer.

Other forms of censorship explore methods to limit the "decency" of materials that can be placed on the Web. The problem here is defining decency. Until (and unless) we can come up with a universally accepted definition, efforts to delimit Web materials by a code of decency will fail. Censorship of the Web, if there is to be any at all, will have to remain the responsibility of the individual viewer or his/her parents.

Chapter Summary

What you can do with what you have learned:

- Recognize the difference between a text-based access method such as Gopher and a multimedia-based access method such as the WWW.
- Recognize a hot link when viewed on a site.

- Follow hypertext and hypermedia links to sites all over the world.
- Recognize the parts of a URL and how the path describes where the information is stored.

The Computer Continuum

- Be aware of why some access links take longer to connect than others, and be aware of the physical path those links must traverse.
- Choose the hardware and software necessary to get on the Internet from home.
- Use search engines to find topics of interest on the Internet.

- Download software, graphics, video segments, and sound clips to your computer.
- Create your own Web page and make it available on the Internet.
- Be careful about sending sensitive financial information on the Internet.

Key Terms and Review Questions

Key terms introduced in this chapter:

Internet 3-22

Gopher 3-22

HTTP (Hypertext Transfer Protocol) 3-22

World Wide Web 3-22

Web 3-22

Read-only 3-22

Medium 3-23

Multimedia 3-23

World Wide Web protocol 3-23

Hypertext 3-23

Hypertext links 3-23

Link 3-23

Hypermedia 3-25

Surfing 3-26

Web pages 3-26

Uniform Resource Locator (URL) 3-26

FTP—File Transfer Protocol 3-26

MAILTO 3-26

FILE 3-26

WAIS 3-26

Telnet 3-26

Internet address 3-26

Domain name 3-26

Subdomains 3-26

Server 3-26

Top-level domain 3-26

Dot 3-27

Path 3-27

Slash 3-27

ISP (Internet service provider) 3-28

Modem 3-29

Hookup fee 3-29

Monthly use fee 3-29

Per-call connection charge 3-29

Web browser 3-30

Hypermedia links 3-30

Microsoft Internet Explorer 3-30

Netscape Navigator 3-30

Web sites 3-31

Add-ons 3-31

Plug-ins 3-31

Search engine 3-31

Spider 3-31

Subject search 3-32

Topic search 3-32

Keyword search 3-32

Concept-based search 3-32

Text analysis engine 3-32

Downloading 3-32

Matching

Match the key terms introduced in the chapter to the statements below. Each term may be used once, more than once, or not at all.

1. _____ This type of Internet communication only accessed textual materials.

2. _____ This communication protocol allows text, visual, and audio information to be accessed and transmitted via the Internet.

3. _____ The vehicle or conduit through which information is communicated.

4. _____ A slang term used to describe the free-form navigation from place to place on the Internet by following hypermedia links.

5. _____ This term refers to two or more types of communication of information simultaneously channeled through several different media.

6. _____ This concept uses the hypertext linking capabilities with other communication mediums, such as sound and pictures.

7. _____ Any word or phrase in an electronic document that can be used as a pointer or link to a related text passage.

8. _____ This refers to any text or image that has been activated as a link to access related material.

9. _____ These links use visual objects and text to be linked to other visual objects, animations, text, or even sound.

10. _____ Links appear in these documents which have been created for World Wide Web viewing.

11. _____ This is the name given to the worldwide standard for expressing the unique address of a specific Web page.

12. _____ This protocol is used for transferring files between computers.

13. _____ This email protocol is used

to send or create an email link.

14. _____ This protocol allows browsers to recognize and display Web pages that have been constructed using this "language."

15. _____ This type of access refers to the ability to view a page, but not being able to make any changes to it.

16. _____ Another term for the domain name.

17. _____ A company that has the capability to connect clients to the Web for a fee.

18. _____ The general name given to software that allows access to the World Wide Web.

19. _____ This is designed and implemented to fill the needs of students who are unable to attend regular classes.

20. _____ This software allows parents to make offensive Web sites inaccessible to their children.

True or False

1. _____ Gopher systems are no longer accessible on the Internet.

2. _____ The concept of hypertext is not a new one. Its use of a visual layout has been useful even back during man's early critical writings.

3. _____ The only links displayed on Web pages appear as highlighted text passages.

4. _____ The World Wide Web is a protocol that not only allows textual information to be accessed on the Internet, but also visual and audio information.

5. _____ The World Wide Web uses multimedia communication.

6. _____ Gopher was, and still is, primarily a text-based system that allows access to some information on the Internet.

7. _____ The prefix or leftmost part of a URL identifies the type of Internet protocol requested.

8. _____ The Internet and the World Wide Web are one and the same.

9. _____ A URL contains the address of the computer you are trying to reach.

10. _____ A URL address for any computer within the United States must contain the two-letter code: us.

11. _____ Because no one owns the World Wide Web, no one includes service charges for accessing the Web.

12. _____ When using a Web browser to view a Web page, hypermedia links are indistinguishable objects on the page.

13. _____ A spider is synonymous with a search engine.

14. _____ Free downloads are exactly that: free!

15. _____ The speed at which a download occurs is only directly related to the speed of your modem.

16. _____ After a download has begun, it can never be interrupted.

17. _____ Many downloads are sent in a compressed format and

need to be decompressed before installation is possible.

18. _____Reading the Readme file that usually accompanies downloads could ultimately save hours of frustration.

19. _____Alpha and beta versions of software are complete and certified dependable by the software authors.

20. _____Unless a document includes specific formatting codes, it cannot be viewed on the World Wide Web as a Web page.

Multiple Choice

Answer the multiple choice questions by selecting the best answers from the choices given.

1. This term is used to describe information being communicated through several different mediums simultaneously.
   a. Medium
   b. Media
   c. Multimedia
   d. Hypertext

2. This term is used to describe any word or phrase in an electronic document that can be used as a pointer to a related passage (restricted to text only).
   a. Medium
   b. Media
   c. Multimedia
   d. Hypertext
   e. Hypermedia

3. Which of the following is not included in a URL?
   a. The type of connection to be made
   b. The Internet address
   c. The name of the Web server
   d. The HTML tags
   e. The domain

4. Which of the following browsers was not mentioned in this chapter?
   a. Internet Explorer
   b. Netscape Navigator
   c. Gopher
   d. NCSA's Apache

5. When searching the WWW, these look for specific requested information.
   a. Web browser
   b. Search engine
   c. Spider
   d. HTML
   e. Tags

6. This will search for sites that have changed or have been recently added to the World Wide Web.
   a. Web browser
   b. Search engine
   c. Spider
   d. HTML
   e. Tags

7. This program allows access to the WWW.
   a. Web browser
   b. Search engine
   c. Spider
   d. HTML
   e. Tags

8. Applying these to a document will allow us to share the document with others on the World Wide Web.
   a. Web browser
   b. Search engine
   c. Spider
   d. HTML
   e. Tags

9. The top-level domain name that would be included in the address of any corporate Web page would be what?

   a. edu
   b. com
   c. gov
   d. mil
   e. org

10. Some examples of this type of communication include CD-ROM, WWW, television, theater, and movies.

   a. Hypertext
   b. Hyperlinks
   c. Multimedia
   d. Medium
   e. Internet

Exercises

1. What is the difference between a text-based accessing method and a multimedia-based accessing method?

2. Which is bigger, the Internet or the World Wide Web? Why?

3. What is the difference between a path and a domain?

4. Check the box indicating the top-level domain identifier for each organization listed.

	org	com	edu	gov
Sony				
The FBI				
Greenpeace				
Harvard				
IBM				
The CIA				
The Salvation Army				
EF Hutton				

5. Mark each of the following as either hardware, software, or other:

   a. Web browser
   b. ISP
   c. Hypertext
   d. Protocol
   e. Modem
   f. HTTP
   g. FTP
   h. Shareware
   i. Search engine

Discussion Questions

1. WWW site names are registered with domain organizations and then owned by the persons who have registered them. Some people have registered as site names the names of other famous people, corporations, and products. They hope to sell them to those people or corporations for a lot of money or possibly place misleading or embarrassing content on those sites. Discuss the ethics of such activity and, if you see this as "wrong," how and what should be changed to prevent this.

2. Discuss possible ways to reward individuals for making the results of their creative efforts (music, books, and so on) available on the WWW.

3. Explain why censorship on the Internet would be hard to police.

4. What implementation issues can you see with online college courses? How could the institution be sure that the person sending in the results was the one who did the work?

5. What social issues can you see with unlimited access to the Web?

6. What business issues can you see with unlimited access to the Web?

7. What legal issues can you see with unlimited access to the Web?

Group Project

A group of four students should pick an area of common interest and create a Web site on the school server. If possible, make use of a Web HTML publishing tool. Each person in the group should pick one of the following job categories and be responsible for recording and organizing information related to his or her area. The four areas are as follows:

Layout and design

Research for content materials

HTML program for the Web page

Logistics for getting Web page up on school system

As a group, ideas for each of these areas should be discussed. Each student should record the group's wishes for his or her area. A general layout and map should be designed by the group.

Web Connections

http://www.cern.ch/

Birthplace of the WWW, updates, and services.

http://www.pcwebopedia.com/

Online encyclopedia of computer technology terms and related sites.

http://www.csd.uwo.ca/~jamie/hypertext-faq.html

Frequently asked questions about hypertext, from use to history.

http://www.dogpile.com

A meta-search engine, searches through more than 20 other search engines including Usenet and FTP databases.

http://www.excite.com/apple/guide/Computing_and_Internet/Internet/Search_Engines/

A list of search engines available, some with editor reviews.

http://www.metacrawler.com/

A search engine that checks results from Lycos, WebCrawler, InfoSeek, Yahoo!, and AltaVista to create a comprehensive hotlist of Web resources for any query.

The Computer Continuum

http://shell.ihug.co.nz/~ijh/

Not only links to many different search engines, but has actual windows to type in your topic and go directly to that search, and has a section on "People" where one can find email addresses.

www.mapquest.com/

Maps from anywhere to anywhere, driving directions, local weather, and so on.

Bibliography

Barrett, Daniel J. *Net Research: Finding Information Online*. Sebastopol: O'Reilly & Associates, 1997.

Gassaway, Stella, Gary Davis, and Catherine Gregory. *Designing Multimedia Web Sites*. Indianapolis: Hayden Books, 1996.

Warner, Janine, Ken Milburn, and Jessica Burdman. *Converting Content for Web Publishing*. Indianapolis: New Riders Publishing, 1996.

Weinman, Lynda. *Deconstructing Web Graphics*. Indianapolis: New Riders Publishing, 1996.

Chapter 9

4000–1200 B.C.	Records of daily transactions are kept on tablets by the Sumerians, the first known civilization.
1801	Punched cards controlled the patterns of weaving in Joseph-Marie Jacquard's loom.
1896	The Tabulating Machine company is established by Herman Hollerith.
1901	The keypunch machine first punches paper cards.
1931	A high school teacher, Reynold B. Johnson, first scores multiple-choice tests by sensing conductive pencil marks on answer sheets.
1967–1968	National Crime Information Center (NCIC) goes online with 95,000 pieces of information in five databases, handling 2 million transactions in its first year.
1971	All 50 states and Washington D.C. can access NCIC criminal data.
1980	The first database program for personal computers, dBase II, is developed by Wayne Ratliff.
1982	The computer is named "Man of the Year" by Time magazine.
1983	5-10 MB hard disk drives are introduced.
1996	NCIC handles 2 million transactions per *day*!
1999	NCIC 2000 is launched, featuring terminals with scanners and digital cameras located in police cars for immediate access.
2005	Human Genome Project completes mapping of all 90,000 or so genes for massive database.

Databases: Controlling the Information Deluge

Chapter Objectives

By the end of this chapter, you will:

- ⊚ Understand the implications of public access to the vast amount of data being generated daily.

- ⊚ Understand the difference between data and information.

- ⊚ Know the definition and uses of a computerized database.

- ⊚ Identify several different methods for collecting data.

- ⊚ Recognize several examples of remote electronic sensing.

- ⊚ Appreciate the FBI fingerprint retrieval system as a highly organized database of a large amount of data.

- ⊚ Understand how statistics are used to analyze data in a database.

- ⊚ Identify how sampling is used to choose data to be analyzed.

- ⊚ Understand how samples can be skewed to give inaccurate results.

- ⊚ Understand how false correlations can lead to erroneous conclusions.

- ⊚ Identify the elements of a DBMS, from field to file.

- ⊚ Identify several advantages of using a DBMS.

- ⊚ Identify several disadvantages of using a DBMS.

9.1 Introduction: Information Overload

The end of the 20th century has often been called the **Information Age**. The process of dealing with information involves first gathering it. Then, one must be able to retrieve the information that has been gathered. Finally, the information is ready for analysis. These three processes are enhanced by a collection of programs integrated together and called a database management system (DBMS). This first section helps understand the magnitude of the problem, and the remaining sections will deal with each of the other topics.

bits & bytes

Online Databases from A to Z
A search for databases on the Internet using Gopher with Veronica turns up more than 5,000 leads. Following are just a few of the online databases.

Amnesty International Statistics
Argoforestry Systems Database at ICRAF
Centre for Information Technology Innovation
Directory of Independent Living Centers
Energy for Rural Development Bibliographic Database
European Commission Host Organization
Global Land Information System
Global Recycling Network
Integrated Service for Information Resources
Latin American Information Systems
Medicine Database
Medieval and Early Modern Data Bank
Movie Database
NASA/IPAC Extragalactic Database (NED) for astronomers
Nucleic Acid Database
On-Line CD Database
Partnerships Against Violence
Publications
Rice Genome Database
Shakespearian Literature Database
Soft-Scape (software development)
World Telephone and Country Area Codes
Worldwide Upcoming Events Database
Zoo Database in Australia

The Information Age

Have you ever wondered why the last third of the 20th century is called the Information Age? The reason is that we are inundated with information: facts, figures, opinions, stories, pictures, records, predictions, and so on. The accumulated knowledge of generations past, present, and future is overwhelming. Up to now, most of that accumulation has been stored on paper!

Indeed, we have amassed so much paper that we could circle the globe with it several times and still have some left over. As if that isn't enough, the amount of time it takes to increase the available quantity of information has shrunk from a number of years, at the turn of the 20th century, to a matter of days now. Every week or so, we have the capacity to double our current store of information.

The Computer Continuum

Think about it …. Currently, there are more than 15,000 magazines, newspapers, radio stations, and television stations—all sources of new information. And, experts estimate that Internet users create a **terabyte** of data daily, an amount equal to 70 million 300 page books per month. Thank heavens a lot of information is duplicated!

Fortunately, we no longer store the bulk of this information on paper. Computer technology provides many types of storage media that are more economical, longer-lasting, and easier to access. This chapter examines the use of computers in three major areas: collecting and manipulating large amounts of data, accessing that data in a timely fashion, and analyzing and formatting it for easy understanding.

A **terabyte** is the amount of computer memory needed to store a trillion bytes of data—that's one thousand million (1,000,000,000,000) bytes, plus.

Data is a given thing or fact, in a raw form.

We will be using the words **data** and **information** throughout this chapter. Although general usage makes the two words interchangeable, each has a specific use in the field of computing.

Computers process data; the resulting information is what people use. An accumulation of useful information can result in people making better decisions—personally, financially, or professionally. Before we can use information, however, we must first collect appropriate data and put it into a form the computer can read. It then must be processed by the computer and stored in a manner that makes sense to a human.

Sir Francis Bacon once said, "Knowledge is Power." The computer puts an awesome amount of information at your fingertips. Merely having access to masses of data, however, does not guarantee the power Bacon envisioned. We need powerful tools to help manipulate data, making it work for us. Today, computer technology provides us with a broad range of analytic and reporting tools. By using them, we can transform data into information that can be understood. The Database Management System (DBMS) was one of the first software applications for doing just this and has remained one of the most versatile.

In order to include whatever data might someday be needed, a database must be very carefully designed. This is often done jointly by a database programmer and the users who will be working with the database. Together, they must answer the following questions.

1. How can we efficiently collect large amounts of relevant data?

Figure 9.1.1

The amount of information we collect and store on paper has become overwhelming.

Figure 9.1.2

Books, magazines, and other print media provide huge amounts of information on any topic.

Information is data repackaged in a meaningful form that a human can understand and use. The repackaging may involve manipulating and organizing the *form* of the data, analyzing and evaluating the *content* of the data, and producing a usable *report* of the results.

2. How can we reliably store that data for later use?
3. Who will use the data?
4. How often will they need to access the data?
5. What format will they need the data in (text, numerical, visual)?
6. How will they use the data?

Over the years, human ingenuity has answered these six questions in many ways. Until the advent of the computer, we collected most data by hand, wrote or typed it onto paper, and stored it in file cabinets. As the data became more complex or numerous, we designed paper forms to make data collection easier and more accurate. Elaborate systems of filing evolved. One such system, for example, the **Dewey Decimal System**, enabled the cataloging of books by subject matter. But even forms and filing systems could not keep up with the ever-growing flood of data needing collection and storage.

Now, let's examine the three major problems of information usage: collection, retrieval, and analysis.

9.2 The Technology for Data Collection

In its simplest form, the collection of data is a task well known to all of us. Suppose, for example, that you wanted to find the best buy in a used automobile. You might collect your own data by finding newspaper ads about autos of interest and comparing their features and prices. Or, instead of collecting your own data, you may choose to purchase a copy of an already prepared paper database such as Consumer Guide's book, *The Complete Guide to Used Cars*. Whichever way you have collected your data, when you have enough you can make a decision and select a car.

Either of these data collection methods would be satisfactory if all you needed were the price and reliability data for a single purchase. What would happen if you wanted automobile prices from all over the country for a project? Or, even more challenging, what if you wanted data from all over the world?

How would you, as a researcher, approach this data collection problem? You might collect the data manually by reading books or magazines.

Figure 9.1.3

Today, large amounts of data are stored electronically.

Figure 9.1.4

Many people think power is synonymous with having information at your fingertips.

The Computer Continuum

You might collect it from Web sites. You might even collect it from databases available at your school's library. Whichever way you collect data, at some point you'll have to organize it so that you can compare, analyze, and make decisions. To do that, you'll need to create a database in a database management system.

In the Beginning There Was Nothing

Early computers provided no means to collect data or to store it from one program execution to the next. You could, however, feed in accurate numerical data and produce accurate calculated results. Each piece of data needed for a particular calculation had to be input during the actual execution of the calculation program. Thus, the earliest form of computer data was collected and stored on paper, outside the computer, and fed in only at the moment when it was needed by the computer's software.

Keypunched Data Cards (Hollerith Cards)

Hollerith cards (you may have seen them as hospital billing cards or class registration cards) enabled the storage of large quantities of data in a form that the computer could read. Each card (see Figure 9.2.2) consisted of 80 columns of digits from 0 to 9. One or more holes could be punched in each column, with each hole removing one of the digits. A code was established which assigned each letter of the alphabet and each punctuation mark a unique number. To enter data on one of these cards, you punched holes in it. The holes in any one column corresponded to the code number of a single character. Only 80 letters or other characters could fit on a card.

Figure 9.1.5

The Dewey Decimal System cataloged books and other nonfiction library materials according to an elaborate numbering system.

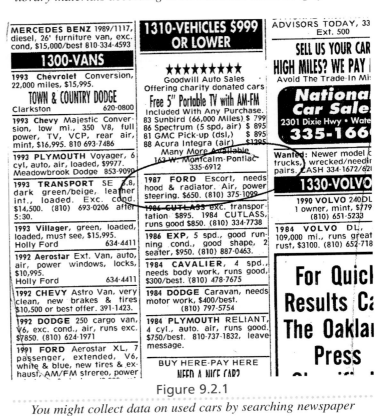

Figure 9.2.1

You might collect data on used cars by searching newspaper want ads.

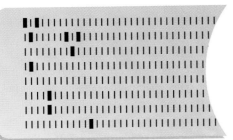

Figure 9.2.2

Part of a Hollerith card.

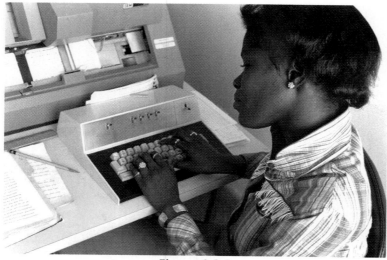

Figure 9.2.3

A keypunch machine was used to enter data by punching holes into a Hollerith card.

QUESTIONS ASKED OF ALL HOUSEHOLDS

PERSON 7

Last name

First name Middle initial

If a RELATIVE of Person 1:
○ Husband/wife ○ Brother/sister
○ Natural-born or adopted son/daughter ○ Father/mother
○ Grandchild
○ Other relative
○ Stepson/stepdaughter

If NOT RELATED to Person 1:
○ Roomer, boarder, or foster child ○ Unmarried partner
○ Housemate, roommate ○ Other nonrelative

○ Male ○ Female

○ White
○ Black or Negro
○ Indian (Amer.) (Print the name of the enrolled or principal tribe.)
○ Eskimo
○ Aleut

Asian or Pacific Islander (API)
○ Chinese ○ Japanese
○ Filipino ○ Asian Indian
○ Hawaiian ○ Samoan
○ Korean ○ Guamanian
○ Vietnamese ○ Other API
○ Other race (Print race)

a. Age b. Year of birth

○ Now married ○ Separated
○ Widowed ○ Never married
○ Divorced

○ No (not Spanish/Hispanic)
○ Yes, Mexican, Mexican-Am., Chicano
○ Yes, Puerto Rican
○ Yes, Cuban
○ Yes, other Spanish/Hispanic (Print one group, for example: Argentinean, Colombian, Dominican, Nicaraguan, Salvadoran, Spaniard, and so on.)

NOW PLEASE ANSWER QUESTIONS H1a—H26 FOR YOUR HOUSEHOLD

H1a. Did you leave anyone out of your list of persons for Question 1a on page 1 because you were not sure if the person should be listed — for example, someone temporarily away on a business trip or vacation, a newborn baby still in the hospital, or a person who stays here once in a while and has no other home?
○ Yes, please print the name(s) and reason(s). ○ No

b. Did you include anyone in your list of persons for Question 1a on page 1 even though you were not sure that the person should be listed — for example, a visitor who is staying here temporarily or a person who usually lives somewhere else?
○ Yes, please print the name(s) and reason(s). ○ No

H2. Which best describes this building? Include all apartments, flats, etc., even if vacant.
○ A mobile home or trailer
○ A one-family house detached from any other house
○ A one-family house attached to one or more houses
○ A building with 2 apartments
○ A building with 3 or 4 apartments
○ A building with 5 to 9 apartments
○ A building with 10 to 19 apartments
○ A building with 20 to 49 apartments
○ A building with 50 or more apartments
○ Other

H3. How many rooms do you have in this house or apartment? Do NOT count bathrooms, porches, balconies, foyers, halls, or half-rooms.
○ 1 room ○ 4 rooms ○ 7 rooms
○ 2 rooms ○ 5 rooms ○ 8 rooms
○ 3 rooms ○ 6 rooms ○ 9 or more rooms

H4. Is this house or apartment —
○ Owned by you or someone in this household with a mortgage or loan?
○ Owned by you or someone in this household free and clear (without a mortgage)?
○ Rented for cash rent?
○ Occupied without payment of cash rent?

If this is a ONE-FAMILY HOUSE —
H5a. Is this house on ten or more acres?
○ Yes ○ No

b. Is there a business (such as a store or barber shop) or a medical office on this property?
○ Yes ○ No

Answer only if you or someone in this household OWNS OR IS BUYING this house or apartment —
H6. What is the value of this property; that is, how much do you think this house and lot or condominium unit would sell for if it were for sale?
○ Less than $10,000 ○ $70,000 to $74,999
○ $10,000 to $14,999 ○ $75,000 to $79,999
○ $15,000 to $19,999 ○ $80,000 to $89,999
○ $20,000 to $24,999 ○ $90,000 to $99,999
○ $25,000 to $29,999 ○ $100,000 to $124,999
○ $30,000 to $34,999 ○ $125,000 to $149,999
○ $35,000 to $39,999 ○ $150,000 to $174,999
○ $40,000 to $44,999 ○ $175,000 to $199,999
○ $45,000 to $49,999 ○ $200,000 to $249,999
○ $50,000 to $54,999 ○ $250,000 to $299,999
○ $55,000 to $59,999 ○ $300,000 to $399,999
○ $60,000 to $64,999 ○ $400,000 to $499,999
○ $65,000 to $69,999 ○ $500,000 or more

Answer only if you PAY RENT for this house or apartment —
H7a. What is the monthly rent?
○ Less than $80 ○ $375 to $399
○ $80 to $99 ○ $400 to $424
○ $100 to $124 ○ $425 to $449
○ $125 to $149 ○ $450 to $474
○ $150 to $174 ○ $475 to $499
○ $175 to $199 ○ $500 to $524
○ $200 to $224 ○ $525 to $549
○ $225 to $249 ○ $550 to $599
○ $250 to $274 ○ $600 to $649
○ $275 to $299 ○ $650 to $699
○ $300 to $324 ○ $700 to $749
○ $325 to $349 ○ $750 to $999
○ $350 to $374 ○ $1,000 or more

b. Does the monthly rent include any meals?
○ Yes ○ No

FOR CENSUS USE

A. Total persons

B. Type of unit
Occupied: ○ First form ○ Cont'n
Vacant: ○ Regular ○ Usual home elsewhere

C1. Vacancy status
○ For rent ○ For seas/rec/occ
○ For sale only ○ For migrant workers
○ Rented or sold, not occupied ○ Other vacant

C2. Is this unit boarded up?
○ Yes ○ No

D. Months vacant
○ Less than 1 ○ 6 up to 12
○ 1 up to 2 ○ 12 up to 24
○ 2 up to 6 ○ 24 or more

E. Complete after
○ LR ○ TC ○ QA JIC 1 ○
○ P/F ○ RE ○ I/T
○ MV ○ ED ○ EN
○ P0 ○ P3 ○ P6 JIC 2 ○
○ P1 ○ P4 ○ IA
○ P2 ○ P5 ○ SM

F. Cov.
○ 1b ○ 1a ○ 7 ○ H1

G. DO ID

Figure 9.2.4

Sample of the mark-sensor form used to collect data during the 1990 U.S. Census.

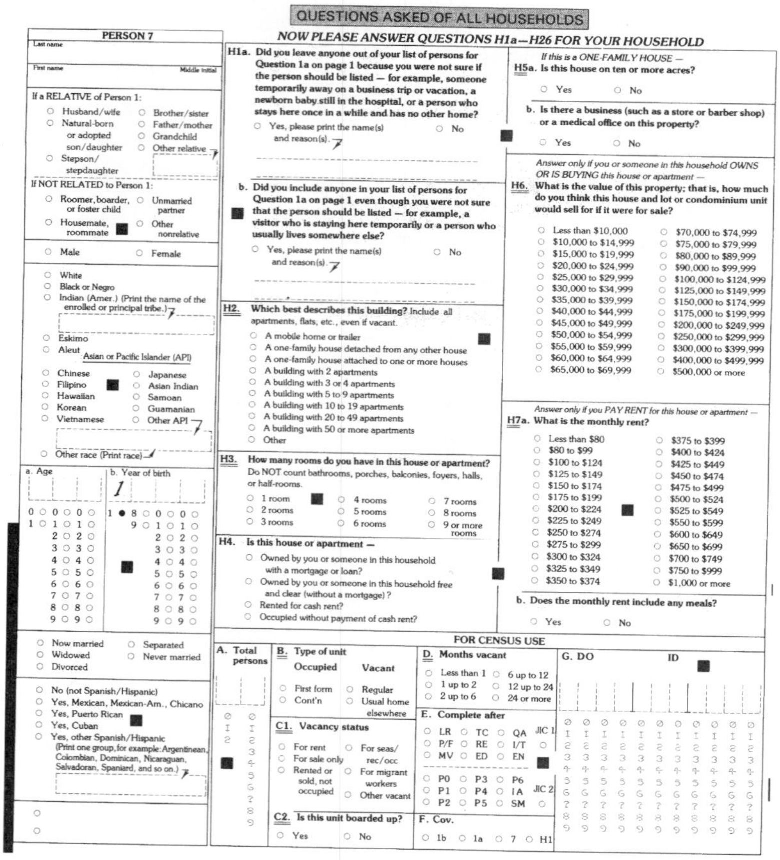

The machine that punched the holes in Hollerith cards was called a **keypunch machine.** Skilled typists, called **keypunch operators**, transcribed the collected data from questionnaires onto the cards. Errors in typing resulted in wasted cards, because once a hole was punched in a card, it (the hole) could not be pasted back in.

Completed cards were then stored in trays in very carefully maintained order. When someone wanted to run an analysis program using a particular collection of data, the entire stack of cards that contained that data was placed in a machine called a **card reader**. The card reader would feed the data into the computer one card at a time by sensing where the holes were in each column on that card. The computer's program could then decode the data needed in the program.

Mark-Sensor Data Collection Sheets

One of the problems of the Hollerith card was that data had to be transcribed from question and answer forms to the cards before it could be used in the computer. What if the data could be collected in a form that the computer could read directly, without the necessity of transcription? That, of course, is the next important development: computer-readable **mark-sensor forms**.

To understand the impact of mark-sensor forms on the data collection and storage process, take a look at one of the world's most important and well-known data collection projects: the U.S. Census.

The usefulness of the computer in gathering data for the U.S. Census is enormous. Needless to say, the mailings to more than 80 million households aren't addressed by hand! Database files of these addresses are kept in computer-readable form until the final list is ready. The mailed questionnaires are themselves machine readable. This enables the persons answering the questions to respond by filling in little printed boxes with a graphite pencil. Because the computer can sense or "read" which of the boxes have been filled in, the computer can

process and store almost all the responses sent in. Transcription is needed only if the responder has used the wrong type of writing implement, filled in too many boxes, or damaged the form in some way.

Remote Electronic Data Sensing

The U.S. Census is certainly a very large data-collection task. But in comparison to other such projects, the amount of data collected is very small. For example, some satellites circling the globe collect millions of times more data in just one day than an entire ten year census! How can that be possible? How can so great a volume of data be collected in such a short period of time? The answer is that the satellite data is collected via **remote electronic sensing**, a method that doesn't directly involve human help. We will look now at two satellites that gather data several hundred miles above the Earth and then send it to Earth via radio.

The satellite called Landsat 4 was launched on July 16, 1982. Landsat 4 can sense an object as small as 30 meters square from 500 miles above the Earth's surface and sometimes can do even better. In fact, a 40-foot square concrete pad at Detroit Metropolitan Airport was recognized by the satellite's system. It also was able to see and transmit the narrow shadow cast by the Washington Monument in Washington, DC. An overview of how Landsat 4 communicates with the Earth is shown in Figure 9.2.6.

The Hubble Space Telescope was deployed into orbit from the space shuttle in 1994 (see Figure 9.2.7). After several repairs and adjustments, it began transmitting high-quality data about outer space. The tremendous amount of astronomical data gathered

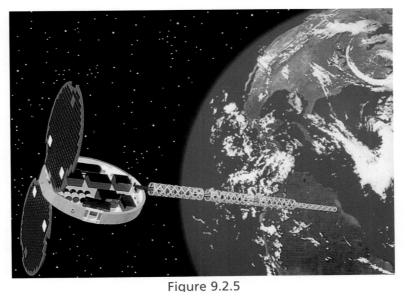

Figure 9.2.5

Simulated image of a communications satellite in orbit.

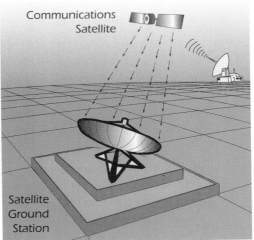

Communications Satellite

Satellite Ground Station

Figure 9.2.6

Overview of Landsat communication with Earth.

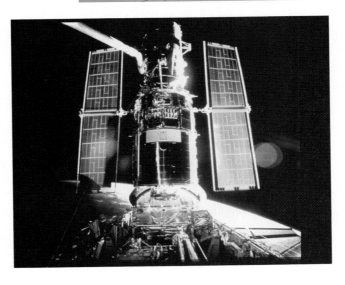

Figure 9.2.7

Solar arrays flank the massive Hubble Space Telescope during deployment from the space shuttle.

by the Hubble Space Telescope is sent back to Earth at a rate of 85 million bytes per second (that is, 85 MB). The images it provides can be retransmitted to scientists all over the world.

Figure 9.2.8

A typical bar code.

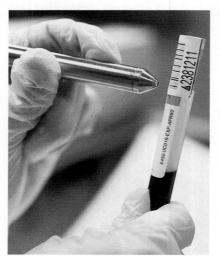

Figure 9.2.9

A bar-code reader.

Bar Codes

Still another data collection innovation made possible through the magic of computers is the **bar code**. A bar code (see Figure 9.2.8) is a series of short black vertical lines, some thick and some thin, that can be sensed or "read" by a computer input device called a **bar-code reader**.

To understand the use of this method of data collection, let's look at the problem of inventory control in a large retail department store. Such a store may have many departments, such as housewares, hardware, men's clothing, toys, and so forth. And each department may carry several thousand different items, in a variety of colors, sizes, and prices.

Before any of these thousands of items is placed on the shelf for sale, certain pieces of information such as brand name, price, size, color, and item number are all **encoded**, or translated, into a unique bar code. The bar code is printed on labels and the information it represents is entered into the computer. Whenever one of the labels is scanned with a bar-code reader, the computer is able to match the item with its information.

When you purchase an item and bring it to the check-out line, the cashier uses a bar-code reader to scan the data on the bar-code label. Immediately, the price of the item appears in the cash register's window. The item's name and price are printed on the receipt tape, along with the quantity you have purchased and any applicable discount. In the computer's memory, the quantity of the item you bought is deducted from the number on hand. Thus an accurate inventory count is maintained for stock replenishing purposes.

In addition to the major advantage of accurate inventory control, bar coding provides several smaller but important fringe benefits. Because the item's price is stored in the computer and accessed by bar code, the cashier does not have to type it in. Therefore, fewer errors can be attributed to inaccurate price entry.

Also, because the price is in the computer rather than in the bar code, changes in pricing do not require changes in labeling. The new price of any item is entered into the computer. When its bar code is scanned, the new price is sent to the cash register window and the receipt tape.

Data Probe Tools

The collection of data electronically, without the error-prone intervention of humans, has carried over into several fields in addition to sales, satellite, and census data. Meter reading is a good example.

In most places using electricity, a meter is placed on the property to measure the actual amount of power used by each customer. A meter reader then comes around once a month to copy the numbers from the meters in his or her territory. The numbers collected by the meter reader determine how much money a particular customer will have to pay.

As population densities grew, especially in urban areas, and as wages for meter readers rose, utility companies found that they were unable to read every meter every month, and that the cost of each meter reading was too expensive. They also experienced a high number of reading/recording errors made by the human meter readers. So they looked for a cheaper, more accurate way to collect power-usage figures.

The solution they found was the **data probe**. A data probe is a key-like instrument which, when inserted into a power-usage meter, will electronically read and record the meter location and usage numbers into a computer. Because the human inserting the key does not have to see or write down the numbers, he/she spends less time at each meter, has fewer opportunities for error, and can visit many more meters in a day. This solved all three problems involving cost and accuracy of readings, and allowed power companies to provide a higher level of service than was possible before.

Voice Recognition Data Entry

The last computerized data collection methodology discussed here is regularly used by regional salespersons and others who travel, but must maintain accurate records and constant contact with databanks at a home office. **Voice recognition data entry** enables people to collect and record data merely by speaking into the microphone of a portable terminal (see Figure 9.2.10). The receiving computer accepts the voice transmission and transcribes it into a form the computer can store.

Figure 9.2.10

A laptop computer can be conveniently used as a remote terminal for voice recognition data entry.

Let's examine the case of a traveling salesperson using voice data entry. After spending a lengthy amount of time examining samples and catalogs, the client is ready to place an order. The salesperson sets up a portable terminal and enters into it the date, time, and customer name. As the client indicates each item and quantity, the salesperson speaks the item number and quantity into a small built-in microphone. When the order is complete, the salesperson types in a brief code. A printer attached to the laptop prints out an invoice, complete with price extensions, discounts if applicable, and total. The salesperson gives the invoice to the client and shuts down the laptop.

9.3 Retrieving the Data

The problem of retrieving data after it has been stored is as complex a problem as collecting that data in the first place. Before computers came along, most data was stored, on paper of course, in file drawers and filing cabinets. Effective retrieval of that data depended on how well the files were organized. If the papers stored in the files were alphabetized, or placed in some other logical order, retrieval could be simple and efficient. If the files were stored in random order, the retrieval could be agonizingly impossible.

Similarly, computer data retrieval also depends on careful organization. In fact, organization of data is the single most important task of information retrieval. The FBI fingerprint database provides an interesting example of well-designed data organization and retrieval.

FBI Fingerprint Processing: A Study in Data Retrieval

Often our society demands an absolute identification of certain individuals, whether for criminal or for security reasons. Because each person has unique fingerprints that do not change throughout life, the fingerprint has become indispensable as an identification aid to law enforcement and security agencies. Let's examine the collection, storage, and retrieval of fingerprint information.

Figure 9.3.1

A typical fingerprint collection card.

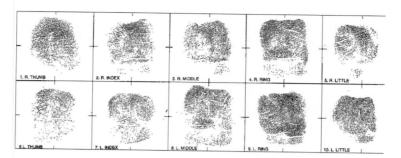

Collection of Fingerprint Data

In Washington D.C., the FBI maintains a database of over 30,000,000 sets of fingerprints. Each set is collected on a special card, with a specific space for each finger of each hand. Anyone who watches police-procedure shows on television has seen the collection process. The subject's fingertips are inked and then applied, one finger at a time, to the collection card. Data concerning the person's name and other information is also entered onto the card. Completed cards are sent to Washington D.C. There the cards are read by a scanning device, which transcribes the information and fingerprint images from the card to the computer's memory. All data from the card (text and images) are now in electronic form.

Storage of Fingerprint Data

Before each set of fingerprints is stored, the scanning device identifies global features and discerns the overall ridge structure of the set. Smudged or unreadable areas are eliminated. The computer operator then readjusts the location and orientation of each fingerprint. Using the ridge structure data from the scanner, the operator computes a center point for the fingerprint, which allows it be properly aligned on the monitor. The computer then compares the newly scanned fingerprints with stored prototype patterns of the different fingerprint types (see Figure 9.3.2). The prototype that most nearly matches the new set determines the major classification for that set.

The sorting process then counts the number of whorl-type patterns on a set of fingerprints and notes which fingers have them. Individual sets of prints are then grouped according to the number and location of whorl patterns their prints exhibit. A person with no whorl-type fingerprints, for example, would be grouped along with all others having no whorled fingers. Another group classification would include all those with only one whorled fingerprint located on the left thumb. A third group is comprised of all those having all whorled fingerprints. Using this classification system, all fingerprint data can be organized into 1,024 different groups, and filed accordingly.

Figure 9.3.2

The six major patterns of the Henry System of Fingerprint Identification.

Retrieving Fingerprint Information

When the FBI receives a request for identification of a set of fingerprints, the unidentified set must first be scanned and classified. It is then compared to other fingerprints in the same classification. When sufficient points of identification are found, a match is declared and retrieved from the database. A final check, performed by a human technician, is performed to verify any matching of fingerprints.

The well-organized storage of computerized fingerprint data, and the increased speed of computer processing, have vastly improved the retrieval time of the fingerprint database and the identification of submitted prints. Before computers came along, 1,400 fingerprint technicians, all working full time, were able to process some 24,000 fingerprint verification requests daily. Today, over 30,000 requests can be processed by fewer than half the technicians.

The FBI fingerprint retrieval system is just one of many examples of very complicated computerized information retrieval systems. All depend, for speed and accuracy, on effective organization of stored data. Others that might be of interest include the Library of Congress Catalog and the information retrieval system used by the Congress and by the executive branch of the U.S. Government. Many articles regarding these two examples have been published.

9.4 The Role of Statistics: Transforming Data into Information

Notice that in the preceding two sections we discussed collecting and storing *data*, but retrieving *information*. That's because whatever we retrieve from a database should be meaningful. The retrieval process concerns the examination, summarization, and manipulation of data into information. The most commonly used method of transforming data into information is **statistical analysis**. Computer applications using statistics include such diverse subjects as the study of heart disease, lung cancer in smokers, average income of a U.S. family, and election outcome predictions.

Statistical ideas are important to database results and usage. Diverse computer applications cannot be fully appreciated without some basic statistical knowledge. This section briefly covers several important statistical concepts.

Percents

A number often quoted and sometimes misunderstood is the statistic called a **percent**. When someone says that 50% of the students in your class are seniors, this should indicate to you that half of the students in the class are seniors (and half are *not*). If there are 30 students enrolled in the class, 15 of them would be seniors, and the remaining 15 would be freshmen, sophomores, or juniors.

A **percent** is special type of fraction. The percentage is the number of parts out of the total of 100 parts that are in question. For example, 25% of 100 people would be 25 people. Also, 20% of 10 dogs would be 2 dogs, or 20/100 of 10.

Probability

It is quite difficult to give a definition of **probability** without seeming like a cat chasing its own tail, but let's give it a try. The concept of probability deals with our ability to predict whether certain events will occur. For example, many of us have heard the weather analysts predict a "50% chance of showers this evening." The prediction is based on the probability that certain patterns of observed weather will continue. Aside from the feeling that weather predictions always seem to be wrong, we should take the prediction to mean that it is just as likely to rain as not to rain. In other words, if we looked back at all the days with a 50% chance of rain over the past year, we should see that about half of the time it actually did rain.

Suppose the weatherman predicted a 50% chance of rain today and tomorrow, and further suppose that it doesn't rain today. Does that mean it will definitely rain tomorrow? Absolutely not!! But, you say, in order to have 50% rain and 50% not rain in two days, it must rain one day and not the other! Why the discrepancy? Weather *predictions* apply to only one day at a time. *Probabilities* tell us that if we look at a large enough number of days where a prediction is 50% chance of rain, about one half or 50% of these days will have rain.

Figure 9.4.1

Statistics are used to analyze collections of data and transform them into meaningful information.

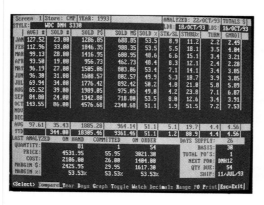

Information on receiving, on-hand and sales is expressed month by month, in either numerical or graphical form, clearly showing important market trends.

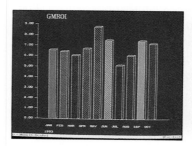

Five primary statistics are constantly monitored and always available: GMROI, Turn, Stock to Sales, Sell-through and Days of Supply.

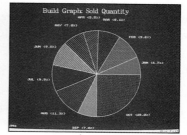

Information graphically displayed helps you quickly interpret the real situation.

Importance of Probability and Percents

As a society, we seem most comfortable making decisions based on numbers. We choose groceries by price and weight, clothing by size, and investments by profits. When we analyze data, we seek ways of expressing that analysis also in numbers. Even business and governmental decisions are based on numeric probabilities that certain events will happen. For example, lenders requesting personal information from a credit bureau are basing their loan approval on the probability (a numeric value!) that the individual will repay the borrowed amount. This probability is a numeric calculation the computer database system makes based on the personal data provided. An error in the data or mathematical calculations of the database program could unfairly cause a borrower to be denied a loan that he or she really has the resources to repay.

The Computer Continuum

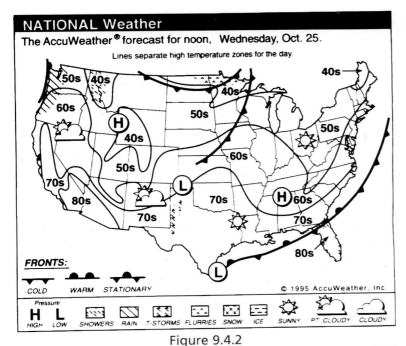

NATIONAL Weather
The AccuWeather® forecast for noon, Wednesday, Oct. 25.
Lines separate high temperature zones for the day.

FRONTS:

COLD   WARM   STATIONARY   © 1995 AccuWeather. Inc.

Pressure
H L   SHOWERS RAIN T-STORMS FLURRIES SNOW ICE SUNNY PT CLOUDY CLOUDY
HIGH LOW

Figure 9.4.2

Weather predictions, often expressed in probabilities, are taken from computer-generated weather maps.

Figure 9.4.3

Sometimes, the weather does not turn out exactly as predicted.

Selecting Data for Statistical Analysis

Often, it is impossible to gather all the data on a particular topic. The Nielsen company, for example, releases a report that rates the popularity of various TV shows. They cannot possibly monitor every TV set turned on in the United States. Instead, they select homes across the country which represent a cross-section of the TV-viewing audience. They connect small computerized boxes to television sets in their chosen representative homes. This sample is then used to rate the top television programs.

Although **sampling** is a very useful technique, a sample must be carefully selected to avoid predetermining statistical results. Suppose, for instance, that some Saturday morning Nielson selected only homes with young children as the representative viewing audience. Needless to say, the cartoon shows would receive very high ratings indeed, giving a far different result than one would expect from a truly representative sample. The better the sample, the better the analysis that will result. If the sample is randomly chosen, we can expect some semblance of a **normal distribution**. But if the sample is **skewed**, or distorted in some way, the data will reflect the distortion. For example, using only the data from monitoring Saturday morning television viewing would not give an accurate list of the top 10 TV shows.

Correlation

We are constantly being bombarded with news reports showing the **correlation** between certain habits and various diseases, such as cancer. A definite correlation or connection exists, for example, between lung cancer, age, and smoking habits.

The analysis needed to investigate this correlation is too complicated to discuss here, and it definitely requires the aid of the computer. Let's analyze instead a much simpler correlation. The lengths of index fingers easily demonstrate correlation. Suppose we pose the following hypothesis:

Sampling is the technique used to predict the total situation using just a few isolated but representative observations.

In a **normal distribution**, 68% of all data values fall within a limited range near the center of the distribution, with the other 32% evenly spread over the top and bottom ranges.

In a **skewed sample**, selection of the group participating in a survey supports some predetermined outcome. A skewed sample gives distorted results because the sample does not match the distribution of the whole population.

A **correlation** is a connection or relation linking two or more pieces of information.

Figure 9.4.4

Supposed you asked each group, "What is your favorite TV show?"
Would you expect the answers to be the same? Why?

Sex	Mean Index
Male	72
Female	68

Figure 9.4.5

Mean index finger lengths for males and females.

False correlation or **false relevance** involves the creation of a cause-and-effect relationship between two facts that seem to be related but are not. Most often, the facts themselves are perfectly true. The statement relating them is what causes the problem.

Hypothesis: There is a correlation between index finger length and whether a person is male or female.

To test this hypothesis, we will measure the length of the index fingers of 100 men and 100 women. Figure 9.4.5 shows the results of separate data for males and females. In general, we see that our hypothesis is proven: Females have shorter index fingers. This is not surprising; our intuition would have led us to the same conclusion because men in general are larger than women. Correlation analysis is really much more complicated than the finger-length example, but the idea contained in this example gives a taste of the real thing.

Sometimes we assume a correlation between two true but unrelated facts. This is called a **false correlation** or **false relevance**.

A classic example is the direct correlation that may seem to exist between eating ice cream cones and drowning while swimming. The correlation is false because there is no cause-and-effect relationship between eating ice cream and drowning.

> **Fact 1:** More drownings occur in the summer.
> **Fact 2:** More people eat ice cream in the summer.
> **False Relevance:** People who eat ice cream are more likely to drown while swimming.

Here is another example.

> **Fact 1:** All human beings breathe oxygen.
> **Fact 2:** All human beings must die sometime.
> **False Relevance:** Oxygen must be toxic, because 100% of those breathing oxygen today will die in the future.

The computer invasion has placed greater attention on statistical analysis of data than ever before. As a result, more people are aware of statistics and are gaining a greater understanding of statistical procedures. The computer's large capacity for data storage encourages a level of statistical accuracy and currency never before possible. Unfortunately, there are negative effects of computerized data analysis: human error and misuse. The most common problem is the misrepresentation of data. Remember: *garbage in = garbage out*! A database is only as good as the data entered and the program used to extract the information. Computers only perform the functions. People enter, program, and explain the results.

9.5 Creating a Custom Database

The Internet and the commercial market provide excellent tools to help you gather general information. Not all information you might want, however, can be accessed through existing databases. What if specific information is needed that is not already in a database?

Let's examine the arrangement of a typical database to understand how the various pieces of that structure are combined to create accessible information. The smallest piece of information accessible in a database is called a **field**, or **data element**. A field contains one particular piece of information. Some examples might be the first name field, the zip code field, and the social-security number field.

A group of fields, all containing information about one instance or individual, is called a **record**. Therefore a record might hold the name, address, phone number, social-security number and salary of one specific individual.

A group of records, all of the same type, is referred to as a **file.** For example, we might have a record for each student in a class. Those records, as a group, would constitute a **Class file.**

It is important that the data in all the records in a given file be organized in the same way. That means two things:

- Every record must have all the same fields as the other records in that file.
- The fields must be arranged in the same way for each record.

Suppose, for example, that the layout for the student record in a class file is the following: *Fname, Lname, Address, City, State, Zip, Phone.* Every record in that file would contain the same list of information, arranged in the same order.

> A **field** is a location in a database that contains one single specific piece of information. For example, the city field would contain the name of the city or town where one specific individual lives.

> A **record** is a collection of related fields or data elements. For example, the name, address, and telephone number of one person could constitute that person's record.

> A **file** is a collection of related records, all the same type, which store information about similar instances or individuals.

Figure 9.5.1

Structure of a typical database.

First Name	Last Name	Street Address	City	State	Zip	SSN	Phone
John	Monroe	222 Alexander	Jefferson	MI	48161	777-00-7676	343-454-5678
Shannon	Jackson	123 Peach Lane	Carleton	MI	48117	313-65-9876	555-321-3452
Abdul	Botswain	22 Circle Drive	Clio	OH	48197	234-56-7890	555-456-1234
Kiernan	Smith	345789 Blanding	Jackson	FL	32075	456-78-9087	555-407-6543
Harmony	Valee	1943 Craig	Springs	CA	98076	654-76-1234	555-407-1234
Mitsu	Yamaha	765 Washington	Alma	GA	87654	777-007676	343-454-5678
Millie	Lintner	88 Sunshine Lane	Flower	HI	98765	313-65-9876	555-321-3452
Kurt	Lauckner	678 Physics Blvd.	Mathma,	MA	12543	234-56-7890	555-456-1234
Joan	Mrazik	123 Applebee	DeBary	FL	98077	456-78-9087	555-407-6543
Rachel	Witte	8907 Arts Drive	Savannah	GA	76543	654-76-1234	555-407-1234
Kristy	King	9876 Dingle	Ardvark	KS	65476	777-00-7676	343-454-5678
Nathan	James	786498 Hwy 66	Daalas	TX	87654	313-65-9876	555-321-3452
Angeal	Bays	East Lake Drive	Seaville	MI	48765	234056-7890	555-456-1234
Jackson	Jones	222 Alexander	Jefferson	MI	48161	456-78-9087	555-407-6543
Sheryl	Lanb	123 Pech Lane	Carlton	MI	48117	654-76-1234	555-407-1234
Art	Piddle	22 Circle Drive	Clio	OH	48197	313-65-9876	555-321-3452

A **database** consists of a collection of information, each dealing with some aspect of a single overall subject. The files might be of similar or very different types. They are connected only by topic and information usage.

A **DBMS (Database Management System)** is an application that allows you to store, organize and retrieve data from one or more databases.

A group of files that are all related to each other, or are all related to the same subject, is called a **database**.

Gathering computerized data and organizing it into fields, records, and files will still not produce the usable results we are seeking. We still need some way of analyzing the data and transforming it into information. If we were to combine these structural elements with a query language and add programs for data modification, statistical analysis, and report formatting, we would have a complete package commonly called a **DBMS (Database Management System)**.

Sometimes referred to just as a *database system*, a DBMS is a powerful software package for storing and accessing data. To understand how such a system works, let's create a small example. Suppose you want to store on computer an index of the compact discs in your own personal music collection. Here's what you would do:

Step 1: Decide what information you might need about each CD. Some of the things you might consider include title, artist's name, recording label, date of issue, titles of selections, and so on. You might also want to list type of music and whether the performer is a vocalist, pianist, jazz band, or chamber orchestra. Each of these pieces of information would occupy one field in the record about one compact disc.

Step 2: After you have decided what information to include, you would then **define the structure** of your database. Commercially available database software packages provide a data definition screen to assist with this task (see Figure 9.5.2).

Step 3: Now you are ready to **enter the information** about each of your compact discs. Because it is important that you enter the information in the correct place and format, your DBMS program includes a data entry screen that guides you through this process. The data entry screen also provides a facility for correcting any errors you might make while typing in your data.

Step 4: You are now ready to reap the benefits of a computerized database. When

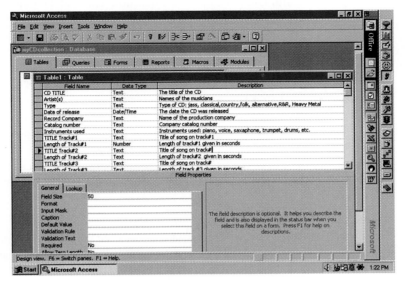

Figure 9.5.2

A data definition screen helps you set up the fields needed to store your data.

you need information from your CD list, a query screen provided by your DBMS software will help you **select exactly the information you wish to extract**. If you planned your data storage carefully in step 1, you should be able to retrieve any combination of information you have entered.

Step 5: As you add CDs to your collection, or perhaps give a few away, you can **update your database** quickly and easily.

Step 6: Finally, you can print out all or any part of your CD information in a format of your choice by using the report writing feature of your database program. You can decide which records to include, what information to display from each record, and how to organize that data. Some DBMS programs can also perform calculations as part of your printed report, providing a count of how many CDs you have in each category of music, or total performance time of a number of selections (if you have included that information in your records).

Database Advantages

Some of the most important advantages of a database and its corresponding DBMS over other less-organized systems of information are as follows:

- **Space saver.** They eliminate redundancy (that is, only one copy of each item of information need exist).

- **Increased accuracy.** One person can control or be responsible for certain data items, thereby lessening chances of human error.

- **Multiple use of data.** More than one department or group of people can use the same information.

- **Data integrity.** Special efforts can be made to make sure data items can't be changed accidentally due to computer failure or human error or malice.

- **Time saver due to search abilities.** The option to look for data by title, keyword, subject, or field.
- **Easy use of data.** Users with different questions can find their answers in one database by changing the question.

Drawbacks of DBMS

We have now had sufficient discussion of databases to understand one of the more important issues facing our society. Collecting information into large and easily accessible databases has raised the public's consciousness on several issues. Some practices make it easy to trick the general public through the misrepresentation of information. Others, like invasion of privacy, pose a personal threat to our freedom and happiness. We will just skim the surface of these issues here. Chapter 15, "Ethics, Electronic Spies, and Privacy," takes a more in-depth look at computers and the ethical dilemmas they present for society.

Misrepresentation of Data

Everywhere we look today, we are assaulted by statistics. Television commercials assure us that a certain product is used by more doctors (more doctors than what? chimpanzees?). A cereal claims to contain 20% less sugar (less than what? maple syrup?). A company complains that its earnings have plummeted by 8.93%! (Is that from an all-time high?) Without a great deal more knowledge than the figures themselves, we cannot possibly know how accurate they are, or how much belief we should put in them.

Invasion of Privacy

With a moment of thought, almost everyone can give an example of an **invasion of privacy**. The computer is facilitating a very powerful means of invading privacy, the extremes of which could easily take the form of events in George Orwell's novel *1984*. Less-exotic examples can be found almost every day in the newspapers and magazines.

Many large databanks can be found within the government. Some of these have been mentioned already, such as the U.S. Census and IRS databanks. In general, these two databanks have a good reputation for honoring the privacy of the individual. However, several IRS employees were disciplined for accessing the personal income tax files of some celebrities and selling the information to tabloids.

The desire to collect all of an individual citizen's data under a single universal identifier, or UID, has already been discussed in Congress. If this were ever done, an authorized operator (with a single request) would be able to obtain an individual's records for tax, military, credit, medical, travel habits (via gas credit-card information and passport usage), and just about any other recorded information imaginable. Indeed, the horrors of *1984* could still become a possibility.

Chapter Summary

What you can do with what you have learned:

- Be aware of the large amounts of data that must be processed each day.
- Use a computer to collect data.
- Use a computer to store data in a DBMS.
- Use a computer to analyze data and print a report of the results.
- Be careful of statistics unless you know for sure that the data sampled and methods used to produce those statistics are correct.

The Computer Continuum

Key Terms and Review Questions

Key terms introduced in this chapter:

Information Age 3-52

Terabyte 3-53

Data 3-53

Information 3-53

Dewey Decimal System 3-54

Keypunched data cards 3-55

Hollerith cards 3-55

Keypunched machine 3-56

Keypunched operators 3-56

Card reader 3-56

Mark-sensor forms 3-56

Remote electronic sensing 3-57

Bar code 3-58

Bar-code reader 3-58

Encoded 3-58

Data probe 3-59

Voice recognition data entry 3-59

Statistical analysis 3-61

Percent 3-61

Probability 3-61

Sampling 3-63

Normal distribution 3-63

Skewed sample 3-63

Correlation 3-63

False correlation 3-64

False relevance 3-64

Field 3-65

Data element 3-65

Record 3-65

File 3-65

Class file 3-65

Database 3-66

DBMS (Database Management System) 3-66

Invasion of privacy 3-68

Matching

Match the key terms introduced in the chapter to the following statements. Each term may be used once, more than once, or not at all.

1. _____The age in which we are living is called this.

2. _____This is a given thing or fact, in a raw form.

3. _____Data repackaged in a meaningful form becomes this.

4. _____This form of a filing system enabled the cataloging of nonfiction books by subject matter.

5. _____This is a collection of interrelated data files or libraries organized for ease of use.

6. _____This type of data storage may come in the shape of a questionnaire.

7. _____This type of data storage needs to run through a card reader to decode the information.

8. _____This type of data storage is used to collect satellite data.

9. _____This type of data storage is used to collect census data.

10. _____This type of data storage is used for inventory control.

11. _____ This type of data storage sometimes has a person mark responses on the form using a graphite pencil.

12. _____ This type of data storage uses a key-like instrument that, after it is inserted into a meter, records the amount of utility service used.

13. _____ This type of data storage enables people to speak into a microphone.

14. _____ This is the most commonly used method of transforming data into information.

15. _____ This special type of fraction refers to the number of parts out of the total of 100 parts that are in question.

16. _____ This technique is used to predict the total situation by using just a few isolated but representative observations.

17. _____ This is the connection or relation linking two or more pieces of information.

18. _____ This is what results when a sample is selected in a way that will result in a predetermined outcome.

19. _____ This involves the creation of a cause-and-effect relationship between two facts that seem to be related but are not.

20. _____ This is a collection of programs that allow immediate access to a database.

True or False

1. _____ We have the capacity to double our current store of information in about a week.

2. _____ The reason why this period of time is called the Information Age is because we are now able to store mass amounts of information on computers.

3. _____ Because the terms data and information are used interchangeably by some, they now have the same meaning.

4. _____ Data is only a part of information.

5. _____ Holes are punched into Hollerith cards to represent some piece of data.

6. _____ Only the Census Bureau uses mark-sensor forms.

7. _____ Bar codes are used exclusively for inventory control.

8. _____ In voice recognition data entry, a person speaks into a microphone attached to a portable terminal. Because voice recognition is very difficult for a computer, it must then be connected to a mainframe computer for decoding.

9. _____ A bar-code reader is needed to "read" bar codes.

10. _____ Keypunch machines are used to encode bar codes.

11. _____ Errors were easily corrected on Hollerith cards.

12. _____ With the advent of the computer being used to process fingerprint information for the FBI, fewer fingerprint technicians were needed.

13. _____ Forecasting the weather is an example of the use of probability to predict an event.

14. _____Although research uses only a sampling of the population, they can still obtain accurate results.

15. _____All samples are unbiased.

16. _____The connection between height and shoe size is an example of correlation.

17. _____False correlation refers to having two related facts, both false, and making a connection between them.

18. _____Kids carry books to school.

_____Books contain a lot of information that kids can learn.

_____It's the books that make kids smart.

_____This was an example of false relevance.

19. _____A record contains all the information pertaining to the one person or instance in question.

20. _____A file may contain many records.

Multiple Choice

Answer the multiple choice questions by selecting the best answer from the choices given.

1. The age in which we are living is called
   a. The Stone Age
   b. The Information Age
   c. The Technological Age
   d. The Second Renaissance
   e. The Industrial Age

2. This is the amount of information the experts say can pass along the Internet in one day.
   a. Byte
   b. Megabyte
   c. Gigabyte
   d. Terabyte
   e. Infinibyte

3. The definition of this term is just that it is a given thing or fact.
   a. Field
   b. Record
   c. File
   d. Data
   e. Information

4. The definition of this term includes taking data and repackaging it in a meaningful form.
   a. Field
   b. Record
   c. File
   d. Data
   e. Information

5. Each field includes a piece of this.
   a. Field
   b. Record
   c. File
   d. Data
   e. Information

6. This is a collection of related data elements.
   a. Field
   b. Record
   c. File
   d. Data
   e. Information

7. This is a collection of related information, all the same type, which contains information about one instance or indi-

vidual.

a. Field

b. Record

c. File

d. Data

e. Information

8. This is a location in a database that contains one specific piece of information about one specific individual or instance.

a. Field

b. Record

c. File

d. Data

e. Information

9. This is a collection of programs that allow direct access to the database.

a. Database Management System

b. Archival Information System

c. Nonstandard System Access

d. Internal Resource System

e. File Backup Interpreter

10. Which of the following is not one of the important advantages of a database.

a. Space saver

b. Increased accuracy

c. Less need for security measures

d. Multiple use of data

e. Time saver due to search abilities

Exercises

1. From the Internet, obtain a list of at least 10 data and document collections you can search to find information on some topic within your major.

2. If your library has a computerized catalog or bibliographic search system, perform a query on any topic of your choice and print out the list of references on that topic. Be sure to include the exact wording of your query at the top of the page.

3. Locate and examine Landsat images from your library resources (for example, *National Geographic Magazine*). Locate the image of a major city or land area that you are quite familiar with and identify recognizable landmarks.

4. Using a sheet of clear white typing paper and an ink pad, make a complete set of your own fingerprints. Identify: (a) Which fingers have the whorl pattern. (b) Which fingerprints are in one of the other categories. (c) Which fingerprints don't fit any of the categories.

5. Carefully read a daily newspaper or weekly news magazine for one week. Cut out or photocopy all articles that you think relate to the privacy issue. Determine whether a computer was involved in each of the articles. Note: A computer-related newspaper will probably contain more of these articles than most regular daily publications. Don't mutilate library copies!

6. Think about the student records databanks at your school. Name one situation where each of the following could be a special advantage. For example, protection of data privacy might be an advantage if you prefer not to let anyone see your grade point average.

a. Elimination of redundancy

b. Control of data

c. Multiple use of data

d. Versatility in representing data relationships

e. Protection of privacy

f. Data integrity

g. Security

The Computer Continuum

7. Design a small-scale database. Be sure to decide what information you need to store in each record and what fields of information you need. Use a DBMS program to define your database and enter 10 records or so.

8. Give five examples of how sampling and correlation are used to give useful results to our society (for example, the correlation between smoking and cancer).

9. Find three examples of large databases that you can purchase on CD-ROMs.

10. Give three examples of false correlation from advertising (for example, TV, magazines).

11. Give three examples of false relevance.

12. Explain how each of the following samples can be skewed:

   a. The percentage of people who own handguns

   b. The percentage of students who commute to school

   c. The percentage of students receiving financial aid

   d. The percentage of armed-forces reserves who go to war

   e. The percentage of students wearing false teeth

13. Explain how the Dewey Decimal System organized the library.

14. List at least three advantages of using bar-code technology for inventory.

15. List two reasons that data probe tools were invented for the power industry.

Discussion Questions

1. Will humankind ever get to the point that the incoming data is just too huge, too unmanageable?

2. Do you think that a UID (universal identifier) that everyone had attached permanently to themselves would be a good idea? If it could be electronically read from a distance would this make a difference? Why or why not? How does this relate to fingerprints and DNA?

Group Project

A group of four students should prepare a survey on a subject of mutual interest. It can deal with student issues or interests, or general information. The survey should be at least 20 questions and can have either yes/no, multiple choice, or numerical answers. If mark-sensing equipment like that used on exams is available, design the questionnaire around that type of gathering system. Have the members of your class (your sorority, and so on) fill out the survey and return it to your group. Use an electronic spreadsheet to chart and analyze the data you collect. Do you see any correlations? Can you express your findings in percentages? Do you think your choice of sample skewed your results? Prepare and give the results in a presentation using an electronic presentation system.

Web Connections

http://www.mbmarktcons.com/mbmarkt/irdinfo.htm

Information on the Internet Resources Database project. Includes details on downloading the software to run it and obtaining the entire database on disc.

http://www.pcwebopedia.com/database.htm

Definition and pictorial demonstration of a database from field to file.

**http://www.yahoo.com/Computers_and_Internet/Software/Databases/
Shareware/**

Links to downloadable database shareware programs.

**http://www.pcwebopedia.com/database_management_system_DBMS.
htm**

Definition and description of DBMS. A lot of links to database suppliers and software.

**http://www-groups.cs.st-and.ac.uk/~history/Mathematicians/
Hollerith.html**

Biography of Herman Hollerith and his contributions to mathematics and computer history.

http://www.taltech.com/Bar_Code/bckb/howabar.htm

How bar-code readers (several kinds are described) read the values from a bar code. Includes informative animation of a beam of light scanning a bar code.

http://www.fbi.gov/2000/ncicinv.htm

Comprehensive site dedicated to the NCIC database of crime information. Very good example of a large database constantly being updated and accessed.

http://www.fbi.gov/publish.htm

Links to FBI publications and statistics organized by year and by type. Good place to obtain actual data by state and by type of crime.

Bibliography

Adriaans, Pieter, and Dolf Zantinge. *Data Mining*. Reading, MA: Addison-Wesley, 1996.

Techniques on how to retrieve data.

Codd, Edgar F. *The Relational Model for Database Management: Version 2*. Reading, MA: Addison-Wesley, 1990.

A book about the relational database model written by the creator and intended for the professional.

Date, Chris C. *An Introduction to Database Systems (The Systems Programming)*. Reading, MA: Addison-Wesley, 1994.

Another giant in the field of databases writes for the professional.

Maxymuk, John, ed. *Finding Government Information on the Internet*. New York: Neal-Schuman Publishers, 1995.

Morville, Peter and Louis Roisenfeld, Joseph Janes. *The Internet Searcher's Handbook*. New York: Neal-Schuman Publishers, 1996.

Chapter 10

1929 First color television signals are transmitted.

1962 Steve Russell, a graduate student at MIT, invents the first video game.

1963 Ivan Sutherland used the first interactive computer graphics in his Ph.D. thesis, "Sketchpad: A Man-Machine Graphical Communications System," which used the light pen to create engineering drawings directly on the CRT.

1969 Alan Kay describes a graphical user interface in his Ph.D. thesis, which designed the first graphical object-oriented personal computer.

1972 Based on the success of the video game Pong, Nolan Bushnell founds Atari.

1972 A brain tumor is found by an experimental computerized axial tomography imager in Wimbledon, England.

1973 The Alto, an experimental PC that uses a mouse, Ethernet, and a GUI, is developed at Xerox PARC.

1975 IBM develops the laser printer.

1979 Sony and Phillips develop digital videodisks.

1984 The MacPaint program gives computer graphics power to the personal computer audience.

1995 First completely computer generated full-length feature movie, *Toy Story*.

2005 Digital cameras outsell 35 mm cameras.

Visual Communication: Gateway to the Brain

Chapter Objectives

By the end of this chapter, you will:

@ Recognize the importance of vision to the communication process.

@ Understand the complexities involved in storing pixels that can be shades of gray.

@ Understand the complexities involved in storing color pixels.

@ Identify digital pictures taken from satellites circling the Earth.

@ Understand how false-coloring is used in image enhancement.

@ Recognize some uses of image restoration.

@ Know the difference between bitmapped and object-oriented graphics and how each is shown visually in both video and print forms.

@ Understand the issues involved with the hidden-line problem.

@ Understand how perspective and shading affect both two-dimensional and three-dimensional images.

@ Recognize how blending can improve shaded surfaces.

@ Know how animation is achieved with many images that differ only slightly.

10.1 Introduction

Consider the five major senses: sight, hearing, smell, taste, and touch. Which of these is most valuable to you? Most people say that sight is their most valuable sense. In fact, the amount of information sent to the brain via the human visual system is incredible. The Stuart Professor of Psychology at Princeton University, Frank A. Geldard, states:

> Of the several senses giving us information about things and events in the world around us, none is richer than the visual one. The eye is the most highly developed of our sense organs, being at once the most complex in structure and the mediator of the most elaborate of our experiences.

Figure 10.1.1

Photograph of a woman.

You have probably heard the old adage: "A picture is worth a thousand words." To help prove the point, look at the photograph of a woman in Figure 10.1.1.

If you have the ambition, write a 1,000-word description of her. After doing this, look at the picture of Figure 10.1.2. It contains the photograph of four women. Can you readily pick out the woman appearing in Figure 10.1.1? You should easily recognize her. To complete this experiment, have someone else read your one thousand-word description and have him or her attempt to identify the woman. Be sure Figure 10.1.1 is out of sight. Chances are your friend can't pick out the woman from your written description without guessing. Of course, it is not fair to use the characteristics of clothing, only the facial features should be considered in the description.

With the power of human vision, it is no wonder that some information going to or coming from the computer (that is, input and output) is designed to take advantage of our visual sense. A major example of this is the huge migration in the mid 1990s from operating systems that use a command-line user interface to those that are **GUIs** (**g**raphical **u**ser interfaces).

Figure 10.1.2

Photograph of four women.

The first part of this chapter deals with existing images and how they are processed and manipulated with the aid of computers. The latter part of this chapter discusses images created using the graphics software tools on computers.

Even so, vision isn't everything. Otherwise, the sharp-eyed hawks and eagles would rule the animal world. Probably the next most important human sense is hearing. The next chapter deals with that topic.

10.2 Processing Existing Images

There are many ways to start examining how computers can be used as regards to visual images. One of the easiest to understand involves in some way modifying or processing images that already exist.

Digitized Images

In section 2.3 of Chapter 2, "Metamorphosis of Information," we discussed the idea of **digitizing** a black and white picture. The images shown there were the simplest type where each pixel is either black or white. **Pixels** are the small equal sized areas that a picture is divided into. In these simple pictures, a single digit binary number could be used to indicate whether a particular pixel was black or white (that is, 1 or 0).

To get more realistic images, it is necessary to have shades between black and white. Each shade is given a number, usually between 0 and 63, 0 and 255, or even 0 and 1,023. The value of the number indicates how light or dark that area is to be shaded. For example, 0 could represent white, 255 black, and 127 would be a gray halfway between black and white.

For color images, more information is needed. In fact, each pixel needs three numbers, each of which represents one of the three primary colors: red, green, and blue. These three numbers specify the amount of red, green, and blue necessary to reproduce the color of the individual pixel. With the **RGB** (that is, red, green, blue) model of color, the right proportions of red light, green light, and blue light are used to get the desired color on a standard broadcast TV monitor. Each pixel usually consists of three rectangles grouped together, yet small enough that you can't see them individually. A full-color picture will result when each group of three rectangles representing a particular pixel is given the right amount of light.

Almost all computers and other digital graphics systems use RGB monitors that display images, but these systems don't use three different numbers. Instead, each pixel's color is derived from a single number. That number contains information regarding the amount of red, blue, and green needed to give a particular color. This is why systems supporting millions of colors look much better than those only supporting 256 colors. Only 8 bits per pixel are needed for 256 colors, 16 bits gives thousands of colors, and the commonly used 24 bits or 32 bits per pixel gives several millions of colors.

Graphics Formats from GIF to JPEG

The most common type of image used by today's computers is bitmapped. These images consist of thousands of pixels, each of which has a number associated with it. How is this pixel information stored in a computer? There are a number of different forms, called file formats, in which these digitized images are stored. In fact, the program Graphic Converter, available in six human languages, converts among more than 100 different file formats. Each of these file formats has strengths and weaknesses. Let's look at just a few of them.

GIF. One of the most common formats is called GIF (Graphics Interchange Format). GIF was created by CompuServe and has two major strengths. First of all it is in common usage, which means it's compatible with almost every computer. Another advantage of GIF is the capability to shrink the size of the graphics file; this is called compression. It makes use of a very fast compression algorithm that can shrink the files by up to a factor of 10. This is very important because graphics files tend to be very large, which leads to inefficiency when used in places like the Internet. A major disadvantage is that it only has 8 bits per pixel, which means only one of 256 colors can be used for any individual pixel. Photographs, in particular, can be degraded from the original form. GIF is especially suited to graphic images like cartoons, but photographic images can still be acceptable. Files with

continues

images in GIF have names that end in GIF, for example, MYDOG.GIF. A more modern file format that follows in the footsteps of GIF is PNG (Portable Network Graphics), which allows either 8 bits or 24 bits per pixel.

TIFF. Computer files that end in TIF or TIFF (Tagged Image File Format) are in a file format that was originally developed by the Aldus Corporation. The major use of TIFF is for large, high-quality or high-resolution images and photographs. It can use up to 96 bits for each pixel and also supports several compression schemes. There are some minor incompatibilities between programs using the TIFF system.

JPEG. Another fairly popular graphics format is JFIF (JPEG File Interchange Format). It is based on a compression scheme called JPEG (Joint Photographic Experts Group). The compression scheme makes use of several decades of research into human vision, which is used to throw out picture information whose absence won't be missed. This type of compression is called lossy compression, because it is removing some of the information each time the image is compressed. JFIF filenames usually end with the letters JPG.

Figure 10.2.1

Two hundred miles offshore in the Gulf of Alaska, using more than 1 million pixels.

Figure 10.2.1 shows an example of a color image printed on paper using colored inks. If this same image were shown on a computer monitor or TV, it would need only about 1 million numbers representing the amount of red, blue, and green light. But unfortunately this is where things get complicated. Red, green, and blue inks won't give the correct appearance. In fact, it is necessary to use four inks: cyan, magenta, yellow, and black. This group of four colors is commonly called **CMYK**, where *K* stands for black. This is called four-color printing and is the most common way to print color. The printed image also has more pixels to make the image appear sharper than is possible on a video monitor. Taking all of this into account, the printed image takes about 5 million numbers to represent Figure 10.2.1.

Many other examples of digitized images are available, but none are more commonly seen than the satellite weather maps appearing on television news broadcasts. Figure 10.2.2, showing Hurricane Andrew, is an example of a typical weather-map image from the GEOS-7 satellite. On August 24, 1992, the eye of this major hurricane hit just south of the Miami, Florida area and caused extensive damage.

A closer look at the Hurricane Andrew image and the weather maps used in most TV weather reports reveals outlines of the continental United States and coastline. When the satellite was digitizing the image from several miles above the earth, these outlines weren't there. How do they become part of the weather picture? As you probably guessed, they are the result of a computer program. By knowing the location of the satellite and the direction it is pointing, the computer program calculates where the continental boundaries lie. The outlines are then made by changing the tiny areas of the picture associated with these boundaries to a contrasting color.

The Computer Continuum

Another series of satellites called the **Landsat satellites** are continuously circling the Earth. They have sent back to Earth millions of pictures since the program first began. These pictures are not typical. They consist of up to seven different pictures of the same area, but are taken at different frequencies, including infrared. It is like having a special camera with different filters, each of which only lets a certain color through.

An example of one of these special pictures is shown in Figure 10.2.3, an image showing Cape Cod. This particular picture uses three of the seven frequencies available from the Thematic Mapper of Landsat 4. It gives a very realistic picture. If you look very closely, you can see the sandbanks and shoals just offshore in shallow water.

All of the examples shown in the first part of this chapter represent the process of digitizing images. The additions, such as the landmass outlines in Figure 10.2.2, represent another aspect of how computers can do more than just take a picture. Sometimes this is referred to as enhancing the image.

Processing Digital Images

Computers are capable of far more than just adding boundaries of continents. The processing of digital images has many specialty areas. Two of the most common are called **image enhancement** and **image restoration**.

A very common example of image enhancement is to change the normal visual colors of an image so as to emphasize detail. This is referred to as **false-coloring**.

This useful technique of false-coloring allows colors to be assigned in any desired way. Figure 10.2.4, for example, is a digital picture acquired on June 11, 1980 from the Nimbus-7 satellite. The false-coloring technique is used to color vegetation red, and bare soil light blue. This coloring reveals that bare soil exists in the heavy farming area on the western edge of the thumb of Michigan, whereas the upper half of the lower peninsula of Michigan is mainly forest. From this image it is easy to understand how satellites can be used to investigate what is growing on the surface of the Earth. Also note the light blue coloring in the lower-left portion of the image. This is the northern tip of the "bread basket" of the United States, where most of the nation's grain is grown.

The second of the image processing techniques discussed here is image restoration. Imagine obtaining clear pictures where only a blur formerly existed, or being able to see something where previously no image existed.

Image restoration is something that most of you have already seen, or at least you have seen its end result. Most of the satellite pictures sent to Earth in digital form must have

Figure 10.2.2

The eye of Hurricane Andrew making landfall in Florida.

Figure 10.2.3

Landsat 4 image of Cape Cod.

Image enhancement is a type of digital image processing whose goal is to highlight or enhance particular aspects of an image or even change the structure of the image itself.

some image-restoration work done on them. The need arises from many sources. For example, electronic "noise" may have resulted in false or incomplete picture information. The computer can be programmed to fill in missing details or change incorrect information as long as the source of the flaw or degradation is known.

Figure 10.2.4

Great Lakes area from the Nimbus-7 satellite. Red represents vegetation, and light blue is bare soil.

Figure 10.2.5

Restoration of license plate image.

An interesting example of image restoration of a different type is found in Figure 10.2.5. The upper photograph is a very fuzzy image of an unreadable license plate. The lower image is a restored version of the same photo. Notice how the letters and numbers are now readable. The computer program that accomplished this was written with the knowledge that the original license plate picture was unrecognizable because of incomplete information. The lack of picture information was due to being too far away.

As a final example of image enhancement, Figures 10.2.6 and 10.2.7 illustrate major changes in the structure of the image. In Figure 10.2.6, there are images of five individuals. Look at them carefully. Now look at Figure 10.2.7, which is a composite of the five original images. The businessman has the hair of the "punk rocker," among many other changes. In fact, on close examination it seems that about the only things remaining of the businessman are his facial features. It makes you wonder whether photographs can be trusted.

10.3 Creating Images: Line Art

The first part of this chapter dealt with the manipulation of pictures already in existence. A real-life image was digitized and then modified, smoothed, or false-colored. This section focuses on creating original pictures.

Figure 10.2.6

Images of five interesting people.

Artists through the centuries have developed a set of fundamental rules for making images. Different sets of rules led to different artistic movements and individual styles. But, there is a set of universal rules that almost all of these schools of thought have recognized. They consist of simple things such as hiding parts of things that wouldn't normally be visible, or violating this principle intentionally. In computer jargon, this particular idea is referred to as hidden-line and surface techniques. In three-dimensional images, it is necessary to know the sources of light that illuminate the objects. In Rembrandt's portraits, for example, he used a particular style of illumination called Rembrandt lighting. Look at any Rembrandt and notice that a light source seems to be located above and to the side of the subject, which leaves a triangle of light on the cheek. This section examines only the most important of these artistic rules.

Figure 10.2.7

Composite image of the five people in Figure 10.2.6.

Because of the complexity of creating images, we will start with the simplest type of line drawings. Two major issues must be addressed when creating images that are made up of only straight and curved lines. The first is to actually create the image, and the second is to display it.

Creating images can be done by using drawing programs that exist for almost every type of computer. These programs have many drawing-related features that help the user create images. There is usually a set of tools for drawing circles, ellipses, rectangles, squares, and curves through several points. Other tools are also usually available, including free-hand electronic pencils and many others. Figure 10.3.1 shows a screen with a caricature in the process of being drawn. Some of the tools used for making this drawing can easily be identified in the menu box along the left side, especially the straight lines and circles.

What are some of the uses for line drawings? The following common applications are just some of the several that use line drawings:

- Map making
- Architectural drawings

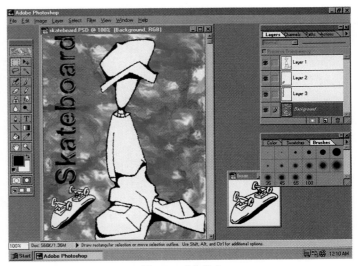

Figure 10.3.1

Screen from the drawing program Adobe Illustrator showing many of the drawing tools available.

- Graphs (for example, a company's profit by year)
- Machine design plans
- Home decorator's layouts
- Model airplane plans
- Aircraft construction blueprints
- City population-density maps

Object-oriented or **vector graphical** images are those that are stored in the computer as lines, curves, or geometric shapes. Formulas are used to indicate how to draw.

Bitmapped or **raster graphical** images in the simplest form are those constructed by individual pixels that are black or white. The pixels can each be shades of gray for photographic-looking images or even colored.

An extremely important distinction should be made here. There are two fundamentally different types of **line drawings**. One is referred to as **bitmapped** or **raster graphics**; the other is **object-oriented** or **vector graphics**. These seemingly complex names describe simple but often misunderstood concepts. Before defining them, let us look at a bitmapped and object-oriented graphic image of the same thing. Figure 10.3.2 shows a simple line drawing of a daisy, done in both forms by a typical graphics program. Note that the bitmapped graphic image is a little uneven. When originally drawn they both looked uneven on the computer screen. However, the bitmapped image printed in the figure has exactly the same pixels that appeared on the coarser computer screen. Therefore, the main drawback with this form occurs when it is necessary to enlarge or manipulate the image. No information exists for the relationship between pixels, so only the crudest manipulations can be done.

Figure 10.3.2a

Images of a daisy in two graphic forms: Bitmapped.

Figure 10.3.2b

Images of a daisy in two graphic forms: Object-oriented.

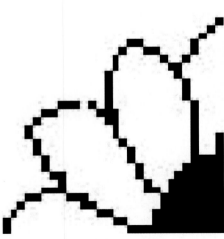

Figure 10.3.3a

Enlargement of two images in Figure 10.3.2a: Bitmapped.

Figure 10.3.3b

Enlargement of two images in Figure 10.3.2b: Object-oriented.

The Computer Continuum

The object-oriented graphics image was handled differently. It was stored in a formula and then redrawn with the printing devices' pixel size, which is much smaller. This makes the curves appear smooth. The main advantage over bitmapped graphics is that the objects can be moved or modified without changing each pixel independently; only the formula has to be modified. A circle of twice the diameter is still a circle, for example.

To further emphasize the difference, suppose the same drawing program is used to make the two original images triple the size of the original drawing. The result in Figure 10.3.3 shows an even greater contrast between the two. Because the bitmapped information of the picture consists of only black and white pixels, the computer has no choice when enlarging the image. It must make each black pixel into nine black pixels, and each white pixel becomes nine white pixels. Because each old pixel is represented by three vertically and three horizontally, the image is three times bigger. However, the object graphics image just draws all lines at the original width, but three times longer.

10.4 Creating Images: Solid Forms to 3D

Although flat, **two-dimensional line drawings** are quite useful, three-dimensional pictures drawn in two dimensions involve more complex concepts that are quite familiar to art students. These concepts include curved surfaces, color, texture, and shading. The first two are probably already familiar, but texture and shading may not be. The texture of a surface can be best explained by example. The surface that looks like wood has a much different appearance than one that looks like fur. It is not hard to see the difference. However, shading is a little more difficult. Artists have worked with shading techniques to produce an endless variety of effects. Proper shading, for example, can make a scene look as if it is in direct sunlight or like a cloudy day. Let's start with simple, **three-dimensional line drawings** displayed on a flat surface such as a piece of paper.

bits
& bytes

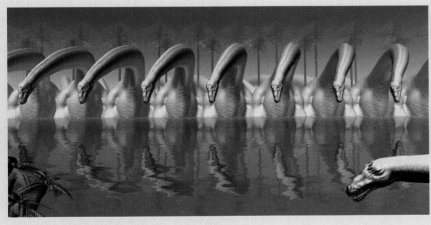

Diplodocuses of the Jurassic in 3D
You may be familiar with the old fashioned 3D viewers from the 1800s. Today, precise image manipulation using computers can produce a 3D effect without a viewer. Tatsuhiko Sugimoto's Creatures is a stereogram produced by Viz Communications. It is constructed using two side-by-side images that fool the brain into thinking the eyes are seeing a single 3D image.

To see a 3D image of a group of the genus diplodocus dinosaurs from the Jurassic period, place a fingertip on the bridge of your nose. While focusing intently on it, with crossed eyes, slowly pull your finger away.

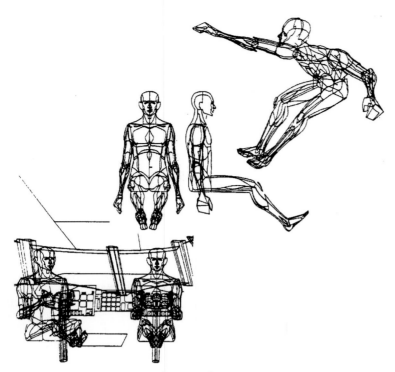

Figure 10.4.1

Studies of an airline pilot in action.

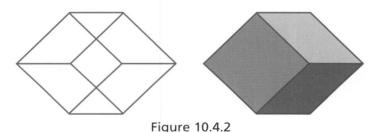

Figure 10.4.2

A box with and without hidden lines showing.

The **hidden-line** or **hidden-surface problem** concerns itself with how to hide the outlines or surfaces of a solid object that shouldn't be seen from the direction of the observation.

Perspective is the quality that allows three-dimensional images to be drawn on two-dimensional surfaces and yet retain the look of a three-dimensional image.

Scenery, objects, and the human figure have all been the subject of computer line drawings. One interesting example involves the representation of airline pilots and an investigation into how their span of reach is affected by cockpit layout. Figure 10.4.1 shows several frames in a series of a pilot reaching for various control switches. By studying this type of image, the engineers who design cockpits of airplanes can see potential problems in the layout of instruments and controls.

There is one rather obvious peculiarity of this line drawing of a pilot in Figure 10.4.1. You can see through him! Is it possible to create better drawings of the pilot, which hide the lines that aren't supposed to be seen? The problem is referred to as the **hidden-line problem**, and is one of the classic problems in computer graphics.

Now, the solution to hidden lines is rather well-defined for most cases. How can they really be hidden if the only things hiding them are other lines? Of course, a little thought will enable us to realize that the lines are really marking the edges of surfaces, and it is these surfaces that prevent us from seeing through the object. Figure 10.4.2 illustrates an object with and without the lines that should be out of sight if the box were opaque.

It's really no problem to remove these lines as long as our viewing direction isn't changed. However, this would be very limiting. In fact, one of the great powers of line drawings in computer graphics is the ability to view an object from different directions. Algorithms have been developed to allow the computer to draw objects as viewed from different directions as demanded by the user. These same algorithms hide the lines that should not be visible from the particular viewing direction.

Perspective is another rather important quality, which must be included to make drawings look realistic—that is, to make the image appear on paper the way it would actually look to the eye. Figure 10.4.3 illustrates a view overlooking some railroad tracks: (a) with perspective, and (b) without perspective.

Using the concepts of hidden-line and perspective, some rather good-looking images can be drawn. Figure 10.4.4 illustrates an architect's line drawing of a home in two different views. Both perspective and hidden-line are very important to this drawing. The computer that made this drawing used information about the dimensions of the home; then when the operator specified the position of the observer, the computer drew the image, taking into account both hidden lines and perspective.

Shading is used to make the image more realistic. Figure 10.4.5 shows an example where the shading is very easy—each complete surface will have the same shading. By examining the figure, it can be seen that the sides facing away from the light source are darker than those facing the light. In this case, the light source is the sun. All scenes that mimic nature must have sources of light illuminating them. These light sources may be the sun, reflections from a surface, artificial lights, or any number of other things.

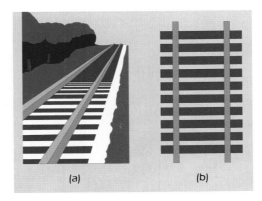

(a)   (b)

Figure 10.4.3

Image of railroad tracks: (a) with perspective, and (b) without perspective.

Shading is a technique used to give the appearance of illumination by some combination of light sources. It is used to make created images look like images humans are used to seeing or to take advantage of these effects.

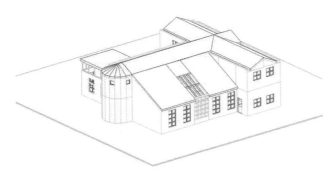

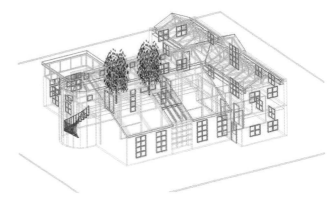

Figure 10.4.4

Architect's line drawing of a home: (a) without hidden lines showing, and (b) with hidden lines showing.

A problem occurs when the object is constructed of **curved surfaces** because there are no flat, discrete surfaces to shade. One solution is to construct the curved surface out of many flat surfaces, as shown in the front view of the face in Figure 10.4.6.

Each of the facets (that is, flat sections) can then individually be shaded as necessary. Figure 10.4.7a shows the face with shading from a light above and to the left. This image is not very realistic, however. It can easily be improved by having the computer smear out or blend in the shading.

Figure 10.4.5

Shading used to give 3D effect to a building.

Suppose, for example, that the region between two facets has shading that is an average of the shadings. The shading can then smoothly vary to the original facet's value at the center of the facet. Figure 10.4.7b illustrates the result of the **smoothing** technique; it looks more realistic.

Many graphics programs are available to the professional illustrator. With these fairly powerful and complex programs, images of very high quality can be created. Incorporating perspective, shading, **texture**, and **color**—along with some illustrator talent—can result in images such as the sports car in Figure 10.4.8. This object-oriented graphics image with color is one of the higher-quality examples of a professional illustrator's work.

Texture is a property of a surface. It is observed and identified by humans through the reflection of the light off the surface. For example, a shiny surface reflects light in a way that sometimes has a mirror-like quality. Rough surfaces, on the other hand, reveal an unevenness.

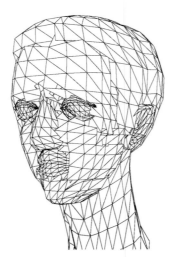

Figure 10.4.6

Construction of a human head from flat surfaces.

Figure 10.4.7a

Shading flat surfaces of the head.

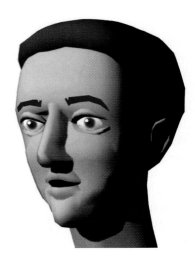

Figure 10.4.7b

Blending facets to give a more natural look.

Figure 10.4.8

Combining professional talent with a high-end graphics program gives spectacular results.

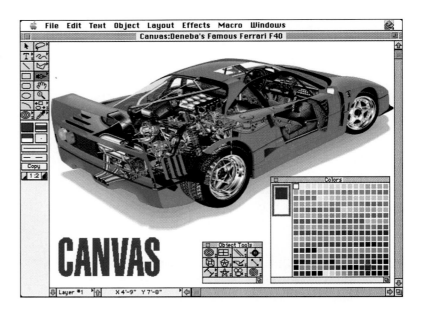

It is important to discuss another aspect of graphics here. Most of the previous images exist in only one view, the one given in the figure. In looking at the architects rendering of the building in Figures 10.4.4 and 10.4.5, however, it seems natural to allow the viewer to look at the building from another position. In fact, the architect's program used to create the building image actually has a three-dimensional description of the building in the computer. This internal description can be used to give pictures viewed from almost any angle chosen by the user of the architect's program. Figure 10.4.9 shows the building from a different perspective. The architect didn't redraw the building; the program redrew it so that it appears as shown from the new direction.

Figure 10.4.9

View of the home from a different perspective.

The Computer Continuum

10.5 Creating Images: Animation

Almost everyone is familiar with the Saturday morning cartoons on television. They portray animated figures that jump, run, swim, drive various contraptions, take pratfalls, get run over, smash and bash each other, and then return the next Saturday morning for more of the same. Who makes these films or videotapes, and how are they made? Twenty years ago, all cartoons had to have the figures drawn by artists. Then the animator would make them move while taking pictures, frame by frame. Now, full-length feature cartoons such as *Toy Story*, shown in Figure 10.5.1, are done completely by computer. To understand the process, it is first necessary to understand how motion pictures work.

If you have ever examined a strip of motion picture film, you probably observed that each of the pictures or frames is almost identical to those surrounding it. However, each frame does change very slightly. By quickly viewing the frames, the objects in the picture seem to move.

Graphics programs on computers can be used to draw these frames. The individual frames can then be stored individually in the computer. Special player programs can be used to view the animation on the computer screen, or they can be recorded on videotape via special hardware attached to the computer.

Figure 10.5.1
A frame from the cartoon movie Toy Story.

bits & bytes

Morphing: Special Effects

Morphing is a graphics technique used in animation. Starting with a beginning image, the technique will distort and change it frame by frame to the predetermined final image with a predetermined number of frames in between. The first commercially successful use was in Michael Jackson's 1991 video "Black or White." In this video, millions of dollars were spent to morph many faces of different races, both male and female, from one to another.

This technique is now available to personal computer users in a program called Morph from Gryphon Software Corporation. The sample shown is a morph from the face of Michelangelos's statue *David* to a second image of his Madonna from *The Pieta*. It then continues with Leonardo da Vinci's *The Virgin of the Rocks*, and then finally to the final form of *Mona Lisa*, also by Leonardo da Vinci.

10.6 Visualization of Information

In section 10.2, many of the images revealed information that was not normally sensed by the human eye. In particular, the false-coloring of satellite images revealed information that couldn't be understood in any other way, especially if it were presented as a series of millions of numbers. This idea of taking any form of information and making it into a picture is called visualization of information. It is one of the fastest-growing areas in computer science. Whether it is blood flow in the heart, turbulence of a jet engine, or even stock market fluctuations, all can be visualized. Let's examine some interesting but simple examples.

One such interesting example involves the display of the population growth of the United States over a period of years. It is easy to read about how the West was settled and how the major population centers grew, but the computer drawings shown in Figure 10.6.1 give the information to the viewer more quickly and with greater understanding. The mountain-like spikes represent population density; the higher peaks represent greater population. In 1870, the effect of the Mississippi River on the population shift westward is striking. Except for the West Coast, which was accessible by water, all the population seems to end at this great river, which acted as a barrier. Looking ahead in time, the 1920 through 1960 illustrations show a lack of population where the Rocky Mountains prevail.

Another interesting feature is found in Figure 10.6.2, where the heavily populated northeastern United States is quite evident. Compare this region with Florida and California. Does this graphic image give you a different perspective? The northeastern U.S. population concentration is quite impressive.

Another interesting example of how three-dimensional line drawings can be used to display information that is otherwise almost impossible to see comes from the medical field. It involves the visual representation of knee noises for use in diagnosing and treating arthritis and other joint disorders. The diagnostic value of the noises made by the moving knee was first recognized in 1880. Unfortunately, the information obtained using a stethoscope was very difficult to interpret, especially if the doctor had to remember how the knee sounded from one week to the next. Add to this the problem of extraneous noise from such sources as skin friction, hand tremor, or snapping tendons. Indeed, the noises of interest were difficult to

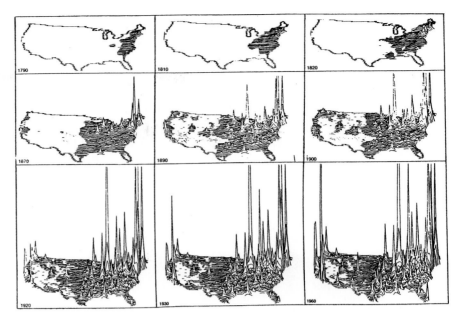

Figure 10.6.1

Population of United States from 1790 to 1960.

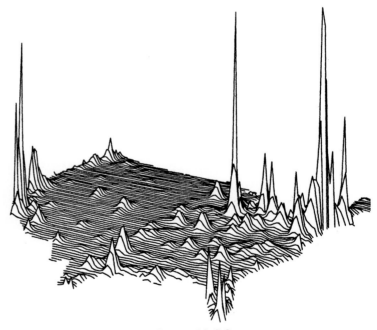

Figure 10.6.2

Population densities of the US in 1979.

hear and discriminate. By using a sophisticated electronic system that canceled out the unwanted noises, researchers were able to isolate the information of interest.

There still remained the problem of recording the information in an easy-to-interpret form. This problem was solved using a computer program, which analyzes the digitized sound information and produces three-dimensional plots of the information. Figure 10.6.3a illustrates the mountain-like plots for a normal knee. Figure 10.6.3b shows a rheumatoid knee. As the patient bends the knee over a period of three seconds (one extension and one flexion), the illustrated data give the frequency of the noise, the position of the knee, and the volume of noise, which corresponds to the height of these "mountain ranges." By looking at the diagrams, the extent and location of the damage to the affected knee can be determined. Then, by recording this information for a particular person over a period of time, the effectiveness or ineffectiveness of drugs and therapy can be determined.

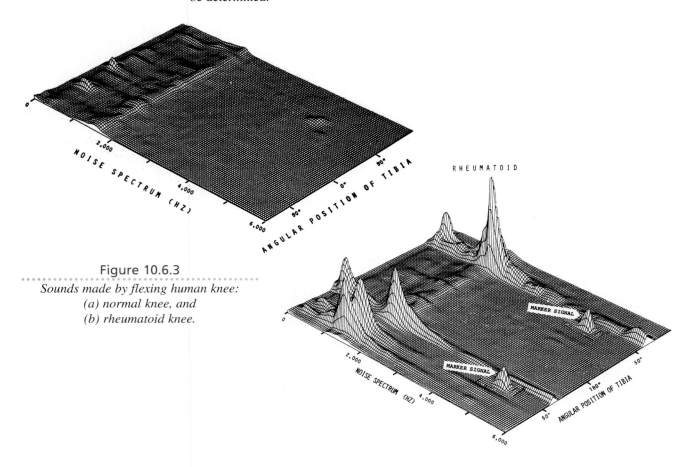

Figure 10.6.3
Sounds made by flexing human knee:
(a) normal knee, and
(b) rheumatoid knee.

A very common technique in visualization of information is false-coloring, discussed in section 10.2. A good example on getting extra information visually is found in the false-colored image shown in Figure 10.6.4. It is a weather image showing how false-coloring can be used to indicate wind speed. This very unusual weather condition, called the train of storms, shows several storm centers, four of which have either hurricane or tropical storm status. In this image, the deep red represents the greatest wind speed, with shading to yellow indicating lesser wind speed. Also note the green outline of the landmasses.

The Computer Continuum

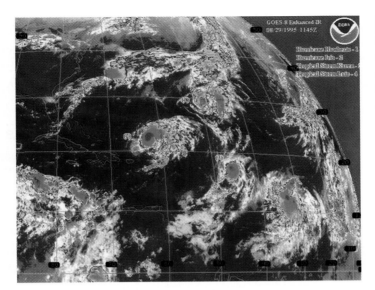

Figure 10.6.4

GOES-8 false-colored image of the train of storms on August 8, 1995; red indicates greatest wind speed.

bits & bytes

Visualization of Heart Blood Flow

Ultrasound imaging uses computers and sound waves to open a "window" into the human body without making an incision. The technology provides visual images constructed from the sounds that reflect off organs in the body. Physicians can measure the size and view the action of the heart, a fetus, liver, kidney, gallbladder, and eye without risk to the patient.

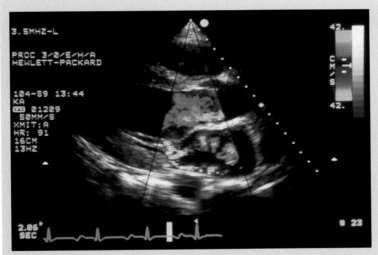

To make an ultrasound "picture," a gel is first rubbed on the skin to improve the sound transmission. Then a device with thousands of transducers that send out sounds higher than normal human hearing is held against the skin.

The transducers, which also behave like small microphones, receive the reflections of the sound from the organs. Each one of the thousands of transducers represent a pixel of the image. The resulting black-and-white image can then be false-colored to make features more obvious. It works just like the sonar used in fish finders or submarines.

Motions of the blood in a heart can even be detected. For example, the figure shows an ultrasound image made by a Hewlett-Packard machine. The blood flow images reveal a heart defect called mitral regurgitation. The blood flowing toward the transducer is colored red, and blood flowing away is blue. The defect can be seen as the red and blue mix.

10.7 Creating Images: Visual Art

Too many exhibitions of art and technology focus on the technology and tend to be razzle-dazzle displays of color and novelty. In this chapter, the emphasis is on the art, not the technology. Because this is a book about computers, however, the artist selected to represent this area makes profound use of the computer.

Attempting to Understand Creativity in the Visual Arts

History abounds with examples of visual artists who have been admired for their creativity. What is creativity? Is it a necessary ingredient of art? These questions should evoke hours of discussion.

Harold Cohen is an artist who contributes some answers to these questions and raises still other new questions. His great success as a painter gives him an insight into the problems of art, with or without technology.

Oliver Strimpel, formerly Executive Director of The Computer Museum in Boston, nicely summarizes Cohen's work in his catalog introduction for the show "The Robotic Artist: AARON in Living Color."

> "I write programs. Programs make drawings." Harold Cohen's matter-of-fact description of his life's work belies the incredible challenge of what he set out to do 25 years ago: nothing less than design a computer that knows how to create Cohen's art, totally unassisted.
>
> By 1969, Cohen had established himself as one of Britain's foremost artists, showing in one-man shows in major museums around the world. With great courage, he turned away from a traditional artist's career to begin working with computers. Using the mainframe and minicomputers of the 1970s at Stanford's Artificial Intelligence Lab, he began to develop the suite of programs that came to be known as AARON.
>
> What is **AARON**? What purpose did this work serve? Cohen has stated that his purpose for working with AARON is to demystify the various functions in art-making that are often labeled as creativity. Many have viewed creativity as inspirational or even romantic; either view is certainly mysterious and unexplainable.
>
> Cohen's work sets out to explore his own mental structures and decision-making processes and incorporate them into the collection of programs called AARON. AARON is then set free to draw what it may draw. The program has only its own resources and the knowledge given it by Harold Cohen. Is it creating? It seems to be!
>
> Examine the scene from a Cohen show in the late 1970s shown in Figure 10.7.1. At this point in the development of the program, AARON expressed itself either on a CRT screen or through various plotting devices. The one shown in the figure is a

Figure 10.7.1

Gallery view from 1970s Cohen Exhibit.

drawing turtle, which moves around the paper on the floor under the control of AARON. The turtle is not really significant to our discussion; however, it is a very novel way of presenting AARON's drawings.

As AARON's proficiency grew, it was capable of drawing plant-like structures and even the human figure. The 1986 drawing shown in Figure 10.7.2 shows three human-like figures and several structures similar to those found in nature. Of course, the program was modified by Cohen to cause it to learn how to draw these structures, as AARON is incapable of learning on its own.

Drawing the human figure was a particularly major accomplishment. A description of the considerations that had to be addressed is given in Cohen's lecture for the NICOGRAPH '85 International Symposium. It reveals some small insight into how Cohen provided AARON with the capability to draw the human figure:

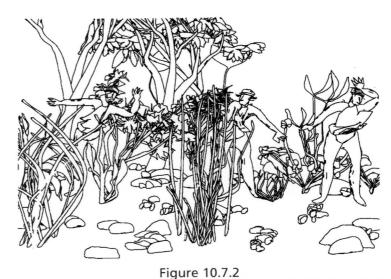

Figure 10.7.2

Plant-like structures and human figures drawn by AARON, 22×30 inches, 1986.

> Structural representations deal with the articulation of the figure: where the joints are, and what the legal range of movements is at each joint. Behavioral representations deal with the figure's perfor-mance: what the different parts have to do in relation to each other so that the figure will move coherently. In other words, AARON does not merely store particular representations of the figure; it knows how to generate an infinite number of plausible examples of the fig-ure from what it knows of the figure's structure and behavior.

> For example, if the figure is balancing on one foot, AARON's rules for the placement of that foot will determine that it must be below the figure's center of gravity. It knows the rules for the use of the free leg in balancing, but these are non-deterministic: that is to say, there is not just one position the leg can occupy. Once an instance of the free leg has been generated, AARON then accesses other rules from which to generate the two arms.

The **rules** referred to in the preceding quotation are what make up AARON's program. It is a way of programming that is commonly referred to as an expert system. Harold Cohen put his own ideas for making art into a set of rules that the program follows. They aren't pre-cise rules, but more like rules of thumb. What this means is discussed in Chapter 13, "Artificial Intelligence and Modeling the Human State."

Figure 10.7.3

AARON drawing with coloring done by Harold Cohen. Oil on canvas 54×72 inches, 1993.

As the reader can certainly recognize, this is a very complex problem. Cohen has also added color to the whole system, which meant teaching AARON some sort of color theory so that it can color its own drawings. The color problem was very dif-ficult and elusive. In fact, before AARON was capable of coloring its own works, Cohen himself colored the drawings. Figure 10.7.3 is an example from the period just before

AARON could color its own drawings. AARON did the drawing in this figure and Harold Cohen added the color.

Having AARON coloring its own image meant designing some means to do the painting. Figure 10.7.4 shows Harold Cohen in his studio with the coloring machine in the process of a drawing. AARON is controlling this painting machine from the computer. Figure 10.7.5 shows AARON's completed painting.

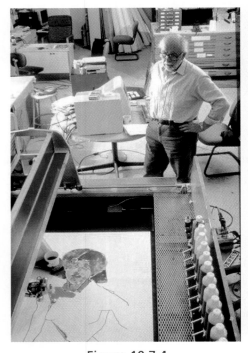

Figure 10.7.4
Harold Cohen in his studio.

Figure 10.7.5
AARON in the process of painting.

Chapter Summary

What you can do with what you have learned:

- Be aware of the large amounts of memory needed to store digitized pictures.

- Recognize false-colored images and features added to satellite images.

- Choose either bitmapped or object-oriented graphics for a particular application.

- Use perspective and hidden lines and surfaces to show the appropriate faces of a three-dimensional image.

- Use blending of shaded surfaces to construct curved surfaces from flat ones.

Key Terms and Review Questions

Key terms introduced in this chapter:

GUI (graphical user interface) 3-78

Digitizing 3-79

Pixels 3-79

RGB (red, green, blue) 3-79

CMYK (cyan, magenta, yellow, black) 3-80

Matching

Match the key terms introduced in the chapter to the following statements. Each term may be used once, more than once, or not at all.

1. _____This is the process of changing a visual image into a form that can be represented within the computer.

2. _____These are the small areas that a picture is divided into.

3. _____This model of color is used to produce the color used in a TV monitor.

4. _____This model of color is used in four-color printing.

5. _____This technique refers to changing the normal visual colors of an image.

6. _____This process entails eliminating known or otherwise unwanted flaws or degradations.

7. _____This process entails processing a digital image to highlight particular aspects of an image.

8. _____This type of image is made up of only straight and curved lines.

9. _____This type of line drawing is made up of individual pixels.

10. _____This type of line drawing allows only crude manipulation of the image.

11. _____This type of line drawing can be modified without changing each pixel individually.

12. _____This type of line drawing has curves that appear smooth.

13. _____When this type of drawing is blown up, lines appear jagged.

14. _____This concerns itself with how to hide lines that should not be seen from the direction of the observation.

15. _____This technique of drawing makes the image appear on paper as it would to the naked eye; close objects appear closer than far objects.

16. _____ This technique is used to show that sides that are away from a light source are darker than those that are facing the light.

17. _____ This is the artist that created a program that could draw.

18. _____ This is the name given to the program that could draw.

19. _____ AARON uses these to determine the structure and behavior of a figure.

20. _____ Currently, who colors in the pictures drawn by AARON?

True or False

1. _____ Most people say that sight is their most valuable sense.

2. _____ Digitized pictures only have black and white pixels.

3. _____ Outlines depicted in maps (satellite images) are placed there by computer programs.

4. _____ Printed books store pixels differently than pictures displayed on TV screens.

5. _____ Color pictures require more memory to store than do black-and-white pictures.

6. _____ Pictures having shades of gray require as much memory as do color pictures.

7. _____ Satellites locate boundaries of countries by locating beacons on the ground.

8. _____ Image enhancement can use false-coloring.

9. _____ False-coloring just means to change the colors of an image.

10. _____ Digitizing an old, cracked image and fixing it would be an example of image restoration.

11. _____ Using the computer to alter a picture that was incomplete for some reason is an example of image restoration.

12. _____ In a bitmapped image, only the formula for the image needs to be changed.

13. _____ Graphic images stored as lines, curves, or geometric shapes are referred to as raster graphics.

14. _____ Bitmapped graphics may have jagged edges.

15. _____ After curved surfaces and color are added to a picture, it can no longer be considered two-dimensional.

16. _____ Perspective is a quality that makes a picture appear to be three-dimensional.

17. _____ Computers can actually draw directly on the motion picture film using lasers or electron beams.

18. _____ Computer graphics can be used to reveal information that is not normally sensed by the human eye.

19. _____ AARON has always colored its own pictures.

20. _____ AARON has a library of several pictures that can be drawn when given a command.

Multiple Choice

Answer the multiple choice questions by selecting the best answer from the choices given.

1. This type of process is used to change the structure of an image.
   a. Image enhancement
   b. Image restoration
   c. False-coloring

2. This is the process that changes the color of an image.
   a. Image enhancement
   b. Image restoration
   c. False-coloring

3. This type of process is used to highlight or enhance particular aspects of an image.
   a. Image enhancement
   b. Image restoration
   c. False-coloring

4. This type of process eliminates flaws or degradations.
   a. Image enhancement
   b. Image restoration
   c. False-coloring

5. Another name for bitmapped graphics:
   a. Bitmapped graphics
   b. Object-oriented graphics
   c. Raster graphics
   d. Vector graphics

6. Another name for object-oriented graphics:
   a. Bitmapped graphics
   b. Object-oriented graphics
   c. Raster graphics
   d. Vector graphics

7. This type of line drawing would probably be used in more professional drawings, such as architectural drawings (may have more than one answer).
   a. Bitmapped graphics
   b. Object-oriented graphics
   c. Raster graphics
   d. Vector graphics

8. This type of line drawing has surfaces that appear smooth (may have more than one answer).
   a. Bitmapped graphics
   b. Object-oriented graphics
   c. Raster graphics
   d. Vector graphics

9. This type of line drawing has surfaces that appear to be made up of individual "spots" (may have more than one answer).
   a. Bitmapped graphics
   b. Object-oriented graphics
   c. Raster graphics
   d. Vector graphics

10. For what purpose is Harold Cohen working with AARON?
    a. To show how creative computers can be
    b. To show how intelligent programmers are
    c. To demystify various functions in art-making that are often labeled creative
    d. To present the inner workings of a computer through visual charts drawn by AARON
    e. To show his own talent as an artist

Exercises

1. Explain why the pixels in a black-and-white image commonly have shades from 0 to 63, 0 to 255, or 0 to 1,023; where 0 is the number representing white, 255 is black, and 127 would be a gray halfway between black and white. Why not 0 to 320?

2. Why is the process of printing color pictures called four-color printing? Explain why four colors are necessary. In theory, isn't it true that to get color it only takes three colors?

3. Look at a TV screen with a magnifying glass. Describe what you see when the set is on and when it is off. Can you identify the pixels? What are the colors used in the pixels, and can you actually see them?

4. Name two categories of image processing and briefly describe them.

5. Which three Great Lakes can be seen in Figure 10.2.4?

6. Looking at Figure 10.2.6, list, if possible, at least two features taken from each of the five people shown in Figure 10.2.7.

7. Think of two or three legal or journalistic ramifications of the ability to produce composite images as shown in Figure 10.2.7.

8. Draw a simple straight-line image of a favorite object on a sheet of graph paper that is 50 squares high and 50 squares wide. When drawing the picture, make sure that the image can be traced without lifting the pencil. List the coordinates of each endpoint of lines in the order determined by the tracing.

9. Draw your own animation using 3×5 index cards. Make a flip book from these cards by stapling them together.

10. Do you think animations that take the facts in a legal case and then make assumptions to fill in details should be used in court cases? Explain both problems and advantages to this type of animation.

11. If it takes 1 bit to store a pixel that can be only black or white, how many bits would be necessary to store a pixel that can be

    a. A shade of gray between 0 and 63?

    b. A shade of gray between 0 and 255?

    c. A shade of gray between 0 and 1,023?

12. Why do color print images take more memory to store than color video images?

13. Explain why object-oriented curves look smoother than bitmapped curves.

14. What is the biggest advantage of object-oriented graphics over bitmapped graphics?

Discussion Questions

1. Why are print colors different from video colors?

2. How does image restoration work?

3. What is your thinking regarding the question of creativity as a necessary ingredient for creating art? How does the computer enter into it? Is AARON really creating?

Group Project

A group of four students should select some event that interests them and create a brochure that announces the event. It should include text, photographs, and drawings. Each person should select one of the following assignments:

- Collect textual information
- Collect photographs (possibly take them)
- Do illustrative drawings for the design
- Be responsible for technical details (printing, digitizing, scanning)

All four should work out the design as a team. Suggestion: Use legal-size paper in horizontal orientation and then fold three times. This will give a trifolded brochure.

Web Connections

http://www.sun.co.jp:8080/960710/feature3/alice.html

Information on Ivan Sutherland, an extremely important figure in computer graphics. Contains links to many pages outlining his work and achievements. Includes a description of the hidden-surface problem.

http://www.sun.co.jp:8080/960710/feature3/cg.html

The first three-dimensional color graphics done on a computer. Requires a browser capable of reading Java applets.

http://www.armytechnology.com/contractors/training/evans/index.html

This army defense-industries site has some pictures created with real-time graphics systems and information on the Evans and Sutherland company that created them.

http://vulcan.wr.usgs.gov/Imgs/Gif/Rabaul/tv_imgs.html

Digitized images from the Rabaul volcano eruption in Papua New Guinea.

http://www.libertynet.org/~dvaa/photos.html

Digitized pictures of astronomical events taken by members of the Delaware Valley Amateur Astronomers club. Pictures of the Hale-Bopp comet, other comets, planets, and nebulas appear.

http://www.lemkesoft.de   or   **http://members.aol.com/lemkesoft**

Individuals working with digital images will find this Macintosh program invaluable for converting among more than 100 different graphic file formats found on computers.

http://www-leland.stanford.edu/~dmiller/gwvis2sml.html

Download animations of current (that day) satellite data from the eastern Pacific Ocean. Works with several types of machines and browsers.

http://twister.sbs.ohio-state.edu/satimages.html

Links to many different views of the continental United States from several different satellites using daily weather information. Includes false-colored (according to current temperature) and infrared images.

http://www.pcwebopedia.com/bit_mapped_graphics.htm

Definition and information on bitmapped graphics. Includes a description of file formats for bitmapped graphics.

**http://www.bergen.org/AAST/ComputerAnimation/
CompAn_Graphix.html**

Information on creating computer-generated animations. Links to all the major issues in computer graphics, including bitmapped, object-oriented, morphing, digitizing, and many more.

http://www-graphics.stanford.edu/demos/

Demonstrations of 2D and 3D computer-generated graphics. Also links to results of graphics-rendering competitions.

http://www.llnl.gov/graphics/

Information on scientific visualization. Includes links to images and movie clips based on visualization.

Bibliography

Kientzle, Tim. *Internet File Formats*. Scottsdale, AZ: Coriolis Group Books, 1995.

A summary overview of file formats for sound, graphics, movies, and an overview of the subject of file compression.

McCorduck, Pamela. *AARON's Code: Meta-Art, Artificial Intelligence, and the Work of Harold Cohen*. New York: W. H. Freeman, 1991.

A complete description of the work of Harold Cohen.

Tufte, Edward R. *Envisioning Information*. Cheshire, CT: Graphics Press, 1990.

Foundation materials with many examples for understanding the ideas of visualization of information.

Tufte, Edward R. *The Visual Display of Quantitative Information*. Cheshire, CT: Graphics Press, 1992.

Tufte, Edward R. *Visual Explanations: Images and Quantities, Evidence and Narrative*. Cheshire, CT: Graphics Press, 1997.

Wolff, Robert S. and Larry Yaeger. *Visualization of Natural Phenomena*. Santa Clara: Telos, 1993.

Chapter 11

<table>
<tr><td>1846</td><td>The Speech Organ, developed by Joseph Faber, performs in London. It produces ordinary and whispered speech.</td></tr>
<tr><td>1876</td><td>The telephone is invented and patented by Alexander Graham Bell.</td></tr>
<tr><td>1895</td><td>First radio signal is transmitted by Guglielmo Marconi.</td></tr>
<tr><td>1959</td><td>Magnetic ink character recognition is used to process checks in a machine developed by General Electric, the GE ERMA.</td></tr>
<tr><td>1962</td><td>Software is developed at Bell Labs to design, store, and edit synthesized music.</td></tr>
<tr><td>1972</td><td>A "blue box" tone generator, to make free phone calls, is built and sold in the dorm at UC Berkley by Steve Wozniak.</td></tr>
<tr><td>1979</td><td>Japan and Chicago test the concept of the cellular telephone.</td></tr>
<tr><td>1983</td><td>MIDI (Musical Instrument Digital Interface) concept is introduced. This concept has been widely accepted and utilized by musicians.</td></tr>
<tr><td>1984</td><td>CD-ROMs are introduced, providing significantly improved storage capacity for digital data.</td></tr>
<tr><td>1990</td><td>The Dragon speech recognition program recognizes 30,000 words.</td></tr>
<tr><td>1992</td><td>First MBone audio multicast is transmitted on the Internet.</td></tr>
<tr><td>2001</td><td>Audio toxic detection meter detects botulism and other food problems.</td></tr>
<tr><td>2003</td><td>Digital audio broadcasting is common (*Wired* magazine).</td></tr>
</table>

Audio Communication Comes of Age

Chapter Objectives

By the end of this chapter, you will:

- ꙮ Recognize the importance of vocal communication.
- ꙮ Understand the difference between speech synthesis and speech recognition.
- ꙮ Identify uses of digital synthesized speech.
- ꙮ Identify limitations of digitized synthesized speech.
- ꙮ Understand how phonemes are used to form words.
- ꙮ Understand how inflection, duration, and elision affect phoneme-produced speech.
- ꙮ Understand how both voiced and voiceless sounds are necessary for speech.
- ꙮ Understand why recognition of disjointed speech is easier than recognition of continuous speech.
- ꙮ Know why a conversational computer is not a reality.
- ꙮ Understand how binary numbers are stored on compact discs and digital audiotape.
- ꙮ Understand how MIDIs aid composers and performers in all aspects of the music industry.
- ꙮ Know how sequencers and patches contribute to a MIDI-produced performance.
- ꙮ Identify audio communication produced by non-humans.

11.1 Audio Communication with Computers

Figure 11.1.1

For most humans, speech is the primary way we communicate with other people.

The five senses—sight, sound, touch, taste and smell—are the instruments we human beings use to communicate with others and our environment. Of these, sight (or vision) is usually considered the most important. Second, and very close in importance, is sound (or audio information). Most of the outside information entering our brains enters through our eyes and our ears. They are, indeed, input devices through which our world communicates with us.

The preceding chapter discussed the various forms of visual communication that have been enhanced, modified, or even created by computers. This chapter explores the effects computers have had on the world of sound.

Forms of audio communication are diverse, ranging from the sounds of nature to the sounds we humans manufacture. A few examples will serve to illustrate this diversity: the thunder of an approaching storm, the myriad calls and whistles of birds, the slamming of a door, the rhythm and melody of instrumental music, and, most important of all to us, the sound of human speech.

This discussion of the effects computer technology has had on audio communication explores three major areas: vocal communication, music, and non-human audio communication.

11.2 The Importance of Vocal Communication

A little thought regarding human communication reveals the importance of speech. Research shows that speech is by far the fastest and most convenient way for humans to communicate. Experiments comparing it with other methods of communication have shown that information is exchanged almost twice as quickly using speech as it is without speech. Try a little experiment yourself. Take an average day and jot down how much information you exchange with others using the most common forms of communication: written, visual (such as pointing fingers or looking angry), and vocal. The results will show that most of the communication you do is vocal.

Most researchers agree that the development of human intelligence is very closely linked to the development of verbal communication and language. Therefore, indeed, vocal communication is worth our attention.

This discussion of computers in vocal communication focuses on two areas of activity: **speech synthesis** and **automatic speech recognition (ASR)**. Questions of **semantics** (meanings) are addressed in Chapter 13, "Artificial Intelligence and Modeling the Human State."

Speech synthesis is the electronic production of sounds and sound patterns that closely resemble human speech.

Automatic speech recognition (ASR) allows computers to recognize and respond to human speech and sound patterns spoken aloud.

The term **semantics** refers to the meanings of words.

11.3 Speech Synthesis: Making a Computer Speak

Electronic synthesis of sound is relatively easy to accomplish. As one of the five basic types of information, sound can be easily represented by a series of numbers. (See

Chapter 2, "Metamorphosis of Information," for review.) Synthesis of human speech should therefore be a matter of translating a group of sounds into their binary numeric equivalents and then reversing the process whenever you wish to reproduce the original sounds. One way to do this is to record a speech selection and then digitize it. Then, when that particular selection of speech is needed, the digitized version is available.

```
2976: EC CF CB F0 30 51 4C 34 1D 07 F6 F5 05 00 C6 9B    ....0QL4........
2992: B6 08 5A 7C 61 23 E9 DF 01 24 26 02 CA A0 9E CB    ..Z|a#...$&.....
3008: FE 08 ED D6 E3 15 4B 5F 41 1C 0C 06 02 09 0D DA    ......K_A.......
3024: 9D 90 CF 2A 6B 72 3E FF E3 F5 19 27 15 C1 AA        ...*kr>...'....
3040: BA D2 D5 C7 BF CD 02 46 5E 47 27 18 17 13 05 01    .......F^G'.....
3056: F3 B8 89 95 EF 39 59 42 1A FB 05 21 27 14 F1 D4    .....9YB...!'...
3072: C8 D4 E6 EF DA BA AF C6 FF 46 65 48 2D 2A 2F 2B    .........FeK-*/+
3088: 21 14 E7 A9 8C B0 07 3C 4C 2A 0D FD 0E 1E 17 02    !......<L*......
3104: E1 CC C8 D9 E6 EF E2 CC C1 DD 11 41 4C 39 28 26    ...........AL9(&
3120: 2A 26 26 11 D8 A4 A9 F5 3B 57 3D 13 F4 00 21 2D    *&&.....;W=...!-
3136: 1A F3 C8 AE BA D7 EB EA DC C7 C8 EF 29 49 3A 21    ............)I:!
3152: 18 18 11 0D 12 E8 9F 80 B0 11 49 58 35 00 E6 09    ..........IX5...
3168: 2F 2D 0A DB B6 B0 C8 DE DD C8 B2 B6 E8 35 5C 4F    /-...........5\O
3184: 2E 1C 1F 26 17 00 02 F9 C0 8C 97 E4 2B 41 42 24    ...&.........+AB$
3200: 0E 24 40 3B 1C F9 CE B5 BB D2 DC D1 C2 BB D2 13    .$@;............
3216: 55 61 49 35 38 36 24 00 EA EF F6 D5 9F 95 CA 10    UaI586$.........
3232: 32 4B 45 25 0F 20 35 31 14 E2 B1 A3 BE D7 CD B3    2KE%. 51.......
3248: B3 DE 22 52 60 52 43 34 2A 1F 0C F0 E0 EB 04 E7    .."R`RC4*.......
3264: AF A2 DB 29 4E 4E 25 F5 FF 31 4B 2D F3 B6 9D B0    ...)NN%..1K-....
3280: CA C9 B6 B2 C2 E9 25 58 66 59 38 1F 14 06 EA D2    ......%XfY8.....
3296: CF E6 18 13 C7 9E D4 27 4D 44 2C 12 14 31 3A 18    .......'MD,..1:.
3312: E4 B3 A3 B0 CD D7 C7 B8 C6 F6 3D 6A 5E 36 1A 11    ..........=↑^6..
3328: 0C 06 F7 DD C3 C2 FA 39 10 B7 A5 EE 3E 6A 5C 2E    .......9....>j\.
3344: 05 14 2F 2D FA C8 9D 9D B5 DF F0 DD D6 F3 23 37    ../-..........#7
3360: 3A 34 1F 0F 15 1B 02 D9 CE D0 E6 1A 2E E3 AE DE    :4..............
3376: 36 48 3E 3A 1A FA 15 30 13 D0 9D 95 B7 B7 01 E5    6H>:...0........
3392: B8 BD F8 32 39 22 15 11 11 1C 12 E6 C9 D1 D6 E9    ...29"..........
3408: 2C 42 EB AC D9 33 41 32 32 17 F5 07 1C 08 D0 B5    ,B...3A22.......
3424: BC CF E6 EC DF BF CB 0D 3E 25 0B 24 33 29 24 12    ........>%.$3)$.
3440: E2 D7 FB 00 FF 26 25 D1 AD F8 4E 3E 1A 28 27 0C    .....&%..N>.('.
3456: 25 3F 27 E4 C2 CD E2 EF E8 D1 A7 B5 05 37 1F 0F    %?'........7..
3472: 32 3C 2F 34 29 03 E9 FF F7 DB E9 14 FC BC C1 0A    2</4)..........
3488: 29 21 3C 50 22 FF 18 29 FD C7 BD C3 C2 BF BB A6    )!<P"..).......
3504: A9 E7 1F 17 1A 45 52 36 2A 30 11 E9 E1 DE B8 B6    .....ER6*0......
3520: EC 16 EA CC 05 44 39 2E 46 3F 03 F2 11 06 D3 BB    .....D9.F?......
3536: C5 BE B2 C1 C8 CC DE 10 26 21 38 4B 41 B1 B0 0C    ........&!8KA&..
3552: E2 CB CD C6 BE D9 12 32 3B 25 15 24 36 41 3A 23    .......2;%.$6A:#
3568: F7 D3 DA EA F3 EA DE D7 E1 F3 04 0F 0C FF FE 16    ................
3584: 28 25 0D EE DD DB E4 EA E9 E8 EA FB 14 39 59 4B    (%...........9YK
3600: 10 06 32 39 17 F6 EC D8 D5 F2 0B 0A E9 DF EF FE    ..29............
3616: FD 04 10 F4 D5 E4 F8 EB D7 D7 E2 E6 EF F6 F7 FC    ................
3632: FC F5 04 2D 48 51 37 05 08 2B 29 0F FE FC E8 E6    ...-HQ7..+).....
3648: FA 0A 09 F4 F4 F4 EA E7 F0 EE D8 CF DD E3 E5 F4    ................
3664: FD F6 EA EA F3 EF E8 E6 04 2B 35 37 50 5C 2A 08    .........+57P\*.
3680: 2B 31 1A 0A 0A FC E9 EF FF 0B FA DC D1 D3 E3 FF    +1..............
3696: 0B ED C9 D2 F4 FD F4 EB E9 E9 EE F1 EC EF 08 18    ................
3712: 1B 25 3D 54 64 5C 22 F4 19 35 1E 02 F4 E1 CC DF    .%=Td\"..5......
3728: F8 F7 E5 DC F0 01 F5 EA E2 D8 CB C7 CF CD D5 E9    ................
3744: F1 E9 DF EF 05 11 18 18 22 33 46 4F 50 4E 28 F6    ........"3FOPN(.
3760: FF 19 18 0E 09 F7 D7 DA 07 28 13 E4 D6 D8 D4 E0    .........(......
3776: EE DC B5 AD D4 E8 DD E3 F1 F6 FA 0B 17 0B 02 0D    ................
3792: 17 1D 27 3C 4F 60 65 3C F1 F6 26 2C 15 F9 EA CD    ..'<O`e<..&,....
3808: DE 12 23 05 CC D6 F4 FE 0D 0C E2 AD AC DB E4 CD    ..#.............
3824: CC DE E5 EC 0F 2B 28 32 49 4D 40 40 4C 42 38 43    .....+(2IM@@LB8C
3840: 32 DC B5 F4 22 11 E3 D3 D0 D4 FE 2E 2A DE CF FE    2..."......*....
3856: 06 F5 EF C9 96 84 A8 C0 A8 A7 CE F1 04 21 3F 40    .............!?@
3872: 39 4D 56 33 15 1F 29 23 2D 35 FE B6 D5 29 2B F4    9MV3..)#-5...)+.
3888: D4 E6 E6 04 3C 3B E4 B0 ED 0B E6 EA E4 BA 93 AB    ....<:..........
3904: DA C2 A7 C8 FA 02 07 3B 5A 4E 59 68 4D 24 2F 4B    .......;ZNYhM$/K
3920: 37 1F 2C 29 D3 B1 08 30 FD D0 E8 E7 CE 0C 3E 13    7.,)...0......>.
3936: D4 F4 2F 13 F7 F2 D6 AA 9C C4 C0 9C AC E0 F7 F7    ../.............
3952: 2F 65 5A 63 79 5D 32 30 49 27 FC 08 27 14 BF AB    /eZcy]20I'..'...
```

Figure 11.3.1

Hexadecimal numeric representation of 1/10 of a second of human speech. Curley Joe saying, "I'm trying to think."

Digitized Recordings of Human Speech

Early attempts at speech synthesis used a recording technique to produce a limited vocabulary of utterances. One device that used this technique was the Texas Instruments Speak & Spell, now no longer available. Designed to teach a child to spell, it could pronounce aloud 230 different words, one at a time. After each word was pronounced, the child pressed the keys corresponding to the spelling of the word. The digitized voice pronounced each letter appearing onscreen and indicated whether the spelling was correct.

More recent devices using the **digitized recording** method of speech synthesis can be heard regularly in department stores and supermarkets. Some cash registers speak aloud each amount of money being entered, as well as the total amount owed, the amount tendered by the customer, and the change due. A few even thank the customer, very politely, for shopping in that store.

Figure 11.3.2

In a computer/language lab, students can hear digital recordings of correctly spoken examples before testing their own pronunciation.

Instructional Language Labs

Instructional language laboratories make especially effective use of digitized speech recordings in pronunciation exercises. Lab students first listen to a correctly pronounced foreign language word or phrase, and then record their own pronunciation of that example. The educational language program then compares the student's pronunciation of each example with the original digitized recording, and analyzes the differences. If the student's recorded pronunciation matches the original, the computer presents a new word or phrase to practice. If the student's pronunciation is not correct, the original digitized recording is replayed so that the student can listen and try again.

Other uses of digitized speech recordings include many commonly available commercial software programs. America Online, for example, a network service, includes a welcoming message spoken aloud. Adventure game programs often congratulate the player on successful completion of a task, or offer spoken clues for solving a problem. And educational programs often offer recorded spoken feedback as well as musical encouragement.

Programming a Talking Cash Register

Although digitized recording is the easiest way to synthesize human speech, the process requires a lot of planning. Let's use the talking cash register as an example. Before we can start synthesizing, we need a very complete list of the words and phrases our cash register must say aloud. This includes words needed to represent amounts of money: numbers such as *one*, *two*, *seven*, *ten*, *twenty*, *sixty*, and so forth, and words such as *dollar*, *dollars*, *and*, and *cents*. We also need some phrases, such as *your total is*, *your change is*, *thank you very much*, and so on. Every word and phrase needed for everything the cash register must say must be included.

Figure 11.3.3

Many late-model cash registers are actually computer terminals, capable of synthesized speech.

After this list is complete, each word and phrase on the list must be spoken by a human and recorded. Each recorded word or phrase must then be individually digitized and stored separately in the computer's memory. The computer controlling the cash register must then be programmed to string together whichever digitized pieces of speech are needed to reproduce a complete utterance. Seven different digitized pieces must be strung together, for example, for a cash register to say, "Your total is ten dollars and twenty-seven cents."

The automated national telephone information service also uses synthesized speech composed of recorded words and phrases. In this case, longer "phrases" may be needed, such as, "this call may be dialed automatically for an additional charge," as well as the numbers from 0 to 9 and words such as "area code" and "the number is." When the information operator locates the number you requested in an electronic directory, the computer reads the number and then strings together the required digitized words and phrases, transmitting them to you via the phone line.

Limitations of Digitized Recording for Speech Synthesis

Some definite problems occur when using this approach to speech synthesis. The 230 words for the Speak & Spell device described earlier occupied about 250,000 bits of memory and were spoken one at a time. They were never grouped as phrases or sentences. To re-create whole sentences of human speech using even a minimal vocabulary of recorded words would take a huge amount of computer memory, to say nothing of an extended period of time. In addition, many words would have to be recorded and digitized more than once. We say words differently at the end of a statement than we do at the end of a question. And words that occur in the middle of a sentence are often spoken with different pitch and volume levels from those that occur at the ends. Therefore several digitized versions of each word might be needed to account for all possibilities. Because the number of words in any human language is enormous (English contains an especially huge vocabulary), the memory needed to store digitized versions of all words in all possible inflections is prohibitive.

Indeed, pure recording and playback is suitable for only a small number of voice synthesis applications. A different approach is obviously needed. Therefore, let us examine another, more useful methodology.

Combining Phonemes to Create Speech

The study of human speech has resulted in the categorizing of various sounds of any given human language into a finite number of units called **phonemes**.

The table in Figure 11.3.4 gives a slightly simplified list of American English language phonemes found in standard prose. Notice that English sometimes uses two letters to spell one sound, and sometimes one written letter might stand for two or more different sounds in different written words.

Difficulties of Phoneme Definition

You may not agree with the number of vowel or consonant phonemes listed in Figure 11.3.4. That's because we do not all say things in exactly the same way. Some speakers make a distinction between the vowels in Mary, merry, and marry, for example, but others don't. Some people think that Wales and whales are spelled differently because they begin with different phonemes; to others, the spelling difference is merely an annoying visual difference, because they pronounce the two words exactly the same way. Such differences in slicing up phonetic reality will become important when we try to teach computers to recognize and understand human speech.

At first, it might seem to be a relatively easy task to construct natural-sounding words and phrases by just stringing together the proper phonemes. Unfortunately, that is not true. Three additional factors have a great affect on how a word or phrase sounds. The first, **inflection**, involves the rising or falling pattern of pitch on an individual phoneme.

Phonemes are the fundamental sounds of any given human language. There may be two or more ways to spell any one phoneme. The phonemes needed to pronounce the word *there*, for example, may also be spelled *their* and *they're*.

The second factor affecting the way a particular word sounds is the **duration** of one or more phonemes. Finally, the two or more phonemes that make up a word or phrase must be spliced so that when one of them ends and the next begins, the connection will sound natural. This is called **elision**.

Figure 11.3.4 *The phonemes of American English.*

Vowels	Consonants			
ee as in bee	p	pea	b	bee
i as in mitten	t	tea	d	Dee
e as in make	k	key	g	gone
eh as in led	f	fee	v	vee
ae as in had	s	see	z	zip
ah as in father	sh	sheep	zh	vision
aw as in small	tsh	chest	dzh	jaw
o as in go	r	rate	m	me
u as in put	y	yet	ëm	chasm
oo as in tool	w	Wales	n	not
uh as in the	hw	whales	ën	Eden
er as in anger	h	he	ng	sing
ai as in while			l	lee
ou as in how			ël	cradle
oi as in toy				
iu as in fuse				

Besides all of this, human speech, controlled by the brain, unconsciously introduces stresses and pauses into our speech. The linguistic rules that determine these are specific to whatever native language we speak, and are learned from childhood. One such habitual rule in American English, for example, involves lowering both pitch and volume for the period at the end of a sentence, but raising the pitch slightly at a comma to indicate that the sentence continues. Rules of this type are very difficult to program into the computer, and therefore make natural speech difficult to synthesize.

The Kurzweil Personal Reader

In spite of the obvious complexity of human speech, several rather respectable speech synthesizers are commercially available. One of particular significance involves a machine that can read printed text out loud! By moving a handheld scanning device over an open page of a newspaper, magazine, book, letter, report, or other printed text, as shown in Figure 11.3.5, a voice will speak the printed words at up to 300 words per minute. The user can cause the machine to read all or part of the page, to back up and repeat portions, to spell particular words, and to record specified parts of text.

Scanning the Document

Optical character recognition (OCR) allows a printed or typed document digitized as a visual image to be converted into a text file in the computer's memory.

The **Kurzweil Personal Reader** is hailed as the biggest breakthrough for the blind since the development of Braille. It consists of two major parts: an **optical character recognition (OCR)** system, and a speech synthesis component. The OCR system can recognize

The Computer Continuum

several hundred different styles of type. Optical character recognition (OCR) is accomplished by a specialized combination of software and hardware. A **scanner** first senses and digitizes the printed image into binary form. The OCR software then converts the bit stream into words and sentences by using the spaces and punctuation of the original written text.

After the OCR software has processed the scanned text, the speech synthesis component of the Personal Reader takes over. It utilizes the phoneme construction of the words to build spoken messages instead of digitizing and recording the hundreds of thousands of words that can be encountered in text material. During this phoneme analysis phase, the Kurzweil Reader uses 40 to 50 phonemes, about 1,000 rules of punctuation, and over 2,000 exceptions to those rules in a special dictionary.

Figure 11.3.5

The Kurzweil Personal Reader.

Ray Kurzweil—Visionary

When Ray Kurzweil formed Kurzweil Computer Products in 1974, he stated, "Our goal was to solve the problem of omnifont (any type font) optical character recognition (OCR) and to apply the resulting technology to the reading needs of the blind as well as to other commercial applications." In achieving this goal, Kurzweil created the world's first print-to-speech reading machine for the blind. The first Kurzweil Reading Machine was introduced in 1976, and is said to be the first commercial product that successfully incorporated artificial intelligence technology.

In 1982 he went on to found Kurzweil Music Systems (KMS). This musical direction was inspired by family musical interests and conversations with Stevie Wonder, a user of the Kurzweil Reading Machine. KMS created the world's first electronic keyboard that had the feel of a real keyboard, and in addition it also accurately re-created the sound of not only a grand piano but other orchestral instruments as well. The K250 was introduced commercially in 1984 and "was considered to be the first electronic musical instrument to successfully emulate the sounds of a grand piano and a wide variety of other instruments: orchestral string instruments (violin, viola, and so forth), guitar, human voice, brass instruments, drums, and many others."

At the same time KMS was formed in 1982, Ray Kurzweil also founded Kurzweil Applied Intelligence (KAI). Its goal was to "master automatic speech recognition (ASR) technology and to integrate ASR with other AI technologies to solve real-world problems."

Ray Kurzweil's creative contributions to the world of sound and artificial intelligence have resulted in many real-world successful applications. The various efforts in speech recognition and music are still actively developing along the cutting edge.

Producing Speech

After a string of phonemes is ready for output, the actual sounds produced are electronically generated. Although the voice production component does not resemble the human vocal system, the sounds it produces simulate those produced by the human vocal tract shown in Figure 11.3.6. Thus it can produce both major types of human sounds: voiced and voiceless. **Voiced sounds** include all vowels and some consonants, such as *b*, *d*, and *g*. Examples of **voiceless sounds** are the consonants *p*, *t*, and *k*. The Personal Reader has separate sound sources that produce voiced and voiceless sounds.

Figure 11.3.6
A cross-section of the human vocal system.

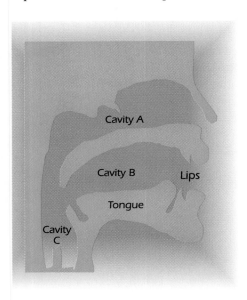

Voiced sounds in human speech are those produced by the vibration of the vocal cords in conjunction with specific positioning of the teeth, tongue, and the lips.

Voiceless sounds in speech are characterized by the lack of vibration of the vocal chords.

Solving a Few Complex Problems

In addition to providing the proper sounds, the Kurzweil Reader deals with many other complex problems to produce reasonably intelligible speech.

One interesting problem involves stringing together the synthesized words to form an intelligible sentence. This involves syntactical rules to apply the proper inflections and accents on words within the sentence. By using rules of this nature, the Kurzweil Reader produces more natural speech than the monotone speech usually ascribed to computers.

The recognition of words and the computations to produce intelligible sound are done fast enough to produce a speech rate of 300 words a minute. The reading and pronunciation of the English language is very complex, so it is quite understandable that mistakes are made. When this happens, the listener will realize something is wrong from the context of the sentence. The Personal Reader can then be backed up to spell the word in question, letter by letter.

This very brief glimpse of speech synthesis is by no means complete. Volumes have been written on the subject. Several things should be clear, however. Spoken language can be broken down into sound units called phonemes. These phonemes can be strung together and pronounced with the proper pitches, accents, and pauses to produce intelligible spoken language, following the linguistic rules we humans use unconsciously. Examples of reasonably good speech synthesizers were discussed. We did not discuss how an electronic circuit could be constructed, which in effect pronounces the phonemes with proper accent and pitch. The latter topic is not appropriate for discussion in this book.

The following topic focuses on whether computers or other machines can recognize speech.

11.4 Analysis and Recognition of Speech

Recognition of speech is inherently more difficult than speech synthesis. To better understand why, let's first look at some examples of problem areas. The following phrases are self-explanatory. Just say each pair out loud several times. Have someone else listen for any problems that may occur in recognizing which version was spoken. Remember that regional accents and speech impediments would complicate the situation even further.

Till Bob rings…
Till Bob brings…

I scream…
Ice cream…

The slip…
This lip…

How can a computer distinguish between similar sounding, but different strings of phonemes?

Complexities of Human Voice Production

Before we discuss possible solutions to the apparent problems that these examples illustrate, let's examine the vehicle that carries the words. The actual sound, which can be thought of as a stream of phonemes, can be visually recorded in what is called a **voiceprint**. Figure 11.4.1 is a voiceprint of a male speaker saying the word *said*. Examine it carefully and notice that it seems to be divided into two major components, in the left and center, followed by a less noticeable minor component on the right. The leftmost component is the *s* phoneme; the one in the center is the *…eh* sound. Finally, on the right, we see the pattern created by the *…d* phoneme. Say the word several times, slowly, to note the three phonemes that make up the sound structure.

If phonemes were the only components of vocal production, we could expect all voiceprints recording the same string of phonemes to look exactly alike. If this were true, voice recognition would be a simpler process.

The mind-boggling truth is this: No two voiceprints are completely identical. That's because the exact sound of each human voice (no matter what it is saying) is determined by at least two qualities: **pitch** and **resonance**. These in turn depend on the unique way each individual voice is formed.

Refer for a moment to Figure 11.3.6. Notice that three rather large cavities occur in the vocal tract, marked in this cross-section as

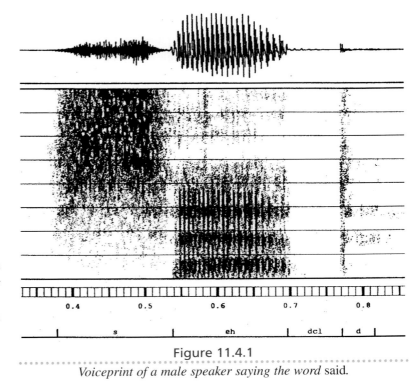

Figure 11.4.1

Voiceprint of a male speaker saying the word said.

Cavity A, Cavity B, and Cavity C. A vocal sound is created by vibration of the vocal chords, two flaps of membrane located below Cavity C in a person's throat. The thickness of the vocal chords largely determines the pitch of the voice produced. Before emerging from the mouth, each vocal sound is amplified, by Cavities A, B, and C. The size and shape of these cavities (sometimes called resonating chambers) determines the resonance, or quality, of the person's voice.

Because each individual has uniquely shaped vocal chords and resonating chambers, each has a uniquely individual voice. The implications for computer voice recognition are clear: If each and every voice is different, and if different individuals pronounce phonemes differently, how can a computer recognize similar words spoken by different people?

Recognizing Disjointed Speech

When words are spoken individually or separately, each chunk of sound represents a single word. Recognizing individual words in a limited vocabulary is not too difficult a problem. In fact, this type of single-word recognizer is available for many home computers.

The simplest systems for recognizing isolated words are restricted to only those individuals who have had a recording session with the computer. The individual must pronounce each word of the limited vocabulary several times. The speech recognition system in effect averages all pronunciations of each word to get a template of that word. After this recording session, the speech recognition system has "learned" its vocabulary and is capable of recognizing any of its limited number of words as long as they are spoken separately by the original speaker. The obvious disadvantages of this type of system are as follows:

- Each person must go through a recording session to train the computer.
- The computer's total vocabulary is usually limited to fewer than 1,000 words spoken by a single individual.
- The process of speaking in disjointed speech is very unnatural.
- Any change in an individual's voice—caused, for example, by a head cold, sinus infection, or dental anaesthetic—may change the voice too much for the computer to recognize it.

More sophisticated computer systems for recognizing **disjointed speech** can distinguish vocabulary words spoken by various individuals, as long as they all pronounced those words with reasonable similarity. Differing regional and foreign accents would not be easily recognized. A system of this type might divide the population of the United States into four groups—northern male, northern female, southern male, and southern female. Even with this division, words such as *nine* and *none* are still sometimes confused by the system.

This doesn't even begin to address the problem of homonyms—words that sound exactly alike—such as *I* and *eye* or *aisle*, *I'll*, and *isle*. Equally difficult for the computer to distinguish are words such as *coke*, *kick*, and *kook*. Figures 7.4.2a, b, and c illustrate the voiceprints for them. Note that the main distinguishing features of each voiceprint are the duration and frequency of the middle phoneme. Time in milliseconds is measured across the bottom of each voiceprint, and the frequency is represented on the vertical axis, with each horizontal line representing 1000 Hertz.

The Computer Continuum

In both types of difficulty, the context in which the words are spoken is needed to discern which usage is meant. The context of a spoken word is also used in a different category of speech recognition—continuous speech.

Recognizing Continuous Speech

Continuous speech is our normal, conversational way of speaking. The words are usually strung together with varying or no pauses between words. An example of this is found in the words *Sue said it* shown in the voiceprint of Figure 11.4.3. The problem of identifying a word in a continuous stream of sound is considerably more difficult than recognizing disjointed speech. The difficulty is distinguishing when one word of a continuous stream ends and the next begins.

The ability of the human brain to recognize the words of continuous speech is not well understood. However, certain things seem to be at work:

- Nonverbal information, such as vocal intonations, and nonacoustic information, such as gestures and facial expressions, are used to fine-tune speech recognition.

- Contextual information helps us clarify confusing similarities and misunderstood words.

- The human brain uses a combination of semantic and syntactic information in recognizing continuous speech.

To date, attempts to mimic the speech recognition abilities of the human brain have fallen short of expectations. The development of a so-called **conversational computer** has been elusive. Until very recently, personal computers did not have the speed or memory size to support the demands of recognizing conversational speech. Therefore older systems provided only very inflexible speech recognition capabilities, recognizing only predetermined phrases by individuals whose speech patterns had been made familiar to the computer. Even within these limitations, recognition accuracy was unreliable, dependent on such factors as microphone placement and ambient noise.

Rapid improvements in both microcomputer performance and speech recognition technology have brought about recent advances in solving continuous speech problems. Several systems have been introduced that allow the computer to be speaker-independent, recognizing input spoken by any individual. One such system is IBM's ICSS (IBM Continuous Speech System.)

When the user opens a compatible application program, ICSS accepts each spoken command as a continuous-stream speech signal through a built-in microphone. The signal is then digitized and stored in the computer's memory in a compressed form. A complex recognition search is applied next. This utilizes comparisons between the digitized input and a set of built-in grammatical rules, phoneme lists, and phonetic models. The search delineates words that the computer can accept as recognizable input within the specific context of the application program being used. After acceptable words have been recognized, the computer can respond to the user's spoken command.

Several problems remain to be solved. For one thing, the number of words recognizable by the computer remains relatively limited. Most systems that

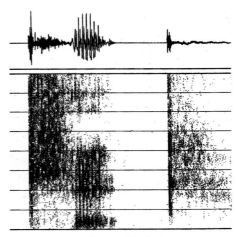
Figure 11.4.2
a) The spoken word kick.

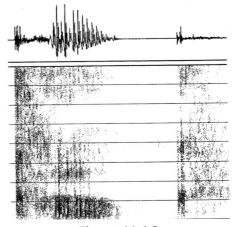
Figure 11.4.2
b) The spoken word coke.

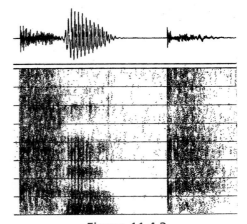
Figure 11.4.2
c) The spoken word kook.

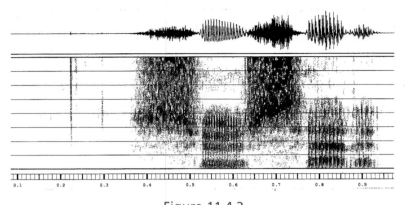

Figure 11.4.3

Voiceprint of a male speaker saying, "Sue said it."

can recognize continuous speech generally have smaller recognition vocabularies than those using discrete recognition. Those with larger vocabularies pay the penalty of slower response time. Larger recognition vocabularies also seem to sacrifice some degree of speaker-independence, often requiring speech training for the user and recognition training for the computer. Therefore, their usefulness is greatly limited.

The complexity of the problem of recognizing continuous speech leads many researchers to believe that it will be many years before a system can come anywhere near matching the human ability of speech recognition. The problem is not made any easier by the pronunciation distortions introduced into common utterances by individual speakers. Here are two examples:

What are you doing?

Whaddarya doin?

Whatcha doin?

Did you eat yet?

D'dya' eatchet?

Jeet chet?

Conversational computer:
A computer that recognizes and understands human conversational speech and can respond meaningfully.

If and when the problems of continuous speech recognition are solved, an even greater problem will still remain. This is the problem of getting the computer system to understand what the sentence means.

Natural Language Communication

The problem is not simple. First, we need to make a system capable of picking out the individual words of continuous speech. Second, the computer system must understand what the words are saying to make use of the information.

One final comment will shed even more light on this complex problem of **natural language communication**. The analysis in the preceding section would seem to indicate that a large part of our problem would be solved if we just separated our words. In fact, the solution seems to be no more complicated than putting the spoken words into print. In doing so, however, a tremendous amount of information is lost. A linguist was once heard to make the following analogy:

Think of spoken language information as analogous to the information absorbed while watching a football game from the 50 yard line. The equivalent written language would then be analogous to seeing only that part of the game occurring between the two 45 yard line stripes. This means that any speech recognition system that merely recognizes words is leaving out most of the information contained in the spoken words. Emotion and other subtleties of meaning would be left out of the system.

11.5 Computers in Music

It is impossible to ignore the impact computer technology has had on the world of music. The advent of the compact disc as a recording/playback device has brought computerized music to every living room and car stereo. Various forms of popular music depend heavily on synthesizers and computerized percussion pads to create the sounds they need. And DAT (digital audio tape) has refined musical recording technology to a fidelity indistinguishable from the original performance. Obviously the contribution computers have made to music and musical performance is worthy of study.

Our discussion of computers in music traces the following progression of computer use throughout the industry:

- Computers as playback devices—compact discs and players, DAT
- Computers as performance instruments—synthesizers, drum pads
- Computers as composers of music for ordinary instruments
- Computers used to compose and perform
- Computers used as an aid in conducting
- Computers as tools in new music areas

Preparing Digitized Sound

Chapter 2, "Metamorphosis of Information," briefly reviewed the process of putting sound into the computer. More formally, this is called representing sound in the computer. Let's review that process.

The easiest way to see how sound is represented in the computer is by examining the typical stereo system. The speakers of a stereo system must be connected with the other parts of the system by a pair of wires. This pair of wires allows a voltage to be applied to the speakers. The instrument used to measure this voltage is a voltage meter, which indicates the amount of voltage in numerical form. Flashlights, for example, typically use 1.5-volt, D-size batteries. This means if a voltage meter is attached to the battery, it will read 1.5. Another example is a car battery. These are usually 12-volt batteries, meaning that if a voltage meter is attached to the car battery, the meter will give a reading of 12.

Now with this voltage meter idea, just imagine that your stereo is blaring away and you decide to look at the voltage on one of the speaker wires. There is a problem with this. Unlike the steady voltage of a battery, the voltage of a speaker wire fluctuates rapidly. This variation is what causes the speakers to vibrate and make sound. To record a piece of sound requires measuring the size of the voltage (for example, the height of the curve) at many points in time so that the same changing voltage can be reproduced just as it was originally played.

As previously pointed out, to represent sounds with frequencies as high as 20,000Hz, 40,000 measurements per second must be taken. Electronic circuits that can read 40,000 voltage numbers per second are commonly available. The actual recordings are not done on the speaker wires. Instead, the recording is done with microphones that convert the sounds they hear to a voltage, which is recorded as a number representing the size of the voltage at that instant. These numbers are stored in binary form in the computer. Where the binary numbers are permanently kept is the next topic.

bits & bytes

Web Browsing: Why the Silence?

Have you ever noticed that Web browsing is primarily a silent activity? You can surf from page to page for long periods of time without ever hearing a sound. Here is why.

Size and quality of sound files: Sound files can be huge—often running to several megabytes in length. They can take several minutes to load on even a fast computer system. Although some types of sound files take less space than others, in general the smaller the file, the shorter the sound clip (in seconds) and the poorer the audio quality. Therefore, if you want to use a long piece of music on your Web page, you must sacrifice quality to keep the file down to a reasonable size. Here's an example: 16.5 seconds of music, recorded at acceptable quality, takes approximately 365KB of space. High-quality sound takes up several times as much space. Low-quality takes less space, but is often unsatisfactory, especially for music.

Sound File Formats: Many Web viewers are confused by the several types of file formats that have been devised for storing digitized sound. To overcome this problem, remember that most were developed for use with a specific computer platform. Here are a few popular sound file formats and the environments they originally ran on:

WAV—Originated with Windows 3.1

AU—Developed by SunAudio for UNIX systems, but now supported by other platforms

AIFF—Originated on the Macintosh

MPEG—Can be played on Windows, Macintosh, and UNIX systems

Hardware and software needs: Older computers and many Windows machines contain only low-quality speakers producing minimal sound. To play back Web sound with reasonable quality, these machines need a sound card and separate speakers. Some of the newer Pentium computers, designated "multimedia" machines, and most Macintosh computers come complete with a decent built-in sound system.

To use a sound file on the Web, you must use a type that your browser can play on its own or with the addition of a helper application called a plug-in. Fortunately, the newer versions of popular browsers can play many of the standard file types (see the preceding list) using built-in utilities such as RealAudio and Netplayer. For more exotic file types, plug-ins are available both as free downloads and commercial products.

Despite these drawbacks, many Web pages can benefit from the addition of sound. A site describing different species of birds, for example, might include samples of bird songs. A musician or band would want a home site viewer to hear samples of their music. And an individual, like you, might want to greet visitors to your site in your own voice. Here are a few tips for effective use of sound on a Web site:

■ If a sound clip is bigger than 500KB, it's too big to use.

■ Stick with good quality. CD and radio quality are acceptable; telephone quality and lower are not worth the time or effort.

■ Stay with simplicity. Don't opt for stereo when mono does the job.

■ Use standard sound file types whenever possible.

The Computer Continuum

Playback Devices: CD Technology

There are two common places to save the millions of binary numbers that are needed to record even a short piece of music. One storage place is the **compact disc (CD)**. Why has this revolutionary form of music recording swept the consumer music field? It's because CDs don't wear out like records and magnetic tape. After the number is recorded, it doesn't change. The only thing that can affect the quality is scratching the surface of the disc so that the numbers can't be read. In addition, compact discs can be produced very inexpensively by the thousands or millions from a master disc.

A microscopic look at the surface of a compact disc would reveal tiny craters or indentations in the surface. An indentation represents a 1, and the lack of an indentation means 0. To retrieve the binary numbers from the disc, a laser beam is reflected off the surface. When the beam bounces off the rough area around a crater, not much light comes back and this means the compact disc player receives a 1. With no crater present, the flat surface of the disc allows the beam to bounce back full strength, indicating a 0. Figure 11.5.1 illustrates the process. The CD player collects 44,100 binary numbers per second from the disc on each of the stereo channels and then transmits the appropriate voltages to the amplifier.

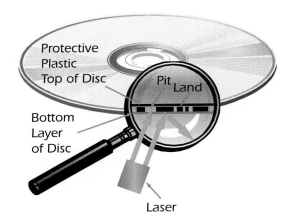

Protective Plastic Top of Disc

Pit Land

Bottom Layer of Disc

Laser

Figure 11.5.1

A schematic representation of a compact disc. The laser beam bounces off a crater and a flat land spot, indicating both a 1 and a 0.

Technically speaking, the CD player is a special-purpose computer. It manipulates binary numbers under a program's control. Granted, it is a very special-purpose computer. You can't even use it for word processing. On the other hand, its special purpose is enjoyed by millions of music lovers everywhere.

Digital Audio Tape (DAT)

The other place where the binary information is commonly kept is the **digital audio tape (DAT)**. The process in this case is to record the binary information onto a magnetic tape. These are not at all like the very popular audiocassette tapes, which store the electrical signals directly on the cassette's tape. Instead, the DAT stores binary numbers on the tape. A spot on the tape magnetized in one direction is a 1, and in the other direction is a 0.

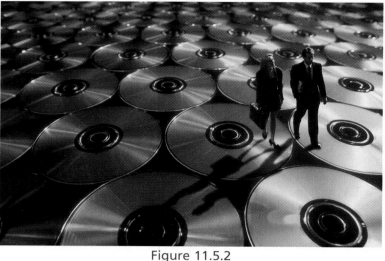

Figure 11.5.2

CDs are now the worldwide standard for recorded music.

Unlike the compact disc that needs special laser equipment to record, the DAT can easily record sound information. This is rather controversial because it means perfect duplications of compact discs can be made onto tape. Piracy of this type has the music recording industry very worried. However, steps have been taken by the recording industry to thwart the copying of CDs or DATs.

Instead of storing the sound information on either CDs or DATs, we could just leave it in a microcomputer or copy it to a computer disk. This can be and is done, but the volume of numbers is really too great to be practical. Also, the sound reproduction features of computers are not as good as typical stereo systems. The microcomputer does have another important part to play besides being a simple playback device like the CD or DAT players (computers), however. This special role is associated with the acronym MIDI.

Performance Instruments

The computer is playing yet another revolutionary role in the music industry, this time in musical performance. Although the role of a CD or DAT was a passive one, merely storing or reproducing what was previously performed, the role computers play as instruments is more active, actually creating the original sound.

Figure 11.5.3

Computers today play an active role in creating the musical sounds we hear.

Musical Instrument Digital Interface (MIDI) (pronounced mid-ee) is an industry-standardized means to connect music synthesizers, electronic drums, and music keyboards to each other, and usually to a controlling computer.

This revolution first surfaced with early drum machines. Percussion sounds were relatively easy to produce electronically, and as consumer demand grew, bigger and better drum machines were developed and perfected. Other instruments such as keyboards and synthesizers, electronic guitars, and other stringed instruments soon followed. Today nearly every contemporary music performance group uses several pieces of electronic equipment to produce their own unique signature sounds during a performance.

The really big breakthrough in music performance was the development of **MIDI** (the Musical Instrument Digital Interface). This musical-instrument standard is so important that the next section is devoted to it. For the moment, however, let's informally define MIDI as an industry-wide standard allowing electronic musical devices and computers to be connected together. This capability has created a revolution in musical performance. Many great performers such as Stevie Wonder, shown in Figure 11.5.4, use this technology.

To use the MIDI interface, a performance group must use specially built MIDI-compatible instruments. Ordinary acoustical musical instruments are not equipped for MIDI connection. Most MIDI instruments produce both the normal audio signal, which can send sound directly to amplifiers and speakers, but also binary signals that are sent to other MIDI instruments, or to computer-controlled sequencers. They must also be able to receive similar signals from other equipment connected to the same MIDI interface. A set of MIDI drum pads, for example, can actually send commands via the MIDI interface to a MIDI piano. The sounds produced would be made by the piano, but controlled by the drumstick's beating.

Some aspects of the MIDI performances are still missing. As traditional instruments are played, the musician does more than just play a note. For a violinist, for example, the angle of the bow and sharpness of the attack on a given note are created by subtle, very individual hand, finger, and arm movements. These gestures are very important in creating the individual sound and quality of a particular violinist's performance. Figure 11.5.5 shows a picture of a violinist with a MIDI violin. Notice the special electronic sensor attached to his forearm and hand. This device is electronically monitoring various wrist and hand movements Tod makes as he plays his cello. The information from the sensor is fed to a computer along with the sound information produced by his computerized cello. The cello is one of many hyper instruments that Tod has developed.

Figure 11.5.4

Stevie Wonder at his Kurzweil synthesizer keyboard.

Composing and Performing Music

Using computers in the performance of music is just the tip of the iceberg of musical uses of computers. Computers in musical composition have roots that go back even as far as Francis Bacon when he conjured up the idea of "sound horses" as described in *The New Atlantis* (1627).

Curtis Roads, the editor of *Composers and the Computer*, points out that the concept of procedural composition (that is, composing using programs) is not new. Guido d'Arezzo used lists of pitches and vowels with rules for assigning them in 1030. Mozart also used special rules in 1770 for musical games. In concept, a computer program is just a set of rules for a computer to follow. This rich heritage is a solid foundation for current twentieth-century efforts at musical composition.

Figure 11.5.5

Violinist playing with a computer-augmented violin.

As a part of composing, the composer must somehow communicate the score or musical ideas to the musicians who are to play the composition. Until recently, most composers had to laboriously hand transcribe their music. It is now possible to use the computer with the appropriate software to do a better job of transcription. In fact, it is even possible to play a MIDI instrument and have the computer record the music that can then be automatically transcribed. Figure 11.5.6 shows part of a score that was first played by the musician on an instrument and recorded in MIDI form. A special program was then used to take the MIDI recording and produce the score shown. The musician had to play each instrument's part of the score separately, accompanied by the parts already recorded in MIDI form.

At the beginning of this section it was noted how important MIDI is in all areas of music. The next section gets right down to the nitty-gritty of MIDI.

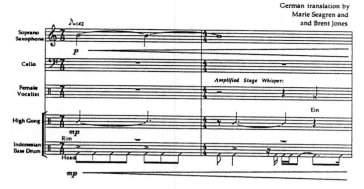

Figure 11.5.6

Part of a musical score recorded and transcribed by the computer.

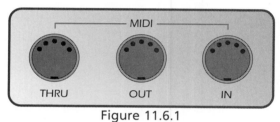

Figure 11.6.1

The three connectors necessary for a MIDI interface.

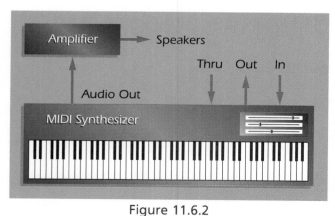

Figure 11.6.2

A MIDI synthesizer, connected to an amplifier.

11.6 MIDI

One of the biggest changes in our musical recording and performance field is due to the musical communication standard that was created in 1982. Called MIDI (Musical Instrument Digital Interface), this standard makes possible communication of audio information between keyboards and drum pads, and from them to a computer-controlled mixer. The results are astounding. Our discussion of computers in music finishes up with an exploration of the MIDI standards and their effects on the music world.

The actual connection made between the computer and instruments is referred to as the **MIDI bus** because it behaves like an electronic expressway, 16-lanes wide. The bus carries electronic binary signals to instruments that are capable of decoding the signals and doing what is commanded. The 16 lanes refer to 16 channels, each of which can be dedicated to a particular instrument or to a group of instruments. The digital data for each channel travels over the MIDI cable so quickly that 65 separate 16-note cords could be played per second using all the attached MIDI instruments combined.

Each instrument connected to the MIDI bus usually has a very small special-purpose internal computer with a built-in memory component. All MIDI instruments have three five-pronged connectors used to connect to the other MIDI instruments or computer via the MIDI bus. Figure 11.6.1 shows these three:

- **IN port.** Used to receive MIDI signals
- **OUT port.** Used to send out MIDI signals
- **THRU port.** Used to send MIDI signals obtained from the IN port on to other MIDI instruments

Using MIDI Instruments

There are several ways to use a **MIDI instrument**. The simplest is to just use the instrument by itself. A MIDI synthesizer, for example, shown in Figure 11.6.2, needs only the connection to an amplifier with speakers and it can be played.

Using a MIDI instrument by itself doesn't fully utilize MIDI features. A slightly more complicated MIDI configuration would be to use one MIDI instrument as a master to a second MIDI instrument, acting as a **slave**. In this configuration, the master not only can play its own notes, but it can also control the slave's notes. Therefore, only one musician is needed to play both instruments simultaneously (see Figure 11.6.3).

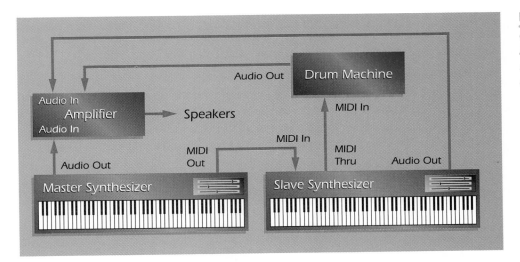

Figure 11.6.3
One way to exploit the benefits of MIDI is to set up a MIDI master/slave configuration.

Using a Sequencer

An even more effective configuration includes a **sequencer**. A sequencer can either be a computer with the proper sequencing software, or it can be a dedicated standalone sequencing device.

A sequencer can be thought of as a tapeless tape recorder. It records all the details of a musical sound (which keys are pressed, how long they are held down, how fast they are struck) and can play back exactly what was played by a human. However, most of its power comes from the fact that the recording can now be edited to change notes (that is, transpose), make tempo changes, and to modify just about everything including the type of sound (for example, change piano sound to that of a flute). A simple MIDI configuration including a synthesizer as master, a drum pad as slave, and a computer as sequencer is shown in Figure 11.6.4.

allows them to be modified, played back, or repeated on demand.

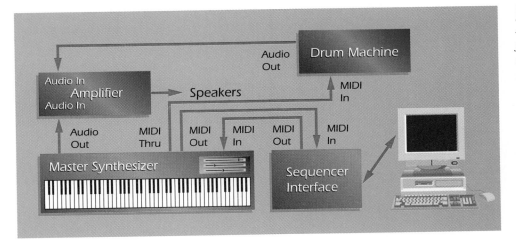

Figure 11.6.4
Another useful MIDI configuration is to attach the master and slave instruments to a computer, which then serves as sequencer.

A **patch** is a MIDI-compatible binary description of a certain customized sound that the performer has prepared in advance. Most synthesizers have libraries of preset sounds stored in the memory of the synthesizer available on demand at any time during a performance.

To make the system more flexible, a general-purpose microcomputer with special software is most often used as the sequencer. This allows some very interesting possibilities. Most MIDI software allows the use of **patches**. They enable the musician to customize the sound that comes out of the musical MIDI system by feeding in binary directions for producing that particular sound. If one section of a performance needs a special sound, for example, the artist can create exactly the right sound in advance and store binary directions for producing it in the memory of the computer or synthesizer. Then the sound can be incorporated into a performance, when needed, as often as desired.

There is yet another very powerful use of a computer-type sequencer. Suppose you would like to produce background music for some of your home videos. Using a sequencer, you could play a MIDI piano on one of the channels of the MIDI system. Then while this is playing back, you could record with a second MIDI instrument on another channel along with the piano. The program that records these two instruments could then play both channels back together in perfect synchronization and enable you to play yet a third instrument along with the first two. At this point, you would have a musical background custom performed by a three-piece combo—you, yourself, and your alter ego. This could be continued until the total piece is done, incorporating, if you wish, the sounds of an entire orchestra.

11.7 Non-Human Audio Communication

Although we have listened to sounds made by non-human creatures for many years, we have only recently begun to realize that we humans do not have a monopoly on meaningful audio communication. Other species of animals have also developed the ability to use specific sounds to communicate specific meanings. With the help of computers, research scientists have identified language skills in a wide variety of animals, from birds, to underwater mammals, to chimpanzees and gorillas. The discussion here focuses on two examples of audio communication in other animals, and the computer's role in their discovery and identification.

Studies of **non-human communication** have certainly not revealed any language skills comparable to those we humans are endowed with. However, many interesting and revealing types of audio communication have been noted. For hundreds of years, for example, humans have been awed by the wail of the loon in the evening around the northern lakes. The loon only has four distinct calls: wail, tremolo, yodel, and hoot. It also uses some combinations of those four. It is well-known that the loon yodel expresses aggression and is given to fend off loons that intrude on their territory. The combination tremolo-yodel shown in Figure 11.7.1 is an example of an aggressive call against an intruding loon.

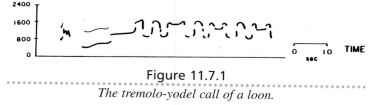

Figure 11.7.1

The tremolo-yodel call of a loon.

The computer can be used not only to record these calls, but also to act in the identification of individual loons—much as voiceprints of humans are also used for identification. These loon-call prints in turn can be used in loon research.

Other animals such as dolphins and whales communicate at audio frequencies; instead of the communication carrying through the air, however, the water of the ocean is the medium. Whale "songs" have been popular as part of pop music and are really part of whale communication. An interesting note is in the basic similarity of the songs of whales that are widely separated. Figure 11.7.2 shows some basic themes in whale songs discovered in the research of Katy Payne. Again, the recording, cataloging, and general research done on the communication of whales is supported by the computer.

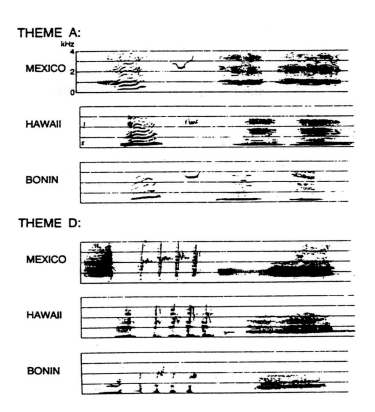

THEME A:

MEXICO

HAWAII

BONIN

THEME D:

MEXICO

HAWAII

BONIN

Figure 11.7.2
Two different themes found in humpback whale songs from widely separated geographic locations.

Chapter Summary

What you can do with what you have learned:

- Recognize digitized speech.
- Use a speech synthesizer to produce the spoken version of text.
- Break an English word into its component phonemes.
- Look at a voiceprint and pick out individual phonemes.
- Configure a MIDI system for your use.

Key Terms and Review Questions

Key terms introduced in this chapter:

Speech synthesis 3-106

Automated speech recognition (ASR) 3-106

Semantics 3-106

Digitized recordings 3-107

Phonemes 3-109

Inflection 3-109

Duration 3-110

Elision 3-110

Kurzweil Personal Reader 3-110

OCR (optical character recognition) 3-110

Scanner 3-111

Voiced sounds 3-112

Voiceless sounds 3-112

Voiceprint 3-113

Pitch 3-113

Resonance 3-113

Disjointed speech 3-114

Continuous speech 3-115

Matching

Match the key terms introduced in the chapter to the following statements. Each term may be used once, more than once, or not at all.

1. _____ This is the electronic production of sounds and sound patterns that closely resemble human speech.

2. _____ This allows computers to recognize and respond to human speech and sound patterns spoken aloud.

3. _____ This term refers to the meanings of words.

4. _____ These are the fundamental sounds of any given human language.

5. _____ The Speak & Spell device used this technique to store and play back speech.

6. _____ The Kurzweil Personal Reader uses this technique to store and play back speech.

7. _____ This refers to the rising and falling pattern of pitch on an individual phoneme.

8. _____ This term refers to the pronunciation of phrases in the form of "dja-know?" or "what-cha-doin?"

9. _____ This device allows written text to be read out loud.

10. _____ This device, used by a Kurzweil Personal Reader, senses and digitizes printed images into binary form.

11. _____ This part of the Kurzweil Personal Reader recognizes different styles of letters on a printed page so that the text can be read out loud.

12. _____ This is the term given to the visible version of a stream of phonemes.

13. _____ The vibration of the vocal chords makes this type of sound.

14. _____ These sounds are characterized by the lack of vibration of the vocal chords.

15. _____ This quality of a human voice is determined by the thickness of the vocal chords.

16. _____ The size and shape of the cavities (chambers) determine this quality of a human voice in one's head.

17. _____ The computer is less likely to recognize speech when spoken in this manner.

18. _____ This storage medium allows the recording of music in the form of binary numbers onto magnetic tape.

19. _____ This storage medium allows the recording of music in the form of binary numbers onto plastic-coated reflective discs.

20. _____ This standard makes possible communication of audio information between digital electronic instruments and computer equipment.

True or False

1. _____ Currently, computers can record only non-human audio sounds.

2. _____ The term given to the computer translating stored binary information into speech patterns is called speech synthesis.

3. _____ The Speak & Spell and the Kurzweil Personal Reader use the same method to store digitized sounds and speak that information out loud.

4. _____ The Speak & Spell and the cash register example use the same method to store digitized sounds and speak that information out loud.

5. _____ Using digitized recordings is as effective and advantageous as using the phonetic method of recording sounds.

6. _____ The scanner is the device that recognizes letters and changes each to its binary format for storage in the computer's memory.

7. _____ OCR software also recognizes parts of pictures and describes them.

8. _____ The Kurzweil Personal Reader is used mainly by the blind.

9. _____ The word *jar* is only made up of voiced sounds.

10. _____ The sound *sh* is voiceless.

11. _____ All human speech, no matter what language, can be represented on a voiceprint.

12. _____ The computer is more likely to recognize disjointed speech than continuous speech.

13. _____ A goal in research is to make a computer not only recognize speech, but to understand what is being said.

14. _____ Both DAT and CDs store binary information.

15. _____ Digital electronic musical instruments are connected to computer equipment using an industry-standard means of connection.

16. _____ MIDI instruments must be connected to a computer before sound can be sent to amplifiers and speakers.

17. _____ Although the computer allows music to be stored in memory and altered, the composer still needs to hand-transcribe the musical notes onto paper.

18. _____ Music played on a digital electronic musical instrument and stored within the computer cannot be altered from its original version.

19. _____ Humans do not have a monopoly on meaningful audio communication.

20. _____ Voiceprints have been used to identify individual animals as well as individual humans.

Multiple Choice

Answer the multiple-choice questions by selecting the best answer from the choices given.

1. Which of the following uses the digitized recording method of speech synthesis?
   a. Instructional language labs
   b. Kurzweil Personal Reader
   c. OCR software
   d. Human languages
   e. Scanner

2. This machine reads printed text out loud.
   a. Instructional language labs
   b. Kurzweil Personal Reader
   c. OCR software
   d. Human languages
   e. Scanner

3. This machine's function is to copy an image and store it in the computer in its digital form.
   a. Instructional language labs
   b. Kurzweil Personal Reader
   c. OCR software
   d. Human languages
   e. Scanner

4. The function of this software is to recognize letters.
   a. Instructional language labs
   b. Kurzweil Personal Reader
   c. OCR software
   d. Human languages
   e. Scanner

5. This is a fundamental sound of any given spoken language.
   a. Phoneme

   b. Inflection
   c. Resonance
   d. Elision
   e. Pitch

6. This is the term given to the splicing together of words or phrases so that when one of them ends and the next begins, the connection sounds natural.
   a. Phoneme
   b. Inflection
   c. Resonance
   d. Elision
   e. Pitch

7. This refers to how a person sounds based on the thickness of the vocal chords.
   a. Phoneme
   b. Inflection
   c. Resonance
   d. Elision
   e. Pitch

8. The size and shape of cavities found in the head characterize this quality of a human voice.
   a. Phoneme
   b. Inflection
   c. Resonance
   d. Elision
   e. Pitch

9. This factor of how a human voice sounds is determined by the rising and falling pattern of individual phonemes.
   a. Phoneme

b. Inflection

c. Resonance

d. Elision

e. Pitch

10. From the group of sounds, choose the one that is voiced.

a. Sh

b. Th

c. F

d. G

e. S

Exercises

1. Give some examples of phonemes in a particular language that give difficulty to those who are learning it as a second language. Try to find examples other than those used in the textbook.

2. Use the library to research and identify the 10–12 phonemes of the Hawaiian language.

3. Identify the African tribe that uses clicking sounds in their speech. Research linguistics books to try to identify its function.

4. Identify several examples of words that sound the same but are entirely different in meaning (for example, aisle and isle).

5. Give several examples in which removing a suffix could lead to a totally different word (for example, rating should be rate and not rat).

6. Identify the phonemes in the words shall, can't, mesmerize, and pumpkin.

7. Write a list of all the talking computers you have encountered. Do you think they use digitized recordings of words and phrases, or do they build their own words from phonemes? Explain your opinion.

8. What issues are involved in having a cash register say, "Your total is $4,622.73."

9. List four difficulties of using phonemes for speech synthesis.

10. Explain the differences between disjointed and continuous speech.

11. Why is continuous speech difficult for computers to recognize?

12. What does a musical instrument need to connect to a MIDI system?

13. List three advantages of the digital instruments over their conventional counterparts.

14. List three advantages of the conventional instruments over their digital counterparts.

Discussion Questions

1. How can you decide whether sound you hear from a cash register or other machine is synthesized speech using phonemes or a prerecorded digitized message?

2. Why is speech recognition more difficult than speech synthesis?

Group Project

A group of four students form a design team to design an ideal audio world for the blind. The team should have at least one blind student. If that is not possible, however, each member of the team will consult with a blind person. The first step shoul be to design a survey form for the blind that includes questions such as the following:

1. What is the most difficult problem you face?
2. What ideas do you have for audio aids of any type?
3. What are some annoying audio problems in your life?

The team should analyze the surveys and come up with a plan for a series of audio conventions and aids to assist the blind. These could include things such as sensors in public places that would activate a message or instructions. The sensor would be switched on by the blind person carrying a small transmitter in his or her shoe or cane. Keep in mind government allocation of the radio frequency spectrum for such devices.

Web Connections

http://www.bell-labs.com/project/tts/voices-java.html

Speech synthesis site. Enables you to type in text and have it spoken in a number of different ways (man, woman, child, raspy, and so on).

http://www.bell-labs.com/project/tts/index.html

Information on Bell Lab's text-to-speech projects. Includes some interesting examples dealing with context and abbreviation.

http://www.speech.su.oz.au/comp.speech/

Many links to speech-related sites. Includes speech synthesis, speech recognition, coding of speech, and more.

http://www.speech.su.oz.au/comp.speech/Section5/speechlinks.html

Links to a multitude of speech synthesis WWW sites, FTP sites, and newsgroups.

http://www.speech.su.oz.au/comp.speech/Section6/speechlinks.html

Links to a multitude of speech recognition WWW sites, FTP sites, and newsgroups.

http://www.itl.atr.co.jp/comp.speech/Section5/Q5.4.html

Links to many speech synthesis sites on the Internet.

http://www.itl.atr.co.jp/comp.speech/Section5/Q5.5.html

Links to speech synthesis hardware and software grouped by platform.

http://mambo.ucsc.edu/psl/smus/smus.html

Pictures of early mechanical speech synthesizers.

http://mambo.ucsc.edu/psl/pslfan.html

Information done on speech recognition by both audio and visual (facial animation) methods. Contains links to several interesting demonstrations.

http://teams.lacoe.edu/documentation/classrooms/patti/teacher/tools/tools.html

Electronic classroom site for assessing elementary student awareness of phonemes.

http://www.whatis.com/ocr.htm

Definition of OCR and links to related sites.

http://www.lantechatl.com/product/cntnuous.wav

Definitions of continuous speech and discrete speech and links to audio demonstrations of each.

http://www.win.tue.nl/2L670/dynamic/cd-rom.html

Good description of the CD-ROM, its history, and how it works.

http://www.pcwebopedia.com/DAT.htm

Definition of DAT and links to related sites. Includes a description of several different types, their storage capabilities, and speed of access.

http://www.OnlineBusiness.com/shops/_midi/BEST_MIDI_Archives. shtml

A lot of links to sites with free MIDI clips. Covers all types of music.

http://www.flexfx.com/

Links to sites with free MIDI clips sorted by music type, sequencer, and synthesizer.

http://www.flexfx.com/musicsof.html

Download software to work with MIDI files.

http://www.harmony-central.com/MIDI/Doc/tutorial.html

Tutorial on MIDI and music synthesis. Includes a description of a PC-based MIDI system and a lot of detail on how it all works.

http://www.geocities.com/SiliconValley/Pines/3119/nindex.html

Links to a number of MIDI files that can be listened to immediately or downloaded to your machine.

http://www.prenhall.com/~plugin/audio.html

Links to consumer, professional, and recording sites. Information for any technical audio enthusiast!

http://www.seaworld.org/sounds/soundfour.aiff

Information about how dolphin sounds are produced. Includes a link to actual dolphin whistles.

http://www.seaworld.org/sounds/contest.html

Animal sounds quiz. Click on a sound, listen, and identify what animal produced it from a list of possibilities.

http://www.onlinebusiness.com/shops/Cool_Graphics.shtml

Music patches and MIDI sound clips.

Bibliography

Keller, Eric, ed. *Fundamentals of Speech Synthesis and Speech Recognition: Basic Concepts, State of the Art and Future Challenges*. New York: John Wiley & Sons, 1994.

Penfold, R. A. *Advanced Midi Users Guide*. New York: PC Pub, 1995.

Penfold, R. A. *Practical Midi Handbook*. New York: PC Pub, 1995.

Chapter 12

Simulation: Modeling the Physical World

Chapter Objectives

By the end of this chapter, you will:

- Know why time compression is necessary to predict the future.
- Understand how the quality of the model used directly affects the quality of the simulation.
- Recognize the uses of simulation.
- Identify whether a model of a system is continuous or discrete.
- Identify whether a model of a system is predictable or probabilistic.
- Identify whether a model of a system exhibits feedback.
- Analyze the Monopoly game simulation as an example of strategy building with a computer.
- Analyze the SimCity simulation as an example of long-term versus short-term planning in a feedback environment.
- Understand how and why validation of a model is done.
- Know how simulation languages make writing simulations easier.
- Identify the specialized hardware necessary for virtual reality.

12.1 Reasons for Simulation

The concept of **simulation** is one of the most important in modern technology. It literally means *to imitate* or *to give the appearance of* something else. Typically, a physical or mathematical model is made to behave like the thing of interest; then by manipulating and working with the model, it is possible to predict, understand, experiment with, and test it, or even use the model for training purposes. A physical model of an aircraft is used in the wind tunnel, for example, to investigate the aerodynamics of the outside shape of its fuselage and wings. Of course, the wind tunnel experiment will not help in designing the cockpit layout for ease of use by the pilots. On the other hand, to investigate the maneuvering of spacecraft by astronauts during docking, a physical model is impractical. In this case a mathematical model that takes into account the gravitational pull of the Earth and other factors is possible. To better understand the whys and hows of simulation, it is quite helpful to look at the major reasons for using simulation. Then detailed examples of simulation become more meaningful.

Herbert A. Simon—Simulating Human Cognition
Born in 1916 in Milwaukee, Wisconsin, and receiving his Ph.D. in political science from the University of Chicago, Herbert A. Simon has had many illustrious honors. The most impressive is his Nobel Prize in Economics awarded in 1978. It was given to him "for his pioneering research into the decision-making process within economic organizations." More fundamentally, he indicated: "My central research interest is in building and testing theories of human cognition, using computer simulation models."

This interest in simulation had its beginnings when Dr. Simon felt that the social sciences needed the same mathematical rigor and foundation that the "hard" sciences found so successful. The desire to accomplish this caused him to comment: "I would prepare myself to become a mathematical social scientist." With his research ranging from computer science to psychology, economics, administration, and philosophy, a major thread tied it all together. The unifying theme was his interest in human decision-making and problem-solving processes, and how these affected social institutions.

Dr. Simon has put a great emphasis in the area of simulating human thinking. By using the tools of computing and techniques of artificial intelligence, he has made great contributions to this area. These efforts started back in 1954 when he joined with Allen Newell to attack the difficult processes in human problem solving by simulating them on the computer. This became a life-long practice as he states: "Gradually, computer simulation of human cognition became my central research interest, an interest that has continued to be absorbing up to the present time."

Forecasting or Predicting the Future

Time compression is necessary when forecasting or predicting the future. It is equivalent to speeding up the clock.

Obviously, in predicting the future some way of compressing time must be possible. Without **time compression**, simulating something like the depletion of the Earth's resources over a period of 100 years would take 100 years, and by then it might be too late to matter!

Therefore, one requirement is to make a model in which time can go faster than actual or real time. A very simple illustration of this concept would be learning how to use a new,

The Computer Continuum

rather complicated clock radio. You would like to become familiar with its operation before letting it take over the responsibility of awakening you for an important day's work. To do this, it is quite easy to turn the clock through a 24-hour period by hand in just a few seconds; the clock's operation during this period can then be observed.

The idea of using a model to predict the future is not unfamiliar. **Prediction** of the outcome of presidential elections, the weather, gross national product, yearly automobile production, the prime interest rate, the population of the United States, an eclipse of the sun by the moon, the price of a stock on the stock market, the pollution of the Great Lakes, flooding of river basins, pollution of the atmosphere, and the deer population in a national forest are all examples of using time compression in simulation. It should be noted, by the way, that not all predictions are correct! A landslide victory of Dewey over Truman was predicted in the presidential election of 1948, for example. As is well known, however, Truman won! On the other hand, some events, such as eclipses of the sun by the moon, can be predicted within seconds of their actual occurrence.

Important Point: Predictions are only as good as the model used in the simulation!

It should be clear that often it is impossible to know everything to include in the models used for simulation. Who could have predicted the rise in oil and gasoline prices before 1992, for example, when Iraq invaded Kuwait?

Simulation of the Inaccessible or Impossible

Many simulations are necessary because it is impossible to gain knowledge in any other way. Observing the collapse of a star, resulting from gravitation, to form a neutron star or black hole is impossible, for example. To understand the collapse of a star, astrophysicists create a mathematical model. Then a computer can perform the billions of calculations to see what happens.

Oklahoma Bombing Simulation

Engineering Animation, Inc. has produced a 3D animated simulation that realistically depicts the detonation that destroyed the Alfred P. Murrah Federal Building in Oklahoma City, Oklahoma, on April 19, 1995. EAI worked with explosive expert Kenneth Waltz and one of the original architects of the Murrah Federal Building, James Loftis, to scientifically depict the detonation and its damage to the building's structure.

After looking at the scene before and after the incident using videos and photographs, Waltz and Loftis combined their experiences to track the bomb's path and show the impact and devastation to the building. Loftis drew on his firsthand knowledge of the structure and design of the building and helped EAI determine the dimensions of the building's structure as well as its surroundings. Waltz determined the force of the shockwave based on his estimate of the bomb's force, and on his years as an explosives investigator.

Five frames from the final result of the animated simulation are shown. They depict the site of the Federal Building as it appeared just after the bomb detonates, unleashing a powerful shockwave and a fireball. The building is engulfed in a cloud of fire, smoke, and dust. As the shockwave penetrates the interior structure of the building, massive concrete floor slabs are pushed upward before they collapse.

It is also sometimes physically impossible to try all the possible combinations or ways of doing things. Intuition may help a chemist select just the right temperature, elements, and proportions to make a new compound. But intuition doesn't always lead to results.

Controlled Experimentation and Testing

Can you imagine what the total cost of developing a large jet airplane would be if it were necessary to build several complete full-size models? As each model was tested, design flaws would be corrected in the next full-size model, but it would take a lot of trials. Obviously, this is not the way to design and develop airplanes. Instead, very complicated mathematical models are run on computers. These models indicate design flaws that can be corrected and the new model can be "flown" or tested in the computer. When all the flaws seem to be gone, a full-sized model can finally be constructed. Of course, it will probably still have some problems, but generally they will be minor and can be corrected as more aircraft are built. This is considerably cheaper in terms of both money and human life.

bits & bytes

Monte Carlo Simulation

This technique, invented by mathematicians von Neumann and Ulam, is used to simulate certain types of real-life systems too complex or expensive to solve in other ways. It is named after the famous casinos at Monte Carlo because it makes use of pure chance to get answers. The military uses Monte Carlo methods in computer programs that simulate battlefield situations.

Jagjit Singh in his book *Great Ideas of Operations Research* shows how a chemical factory with only two loading docks for trucks can improve efficiency. When first observed, the situation has daily waiting times for trucks of 96 hours, and unloading crews of 50 man-hours. By using Monte Carlo simulation, the effect of building extra loading bays and/or hiring more personnel can be examined without the cost of actually making the changes. In this particular example, it was found that by building an extra loading dock the daily waiting time of trucks was reduced to 25 hours, although the loading crews idle-time increased to 76 man-hours daily. Because personnel hours are cheaper than truck hours, however, the extra loading dock would be a good decision. In this situation, and many others like it, the Monte Carlo simulation can determine in advance the effects of changes, while costing relatively very little.

Figure 12.1.1 shows an example of how computer simulation can be used to test a new type of bridge railing. Instead of crashing several dozen automobiles at various angles and speeds, which is both costly and dangerous, it is possible to give the computer program the information. The program will draw individual frames for an animated "cartoon." Researchers can then study the films and make necessary changes. An important point to remember is that testing the simulated model of a complicated system is sometimes more feasible than testing the real thing.

Sometimes, of course, computer simulation is not the best method for developing a new product design. It is much cheaper and quicker to design a flying disk for playing Frisbee by building several versions, for example. Then the best design is chosen on the basis of a test of the actual flying disk.

Another very important aspect of simulation is experimentation. It is sometimes disastrous to experiment on the actual system being tested. The U.S. economy, for instance, is very sensitive to changes in certain areas. Yet the federal government has the power to change taxes and prime interest rates, regulate rates for railroads and automobile gas mileage requirements, and control many other critical variables. How does the government decide to make a change in some sensitive areas? As you might guess, many decisions are made on the basis of how models of various parts of the U.S. economy behave. Unfortunately, the models don't seem to describe accurately how the economy really works. This is because so many unknown and unpredictable events affect the economy; therefore, no model of the U.S. economy can be entirely complete. How could something like the death of President Kennedy be predicted, for example? How could the effect of his death be incorporated into any model?

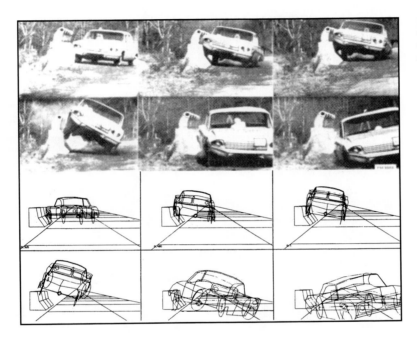

Figure 12.1.1

Simulation of an auto crash.

Education and Training

Among the most valuable uses of computer simulations are **education** and **training**. The following examples show how simulations allow greater flexibility and are often better than traditional methods for education and training.

It is often quite difficult to give the benefit of years of experience to people learning some complex skill. Diagnostics in medicine takes years of experience, for example, usually done on the job. But the simulation of patient-doctor relations can be extremely useful. One such simulation involves an interactive situation between the prospective doctor and a simulation that models an emergency. By typing into a computer, the doctor can request the vital signs such as pulse and temperature of the simulated patient. The time element is also incorporated; if the doctor takes too long, the "patient" dies! Records of how well the prospective doctor diagnosed and treated the various "patients" can be kept for progress reports.

Another interesting example of simulation involves management of salmon runs. Control over how many salmon are allowed up a stream or river to spawn must be exercised so that there aren't large fluctuations in population from year to year. Uncontrolled situations can yield bumper-crop years followed by lean runs. It is much better to have a steady, controlled growth of the fish population. Unfortunately, to gain experience in managing a fishery for 10 years takes 10 actual years, unless a simulation is used. A student of wildlife management can gain a similar experience in a matter of days or weeks, depending on the instructional pace.

To emphasize the vast number of applications where simulation is used, Figure 12.1.2 lists several areas of current simulation activity.

Aircraft Landing Simulation

Some of the more exotic interactive simulations appear in military training. Aircraft simulation is one that is particularly intriguing. The figure shows four snapshots from a training session of a jet landing on an aircraft carrier. The person at the controls of the imaginary moving airplane causes the picture to change. This particular system can also include other moving aircraft to simulate even more complex events. The pilot sees the other aircraft and has to make decisions, which in turn affect the picture being shown. This constitutes a good example of a feedback loop as described in the beginning of the chapter. It enables pilots to have preliminary flight training at considerably less cost than practicing with real aircraft. Evans and Sutherland developed the software for the interactive landing.

Figure 12.1.2

Areas of simulation activity.

Nuclear Power Plant	Bus Scheduling	Library Layout Design
Fish Farm Management	Airline Maintenance	Airport Design
Health Care Delivery	Job Shop Scheduling	Bank Teller Scheduling
Traffic Light Timing	Harbor Design	Electronic Circuit Design
Steel Mill Scheduling	Ambulance Dispatching	Consumer Brand Selection
Financial Forecasting	Inventory Reordering	Mail Distribution
Sales Forecasting	Police Response	Facility Layout
Railroad Operations	Election Predictions	Weather Prediction
Armed Forces Logistics	Urban Traffic System	Human Heart Functions
Space Shuttle Re-entry	Manufacturing	Sailboat Hull Design
Nuclear Waste Disposition	Ship Pilot Training	Auto Suspension System
Taxi Dispatching		

The Computer Continuum

12.2 Models of Systems

The word **model** has been used over and over again in the previous paragraphs. What is a model? As mentioned in the beginning, the model of a thing or system is something that fakes or gives the appearance of the system in question. There are many types of models, both physical and computer simulated. All these share some general characteristics.

Models can be characterized as **continuous** or **discrete systems**; a combination of continuous and discrete systems is also common. Models of continuous systems are those for which the observable characteristics vary in a smooth or continuous manner.

In simulating the landing of a rocket on the moon, for example, the quantities such as velocity, engine thrust, and deceleration are all smoothly varying. In other words, these quantities don't jump from one value to another value, but change smoothly from one to the other.

A simple example of a discrete system is the modeling of traffic at an intersection. There can be 1 or 23 cars passing through the traffic light, but not 1.5 or 7.6 cars. Fractions of cars don't make any sense. The number of cars "jumps" in units of one car.

Models of systems can also be categorized as being either **predictable** or **probabilistic**. The mathematical model of the solar system used to predict the eclipse of the sun by the moon is predictable. This is also true of the model of the orbit of a satellite.

Probabilistic systems, on the other hand, are those that are not predictable. The model for a roulette wheel is completely unpredictable, for example (unless, of course, it is dishonest). The model for traffic flow in the downtown area of a city is also probabilistic. It is almost impossible to predict when a shopper will decide to go home.

Another characterization of system models is the feedback versus nonfeedback feature. Feedback is a general term denoting the feeding back or recycling of actions or results of a model as input to itself. An automobile driver system is of the feedback type, for example. When a driver tries to avoid an object in the road, as in Figure 12.2.1, a turn away from the object is started. The eyes of the driver feed back information about how the turn is progressing. If the turn isn't sharp enough, the driver increases the turn. This system of recycling information is just one of the many human feedback examples. It is often referred to as a feedback loop. The figure of the driver illustrates a closed feedback loop. If the driver were suddenly blinded by the glare of the sun, the **feedback loop** would be opened, probably resulting in an accident.

Figure 12.2.1

Driver feedback loop during an emergency turn.

As you might guess, these classifications are not always easy to determine. In fact, some of the more complicated models have combinations of all the previously discussed characteristics: discrete and continuous, predictable and probabilistic, feedback and nonfeedback. To better understand some of these characteristics, a look at two examples in detail will be most helpful. First, we look at the game of Monopoly and then at an example of world resource and environment management.

12.3 Monopoly Game Simulation

A vast number of applications for simulation exists, but none will have a more familiar setting than simulation of that world-famous game Monopoly. Invented by Charles

Darrow in 1933, Monopoly is now marketed in 25 countries and has sold more than 80 million sets in the United States alone.

This section investigates a simulation that will help develop some winning strategies for the game of Monopoly. The ideas first appeared in an article "How to Win at Monopoly," by Irvin R. Hentzel.

Moves by each player are controlled by the random toss of dice or instructions given by randomly shuffled cards; the game is probabilistic. It is also discrete rather than continuous. Is there any feedback in the system? It depends, of course, on how the system is defined. If the system includes the players, there is definitely feedback. As moves are made, the players observe the game's progress and then make decisions on what properties to buy, and so on. If, on the other hand, the system is defined not to include the players but only the dice tosses and board play, it does not have a feedback loop.

The simulation considered here will model only the board play; in other words, the model will do no decision making. Using a general-purpose computer, a program can be written that carries out all the basic play of the game: tossing dice, moving pieces on the board, allowing property purchases, checking ownership for possible rent payment, drawing Chance or Community Chest cards, and all other relevant aspects of the game. A group of players can then sit around a terminal and let the computer toss the dice and perform other functions, while they make decisions about whether to buy property. As most players would probably agree, the presence of the actual board and money is more satisfying than having the computer simulate them. But remember, this is an exercise to illustrate how computers can be used to simulate systems! A detailed list of activities necessary to simulate the game of Monopoly follows:

- Toss dice
- Move game pieces
- Allow real estate purchases
- Allow hotel purchases
- Allow house purchases
- Draw Chance card if necessary
- Draw Community Chest card if necessary
- Toss second time if doubles
- Toss third time if doubles on second toss
- Go to jail if third toss is doubles
- Collect $200 upon passing GO
- Check for rent payment
- Keep records of each player's assets (cash and real estate)
- Allow mortgaging
- Get out of jail on doubles
- Get out of jail after third toss
- Go to jail if player lands in Go to Jail square
- Pay luxury tax when landing on Luxury Tax square
- Pay income tax when landing on Income Tax square

To understand the process of writing a program to play Monopoly, a look at a part of the problem is useful. Let's examine the problem of getting out of jail.

The general flow of play is best illustrated by a flowchart as shown in Figure 12.3.1. It represents the process of getting out of jail.

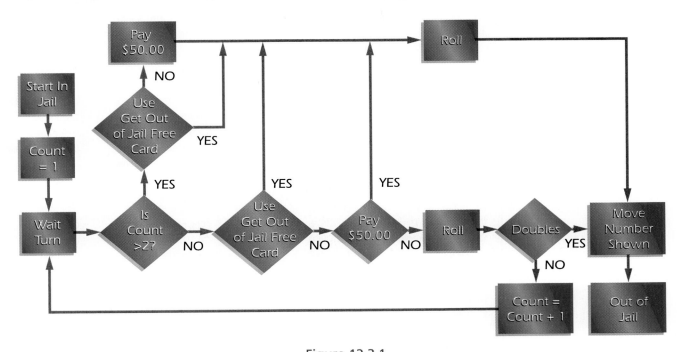

Figure 12.3.1

The flow of play, showing getting out of jail.

To develop strategy for Monopoly, certain types of information about the game are absolutely necessary. What information is necessary to help decide whether to build houses evenly on two or more of your monopolies, for example, or to build up only one of them? Of course, if you knew that your opponent is 30 percent more likely to land on one of them, it is obvious that this monopoly should be developed first. Obtaining these probabilities is somewhat difficult from a purely theoretical point of view. But if we could simulate the play of many games and record how often each of the properties were landed on, we would have the information necessary. Figure 12.3.1 is only part of the general scheme for a computer program that would play Monopoly. A complete flowchart of all the details is too much to consider here. Mr. Hentzel describes it as follows:

> The computer program … was used to compute the various probabilities necessary for mathematical analysis of Monopoly. The initial step in the program involves the determination of an assigned probability—the probability that a player will be on a particular square at the beginning of his turn. There are 40 squares a player can occupy, and, for calculation purposes, these are numbered in the direction of play. There are also three stages of being in jail.

> There is another adjustment to be made, however, before the computer can consider the first roll of the dice. This is to cover the possibility that a player begins his turn in jail, and gets out during that turn. He may do so by paying a $50 fine to the bank or by throwing doubles.

If a player pays the fine, he will move to Just Visiting before throwing the dice. To account for this possibility, we add the assigned probability that a player began the turn in jail to the assigned probability of Just Visiting. If a player in jail elects not to pay, he has a one in six chance of throwing doubles and escaping. This probability is spread among the six squares on which he could land if he did throw doubles. The probabilities for landing on squares 12, 14, 16, 18, 20, and 22 are each increased.

Figure 12.3.2

Probability of landing on each square.

1 Mediterranean	.0238252	23 Indiana	.0304690
2 Community Chest	.0210683	24 Illinois	.0355236
3 Baltic	.0241763	25 B. & O. Railroad	.0343378
4 Income Tax	.0260343	26 Atlantic	.0301120
5 Reading Railroad	.0332449	27 Ventnor	.0298999
6 Oriental	.0253014	28 Water Works	.0314613
7 Chance	.0096756	29 Marvin Gardens	.0289385
8 Vermont	.0259620	30 Go to Jail	.0000000
9 Connecticut	.0257326	31 Pacific	.0299534
10 Just Visiting	.0253909	32 North Carolina	.0293420
11 St. Charles Place	.0303370	33 Community Chest	.0264392
12 Electric Company	.0310260	34 Pennsylvania	.0279291
13 States	.0258042	35 Short Line Rail.	.0271871
14 Virginia	.0287890	36 Chance	.0096825
15 Pennsylvania Rail.	.0312800	37 Park Place	.0244447
16 St. James Place	.0318117	38 Luxury Tax	.0243572
17 Community Chest	.0272474	39 Boardwalk	.0294734
18 Tennessee	.0334833	40 Go Jail Probabilities	.0345904
19 New York	.0333734	J(1) Sent to Jail	.0444049
20 Free Parking	.0335340	J(2) In Jail 2 Turns	.0370041
21 Kentucky	.0310290	J(3) In Jail 3 Turns	.0308368
22 Chance	.0124010		

After running the Monopoly program through several thousand turns of play, the probabilities for landing on the various squares were calculated by Henzel's simulation and are as shown in Figure 12.3.2. The calculations assumed that all Chance and Community Chest cards are in play and also that players elect to throw doubles to get out of jail.

Examining this table, you see that the property most often landed upon is square number 24, Illinois Ave., but there are several other properties with probabilities close to this value. In fact, the top five properties most often landed on are Reading Railroad, Tennessee, New York, Illinois, and B. & O. Railroad. At first glance, one might tend to think that these are obvious candidates for ownership and development. However, what should be kept in mind is not merely how often an opponent may land on the square, but also how much it costs to develop the property and the return on that investment. A study of the expected return on investment is really necessary.

To calculate the return on investment, taking into account the probability of landing on that particular property, you need only multiply the probability of landing on a property by its rent; do this for each property in a monopoly and sum the results. Of course, the rent varies with how many houses or hotels are present. Figure 12.3.3 shows the yellow Monopoly deeds, for example, for which rents are $22, $22, and $24.

The Computer Continuum

Figure 12.3.3
Yellow Monopoly deeds.

As houses or hotels are added, the rents go up. Calculating with all the details for each house added to the group, a graph such as the one shown in Figure 12.3.4 would result.

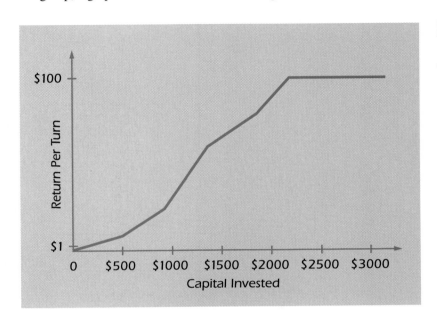

Figure 12.3.4
Yellow monopoly's return per turn versus capital invested.

Note that a maximum of three hotels can be erected on the yellow monopoly, one on each property. Therefore, even though additional capital is available, only $103.74 can be expected as return per turn from $2,250 capital invested.

Doing this calculation for all the monopolies results in Figure 12.3.5. Examination of this figure will help you develop two strategies for winning Monopoly.

Developing a Winning Strategy

On examining Figure 12.3.5, you see that for small amounts of investment capital, railroads are a good investment. Suppose, however, that $2,000 of investment capital was available; then the expected return from railroads is only about $30, whereas investing the additional monies in the yellow monopoly would yield $103.74, and the green monopoly would yield an expected return of $87. It seems that a player's investment plan depends on how much money he/she has available or will have available for capital investment.

This leads to a somewhat obvious pair of strategies: the Peasant and Tycoon Strategies. A player should first estimate how much money can be raised over the course of the game. The Peasant Strategy assumes only small amounts of money will be invested for development. Looking at Figure 12.3.5, you see that the orange monopoly reaches a maximum expected return with only $1,500 invested. It also has good expected return at lower capital investments; although at $500 capital investment, it seems as though the railroads and light-blue monopolies would be more desirable. Nevertheless, the idea in the Peasant Strategy is to invest small amounts early in the game.

Figure 12.3.5

Return per turn as a function of capital investment on all the monopolies.

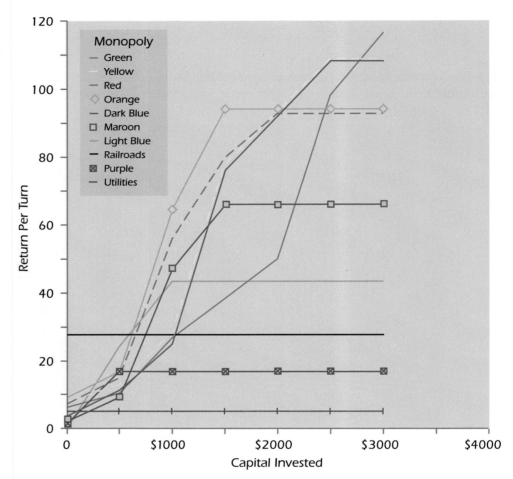

The Tycoon Strategy, on the other hand, assumes large amounts of investment capital will be available during the course of the game. The green monopoly has the highest return on investment, although it doesn't reach this large value until over $2,500 is invested. In fact, at $2,000, the yellow, red, orange, and dark-blue monopolies all have better return on investment. The Tycoon tactics involve delay of development and blocking of your opponent's development until sufficient funds are available.

This analysis doesn't treat the more complicated problems of multiple monopoly ownership. A more complex simulation could, of course, be developed which would shed light on winning strategies for players owning multiple monopolies. These types of analyses could become very complex indeed.

12.4 SimCity: Simulation of City Planning

SimCity is called a game. If your definition of a game is an amusement or pastime, however, SimCity is more than a game. It is rich in the details needed to do real city planning, which is not surprising. The influences on the author Will Wright range from Stanislow Lem's science-fiction anthology *The Cyberiad* to the indirect influence of Dr. Jay Forester of MIT, a world-renowned pioneer in dynamic modeling of urban environments. *The Cyberiad* involves the adventures of Trurl and Klapaucius, two of the greatest city builders in the universe. Because the objective of SimCity is to build cities, these influences are noteworthy. SimCity was first released in 1987.

Overview of SimCity

The basic thesis is that the player will build and run a city. But, there is the option of starting with a ready-made city. Of course, when starting from scratch building a city you must create everything. Either way, all the attributes of managing a city are well represented. These include things such as planning and maintaining the infrastructure, where the infrastructure includes the usual things such as power, water, and transportation.

A very nice feature that makes the game challenging is that as time goes by the power plants wear out and the roads become impassable. This means planning on replacements and repairs is necessary. There are a large number of choices regarding power plants as shown in Figure 12.4.1. Demands on water and power also have to be dealt with in ways that allow the city to grow. As the city grows, expansion must be done with appropriate zoning into residential, industrial, and commercial areas so as to attract Sims, the citizens that inhabit the city. If Sims don't move into the city, the city could collapse. Built in to the game are many of the common factors fundamental to today's cities, including supply/demand, tax sensitivity, quality of life, and other normal factors that influence city growth and development.

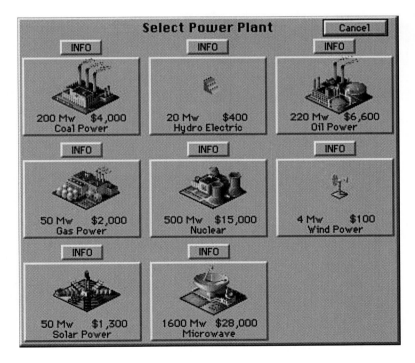

Figure 12.4.1
Choices of power plants in the year 2026.

Disasters are another feature included in the game. These disasters make the game more challenging in the sense that recovery from flood, fire, air crash, tornado, earthquake, monster, hurricane, and rioters takes skill to keep the city running. Each of these disasters has severe consequences, but a healthy city will survive. When a fire disaster occurs, for

Figure 12.4.2

The city Happyland with both fire and monster disasters occurring.

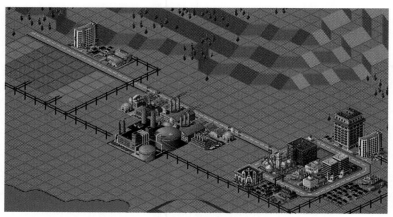

Figure 12.4.3

The effect roadways have on the growth of a city.

example, the proper preparation would have been to make sure that an adequate number of fire stations are operational. Neophytes can turn off disasters, however, which makes SimCity easier to play. Figure 12.4.2 shows both fire and monster disasters.

Consistent with all cities is the ability to tax and then spend the revenue on building schools, hospitals, recreation areas, seaports, roads, power plants, airports, police departments, fire departments, and many other things. But, it is also true that if the taxes are raised too high, people will move away and the city will shrink. This will lead to all the problems that can be seen in today's cities.

The model used to simulate the cities of SimCity is one that truly exhibits some interesting properties of all cities. As an experimental investigation of certain aspects of the model, a new city can be constructed with two commercial zones. However, one of the zones will have very good access through a road completely surrounding it. The other will only have a single road going along the side. Figure 12.4.3 shows that after 10 years, the commercial zone with the better access has a much larger residential community that has formed around it. Both commercial zones had the same amount of property zoned residential around them. This shows that the SimCity model seems to follow the normal course of development experienced in real life. This example also helps to reinforce a variation of an old adage: "Build a good city, and they will come." It implies that if planning is done correctly by today's standards, people will inhabit the city and both industry and commercial activity will flourish.

Planning Details in a Feedback Environment

There are so many details to master when planning a city. To get an idea of one aspect of this, take a look at an existing city in SimCity 2000 called Happyland. The roadways and other transportation have already been done, but the water supply is minimal. A series of three screen shots from SimCity's Happyland are shown in Figure 12.4.4.

In Figure 12.4.4a, the city of Happyland has grown to include residential, commercial, and industrial development. To see how the original zoning was done, the zoning view shown in Figure 12.4.4b shows high-density residential (green), city/government (orange), dense commercial (blue), light residential (greenish tan), and land not zoned (tan). After zoning is done, the Sims—citizens who inhabit the city—will make use of the land according to the zoning restrictions. However, several factors do affect development. These include access, water, power, and even desirability. Land zoned residential next to a coal-burning power plant will not develop as fast, for example. The water factor can enter into development when the supply is limited, as is the case with new development. Only minimal water is automatically supplied when the Sims build, but the infrastructurefor water is supplied. This underground water-piping infrastructure is shown in Figure 12.4.4c. The pipes are shown in the figure, as are some water pumps, which were added to supply the extra water that appears in blue.

It is interesting to note the complexity of this simulation by examining the water systems. As was already indicated, the Sims built the underground water systems as the land was developed for residential, commercial, and industrial properties. The supply of water to existing water pipes can be done in several ways. Pumps may be added, as was done in Figure 12.4.5c. The color blue in the pipes indicates water flow. The pumps are wells when installed individually away from fresh water, but they depend on the water table, which is lower in the dry season. When placed near freshwater rivers and lakes, the pumps produce three times more water, unless next to saltwater, where they produce the same as inland wells. A desalinization plant is needed to treat saltwater used for drinking. One way to deal with water shortages is to build water-treatment plants to clean and recycle the water. Another strategy involves using water tanks to store water during the wet season for use in the dry season.

Water has other uses. It can help development by providing transportation and shipping. Recreation can also be developed on the waterfront. Recreational areas, stadiums, parks, and green space provide a quality of life that attracts people and will allow the city to flourish.

Strategies and the Model

Strategies of many types can be used to play this game. However, some general ideas of long-range goals should be kept in mind. Suppose, for example, that the long-term objective is to grow the population as large as possible. In this case, game designers indicate that you should "zone densely, keep control of crime, and watch the newspapers for public opinion and important inventions." Other possible objectives

Figure 12.4.4a
Happyland as you take over as mayor.

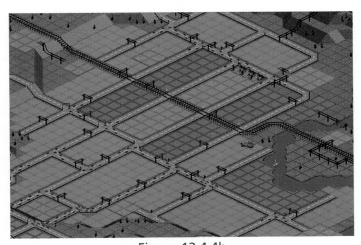

Figure 12.4.4b
The zoning of Happyland.

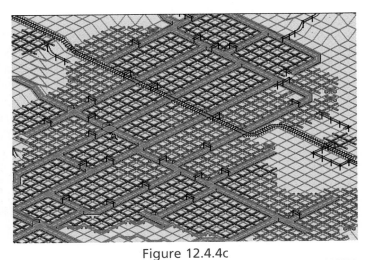

Figure 12.4.4c
The water system infrastructure with pumps added.

Chapter 12: Simulation: Modeling the Physical World

include maximizing city income, or even creating an ideal city to live in. The last objective is of a personal nature, but it's your choice.

The model itself is contained in the algorithms that control the interactions between the things that you create. The basic things that should be created are as follows:

- A residential zone where the Sims will live
- An industrial zone where the Sims will work
- A commercial zone where the Sims will shop and conduct business
- A power plant to supply power for all these areas
- Power lines to bring power to the various areas
- A transportation infrastructure so that the Sims can get from place to place

With these basic things, the city will grow. The model has much more to it than the basics. The additional things that make SimCity even more complex are the algorithms that take into account the following:

- Zoning that has different density levels
- Multiple means of transportation including subways, trains, water, and air
- A water system including pumps, tanks, reclamation, and desalinization
- Landscaping for quality of life
- Police and fire stations
- Schools
- Recreational facilities

In the analysis of any model, several attributes of importance were identified in the beginning of this chapter. In particular, feedback was identified as one that adds complexity in a rather unique way. SimCity has feedback incorporated at many levels. As your city is growing, for example, some decisions are made on the basis of what you see happening. The feedback is actually quite complex and has many feedback loops, which make the game exciting and eventful. As each decision is implemented, its effects ripple through the city.

Another more complex idea not mentioned earlier is a part of the model that is recognized by urban planners as the most impressive part of SimCity. Inside the program itself is an algorithm that implements something called the traffic density model. The traffic density model uses a technique referred to as recursion. Simple formulas aren't used to obtain the traffic density in a single calculation. Although too difficult to go into here in this discussion, recursion is used extensively by computer scientists. But the outcome of the traffic density model is something that we can all identify with. It relates to the fact that traffic always seems to expand to fill new roads and freeways. This is something everyone has experienced!

12.5 Design and Implementation of Computer Simulations

Before any simulation is designed or implemented, its purpose must be established. Usually it is necessary to simulate an event or physical object to solve some particular problem. Sometimes there are other reasons, such as the need to train with lifelike

The Computer Continuum

conditions. Whatever the objective, a simulation must have a reason for existing—whether it is for education, problem solving, entertainment, or even high-level governmental decision making. After the goals have been generally established, the total system must be defined and analyzed so as to make apparent the interrelationships or interactions among its various parts. Then the goal should be completely restated in terms of the analysis just completed. Two simulation experts, Adkins and Pooch, point out four basic tasks to be performed in setting up a computer simulation:

1. Determine that the problem requires simulation. The critical factors are the cost, the feasibility of conducting real-world experiments, and the possibility of mathematical analysis.

2. Build a model to solve the problem.

3. Write a computer program that converts the model into an operating simulation program.

4. Use the computer simulation program as an experimental device to resolve the problem.

As has already been pointed out, a simulation is only as good as its model. To prevent the possibility of erroneous results from a simulation, the model must be **verified** or **validated**. This should be done with any simulation.

> A model is said to be **verified** or **validated** when it is proven to be a reasonably accurate representation of the system being simulated.

Imagine spending millions of dollars on a traffic-flow simulation, only to find out that it doesn't model the actual situation of interest. This was the unfortunate outcome for a real city that installed a complete traffic-flow system based on a computer simulation. When the system was turned on, the city had the worst traffic jam in its history.

Sometimes historical data can be used to validate models used for prediction. Start the simulation at an earlier time, for example, and see whether it predicts the situation at present. If the simulation predicts what actually happened, the model is probably a useful instrument.

Simulation Languages and Modeling Systems

Simulations can be written in any number of computer languages, such as Visual BASIC, Smalltalk, C++, Pascal, and others. Even electronic spreadsheets can be used to develop very sophisticated simulations. For very complex simulations, however, these general-purpose languages are sometimes too difficult to work with because they offer too few tools to the programmer.

To make writing simulation programs easier, several simulation languages have been invented. What is a **simulation language**? An analogy with automobile repair might help explain what is meant by simplifying the writing of simulation programs. Imagine trying to fix an automobile engine with just two screwdrivers and an adjustable wrench rather than a complete set of mechanics' tools. This may be an extreme analogy, but should get the point across.

A new type of simulation-modeling system has surfaced over the past few years. It is very closely connected to the concept of object-oriented programming systems. These modeling systems usually have a graphics orientation. One example is a program called **Extend**, which is a general-purpose, library-based simulation program created by Imagine That, Inc. The programmer can build libraries of icons that represent the behavior of elements in the system being modeled. Figure 12.5.1 shows the classic predator/prey problem as modeled in Extend.

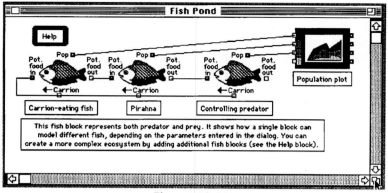

Figure 12.5.1

The program representing the predator/prey problem.

In this case, three types of fish are in the pond. The rightmost fish icon represents the group of controlling predators, the middle fish icon represents the piranhas, and the leftmost fish icon represents a carrion-eating fish. The lines drawn between the icons represent the actual programming of the simulation. The line between the controlling predator and piranha, for example, shows the relationship between them (that is, the controlling predator eats the piranha). The characteristics of the piranha can be seen by selecting it on the screen as shown in Figure 12.5.2, where the piranha icon is shaded.

On the Extend screen in Figure 12.5.2, the programmer can select the beginning number of piranha, average breeding time, average number of offspring, and several other characteristics.

Starting with 50 carrion eaters, 2 piranha, and 2 control predators, Figure 12.5.3 shows the population changes for each of the fish over a period of 100 days.

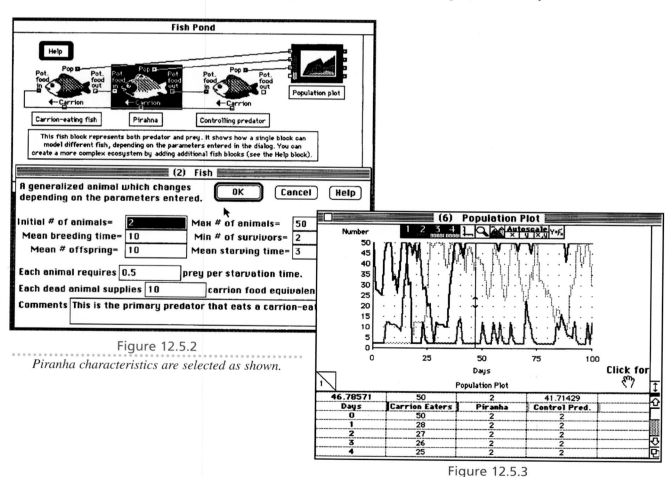

Figure 12.5.2

Piranha characteristics are selected as shown.

Figure 12.5.3

Fish pond population cycle over 100 days.

The control predators multiply because of the large supply of food. Because the carrion-eating fish are the food, their numbers fluctuate until at about 20 days the carrion-eating fish population is only two fish. At this point, the control predator's population is about 13 and the piranha's population is over 40 fish. The top line of numbers in the box at the bottom of Figure 12.5.3 shows that at 46.78571 days, there are 50 carrion eaters, 2 piranha, and 41.71429 control predators. The fraction of fish can't really exist and is due to the equations used to model the fish pond.

The Extend simulation program can be used for many other simulations. It is not restricted to population studies. Another interesting example involves the simulation of a bank's counter service. Suppose you are responsible for designing a new bank. How many teller windows should be constructed? It depends on how many customers are to be served and also what services they need. In the example simulation shown in Figure 12.5.4, three tellers will service customers with needs shown in the "Decide Task" window.

Note that not only is the percent of the different kinds of services specified, but also how long each service takes is entered. These various parameters can be changed to fit the situation.

In Figure 12.5.5, two other windows of information are visible. One enables the programmer to specify the speed at which the various tellers work. The other window shows a plot of the number of customers standing in line waiting for a teller (lighter plot) and the total number of customers that have been serviced and then left the bank (darker plot) over a period of 60 minutes. The largest number of people standing in line was six at about 47 minutes from the start of the simulation.

After examining the plots of several runs of the simulation, the designer can make decisions about how many tellers should be working and other appropriate considerations.

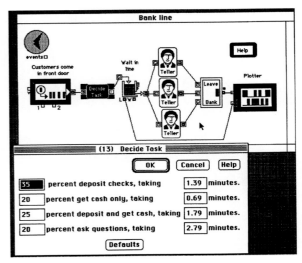

Figure 12.5.4

Bank teller simulation with three tellers.

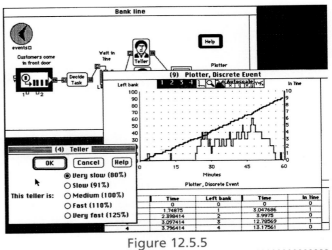

Figure 12.5.5

Bank teller simulation with teller information and plots.

12.6 Virtual Reality

The need for simulating the image of things that we see in everyday life is growing each year. Both industry and the military need to train people in the use of complex systems. The demands for new and unusual entertainment are endless. These are only two out of hundreds of uses of a new area called **virtual reality** or **artificial reality**.

The view is usually obtained through a special headset, which consists of a miniature TV set for each eye, worn like oversized glasses. The visual images seen by the wearer of the headset are totally fabricated by the computer. With the proper sensors attached, the viewer can interact with and move around in an imaginary world. Other senses such as hearing, touch, and smell are sometimes also included in a limited way. Virtual reality systems are being developed so that individuals can share the same imaginary

Virtual reality and **artificial reality** are catchall names describing a situation in which an individual has a three-dimensional view into a world that doesn't exist except in the computer.

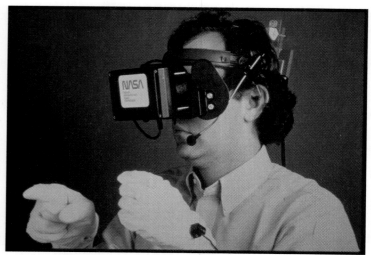

Figure 12.6.1

Virtual reality headset and special gloves.

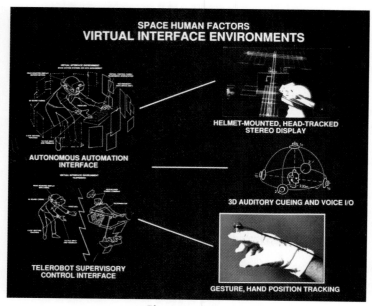

Figure 12.6.2

Virtual interface environments for humans.

environment with others. Science-fiction author William Gibson in his book *Neuromancer* generalizes this virtual or artificial world, calling it **cyberspace**. Cyberspace is a fictional place where millions of people can simultaneously visit and interact. Back down to earth, let's examine the current capabilities and uses of virtual reality.

Fundamentals of Virtual Reality

A virtual reality system consists of very sophisticated software and some specialized hardware. The minimum hardware would be a viewing system. This must deliver a three-dimensional image to the individual. Figure 12.6.1 shows a person wearing a special headset, which consists of small TV-like screens, one for each eye.

A computer generates a left-eye picture and a right-eye picture. The illusion of three dimensions is relatively easy to create: All that is needed are a few well-chosen cues and the brain can fill in the details. The next major thing needed is a way to interact with the virtual space. Most virtual reality headsets have sensors that can sense when the wearer turns his/her head; this causes the scene being viewed to shift just as a real scene changes when we move our heads. Another common interaction device is a special glove worn by the viewer. The glove is also shown in Figure 12.6.2. It has a series of sensors connected to the computer. Hand gestures with the glove may be translated to equivalent movements of a virtual hand in the virtual scene. Another possibility is that pointing your finger causes motion in the direction being pointed at.

Bodysuits with a series of sensors can be used in some virtual reality systems to feed navigation information into the system. The Lycra suits have many sensors, which send body movement information to the computer. You could walk around in the virtual world. All these devices are very expensive. The special gloves cost several thousands of dollars, and the bodysuit ten times as much.

A great deal of research is being done at NASA-Ames. Several of the virtual interface environments being researched are shown in Figure 12.6.2.

Uses of Virtual Reality

There are many possible business applications for virtual reality, among them interior design and architecture. Imagine yourself trying to design a new kitchen. You must pick out all the colors and arrangements of a sink, refrigerator, stove, counter, and cupboards. The Matsushita company in Japan has a virtual reality system that enables customers to see a virtual kitchen, which can be changed to suit their tastes. This way, the customers can see the prospective kitchen before they buy it, no surprises!

A more scientific application has started at the NASA-Ames Research Center. Michael McGreevy, director of the VIEW project at NASA, predicts that by 2008, unmanned Mars probes will have collected enough data about the surface to make virtual representations of the planet. This means that a replica would exist inside a computer (that is, a virtual Mars's surface). By 2015, he says they could have virtual representations of the landing sites for the astronauts to practice on.

Virtual Surgery

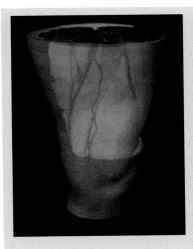

Imagine the following scenario: You are in Alaska and have an accident. Your condition requires expert surgery of a very peculiar nature. An expert surgeon is located in Los Angeles, but you can't be moved and it is impossible for the surgeon to travel to Alaska. This situation is where the "virtual surgery station" can come to the rescue. Researchers are now making it a reality.

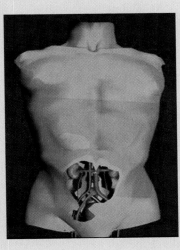

Researchers have developed surgery-training workstations with a video monitor and special hand manipulators. Combined with features of a human body in its memory and special software, the surgeon can use this workstation to practice various types of surgery. After training on this surgery station, a switch can be flipped and now the surgery station becomes a remote surgery facility. This means the surgeon can sit at the surgery station with its manipulators connected via satellite communications to the operating room in Alaska. As the surgeon from Los Angeles moves, the scalpel robotic-like devices in Alaska do the job.

The two images shown here are from High Techsplanations' virtual surgery system. The human torso can be "touched" by the surgeon using the hand manipulators. Organs in the body have "properties" that will respond by changing shape when poked, and so on. The other image is that of a thigh reconstructed from the "visible human." This model will have a virtual gunshot wound created for medics to train treating wounded soldiers. This makes it unnecessary to shoot animals in the leg for practice.

Back on earth, but just as extraordinary, is the suggestion by Warren Robinett of the University of North Carolina that it is possible that an obstetrician could see virtual images created from an ultrasound scanner's data. Speaking of an expectant mother, he said, "It would be like shining a little x-ray flashlight around inside her belly." The fetus could be carefully examined for any position problems or other important details.

Chapter Summary

What you can do with what you have learned:

- Be careful about believing the results of every simulation or prediction.

- Choose to simulate a problem using a verified model rather than testing the real thing.

- Make informed decisions while playing Monopoly.

- Understood the complexities of simulating the management of a city.

Key Terms and Review Questions

Key terms introduced in this chapter:

Simulation 3-134

Time compression 3-134

Prediction 3-135

Simulating the inaccessible 3-135

Simulating the impossible 3-135

Controlled experimentation and testing 3-136

Education 3-137

Training 3-137

Model 3-139

Continuous system 3-139

Discrete system 3-139

Predictable system 3-139

Probabilistic system 3-139

Feedback loop 3-139

Monopoly simulation 3-139

SimCity 3-144

Verified 3-149

Validated 3-149

Simulation language 3-149

Extend 3-149

Virtual reality 3-151

Artificial reality 3-151

Cyberspace 3-152

Matching

Match the key terms introduced in the chapter to the following statements. Each term may be used once, more than once, or not at all.

1. _____ The literal definition of this is "to imitate or to give the appearance of something else."

2. _____ This is the equivalent of speeding up the clock.

3. _____ An example of this type of simulation would be to observe the collapse of a star, resulting from gravitation, that results in the formation of a black hole.

4. _____ An example of this type of simulation would be to observe the U.S. economy after making sensitive changes in certain areas.

5. _____ An example of this type of simulation would be to observe how well a new type of bridge railing would withstand an impact of different size vehicles from different directions and at different speeds.

6. _____An example of this type of simulation would be to have a doctor identify a treatment plan based on symptoms displayed in a program that simulates an emergency room in a hospital.

7. _____An example of this type of simulation would be to have a pilot fly a simulated jetliner in adverse conditions based on actual data from previous flights.

8. _____This model has quantities that vary smoothly or in a continuous manner.

9. _____This concept is necessary when forecasting or predicting the future.

10. _____This fakes or gives the appearance of the system in question.

11. _____This model can predict exactly what will happen.

12. _____This model contains unpredictable features.

13. _____This model has quantities that vary in steps or jumps.

14. _____This model generates results, which it feeds back as more input for the simulation.

15. _____This means that the model is proven to be a reasonably accurate representation of the system being simulated.

16. _____This is another name for verified.

17. _____This general name is given to a type of language often used to create simulation programs.

18. _____This is a specific example of a simulation language that is a general-purpose, library-based simulation program.

19. _____This gives an experience into a three-dimensional world that doesn't exist except in the computer.

20. _____This is another name for virtual reality.

True or False

1. _____Simulations are created so that predictions can be made.

2. _____Predictions are only as good as the model used in the simulation.

3. _____We need to compress time in most simulations so that we don't have to wait, sometimes years, to see the outcome of the simulation.

4. _____Before creating the simulation, we need to know as much as possible about the model in question.

5. _____Simulating car crashes using a computer has proven to be more costly and less feasible than using the real thing.

6. _____The earth's orbit around the earth is an example of a continuous system.

7. _____The time the "sun will rise" in the morning is an example of a probabilistic system.

8. _____The game of Monopoly is an example of a probabilistic system.

9. _____Counting the number of cars as they pass through an intersection is an example of a discrete system.

10. _____The game of Monopoly is an example of a model that is both discrete and pre-dictable.

11. _____A simulation must have a reason for existing.

12. _____A simulation program can never be proven to be a reasonably accurate repre-sentation of the system being simulated because changes always seem to occur to the simulation itself.

13. _____Simulations are created using the same kinds of lan-guages as other programs (there is no difference in the type of language used.)

14. _____The SimCity program enables the user to design or alter zoning and utility pro-jects for make-believe cities.

15. _____Part of the design and implementation of a com-puter simulation program is to determine whether the problem really requires a simulation in the first place.

16. _____Using the Extend program, icons can be used to repre-sent elements of a system being modeled. These icons can then be manipulated to show the effects of the changes to the model in question.

17. _____The Extend simulation is restricted to a predator/prey environment.

18. _____To have a virtual reality experience, you would need to wear special equipment.

19. _____Virtual reality is an individ-ual experience, where the computer interacts with one person at a time.

20. _____Virtual reality is conducted in a three-dimensional envi-ronment.

Multiple Choice

Answer the multiple choice questions by selecting the best answer from the choices given.

1. This is the same as speeding up the clock.
   a. Time compression
   b. Prediction
   c. Simulation of the inaccessible or impossible
   d. Controlled experimentation and testing
   e. Education and training

2. This type of simulation helps people learn some complex skill that would otherwise be dangerous if "learning by doing" was taking place.
   a. Time compression
   b. Prediction
   c. Simulation of the inaccessible or impossible
   d. Controlled experimentation and testing
   e. Education and training

The Computer Continuum

3. This type of simulation enables people to manipulate designs based on very complicated mathematical models.

a. Time compression

b. Prediction

c. Simulation of the inaccessible or impossible

d. Controlled experimentation and testing

e. Education and training

4. This type of simulation enables people to gain insight into models that would be unobtainable in any other way.

a. Time compression

b. Prediction

c. Simulation of the inaccessible or impossible

d. Controlled experimentation and testing

e. Education and training

5. This is the whole purpose behind creating simulations! Without altering the simulation with different inputs such as changes in the weather, this would not be possible.

a. Time compression

b. Prediction

c. Simulation of the inaccessible or impossible

d. Controlled experimentation and testing

e. Education and training

6. This model has quantities that vary smoothly.

a. Continuous system

b. Discrete system

c. Feedback loop

d. Predictable system

e. Probabilistic system

7. This model has unpredictable features.

a. Continuous system

b. Discrete system

c. Feedback loop

d. Predictable system

e. Probabilistic system

8. This model feeds back input to itself.

a. Continuous system

b. Discrete system

c. Feedback loop

d. Predictable system

e. Probabilistic system

9. This model has quantities that vary in steps or jumps.

a. Continuous system

b. Discrete system

c. Feedback loop

d. Predictable system

e. Probabilistic system

10. This model results in outcomes that can be foreseen.

a. Continuous system

b. Discrete system

c. Feedback loop

d. Predictable system

e. Probabilistic system

Exercises

1. Which of the following simulations must use time compression to be useful?

a. Aircraft landing simulation

b. Simulation of the Earth's weather

c. Simulation of fish hatchery management over a decade

d. Automobile engine simulation

e. Simulation of star formation

f. Simulation of a nuclear reactor meltdown

2. All the following simulations are subject to predictions based on uncontrollable random events. For each example, name one possible event that could cause the simulation to go awry.

   a. Simulation of a presidential election

   b. Simulation of automobile traffic flow in a city

   c. Simulation of a dial-a-ride city bus system

   d. Simulation of the steel industry to predict demands

   e. Simulation of a university's financial operations

3. Give an example not mentioned in the book that illustrates each of the following:

   a. Simulation of the inaccessible or impossible

   b. Simulation for controlled experimentation or testing

   c. Simulation of education and training

   d. A continuous system

   e. A discrete system

   f. A probabilistic system

   g. A predictable system

4. Simulate the process of tossing a die

   a. using a computer.

   b. by putting six slips of paper numbered 1 through 6 into a hat and drawing out one of them.

   c. by using the number on a license plate, dividing by six, and then taking the remainder plus one as the "die toss."

   d. by dividing a sheet of paper into six equal square areas and numbering them 1 through 6. Toss a coin onto the paper. The number of the square that the majority of the coin covers is your "die toss."

5. Discuss the results of exercise 4. Do they seem to be equivalent to an actual die toss?

6. Simulate the tossing of a coin

   a. using a real coin.

   b. by writing a program to simulate the tossing of a coin. Hint: Use the random number generator.

   c. by putting two slips of paper with *head* written on one and *tail* written on the other into a box, and drawing out one of them.

   d. by dividing a sheet of paper into as many squares as is convenient. Label half of them with an *H* and the other half with a *T*. Toss any object small enough to fit within the squares onto the paper. The toss will represent heads or tails, depending on which square the majority of the object covers.

7. Suppose a certain machine can give you a random number (x) between zero and 1 (for example, .42317, .71123, .00121, .98791, and so on). Assume that the random numbers are evenly distributed (that is, just as many less than .5 as there are greater than .5).

   a. Show how a random 0 or 1 can be obtained from x.

   b. Show how a random number 1 through 6 can be obtained from x.

8. List three examples of systems that can be viewed as both continuous and discrete. For example, the traffic flow in a city can be viewed in two ways. The actual motion of a car accelerating and decelerating is continuous, whereas the number of cars going through an intersection is discrete.

9. For each of the following examples, describe one factor that would keep the system from being predictable. For example, we can't predict the time of a

transatlantic balloon flight, because the wind speed cannot be exactly predicted.

a. Grocery store cash register checkout line

b. Movement of the earth around the sun

c. Changes in the stresses of skyscraper structure

d. Growth and decline of the fish population in a lake

e. Launching a rocket on the moon

f. Simulation of an aircraft in flight

g. Simulation of cancer cell growth

h. Simulation of a computer system

i. Simulation of a mouse in a maze

j. Simulation of an automobile engine

k. Simulation of the game of Monopoly

10. Find two examples that involve feedback.

11. Name several areas where simulation has been applied but has had relatively little success (for example, weather, some city traffic simulations).

12. Write a short paragraph describing an example of an event from current news media (newspaper, magazine, radio, TV) that illustrates the unpredictability of normally predictable situations.

Discussion Questions

1. How much importance should be put on simulation of the U.S. economy?

2. Can a model be both continuous and discrete? Give an example.

3. Is the competing cities approach shown in Figure 12.4.3 better than investigating each city's organization independent of the other? Remember that the two cities in Figure 12.4.3 compete against each other for citizens.

4. Describe a virtual reality system to simulate attending a standard lecture class. Could you learn this way?

Group Project

A group of four students should design a series of experiments investigating the model underlying the SimCity simulation. Figure 12.4.3, for example, illustrates the effect that roadway access has on two cities' development. Each person should pick two effects to investigate. The group should meet to decide on the best city model that all experiments will use. Note that the two cities in Figure 12.4.3 have the same areas zoned commercial and residential; they differ only by the roadway access. Industrial zoning was placed exactly between the two cities. Ideas for investigation might include the effects of the following: recreation, taxation, mass-transit, airports, and many more. Before doing the experiments, the group should meet and review each other's proposed plan. Experiments on the cities already developed in SimCity may also be used as a starting point.

Web Connections

http://ssb-www.larc.nasa.gov/fltsim/index.html

Flight simulation site of NASA's Langley Research Center. Explanation of how flight simulators are used and links to related sights.

http://compsimgames.miningco.com/

Links to many online computer simulations, some based on your existing simulation software. Includes links to download free flight simulator software.

http://shnet1.stelab.nagoya-u.ac.jp/omosaic/simulation.html

Many links to results of simulations studying the interaction of the solar wind with the earth's magnetosphere.

http://www.opsd.nos.noaa.gov/tp4days.html

Links to tidal predictions for U.S. coastal stations for the next six months.

http://www.opsd.nos.noaa.gov/about2.html#ABOUT

Information on tides, and how and why tide predicting machines work.

http://www.paradigmsim.com: 80/about_psi.html

Information on the Paradigm company, which produces visual simulation and virtual reality software.

http://www.pcwebopedia.com/simulation.htm

Definition of simulation and links to many simulation software producers.

http://www.monopoly.com/

Main site for Monopoly information based on the CD-ROM version.

http://www.inactive.demon.co.uk/monopoly/index.html

Statistical analysis of the UK version of Monopoly. Includes information on how the analysis was done. Source code for the program is also available.

http://www.radiationphysics.com/hmonopoly/

A downloadable version of Monopoly designed for the health field. Print actual game board, cards, and rules.

http://www.nextorbit.com/co/main/webpages.htm

Many links to SimCity 2000 pages on the Internet rated as to quality.

Bibliography

Brady, Maxine. *The Monopoly Book*. New York: David McKay Company, 1974.

Darzinskis, Kaz. *Winning Monopoly*. New York: Harper & Row, 1985.

Lem, Stanislaw. *The Cyberiad*. New York: Harcourt Brace Jovanovich, 1985.

Wilson, Johnny L. *The SimCity Planning Commission Handbook*. New York: Osborne McGraw-Hill, 1990.

PART IV

EMPOWERMENT: EXTENDING OUR LIMITS

C h a p t e r   13

1859 The principle of natural selection and its influence on the evolution of species is explained in Charles Darwin's *The Origin of Species*.

1920 Karel Capek uses the word *robot* (derived from the Czech word for compulsory labor) in his play *Rossum's Universal Robots*.

1937 The concept of the Turing Machine is introduced in Alan Turing's paper "On Computable Numbers."

1950 The Turing Test of machine intelligence is put forth by Alan Turing.

1956 The concept of artificial intelligence is developed by John McCarthy and Marvin Minsky and others attending a conference at Dartmouth College.

1959 The programming language Lisp (list processing) for artificial intelligence applications is developed by John McCarthy.

1959 A checker-playing program by Arthur Samuel performs as well as some of the best players of the time.

1960 The Perceptron computer at Cornell University learns by trial and error through a neural network.

1961 The first industrial robot is patented by George C. Devol. Its first use is to automate the manufacture of picture tubes for televisions.

1994 The use of DNA as a computing medium is demonstrated by Leonard Adleman of the University of Southern California.

2050 Raymond Kurzweil predicts that a computer will pass the Turing Test.

Artificial Intelligence and Modeling the Human State

Chapter Objectives

By the end of this chapter, you will:

@ Recognize early attempts at machine intelligence.

@ Understand how a computer's intelligence is tested with Turing's test.

@ Identify semantic networks, frames and scripts, and expert systems as imperfect attempts to model the activities of the human brain.

@ Understand how models of the human brain make use of knowledge acquisition, knowledge retrieval, and reasoning.

@ Understand how heuristics limit the search possibilities when trying to solve a problem.

@ Recognize that exhibiting common sense is an attribute of very few computer programs.

@ Identify how recognizing printed letters and speech recognition fall into the category of pattern recognition.

@ Appreciate how game-playing computer programs have aided in our understanding of how humans make similar decisions.

@ Know some of the problems related to natural language understanding by a computer.

@ Identify the basic premise of the genetic algorithm as solving all types of problems using a model of evolution.

13.1 What Is intelligence—Artificial or Not?

When the word **intelligence** is mentioned, almost everyone immediately thinks about human intelligence. For thousands of years, the human species has wondered over the complexity of the human brain and what it represents. Only recently has the scientific community begun to unravel its secrets. This chapter's purpose is to show the attempts at creating intelligent systems using the computer and to get some very small insight into the working of the human brain. A look at history is probably a good place to start this exploration.

It is known that about 400 B.C. the Greek philosopher Plato's teachings included a theory that a perfect heaven rained down ethereal spirits that entered the body and were concentrated by the brain to produce semen. His logic was that semen obviously transferred the soul of the male into the female, causing pregnancy. Plato's student Aristotle didn't do much to improve on this theory; in fact, he concluded that the heart must contain the soul, and the brain's function was merely to cool the blood.

Other ideas of intelligence surfaced in the 1700 and 1800s, when an object having human form would seem to mimic the intelligence of the human. In particular, **Maillardet's Automaton** (Henri Maillardet, 1805) was a drawing machine disguised as a young boy. Incidentally, for many years Maillardet's Automaton was dressed as a lady in green, but has since been restored to its original male form. The small boy shown in Figure 13.1.1 kneels on a very large box that contains the bulk of the complex drawing machine's levers, ratchets, cams, and other mechanical parts. It could draw several complex images, one of which is shown in Figure 13.1.2. Because of its human form and the fact that it could draw such complex images, a certain feeling of intelligence was ascribed to the machine. Maillardet's Automaton now resides in the Franklin Institute, a museum in Philadelphia.

Figure 13.1.1

Maillardet's Automaton as restored to the little boy.

Figure 13.1.2

Sailing vessel drawn by Maillardet's Automaton.

There are many other unusual, incorrect, or misleading examples of the attempt to understand intelligence, but it is more fruitful to return to the scientific investigation, which was more on the track of reality.

The nervous system was discovered, but not understood, by Galen while treating fallen gladiators. He discovered that gladiators with damaged spinal cords lost feeling in certain limbs, but that they could often regain use of them. It was then Galvani who used Benjamin Franklin's findings about static electricity to show the famous jumping frog legs that indicated the electrical nature of the nervous system: The shocks from static electricity stimulated the nerves, causing the frog's muscle tissue to think the brain had sent the signal to contract.

Subsequently, the human central nervous system was found to be a very intricate continuous network of billions of **neurons**. The long axons that run throughout the body send communications by both electrical and chemical means. These interconnected neurons, called **neural nets**, stretch from the innermost portions of the brain all the way out to the sensory organs, such as the eyes and ears. In a certain way, the power of humans to perceive (for example, touch, hear, see, taste, and smell) is not just in the brain, but is spread throughout the body in the simultaneously operating neural nets associated with the various sensory organs. In effect, therefore, the mind is not all in the brain! Later in this chapter, we will discuss the construction of intelligent systems modeled after the brain's neural networks. In the meantime, it would help our current understanding of intelligence to discuss criteria for intelligence and also to compare the human brain with the computer. The latter is necessary because ultimately a discussion of computer or machine intelligence (commonly referred to as **artificial intelligence** or AI) must be addressed. The major question boils down to this: Can machines think? Before pursuing this weighty question, a discussion of intelligence is necessary.

What does it mean to be intelligent? The brilliant British mathematician Alan Turing (1912–1954) proposed a test, now referred to as **Turing's Imitation Game**. In its final form, the imitation game is essentially an intelligence test of the computer. In phase one, it consisted of having a man and a woman separated from a human interrogator as shown in Figure 13.1.3.

Interrogator

Truthful Woman   Lying Man

Figure 13.1.3

Phase one of Turing's test in operation.

The interrogator communicated with both individuals via a terminal-type device with a keyboard and a display to show the responses. The interrogator was to type questions addressed to either party without knowing which was receiving the question. By observing the responses, the interrogator's goal was to try to identify which was the man and which was the woman. The rules of the test required the man to try to fool the interrogator into thinking he was the woman. Meanwhile, the woman tried to convince the interrogator that she was indeed the woman.

In phase two of the imitation game, the man was replaced by a computer as shown in Figure 13.1.4. If the computer could fool the interrogator as often as the man did, it could be said that the computer had displayed intelligence.

Figure 13.1.4

*The Imitation Game
phase two.*

Interrogator

Truthful Woman   Computer

Putting aside the question of whether computers possess intelligence now or will possess it in the future, it is useful to compare the human brain with the current computers. The brilliant information theorist Claude E. Shannon made the five comparisons shown in Figure 13.1.5.

Figure 13.1.5

Claude Shannon's five comparisons between the human brain and the computer.

1. **Differences in size.** The brain has a million times more parts than even a super-computer.

2. **Differences in structural organization.** The seemingly random local structure of nerve networks differ vastly from the precise wiring of a computer.

3. **Differences in reliability organization.** The brain can operate reliably for decades without really serious malfunctioning, even though the components are probably individually no more reliable than those used in computers.

4. **Differences in logical organization.** The differences here seem so great as to defy enumeration. The brain is largely self-organizing. It can adapt to an enormous variety of situations tolerably well. It has remarkable memory classification and access features. In contrast, our digital computers do only a few narrowly defined tasks well, such as doing long chains of arithmetic operations where a digital computer runs circles around the best humans. When we try to program computers for other activities, their entire organization seems clumsy and inappropriate.

5. **Differences in input-output equipment.** The brain is equipped with beautifully designed input organs, particularly the ear and the eye, for sensing the state of its environment. Our best artificial counterparts seem pathetic by comparison. On the output end, the brain controls hundreds of muscles and glands. The two arms and hands have some 60 independent degrees of freedom. Most of our computers, indeed, have no significant sensory or manipulative contact with the real world, but operate only in an abstract environment of numbers and operations on numbers.

As the preceding figure points out, a major question in the field of artificial intelligence is to determine whether machines can think. The following sections examine many areas of research and application to give some background for answering this question.

13.2 Fundamental Concepts in Artificial Intelligence

To appreciate the complexity of the how humans store information and manipulate it, this section examines some attempts to model this capacity. It should be emphasized that these are human attempts to model something that is not completely understood.

Modeling the Human Knowledge System

Intuitively it is clear that there are some necessary requirements for thinking. In fact, it seems plausible that thinking needs some basis on which to think. In other words, thinking involves using some knowledge (for example, facts, processes) about the circumstance in which the thinking is done. There must be something to think about! When you think about going out for a dinner at some exclusive restaurant, for example, many things must be known. Here are just a few of the thousands of them:

What clothes to wear

What are clothes

Dinner means eating

Other people involved

Who is going to pay

Do you have enough money

Take a shower

Brush your teeth

How to get to the restaurant

When do you leave (what is time)

Literally thousands of small facts and situations must be known in order to think about going to dinner. How do humans keep all this knowledge in their brains, and how do they access it? This is a most difficult question. It is not known how the human brain maintains its base of knowledge or how it actually works. Certainly the body of knowledge applicable to any given situation is large, and the thought network connecting that knowledge is complex.

Marvin Minsky—A Leader in AI
Since the early 1950s, MIT Professor Marvin Minsky has been working to understand various aspects of human intelligence. He co-founded the MIT Artificial Intelligence Laboratory in 1959 with John McCarthy. In the early years, the problems of how humans play games such as chess were thought to be the difficult

continues

Semantic networks are designed after the psychological model of the human associative memory.

Frames and scripts: Frames are attempts to create descriptions of objects and events in the environment, which pertain to the knowledge in question. Scripts describe activities involving the knowledge in question, and also supply possible outcomes and scenarios.

One way to study complex systems is to build a working model of the system, and observe it in action. Several major approaches are used to model the human knowledge system. They all make use of knowledge as just discussed. It cannot be said that any of them approaches the way the human brain works, because it is not known exactly how the brain works. We will examine three of the approaches considered reasonably accurate representations of some of the thinking patterns of the human brain. None pretends to be a complete model of all brain activities.

Semantic networks consist of objects, concepts, or situations that are connected by some type of relationship. Examine the following sentence, for example:

A daisy is a flower.

The relationship between the concept daisy and the concept flower is expressed in English by the words *is a*. The words *is a* are so significant in a semantic network that they are usually written "isa." We might label this type of relationship membership. A daisy is a member of the group of objects included under the title flower. A semantic network is made up of a series of these interconnected relationships.

A small part of a typical semantic network relating a man named John to his belongings is shown in Figure 13.2.1. Notice how the network describes the relationship between John and his environment.

A second technique used to get knowledge represented in a computer is referred to as **frames and scripts**. The knowledge is stored in a series of frames of reference, and the knowledge on how to act in this frame of reference is contained in a script. Just imagine yourself going to a restaurant. What knowledge is necessary to participate as a

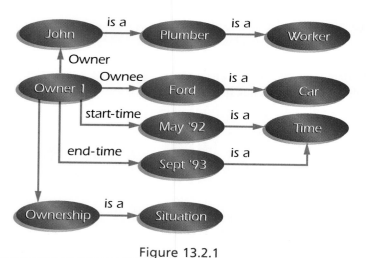

Figure 13.2.1

Simple example of a semantic network.

normal human being in this context? The frames-and-scripts approach tries to put all this knowledge in a computer program so that the computer will respond in a way similar to the way the human would respond. Figures 13.2.2 and 13.2.3 are short examples of such a frame and script.

Figure 13.2.2

The generic restaurant frame.

Generic RESTAURANT Frame

Specialization-of: Business-establishment

Types:

    Range: (Cafeteria, Seat-yourself, Wait-to-be-seated)

    Default: Wait-to-be-seated

    If-needed: IF plastic-orange-counter THEN fast-food
                    IF stack-of-trays THEN cafeteria
                    IF wait-for-waitress-sign

                    OR reservations-made,

                    THEN Wait-to-be-seated.
                    OTHERWISE Seat-yourself.

Location:

    Range: an ADDRESS

    If-needed: (Look at the MENU)

Name:

    If-needed: (Look at the MENU)

Food-style:

    Range: (Burgers, Chinese, American, Seafood, French)

    Default: American

    If-added: (Update Alternatives of Restaurant)

Times-of-operation:

    Range: A time-of-day

    Default: Open evenings except Mondays

Payment-form:

    Range: (Cash, Credit Card, Check, Washing-Dishes-Script)

Event-sequence:

    Default: Eat-at-restaurant script

Alternatives:

    Range: All restaurants with same food style

    If-needed: (Find all restaurants with the same food style)

Figure 13.2.3

Eat at a restaurant script.

EAT-AT-RESTAURANT Script

Props:	(Restaurant, Money, Food, Menu, Tables, Chairs)
Roles:	(Hungry-persons, Wait-persons, Chef-persons)
Point-of-view:	Hungry-persons
Time-of-occurrence:	(Times-of-operation of restaurant)
Place-of-occurrence:	(Location of restaurant)

Event-Sequence:	First:	Enter-Restaurant Script
	Then:	if (Wait-to-be-seated-sign or Reservations)
	Then	Get-maitre-d's-attention script
	Then:	Please-be-seated script
	Then:	Order-food-script
	Then:	Eat-food-script unless (Long-Wait) when Exit-restaurant-angry script
	Then:	Pay-for-it-script
	Finally:	Leave-restaurant script

A third type of knowledge representation is done in the form of a set of rules. These systems use rules to store the knowledge, and that is why they are commonly called rule-based systems. Because the rules are usually gleaned from experts in the field being represented, they are often referred to as expert systems. A rule in an expert system that deals with everyday events, for example, might be the following:

IF (it is raining AND you must go outside)

THEN (put on your raincoat)

Because **production systems** attempt to emulate the experts in a particular endeavor, they have proven to be the most useful and widely used knowledge model in the commercial world. A discussion of expert systems is presented in a later section of this chapter.

The primary objective of this section was to discuss the problem of knowledge representation and the design of several models of the human knowledge system. For any of these models to work, it must be able to make use of this knowledge in three different ways:

1. **Knowledge acquisition.** There must be some way of putting information or knowledge into the system, because it is impossible to do anything without a base of information.

2. **Knowledge retrieval.** The intelligent system must be able to find the knowledge when it is wanted or needed. It does this by searching through the knowledge base.

3. **Reasoning.** The system must have the capability to use that knowledge through a mysterious process called thinking or reasoning.

The following sections examine these three important intelligence functions in more detail.

Knowledge Acquisition

A fact, such as bees can sting, is an example of the simplest type of knowledge that can be acquired. Other types of knowledge, such as ideas, concepts, and relationships are much more difficult for humans (or machines) to acquire. The idea that provoking bees causes them to sting, for example, could be inferred from the idea that teasing a dog results in being bitten. Before such an inference can be made, however, the dog-teasing idea must be integrated into the existing knowledge base, and the reasoning process called inference must be learned.

To better understand the process of knowledge acquisition, let's explore how a human being "learns" a seemingly simple concept: the definition of a class of objects called "chair."

Actually, by the time you were in second or third grade, you already had a clear idea of what a chair was. If someone showed you a group of furniture items, you could pick out the chairs in the group unerringly. Suppose you had to describe a chair to some extra-terrestrial being who had never seen one? What would you say? Here's a possible definition of chair:

> **Chair:** An object with four legs, a back, and a flat surface that you can sit on.

That sounds great—very functional and descriptive. It's certainly a good enough definition for the object we are talking about. Right? Let's send our extra-terrestrial out to prove he's learned the concept of chair by pointing out some chairs he sees. Figure 13.2.4 illustrates three objects that our extra-terrestrial student identifies as chairs. A brief look will show you that his understanding of chair is imperfect. The middle object is not a chair, but a sofa. We had better rewrite our definition so that sofas and other objects similar to chairs, but not exactly like them, are left out. Here's our second try:

> **Chair:** A thing with four legs, a back, and a flat surface that one person can sit on at a time.

There! That's better. The sofa is now eliminated from our definition, as are settees, love seats, and benches.

Figure 13.2.4

Three examples of four-legged objects that we can sit on.

Figure 13.2.5

Several chairs that do not mach our current definition.

Don't get too satisfied with the corrected definition. It is still not adequate. True, we have narrowed the definition to eliminate several objects that do not belong in the category called chairs. But is it broad enough to allow our extra-terrestrial student to recognize all examples of chairs? A quick look at Figure 13.2.5 will show you that we are not yet done with our definition. These are chairs that our learner has failed to recognize, because they do not fit our definition very well. One has no back, one has a pedestal rather than legs, one has rockers, one has a platform rather than legs, and the last defies description, but is still a chair.

Here's a definition from *The American Heritage Dictionary of the English Language* that comes close to accommodating most of the pictures in Figure 13.2.5.

> **Chair:** A piece of furniture consisting of a seat, legs, and back, and often arms, designed for one person.

Even this definition, however, does not adequately describe all examples of the concept chair. It is, in fact, impossible to devise a definition that describes all possible chairs while excluding objects that do not belong in this classification. The extra-terrestrial learner might still have difficulties identifying a wheelchair, for example, or a chair lift.

At this point, we have defined chair to the best of our ability, and we have pointed out many examples for our student to see. We must now count on his native intelligence to be able to generalize the concept to include other examples, by comparing each new chair to the examples stored in his memory. This ability to generalize, and to apply old definitions to new objects, is an important form of intelligent learning, or knowledge acquisition.

Knowledge Retrieval by Searching

After knowledge has been acquired and stored in one's memory, the next task of intelligence is to be able to retrieve that knowledge and use it to solve problems. One way in which this is done is searching the built-up knowledge base for the appropriate tidbits of information, and then relating them to the problem to be solved. The next discussion centers on ways in which a knowledge base can be searched to find information needed in solving a problem.

Brute-Force Search

Many advances in artificial intelligence have consisted of searching for ways of solving a problem and choosing among possible solutions for what seems to be the best solution. In playing the game of **hexapawn**, for example, computers can make decisions on what move to make based on looking at (that is, searching) all possible moves, and then selecting the best, whatever that means. The game hexapawn is played on a 3×3 board with three white pawns and three black pawns. They start on opposite sides of the board and move just like chess pawns, which means they can move forward onto an unoccupied square or they can move diagonally to an adjacent square occupied by the opposite color; the opposing pawn is then removed from the board. Whichever color reaches the opposite side first wins the game.

To explore the hexapawn example further, examine Figure 13.2.6, where all possible moves have been outlined in what is referred to as a game tree. This is part of the knowledge base for playing hexapawn. Note that some moves are equivalent to others. The first move, for example, moving the white pawn on either edge forward, is the "mirror image" or essentially the same move. This is due to the symmetry of the nine-square grid used in the game. The game tree shows only the different moves (that is, all equivalent moves are not shown).

The searching strategy might be to look for all moves that lead to a win, evaluate them, and choose the best move. This means there must be some way to decide which is the best move. The main point here, however, is to examine the searching aspect of the problem. So, let's not worry about the best move at this time. A player examining the game visually, and thinking about the possible moves, is equivalent in many ways to a computer searching for the next move to make. The number of moves is small enough that they can

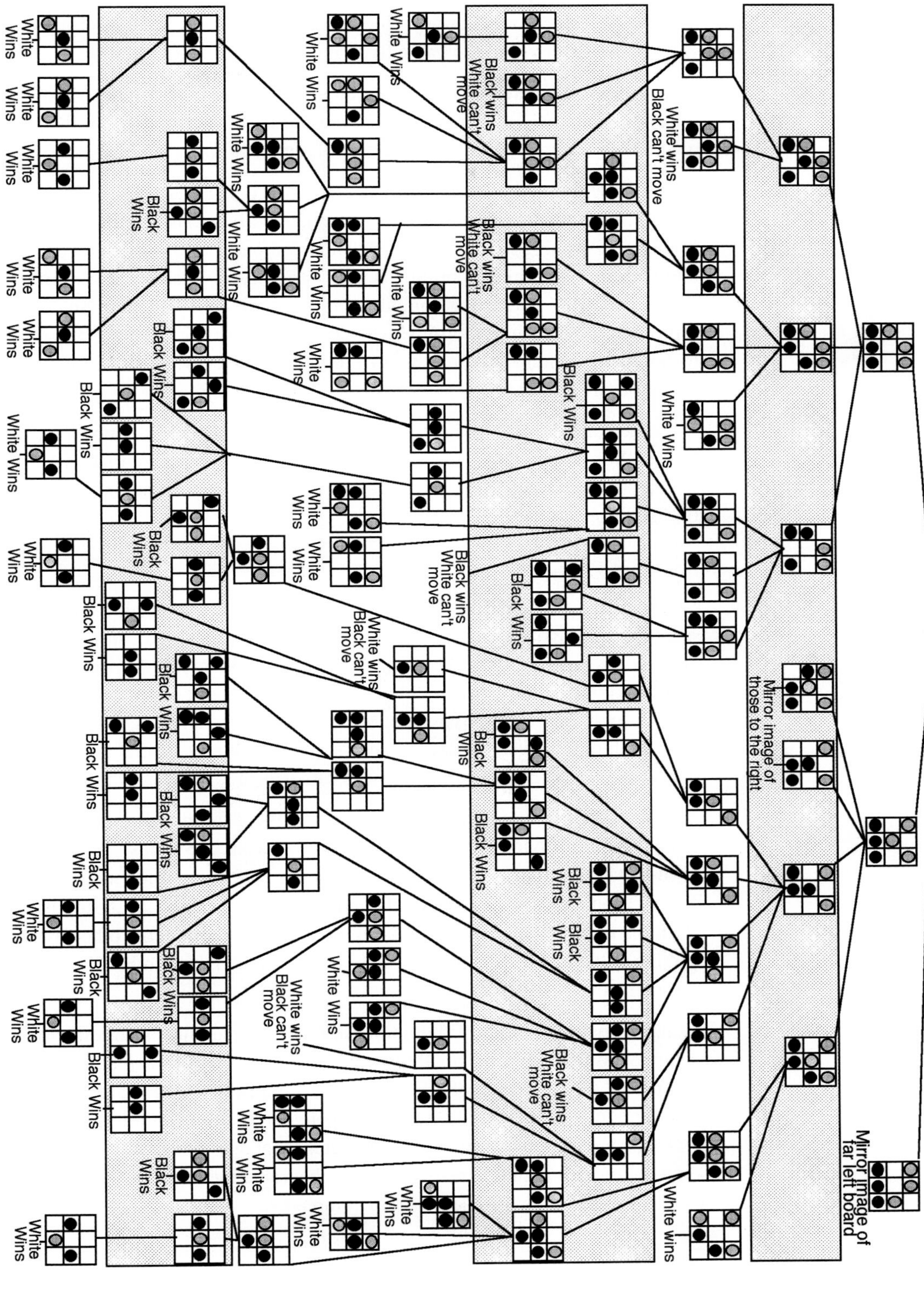

Figure 13.2.6
Hexapawn game tree.

easily be written down and, therefore, stored in a computer. For more complicated games, such as chess, the complete game tree would be much too large to put into a computer all at once. Searching, in essence, is looking at all the appropriate information or knowledge (for example, moves in the game tree) and selecting one of them.

In a certain sense, searching is done on the knowledge representation of the system in question. Technically, there are many ways to do the searching. For the purposes of this chapter, however, it is only necessary to understand that searching is being done.

It should be pointed out that this concept of searching is necessary when trying to create intelligent computers. How does this compare with human intelligence? Does the human brain use searching in the same way as the computer? How the human brain examines and identifies solutions to problems isn't currently understood. It certainly doesn't search in the same way as existing computer programs do. The human brain probably does not represent knowledge in the same way as described in this section. However, these are the techniques researchers currently have found necessary when simulating knowledge representation in computers.

Only the simplest of intelligent computer programs work with knowledge bases that can be searched completely. More complex systems, such as those that diagnose individuals who are prone to heart attacks, or chess-playing programs, must use "rules of thumb" to find solutions to problems.

Heuristic Searching

Heuristics are rules of thumb that are used to limit the number of items that must be searched in solving a problem. These rules of thumb are not guaranteed to lead to a solution.

The concept of **heuristics** or **rules of thumb** is important when a complete or exhaustive search of all possible situations is impossible. The hexapawn game has only several hundred moves, and these can be reduced because of symmetry. Suppose we tried to write out the complete game tree for chess. There are 10,120 possible chess plays. This is a huge number and can't possibly be written down or even searched through. Instead, some rules of thumb are used to greatly reduce the possible plays that are examined. One such rule is to search only a few plays ahead rather than all the way to the end of the game.

Another example should help you understand the difference between a brute-force search of all possibilities and the use of heuristics in a search. Suppose you are visiting a small town and would like to visit the local museum. The brute-force method would consist of driving around, exploring all streets until you find the museum. A heuristic approach might be to drive down streets looking for Main Street or some other likely major street that looks like the town's main street, because the museum in small towns is usually on the main street downtown.

Using heuristics or rules of thumb doesn't always guarantee a solution to a problem. Just imagine the museum in a small town that is located out of town at the nature center. This absence of a guaranteed solution should be contrasted with the algorithmic solutions to the problems in Chapter 3, "From Stonehenge to the Supercomputer." These algorithmic solutions are usually expressed in computer languages and give precise details on how to get a solution. It's guaranteed! Therefore, heuristic methods are quite a change from the usual way of solving problems using computers.

Reasoning

With the ability to gather knowledge and represent it in our brain, the next step is to retrieve and reason with the knowledge. Reasoning is what we humans do when we solve problems. In the field of artificial intelligence, two types of reasoning are commonly

The Computer Continuum

used: shallow reasoning and deep reasoning. Shallow reasoning is based on heuristics (intuition) or rule-based knowledge. Deep reasoning deals with models of the problem obtained from analyzing the structure and function of component parts of the problem. Humans commonly apply deep reasoning, but computers for the most part use shallow reasoning.

Reasoning is a difficult and important area of study in artificial intelligence. Just a few of the commonly known patterns of human reasoning include the following: probabilistic reasoning, fuzzy reasoning, inductive reasoning, and deductive reasoning.

The field of AI has also been challenged to consider another problem: How can the knowledge base be built up so that there is sufficient knowledge to reason with? It would be too time consuming or impossible manually to put all the knowledge of even a five year old child into the computer. One approach to the problem is to develop programs that learn.

Learning Systems

With some thought it becomes clear that to build the knowledge bases by whatever means can be very tedious. For computer programs to become truly intelligent, they must be capable of learning on their own. After all, learning is one of the most prized attributes of intelligence. A commonly accepted classification scheme for learning is summarized as follows:

1. **Rote learning.** This corresponds to the memorization of facts, such as memorizing multiplication tables.
2. **Learning by instruction.** This is similar to the student/teacher relationship found in any classroom.
3. **Learning by deduction.** In this classification, deductive inference is used to transform knowledge into other forms. Deduction consists of drawing conclusions from certain premises. For example: All cats are animals; this is a cat; therefore, this is an animal.
4. **Learning by induction.** Inductive learning consists of several subcategories: learning by example, learning by experimentation, learning by observation, and learning by discovery.
5. **Learning by analogy.** This combines both deductive and inductive learning. In the case of the bee sting discussed earlier, being bitten by the teased dog could have made the individual learn not to tease bees.

These types of learning are used in writing intelligent computer programs that are capable of learning. Sometimes this concept is referred to as machine learning.

A very simple and somewhat trivial example of a learning system is found in a modification of the hexapawn game. Suppose the game tree of Figure 13.2.6 were enlarged so that a small container can be placed on each board diagram. Assume that the computer takes black. You will be the white player. After each move, put a red button in the box corresponding to the move that is made. If the computer wins, replace each red button with a dried pea. If you win, however, remove the red buttons and don't replace them with the peas. During each subsequent game, when the computer chooses a move, it should select the path that has the most peas in the boxes. If there are not any peas, or if all paths have the same number of peas, then randomly choose between them. Eventually, the computer will choose paths that lead to winning. It is learning!

Common Sense

It is interesting to note that when the field of AI was in its infancy back in the late 1940s and 1950s, the problems that seemed to be the most difficult, such as playing chess, turned out to be relatively simple.

Contrary to this frame of mind were those of an informal research group from the mid 1970s called the Frames Group located in Berkeley, California. They would devote the first half-hour of their meetings to watching the TV program *Mork and Mindy*. Mork was an alien from the planet Ork and possessed remarkable reasoning powers. Because of his background, however, he didn't have an earthling's common sense. In one program, for example, Mork threw an egg in the air and said, "Fly, little bird, fly!" It so happened that on Ork space ships were egg shaped and Mork, reminded of them, thought the egg could fly. Of course viewers watching the program thought this to be very funny. It was this constant misunderstanding or lack of common sense that made the program so amusing. The program was understandably funny because Robin Williams played Mork.

The concept of common sense is multifaceted. There are common-sense facts that must be in the knowledge base, and also common-sense reasoning must be included to make inferences from the knowledge base. Grappling with this area of AI has been exceedingly difficult.

bits & bytes

CYC - A System with Common Sense
Douglas Lenat and others have worked several years to develop a knowledge base for common-sense reasoning called CYC (enCYClopedia). The project was started in 1984 at MCC (Microelectronics and Computer Technology Corporation) in Austin, Texas. Ultimately the knowledge base will have about 100,000,000 axioms. Another way of looking at its size is to compare it with the human brain's capacity. In fact, CYC will have slightly less information than estimates of the human brain's capacity. CYC's knowledge base includes not only facts, rules, and classifications, but also partial solutions to problems involving goals, desires, concepts of time, and everyday life events. These include money, buying and shopping, containers, and many common everyday things. Only a small part of the knowledge base deals with facts such as famous people and battles. Using this knowledge base, CYC can make common-sense decisions and observations.

13.3 Pattern Recognition

As you probably inferred from the title of this section, it must certainly concern the recognition of visual objects. Also, sound patterns made in human speech, for example, and smell or taste patterns all have the same things in common. Namely, they have in common the human brain's ability to understand or recognize the relationship among the various parts of the pattern. **Pattern recognition** using computers has been applied in many areas. Some of the more interesting are listed in Figure 13.3.1.

To get some idea of how computers are taught to recognize patterns, it is necessary to look at some examples. It should be emphasized that the human brain does not function in the same way as these examples.

- Robot vision
- Speech recognition
- Fingerprint identification
- Face identification
- Handwriting identification
- Optical character recognition (OCR)
- Weather data analysis
- Surveillance satellite object identification

Figure 13.3.1

Areas where pattern recognition is used.

The Computer Continuum

In fact, some progress has been made in determining how the human brain recognizes visual patterns. The approximately 100 million retinal rod cells in the eye continuously receive visual information from the environment. It would be impossible for even the human brain to handle or store the resulting stream of information, much less a multimillion-dollar supercomputer. Instead, the multiple layers of cells cause resonances or reinforcement to occur with similar past experiences or patterns. As stated in *Cognizers* by Johnson and Brown:

> The raw data is treated as a continuous stream from which patterns can be extracted by association. As the senses take in information, they cause it to vibrate against a background of sympathetic resonances wrought from encoded memories of similar past experiences. The raw sense data combined with the associations from the past then resonate forward and backward in the mind until a coherent image forms, whereupon the conscious mind is notified. In the conscious mind, both current recognized patterns and a mixture of associations from past experiences congeal into emotional opinions enforced by hormones and subsequently acted out.

Now take a look at the more mundane approaches used in artificial intelligence. In particular, let's briefly examine two relatively easy-to-understand applications. The first involves the identification of printed letters; the second deals with speech recognition.

Recognizing Printed Letters

The process of recognizing simple printed letters is not as easy as one might think. One of the first problems is to put the letter into some standard position and size. As shown in Figure 13.3.2, the letter may need translation, sizing, and rotation to be put into a standard position and size. It is also necessary to note that the letter could be in any one of several fonts or styles, as illustrated in Figure 13.3.3. But this is just the beginning. The recognition of the individual letters that are similar, such as *Q* and *O*, add even more difficulty. All sorts of techniques have been used to make the character recognition programs work quite well.

Character recognition is a standard addition to many commercial products. In fact, most fax modems include a program that will take the bitmapped image of a fax and convert it to ASCII codes. This will then allow working with the text in the normal fashion. It also results in storage savings when files are more than 100 times smaller in the ASCII or text file format.

Speech-Pattern Recognition

Because humans can communicate about twice as fast speaking as compared to using a keyboard, it is no wonder that speech recognition is an important research area of artificial intelligence. Communication directly with the computer would remove the keyboard, which is one of the major obstacles in human/machine communication. It is also one of the most elusive areas of study. However, commercial products that can recognize continuous speech are now appearing on the market. The difficulty is that there seem to be so many important factors that make up human speech recognition.

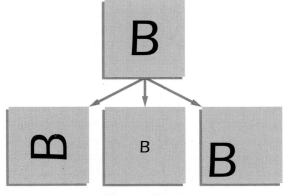

Figure 13.3.2
Letter positions and orientations.

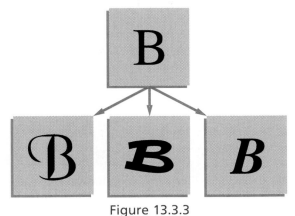

Figure 13.3.3
Letter fonts and styles.

Problems in speech recognition start with the most obvious. The accents of individuals from, for example, Brooklyn or Texas complicate any efforts to recognize English speech. A further complication is the fact that most speech is spoken continuously. As we speak, the sound normally comes out of our mouths with no breaks between the words. In the chapter on audio communication, the discussion concentrated on creating continuous sound by using sound chunks called phonemes. Now the problem is to recognize the words.

With single words, the number of possible phoneme matches is significantly reduced. In fact, single-word, speech-recognition systems are quite common on microcomputers. Unfortunately, almost all these single-word recognition systems must be trained. This means the individual who is going to talk to the computer must pronounce each word to be recognized by the computer several times. The computer then makes a template for each word, which is like an average of those pronunciations for the word. Most of these microcomputer systems have an accuracy of over 95 percent, but they are usually limited to less than 100 words. It should be noted, however, that in everyday English speech, individuals use about 10,000 different words. Newer systems will recognize the Midwestern dialect of English without training, but they can't handle continuous speech.

Achieving continuous speech communication with the computer has turned out to be much more difficult than suspected. The context of the conversation gives many clues to the words being pronounced. Whether the word *I* or the word *eye* was pronounced in a conversation must come from the context of the sentence, for example. Even words such as *quick*, *lick*, *chick*, *sick*, *click*, and *pick* could be easily confused if some noise interfered at just the instant when the slight differences are enunciated. Then there is the classical sentence in continuous speech recognition research: Did you eat yet? This is sometimes pronounced "jeetyet." Yet another example of two sentences that would be extremely difficult for the computer to differentiate are from Johnson's book *Machinery of the Mind*:

He walked to the store.

He walked to this door.

As farfetched as some of these examples seem, they are not that uncommon.

Putting these complications together with the differences of pronunciation by different individuals makes continuous speech recognition a very formidable problem. And, as formidable as the previous examples suggest, this is less than the tip of the iceberg. The next major stage, beyond just knowing what words were pronounced, is to know what they are saying. Section 13.5 deals with the understanding or semantics of human communication.

13.4 Game Playing

In the early days of artificial intelligence, researchers thought that teaching computers to play games such as chess would enable them to understand something about human intelligence. After all, it is well-known that playing complicated games such as chess takes a great deal of intelligence. It seems to follow that understanding how to make a computer play chess would be a step in the direction of how to make computers smart or intelligent. In fact, it is relatively easy to write programs to play chess, but it is very difficult to go beyond game playing and into the realm of human intelligence. However, teaching computers to play games is still an important area of artificial intelligence research. It has led to many refinements in solving AI problems.

The Computer Continuum

The major problem facing game-playing programs is how to make the moves. This involves processing or searching many moves and making the best move possible. As seen in Section 13.2, the hexapawn game involved a relatively small number of possible moves in any particular situation. All moves are shown in the hexapawn game tree of Figure 13.2.6. The diagram is called a tree because of the similarity to real trees, branches, and leaves. This relatively small game tree means that all possible move results can easily be analyzed.

Remember that hexapawn is played on a 3×3 square game board. The two players alternate turns making a single move. The game starts with each player having three pawns lined up on opposite sides of the board. The pawns move just like the pawns in the game of chess, which means they can only move forward one square at a time to an empty square. Also, a move one square along the diagonal onto a square occupied by an opponent eliminates that pawn. An opponent's piece may not be taken by moving straight forward. And finally, to win the game a player must be the first to reach the opposite side of the board.

By adding some rules of thumb or heuristics, decisions can be made by the computer program as to what is the best next move. Two simple-minded heuristics for the hexapawn game might be the following:

1. If an opponent is diagonally opposite any of your pawns, take the opponent's piece.

2. If any move will result in winning, make that move.

In certain situations, these two heuristics could cause some poor moves to be made. Figure 13.4.1, for example, shows a situation where black or white might win depending on how black moves. Assume the computer is black. If the rules of thumb or heuristics were followed in the order they are written in the preceding list, black will take white's far-right piece, leaving white the next move to win. If the order of the heuristics is reversed, however, black immediately moves to win. Instead of using the rules in order, what is usually done in a case like this is to give a desirability factor or number to each kind of move. Making a move that wins would be worth more than making a move that takes an opponent's piece. After looking at all the moves, the one chosen should have the largest desirability factor or number.

Creating the heuristics that make a smart program is difficult. But in hexapawn, the complete game tree can be examined. This makes the process of developing strategy easier, because there are relatively few moves that can be made. Games such as chess are much more complex, however.

As stated earlier in the chapter, there are about 10,120 different chess game board situations, far too many for any computer program even to store in its memory, much less analyze them. The heuristics and searching involved in a game such as chess are far too complex to discuss here. A little history of computer chess will have to suffice.

In 1974 a program called MacHack written by Richard Greenblatt of MIT was the first computer to compete in a chess tournament. The U.S. Chess Federation gave the program

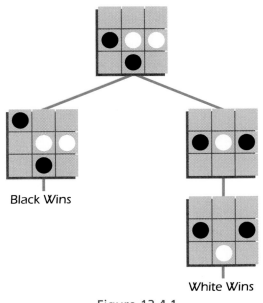

Black Wins

White Wins

Figure 13.4.1
A particular hexapawn game situation.

a rating of 1400–1450, which is a Class C chess-player ranking. This was just a beginning.

The first round in the human versus computer competition was won by a computer in 1997 when world-champion chess player Garry Kasparov conceded victory to the IBM program called Deep Blue. The score was 3.5 points to 2.5 points. Kasparov had beaten Deep Blue the preceding year 4 points to 2, but IBM engineers had improved the program. It is commonly realized now that chess was a relatively easy problem, and things such as common sense are really difficult.

Another interesting historical note is the challenge issued by David Levy of the United Kingdom. In 1968 he bet 500 British pounds that no computer would beat him in chess within the next 10 years. Levy won the 1978 match 3.5 points to 1.5. The Fredkin Prize was another interesting monetary prize offered to the first chess-playing program to defeat a human Grandmaster of chess. In the spring of 1997, IBM's Deep Blue chess program defeated Garry Kasparov as mentioned earlier. The Fredkin Prize was awarded to three IBM employees who split the $100,000.

It should be strongly emphasized that all these chess-playing programs don't play chess in the same way as humans do. The fastest of them is capable of processing 200,000 positions per second. This is thousands of moves more than humans can possibly analyze; yet the best chess players still commonly beat most computer programs.

13.5 Natural Language Communication

As mentioned in a previous chapter, the semantics or meaning of the words being spoken is the goal in communication. It is necessary to have the computer understand the meaning, not just the words themselves. For example,

The bark was irritating!

is a sentence whose individual words don't tell the real story. Understanding the words such as *irritating* is not simple, because the sentence implies that there is an individual who was irritated. The computer would somehow have to determine this along with the understanding of the word *bark*. Is it the bark of a tree or the bark of a dog?

In the 1950s, it was optimistically assumed that it would be relatively easy to have computers translate from one language to another. The semantic problem has certainly dulled this optimism. A classic example known as the Bar-Hillel paradox illustrates an even more difficult semantic problem:

The pen is in the box.

The box is in the pen.

These sentences convinced the linguist Yehoshua Bar-Hillel after nine years of struggling with the semantic problem that computer translation of languages is impossible. The sentences have identical syntax, yet the meanings can be interpreted completely differently. Most individuals interpret the first sentence as saying the writing instrument is in the box, while the meaning of the second sentence is that the box is in the playpen.

A rather confusing example in the area of communication and understanding was invented by Joseph Weizenbaum of MIT. In 1965 he wrote a program called Eliza, which simulated the conversation style of a Carl Rogers-type therapist. This method of therapy is still used in treating cases ranging from mildly misbehaving children to psychotic adults.

In it the therapist mirrors the patient's conversation in a positive manner. The Eliza program turned out to fool a lot of people, some who refused to believe it was just a computer communicating with them. Figure 13.5.1 is a conversation with Eliza reported in a paper by Weizenbaum in the January 1966 *Communications of the ACM*.

All men are alike.

IN WHAT WAY

They're always bugging us about something or other.

CAN YOU THINK OF A SPECIFIC EXAMPLE

Well, my boyfriend made me come here.

YOUR BOYFRIEND MADE YOU COME HERE

He says I'm depressed much of the time.

I AM SORRY TO HEAR YOU ARE DEPRESSED

It's true. I am unhappy.

DO YOU THINK COMING HERE WILL HELP YOU NOT TO BE UNHAPPY

I need some help, that much seems certain.

WHAT WOULD IT MEAN TO YOU IF YOU GOT SOME HELP

Perhaps I could learn to get along with my mother.

TELL ME MORE ABOUT YOUR FAMILY

My mother takes care of me.

WHO ELSE IN YOUR FAMILY TAKES CARE OF YOU

My father.

YOUR FATHER

You are like my father in some ways.

WHAT RESEMBLANCE DO YOU SEE

You are not very aggressive, but I think you don't want me to notice that.

WHAT MAKES YOU THINK I AM NOT VERY AGGRESSIVE

You don't argue with me.

WHY DO YOU THINK I DON'T ARGUE WITH YOU

You are afraid of me.

DOES IT PLEASE YOU TO BELIEVE I AM AFRAID OF YOU

My father is afraid of everybody.

WHAT ELSE COMES TO YOUR MIND WHEN YOU THINK OF YOUR FATHER

Bullies.

DOES THAT HAVE ANYTHING TO DO WITH THE FACT

THAT YOUR BOYFRIEND MADE YOU COME HERE

Figure 13.5.1

A conversation with Eliza.

The last statement by Eliza is very convincing. The techniques used to write the program, however, are really quite simple. For example, the exchange:

Well, my boyfriend made me come here.

YOUR BOYFRIEND MADE YOU COME HERE

is a simple translation of the word *my* to *YOUR* and the word *me* to *YOU*. That is one of the simpler techniques. When no standard sentence pattern can be matched, the program will randomly pick some previously recorded information. This is what happened in the last sentence in Figure 13.5.1. When humans see this type of response, however, they immediately think the computer really understands. But nothing could be further from the truth. In fact, Weizenbaum was so upset with people believing in his program that in 1976 he wrote the book *Computer Power and Human Reason*. In it he states:

Science promised man power. But, as so often happens when people are seduced by promises of power … the price actually paid is servitude and impotence.

Failures in Natural Language Translation

In the early years of artificial intelligence, there was an overabundance of optimism, especially in the area of language translation. It was thought that only a few years work and computer programs would be able to translate from Russian, Chinese, or any other language to English, or vice versa. However, difficulties started to show themselves in sometimes humorous ways. An early attempt was made to translate the following English expression, for example:

The spirit is willing,

but the flesh is weak.

The translation to Russian had the humorous result:

The vodka is strong,

but the meat is rotten.

These early results were not encouraging. Through hard work and better understanding, however, language translation programs have come a long way.

13.6 Expert Systems

Expert systems are commercially the most successful domain of artificial intelligence. These computer programs mimic the experts in whatever field the programs were written to be experts. Systems are designed to be experts in many fields, such as the following:

Auto mechanic expert

Cardiologist expert

Organic compounds expert

Mineral prospecting expert

Infectious disease expert

Diagnostic internal medicine expert

The Computer Continuum

VAX computer configuring expert

Engineering structural analysis expert

Audiologist expert

Telephone network expert

Delivery route-finder expert

Professional auditor expert

Manufacturing expert

Pulmonary (lung) function expert

Weather forecasting expert

Battlefield tactical expert

Space-station control/life support expert

Civil law expert

Oil-rig drilling expert

Toxic materials expert

Expert systems are also called **rule-based systems** because the expert's expertise is built in to the program through a collection of rules. The desired result is that the program functions at the same level as the human expert.

The list goes on and on. Several thousand expert systems of various capabilities exist. Some of these are trivial microcomputer-based experiments, but many are important commercial successes.

XCON, for example, was an expert system used by the Digital Equipment Corporation to help configure the old VAX family of minicomputers. When customers bought a computer, the system was customized to their needs. This means of the thousands of combinations available for the VAX family of computers, the salesperson must pick all the proper cables, connectors, interface boards, and software that will work with the customer's choice. This was a very difficult job until the expert XCON was created. Using XCON, the salesperson indicates what hardware/software capability and layout the customer wants. XCON then fills in all the details by specifying cables and other parts needed to make it work.

Even the fine arts have an expert system. In section 10.7, Harold Cohen's program **AARON** is an expert system. AARON is an expert in drawing human figures in a garden-like setting. Also, it has rules on how to draw human figures. Cohen stated in an invited paper for the annual meeting of the American Association for the Advancement of Science (1985):

> AARON knows what the parts of the human figure are and how big they are, where the joints fall, and what the permissible range of articulation is at each joint. A functioning figure is not merely a collection of independently moving parts, however, and the program knows how the movement of the parts has to be coordinated so that the figure doesn't fall over. It knows, for example, how a person uses one leg to balance the weight of the torso when standing on the other foot.

Rule-based systems or **expert systems** are knowledge bases consisting of hundreds or thousands of rules of the form: IF (condition), THEN (action).

The rules that make up an expert system are typically of the following form:

If (some condition), then (some action).

For example,

If (gas near empty AND going on a long trip),
    then (stop at gas station AND fill the gas tank
    AND check the oil).

Typical expert systems will have thousands of these **rules**. In fact, the XCON expert system has over 10,000 rules that help in the layout and assembly of well over 400 parts and components.

Structure of an Expert System

Aside from the obvious human communication link to an expert system, there are two major parts: the knowledge base (set of rules), and the inference engine (rule interpreter). The simple expert systems have only rules of the type just shown. With possibly thousands of these types of if/then rules, a controlling program is needed to interpret the rules. This is the **inference engine**. The inference engine will go through the knowledge base and find all the rules that have the "condition" (*if* part) satisfied. Then it will use the "action" part (*then* part) and look for all the additional rules that have it as a condition. This goes on until it can't find any more rules that have the current conditions. The final action part of the if/then is the answer from the expert system. The following shows a simplistic situation, for example:

Rule #1: IF (it's raining outside), THEN (get an umbrella).

Rule #2: IF (getting an umbrella), THEN (go to umbrella rack).

Suppose our extremely simple two-rule expert system was given the condition "it's raining outside," the inference engine would see that the condition in Rule #1 is satisfied, but no others. It would then make a second round using "get an umbrella" as the condition. The inference engine would then see Rule #2 and respond with "go to umbrella rack." Using this last response as a new condition doesn't give any further results. Therefore, the final response to "it's raining outside" would be "go to umbrella rack."

Many other factors make this simplistic example almost incorrect. But the essence is there. The complexities become involved when there is uncertainty as to which rule to use. Probability can then be invoked to use the best rule.

The preceding example used what is referred to as forward chaining, which means going from a rule's condition to a rule's action and using the action as a new condition and so on. Another concept called backward chaining goes in the other direction, looking for conditions that have certain actions.

Medical doctors, in effect, use both forward and backward chaining. When going to the doctor with some medical problem, for example, the first thing you would do is to tell the doctor the symptoms (for example, stomach pain). The doctor will come up with a tentative diagnosis—let's say an ulcer. This would be forward chaining. The doctor then may ask whether you have eaten a green apple (he knows green apples give stomachaches), which would be backward chaining. In a diagnosis, this is done literally hundreds of times in every patient's visit. But the doctor doesn't look at all rules, only the most likely. The doctor wouldn't ask whether you had just been shot in the stomach, for example, because that would have been obvious.

Bots and Intelligent Agents

As our world gets more and more complex, it is difficult for the average citizen to always know the right thing to do. It can be dangerous, for example, to sell your own house. If you forget even a single important word in the contract, the buyer may back out or force you to pay for something not precisely indicated. That's why there are real-estate agents, insurance agents, and other types of experts in certain areas.

The Internet has already produced the precursor of the intelligent agent. Called *bots*, as in robots, they do menial tasks such as roaming the World Wide Web looking for things. As the following names indicate, they come in many different forms: web robots, spiders, wanderers, worms, cancelbots, modbots, softbots, userbots, taskbots, chatterbots, knowbots, mailbots, bolo bots, warbots, clonebots, crashbots, floodbots, annoybots, hackbots, Vladbots, Turing bots, gossipbots, gamebots, conceptbots, roverbots, skeletonbots, spybots, spambots, and many others. The bots don't have the intelligence expected of the intelligent agent. However, bots that provide services and act as intermediaries between computers and humans could be considered a bottommost class of intelligent agents.

The AI community is now developing computerized agents using the model of the human intelligent agents. Alan Kay in his Knowledge Navigator proposed an early classic example of such an agent. His agent was to be a personal assistant that had access to electronic communications. In a simulation of how this agent might behave, the agent took phone calls, made appointments, and would do tasks such as locating individuals by phone or finding research materials. The agent appeared as a talking human form on the monitor screen of the computer. The human would give verbal instructions to the agent in continuous speech, and the agent would respond as if it were human. Other researchers have proposed agents that scan the Internet for things of interest to the owner of the agent. This agent would then report back its findings.

13.7 Neural Networks

Curiosity about the human brain was discussed at the beginning of this chapter. In the many years since Plato and Aristotle, this curiosity has been piqued even more. Researchers who study the brain have found some very interesting and complex structures. One of the most fundamental of these structures is the nerve cell or neuron that is the basic building block of the brain. There are several specialized types of neurons, but they all have the same basic structure as shown in Figure 13.7.1.

Figure 13.7.1

The basic structure of an animal neuron.

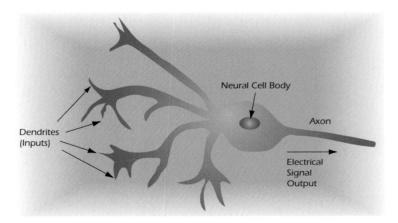

The neuron has several inputs and one output. This means it can receive information from many other neurons, but only gives out a single signal. In fact, it has been found that neurons can receive input signals from 100,000 to 200,000 other neurons. These inputs are electrical pulses from other neurons, which can pulsate up to 1,000 times per second. The single output of a neuron (axon) is also electrical and can be connected to several thousand other neurons. Researchers' estimates of how many neurons are in the brain vary from 10 to 100 billion neurons. The brain can grow new connections and dissolve others when these others are insufficiently used.

For many years researchers have been trying to build artificial brains. It should be emphasized that these artificial models of the brain are not copies of a human brain. About the only connection between the human brain and the researchers' models is the concept of the neuron. Researchers don't try to duplicate the human brain for many reasons. One is that it is too complicated. Also, the brain's details are still not completely understood. In fact, it should be noted that the vast capability of the human brain is still far beyond the computers we have today. It is estimated that one of the most powerful supercomputers (that is, the Connection Machine) has only enough speed and memory to give it a little less brainpower than a leech's.

The artificial models of the brain are of two distinct types. One is electronic; the other is software running on a computer. The electronic version has electronic circuits that behave like the neurons, whereas the software version runs a program on a computer, which simulates the action of the neurons. Most research is done using the software approach. The following discussion pertains to either approach.

Model of a Neural Network

An **artificial neuron** shown in Figure 13.7.2 looks in principle very much like the real neuron. It has many inputs and one output.

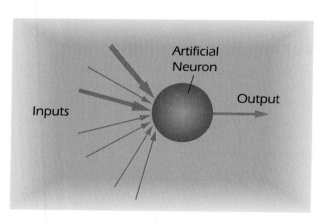

Artificial
Neuron

Output

Inputs

Artificial neurons, commonly called **processing elements**, are modeled after real neurons of humans and other animals.

What are the inputs to the artificial neuron? The inputs are signals that are strengthened or weakened (that is, weighted), just as a real neuron's inputs are weighted. The width of the input line in Figure 13.7.2 indicates how much of the signal gets through to the neuron's center, where the signals are combined. Thick lines mean more of the signal gets through than for thin lines. If the sum of all the inputs is strong enough, the neuron will fire, which means it puts out a signal to the output. In the case when a real neuron fires, it sends out a signal over its axon to other neurons. Several neurons connected together are referred to as a **neural network**.

The first neural networks of the 1950s were very simple single layers of artificial neurons. Figure 13.7.3 shows a very simple single layer of two neurons with three inputs. Note that all three inputs are connected to both neurons with different strength connections. Input 1, for example, has a stronger connection to Neuron 2 than it does to Neuron 1. This can be seen by the width of the lines connecting Input 1 to the neurons. In other words, Input 1 has more effect on Neuron 2 than it does on Neuron 1.

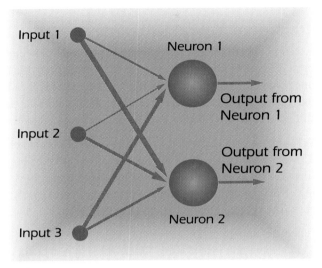

Figure 13.7.3
A single-layer neural network with only two neurons and three inputs.

The single-layer neural networks didn't have much success. In fact, advances in the field came almost to a standstill after the book *Perceptrons* by Minsky and Pappert showed (in the late 1960s) the limitations of the approach used in neural networks. However, some researchers still pursued the neural-network concepts. When the multilayer networks were created, progress was astounding. One of the more common types of neural-network architectures is the three-layer neural network. Figure 13.7.4 shows a three-layer neural network. It has an input layer, an output layer, and a hidden layer. This is a very simple example; most neural networks have many more neurons.

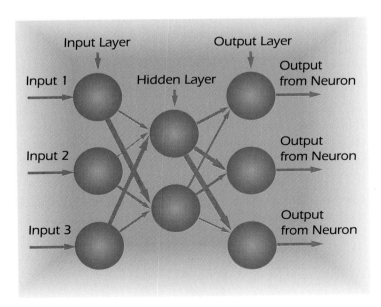

Figure 13.7.4
A three-layer neural network with three input neurons, two hidden-layer neurons, and three output neurons.

The connections made between the neurons in Figure 13.7.4 follow the rule that each neuron in one layer connects with all the neurons in the following layer with some weighting strength. Many other ways of connecting the neurons are possible, however. The neurons at the output layer could feed back to neurons in previous layers, for example, or input-layer neurons could be connected directly to output-layer neurons, or some of the connections could be left out altogether. Many of these various possibilities have been tried by the researchers with both successes and failures.

Training a Neural Network

A neural network does not have any knowledge in the beginning. Many techniques have been designed to impart knowledge to a neural network so that it can function. To better understand the process of training neural networks, let's look at both traditional programming and the expert systems that were discussed in the preceding section. Nelson and Illingworth, in their book *Neural Nets*, make an interesting observation.

When writing a program, the problem must be completely specified before programming. The programmer analyzes the starting information or inputs (for example, a corporation's financial data) and the desired results (for example, how much can be spent on advertising). The process of programming is to specify precisely how every situation is to be handled. The program takes care of every event that can be foreseen by the programmer.

When developing an expert system, the programmer develops a set of rules that take a certain input and give a result. These rules form a chain of relationships between the input and output. But again, the programmer has to make sure all the rules are in the system for it to function properly. In this case, the rules can be more general so that the specification isn't as precise as in writing a program.

By complete contrast, a neural network must be trained. There are no program steps or rules that a programmer must put into the network. In the beginning, no information is in the network. At the start of training, the weights or strengths of the connections between neurons are often randomly assigned. The neural network learns from experience by using many actual examples of inputs and expected outputs. This is much the same way humans do some types of learning.

Supervised training occurs when the neural network is given input data, and then the resulting output is compared to the correct output. The strengths of the connections between artificial neurons are then modified so as to minimize the difference or error in succeeding input/output pairs.

The most common process for training a neural network is called **supervised training**. The process involves getting many examples of both input and output data from the area of interest—for example, credit information on an individual (that is, input) and whether he repaid loans or defaulted (that is, output). The credit information on many individuals and their records of payment are referred to as a training set.

An example of a very successful type of supervised learning is called back propagation. This method of learning is divided into two phases. In phase one, the inputs are applied to the network, and the outputs compared with the correct output. In phase two, the resulting information about any error is fed backward through the network, adjusting the connection strengths to minimize the error.

There are many other types of learning rules and training schemes, but it is time to look at what all this means. On to some real-world examples!

The Computer Continuum

Neural Networks in Action

Out of the hundreds of examples, we will take the time to examine only two successful neural networks. The first is called the Mortgage Risk Evaluator. Data from several thousand mortgage applicants was used to train a neural network. This was done by applying each individual's credit data and loan result (that is, paid on time or default), one by one in pairs. This training took many hours. The patterns for a successful loan or default of the mortgage were contained in the data. By using the patterns inherent in the data, the neural network's weights were adjusted so that the output closely matched the actual output. Now, when a new applicant for a mortgage is entered as input to the neural network, the learned patterns will determine whether the person is a bad credit risk. The company that wrote the program, Nestor, even put in options to make the network conservative or optimistic. The success of the product was clear when a California financial institution began using the Mortgage Risk Evaluator neural network. The *New York Times* reported that a test revealed the California company would have had a 27 percent increase in profits if they had been using the neural network the preceding year.

The second example, SNOOPE, is a combination expert system and neural network. It was designed to detect plastic explosives in luggage at airports. Plastic explosives give off a characteristic pattern of gamma-ray emissions that can be detected by the SNOOPE machine. One of these $1.1 million machines was installed at New York's JFK International Airport in 1989; it can handle 10 pieces of luggage per minute. Unfortunately, at least two and a half pounds of the plastic explosive must be present for detection. Therefore, it is unlikely that the SNOOPE system would have detected the small amount of explosive that was the probable cause of the crash of Pan American World Airways Flight 103 over Lockerbie, Scotland, in 1988.

13.8 Complex Adaptive Systems

Examples of **complex adaptive systems** are everywhere. The vast majority of them relate to living systems. Research on them has reached into many areas from the weather to predicting the stock market.

Complex adaptive systems are rather hard to define in a precise way. There are many examples of them, however, such as ant colonies, communities of bees, economies of nations, the world economy, political systems, cultural systems, the ecological system of an isolated island, and the ecological system of the world.

In spite of the difficulty in defining a complex adaptive system, some definite themes can be identified:

- They are nonlinear systems. What is meant by the term *nonlinear* is not easy to explain without recourse to mathematics. But, we can say that the solutions to them are almost impossible to find except through the use of the computer. Most things in our world are nonlinear. Very small changes in a situation may result in completely different outcomes.

- They are parallel rather than serial (for example, like a supercomputer rather than a von Neumann computer, but even more complicated).

- They are evolutionary with natural selection involved (for example, Darwin's theory of natural selection).

Figure 13.8.1

Termite mound found in Australia.

- They have emergent behavior. This is totally unpredicted, but significant behavior.
- The basis of the complex system contains some very simple rules. Each one of the thousands of parts of a complex system abides by these very simple rules.
- They are self-organizing. This means through various interactions, the individual parts will organize themselves much as ant colonies have developed.

Termite colonies in Australia are a beautiful example of a complex adaptive system that is reasonably easy to understand. The mounds built by the termites can be several feet high, as shown in Figure 13.8.1. Each termite has certain abilities that follow a rather simple (compared to humans) set of behaviors. These behaviors can be modified over time by the chemistry of the mound.

The mounds are magnificent structures that seemingly just happen. There are no architectural plans or an engineering firm to guide its construction. Through the behavioral characteristics of the individual termites, however, the structure gets built. The termites just follow their simple set of rules. This is an emergent behavior of the colony of termites.

One very interesting emergent result is that the mounds have a form of air conditioning. The cooler air from below ground is circulated up through the mound. A complex air duct system emerges during construction.

It is tempting to think of the termite mound as being somewhat isolated from the surrounding landscape. To the contrary, they are integrated into a surprisingly interdependent community. They affect the types of plant that can grow above ground near the mound, and populations of mites and springtails flourish in the surrounding environment. On the other hand, the concentration of fungus spores and humus declines.

Chaos

The word **chaos** is used to describe a situation where things seem unorganized and unpredictable. Tiny changes in the starting point (for example, a small change in temperature) produce solutions to a problem that seem to have almost random or chaotic, unpredictable results. This sensitivity is sometimes referred to as the butterfly effect, which refers to the fact that a flip of a butterfly's wing could be the "seed" that starts a hurricane.

In analyzing the chaotic behavior of certain systems, however, some structure is indeed found. The understanding of these behaviors is beyond this discussion. To get just a taste of the difficulties in learning about chaos, it is revealing to look at some of the names used in describing it. They include terms such as attractors, strange attractors, bifurcation, deterministic chaos, state space, simulated annealing, fractals, and many more.

In the process of simulating these systems on a computer, it is found that under certain conditions, things are totally predictable and there is no evidence of chaotic results. With changes in the conditions, chaotic results start to exhibit themselves. This is the point where interesting things begin to happen. In fact, it has often been said that life exists at the edge of chaos. This is the region of activity where self-organizing begins and interesting behaviors occur. It is for this reason that scientists are very interested in understanding chaotic systems. They may help explain concepts of life on earth.

Artificial Life

What is life? Philosophers, religious experts, scientists, and many others have argued for hundreds of years over its definition. Rather than get into the problem of trying to precisely define life, it is probably more fruitful to take a broader view. Almost everyone would probably agree that stones or pebbles do not possess life. At the other extreme, everyone probably agrees that humans are alive and possess that mysterious thing called life. In between there are things such as lichen, trees, sea slugs, worms, bees, ants, cockroaches, turtles, monkeys, dolphins, whales, and many other forms. In addition, most humans would agree that these various forms possess life to differing degrees, more than stones but less than humans possess. The argument begins when we try to identify the point at which we say something is alive. It is probably most reasonable to accept what biologists see as the lowest forms of life, viruses and simple bacteria.

How does the computer enter into all of this? Later in this section, the discussion focuses on the computer as the tool used to study and support forms of life that are not carbon based, but silicon based. These forms of life are called **artificial life** or **a-life**. Because computers are constructed from components whose main ingredient is silicon, the common substitute term for artificial life or a-life is silicon-based life. Some argue that the first forms of artificial life are already here in the form of computer viruses. Several hundred computer viruses possess many of the attributes of the common cold viruses that we all know about.

To give further credibility to this new field of artificial life, it is revealing to note the intellectual caliber of individuals concerned with this field. Some of the brightest minds of this century have been involved. Heading the list is John von Neumann, the person most often identified with the invention of the stored program digital computer. When von Neumann knew he was going to succumb to cancer (he died in 1957), he worked on two areas that were extremely important to him, one of which was the technology of life. He wanted to create a theory that encompassed both biology and computers.

His interest alone may not be sufficient reason to think of a-life as important. Other names connected with this field may indicate something worthwhile indeed exists, names such as Alan Turing, Steven Wolfram, Ed Fredkin, Stuart Kauffman, Arthur Burks, Murray Gell-Mann, Heinz Pagels, E. O. Wilson, John Holland, Christopher G. Langton, Norman Packard, James Doyne Farmer, Roger Penrose, Freeman Dyson, Norbert Wiener, John G. Kemeny, and E. F. Codd. The connection of these individuals is found through the many areas closely related to a-life, such as complex adaptive systems, nonlinear systems, chaos, and the genetic algorithm. It is necessary to look at some of these areas to better understand the a-life concept.

The Genetic Algorithm and Genetic Programming

As the name implies, the **genetic algorithm** or **simulated evolution** mimics the processes in the genetics of living systems. It was created by John Holland of the University of Michigan in the mid 1960s, and is meant to be a general solution to all types of problems. The most important point to make in this discussion is this: Evolution creates the final

Artificial life or **a-life** is the name given to phenomena in computers that have attributes of life. Currently, a-life systems have simple rules followed by each of the thousands of constituent parts. With thousands or millions of interactions, it is impossible to predict what behavior will emerge (that is, emergent behavior).

The **genetic algorithm** or **simulated evolution** is a searching method based on the principles of genetics and evolution. It includes the equivalents of mutation, crossover, and chromosomes found in human genetics.

result; there is no human programmer. A human puts together the system and specifies the desired result, but the details on how it is done are left to evolve.

An example illustrates the diversity of the genetic algorithm and its derivatives. John Koza, one of John Holland's students, developed a system that had tree-structured chromosomes, in contrast to the string-shaped chromosomes of humans. Using some basic astronomical data, his system came up with Kepler's third law of planetary motion ("the cube of a planet's distance from the sun is proportional to the square of its period"). More interestingly, on the way to "rediscovering" Kepler's third law, Koza's system found a solution that Kepler had published 10 years earlier than his final one.

A difficulty with the genetic algorithm is that a coded representation of the problem must first be constructed in fixed-length character strings. This means the details of what the problem consists of must be known intimately. Then, with this knowledge, the detailed representation of the problem can be put into the computer for the genetic algorithm to work on.

Genetic programming is a technique that follows Darwinian evolution. The evolution takes place directly on the programs in the population that are striving to reach the goal specified by the programmer.

Koza went on to develop something called **genetic programming**. It is similar to genetic algorithm only in a general sense. They both use the concepts in Darwinian evolution. Genetic programming has somewhat less structure in the sense of organization restrictions to things such as fixed-length character strings representing the problem. In effect, no limitation on some predetermined length is given. The representation is a program that can be of any length.

An example of genetic programming from Koza's work is creating a program to play the game Pac Man. The Pac Man game consists of the Pac Man that gains points by eating food, fruit, and the monsters when they are in a vulnerable state. The four monsters can eat the Pac Man, whom they pursue, but with a limited attention span. The person controlling the Pac Man tries to get a high score. In Koza's example, the computer takes the place of the human and tries to obtain a high score.

This example was done using a group of 15 primitive tasks, three of which are as follows:

■ GA—Retreat-from-Monster-A, which causes Pac Man to retreat from the nearest monster

■ AFOOD—Advance-to-FOOD, which causes Pac Man to advance to the nearest uneaten food dot via the shortest path

■ AFRUIT—Advance-to-FRUIT, which causes Pac Man to advance to the nearest moving fruit using the shortest path

Each of these primitive tasks is implemented with several programming steps. The whole system is done in a programming language called Lisp. The nature of the Lisp language lends itself to genetic programming. Why this is true would entail a more detailed understanding of not only Lisp, but also the details on how genetic programming works. The bottom line is that each primitive task consists of several programming instructions needed to implement it.

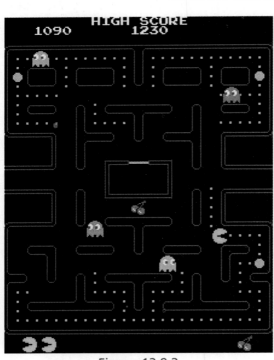

Figure 13.8.2

A sample screen of the Pac Man game in action.

The simulation of the Pac Man game begins with the random generation of 500 programs. Each of them is run and a portion of highest scoring programs are kept. Some of them have an instruction or two randomly changed; others are split into parts that are swapped with another program. The new set of 500 programs is run again, and the process starts all over again.

After 35 generations, one particular Pac Man program emerged and scored 9,240 points. For anyone who has played the game, this is a respectable score! It is truly remarkable that following the Darwinian theory of evolution, a programming technique could result in such a sophisticated program.

A quotation from theoretical biologist Stuart Kauffman is a good way to end this section. He says, "Artificial life is a way of exploring how complex systems can exhibit self-organization, adaptation, evolution, co-evolution, metabolism, all sorts of stuff. It is mimic of biology, although biologists don't know it yet. Out of it will emerge some sort of strange companion theory to biology … a particular substantiation of how living things work. This emerging discipline may be getting at what the logical structure is for living things."

Chapter Summary

What you can do with what you have learned:

- Choose between a brain and a computer in a number of areas.
- Model some processes of the human brain with semantic networks, frames and scripts, or expert systems.
- Be wary of computer programs that insist that they exhibit common sense.
- Be aware of the many problems associated with natural-language understanding by a computer.
- Choose an expert system to aid in decision making based on a perceived expert's knowledge of a particular system.
- Pick a neural network for implementing situations where continual learning is necessary.
- Recognize complex adaptive systems, chaos, artificial life, and the genetic algorithm as ongoing research areas in artificial intelligence.

Key Terms and Review Questions

Key terms introduced in this chapter:

Intelligence 4-6

Maillardet's Automaton 4-6

Neurons 4-7

Neural nets 4-7

Artificial intelligence 4-7

Turing's Imitation Game 4-7

Semantic networks 4-10

Frames and scripts 4-10

Production systems 4-12

Knowledge acquisition 4-12

Knowledge retrieval 4-12

Reasoning 4-12

Brute-force search 4-14

Hexapawn 4-14

Heuristic searching 4-16

Heuristics 4-16

Rules of thumb 4-16

Learning systems 4-17

Rote learning 4-17

Learning by instruction 4-17

Matching

Match the key terms introduced in the chapter to the following statements. Each term may be used once, more than once, or not at all.

1. _____This object had human form and mimicked human intelligence by having the capability to draw several complex objects using a combination of levers, ratchets, cams, and other mechanical parts.

2. _____The human central nervous system was found to be a very intricate continuous network of billions of these.

3. _____These are interconnected neurons that stretch from the innermost portions of the brain all the way out to the sensory organs.

4. _____This is another name for computer or machine intelligence.

5. _____This model of thinking patterns of the human brain is designed after the psychological model of the human associative memory.

6. _____This model of thinking patterns of the human brain is a combination of descriptions and activities involving the knowledge in question.

7. _____This model of thinking patterns of the human brain is an emulation of an expert in a particular endeavor.

8. _____This model of thinking patterns of the human brain consists of hundreds or thousands of rules of the form: IF condition, THEN action.

9. _____This deals with the way of putting information or knowledge into the system.

10. _____This deals with the capability of the system to be able to find the knowledge when it is wanted or needed.

11. _____This deals with the capability of the system to use knowledge through a process of thinking or reasoning.

12. _____This type of search looks everywhere for the solution to the problem at hand.

13. _____This search limits the number of items that must be searched in solving a problem (selectively searching using rules of thumb).

14. _____If this search technique is used, it is not guaranteed that a solution to the problem will be found.

15. _____This is what we do when we solve problems.

16. _____This area of AI includes the recognition of letters and sounds.

17. _____This simple game illustrates the problems facing game-playing programs, including how computers choose to make the moves they do.

18. _____This type of communication is the goal of AI programmers. The goal is not only to have the capability to recognize words, but also understand their meanings.

19. _____XCON and AARON are examples of this area of artificial intelligence.

20. _____This name is used to describe the situation where things seem unpredictable and chaotic.

True or False

1. _____A feeling of intelligence was ascribed to Maillardet's Automaton because it could draw complex images.

2. _____It was not until the twentieth century that scientific investigation into the nervous system took place.

3. _____The mind is not all in the brain. (Human perception is spread throughout the body in simultaneous-operating neural nets associated with the various sensory organs.)

4. _____The purpose of Turing's Imitation Game was to test the intelligence of the interrogator.

5. _____A supercomputer has more parts than a human brain.

6. _____Computers need to be wired in a precise order, but the human brain has a seemingly random order.

7. _____Programming computers seems clumsy and inappropriate when compared to the largely self-organizing adaptability of the human brain.

8. _____Semantic networks are reasonably accurate representations of some of the thinking patterns of the human brain.

9. _____ The rules that make up an expert system are usually gathered from experts in the field being represented.

10. _____ Every search routine performed by the computer will eventually find what the computer "thinks" is the answer to the problem.

11. _____ In a learning system, someone needs to manually input all the information needed by the computer to solve a problem.

12. _____ Common sense is less difficult for the computer to learn than playing a good game of chess.

13. _____ The programs that recognize text are extremely massive. They need a supercomputer to perform even the simplest character recognition.

14. _____ There has not and will never be a computerized champion chess player.

15. _____ It is difficult to program a computer to recognize the meaning of the words we speak.

16. _____ An expert system needs only a good set of rules to be an expert in any field.

17. _____ Researchers in AI have been striving to create a copy of the human brain to use as computer memory.

18. _____ Each neuron can receive only one input signal.

19. _____ In the same way that expert systems are trained, neural networks need a set of rules that take a certain input and give a certain result.

20. _____ Artificial life is the name given to phenomena in computers that have attributes of life.

Multiple Choice

Answer the multiple choice questions by selecting the best answer from the choices given.

1. This type of learning combines both deductive and inductive learning.
   a. Rote learning
   b. Learning by instruction
   c. Learning by deduction
   d. Learning by induction
   e. Learning by analogy

2. Learning by example and learning by observation are two of the subcategories of this type of learning.
   a. Rote learning
   b. Learning by instruction
   c. Learning by deduction
   d. Learning by induction
   e. Learning by analogy

3. This type of learning corresponds to the memorization of facts.
   a. Rote learning
   b. Learning by instruction
   c. Learning by deduction
   d. Learning by induction
   e. Learning by analogy

4. This type of learning is similar to the student/teacher relationship found in any classroom.
   a. Rote learning
   b. Learning by instruction
   c. Learning by deduction
   d. Learning by induction
   e. Learning by analogy

5. This type of learning draws conclusions from a given set of facts.
   a. Rote learning
   b. Learning by instruction
   c. Learning by deduction
   d. Learning by induction
   e. Learning by analogy

6. These are commonly called processing elements.
   a. Artificial life
   b. Artificial neurons
   c. Chaos
   d. Complex adaptive systems
   e. Genetic algorithm

7. Some themes that identify this system include the fact that they are nonlinear, evolutionary with natural selection involved, have emergent behavior, and are self-organizing.
   a. Artificial life

b. Artificial neurons
c. Chaos
d. Complex adaptive systems
e. Genetic algorithm

8. These produce systems that are almost random with unpredictable results.
   a. Artificial life
   b. Artificial neurons
   c. Chaos
   d. Complex adaptive systems
   e. Genetic algorithm

9. These systems have thousands or millions of interactions. It is impossible to predict what behavior will emerge.
   a. Artificial life
   b. Artificial neurons
   c. Chaos
   d. Complex adaptive systems
   e. Genetic algorithm

10. This searching method includes the equivalent of mutation, crossover, and chromosomes found in human genetics.
   a. Artificial life
   b. Artificial neurons
   c. Chaos
   d. Complex adaptive systems
   e. Genetic algorithm

Exercises

1. List several other facts that must be known and understood (whatever that means) before you could go out to dinner at some exclusive restaurant.

2. Write out 50 of the simple facts and actions that you think are necessary to start the day as you get up in the morning.

3. Explain why the mirror images in the game tree for the hexapawn game aren't necessary to complete the game for all possible moves.

4. In teaching the computer to play hexapawn, what would be the quality of the learning the computer is doing if you intentionally let it win with your poor strategy? Explain.

5. Draw the game tree for the game of Nim. Nim is a two-person game played with three piles of sticks or similar objects. There are 1, 2, and 3 sticks in each of the respective piles. The two players take turns selecting a pile and the number of sticks to take from it. At least one stick must be taken on each turn. Sticks can be taken from only one pile each turn. The player who takes the last stick is the loser.

6. There is a simple trick that will enable the first player in Nim to win every time. This player must always select a number of sticks so that the total number of sticks remaining is an odd number. Try this strategy out on some opponent who doesn't know how to play the game.

7. Make a list of at least six words that sound almost alike (for example, quick, lick, chick, click, pick, sick).

8. Make a list of at least three words that sound identical but mean something entirely different (for example, I and eye).

9. Think of two sentences that would give a computer problems in speech recognition because they sound the same. For example,

   He walked to the store.

   He walked to this door.

10. Do machines think? Why or why not?

11. Explain the difference between knowledge acquisition and knowledge retrieval.

12. Why is searching necessary in knowledge retrieval?

13. Which area of artificial intelligence enjoys the most commercial success?

Discussion Questions

1. In Turing's Test called the Imitation Game, why is it necessary to have two phases? Why not just have a computer and a human, and the interrogator try to tell them apart?

2. The Eliza program was written to act like a Rogarian psychoanalyst. Do you think it is ethical to use modernized versions of this program to provide low-cost counseling?

3. Based on Shannon's comparisons of the brain and the computer, analyze each item and conclude whether the computer or human brain is best? Defend your answer.

4. What is *your* theory on how the human brain searches for a particular piece of information? Can you explain the phenomena of trying to remember and failing, and then suddenly later the needed fact jumps into your consciousness?

5. Do any of the many examples of robots in the movies (Data from *Star Trek*, R2D2 and C3PO from *Star Wars*, and so on) exhibit what this book calls artificial life? Defend your answer.

Group Project

A group of four students should select a simple task such as making oatmeal for breakfast, answering a phone, or moving a box from floor to table. Each member will look at various aspects of the task such as description/definition of items encountered (for example, oatmeal box), processes needed (for example, pick up box), dissecting the task into

The Computer Continuum

related components, and coordinating the work of the other three members of the group. With this knowledge, create a semantic network of relationships between things. It may even be necessary to create new types of relationships. Act out a typical scenario involving the task in front of the class. As the demonstration is carried out, a verbal commentary should be given by one or more members of the group.

Web Connections

http://www.cs.reading.ac.uk/people/dwc/ai.html

The WWW virtual library of artificial intelligence housed in the United Kingdom. Includes many links to research sites, newsgroups, programming languages, commercial sites, journals, and other information.

http://www.cs.cmu.edu/Groups/AI/html/repository.html

Carnegie Mellon University's artificial intelligence repository. Includes links to AI resources, including the complete text of a Lisp book.

http://www.labs.bt.com/innovate/speech/laureate/index.htm

Description of a text-to-speech project that attempts to make the spoken language less robotic and more human sounding. Includes an interactive choice where you type in a line and the sound file is created and spoken.

http://www.nlm.nih.gov/research/umls/META3.HTML

Description of a semantic network in use by the medical community in the Unified Medical Language Project to attempt to codify the language used by professionals.

http://vvv.com/ai/demos/whale.html

Online whale-watching expert system that can be downloaded to your computer.

http://www.cee.hw.ac.uk/~alison/ai3notes/subsection2_6_2_3.html

Good definition of heuristic search and links to related ideas.

http://forum.swarthmore.edu/~jay/learn-game/index.html

Machine learning as it relates to game playing. A lot of links to actual games that learn and relate information.

http://www.radonc.uchicago.edu/IWDM/IWDMa25.html

Site describing a neural network used to detect information from mammograms.

http://alife.santafe.edu/

Artificial life online. A lot of links to a-life–related sites.

http://www.cs.cmu.edu/afs/cs.cmu.edu/project/oz/web/oz.html

Oz Project home page at Carnegie Mellon University. Oz attempts to study artificial worlds in a number of different ways.

http://lslwww.epfl.ch/%7Emoshes/ga.html

A brief introduction to genetic algorithms. Includes a link to a Java applet that visually runs the genetic algorithm explained on the main page.

Bibliography

Johnson, R. Colin and Chappell Brown. *Cognizers—Neural Networks and Machines that Think*. New York: Wiley, 1988.

Johnson, George. *Machinery of the Mind*. Redmond: Tempus, 1986.

Koza, John R. *Genetic Programming—On the Programming of Computers by Means of Natural Selection*. Cambridge: The MIT Press, 1992.

Kurzweil, Raymond. *The Age of Intelligent Machines*. Cambridge: The MIT Press, 1990.

Langton, Christopher, ed. *Artificial Life—An Overview*. Cambridge: The MIT Press, 1995.

Levy, Stephen. *A-Life*. New York: Pantheon Books, 1992.

Minsky, Marvin. *Society of Mind*. New York: Simon and Schuster, 1986.

Simon, Herbert A. *The Sciences of the Artificial, 3rd Edition*. Cambridge: The MIT Press, 1996.

Chapter 14

Pushing the Envelope of Human Potential

Chapter Objectives

By the end of this chapter, you will:

@ Recognize how the "education factory" influenced society's impression of education.

@ Understand how microcomputers have changed the educational system to date.

@ Understand why computer learning appeals to all types of learners.

@ Understand how the computer can be used to teach cognitive skills, psychomotor skills, and social-interaction skills.

@ Appreciate how the focus of education has moved from the teacher imparting knowledge to the student actively learning a topic.

@ Recognize how the use of CD-ROMs, local area networks, and the Internet have broadened the range of possible learning activities.

@ Understand how distance learning can benefit an absent learner.

@ Know how presentation technology has produced items of special use to educators and trainers.

@ Appreciate how the Information Age classroom will differ from the traditional classroom.

@ Recognize the rewards of the Information Age classroom for the learner.

14.1 Introduction

Education and training are perpetual needs of our society. Whether it is learning how to solve the infamous story problems of algebra or how to sail a boat, information and technique must be transferred from one individual who has the knowledge to another who needs it. Skills for applying that knowledge to other situations, and for problem solving, are also passed along to the individuals being trained. Thus, each person can increase his/her thinking abilities and become more creative in the learning process, as well as more knowledgeable.

14.2 Historical Perspective: The "Education Factory"

Our educational system, developed during the Industrial Revolution—the late 1800s and the first half of the twentieth century—was built on the **factory model**. Students entered the system at age five or six, were processed through several stages, and emerged 12 years later as finished products—workers with the knowledge, facts, and skills needed for jobs in industry and agriculture.

Despite major societal developments as we approach the twenty-first century, our educational system remains fundamentally unchanged. We can characterize the **education factory** of the last half of the twentieth century with the following descriptions:

Figure 14.2.1

In the traditional "education factory" classroom, the teacher presented information to neatly arranged rows of students.

Figure 14.2.2

Tests are given periodically to check student learning and understanding.

1. The teaching/learning environment assumes that all students need to learn the same things, and that all students learn in the same way, and at the same pace.

2. The teacher's responsibility is to pour knowledge into students, while periodically checking that each student achieves and maintains an acceptable knowledge level.

3. For teaching and learning to take place, students must spend class time sitting quietly in straight rows, listening to their teachers. They then must study individually to absorb facts provided in class, and to perform well on knowledge checks (tests).

The Microcomputer Explosion

In 1975, the first commercial microcomputer, the **Altair 8800**, became generally available. You could purchase one, completely assembled, with 4KB of memory, for under $1,000. Of course, little or no software had yet been written for it. Any program you needed, you had to write for yourself. For that reason, the Altair and other early microcomputers were shipped with the **BASIC** programming language installed in ROM memory. Despite the lack of commercially written software, educators were quick to make use of this new, relatively inexpensive computer in their work.

Figure 14.2.3
Who could guess that the first Apple computer, pictured here, heralded an educational revolution?

Within the next few years, the **Commodore Pet**, Atari, and **Apple** microcomputers were introduced, and the microcomputer explosion was on its way (see Figure 14.2.3). Literally dozens of cheap, small, and easy-to-use microcomputers appeared on the market. By 1980, mainframe giant IBM awoke to the possibilities of the small-computer market and brought out the **IBM PC** in 1981 and **PC Jr.** in 1982 (see Figure 14.2.4). Apple continued to improve its original Apple II series of computers, and in 1984 brought out a new market contender: the **Macintosh** (see Figure 14.2.5).

Figure 14.2.4
IBM intended its PC Jr. for the home and school environments.

Figure 14.2.5
Early Macintosh computers were the first to incorporate the use of a mouse into commercially viable machines.

Chapter 14:   Pushing the Envelope of Human Potential

Figure 14.2.6

By the early 1990s, thousands of educational programs had appeared on the commercial market.

As the number of microcomputers in both education and personal use continued to expand, the number of commercially available programs grew also. By the early 1990s, literally hundreds of thousands of computer programs had been written to serve almost every conceivable educational purpose. Both expensive and cheap software packages were available to address any content area or skill-based learning need.

Of necessity, most instructional programs were textual in nature at the beginning of this decade. Audio and video files (especially in color) required speed and memory capabilities so costly that most educational and home microcomputers did not include them. Audio expression included short and sometimes crudely designed sound clips, and brief, tinny-sounding music. Both often added more to the entertainment value of the software than to its instructional effectiveness.

Over the past two or three years, computer processing speed and memory capacity have caught up with the development of video and audio technology. Therefore full-dimensional sound and full-color video action can now be incorporated into the computer learning environment. The result is a more learner-centered experience, easily customized to each student's abilities, thought processes, and imagination.

Figure 14.2.7

More recent educational programs, such as World Atlas, incorporate a graphical user interface and background sound into the learning experience.

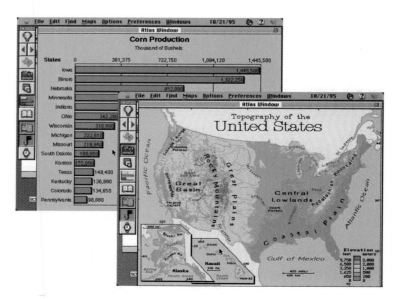

The Computer Continuum

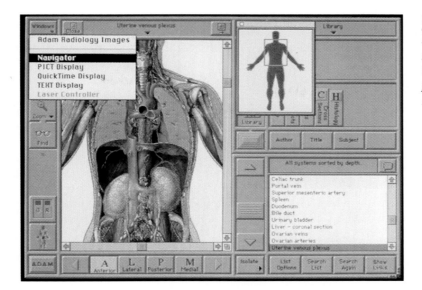

Figure 14.2.8

Realistically accurate graphics greatly enhance the learning experience provided by Adam: The Inside Story.

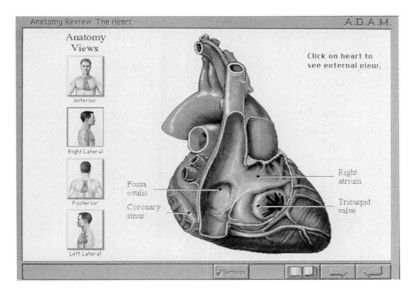

Availability of software and the constantly growing capabilities of the microcomputer have together made computers a viable and realistic tool for education. They provide the vehicle through which properly developed software will make incredible changes in our methods of education and training. In fact, many educators believe that formal schooling as we know it today will not exist very far into the twenty-first century. Of course, our education system moves slowly. It took 70 years for the overhead projectors and 35mm slide shows to gain universal acceptance as teaching tools. Nevertheless, inroads are being made. The acceptance of change is increasing along with the rate of change. As microcomputers continue to incorporate new technologies into the educational process, they will become the innovative impetus so vastly needed in our educational system.

Seymour Papert:
A Visionary Looks at Kids, Computers, and Learning

Philosopher, mathematician, and pioneer researcher of artificial intelligence, Seymour Papert is internationally recognized as a visionary concerning how computers can revolutionize learning. At a time when educational values and methodology have been questioned from all sides, Papert enjoys a truly outstanding reputation. His advice on technologically based educational methods has been sought internationally by governments and governmental agencies in Africa, Asia, Europe, Latin America, and the United States.

Born and educated in South Africa, Papert enjoyed a global education, earning degrees from the University of Witwatersrand (South Africa), Cambridge University (United Kingdom), and worked with Jean Piaget at the University of Geneva (Switzerland). This last collaboration led him to consider using mathematics to study how children learn and think. In the early 1960s, Papert moved to MIT (The Massachusetts Institute of Technology) in Boston. There he began his most important work.

Papert feels that the most important things children can learn are the art of learning and the art of managing their own discoveries. His early efforts at child-based learning resulted in his invention of the LOGO Computer Language, a computer environment designed to give children control over the new technology surrounding them. Papert's ideas about education moved him into national prominence with the publication of *Mindstorms: Children, Computers and Powerful Ideas* (1980). Other books—*The Children's Machine: Rethinking School in the Age of the Computer* (1992) and *The Connected Family: Bridging the Digital Generation Gap* (1996)—along with more than 60 scholarly papers and several hundred lectures and presentations, have made Papert the world's leading thinker on the future of education and the place of technology in that future.

14.3 Why Can Computers Teach?

Even outside the formal educational setting, a vast amount of education and training is done using microcomputers. Government and businesses need to train personnel (for example, sales people, computer programmers, assembly line workers, and managers). Corporations maintain complex computer training programs to teach everything from word processing and **CAD/CAM (computer-aided design and manufacturing)** to interviewing techniques and personnel selection. Individuals find microcomputers to be an effective tool for personal enrichment and intellectual development. Educational applications of computer technology seem endless. As computers invade more and more educational realms, a major question becomes apparent: What makes the computer such an effective teaching/learning tool? Why can computers teach?

To begin with, most people like to learn with computers. They find computers to be innovative, interesting, and challenging. Because today's computers incorporate sound, visual images, and motion, many different types of learners can relate to them. Some people learn best when they see something, for example. For them, computers can present video clips and animated moving models as part of the teaching/learning experience. Other people learn better by listening than by seeing. To accommodate these learning styles, computers can incorporate a wide variety of sounds, including accurate reproduction of human speech, into every lesson. In fact, computer learning has something for everyone—a major reason for computer effectiveness.

Another reason computers can be used to teach is cost. Microcomputers, in the long run, are cheaper than human beings. Despite their high initial-purchase and setup cost, computers cost less, over the years, than teachers do. Teachers need salary, retirement funds, medical benefits, and so on. These are costs that must be paid, month in and month out, over the entire time the teacher is in service. Although it is true that teachers are not in the highest-paid profession in the world, the annual salary of a single teacher would purchase several microcomputers and enough software to equip a small lab. True, computers have ongoing costs, too. They must be serviced, and both hardware and software need regular update and replacement. Nevertheless, computers cost significantly less per learning hour than their human counterparts.

Figure 14.3.1

People like to learn with computers.

Yet another reason computers can teach is flexibility. Not even the best human teacher can be expert, or even adequately knowledgeable, in every field. The result is that in some schools, especially small ones with relatively few teachers, the level of learning across the curriculum can be uneven. It stands to reason that a teacher can teach better (and students learn more) in those areas where he/she has greater in-depth knowledge. This is not so with the computer. With well-chosen software and networking capabilities the computer can become an expert in anything and everything. Load up the appropriate program or log on to an appropriate Web site, and the computer is ready to help you learn. Instant expertise on any subject, and unlimited knowledge resources to back it up! Amazing!

14.4 What Can Computers Teach?

Now there's an easy question! The answer is EVERYTHING!

Define *Everything*

Most often, we tend to categorize learning in one of two ways. We can group learning experiences by age or grade level (that is, elementary, intermediate, secondary). Or we might choose to divide learning into content areas such as History, Physics, French, and so on. Neither of these classifications offers any insight into what computers can or cannot teach. Computer instruction can be used for any age group and any subject matter. Therefore, we must use a classification method that cuts across grade-level and subject matter boundaries. Using this new classification, we can group all education and training into three major categories:

- **Cognitive learning**
- **Psychomotor skills**
- **Social interaction**

Let's define these categories and examine the role played by computers in each.

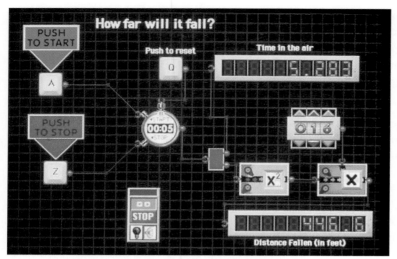

Figure 14.4.1

In the Widget Workshop, students test scientific concepts, such as gravity, by interactively controlling an onscreen simulation.

Cognitive Learning

It may help in understanding this category to know that the word **cognitive** comes from the Latin word for think. Actually, there are two subclassifications within cognitive learning: **knowledge** and **thinking skills**. Of the two, the knowledge area gets the most attention in our current school systems. Knowledge is the easiest type of learning to define and the easiest area in which to demonstrate achievement. Facts, figures, dates, comparisons, causes and effects, meanings, spelling, and so on are all examples of knowledge.

Unfortunately, our education system, to date, has not done as thorough a job in the teaching of thinking skills. These include the ability to analyze and solve problems, to give directions, to apply criteria, and to utilize acquired knowledge in new situations. In general, these skills are much more difficult to teach than facts and figures, and much more difficult to learn or demonstrate learning achievement.

Huge numbers of computer programs have been written to enhance cognitive learning. They add interest to the presentation of new material, as well as provide an individually interactive way to review and practice what has been previously taught. Math facts, new vocabulary, and historical dates are just a few samples of subjects well suited to computer-guided practice. In addition, the microcomputer has proven tireless in giving students endless numbers of problems to solve, words to define, and questions to answer, thus allowing each student to study and check for content mastery at an individually appropriate pace.

Figure 14.4.2

Vette requires the user to combine quick hand-eye coordination with sound common sense to simulate a ride through San Francisco's hilly streets.

Psychomotor Skills

A second category of education and training involves the psychomotor skills. The term psychomotor refers to the relationship between the brain and the muscles. Therefore, psychomotor skills are those that require coordination and neuromuscular coordination.

Microcomputers exceed our expectations as teaching tools for this category of education. Some of the available instructional software in this area is aimed at increasing general muscular control. Examples include the many arcade and computer games, which develop eye-hand coordination and rapid response. Other software focuses on training for specific tasks. An impressive example is astronaut training for manual maneuvering of spacecraft. Of course, not all programs are designed to develop coordination and skills. Some are analytic, capable of examining a maneuver to detect flaws. An example of this kind of educational software is a program that provides dynamic computer analysis of a golf swing, or a speech articulation problem.

Social Interaction

Finally, we have the education category dealing with interpersonal skills and social interaction. All activities that involve the development of successful relationships with other people are included here. This is the hardest area to define and, therefore, the hardest area to teach. It is also the most difficult area to quantify. Some of the topics included are working with others (teamwork), winning and losing (competition), management skills, and leadership skills. Social values and emotional response are developed within this area. Although this third category has been less often addressed by the computer than the other two, there are still some interesting applications. There are, for example, many educational simulations in which the players must cooperate to survive. There is even a game called Terrorist in which the player must negotiate with terrorists to save human life and property.

Programs of greatest value in teaching social interaction are those combining the microcomputer with video and audio technology, to produce **interactive multimedia** experiences. Still a relatively new methodology, it has already produced some exciting educational applications in the areas of management styles, negotiation skills, and stress management.

It is probably obvious that the three categories are seldom independent. Learning to play any sport, for example, requires all three: cognitive knowledge, including the rules and problem solving for planning strategy; psychomotor skills for the actual playing; and interpersonal skills to build teamwork and the competitive spirit.

Before we dismiss this issue, however, let's back up and take another look at the question:

What Can Computers Teach?

By asking what computers can teach, we are assuming that a traditional teacher/student relationship exists, with the computer acting as (or replacing) the teacher. Reality could hardly be further from the truth.

The traditional teacher selected what students needed to know according to a prescribed curriculum. After specific knowledge was chosen, the teacher's job was to teach the

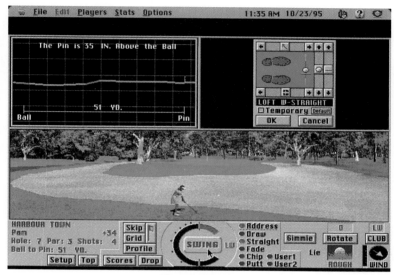

Figure 14.4.3

LinksPro, a golf program, helps the player improve his/her game by adjusting club choice, stance, and shot type to specific holes on simulated courses.

Figure 14.4.4

Working together to share computer resources helps develop team-work, an important social interaction skill.

Figure 14.5.1

Our educational goals and dreams must expand to fit the new century.

selected topics. Students sat passively by and accepted (learned) what was taught.

In our new-type educational environment, the situation is different. Students are presented with tasks to complete or problems to solve—sometimes defining the problem is part of the task. With the guidance of a teacher, the student may explore several means of approaching the problem for the best possible solution. Exploration may involve several different activities. The computer is used both as a resource for information and know-how and as a tool for completing the task and presenting results. Decisions on how to get from the initial task to its conclusion must be made by the student, using the tools and resources available.

Therefore we must rephrase our initial question before we continue further. Using the word *teach* places responsibility on the computer. In our information age classroom, responsibility falls on the student: The student must actively learn. So the title for the next section must be:

14.5 What Can Computers Help Us Learn?

As society moves more inexorably into the twenty-first century, we need to redesign not only our learning environments, but our educational goals as well. The education factory's primary goal was the transfer of knowledge from one generation to the next. The educational goals of the Information Age, however, need to focus on the development of skills that enable us to define tasks, find and utilize information, and deal effectively with the rapidly changing world our technology has evolved.

Here are some of the areas in which computer-aided learning can help us achieve these goals:

1. **Reading/writing literacy:** The growth of technology has not eliminated the need for basic literacy skills. The necessity for reading and writing skills has increased. We cannot even use the computer as a learning resource without being able to read what is onscreen. Computer programs exist in this area for students at

every level, helping them to increase the speed and comprehension level of their reading, learn new vocabulary, organize ideas, express themselves clearly in writing, and present their ideas to others in various forms.

2. **Ability to apply math concepts to solve problems:** Many of us resent the amount of time we have had to spend learning things such as algebra, square roots, geometry, and fractions. But even today, when most people can access a calculator, we need math skills. More important than the skills themselves, however, is the ability to apply those skills to our environment. Computer games and simulations can help us understand mathematical concepts (not just do calculations) and use them as a tool in solving problems relevant to our own experiences.

3. **Ability to analyze situations and determine appropriate actions:** In the past, educators assumed that by doing math problems (especially story problems) students learned to think, analyze tasks, and find solutions. Although mathematical concepts do help in many situations, they do not necessarily teach people to solve all kinds of problems. We all face many decisions every day, whose solutions do not depend on mathematical choices. Using simulation techniques, computers enable us to make choices and experience the effects of those choices without harm to ourselves, our environment, or others. We can even "undo" our decisions and try new ones to seek better outcomes (which we can seldom do in real life).

Figure 14.5.2

This computer lab environment lends itself to group problem solving as a learning technique.

4. **Technological familiarity:** In the Information Age world, computers will continue to proliferate like telephones or automobiles. To function effectively in that world, we must learn to use all the information-manipulating tools available, from pencils to networked computers. Not only must we learn to handle the tools, but we will need to understand their underlying concepts and limitations. Only when we divest computers of their aura of magic can we view them critically. Then, and only then, will we reap their benefits and avoid their risks.

5. **Local and global communication skills:** Today's technology has caused us to re-examine the definition and scope of the communication concept. In an era dependent on information flow, communication skills are the skills of survival. They include, of course, the traditional skills of speaking and writing, as well as the newer networking skills that allow us to communicate both locally and globally via computer.

Information Age Music Class—From the New World

The study of classical music "ain't what it used to be." In the education factory, classical music was placed on a pedestal and taught as a monument. One listened in silent reverence or hated it completely. Music appreciation classes were long sessions where the teacher explained symphonic form, and followed that by playing endless tapes. At some point, after you had listened to enough examples, you somehow became a cultured individual, with a fine taste for the classics.

continues

bits & bytes

Boring, says Robert Winter, distinguished music professor, former head of the music department at UCLA, classical music scholar, and master of the art of multimedia. Instead, Winter designs CD-ROM programs for today's appreciation of music. Let's see how an information age classical music session might go, using a recent Winter CD-ROM program on Antonin Dvorak's *From the New World* symphony.

You adjust your computer's sound system, load in the Dvorak disc, and double-click on the disc's icon. The opening screen shows a picture of Dvorak and a table of contents. Listed are topics of historic and cultural significance, a glossary of relevant musical terminology, and an annotated bibliography. You can choose to analyze the make-up of the orchestra, read reviews, or listen to all or part of the symphony.

While you listen you might choose to view the score, either in its formal, printed form, or as musical sketch in the composer's own handwriting. You could study the music themes of the piece or its rhythmic structure. Perhaps you might want to switch back and forth from the analysis to the performance, or understand a bit about the social milieu in which Dvorak lived. You might even want to know something more about the composer himself—he was considered wild in the 1890s.

Most important, you can do all these things, or none of them, at your own pace and your own choice. You can review, or not, more than 800 pages of original historical documents. You have at hand a library of scholarly information, a stack of fine recordings, and a superbly knowledgeable guide. Sitting at your computer, your head buzzing with information, ideas and music, you feel you're in a room with records, books, scores, and an exciting teacher—all right there with you, and every bit of it is available to you at the click of a mouse.

Figure 14.5.3

Some possible careers of the past have all but vanished today ... replaced by others that never existed before the computer revolution.

6. **Cultural awareness:** With so many human activities becoming seemingly dependent on technology, we must never lose sight of those things that are essentially human. Computer advances such as CD-ROM and the World Wide Web have made exploration of humanistic topics such as music and the arts, history, sociology, and psychology especially accessible.

7. **Learning how to learn:** Just as the jobs people trained for in the nineteenth century no longer are as important now (blacksmiths, buggy builders, telegraph operators, to name a few), many of the jobs of the future do not yet exist (see Figure 14.5.3). Because of the speed of societal change we experience today, tomorrow's workers will not have time to learn new jobs in advance. The skills they learn will be obsolete before they can be applied in the workplace. (That is already true of computer-related technological skills today!) Therefore, tomorrow's workers will have to know how to learn as they go along, often on their own, without training.

14.6 How Do Computers Help Us Learn?

Recent computer advances broaden the computer's effectiveness as a learning tool. This technology includes the **CD-ROM**, **local area** networks (**LANs**), and the **Internet**. The advances are changing the way learning is done. The most extreme example of this is distance learning.

CD-ROM

The major significance of CD-ROM technology is that it allows immediate accessibility to large amounts of interrelated digitized data, on demand. In the past, student resources were limited to whatever books and so on were in the classroom, whatever materials the teacher brought in, and of course, the teacher. Other resources such as encyclopedias, microfiche, and periodicals in the library were unavailable until the student got to them.

Because of its large capacity, a single CD-ROM disc might contain, in addition to the project or activity assignment, a wealth of books and articles, sound and video clips, helpful hints, and enrichment materials, all on hand for immediate use. Therefore, an individual student can ask questions, get definitions and examples, see historical enrichment, try alternative solutions, and explore related topics, bounded only by his or her interests and capacity for learning.

Local Area Networks

The use of local area networks has brought about three major advances to learning technology:

Figure 14.6.1

CD-ROM technology allows immediate accessibility to large quantities of interrelated information.

- **Increased flexibility of lab use:** Because all machines in a given lab are connected, students have better access to uncorrupted software, both on an individual and group basis. If the particular program a student wants to use becomes corrupted, infected with a virus, or is accidentally deleted, a clean copy can be quickly downloaded and installed to that lab station from the lab's network server, saving the student both time and wasted frustration. An added benefit to serving a lab via local area network is that students working together can collaborate and help each other (if encouraged to do so) learn the technology.

- **Decreased software and hardware costs:** Because many courseware development companies have instituted network pricing for their products, schools can experience substantial savings in a networked lab over the cost of many single copies of the same package. Having Web browsers and Internet access on the network's file server also cuts installation and telephone line costs. With stand-alone computers, each workstation in a given lab needs its own telephone line and modem for Internet access. A networked lab needs only one phone line connected to the server, with multiple client browsers sharing the access. Both initial and monthly savings are substantial.

- **Ease of software maintenance:** Suppose you have 30 computers in a student lab, all networked via a LAN to a file server using resident multi-launch programs. With proper configuration and password protection, software could be easily changed or maintained because only one copy needs to be modified. If network software needs to be upgraded, for example, the task merely involves upgrading one set of software—the one on the file server. After that

Figure 14.6.2

A networked classroom increases the flexibility and ease of maintenance for both software and computers.

has been upgraded, all networked stations can access the new versions from the file server. The lab would realize great savings in time and cost; upgrading and reloading software are time-consuming tasks for lab supervisors and employees.

Even if software in a networked lab is single-user software resident on each workstation, the network provides a way to cut the time and money consumed by maintenance. If the software at a particular workstation crashes, it can be downloaded from the file server quickly and effortlessly, again short-cutting the time-consuming reloading task.

The Internet

Although the Internet has existed for several years, only recently has it developed into the popular educational and personal tool it is today. Until now, the only information accessible through the Internet was textual—information you could read from your screen or download to your computer. Current technology has allowed the Internet to become a source for color graphics, video segments and sound clips, as well as text. Microcomputer speed and memory capacity make downloading such materials possible, and user-friendly graphic interface software, such as Netscape Navigator and Internet Explorer, makes accessing them easy and fun. As a result, the possibilities for Internet use in education are remarkable and limitless:

- The Internet can be searched by any student, at any grade or age level.
- Resulting materials can be used as a resource for any learning activity in any subject area.
- Surfing (browsing) the Web encourages development of creativity and intellectual curiosity.
- The free-form style of World Wide Web information can support any teacher's instructional strategy, and any student's learning style.
- Because information on the Internet is updated continuously, it provides a virtually limitless educational resource, easily adaptable to the needs of the Information Age school.

Distance Learning

Distance learning is an unsupervised, independent mode of education where students do not meet in a classroom but "meet" via interactive video, email, the Internet, and real-time electronic communication.

Distance learning is not a new concept. Correspondence courses, credits-by-exam, and even visiting teachers have long served the educational needs of students who are hospitalized, living in rural communities, or otherwise unable to attend regular classes. Why then include it in a section on new technology? Computer and video technologies have totally revolutionized distance learning. Networks, CD-ROMs, and the Internet have transformed it from a poor substitute for "real" school into a viable and respected learning methodology.

Here are some of the reasons for the success of the transformation:

- **Interactive video** enables distance students to get the same lectures available to in-class students, and to participate in post-lecture discussion and questioning.
- Wide area network use of telephone lines enables students with computers and modems to receive assignments and helpful handouts from the teacher.
- CD-ROMs and the Internet provide nearly endless resources of up-to-date information for completing projects and assignments.

The Computer Continuum

- **Electronic mail** enables distance students to submit completed assignments electronically and to receive timely critiques of their work.

- Review, test, and exam questions can be answered **online**, giving students immediate feedback and scoring.

- Real-time electronic written conversation can put the student in direct communication with the teacher for conferences and immediate response to questions.

Distance learning is not suitable for everyone. It is most successful for adults or for students with the self-discipline needed to complete unsupervised independent work.

Presentation Technology

Both traditional and information age learning environments rely heavily on the presentation of ideas and information. Teachers present new material to students; students present reports, conclusions, and solutions of problems to the teacher and their classmates. Information exchange is an inescapable part of the teaching/learning experience.

Figure 14.6.3
Presentation technology enables the teacher to present new information more effectively.

We have long known the value of visual enhancement to presentations. Think of the many times you have seen a speaker use a blackboard, flip chart, overhead projector, slides, charts, or models.

Here are a few of the ways current technology has enhanced the use of visual presentation materials:

- The development of **presentation software** has combined tools for outlining and word processing (including spell-checking) with layout, drawing, and graphics tools, enabling anyone to create professional-looking visuals for a presentation.

- Some software also incorporates online visual presentation capability. These packages can store in memory all the visuals needed for a presentation. The speaker can then, at the touch of a key or mouse button, switch from one visual to the next, adding fades, dissolves, layers, and other graphic effects for more impact and appeal.

Presentation software allows users to create text and color graphics presentations with animation and sound effects.

- **Computer video recorders** (special still cameras) can capture any image from the monitor, in full color, and digitize it for later use.

- **Computer projection panels**, both color and monochrome, allow use of an overhead projector to display whatever is on the computer's monitor on a screen.

14.7 The Information Age Classroom

In contrast to the education factory of the twentieth century, the schools of the twenty-first will become less teacher-centered and more focused on each individual student. Here are some of the characteristics of the **Information Age classroom** we can expect to see:

1. Rooms full of students all facing the teacher, listening carefully and taking tests, will vanish. Instead, classrooms will be equipped with a wide variety of learning and activity stations, some suited for groups, some for individual work, and all with computer and Internet access.

2. The teacher's role will change from that of primary source of knowledge to primary guide to resources and their usage. Teachers will work with each student or activity group individually, guiding them in selecting appropriate resources, and seeking solutions to problems.

Figure 14.7.1

In the Information Age classroom, teachers will work with each student or group individually.

3. Every student will follow a unique program of experiences best suited to his or her educational needs. When interests and abilities overlap, students will work in small groups on specific activities.

4. Dictionaries, encyclopedias, and other knowledge resources will be instantly available on demand, online. Students will be able to access both local and international resources using computers and the Internet.

5. Students will demonstrate mastery through presentation of projects and demonstration of problem-solving activities and experiences, rather than by regurgitation of facts on tests.

The Computer Continuum

On the whole, students will have to work harder in the Information Age classroom. The burden of acquiring an education will shift to them from the teacher. The rewards, however, are worthwhile:

- A meaningful, challenging learning environment customized to each person's needs and interests
- Emphasis placed on individual abilities and goals
- A population able to cope with the rapid changes characteristic of a highly technological society

A Computerized CPR Tutorial

The American Heart Association, in conjunction with a computer company called Actronics, developed an interactive computer training system to teach cardiopulmonary resuscitation (CPR). CPR is a technique used to sustain the life of a heart attack victim by using external pressure to manipulate the heart while also providing fresh oxygen to the lungs. The technique can be continued indefinitely until help arrives or the victim's heart starts beating normally again. It can save thousands of lives.

The CPR tutorial was designed to replace human instruction with a completely automated computerized learning system, which could provide the following:

- Accommodating and responsive instruction in basic concepts
- Hands-on instruction with mannequin to develop mechanical skills
- Visual and audio feedback based on performance
- Easy operation for the average person
- Training to pass the American Heart Association's performance test

The CPR training system consisted of an intricate human mannequin equipped with multiple sensors, videodisk technology, and a random access voice-playback system. All components were controlled and coordinated by a computer.

The picture shows the CPR training system in action and a "naked" mannequin showing its sensor arrangement. The sensors continuously check the student's progress in three major areas: opening the victim's airway, ventilating the victim (that is, mouth-to-mouth resuscitation), and performing external chest compression.

Context-sensitive graphic images and video demonstrations lead the student through each step of the process. Data collected while a student is working forms the basis for individual evaluation and helpful feedback. In addition to evaluating each student's technique, the system provides suggestions for improved performance.

Chapter Summary

What you can do with what you have learned:

- Identify important educational microcomputers.
- Find an educational computer program for almost any topic.
- Analyze learning into different types.
- See how computers can be used to bring education into the Information Age.
- Use a LAN for quick update and maintenance of software.
- Look on the Internet for any topic of interest.
- Investigate a new area of interest in a distance-learning environment.

Key Terms and Review Questions

Key terms introduced in this chapter:

Education factory 4-46

Factory model 4-46

Altair 8800 4-46

BASIC 4-47

Commodore Pet 4-47

Apple computer 4-47

IBM PC 4-47

IBM PC Jr. 4-47

Macintosh 4-47

CAD/CAM (computer-aided design and manufacturing) 4-50

Cognitive learning 4-51

Psychomotor skills 4-51

Social interaction 4-51

Cognitive 4-52

Knowledge 4-52

Thinking skills 4-52

Interactive multimedia 4-53

CD-ROM 4-56

LAN (local area network) 4-56

Internet 4-57

Distance learning 4-58

Interactive video 4-58

Electronic mail 4-59

Online 4-59

Presentation technology 4-59

Presentation software 4-59

Computer video recorders 4-60

Computer projection panels 4-60

Information Age classroom 4-60

Matching

Match the key terms introduced in the chapter to the following statements. Each term may be used once, more than once, or not at all.

1. _____During what period of time did our educational system develop?

2. _____On which model was our educational system built?

3. _____Which microcomputer was the first to incorporate the mouse?

4. _____What was the name of the first microcomputer?

5. _____ This category of learning contains the subcategories of knowledge and thinking skills.

6. _____ This category of learning has activities that involve the development of successful relationships with other people.

7. _____ This category of learning includes the ability to analyze and solve problems.

8. _____ This category of learning includes behaviors that deal with neuromuscular coordination.

9. _____ This category of learning develops social values and emotional response.

10. _____ Topics included in this category of learning include management skills and leadership skills.

11. _____ Computer programs in this category of learning are designed to develop coordination and motor skills.

12. _____ Computer programs written to review and practice what has been previously taught fall into this classification of learning.

13. _____ An example of a program that relates to this category of learning might be a program that provides dynamic computer analysis of a golf swing or one that helps with a speech articulation problem.

14. _____ Topics in this category of learning include those that work with others.

15. _____ Social interaction uses these experiences that include a combination of microcomputers, video, and audio technology.

16. _____ The major significance of this technology is that it allows immediate accessibility to large amounts of interrelated digitized data on demand.

17. _____ Because of this, three major advances to learning technology have occurred; one of which is the availability of connected machines to have better access to software.

18. _____ This enables distance students to get the same lectures available to in-class students, and to participate in post-lecture discussion and questioning.

19. _____ This enables distance students to submit completed assignments electronically and receive timely critiques of their work.

20. _____ This tool enables anyone to create professional-looking visuals for a presentation.

True or False

1. _____ The first microcomputers had abundant commercial software available.

2. _____ Early on, if a teacher wanted a computer to do something, she or he had to program it.

3. _____ IBM never intended its microcomputers to be used in the home or school.

4. _____Today, very few programs are written with educational purposes in mind.

5. _____The reason why early programs were text-based with little sound is because of the difficulty to write programs back then.

6. _____People like to learn with computers.

7. _____A computer can be an expert in any field.

8. _____Computers can be used in education because computers are cheaper than human beings.

9. _____It is common to find educational computer programs that fall neatly into one of the categories of learning.

10. _____We can assume that a traditional teacher-student relationship exists when the computer is acting as (or replacing) the teacher.

11. _____Educational goals from the current factory model need to be redefined to fit new goals of the Information Age.

12. _____One way to achieve the educational goals of the Information Age is to increase the speed and comprehension level of reading of students.

13. _____Because of the advancement of computers and calculators, it is no longer necessary to excel in math.

14. _____Learning to solve math problems (especially story problems) can teach people to solve all problems that can arise in life.

15. _____Solving problems that arise in simulation programs can make us better prepared to solve similar problems in real life.

16. _____In the Information Age, computers will continue to be part of our lives.

17. _____In the Information Age, we will need to communicate with each other not only face to face, but also globally via the computer.

18. _____The CD-ROM is an example of a computer advancement that has broadened the computer's effectiveness as a learning tool.

19. _____One of the three major advances to learning technology that have occurred because of local area networks is the decrease in the cost of software to schools because of the ability to share one copy of purchased software to all computers on the network.

20. _____Having a network can cut down the amount of the laboratory's downtime when crashes occur.

Multiple Choice

Answer the multiple-choice questions by selecting the best answer from the choices given.

1. An example of this type of category of learning would be an astronaut training for manual maneuvering of a spacecraft.

   a. Cognitive learning
   b. Psychomotor skills
   c. Social interaction

2. Of all the categories of learning, this one is the hardest to define and to teach.

   a. Cognitive learning

   b. Psychomotor skills

   c. Social interaction

3. This category of learning comes from the Latin word for *think*.

   a. Cognitive learning

   b. Psychomotor skills

   c. Social interaction

4. Computer-guided practice programs such as reviewing math facts, historical dates, and vocabulary fall into this classification of learning.

   a. Cognitive learning

   b. Psychomotor skills

   c. Social interaction

5. This category of learning deals with the development of interpersonal skills.

   a. Cognitive learning

   b. Psychomotor skills

   c. Social interaction

6. The computer programs that pertain to this category of learning are those that are aimed at increasing general muscular control.

   a. Cognitive learning

   b. Psychomotor skills

   c. Social interaction

7. An example of this category of learning is the golf program that helps the player improve his/her game by adjusting club choice, stance, and shot type to specific holes on simulated courses.

   a. Cognitive learning

   b. Psychomotor skills

   c. Social interaction

8. These can be answered online, giving students immediate feedback and scoring.

   a. Interactive video

   b. Wide area network

   c. CD-ROMs

   d. Electronic mail

   e. Review, test, and exam questions

9. One of these can provide nearly endless resources of up-to-date information for completing projects and assignments.

   a. Interactive video

   b. Wide area network

   c. CD-ROM(s)

   d. Electronic mail

   e. Review, test, and exam questions

10. This can enable distance students to submit completed assignments electronically and to receive timely critiques of their work.

   a. Interactive video

   b. Wide area network

   c. CD-ROMs

   d. Electronic mail

   e. Review, test, and exam questions

Exercises

1. Why did BASIC become so important to the field of educational computing?

2. Describe how the use of video and audio has evolved in educational computing.

3. List three reasons mentioned in the book why computers can be used to teach.

4. Name three specific computer learning programs for each of the categories of education and training named in the text.

5. Make a list of 10 different pieces of educational software. You can find them at home, in your school, at a computer store, or reviewed in a magazine. For each one, determine what teaching strategy or strategies it contains.

6. Pick a somewhat simple task to teach a fellow student. Now write out in detail a flowchart that takes into account all possible situations. Refer to Chapter 5, "Computer Languages: Empowering Algorithms," for an example.

7. Visit a video arcade game parlor and make a survey of all the video games that seem to be teaching something other than just eye-hand coordination.

8. For each of the following goals of teaching, find a computer program that seeks to fulfill that goal. List the name of the program, the manufacturer, and the cost. Give a short (one paragraph) description of how the program meets the goal:

    a. Reading/writing literacy

    b. Ability to apply math concepts to solve problems

    c. Ability to analyze situations and determine appropriate actions

    d. Technological familiarity

    e. Local and global communication skills

    f. Cultural awareness

    g. Learning how to learn

9. Should government censor games such as Mortal Kombat? Does the same logic apply to movies, books, videos, and other forms of communication?

10. From one of the computer magazines in the library or by searching the Internet, find out the names of the top-selling multimedia CD-ROMs.

Discussion Questions

1. What if the mouse had not been developed? Are there any other input devices that could fill that gap?

2. Will computers put teachers out of work? Why do you think so?

3. How can computers be used with a classroom full of learners with varying rates of attention?

Group Project

A group of four students should select one of the grade level areas such as elementary, middle school, high school, or college and research software availability at that level. Each person should select one of the subject areas of the chosen level. Examine presentation and techniques used in the software and give a general critique. The group should meet to combine common elements found in the research results and then create a summary report. If possible, use a presentation program such as PowerPoint to make the report to the class.

The following are suggested topics that can be researched via the Internet and by examining software catalogs for the best software to teach them. If possible, try them yourself before making your review.

Level	Topics
2nd–4th grade students	Spelling of English words
2nd–4th grade students	How seeds germinate
2nd–4th grade students	Mathematical facts
2nd–4th grade students	Social responsibility
6th–7th grade students	Spelling of English words
6th–7th grade students	How seeds germinate
6th–7th grade students	Mathematical facts
6th–7th grade students	Social responsibility
10th–12th grade students	Spelling of English words
10th–12th grade students	How seeds germinate
10th–12th grade students	Mathematical facts
10th–12th grade students	Social responsibility

How do the software packages for teaching the same subject at different ages differ? How are they alike?

Are there some specific types of software that are more expensive than the rest?

Which are the best, in your opinion?

Web Connections

http://www.edb.utexas.edu/coe/depts/ci/bilingue/resources.html

A lot of links to bilingual education sites.

http://seawifs.gsfc.nasa.gov/ocean_planet.html

Presentation of the Smithsonian Institution on the Ocean Planet.

http://www.si.edu/organiza/museums/ripley/eap/

Smithsonian Institution site outlining an online presentation of Revealing Things, designed to look at things humans create and use that give insight into the society of the time.

http://whales.ot.com/

Information on whales and whale watching. Follow a teacher as she goes on a whale-watching cruise.

http://www.seaworld.org/sounds/contest.html

Animal sounds quiz. Click on a sound, listen, and identify which animal produced it from a list of possibilities.

http://liftoff.msfc.nasa.gov/

Space exploration site with links to sites where you can find your age or weight on other planets or where MIR space station is at the moment. Fun!

http://liftoff.msfc.nasa.gov/RealTime/JTrack/

Links to tracking spacecraft (such as MIR and Hubble), weather satellites, amateur radio satellites, and search-and-rescue satellites.

http://education.indiana.edu/cas/tt/tthmpg.html

Great page with suggestions, comments, and lesson plans for teachers of elementary and secondary students on a wide variety of topics. Presented in both cartoon form and text form. This is a wonderful resource.

http://www.house.gov/eeo/

Home page of the Committee on Education and the Workforce in the United States House of Representatives. Up-to-date information on current issues in education being considered by the House. Includes links to current floor activity and the daily schedule of this committee.

http://www.loc.gov/

Home page of the Library of Congress. Many links to interesting sites including current displays and how to research a topic using the site.

http://www.mrtc.org/~twright/quizzes/quizcenter/quizmaker.html

Tool for making online quizzes. Very easy directions for creating a quiz and having your students take it online. Try this one!

http://www.u.arizona.edu/ic/edtech/wave.html

A paper on adult education and how learning is done by adults. Good references to how technology and computers can aid this process.

http://ourworld.compuserve.com/homepages/jmtaylor/links.htm

Links to a myriad of sites for distance learning aimed at adult students. Many kinds of education are represented, from casual knowledge to doctoral degrees.

Bibliography

Alessi, Stephen M., and Stanley R. Trollip. *Computer-Based Instruction: Methods and Development*. Upper Saddle River, NJ: Prentice Hall, 1991.

Bauer, Jo Anne et.al. *Beyond a Technology's Promise: An Examination of Children's Educational Computing at Home*. New York: Cambridge University Press, 1994.

Collis, Betty ed. *Children and Computers in School*. New York: Lawrence Erlbaum Associates, 1996.

Eastmond, Daniel V. *Alone but Together: Adult Distance Study Through Computer Conferencing*. New York: Hampton Press, 1995.

Land, Michael, and Sandra Turner. *Tools for Schools: Applications Software for the Classroom*. New York: Wadsworth Publishing Company, 1996.

Maddux, Cleborne D. *Educational Computing: Learning with Tomorrow's Technologies*. New York: Allyn & Bacon, 1996.

Papert, Seymour. *The Children's Machine: Rethinking School in the Age of the Computer*. New York: Basic Books, 1994.

Perkins, David N. ed. *Software Goes to School: Teaching for Understanding with New Technologies*. London: Oxford University Press, 1997.

Porter, Lynnette R. *Creating the Virtual Classroom: Distance Learning with the Internet*. New York: John Wiley & Sons, 1997.

Chapter 15

Ethics, Electronic Spies, and Privacy

Chapter Objectives

By the end of this chapter, you will:

- Recognize the ethical issues involved in using computers in the electronic world.

- Appreciate how the use of a computer has added new possibilities to the list of crimes.

- Understand how trojan horse and salami-slicing programs can be used to steal money and goods.

- Understand how piggybacking and data diddling can be used to steal information or services.

- Recognize methods of protecting a computer from computer crime.

- Understand the motivation for pirating software and appreciate the scope of the problem.

- Understand the techniques used by illegal hackers and appreciate the simplicity and ease with which some hacking methods are completed.

- Know the damage a computer virus can cause and how to use a vaccine or disinfectant program to find and eliminate such viruses.

- Understand how inaccurate, incomplete, or poorly maintained information in databases can inadvertently invade individual privacy.

- Know how credit doctors steal identities for their clients.

15.1 Vulnerability and Technological Abuse

In the relatively short span of 45 years, humans have come to rely on computers as the controlling force in our everyday lives. The government, health care, the manufacturing industry, education, research, commerce, finance, military defense, transportation, distribution, and personal and public communication all rely on computers and related software systems to function. If we suddenly removed computer technology from these institutions, life as we know it would come to a grinding halt.

Why the Phones Stopped

On January 15, 1990, the AT&T long-distance network of 114 switching centers throughout the United States went dead for almost nine hours. The cost to business nationwide was measured in the hundreds of millions of dollars. It was inconceivable that the company noted for its extremely reliable software could have a software problem of such immense proportions. In reality, it came down to a single line of the program that had never been executed (and therefore never tested) because the conditions were never exactly right to cause that part of the program to be accessed. Each center having trouble was running a copy of the tainted program that day.

Indeed, our dependence on high-tech systems swells daily, and will continue to do so as we rush into the twenty-first century. As our trust in computers grows, our vulnerability to their abuse grows also. Unfortunately, the machine on which we rely so heavily has displayed its dark side over the past several years, showing it to be the vehicle for a broad range of bothersome activities.

Radiation Treatment Gone Berserk

The use of radiation in the control of cancers is quite common. Typically, beams of electrons are aimed at small affected areas of the body, building up a therapeutic dose of between 4,000 and 6,000 rads delivered in 20 or 30 treatments over a period of a month or more.

In 1985 and 1986, a subtle software error in the programming of a Therac-25, a multi-million dollar radiation machine, caused some individuals to receive single doses of radiation of between 17,000 and 25,000 rads. The results were tragic. Within several months, the malfunctioning machine had burned a number of patients, left others with partial paralysis, and killed one person. Previously, the machine had been running at several hospitals throughout the country without a problem.

This chapter examines some important issues inherent in our electronic world—issues caused by our very dependence on computers and by their vulnerability to system failure and to human abuse. These include the following:

- Use of computers to commit crimes
- Unauthorized use of hardware
- Data theft
- Sabotage
- Theft (piracy) of software
- Individual privacy

The Computer Continuum

Interlaced with these sociotechnological issues is an ethical one. How can we define, for novices and professionals alike, appropriate interactions with each other and with the machines themselves? Here are some ethical concerns to be considered:

- At what point does collection of data become an invasion of privacy?

- What constitutes misuse of information?

- Who is responsible for data security?

- Are so-called 'victimless crimes' (such as those against banks) as serious as crimes with human victims?

- Is copying software a form of stealing?

- Are hackers criminals or protectors of our civil liberties?

- How should we deal with the creators of viruses?
  and finally,

- Should there be a code of ethics to control computer use and protect the rights of all? If so, who should define that code, and how can it be enforced?

Figure 15.1.1

At what point does storage of personal data become an invasion of privacy?

Factual Reporting or Deception?

Controversy surrounded O.J. Simpson's arrest and prosecution for the murder of his ex-wife, Nicole Simpson, and Ronald Goldman—the media trial of the 90s. *Time* magazine's June 27, 1994, article featuring an enhanced mug shot of Simpson on the cover of the magazine was sharply criticized for its sinister portrayal. Dark shadows had been added to the mug shot photo. Opposing journalists and others claim the changes were racist and deceptive. *Time* defended photo alteration on the grounds that image enhancement is art appropriate for a cover of the magazine. According to *Time* editors, they alter cover photos on a regular basis and page three notes when the cover is a photo illustration. *Newsweek* published an unaltered O.J. mug shot on its June 27 issue.

Media policies regarding photo enhancement are set by each organization. The National Press Photographers Association guidelines state that editorial and/or hard-news pictures should not be altered like an advertisement. Yet, image enhancement of editorial and hard-news photos is done. The following are just some examples:

- *National Geographic* shifted one of the Great Pyramids of Egypt so that the photo would fit on its cover.

- The *Orange County Register* made the sky bluer in a smoggy picture of Los Angeles and in another photo closed a young boy's zipper that was open at the time the photo was taken.

- The *St. Louis Post Dispatch* deleted a Diet Coke can from a photo of the paper's office celebration.

Norway requires that all photo illustrations or manipulated photos be marked by a box with the icon "M." Currently, most U.S. publishers indicate that a photo is enhanced on another page in the publication. How should the United States address these issues? Should it be through self-regulation, litigation, or photo branding similar to Norway?

15.2 High-Tech Crime: The Computer as a Criminal Tool

Unfortunately, helpful tools can be used to support criminal as well as legitimate activities. Just as fire can either provide heat or destroy homes, computer technology can either create ideas or steal them.

Because of their scope and power, computers have provided both law-enforcement professionals and criminals with opportunities that have never existed before. The FBI, for example, now uses its home page on the World Wide Web (**http://www.fbi.gov**) as a powerful weapon against crime and criminals. The first several screens give information about the Bureau, its personnel, and its activities. Another screen lists persons currently suspected of criminal activities. Other screens, still accessed through the FBI home page, tell readers how to protect themselves from some types of computer crimes. Before the Internet and the Web, the most common place used by the FBI to display information about criminal activity was on post office bulletin boards across the country.

Criminals have used much greater ingenuity in finding ways to use computers in crime. Every new technological advance has served as an open invitation for the development of a new type of crime. ATMs (automated teller machines), EFTs (electronic fund transfers), and cellular phones have all provided new platforms for theft and fraud.

In fact, computer crime has become an expensive national phenomenon. In 1988, an accounting firm in Cleveland reported that computer crimes cost U.S. companies between $3 billion and $5 billion *per year*! That was over a decade ago. Imagine what that figure must be now if computer crimes have proliferated at the same rate as computers.

What Is a Computer Crime?

What illegal activities are we talking about here? Well, we have found three different definitions for computer crime:

1. A **computer crime** is any criminal act that has been committed using a computer as the principle tool.

   For our purposes, this definition is much too broad. What if a thief gained access to your house by tossing a computer mouse through your window and breaking the glass? What if a person wanted to kill someone and hit his victim over the head with the nearest heavy object—a computer keyboard? Would either of these be a computer crime? We don't think so. So let's examine a second definition:

2. A **computer crime** is an illegal activity that could not take place without a computer.

   Well … that's a little better. If definition (1) was too broad, then (2) is perhaps too narrow. Under this definition, computer crimes would require computer expertise and skill in their implementation. Experience tells us that many, many "computer crimes" have needed very little skill, relying instead on opportunity and determination. So let's try one more:

3. A **computer crime** is any illegal activity using computer software, data, or access as the object, subject, or instrument of the crime.

   This "middle-of-the-road" definition better suits our purposes, providing a broad umbrella under which we can study the several types of crime computers are used for every day.

High-Tech Heists

Theft of Money. By far, the great majority of computer crimes fall under the general category of theft. The heist can take any one of several forms. Most popular, of course, is the theft of money. Consider this example:

> On Christmas Eve a few years ago, a 26-year-old bank clerk used SWIFT, an international electronic funds-transfer system, to divert two large corporate bank deposits. The money, totaling over $15 million, was sent to a secret account the clerk had opened in Switzerland. A few days later, the clerk flew to Switzerland to claim his stolen funds. Imagine his disappointment when he found that an unforeseen computer malfunction had interrupted one of the transactions. The service interruption caused by the malfunction was noted on a security screen. Instead of collecting a generous Christmas bonus, the clerk got instead a prolonged vacation in a federal prison. In a perfect example of poetic justice, the criminal was caught by the same computer that he used to perpetrate the crime.

Theft of Goods. Another form of theft freely adapted to technological crime is the theft of goods. This type of crime uses the computer to track goods and alter computer inventories, redirecting products to a safe location—from which they can be sold for cash. Here's an example:

> Suppose you order a shipment of electronic equipment for your company. When the shipment arrives, you find it has been incorrectly packed and that what is in the box is not what you ordered. Following directions on the packing list, you dial a touch-tone customer-service line. You are told to return the parcel to a warehouse address

and to charge shipping costs to the manufacturer's UPS account. Of course, you follow instructions. What you don't know is that computers have befuddled both the company's inventory records and its shipping charges. The manufacturer will never again see his goods because the thief runs a catalog sales business from that warehouse.

Figure 15.2.3

Computerized inventories can be manipulated to mask illegal sales of goods from a warehouse.

The trojan horse involves the insertion of false information into a program to profit from the outcome.

Salami-slicing involves spreading the haul over a large number of trivial transactions, like slices of salami in a sandwich.

Thefts of money and goods by computer have become so prevalent that some specific techniques for implementing these crimes have surfaced. Two noteworthy techniques are the **trojan horse** and **salami-slicing**.

The two scenarios already described illustrate the trojan horse technique. Here is a classic example of salami-slicing:

A bank clerk had the job of updating customer accounts by running the program that added daily interest to all savings. As part of the program, each new total was rounded to two decimal places before being recorded. If a total had come out to $1,406.4544290, for example, the recorded total would be $1,406.45. The clerk inserted a line into the program diverting the rounded-off amount (in this case, .0044290, nearly half of a cent) into a secret account of his own. That's a thin slice of salami indeed, but the secret account added thousands of them a day. There were several millions in the account by the time the theft was discovered.

Theft of Information or Services. A third form of computer crime involves the theft or unauthorized use of information and electronic services. An important technique involves **data diddling**.

Figure 15.2.4

Each individual transaction in a salami-slicing theft is as thin as the slices of meat on this sandwich.

4-74

The Computer Continuum

In the following example, data diddling was used to redirect phone use charges to someone else's number:

> In 1997, the *New York Times* reported that 18 residents of New York were arrested for stealing mobile communication services. They had reprogrammed the microchips in their cellular phones so that calls could be made at no charge. At the time of the arrest, this fraud was costing the local cellular phone company nearly $140,000 per month.

Data diddling involves swapping one piece of information for another of the same type.

Figure 15.2.5

Cellular telephone users are often the target for fraud and illegal telemarketing scams.

The several thefts discussed so far have had one thing in common: in each crime, the computer was an important tool in perpetrating the heist. The types of thefts themselves were not new.

Although banks and moneyed individuals are the chief targets of computer criminals, governments, charge card users, communication providers, and insurance companies are also highly vulnerable. Can they protect themselves from the unprecedented onslaught of computer criminals?

The growth of computer crime calls for the development of new kinds of security measures. These are costly, both in financial and computer resources, and companies have been slow in implementing them. Nevertheless, security can be improved relatively easily by adopting some common-sense measures. Here are a few:

- Protect all data, programs, and system access by **password**.
- Issue passwords to as few people as possible and to no outsiders.
- Make passwords less obvious and less memorable: Avoid family names, pet names, or company partners' names. Avoid birth dates and holiday dates.
- Avoid using common "cuties," such as *money*, *taxes*, *sex*, *love*, and *genius*, as your password. These were all on a common passwords list compiled in the early 90s.
- Change passwords frequently. This will minimize the chance that someone who learns your password today can use it in the future.

15.3 Software Piracy

Let's face it. The computer industry has changed drastically over the past several years. The cost of computer hardware has spiraled continuously downward, with the same number of dollars able to purchase more and more computing power over the years.

- In 1984, $2,500 purchased an Atari 800 computer, with 16KB of RAM memory, one floppy-disk drive, no hard drive, and an adapter that enabled you to use your color television as a monitor.

- The same $2,500 in 1998, less than 15 years later, got you a 200MHz Pentium II–powered machine, with 16MB of RAM, a high-density floppy drive, a CD-ROM drive, and two or more gigabytes of hard drive space. A high-resolution color monitor and sound adapter and several hundred dollars worth of software were also included.

- Today, the same amount of money would give you an even more powerful computer system.

Because of these hardware changes, the importance of software is on the rise. Without software (sets of instructions written by human beings), computers are little more than useless lumps of silicon, metal, and plastic. Therefore, much of the industry's excitement and money is centered on the software market. In fact, the total world market for software soars somewhere near the $100 billion mark. As a result, the illegal copying of computer programs, called **software piracy**, has become a major growth industry.

Exactly What Is Software Piracy?

Actually, a clear, simple definition for software piracy already exists (see margin definition!).

> **Software piracy** is the unauthorized copying or use of software for which you have not paid the appropriate licensing fee.

The key phrases here are *unauthorized* and *appropriate licensing fee*. When you purchase a piece of software, you usually get a box containing some books (called **documentation**) and one or more disks. No matter how much you paid, however, you do not own the program. The money you paid was actually a licensing fee. This gives you authorization (called a **license**) to copy the program onto your own machine and make personal use of it. When you open the package containing your disks, you agree to abide by the terms of the license.

The program you "bought" is actually owned by the company that developed it or paid for its development. For a fee—the price you pay for the software—the owner of the software allows you to use it. This is called licensing. The practice of software licensing dates back to the early 1960s. The rights of software ownership were formally defined and protected by the **U.S. Computer Software Copyright Act of 1980**. Under this legislation, computer programs are copyrighted as "intellectual works." Therefore, computer programs fall into the same class as books and magazines. It is illegal to use or copy any of them without the copyright holder's written permission. Many questions have arisen since 1980, and the Copyright Act is under constant re-examination and re-interpretation. But its basic premise is the same: Unlicensed use and copying constitute software piracy, and as such, are illegal.

How Big a Problem Is Software Piracy?

In a word, the problem is ENORMOUS! The U.S. Software Publishing Association estimated in 1990 that its members lose $4–6 billion a year because of software theft. Lotus, Inc., the developers of the popular *Lotus 1-2-3* and the *Lotus Suite*, claims that over half of its potential sales in the early 1990s was lost to pirates—at a loss to the company of over $160 million every year. MicroPro, the company behind *Wordstar*, estimated that during the same time period, two or three illegal copies of the program existed for every one that was legally purchased. If you multiply these figures by the number of programs on the market today, you will get an idea of the scope of the piracy problem.

Although software piracy has yet to be conquered, the SPA (Software Producers Association) is making terrific inroads in combating it. Clearer, more precise statements of intellectual property rights and licensing have heightened awareness of piracy throughout the private and corporate sectors. In commerce, education, industry, and even government offices and labs, increasing evidence shows a gradual reduction in the mass copying of software packages. In schools and computer clubs, long-time bastions of casual software piracy, attitudes are changing. No longer is it common for entire school districts to make a few copies of an application package available on every machine in the district. Instead, a much more serious approach to software copyrighting prevails. The result is a national trend toward "being legal" with software—purchasing sufficient licenses of each application program to cover the number of machines that actually use it. The problem of piracy is not yet solved, but conditions are definitely improving.

15.4 Hacking

There are nearly as many definitions for **hacking** as there are **hackers** and their victims. Let's list just a few:

- **Hacking** means the same as software troubleshooting—if you can make a program work despite the frustrations of others, you are a hacker.

- **Hacking** is problem solving using the computer. Under this definition, a hacker is a person who has to see whether some task is possible.

- **Hacking** is delving into the workings of a computer and its software to learn as much as possible about it.

- **Hacking** is trying to discover information by malicious persistence in poking around existing data sources.

- **Hacking** is discovering and using other people's passwords, often without permission.

Each of these definitions has at least some validity. Some seem to describe hacking as a perfectly legal, and even noble activity. For our purposes here, however, our discussion is limited to the use of hacking techniques for illegal purposes. The term often used to describe illegal hacking is **cracking**.

- **Cracking** is breaking into other people's systems for either fun or profit or with intent to commit blackmail or sabotage.

Gang War in Cyberspace

Two groups of youths turned an adolescent hobby into a 23-page federal indictment. The cyberspace gangs, the Masters of Deception (MOD) and the Legions of Doom (LOD), were made up of extremely smart young men who clashed over typical cultural differences. The *D* in either gang's name could never stand for *Dumb* (even though most were failing traditional high school). The warfare began in 1989.

continues

bits & bytes

They were self-taught computer whizzes. Each night they explored cyberspace to learn all they could about computers and information systems. No teacher could ask for more motivated or creative students. They used trial and error and picked the brains of experts until they graduated into experts themselves.

In 1989, Phiber Optik, alias Mark Abene, age 17, was inducted into the LOD gang because of his expertise on telephone system hacking. Erik Bloodaxe, alias Chris Groggans, age 20, was LOD's leader. LOD had an unofficial creed that member hackers should not share system secrets with just anyone and that they should be courteous. Phiber Optik believed the opposite: He freely shared system secrets and belittled inferior hackers. As a result, Phiber Optik was soon kicked out of the LOD.

In response to Phiber's expulsion, Acid Phreak founded MOD as a joke. Acid Phreak, Outlaw, and Corrupt were a group of hackers who were protégés of Phiber Optik. MOD was a joke until an LOD member made racial slurs about Corrupt during a telephone conference bridge. The racial slur united the inner city New York boys of MOD against the Texans.

A telephone conference bridge is when three-way calling services are hacked into for free. The hackers set up a daisy-chain in which many hackers from Europe to the United States all talked simultaneously in a single phone session.

The MOD group began attacking Bloodaxe's telephone lines. Bloodaxe retaliated by translating the Internet file/document "The History of MOD" into jive-talk. Shortly after, Bloodaxe decided to go straight and start a firm called Comsec Data Security, a computer security firm. Comsec Data became somewhat successful and, therefore, a new target for the MOD boys. The gang quietly began eavesdropping on Comsec's business.

A prospective customer called Comsec for help in finding out who was playing with his phone lines. Groggan's told the customer he thought it was MOD. During Groggan's conversation with the customer, Corrupt called and said it did sound like something MOD would do! Groggan was furious when he realized Corrupt had been listening to the conversation. Who would hire a computer security firm that couldn't keep its own lines secure, and what had MOD broadcasted about Comsec and its clients? He called the FBI.

The FBI already was watching MOD and monitoring their phone lines to build a case. Groggan's information and statements were valuable. In all, 11 counts and charges of illegal computer intrusion were filed against Phiber Optik and his pals.

The irony of the whole affair is that MOD never hurt anyone's system. Their biggest transgression was the thousands of dollars in revenue lost by telephone companies and businesses for MOD's illegal telephone usage. (The LOD also illegally tapped into the phone companies and corporate systems.) Many experts believe their antics had a benefit: They revealed the weaknesses in their victims' computer systems and thereby allowed the corporations to fix their fences before someone really dangerous trespassed to steal trade secrets. Money for personnel and processing time was well spent protecting the companies' data—it was not a loss, as stated in the indictment charges.

LOD, MOD, and Comsec no longer exist. Most of the gang members are now gainfully employed by various computer and information system firms (hacking was excellent job training). Phiber Optik served the longest time in jail, 18 months.

Who Are Crackers and Why Do They Hack?

Some hackers see themselves as adventurists, approaching computers as new adventures that are full of fun and excitement. For them, the primary appeal of hacking is the intellectual challenge it presents. Guessing passwords and bypassing file protections pose intriguing problems that some individuals will go to huge lengths to solve. **Crackers**, those who hack maliciously, have additional, more personal motives. Some, for example, are disgruntled ex-employees, using the computer as an instrument of vengeance. Here are two examples:

- An employee who had been recently fired (unfairly, he felt) planted a **logic bomb** in the company's main computer. He then threatened to trigger it unless the company paid him a weekly salary of $350 until he found another job. If triggered, the bomb would have erased sensitive information from the databank, jeopardizing the company's future operations. Fortunately for the company, an internal electronic "bomb squad" located and removed the software bomb. The former employee was later arrested.

- A low-level programmer at a large software company had reason to suspect that she was about to be fired. While still on the job, she wrote a little routine to check employee records daily to see whether her ID number was still there. She secretly embedded her routine into the company's software system. As long as the programmer's ID number remained in the file, the logic bomb did nothing. If her number were removed, meaning she was no longer an employee, the logic bomb would be triggered, destroying important pieces of the company's software and data files.

A **time bomb** or **logic bomb** is a software routine that can be triggered at some later time by the computer's clock or by a predetermined combination of events.

Figure 15.4.1

A time bomb program lurks in a computer's system, ready to destroy files at a predetermined time or when a certain event occurs.

More than anything, however, computer crackers hack as an expression of power. Psychologists have defined the cracker personality as a basically competent intellect with severe social inadequacies. We sometimes refer to these people as "nerds." Unable to function well in the complex relationships of human interactions, they turn more and more to computer interactions for personal gratification. Becoming crackers, they measure success in terms of the power they wield—power over the technology they abuse, power over the humans they outsmart, and power over the institutional and corporate entities they damage. They have the potential to cause massive societal damage and few skills in understanding the enormous human costs of their acts.

Scavenging is searching through stray data and electronic garbage for clues that might unlock the secrets of a targeted computer system.

Contrary to popular belief, the great majority of hacking involves minimal intellectual challenge or computer expertise. Although some system penetrations display incredible ingenuity, most rely on a few basic characteristics: excessive determination on the part of the hacker, reliance on human fallibility, and hours of tedious drudgery. Armed with only a minimal set of equipment—a computer, a modem, and some communications software—the hacker intending to cause harm relies heavily on three or four techniques to identify and penetrate new computer systems. By far the easiest technique is **scavenging**.

Figure 15.4.2

Scavengers search the computer's electronic trash seeking clues to unlock the secrets of its data and system.

From the comfort of his home (Did you know than over 85 percent of all known hackers have been male?), the hacker browses known systems and networks for bits and pieces of data garbage that might in the future provide some clue or insight into system penetration. Among useful tidbits might be descriptions of password systems and security plans, information about corporate hardware and software, and even descriptions of successful hacks. The tidbits thus gleaned are organized and stored (electronically, of course) for later use.

Another very common attack technique is **password guessing**. As mentioned earlier, computer users are amazingly unoriginal in the selection of passwords. A determined hacker often has to go no further than persistently checking the most commonly used passwords on known user accounts: names or initials of pets, friends, spouses, children; birth dates or sequential strings of letters or numbers (qwerty, asdf, abcde, and 12345, for example); and popular "cutesy" words (sex, love, word, fred, god, and genius, for example). It is surprising how much sensitive data can be accessed through the use of such common passwords.

Still another popular technique requires adding a special feature to the communication system. Called an autodialer, this program will systematically dial all possible combinations of telephone numbers within a given numeric range. Thus while the hacker eats, sleeps, or watches TV, his computer can target the particular area where a large computer installation is suspected to exist. It just dials all numbers in the area, one at a time. Most of these calls will be answered by humans, answering devices, or fax machines, and many will go unanswered. A few, however, will reach the carrier tone of another computer's modem. Those numbers are stored, and the cracker can later get to work accessing that system.

A last word about computer cracking, and then we will move on. Apart from the simple identification of target systems and guessing of passwords, there are few ways a hacker can access a system from the outside. Most system penetrations are assisted by some form of inside aid. In universities, a cracker need only spend time in a computer lab.

The Computer Continuum

Sooner or later (and more often sooner) an unsuspecting student will leave without logging off the network. Pay dirt! The hacker just sits down at the terminal and has full access to the system by **piggybacking** on a legitimate user. The ease with which this is accomplished should remind us that much responsibility for illegal hacking lies with the casualness of computer users and network administrators alike. Hacking will be controlled only if we protect computer assets more seriously.

15.5 The Virus Epidemic

Among the most malicious products of computer hackers today is a group of programs designed to create havoc and destroy data wherever they go. The term used to describe such a program is **virus**. Let's spend a few minutes examining what a virus is and how it works.

What Is a Computer Virus?

A **virus** is a self-replicating program that may cause damage—generally hard disk erasure or data file corruption. It infects other programs, floppy disks, and hard disks by copying itself to them. Operating systems and "boot" segments of disks are especially susceptible to viral damage. Some viruses are harmless, merely informing the user that the system has been infected without doing any damage. They serve as a warning to the user that a more serious infection could just as easily have happened without detection. Other viruses, of course, are far from harmless.

Why would anyone go to the trouble of creating a virus and inserting in into an infectious situation if no harm was intended or caused? Like other hackers, virus writers seek intellectual release from boredom. Although many remain anonymous, they still seek recognition of their computer-controlling skills and acknowledgment for their computer prowess. Impotent viruses are the virus creator's way of demonstrating power without causing lasting harm. If we add malicious intent to cause damage to intellectual boredom, the result could create havoc in the computer community.

The most obvious and common way to infect a system is to piggyback a virus onto legitimate programs so that the virus can be transported on storage media such as tapes, floppy disks, and hard disks. In addition, a piggybacked virus can be transported via network links, bulletin boards, and electronic mail. As long as the virus appears to be part of a legitimate program or can attach itself to legitimate programs, its spread to other systems and users is assured.

■ A particularly malicious virus, later referred to as the Lehigh virus, was discovered at Lehigh University in Bethlehem, PA, late in 1987. After the virus infected a hard disk, it checked all other disks inserted into the machine. If it found uninfected system files on the disk, the virus copied itself to them. When an infected disk was

Figure 15.4.3

A cracker's main technique involves searching for the key to unlock a supposedly secure computer system.

Piggybacking involves invading a communication system by riding in behind a legitimate user with a password.

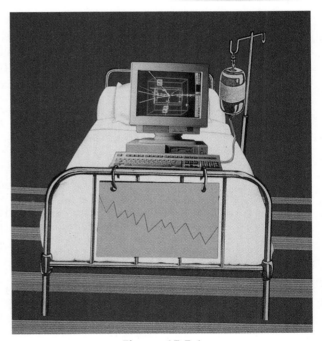

Figure 15.5.1

Many serious computer illnesses can be traced to an electronic virus.

copied for the fourth time, the virus destroyed all data on the disk, after first attaching itself to the new copy.

A simple and effective variation on the virus theme is to combine the qualities of the time bomb and the virus, producing a program that begins its self-replicating damage on a specific date or destroys a system only after a predetermined time lapse. This was the modus operandi of the so-called Jerusalem (Friday the 13th) virus.

■ First signs of a full-scale viral infection were noticed on Israeli computers when programs that had run thousands of times with no problem suddenly became too large to fit into available memory. The virus appeared to work by copying itself into memory and then attaching itself to any other program the user might subsequently execute. Over a period of time, the virus seemed to mutate, exhibiting different effects at differing intervals. During its second year, for example, the virus would wait for 30 minutes after the machine was turned on and then slow the machine down to one-fifth its normal speed. Later, the virus would cause different sections of the screen to scroll (jump up and down) uncontrollably. But whenever the date was Friday the 13th, any program on the infected disk that was executed was destroyed.

It is estimated that the Jerusalem virus infected some 20,000 machines before it was stopped. That brings up the final consideration of this section: How can you stop a virus?

Vaccines and Disinfectants

A **vaccine** is a program that searches your disk for viruses and notifies you of any that were found.

With computer viruses, as with those that affect human health, an ounce of prevention is worth a pound of cure. Therefore, the best way to stop the effects of a virus is to prevent it from invading your disks. One way to do this is to make periodic use of a preventative virus checker, called a **vaccine** or **disinfectant**.

Some vaccines can search for and identify a wide variety of different viruses. Others, which are more restrictive, can detect only a single virus. Unfortunately, most virus-detection programs do not eradicate a virus on contact. They can pinpoint the exact location of a virus and identify what software has been infected but can eliminate the virus only by erasing the infected programs from the disk.

After a particular virus has been detected, it can be isolated by moving other programs on the infected disk to new storage media. After other software has been secured, the infected disk can be erased and reformatted for later use.

Of course, the best protection you can get is never to allow the virus to reach your disks. There are three simple and effective ways to protect your disks and system:

1. Always write-protect your system-booting disks. This will prevent viruses from copying themselves to your operating system and from there to your hard disk.

2. Use a vaccine to check every previously used disk—*every time*—before placing it into your machine.

3. Use a minimal system to run your virus checker on any shareware program or any software you download from a network or bulletin board. It pays to be careful.

15.6 Invasions of Privacy

As various computer databanks are being integrated and easy access is available by more and more agencies, abuses and mistakes involving privacy are inevitable. The NCIC

(National Crime Information Center) is an example of a very large database that has resulted in problems, such as mistaken identity and incomplete information updating. The following example is just one of many:

A Nevada businessman on his way home from a trade convention was recently stopped by police for failure to dim his headlights. As part of their regular routine, the police radioed a query to the NCIC (**N**ational **C**rime **I**nformation **C**enter) databank seeking information about the businessman. Within moments, the NCIC response revealed an outstanding warrant for grand theft issued in Tempe, Arizona, for his arrest. The police handcuffed and arrested the businessman and brought him in.

Figure 15.6.1

Has NCIC fingered the right person?

Ultimately, the information about the arrest warrant was proven wrong, but not before the businessman spent the night in the Tempe jail. In fact, not only was the information incorrect, but it was also six months out of date. The NCIC file originated when the Nevada businessman had repossessed a trailer that he had sold. The person who had originally purchased the trailer had filed the charge of grand theft. The charges were later dismissed in court, but the NCIC file containing the warrant information had never been updated.

Inadvertent Encroachments

Thousands of individuals every year become victims of erroneous or misapplied computer-based information. The preceding example is only one case, but it clearly illustrates the impact computer information and databases have on our lives. It also demonstrates the blind faith we place on computer-based records. Even skeptics, who question every word spoken by a human being, will accept at face value information supplied by a computer. Like the police in the anecdote, we tend to act without questioning the accuracy of the information. The result is predictable. Individual privacy and quality of life is disrupted.

Privacy infringements are caused by inaccurate and out-of-date computer information in every major database existing today. The Nevada businessman ran into trouble with NCIC, a government-supported police databank. The next two examples involve private databases.

A company based in California provides a special information service to landlords. The company collects information from all over the state on court cases involving landlord/tenant complaints. Landlords pay the company an annual fee to identify potentially high-risk tenants who have been sued by landlords in the past. From the landlord's position, this seems like a reasonable precaution to take. Let's take a look at it, however, from the potential tenant's point of view:

Jane Smith (a pseudonym) rented a Los Angeles apartment. When she moved in, she found that it was infested with cockroaches and rodents. The landlord refused to deal with the problem, so Smith gave him 30 days notice that she was leaving. The landlord countered with an eviction notice. Smith went to court with documentary evidence, but the landlord failed to show up, and the case was dropped.

Several years later, Smith was still being refused rented accommodation because the rental information company's computer showed that she had once been served with an eviction notice. Unfortunately for Smith, she had no idea such an information service existed, nor that it was spreading incomplete and inaccurate information about her rental history.

Let's examine one more example of what can go wrong when we rely on computer-based record keeping and surveillance. This one involves a large, privately owned credit bureau.

A woman in Illinois—we'll call her Betty—believed she had a respectable credit record. When she applied for a $75,000 mortgage, however, the lender informed her that she had accumulated too much debt to be considered. Credit bureau records showed balances in excess of $5,000 on several major credit cards, large revolving credit accounts in department stores, and an outstanding delinquent loan of $34,000 for a new sports car.

None of these accounts actually belonged to Betty. She had no balance on her two credit cards and owned her four-year-old Chevy outright. The bad credit history belonged to some other person!

By the time Betty's problems were cleared, the house she wanted had been sold. She will probably never get a major loan because her credit rating shows she was denied a mortgage because of a poor lending history.

Figure 15.6.2
Too often, information residing in some electronic file cabinet is searched and used against unsuspecting victims.

It doesn't take much thought to identify at least one problem inherent in trusting inadvertently inaccurate computer information: the problem of identifying individuals correctly. If you have the habit of varying how you give your name (using initials sometimes and the entire first name at other times) or if you have changed your address, you are a prime candidate for errors in identification. On top of this, mistakes by operators in entering data further increase the risk of error. Mistaken identities are a real problem and are one of the major reasons why credit reporting agencies are said to treat individuals unfairly.

All three of the scenarios described previously had one thing in common: A person's life was disrupted inadvertently. No one meant to cause harm, and no one could be directly blamed for the consequences. The individuals involved were the victims of poor database maintenance, incomplete data, and mistaken identity, all common in our age of high-tech information.

As a final comment on this issue of databanks and privacy, we should question the relevancy of some information being maintained in many types of government and private data banks. Is it *relevant* to maintain information regarding an individual's housekeeping standards, sexual preferences, personal grooming, political affiliations, social or religious associations, or drinking habits? Most of us would probably say no. Yet this information, too, is often used in ways that intrude on individual lives and privacy.

The Computer Continuum

In the next section, we take a brief look at things that can happen when information technology *deliberately* disregards personal privacy. The resulting gains (and there are some significant ones) are always purchased at the cost of someone else's personal pain.

Deliberate Acts of Intrusion

Before we examine a few examples of deliberate invasions of personal privacy, we should note that none of these were done for the purpose of causing someone pain or inconvenience. They describe generic instances of high-tech surveillance in the workplace. Many of the invaders would explain their actions in terms of increased productivity, quality control, and good management practices. Nevertheless, unprecedented denial of privacy is their result. See what you think:

- **Nursing:** Hospital care is no longer measured in terms of patient benefits, but in units of time. Many nurses are monitored. They carry boxes on their belts that track the amount of time used for each procedure with a patient. Don't be surprised if nurses seem to lack bedside manner; they can't overstay their time limit.

- **Trucking:** Where can people get a better sense of independence and freedom from supervision than barreling across the great plains, completely on their own? Think again! At the end of a long run, the trucker pulls into the company terminal. While the rig is being serviced, a little computer tape is removed from the engine. The tape tells the supervisor what the average speed and gas mileage were, how many stops the truck made, where his stops were, and a lot more. In addition, some trucks are now monitored by satellites. If the trucker is speeding, he gets a phone call in the truck (and often a fine).

- **Hotel Housekeeping:** The maids at the hotel you stay at are probably monitored. Your maid punches her employee code into the phone when she enters your room and again when she leaves it. This provides her supervisor with a detailed log of her speed of performance, as well as a detailed log of her movements throughout the day.

These are only three scenarios. Many, many employers regularly disregard workers' privacy rights in the name of accountability and efficiency. Their intentions are good, but the methods used are a disaster.

Figure 15.6.3
Many employers invade their workers' privacy in the name of efficiency and effectiveness.

Privacy and Personal Freedom
It's not just Big Brother who may be watching you; it may be a neighbor, your boss, a merchant, or some stranger getting a cheap thrill. These unseen spies may do nothing with the information (this is called lurking on the Internet); or, if their ethics disagree with your behavior, turn you in; or they may use it to their advantage—blackmail. Eavesdroppers can tap into radio scanners, baby monitors,

continues

cellular phones, financial transactions made by computer, email messages, and voice mail. Is privacy a dead issue on the electronic roadway? You decide.

- In Michigan, a woman overheard on her cellular phone a conversation between two people plotting a murder on their cellular phones. She called the police, prevented a murder, and received 15 minutes of fame for her good deed.

- A married male employee for the McDonald's corporation was having an affair with a female colleague. The lovers whispered sweet nothings to each other on the company's voice mail. The supervisor listened to the voice mail recordings, fired the male employee, and played the messages to his wife. McDonald's argued that the voice mail system is their property and that the affair was on company time, so they had a right to screen the recordings.

- Borland International, Inc. and Symantec Corporation, two large competitors in the software business, are in court over evidence from electronic mail (email) messages of a former Borland employee. Borland claims Symantec is guilty of stealing trade secrets/corporate espionage. Borland read an executive's email after he defected to Symantec and found ongoing communications prior to his resignation with Symantec that led to the charges.

The Electronic Communications Privacy Act (ECPA) of 1986 was designed to protect one's privacy when using electronic forms of communication. However, company policies regarding the monitoring of voice mail and email overrule the protections of the ECPA. And, although the woman who caught the individuals plotting the murder was in violation of the ECPA—she should have hung up the phone immediately upon hearing the conversation—she was not prosecuted. However, the conspirators were prosecuted and convicted.

A **credit doctor** is a person who can cure your low credit rating by stealing a good credit history and selling it to you to replace your bad one.

Not all invasions are well intentioned, as these anecdotes show. Some computer criminals make their fortunes by stealing the private information of one group of people for the financial benefit of another. A good example is the **credit doctor**.

In many ways, the modus operandi of the credit doctor is similar to that of the most malicious hacker. Generally, credit doctors bribe some employee of a credit bureau to gain a password into their computer system. They then log on to the system from a personal computer and search for someone with a good credit history who happens to have the same name as their client. The doctor copies the information associated with this good-credit person, including the social security number, and supplies it to the client. Instantly, the client has access to easy loans and credit cards. If an inquiry is made, the client merely gives the new social security number, and an A-1 rating is returned.

The main discussion of this chapter concerns problems caused by our societal addiction to computers and to communications technology. These problems, computer crime and invasion of privacy, are only symptomatic of the greater issue facing us: How can we protect the rights and freedoms of ordinary citizens, while at the same time controlling criminal elements and protecting us from a long progression of database errors? Of course, there can be no guarantees. Nothing in life is guaranteed. But the first step to solving any problem is being aware that it exists. The second step is understanding its consequences. All else must follow from that.

Chapter Summary

What you can do with what you have learned:

- Define what is meant by a computer crime.

- Recognize the major types of techniques used in committing a computer crime.

- Purchase a license to use software, not the software itself.

- Be wary of illegal hackers and software produced by them.

- Recognize the techniques used by illegal hackers.

- Use a vaccine or disinfectant program to spot and destroy viruses.

- Be careful how you identify yourself to limit the possibility of mistaken identity.

Key Terms and Review Questions

Key terms introduced in this chapter:

Computer crime 4-75

Theft of money 4-75

Theft of goods 4-75

Trojan horse 4-76

Salami-slicing 4-76

Theft of information or services 4-76

Data diddling 4-76

Password 4-77

Software piracy 4-78

Documentation 4-78

License 4-78

U.S. Computer Software Copyright Act of 1980 4-79

Hacking 4-79

Hacker 4-79

Cracking 4-79

Cracker 4-79

Logic bomb 4-81

Time bomb 4-81

Scavenging 4-82

Password guessing 4-82

Piggybacking 4-83

Virus 4-83

Vaccine 4-84

Disinfectant 4-84

Invasion of privacy 4-84

Credit doctor 4-88

Matching

Match the key terms introduced in the chapter to the following statements. Each term may be used once, more than once, or not at all.

1. _____This term is given to any illegal activity using computer software, data, or access as the object, subject, or instrument of the crime.

2. _____This type of theft uses the computer to track goods and alter computer inventories, redirecting goods to another location.

3. _____This type of theft may use electronic funds-transfers to redirect funds.

4. _____ This computer crime involves invading a communication system by riding in behind a legitimate user with a password.

5. _____ This computer crime involves spreading the haul over a large number of trivial transactions.

6. _____ This computer crime involves the insertion of false information into a program to profit from the outcome.

7. _____ This computer crime involves swapping one piece of information for another of the same type.

8. _____ By keeping this private, you are ensuring that no one will be able to access the computer "in your name."

9. _____ This is the term used to represent the collection of books that comes with software.

10. _____ This is what you actually purchase when you buy software. It gives you the authority to use the software. You do not own it.

11. _____ This legislative act protects the rights of authors of computer programs.

12. _____ This is the act of breaking in to other people's systems for either fun or profit or with intent to commit blackmail or sabotage.

13. _____ This is a software routine that can be triggered at some later time by the computer's clock or by a predetermined combination of events.

14. _____ The technique used here entails persistently checking the most commonly used passwords on users' accounts, including their birthdays (backward or forward), mothers' maiden names, children's names, pet names, spouses, friends, and more to guess a person's password.

15. _____ This is searching through stray data and electronic garbage for clues that might unlock the secrets of a targeted computer system.

16. _____ This possibly destructive program can cause major damage to computer operating systems, applications, data, or memory.

17. _____ Hackers write these. Some are written as a release from intellectual boredom or to demonstrate power over the computer. Many are not intended to do harm, but get away from the hacker.

18. _____ This is a program that searches your disk drives for viruses and notifies you if any were found.

19. _____ This should be used on disks that have been inserted into another computer before being allowed to be accessed on your computer.

20. _____ This is the term given to a person who steals credit information for those who replace their credit history with someone else's.

True or False

1. _____ According to the book, hitting someone over the head with a computer keyboard would constitute a computer crime.

2. _____ According to the book, anyone who commits computer crime is required to have computer expertise and skill in the implementation of the crime.

3. _____ According to the book, a computer crime requires the use of computer software, data, or access as the subject, or instrument, of the crime.

4. _____ The most popular form of theft under the category of computer crime is the theft of money.

5. _____ One way computers are used to commit crimes is the redirecting of products to a location where the thief can get them and sell those products for cash.

6. _____ The computer crime called salami-slicing is used for profit. Obtaining money using an electronic funds-transfer is one example.

7. _____ Redirecting products to another location for a thief's profit is an example of a trojan horse.

8. _____ Redirecting phone use charges to someone else's number is an example of data diddling.

9. _____ Unless the software states that you can make a copy for archival purposes only, even making a backup copy of software is illegal.

10. _____ Rights of ownership of software as "intellectual works" was given under the U.S. Computer Software Copyright Act of 1980.

11. _____ If a piece of software is downloaded from the Internet, and the software says that it is free, it is assumed that the software is not copyrighted.

12. _____ The copying of software is commonplace. Therefore, software companies don't worry about it; they just raise their prices for the software.

13. _____ All the definitions of the word *hacker* refer to a person who commits an illegal act with the computer.

14. _____ Some activities performed by hackers can be extremely dangerous to computer systems.

15. _____ Time bombs or logic bombs are placed on computer systems by hackers.

16. _____ One way hackers get onto computer systems is by guessing passwords. Therefore, it is a good idea to select a password that would be difficult for the hacker to guess.

17. _____ Viruses can be self-replicating, which is how they are spread from computer to computer.

18. _____ Vaccines automatically find and destroy all viruses.

19. _____ One way to protect your computer from viruses is to disallow anyone (including

yourself) from inserting disks into your disk drive after they have been inserted into any other computer.

20. _____ Although not common, it is possible to steal a good credit history from one person and let another use that good credit history to obtain credit.

Multiple Choice

Answer the multiple choice questions by selecting the best answer from the choices given.

1. This general term encompasses all illegal activity using computer software, data, or access.
   a. Computer crime
   b. Data diddling
   c. Piggybacking
   d. Salami-slicing
   e. The trojan horse

2. An example of this type of computer crime would include anything that involves the insertion of false information into a program to profit from the outcome.
   a. Computer crime
   b. Data diddling
   c. Piggybacking
   d. Salami-slicing
   e. The trojan horse

3. An example of this type of computer crime would include the insertion of a line within a program to divert the parts of each cent that are otherwise overlooked into an account set up by the hacker.
   a. Computer crime
   b. Data diddling
   c. Piggybacking
   d. Salami-slicing
   e. The trojan horse

4. This type of computer crime involves invading a communication system by riding behind a legitimate user with a password.
   a. Computer crime
   b. Data diddling
   c. Piggybacking
   d. Salami-slicing
   e. The trojan horse

5. This type of computer crime involves swapping one piece of information for another of the same type.
   a. Computer crime
   b. Data diddling
   c. Piggybacking
   d. Salami-slicing
   e. The trojan horse

6. An example of this type of computer crime is the act of identifying a cellular phone frequency and other identifying characteristics, which are then used to "clone" another phone to be used with that same identification information. The person owning the phone is sent the bill for the air time charges.
   a. Computer crime
   b. Data diddling
   c. Piggybacking
   d. Salami-slicing
   e. The trojan horse

7. Which of the following is not a good way to handle passwords?

   a. Issue passwords to as few people as possible.

   b. Avoid common passwords, such as money, taxes, love, genius, and god.

   c. Change the password frequently.

   d. Post the password in a prominent location for all to see.

   e. Make passwords less obvious and less memorable.

8. This term refers to the unauthorized copying or use of software for which you have not paid the appropriate licensing fee.

   a. Documentation

   b. License

   c. Software piracy

   d. Freeware

   e. Shareware

9. This is actually what you buy when you purchase a piece of software.

   a. Documentation

   b. License

   c. Software piracy

   d. Freeware

   e. Shareware

10. This is the legislative act that was passed that protects the ownership of software.

   a. The Copyright Act of 1980

   b. The Software Copyright Act of 1980

   c. The Software Act of 1980

   d. The Warren Papers of 1980

   e. The Legislative Bill of 1980

Exercises

1. Find an URL that gives information on a new (not mentioned in the book) example of each of the following:

   a. Theft of money

   b. Theft of goods

   c. Theft of information or services

2. Give three different definitions of *hacking*.

3. Do you think software piracy is a form of stealing? Explain your answer.

4. Do you think people who write virus programs should be punished? How?

5. How can we strike a balance between maintaining good records and protecting student privacy?

6. Do you think it is an invasion of your privacy to include your name on an honors list (for academic excellence, for example)?

7. What do you think will be the effect of the World Wide Web and the growth or control of computer crime?

8. Explain how a trojan horse heist works.

9. In the field of computer crime, what is salami-slicing?

10. The term *piggybacking* is used three times in this chapter. Explain how the references differ.

11. What are you actually getting when you purchase a commercial software product?

12. What are the differences between shareware and freeware?

13. What is a logic bomb?

14. How might a hacker use the technique of scavenging?

15. Exactly what is a virus, and how does it work?

16. How can you protect your disks from viruses?

17. What are the two types of viruses? Explain what each does and how each works.

18. Explain how a credit doctor works.

Discussion Questions

1. Are hackers a poor, misunderstood group; individuals who should be incarcerated; or something in between? Why do you think so?

2. Why are viruses so easily spread?

3. Where are your medical records kept? What information is in your hospital medical records? How private are they? A visit to the hospital usually entails signing a release of your records for insurance purposes. What happens then? Does an employer have a right to see your medical records? (Note: Employers usually pay for your health insurance.) A health insurer usually has complete access to your medical records, regardless of how personal they may be.

4. How have computerized issue-tracking systems changed election campaigning?

Group Project

A group of four students should decide on four areas of business that can be taken from the following list:

Retail sales in small businesses

Accounting offices in corporations

Academic department offices in a university

Administrative offices in a university

Copy centers

Programming departments in corporations

Health profession offices

Contact 10–20 computer professionals working in each area. Without revealing their identities, collect answers for the following questions:

Have you ever knowingly used pirated software? If not, would you use it given the chance?

Have you ever used software that you later found out was pirated?

Have you ever let someone else make a copy of your legal software, knowing that he or she was not going to pay for it? If not, would you let someone do so?

Have you ever "turned in" someone for using or pirating software? If not, would you turn someone in if the opportunity presented itself?

Collect your results and see what conclusions you can make about the data that you have collected. If possible, use a presentation program such as PowerPoint to make the report to the class.

Web Connections

http://www.fbi.gov/

Links to crime information, reports, and crime protection.

http://www.cs.purdue.edu/coast/

Home page of Computer Operations, Audit, and Security Technology (COAST), a research laboratory in computer security at Purdue University. Links to ongoing projects and an archive of security-related sites.

http://www.copyright.com/

Home page of the Copyright Clearance Center, a not-for-profit organization created at the suggestion of Congress to help organizations comply with U.S. copyright law. Includes links to sites relating to reproduction rights in other countries.

http://lcweb.loc.gov/copyright/

The U.S. Copyright Office home page. Up-to-date information on current copyright issues.

http://www.cyberspacelaws.com

Home page of Cyberspace Laws, with links to sources and information on a number of related topics, including encryption, security, privacy, crimes, and ethics.

http://www.symantec.com/avcenter/

Antivirus center of Symantec Corp. Includes links to articles on related topics and information on upgrades for antivirus software.

http://www.pcwebopedia.com/antivirus_program.htm

Definition of and information on programs to combat viruses. A lot of links to sites with antivirus software for many platforms.

Bibliography

Biggar, Bill, and Joe Myers. *Danger Zones: What Parents Should Know About the Internet.* New York: Andrews & McMeel, 1996.

Forester, Tom, and Perry Morrison. *Computer Ethics: Cautionary Tales and Ethical Dilemmas in Computing.* Cambridge: MIT Press, 1993.

Garson, David G. *Computer Technology and Social Issues.* Hershey, PA: Idea Group, 1995.

Greenia, Mark W. *Computer Security and Privacy: An Information Sourcebook— Concepts and Issues for the 21st Century.* London: Lexikon Services, 1998.

Icove, David J., et al. *Computer Crime: A Crimefighter's Handbook (Computer Security).* Sebastopol, CA: O'Reilly & Associates, 1995.

Judson, Karen. *Computer Crime: Phreaks, Spies, and Salami Slicers (Issues in Focus).* New York: Enslow, 1994.

Kane, Pamela. *PC Security and Virus Protection: The Ongoing War Against Information Sabotage.* New York: IDG Books Worldwide, 1994.

Littman, Jonathan. *The Fugitive Game: Online With Kevin Mitnick*. Boston: Little, Brown & Company, 1997.

Mayo, Jon. *Bigelow's Computer Virus Pocket Reference*. New York: McGraw-Hill, 1998.

Orwell, George. *1984*. New York: Mass Market Paperback, 1990.

Pipkin, Donald L. *Halting the Hacker: A Practical Guide to Computer Security*. New Jersey: Prentice Hall, 1997.

Shimomura, Tsutomu with John Markoff. *Takedown: The Pursuit and Capture of Kevin Mitnick, America's Most Wanted Computer Outlaw—By the Man Who Did It*. New York: Hyperion, 1996.

Spinello, Richard A. *Case Studies in Information and Computer Ethics*. New Jersey: Prentice Hall, 1997.

GLOSSARY

Selected Solutions

Chapter 1: Computers: A First Look

Answers to Matching Questions

1. Computer
3. Memory
5. Central processing unit
7. Mechanical computer
9. Electronic computer
11. Digital computer
13. General-purpose electronic digital computer
15. Program

Answers to True or False Questions

1. False   (This counting device holds only information.)
3. True
5. False   (The floppy disk is a physical device that stores programs. It is considered "hardware.")
7. True
9. False   (The more values that are possible, the greater the chance an error could occur.)
11. False   (The examples given had purposes that were predetermined by the manufacturer. These fall into the special-purpose category.)
13. True
15. True

Answers to Multiple Choice Questions

1. A
3. D
5. D
7. A
9. C

Chapter 2: Metamorphosis of Information

Answers to Matching Questions

1. Transformation of information
3. Binary circuits
5. Binary
7. ASCII
9. Control character
11. Pixel
13. Grayscale
15. Voltage
17. Hertz
19. Sequential access

Answers to True or False Questions

1. True   (Numerals refer to the symbols being used. Numbers refer to the values represented.)
3. True
5. False   (Each set of standard codes was created by different groups of people. Therefore, each group created a different set of codes.)
7. False   (Both 1s and 0s are equally important. The computer needs to account for all pixels.)
9. False   (Each pixel in a color picture needs three values: one each for hue, saturation, and grayscale. Grayscale pictures need only one value per pixel, the amount of ink at that pixel.)
11. True
13. True
15. False   (Although the manufacturer could be deemed important, the type of access is what we were looking for here.)
17. False   (It would take over an acre to store the information on electronic circuits versus storing it in a typical computer media room using optical mass storage media.)
19. True

Answers to Multiple Choice Questions

1. D
3. C
5. C
7. C
9. D

Chapter 3: From Stonehenge to the Supercomputer

Answers to Matching Questions

1. Program
3. Stored-program computer
5. Algorithm
7. Algorithm
9. Input/Output units
11. Loader
13. Microcomputer
15. Minicomputer
17. Minicomputer
19. Mainframe computer

Answers to True or False Questions

1. False   (Machine-language programs are already in binary form.)
3. True
5. True
7. True
9. True
11. False   (The CPU performs a nondestructive reading of memory. The instruction remains in memory even after it has been executed!)
13. False   (The programmer can choose where data is stored by naming individual memory locations. This may not be wise. It is usually not done. Doing so may destroy necessary information, such as program instructions previously stored there!)
15. True
17. True
19. False   (Although the textbook discusses only the Motorola PowerPC chip and the Intel Pentium chip, other companies also produce microprocessor chips.)

Answers to Multiple Choice Questions

1. B
3. C
5. E
7. C
9. A

Chapter 4: Operating Systems: The Genie in the Computer

Answers to Matching Questions

1. Operating system
3. Altair 8800
5. Words
7. Voltage pulse
9. Parallel
11. Interface
13. Drag and drop
15. Shell
17. Hierarchical file system
19. Disk cache

Answers to True or False Questions

1. True   (Only the rudimentary part of the operating system is found in the ROM.)

3. True

5. True

7. False   (The voltages are not constant. Voltage pulses are applied for a short period of time, millionths of a second to send information from one place to another within the computer.)

9. True

11. False   (Command-line commands are not intuitive. Each command must be spelled correctly, in the right order, using the proper punctuation. This takes longer to learn than GUI commands.)

13. True

15. False   (Disk cache holds only pieces of programs in RAM that it needs to repeatedly retrieve from the disk drive. Files that are saved to disk are saved to disk. In RAM disk, entire contents of a disk may be placed in RAM. It no longer accesses the disk drive. Any alteration to a file does not alter the file on the disk.)

17. False   (Multiprocessing refers to computing being done with more than one CPU.)

19. False   (A server's function is to serve and control the interactions of other computers on a network. This includes sharing resources such as programs, data, and hardware.)

Answers to Multiple Choice Questions

1. A

3. D

5. C

7. A

9. D

Chapter 5: Computer Languages: Empowering Algorithms

Answers to Matching Questions

1. Human language

3. Syntax

5. Translation

7. Machine code

9. Assembly language

11. Fifth-generation language

13. Query language

15. Translated

17. Source code

19. Algorithm

Answers to True or False Questions

1. True

3. False   (Each assembly-language instruction produces one line of object code.)

5. True

7. True

9. False   (Both translators may produce several lines of object code from one instruction.)

11. False   (Data is a given thing or fact. Information takes data and repackages it into a meaningful form.)

13. True

15. False   (Alpha testing is done in-house, by a team of programmers.)

17. True

19. True

Answers to Multiple Choice Questions

1. C

3. B

5. D

7. A

9. E

Chapter 6: Networks: Everything Is Connected

Answers to Matching Questions

1. Infrared

3. Network links

5. Baud rate

7. Synchronous transmission

9. MAN

11. Half-duplex transmission

13. Protocol

15. HTTP (Hypertext Transfer Protocol)

17. Server

19. Email

Answers to True or False Questions

1. False   (Smoke signals, drums)

3. False   (Twisted pair, coaxial cable, fiber-optic cable, and space)

5. True

7. True

9. False   (Properties depend on the type of communication channel being used.)

11. True

13. False   (Wireless, and those not directly connected)

15. False   (Collection of linked networks versus those under the rules of TCP/IP)

17. False   (Packets are packaged and repackaged as they travel along the Internet.)

19. False   (Legislative changes were cited in the text.)

Answers to Multiple Choice Questions

1. D

3. E

5. B

7. C

9. C

Chapter 7: The Internet: Communication with the World

Answers to Matching Questions

1. ARPAnet

3. Packet

5. CSnet

7. Archie

9. Milnet

11. Internet address or IP address

13. MOO

15. Virus

Answers to True or False Questions

1. False   (The Defense Department gained ownership in 1975 after ARPA wanted to sell it off.)

3. True

5. False   (Although many Gopher systems that access databases of information are being transferred to the World Wide Web, they still exist.)

7. False   (Some used TCP/IP; others used the Network Control Protocol.)

9. True

11. True

13. True

15. True

Answers to Multiple Choice Questions

1. B

3. C

5. C

7. D

9. D

Chapter 8: The World Wide Web: Expanding the Global Community

Answers to Matching Questions

1. Gopher

3. Medium

5. Multimedia

7. Hypertext

9. Hypermedia links (or hyperlinks)

11. URL (Uniform Resource Locator)

13. MAILTO

15. Read-only access

17. ISP (Internet service provider)

19. Online course

Answers to True or False Questions

1. False   (Although many Gopher systems that access databases of information are being transferred to the World Wide Web, they still exist.)

3. False   (Although links can appear as highlighted text passages, it is much more than that. Links can also appear as images, buttons, or icons.)

5. True

7. True

9. True

11. False   (Internet service providers usually charge a fee.)

13. False   (Search engines look for specific requested information. A spider searches for sites that have changed or have been recently added to the WWW.)

15. False   (Not only is it tied to the speed of the modem, but it is also tied to the sending modem and to the amount of network traffic encountered.)

17. True

19. False   (These versions are still in the testing phase.)

Answers to Multiple Choice Questions
1. C
3. D
5. B
7. A
9. B

Chapter 9: Databases: Controlling the Information Deluge

Answers to Matching Questions
1. Information Age
3. Information
5. Database
7. Keypunched data cards or Hollerith cards
9. Mark-sensor form
11. Mark-sensor form
13. Voice recognition data entry
15. Percent
17. Correlation
19. False correlation or false relevance

Answers to True or False Questions
1. True
3. False   (Although the terms data and information are used interchangeably by some, they do have different meanings.)
5. True
7. False   (These bar codes have also been beneficial for the reduction of errors made by cashiers because the prices are already in the computer.)
9. True

11. False   (Cards that had errors needed to be repunched.)

13. True

15. False   (Those samples that are biased are called skewed samples. The sample is chosen that would support some predetermined outcome.)

17. False   (It refers to having two unrelated facts, both true, and making a connection between them.)

19. True

Answers to Multiple Choice Questions
1. B
3. D
5. D
7. C
9. A

Chapter 10: Visual Communication: Gateway to the Brain

Answers to Matching Questions
1. Digitizing
3. RGB
5. False coloring
7. Image enhancement
9. Bitmapped or raster graphics
11. Object-oriented or vector graphics
13. Bitmapped or raster graphics
15. Perspective
17. Harold Cohen
19. Rules

Answers to True or False Questions
1. True
3. True
5. True
7. False   (Boundaries are located as a result of computer programs.)
9. True
11. True
13. False   (Object-oriented or vector graphics store formulas for shapes.)

15. False (Two-dimensional objects appear flat. They can have color and curved surfaces.)

17. True

19. False (Harold Cohen painted the earlier works; AARON just drew the line art.)

Answers to Multiple Choice Questions

1. A
3. A
5. C
7. B, D
9. A, C

Chapter 11: Audio Communication Comes of Age

Answers to Matching Questions

1. Speech synthesis
3. Semantics
5. Digitized recordings
7. Inflection
9. Kurzweil Personal Reader
11. OCR (Optical character recognition)
13. Voiced sounds
15. Pitch
17. Continuous speech
19. CD (Compact Disc)

Answers to True or False Questions

1. False (All types of sounds can be digitized by a computer, including human, nonhuman, and musical sounds.)

3. False (The Kurzweil Personal Reader uses phoneme structures; the Speak & Spell uses digitized recordings.)

5. False (Several versions of the recorded words would be needed to account for all possibilities of their use to account for inflection and duration.)

7. False (OCR software tries to recognize text only.)

9. True

11. True

13. True

15. True

17. False (The software automatically transcribes the music.)

19. True

Answers to Multiple Choice Questions

1. A
3. E
5. A
7. E
9. B

Chapter 12: Simulation: Modeling the Physical World

Answers to Matching Questions

1. Simulation
3. Simulation of the inaccessible or impossible
5. Controlled experimentation and testing
7. Education and training
9. Time compression
11. Predictable system
13. Discrete system
15. Verified or validated
17. Simulation language
19. Virtual reality or artificial reality

Answers to True or False Questions

1. True

3. True

5. False (Using real cars is more expensive and dangerous to human life. Animations can be made, and researchers can watch the film and make necessary changes.)

7. False (Sunrise is a predictable system. Almanacs and weather forecasters can tell the time of sunrise from any point on the planet.)

9. True

11. True

13. False (This is half true, but not totally. Some simulations use common programming languages. However, the larger, more complex models often use a special programming language, called a simulation language, to create simulation programs.)

15. True

17. False   (The Extend simulation program can be used in many different types of situations. An example of a bank's counter service was given.)
19. False   (Virtual reality can be shared with other people. These people can be found in the same "cyber-space.")

Answers to Multiple Choice Questions
1. A
3. D
5. B
7. E
9. B

Chapter 13: Artificial Intelligence and Modeling the Human State

Answers to Matching Questions
1. Maillardet's Automaton
3. Neural nets
5. Semantic networks
7. Rule-based (or expert system or production system)
9. Knowledge acquisition
11. Reasoning
13. Heuristic search
15. Reasoning
17. Hexapawn
19. Expert systems

Answers to True or False Questions
1. True
3. True
5. False   (The brain has more parts than even a super-computer.)
7. True
9. True
11. False   (Learning systems learn. They build up their own knowledge bases.)
13. False   (Most fax machines that can be connected to a microcomputer come with software that will recognize text.)
15. True

17. False   (Researchers have tried to emulate the concept of how neurons work; they have not tried to copy the human brain.)
19. False   (The neural network does not have a base of knowledge. The neural network must learn from experience by using many actual examples of inputs and expected outputs.)

Answers to Multiple Choice Questions
1. E
3. A
5. C
7. D
9. A

Chapter 14: Pushing the Envelope of Human Potential

Answers to Matching Questions
1. Industrial revolution
3. Macintosh
5. Cognitive learning
7. Cognitive learning
9. Social interaction
11. Psychomotor skills
13. Psychomotor skills
15. Interactive multimedia
17. Local area networks
19. Electronic mail

Answers to True or False Questions
1. False   (The first microcomputers came with only BASIC.)
3. False   (The PC Jr. was created intentionally for home and school.)
5. False   (Audio and video files needed more speed and memory than the early computers were capable of.)
7. True
9. False   (Most of the time, educational programs fall into more than one of the categories of learning.)
11. True
13. False   (We still need the math skills and the ability to apply those skills to our environment.)

15. True

17. True

19. False   (It is illegal to share a single purchased piece of software with the entire network!)

Answers to Multiple Choice Questions

1. B

3. A

5. C

7. C

9. C

Chapter 15: Ethics, Electronic Spies, and Privacy

Answers to Matching Questions

1. Computer crime

3. Theft of money

5. The salami

7. Data diddling

9. Documentation

11. U.S. Computer Software Copyright Act of 1980

13. Time bomb (or logic bomb)

15. Scavenging

17. Virus

19. Vaccine (or disinfectant)

Answers to True or False Questions

1. False   (The use of the keyboard in committing the crime is not what was intended in the definition of "computer crime.")

3. True

5. True

7. True

9. True

11. False   (Even free software can be copyrighted.)

13. False   (Some definitions of "hacker" do not include illegal activities.)

15. True

17. True

19. True

Answers to Multiple Choice Questions

1. A

3. D

5. B

7. D

9. B

Glossary of Terms

3D rendering program—A program that provides tools to give perspective, light sources with appropriate reflections, and a point of view.

4th generation language—Any of a number of types of programming languages aimed at simplifying the task of imparting instructions to a computer. Most are associated with a particular applications package.

Abacus—A calculating device that only holds information.

Accelerator board—This optional internal set of chips speeds up the processing of the computer.

Access time—1) The time it takes to get information from a device; or 2) the time it takes to put information into the device.

Accumulator—This part of the arithmetic unit found in the CPU acts as a holding place for results of calculations.

Acronym—A word formed from parts of several words. This makes is easier to communicate complete phrases with a single word (for example, FBI = Federal Bureau of Investigation).

Address—A numeric value identifying the location of a unit of information in internal storage.

AI (Artificial Intelligence)—A branch of computer science involved with using a computer to learn from experience by storing information and applying it to new situations. Currently, there are several areas of research within the scope of artificial intelligence.

Algorithm—A detailed description of the exact methods used for solving a particular problem. It is essentially the solution to the problem and is usually implemented by a program. It should solve the stated problem in all situations.

Alphanumeric—A general term referring to alphabetic letters (*A* through *Z* and *a* through *z*), numeric digits (0 through 9), and special characters (+, -, /, *, $, (,), and so on) that a computer can process.

Alpha testing—The first stage in testing of a software program. This is normally done within the company that created the program.

Alpha version—This term refers to what could be termed a "first draft" of a program. It is usually only circulated within the company that created it.

Analog computer—A computer that functions in continuously varying quantities and produces results that vary continuously.

Analog signal—A signal that varies directly with the input, such as a mercury thermometer or voice signal on the telephone line.

Analog-to-digital converter—An input device for changing analog signals into digital form. In other words, a converter that changes the magnitude of voltages into numbers that can be read by a computer.

Animation—The construction of images that appear to move, by rapidly presenting sequential pictures that vary slightly from one to the next.

ANSI (American National Standards Institute)—An organization that develops and maintains programming language standards for use by industry and computer manufacturers.

AppleTalk—Apple Computer's local area network scheme.

Application—A program developed for a special purpose such as word processing, graphics, and so on.

Application generator—A program that enables the user to specify a problem and describe the desired results. The program is then created by the application generator.

Archie—The name of an automated search service on the Internet. It gets its name from the shortened form of *archive*.

Archival information—A type of storage or memory used to store large quantities of information for long periods of time.

Argument—See **Operand**.

Arithmetic instruction—One type of instruction used for computations.

Arithmetic operator—A symbol or combination of symbols used in a statement that manipulates arithmetic expressions.

Arithmetic unit—The part of the CPU where arithmetic is done.

ARPA (Advanced Research Projects Agency)—A federal government research branch that influenced the formation of the Internet.

ARPAnet—The early network formed by ARPA to connect researchers. It was the backbone of early Internet development.

Array—A group of values that are assigned a single variable name and are of the same data type.

Artificial neuron—Also called processing elements. Basic building blocks of a neural net modeled after real neurons of humans and other animals.

ASCII (American Standard Code for Information Interchange)—A standard 7-bit code that represents letters, numbers, and special characters in the computer's memory.

ASR (Automatic Speech Recognition)—Allows computers to recognize and respond to human speech and sound patterns spoken aloud.

Assembler—A computer program that translates or converts an assembly language program into machine language so that the computer can then execute it.

Assembly language—A low-level programming language that closely resembles machine code language. The programmer can use mnemonic instruction codes, labels, and names to refer directly to their binary equivalents.

Assignment operator—A symbol or combination of symbols used in an assignment statement.

Assignment statement—An operator in programming languages that stores the value on its right in the memory location(s) on its left: x:=2 in Pascal, x=2 in FORTRAN, and so on.

Asynchronous transmission—Information is sent down the communications channel character by character.

Backward chaining—The act of going from a rule's action to find a rule's condition.

Bandwidth—It is a measurement of the capacity of a network and is usually given in bits per second.

Bar code—Found on most consumer products, a bar code is a series of parallel lines of varying widths and at varying distances from each other. These strips are machine readable by a scanner and indicate information about the product such as price, brand, and size. They can also be used in noncommercial areas to store other information.

Baud rate—The number of times per second that the state of a communication device or line can be changed.

BBS (Bulletin Board System)—It is a special purpose database that usually resides on a single computer and is accessible over the telephone lines or through a computer network. Its purpose is to provide information to the person who accesses it and enable him to put his own information into the BBS for others to access.

BCD (**B**inary **C**oded **D**ecimal)—A way of representing numbers in a computer that allows for exact arithmetic.

Beta testing—The second stage in testing of a software program. The company sends an isolated number of sophisticated users copies of this version to test for errors.

Beta version—This term refers to what could be termed a "second draft" of a program. It is usually only circulated to selected individuals, but is sometimes offered free to the public. This allows the program to be tested in a multitude of different environments.

Binary—Base 2 numeric system.

Binary circuit—An electronic device that assumes only two states or conditions.

Binary number—A number made up of the symbols 1 or 0.

BIT (**B**inary dig**IT**)—The smallest unit of information that a computer can recognize. It is represented by an electronic pulse; the presence or absence of a pulse is represented by a 1 or a 0.

Bitmapped graphics—Graphics constructed of individual pixels that are black and white, shades of gray, or colored. If it is necessary to reduce or enlarge the image, only the crudest manipulations can be done.

Block—A group of records, words, or characters that have been placed in an input/output medium and transferred to or from the central processing unit.

Boolean data—Data that can take on only two values, TRUE or FALSE. It is named after George Boole, a mathematician.

Booting—Turning on the computer and starting the operating system.

BPS (**B**its **P**er **S**econd)—The number of bits per second transmitted over a communications line.

Bridge—A device that connects two or more segments of a network.

Browser—In reference to the Internet, it is a program that follows the rules of a protocol and enables the user to search the Internet. Mosaic and Netscape, for example, are browsers used to search the World Wide Web.

Bug—An error or problem that arises with a computer or a program.

Bulletin board—An electronic messaging system that may be open to many people at the same time. These messages may be a response to a question, a picture, or an application program. Some bulletin board services have teleconference capabilities that enable people to talk together simultaneously.

Bus network—Consists of a continuous wire to which all nodes on the network are attached. All nodes can detect all messages sent on the bus.

Byte—A unit of storage in a computer used to hold a set of bits (usually 8, 16, or 32, depending on the computer). A byte can hold the binary code for a letter, a digit, or a special character. Each byte in a computer's internal storage normally has a separate location or address.

Cache memory—A section of RAM set aside for accessing by the CPU without the delays usually associated with slower memory areas.

CAI (**C**omputer **A**ided **I**nstruction)—Combinations of techniques and strategies used to create effective educational software.

Calculator—An electronic device that may be special purpose (usually arithmetic) or general purpose (can run programs and be connected to other devices).

Card reader—An input device that reads information by sensing the holes on punched cards. The information read is transferred into the computer's memory.

Cassette tape—A plastic cartridge that contains a length of magnetic tape on which programs and data may be stored.

CD (**C**ompact **D**isc)—A circular object containing digital information recorded and played back by laser.

CD-ROM (**C**ompact **D**isk–**R**ead **O**nly **M**emory)—A large capacity memory storage device that uses a laser to read and write data.

Central tendency—An indicator used to give the value about which a group of numbers tends to center.

Chaos—Used to describe a situation where things seem unpredictable and chaotic. In practice, chaos systems begin with minor effects that may create major effects.

Character data—Data expressed as a single character or a string of characters. Each character may be a letter, a punctuation mark, or other special character, a digit, or a space.

Character set—All symbols that are available in an encoding scheme used when storing characters inside a computer.

Character string—A data structure composed of individual characters that have been lined up in a specific sequence.

Chat rooms—A place on the Internet where you can communicate with others in real time. Services such as America Online and CompuServe provide chat rooms for their subscribers.

Chip—A miniaturized group of electronic circuits placed on a "chip" of silicon.

Clip art—Computerized images available for inclusion in documents.

Coaxial cable—A two-wire cable where one of the wires is formed in a tube of fine wire and the other runs down the center of the tube. The outer "wire" acts as a shield from electrical interference.

Cognitive learning—Acquisition of knowledge or of thinking skills.

Cold boot—Starting up the computer by turning the power on. The operating system in ROM looks for and loads the remaining parts of the operating system into RAM.

Command language—A set of procedures for instructing a database management system to perform manipulations, comparisons, and operations on its data.

Command line—An operating system interface in which commands are typed on a keyboard.

Comment—Explanation written in English by the programmer to clarify the individual steps in a program. These statements are meaningless to the computer.

Communication cycle—Process where one entity relays information to another. In turn, the other entity decodes that information and relays feedback back to the first.

Communications channel—The path over which data travels from its source (creator) to the destination (receiver).

Competition—Students are encouraged to outperform each other, or to better an existing standard.

Compiler—A translation program that rewrites high-level instructions into binary instructions (also known as machine code), which are then ready for execution. The entire program is translated before execution.

Complex adaptive system—It is a system that has most of the following characteristics: nonlinear, works in parallel, evolutionary, based on simple rules, self-organizing, and emergent behavior. Most of the examples of these systems have what we call life, whether it is in the form of plant, animal, or bacterium. However, the stock market and political systems are also complex adaptive systems.

Compressed format—This refers to a computer file that has been made smaller to make it easier to send and receive. It could be a picture, program, segment of sound, or any of the five basic kinds of information.

Compression—It refers to the compression of any binary files. This means making them smaller without losing information. To be used, they must be expanded to the original form.

Computer—A device that takes information in one form, uses it, and produces a different form of information that is related to (but not the same as) the original.

Computer crime—Any illegal activity using computer software, data, or access as the object, subject, or instrument of the crime.

Concatenation—The process of joining one character string with another.

Concordance—An index in alphabetic order that contains all major words in a text and shows the contextual occurrence of each word.

Conditional statement—A computer instruction that allows the computer to decide which of two or more alternative sets of instructions to execute.

Conference (computerized) or **teleconference**—It is an electronic meeting that can take place at the convenience of the participants. A network is necessary for a conference to function.

Constant—A fixed or invariable value or data item.

Content lecture—Involves the presentation of new material as exposition by the teacher often accompanied by illustrations and outlines on the chalkboard or overhead projector.

Context switching—Switching from one application to another.

Continuous—Having quantities that vary smoothly or in a continuous manner.

Continuous speech—Words strung together with varying or no pauses between words.

Continuous system—A model that has quantities that vary smoothly or in a continuous manner.

Control character—A special character used to control communication between different computers or between a computer and a device.

Control instruction—One type of instruction that changes the order of a program's execution.

Control statement—Used to alter the sequence of instructions executed. Includes conditional and iteration statements.

Control structure statement—Any statement that determines the order in which other statements are executed. Common control statements include FOR statements, for repeating or looping, IF-THEN-ELSE statements for making a two-way decision, and CASE statements for multiple-way decision making.

Control unit—The part of the CPU that contains the Instruction Register and the Program Counter. This unit carries out the operation given by the opcode in the instruction register and controls the flow of commands through the CPU based on the contents of the program counter.

Conversational computer—A computer that recognizes and understands human conversational speech and can respond meaningfully.

Correlation—A connection or relation linking two or more pieces of information.

Count-controlled loop—This type of iteration statement enables the user to execute a group of statements a predetermined number of times.

Courseware—Teaching and learning materials developed on a computer, using the computer as a primary teaching/learning tool.

CPU (Central Processing Unit)—The collection of hardware pieces responsible for controlling all activities of the computer system, for performing all calculations, and executing all instructions. Sometimes called the "brain" of the computer.

Crash—An unplanned shutdown or failure of the computer to operate.

Cross-reference—A list that shows each name used in a computer program along with the number of the statement in which it is defined and the number of each statement that refers to it.

CRT (Cathode Ray Tube)—A device that resembles a television screen and acts as an output device.

CSNET—The Computer Science Network was an early network that provided email and Internet access to computer science departments at colleges and universities.

Cursor—An indicator on the screen that tells you where you are typing.

Cyberspace—A fictional place where millions of people can simultaneously visit and interact.

DAN (Desk Area Network)—A network that connects devices within a single computer, such as the display, a camera, disk drives, CD-ROM drive, and other such devices.

DARMS (Digital Alternative Representation of Musical Scores)—A graphic representation of music based on the position of symbols on a staff.

DAT (Digital Audio Tape)—Similar to a cassette tape in form. Information is stored digitally.

Data—A given thing, a fact. Often used to mean the facts that will be given to the computer to be processed. Technically, *data* is plural, and the singular is *datum*. However, *data* is now often used as a singular form.

Databank—A comprehensive collection of libraries of data, usually holding archival information not often accessed.

Database—A collection of interrelated data files or libraries, or a databank, organized for ease of access, update, and retrieval.

Database system—Also called an information management system. Organizes information so that it can be stored, retrieved, analyzed, and printed in report form.

Data bits—In telecommunication, the number of bits in each segment of the transmission that carry the information being sent. Data, parity, and stop bits usually total 9.

Data diddling—Swapping one piece of information for another of the same type.

Data integrity—Data that has not been mistakenly or maliciously altered is said to possess integrity.

Data movement instruction—One type of instruction that moves information within the computer.

Data probe—The collection of data electronically by inserting an instrument into a device designed to output information in this fashion.

Data structure—A method of organizing data. Some common data structures are arrays, character strings, records, lists, files, and stacks.

Data type—A way of specifying how data will be stored in memory. Examples include integer, real, character, and Boolean.

DBMS (DataBase Management System)—A set of computer programs that controls the creation, maintenance, and utilization of the databases and the data files of an organization. The DBMS allows direct and immediate access to the database.

Debug—To find and correct mistakes in a program.

Decimal system—Base 10 numeration system generally used by our society in our daily lives.

Declaration statement—In a programming language, it is a statement that defines or describes which data types and structures will be used in a particular program.

Decompressing—This is the process of returning a file from its compressed form back to the original form.

Dedicated program—A program that has been designed to perform a specific task.

Demonstration—Shows the student a new set of skills, or illustrates some new concepts.

Desktop publishing program—Specialized computer software to lay out text and graphics as well as font manipulation for printing.

Device independence—The ability to add an input, output, or storage device to a computer system by modifying only the I/O manager of the operating system without altering other software.

Digital computer—A computer that functions in discretely varying quantities and produces results that are also discretely varying.

Digital photo system—A service that takes slides or pictures, digitizes them, and stores them on some computer-accessible memory device.

Digital signal—A signal expressed in binary digits, such as the data passed from the computer to a terminal, or encoded on a compact disc.

Digitize—To convert data such as a photograph into binary numbers.

Digitized image—A picture that has been translated into digital form.

Digitizer—A device used to convert a picture to numeric form.

Direct-link network—This refers to a network such as the telephone switching system, where a direct link is formed between two communicating parties.

Discovery learning—See **Learning by doing**.

Discrete system—A model having quantities that vary in steps or jumps.

Disjointed speech—Words spoken individually or separately with definite pauses between words.

Disk (diskette)—A flat, circular platter coated with a magnetic material on one or both sides. The plate is capable of holding magnetized spots representing binary numbers and codes. This plate rotates so that data can be stored or retrieved by one or more of the heads that then transfer the data to and from the computer. A disk can be either floppy or rigid (hard).

Distance learning—An unsupervised, independent mode of education where the students do not need to meet in a classroom, but "meet" via interactive video, email, the Internet, and real-time electronic communication.

Distributed processing—Involves using a network to allow a single entity to decentralize its computing needs over several interconnected computers.

Distribution—In statistics, the property of a group of numbers described by the relative number of occurrences of each possible value.

Document formatting—Those actions taken that affect the appearance of the document, such as setting margins and tabs, using type effects, justifying text, and so on.

Documentation—The manual or instructions that come with most software programs and pieces of hardware. Some software programs have the documentation on disk. Also, the comments included in a computer program help the programmers who work on the program.

Domain name—This is the name assigned to a computer on the Internet. For example, **whitehouse.gov** is the domain name when sending email to the White House in

Washington, D.C. The complete address for sending email to the president is **president@whitehouse.com**.

DOS (**D**isk **O**perating **S**ystem)—An operating system for which a disk is the principal storage medium for files, programs, and so on.

Dot-matrix printer—A printer that uses a pattern of closely spaced dots that can form letters, numbers, or other symbols.

Downloading—The process of receiving a copy of a program, document, or file from another computer. **Uploading** is the process of sending a copy of a program, document, or other file to another computer.

Drawing program—Used to create images instead of manipulating existing images.

Drill and practice—Programs that lean heavily on question-and-answer teaching strategy, sometimes adding an element of competition.

Driver—Program to transfer information between RAM and a piece of hardware.

Drum—A storage device that uses magnetic recording on a rotating cylinder.

Drum plotter—An output device for creating hard-copy graphics in which a continuous sheet of paper rolls over a cylinder beneath one or more pens.

EBCDIC (**E**xtended **B**inary **C**oded **D**ecimal **I**nterchange **C**ode)—A standard coding method used to represent numbers, letters, and special characters, traditionally used on mainframe computers.

Edge detection—Identifying the edges of objects is necessary to separate objects from their backgrounds.

Electronic books—This is a new genre of books on the computer. Normally they present more than just electronic pages of text, and many use hypertext and hypermedia.

Electronic computer—A device constructed from transistors that use electricity to function.

Electronic mall—This is the equivalent of a shopping mall on the World Wide Web.

Electronic spreadsheet—A computerized ledger page arranged in columns and rows.

Elision—The two or more phonemes that make up a word or phrase must be spliced so that when one of them ends and the next begins, the connection will sound natural.

Email (**E**lectronic **M**ail)—The software used to send messages from one user to another on a computer system or network; also, the messages sent by such software.

Emoney—Used interchangeably with ecash, digicash, and cybercash; it is money that can be used over the Internet. It only exists in electronic form.

Enterprise IP Network—It is a TCP/IP network that operates inside a corporation.

Ethernet—A very fast local area network protocol.

Executable statement—A command telling the computer to carry out a particular action or manipulation.

Execute—To perform the instructions in a computer program.

Expert system—A system consisting of rules and an inference engine, which when given input can make decisions based on the rules. Also called a production system.

Expression—A constant or variable, or the statement of one or more arithmetic operations to be performed on constants or variables.

False coloring—Assigning different colors to specific shades of gray in a grayscale image to make it more understandable to human eyes. Also called pseudocoloring.

False relevance—A statement that a cause-and-effect relationship exists, when the two facts involved seem to be related but are not.

Feedback loop—The use of the output of a computer program as input to another phase of the same program, especially for self-correcting or control purposes.

Feedback system—A model that reacts to input.

Fetch and execute cycle—The operation in which an instruction is moved from internal storage to a special register for decoding and is then executed.

Fetching instructions—The first state in processing an instruction, in which the instruction is copied from memory into the CPU and decoded.

Fiber-optic cables—This is a cable made of fine strands of glass fiber that carries digital signals using pulses of light rather than electricity.

Field—1) An instruction has two parts: opcode and operand. Each part is called a field; 2) A location in a database that contains one single specific piece of information.

File—A collection of records or data designated by name and considered as a unit by the user, usually stored on disk. A file, of payroll records, for example, can consist of a record for each employee, showing pay rate, deductions, and so on.

File server—A computer dedicated to providing files to other computers on the network.

Film recorder—An input unit that records the digitized version of a 35mm color slide.

Filtering software—In reference to the Internet, it is software used to filter out access to undesirable Web sites on the Internet.

Floppy disk—A circular platter that has been coated with a magnetic material with concentric tracks. The flexible disk is stored in a paper or plastic envelope. The entire envelope is inserted in the disk unit of the computer. Floppy disks are a low-cost storage medium used widely with minicomputers and microcomputers.

Flowchart—A series of visual symbols that represent the logical flow of a program.

FOR loop—In BASIC, a loop that is iterated (repeated) a certain number of times.

Formatter—A program that conducts the formatting of a disk.

Formatting a disk—Also called initializing a disk. Setting up a disk to be used by a particular operating system. Note: Formatting a disk *erases* everything that is currently on the disk.

Formula—A feature of an electronic spreadsheet that gives the user the ability to perform calculations directly within the spreadsheet.

FORTRAN-77—(**FOR**mula **TRAN**slator, 1977 standard) An early high-level computer programming language that is most widely used to perform mathematical, scientific, and engineering computations.

Forward chaining—The act of going from a rule's condition to a rule's action, and using the action as a new condition, and so on.

Fourth-generation language—Computer programming languages such as application generators, query languages, report writers, and data manipulation languages that make it easier for humans to program for a specific purpose than such languages as FORTRAN and Pascal.

Frame—A description of various properties and scripts needed to represent a generalized situation in artificial intelligence.

Freeware—Software that is totally free. It is legal to copy and distribute this software, although no support is provided by the author.

FTP—The File Transfer Protocol is an Internet service used to transfer files from one computer to another. Many FTP servers offer access to public files under the username *anonymous*.

Full-duplex transmission—A type of communication channel or line that allows transmissions in both directions simultaneously.

Fully connected topology—This term refers to a network in which every node has a connection to all other nodes.

Function—A subprogram designed to perform a specific task and return a single value.

Functional programming language—Often used for special-purpose computers to solve problems that apply to systems such as thermostatic controls or security devices.

Gaming—Combining the enjoyment and competition of playing a game with specific educational content.

Gateway—A computer that connects to different networks and provides a gateway from one to the other. Digital communications flow through the gateway.

General-purpose computer—A computer that can be used in many situations and for many different and unrelated tasks.

General-purpose electronic digital computer—A device constructed of binary electronic circuits that accepts many kinds of information, changes it in a way that is controllable by humans, and presents the results in a way controllable by humans.

Genetic algorithm—Mimics the processes in the genetics of living systems. Meant to be a general solution to all types of problems.

Gigabyte—A unit of storage containing 1,073,741,824 bytes (about one billion bytes).

Gopher—It refers to a service that allows communication on the Internet. It was created at the University of Minnesota, home of the Golden Gophers.

GOTO statement—In BASIC, the statement that provides for an unconditional transfer of control.

Grammar checker—Enables the user to find syntax errors in text and sometimes suggests corrections.

Graphics—Visual images that are not primarily text.

Grayscale—A method of storing pictures in a computer where each pixel contains a value for a shade of gray.

GUI (Graphical User Interface)—An operating system interface represented in pictorial form, usually accessed with a mouse.

Hacking—Any unauthorized computer- or data-related activity not sanctioned by an employer or the owner of a system, database, or network.

Half-duplex transmission—A type of communication channel or line through which data can be transmitted, but in only one direction at a time.

Hard-copy device—A device used to display information by typing or printing on paper. The paper holds a permanent record of the information.

Hard disk—A circular platter that has been coated with a magnetic material with concentric tracks. The nonflexible disk is stored in a special housing or within the main "box" with the CPU. Hard disks are a medium-priced storage that is used widely with minicomputers and microcomputers.

Hardware—The electronics and associated mechanical parts of the computer. Each has a physical presence. (You can see, feel, or touch it.)

Hertz—A measure of the frequency of a sound or electrical signal, expressed in cycles per second.

Heuristic—A rule of thumb (a nonrigorous rule) that often gets a correct result, but is not guaranteed to do so.

Hexadecimal—Base 16 numeration system commonly used in computers.

Hexit (HEXadecimal digIT)—One symbol of the hexadecimal system.

Hidden-line problem—A line in a graphic image that would not be visible if the surfaces closer to the viewer were opaque.

High-level programming language—A programming language that is independent of specific hardware. Programs of a high-level programming language require a compiler or interpreter.

Hollerith card—Keypunched cards used to hold information.

Hologram—A multidimensional photograph on a film storage medium, made with laser beams, and containing a 3D image of a physical object.

Host—A computer that accepts remote logons.

HTML (Hypertext Markup Language)—It is a language used for World Wide Web authoring and provides hypertext and hypermedia links.

HTTP—The Hypertext Transport Protocol refers to a set of rules used by computers to communicate with TCP/IP and on to the WWW. HTTP often refers to the program that implements the protocol and resides on all computers of the WWW.

Hub—It is a device that connects several computers in local areas and in some ways replaces a LAN.

Hypermedia—It carries the concept of the linking in hypertext to all media. This includes audio, animation, video, visual, and other media.

Hypermedia links—These are links associated with media other than text. They have actions similar to hypertext links.

Hypertext—It is a form of text that has a certain interactive component. Individual words have links to additional related material that could be located anywhere. The link contains information on how to get to the related material.

Icon—A small graphic picture representing objects or commands.

Image enhancement—A type of processing of digital images whose goal is to highlight or enhance particular aspects of an image or to change the structure of the image itself.

Image manipulation program—Enables the user to change the appearance of an image.

Image processing—The act of modifying an image. The two major categories are image restoration and image enhancement.

Image restoration—The elimination of known image flaws or degradations.

Imitation Game—Also known as Turing's Test. This interrogation of the computer was designed to test for intelligence.

Index—1) A list giving the identifier of a record and the location where the record can be found; 2) An amount to be added to the starting location of a table to locate a specific element within a table.

Inference engine—The part of an expert system that interprets the rules in the knowledge base.

Infinite loop—A set of computer instructions that repeats forever.

Inflection—Involves the rising and falling pattern of pitch on an individual phoneme.

Information—Data repackaged in a meaningful form.

Information extraction—This process uses human/computer interaction to present pictorial data in a form that aids the human in extracting information.

Infrared—A frequency of light of slightly shorter wavelength than humans can perceive. It is used for wireless line-of-sight communications between things such as keyboards and computers.

Initializing a disk—See **Formatting a disk**.

Input—Information put into a communication system for transmission or into a data processing system for processing.

Input unit—Any machine device that allows entry of commands or information into the computer. An input unit can be a keyboard, tape drive, disk drive, microphone, light pen, digitizer, electronic sensor, and so on.

Input-output instruction—One type of instruction or statement (I/O statement) that moves information in and out of the computer.

Instruction—Contains an identifying code (operation code) that tells the computer which operation is to be performed and the location in memory (operand) where the data can be found.

Instruction decoding unit—This part of the CPU decodes instructions.

Instruction register—This part of the control unit found in the CPU is where an instruction is placed for analysis by the instruction decoding unit.

Instruction set—Those commands in a programming language that the computer can understand.

Integer data—Numeric data not containing a decimal point.

Interactive dialog—An advanced form of tutoring that asks substantial questions and interprets student results in terms of learning achievement.

Interactive multimedia—It is communication that uses visual and audio forms to supply information to a human, but it also requires the interaction from the human observer. It is two-way communication.

Interface—1) The device used to connect a computer with its peripherals; 2) In reference to *user interface* or *graphical user interface*, it is what the person working with the computer sees and experiences when using the computer.

Internet—The Internet is the informally organized system of all computers that communicate using the TCP/IP protocol. It spans the world and contains hundreds of thousands of computers.

Internet address—Sometimes called the IP address, it is a unique number that identifies each computer attached to the Internet.

Interpreter—A translation program that converts a higher-level language program into machine code, one line at a time, and executes the line immediately.

Intranets—This is a term used to describe networks that are wholly within a corporation or organization and are based on the same TCP/IP protocol as the Internet.

I/O bound (**I**nput/**O**utput bound)—A characteristic of running a program (a process) that spends most of its time waiting for input or output to occur.

IP (**I**nternet **P**rotocol)—It is the network protocol used by the Internet. IP along with TCP (Transport Control Protocol) consists of over 100 protocols. This suite of protocols is referred to as **TCP/IP**.

IRC—(**I**nternet **R**elay **C**hat)—An Internet service that consists of chat rooms where people communicate through "channels" in real time. If you have signed into a chat room, you will see all the comments typed by others who are also in that chat room.

ISP (Internet Service Provider)— A company or organization that offers a connection to the Internet.

Iteration statement—The part of a loop that designates a statement or sequence of statements to be repeated.

JPEG (Joint Photographers Expert Group)—A file-compression scheme used to compress visual-image files on the computer (see **Compression**).

K (Kilobyte)—A unit of storage holding 1,024 bytes.

Kernel—A small portion of an operating system permanently resident in main memory or read-only memory, and which is responsible for the most critical activities of the system.

Kiosk—A computer-controlled kiosk or information center is a standalone information center that is often located in public places. The main purpose is to supply information to those passing by.

Knowledge acquisition—Using input (human senses, computer input units) to collect a base of information.

Knowledge base—A list of pertinent information on a given topic.

Knowledge retrieval—Efficiently finding information stored in the knowledge base.

Label—A name given to identify a memory location.

LAN (Local Area Network)—A group of interconnected computers that are all within a short distance of each other (typically within one room or building).

Language processor—A general term for any assembler, compiler, or other routine that accepts statements in one language and produces equivalent statements in another language.

Laser—A device capable of producing a tightly-packed, narrow beam of high-intensity light.

Laser disc—See **Video disc**.

Laser printer—A printer that produces output of a much higher quality than a dot-matrix printer.

Learning by doing—Also called "discovery learning." The teacher assigns a task to the student and offers little or no instruction.

Library—A collection of programs, routines, source statements, or executable programs that may or may not be accessible to all users of the computer.

Light pen—This pen-like input unit enables the user to point at an object on the screen and activate the object so that it can be manipulated.

Link—A physical connection between nodes of a network. It may consist of wire, infrared, microwave, and/or fiber-optic types of communication.

Loader—A program or module within the operating system that places into main memory the code of a program that is stored on a disk, magnetic tape, paper tape, or the like. It will also place the address of the first instruction to be executed into the program counter.

Loading a program—The process of copying a program or data that is found on an input device into the computer's memory.

Logic—The processing part of a program algorithm.

Logic bomb—See **Time bomb**.

Logic error—A mistake in the steps used in an algorithm. An error results when steps are left out, unnecessary, or out of order.

Logical or comparison instruction—One type of instruction used in decision making.

Logical programming language—This language uses a series of If...Then statements to solve problems.

Loop—A sequence of instructions repeated one or more times when the program is executed.

Low-level programming language—A computer programming language that is hardware dependent, written for a particular type of computer with a particular CPU.

LSI (Large Scale Integration)—The combining of approximately 1,000 to 10,000 circuits on a single chip. Examples of LSI are memory chips, microprocessors, calculator chips, and watch chips.

Machine language—The form that all instructions must be in before the computer can execute them. It consists of binary numbers or binary code. Programs in other programming languages must be converted to machine language before the computer can understand the code.

Machine learning—The concept of using computer programs that are capable of learning.

Magnetic tape—A plastic tape having a magnetic surface, which can be magnetized in spots that represent binary numbers and codes.

Maillardet's Automaton—A mechanical drawing machine created in 1805. It was considered to have some intelligence at the time because it had the appearance of a boy.

Mainframe computer—A large computer characterized by multiprocessing and a high price.

MAN (Metropolitan Area Network)—A network technology that is very fast and can span areas as large as a major metropolitan area.

Mark-sensor form—A sheet of paper with areas to be colored in by a user to indicate specific responses to questions. The computer can then sense where the marks have been made on the sheet.

Math coprocessor—A microprocessor chip that allows intricate calculations to be performed.

Matrix, The—Consists of all computers and networks that have the capability of exchanging electronic mail.

Mean—The sum of a group of numbers divided by how many numbers are in the group.

Mechanical computer—A computer constructed of a combination of levers, springs, gears, cranks, pulleys, and so on.

Median—The number that divides a group of numbers in half. Half the numbers are below it, and half above it.

Megabyte—A unit of storage containing 1,048,576 bytes (about a million bytes).

Memory—Any portion of a computing system where information to be used by the computer is kept for recall. Each item in memory has a unique address that the central processing unit can use to retrieve information.

Memory-mapped display—A listing of the locations in RAM or ROM of various programs.

Microcomputer—A small computer designed for a single user. A microcomputer typically fits on a desktop or even in a briefcase. It is comprised of a central processing unit, input/output units, and a power supply.

Microprocessor—The entire contents of a CPU designed to fit on one single chip.

MIDI (Musical Instrument Digital Interface)—An industry standard for connecting music synthesizers, electronic drums, and music keyboards to each other and usually to a controlling computer.

MIDI bus—The actual connection made between the computer and musical instruments.

Milnet—The military network was originally part of ARPAnet and used for non-classified military communication.

Minicomputer—A medium-sized computer characterized by a higher-performance level than microcomputers, more powerful instruction sets, a higher price, and a wide selection of available programming languages and operating systems.

Mnemonic—An abbreviated name that reminds one of the full name, such as *sub* for *subtract*.

Mode—The value that occurs most frequently in a group of numbers.

Model—A simulation that fakes or gives the appearance of the system in question.

Modeling—1) Students are guided in building and studying a model; 2) Students enter into an already developed simulation and study it from within.

Modem (MODulator—DEModulator)—It is an electronic device that takes the binary data from the computer and converts it to a form (modulates) that can be sent over telephone lines. The receiving end modem then converts it back to a form the computer can use (demodulates).

Module—A section of a program that may be written, compiled, and catalogued as a unit and later combined or linked to other parts.

MOOs—(**M**ultiuser **O**bject-**O**riented **s**ystems)—Role-playing games that use object-oriented software technology and are played over the Internet.

Mouse—An input unit used to send information to a computer. Usually involves a roller ball that manipulates an icon onscreen.

MPEG (Motion Picture Experts Group)—It is a video-compression scheme specifically for digitized video playback on computers. MPEG requires hardware for the decompression.

MS-DOS—A widely used operating system developed by Microsoft Corp.

MUDs (Multi-User Dungeons)—Role-playing games played over the Internet.

Multimedia—It is the use of more than one medium or means to communicate information. For example, a presentation with audio, video, and still images is a multimedia presentation.

Multimedia presentation system—A system that incorporates elements such as sound, videotape, slides, and so on into a presentation.

Multiprocessing—Computing done with more than one CPU. Also called **parallel processing**.

Multiprogramming—Running two or more programs at the same time on the same computer.

Multitasking—A complicated form of multiprogramming where one task is continued in the background while another is working.

Nassi-Schneidermann Chart—A schematic representation of the organization of a process or computer program, shown by symbols of different shapes arranged within a large rectangle.

Natural-language communication—The process of having the computer understand normal spoken language.

Natural-language processing system—The processing of natural language by a computer to facilitate communication between humans and the computer.

Network—It consists of communication channels connecting a collection of computers, terminals, printers, switches, and other devices. All these devices will be referred to as **nodes**.

Network architecture—The logical connections and organization of the software that will run the network.

Network protocol—The collection of programs written to follow the rules for communication according to some prearranged scheme.

Neural network—An interconnected collection of neurons.

Neurocomputer—A computer wired to simulate a neural network.

Neuron—An individual nerve cell capable of receiving input from the environment or other cells and transmitting output to other neurons or to muscles and organs.

Nibble—A unit of storage usually containing 4 bits.

Node—A device with its own personal address on a network, which can send or receive information over the network.

Nondestructive reading—Reading data from a storage location without changing or deleting the data.

Nonprocedural programming language—A type of language that expresses a computer problem's solution as a series of tasks to be accomplished.

Normal distribution—Data exhibiting a pattern as found in nature. The popular range of values tends to center around the average and forms a "bell curve." Approximately 68 percent of the data fall within a limited range near the center of the distribution.

NSFnet (**N**ational **S**cience **F**oundation **net**work)—Commonly recognized as the original backbone of the Internet.

Number crunching—The manipulation of numeric data into useful calculated results.

Object-oriented graphics—Those which are stored as lines, curves, or geometric shapes. The main advantage over bitmapped graphics is that objects can be moved or modified easily.

Object-oriented programming language—This type of language resembles the human way of thinking in that it works on objects and their associated tasks.

OCR (**O**ptical **C**haracter **R**ecognition)—Allows a printed or typed document digitized as a visual image to be converted into a text file in the computer's memory.

Offline—A term used to refer to processing while not directly connected with the computer.

Online—A term used to refer to the equipment or devices that are connected to the computer while you are using it. These devices input and process information directly with the CPU of a computer.

Opcode (**OP**eration **code**)—1) A code used to represent a specific operation of a computer; 2) The part of an instruction that tells what operation is to be performed.

Operand—1) A unit of data on which an operation is performed; 2) The part of an instruction that tells where to find the data or equipment to be operated on.

Operating system—A collection of programs that not only makes the computer easier to use, but also allows the most efficient use of this expensive resource. It moves information around the computer.

Operation—A defined computer activity that has been specified by a single computer instruction or high-level language statement.

Operator—A word or symbol that tells the computer what to do in a particular data manipulation.

Optical character recognition—A method of reading characters by machine directly from a printed document and translating them into machine-readable form to be used by a computer.

Order—To put items in a given sequence.

Outliner—A program designed to help a writer organize thoughts and produce better-quality documents.

Output—Information produced by a computer from specific input.

Output unit—The output unit is a machine that transfers programs or information from the computer to some other medium. An output unit can be tape, disk memory drives, computer printers, typewriters and plotters, the computer's video display screen, robots, and so on.

Packet—A collection of bytes containing various types of information that usually includes where it came from and the address of where it's going. An Internet packet is called an IP datagram.

Packet-switching—The process of moving packets in a network from node to node until the destination is reached. The Internet uses packet-switching.

Paper-tape reader and punch—Machines that process a narrow continuous strip of paper in which punched holes record numeric and alphabetic information for computer programming.

Parallel—1) A transmission format in which all the elements of a word (several bits) or message are sent simultaneously; 2) In reference to **parallel processing**, it is the simultaneous processing of two or more program statements. This implies a computer system with more than one CPU.

Parity bit—A bit used to verify that the data bits have remained unaltered.

Passive multimedia—It is communication that uses visual and audio forms to supply information to a human. It is one-way communication, from the medium to the viewer, and it usually refers to electronic media used in the context of computing.

Password—Secret word or phrase used to prevent unauthorized people from accessing computer accounts, files, or equipment.

Patch—A customized sound that the performer has prepared and stored in a MIDI-compatible form.

Pattern recognition—The field of AI that concentrates on computer recognition of visual objects.

PC (Personal Computer)—A name commonly given to microcomputers.

Pedagogical techniques—Techniques used to go about the process of teaching.

Percent—A special type of fraction that represents the number of parts out of a total of 100 parts.

Peripheral—Any piece of hardware that is *not* a part of the basic computer (for example, disk drives, printers, plotters, graphics tablets, mice).

Perspective—Alteration of the relative sizes and shapes of objects in an illustration to make it appear three-dimensional.

Phoneme—A basic sound category in a spoken language.

Piggybacking—Invading a computer system by riding in behind a legitimate user with a password.

Pirated software—Software that a user does not have a legal right to have or use.

Pitch—The sound of a human's voice, determined by the number of cycles per second of a particular sound's vibration. The more vibrations per second, the higher the pitch.

Pixel—An acronym for **pic**ture **el**ement, the building blocks of a computer picture. For simple pictures, each pixel is either black or white.

Plotter—An output device that produces line drawings with one or more pens of varying widths and colors, which is/are under the control of a computer.

Plug-ins—This is software that can be added to a browser to give it additional capabilities, such as playing sounds.

Point-to-point network—This is a network where the connection is direct rather than indirect. With PPP (Point-to-Point Protocol) or SLIP (Serial Line IP) software, TCP/IP traffic can travel over the direct link.

Predictable system—A system whose model can predict exactly what can happen.

Presentation software—It is an application or program that assists in creating a multimedia presentation. It usually includes the capability to create text and color graphics presentation with some simple animation and sound effects.

Primary memory—The main electronic memory used by a computer where a program and related data reside when being executed by the computer.

Probabilistic system—A system whose model contains unpredictable features or events.

Probability—A numeric value given to a prediction of whether an event will occur.

Problem—A task to be completed by a computer. The task must be possible within the capabilities of the computer involved.

Problem solving—The teacher presents a problem and then, step by step, guides the student through its solution.

Procedural programming language—A type of language that expresses a computer problem's solution as a series of discrete instructions or steps.

Procedures—1) A sequence of steps performed to solve a problem; 2) A subprogram in Pascal.

Process control—The control of some process by computer in real time.

Processing element—The smallest logical unit in a computer, equivalent in a neural network to a single neuron.

PRO DOS—An operating system designed for microcomputers.

Production system—See **Expert system**.

Program—A collection of commands or instructions for the computer to perform one by one. The programmer types in instructions for a certain task, and the computer follows these instructions precisely.

Program counter—This part of the control unit found in the CPU contains the address of the next instruction to be executed.

Programming language—A language used by humans to communicate with computers.

PROM (Programmable Read-Only Memory)—A memory that is not programmed by the manufacturer, but rather by the user. After the user has programmed the memory, it behaves much the same as ROM—that is, it can be read as many times as desired, but it cannot be written into.

Prompt—A character, word, or series of words to signal a user to give some command or other input.

Protocol—In reference to networks, a protocol is set of rules that must be followed by computers for them to communicate.

Protocol suite—A collection of programs that implements the protocols that the programs implement.

Pseudo-coloring—See **False coloring**.

Pseudocode—A verbal shorthand method of detailing the steps of a program.

Psychomotor skills—Physical coordination and neuromuscular learning.

Punch card—A stiff paper card with small rectangular holes punched in patterns that denote numeric values and alphanumeric codes. Each card has 12 rows and 80 columns of possible hole locations. Punch cards are especially used in the older mainframe computers.

Query language—A fourth-generation computer language developed specifically to ask questions and request information from databases.

Question and answer—A strategy that presents a series of questions for the student to answer.

RAM (Random Access Memory)—A part of the main memory of the computer. Its contents are not permanent and can be changed. If the power shuts off, RAM loses everything that was stored in it.

Random access—The capability of accessing memory without having to examine all the other information.

Real data—Numeric data containing a decimal point.

Real-time processing—Computing that involves humans interacting with the computer in a situation where quick or timely return of results is important.

Reasoning with knowledge—The process of manipulating or generalizing previously stored knowledge.

Record—A collection of data items related to one person or item, which are stored on a disk or some other type of storage medium and may be recalled as a unit. A record can be composed of elements of different types.

Relational operator—A symbol that instructs the computer to make a comparison between two values of the same data type.

Reliable program—Must be able to produce correct results with every possibility of appropriate data.

Remote electronic data sensing—Using a satellite to collect data from a great distance.

Report writer—A program that takes information from a database and produces interactive, usable output.

Resonance—The reverberation of amplification of the voice in the cavities of the vocal tract. The larger the cavities, the deeper or richer the resulting resonance.

Ring network—This network consists of nodes connected together to form a circle.

Robust program—Must be able to detect execution errors. It may warn the user and allow the error to be corrected or terminate the run.

ROM (**R**ead **O**nly **M**emory)—A part of the main memory of the computer. It is permanent memory that cannot be changed unless you replace it.

Router—A network node connected to two or more networks, which forwards the packets from one network to another.

Routine—A self-contained collection of program statements that perform some very specific subsection of an overall program. The same routine may be invoked numerous times within the same program. Therefore, it is useful to separate routines from the main body of a program so that routines can be invoked many times without the necessity of typing in their statements many times (that is, the statements will be executed repeatedly).

Sample—The data collected from a group of possibilities.

Sampling—A technique used to predict the total situation by selecting a few instances to represent a larger group.

Scanner—An input unit that digitizes an image or text.

Scavenging—Searching through stray data and electronic garbage for clues that might unlock secrets of a targeted computer system.

Scheduler—A part of the operating system that is responsible for scheduling (that is, determining the order in which resources, especially CPU and memory, will be assigned to process jobs).

Script—A set of definitions of props, roles, point of view, time of occurrence, place of occurrence, and event sequence used in artificial intelligence to describe what happens in a particular situation.

Scrolling mode—A method of displaying information on a cathode ray tube (the user's screen) by adding new lines to the bottom of the screen while letting old lines roll or fall off the top.

Search engine—This term most commonly refers to WWW programs that provide the capability of searching the Internet for information. It is done using keywords.

Searching—Looking at all appropriate information or knowledge and selecting one instance.

Secondary memory—Memory units such as a floppy disk or hard disk that are used to store information to be loaded into RAM when needed.

Semantic network—A representation of reality in artificial intelligence that consists of objects, concepts, or situations connected by some type of relationship.

Semantics—The exact content (meaning) of a language unit. In computer language, it refers to the commands you wish the computer to perform.

Sequencer—Either a computer or a separate sequencer that acts as a recording device. It allows the modification of the music after it is stored.

Sequential access—Allows the desired information to be obtained from memory by starting at the beginning of a list of information and then proceeding item by item until it is reached.

Serial—A transmission format in which data is sent bit by bit in a stream.

Server—Usually a dedicated computer that is part of a network. A server's hard drive contains files that are "served" to whatever requests them. The server normally also runs the networking software that implements the network's protocols, which means it manages the network.

Shading—Assigning a grayscale value to a face of a solid.

Shareware—Software that is legal to pass and copy. The receiver is allowed to try it and is expected to send money to the author if he/she keeps it.

Show and tell—The teacher assigns a student the task of explaining or describing something to others. This sharpens communication and group-interaction skills.

Simplex transmission—Transmission in which information can flow in only one direction, such as that between the keyboard and the computer.

Simulation—A computerized reproduction, image, or replica of a situation or a set of conditions. Often used to model or mimic a real-life situation. Simulation enables the user to react or experiment without endangering life or property.

Simulation language—A special-purpose computer language used to write simulation programs.

Single alternative decision structure—A conditional statement where a condition is evaluated and action is taken only in the true case. If the condition is false, the program continues.

Skewed sample—Data that is distorted and misrepresents the total population.

Social interaction—The communication that occurs during relationships among people.

Software—The instructions that control the hardware and cause the desired thing to happen.

Software piracy—The unauthorized copying or use of software for which you have not paid the appropriate licensing fee.

Special purpose computer—A computer designed to be used in a very limited way.

Speech recognition—A computerized system designed to identify spoken words.

Speech synthesis—The electronic production of sound and sound patterns constructed by a computer from a series of numbers previously stored in the computer's memory in digitized form.

Speech synthesizer—A special-purpose computer to produce spoken words.

Spelling checker—Software that enables the user to select appropriate spellings and make needed corrections.

Spider—A spider refers to a program that follows links on the WWW and records words on Web pages and follows any links found at a Web site.

Standard deviation—The amount above and below the most common value of a normal distribution, which 68 percent of all measurements lie within.

Star network—This network consists of nodes connected to a central node.

Startup disk—A disk containing an operating system and sometimes a self-starting application program.

Stored program computer—A computing device with a memory that contains both a program and the information needed for computing by the program.

Structured programming—An approach used in the process of designing and coding of computer programs. The top-down analysis and design strategy is used to break the major problem down into smaller and smaller logical steps. Another strategy that is used is to determine where all the program logic can be reduced to a combination of three patterns: sequence, repetition, and selection.

Subprogram—A part of a larger program. Usually, a subprogram can be translated into machine language independently of the remainder of the program.

Subroutine—A subprogram in the form of a named group of statements within a program, which performs a specific task and can be invoked, or called, by its name.

Supercomputer—A large computer characterized by incredible speed of processing and multiple CPUs.

Supervised training—This occurs when the neural network is given input data and the resulting output is compared to the correct output. The strengths of connections are adjusted as necessary.

Surfing the Web—A slang term used to describe the free-form navigation from place to place on the Internet by following hyperlinks of the WWW.

Switch—A node that connects networks of the same type.

Synchronous transmission—Information is sent down the communications channel in groups or blocks.

Syntax—The grammar rules of a natural or computer language.

Syntax error—A mistake violating the grammar rules of a computer language. Typing errors usually fall into this category.

System crash—See **Crash**.

Systems analysis—The study and planning of systems, especially business computer systems.

Systems programming—The development of system programs that form the operating system of a computer. System programs are written to control the computer and its related equipment (for example, the programs that start and stop jobs or find data on a tape or disk).

Systems programming language—A special-purpose programming language designed to meet the needs of constructing systems software—that is, operating systems, file systems, language-translator systems, utility systems, and database systems.

TCP/IP—TCP (Transport Control Protocol) with **IP** (Internet Protocol) consists of over 100 protocols. This suite of protocols is referred to as TCP/IP.

Teleconference—An electronic meeting held over a computer network that can take place at the convenience of the participants.

Telnet—This is a remote logon service for Internet access. It allows a remote computer to connect to a computer that is part of the Internet and thereby gain Internet access.

Template—A predesigned format for a graphic image, text document, presentation slide, and so on.

Terabyte—A unit of storage containing about one trillion bytes.

Terminal—A point in a computer system through which information can either enter or leave, usually consisting of a monitor, keyboard, and some local memory devices.

Text entry—Typing a document, checking it for spelling errors, and modifying text by inserting or deleting.

Text-processing programs—Electronically creates and corrects text without the use of paper, except for final output.

TFTP—Trivial File Transport Protocol allows the use of Telnet for remote logon, SMTP (Simple Mail Transfer Protocol), and email communication.

Time bomb—A software routine that can be triggered at some later time by the computer's clock or by a predetermined combination of events.

Time compression—Shortening the time a simulation takes compared to the time required by the actual activity.

Time sharing—A form of multiprogramming in which the different programs in memory belong to a number of human users who interact directly and simultaneously with their own programs from their terminals that are connected to the computer.

Token Ring—Invented by IBM, the token-ring concept uses a token, which is a special piece of information that is passed around the nodes of a ring network. An individual node can send information on to the ring network only when it possesses the token.

Top-down analysis and design—A method of writing computer programs, starting with the main idea or problem and refining it until it has been broken down into smaller, more manageable and distinct modules.

Top-level domain—In the domain name of an Internet address, the rightmost subdomain, called the top-level domain, identifies the type of organization owning the computer. For example, in the address president@whitehouse.gov, the top-level domain is gov.

Total immersion—The student is totally immersed in an environment conducive to learning particular subject matter.

Training—Presenting input to a computer program that, together with proper feedback about the program's output, enables the program to alter its assumptions or responses to later input.

Translation—The porting of ideas, instructions, and concepts from one language form to another.

Tree network—This hierarchical network consists of nodes connected at more than one level. Several nodes may be connected to a single node forming the next level.

Trojan horse—An unwanted program distributed by being hidden within a more-desirable program.

Turing's Test—See **Imitation Game**.

Tutorial—A program that presents material and tests understanding. The material and rate of presentation are adaptable, and the order of presentation can be altered according to student responses.

Twisted pair—This refers to a pair of wires twisted together to help reduce electrical interference. Twisted pair are sometimes used to connect LANs.

UDP (**U**ser **D**atagram **P**rotocol)—Provides a less-reliable channel than TCP to programs running on the computer where it resides. Used mainly for audio- and video-related information that can tolerate small errors. A datagram can be thought of as a message.

UNIX—A popular interactive operating system developed by the researchers at AT&T Bell Laboratories.

Uploading—See **Downloading**.

URL (**U**niform **R**esource **L**ocator)— The name given to the worldwide standard for expressing the unique address of a specific Web page.

Usenet—A term used to describe a group of computers that exchange network news. They often make use of the Internet, but sometimes they use the telephone system.

User friendly—A term given to a program that is easy for a person to use.

Vaccine—A program that searches your disk for viruses and notifies you of any that were found.

Variable—A named storage location that contains a value that can change during program execution.

Verified model—A model proven to be a reasonably accurate representation of the system being simulated.

Veronica—A Gopher keyword search program that allows searching Gopher space for Gopher menus that have those words.

Version—A number assigned by the manufacturer of a software program. It designates the continuing revision process of programs.

Video disc—An analog medium of storage, usually optically encoded, on a platter that stores high-quality visual images; these images are then read by a video-disc player used as a peripheral device with computers.

Viewpoint—This graphic technique enables the user to view an object from various directions.

Virtual memory—An operating system feature that allows running programs that would otherwise be too large to run in the available RAM.

Virtual reality—A situation in which an individual has a three-dimensional view into a world that doesn't exist except in the computer.

Virus—An unwanted program that spreads by attaching itself to other legitimate programs.

VLSI (**V**ery **L**arge **S**cale **I**ntegration)—Similar to LSI, but on a scale that made possible the personal computer.

Voice recognition data entry—The collection and recording of data by speaking into a microphone of a terminal.

Voiced sound—Phonetic sounds produced by the vibrating of the vocal cords in the absence of aspirated air. Examples include b, d, and g.

Voiceless sound—Phonetic sounds characterized by the lack of vocal cord vibration. Examples include p, t, and k.

Voiceprint—A visual representation of the sound frequencies made by a person speaking.

Voltage—A numeric value given to an amount of electrical power measured in volts.

von Neumann computer—A stored program computer named after John von Neumann.

WAIS (**W**ide **A**rea **I**nformation **S**erver)— Internet automated search service that allows searching for documents containing keywords or phrases.

WAN (**W**ide **A**rea **N**etwork)—It consists of a number of computer networks, including LANs, connected by communication channels of many different types.

Warm boot—Reloads the operating system into RAM without disrupting power to the disk drives or power supply.

Web—Web is a slang word representing the World Wide Web.

Web browser—A program that enables the user to browse or look around. A Web browser enables users to browse or navigate the WWW.

Web page—A document that may consist of images, sound, or text, and whose display to a WWW browser is controlled by HTML.

Web site—This consists of a group of related Web pages.

What-if forecasting—Allows examination of theories of the future on an electronic spreadsheet.

Word—A set of bits considered as a unit. It is a unit of memory, usually consisting of 1 or more bytes.

Word processor—1) A computer system designed to create, modify, and produce documents, letters, and manuscripts using electronic text-editing software and equipment; 2) A text-processing program.

Workstation—A subcategory of computers that lies between microcomputers and minicomputers, typically connected to other computers and storage devices through a network. It is used by one person at a time.

Worm—An unwanted program that spreads itself without being hidden inside or attached to another program.

WWW (World Wide Web)—A communications protocol that allows multimedia access to the Internet.

WYSIWYG (What You See Is What You Get)—A feature of a text-manipulation program where what is seen onscreen is what is printed on paper.

Photo Credits

Chapter 1

Chapter 2

Chapter 3

3.4.5   Courtesy of IBM

3.4.6   Courtesy of Sun Microsystems

3.4.8   Courtesy of Thinking Machines Corporation

Chapter 4

4.1.1   Christopher Lauckner

4.2.2   Christopher Lauckner

4.3.1   Courtesy of Microsoft Corporation

4.3.2   Courtesy of Apple Computer

4.4.1   Mason Morfit/FPG

John McCarthy   Courtesy of The Massachusetts Institute of Technology

Chapter 5

5.2.1   Wernher Krutin/PHOTOVAULT

5.2.2   ©TSM/Jon Feingersh, 1997

5.2.3   ©TSM/T&D McCarthy, 1997

Grace Hopper   Courtesy of Navy Office of Information

Chapter 6

6.1.1   Courtesy of Virtual Vineyards

Courtesy of the New York Stock Exchange

Courtesy of the Hewlett-Packard Company

6.1.2   Cave: Jean Clottes/Sygma

Drums: Deborah Davis/Photoedit

Stagecoach: Hamilton Projects, Inc.

A.G. Bell: Mark Marten/PhotoResearchers, Inc.

6.2.1a   ©TSM/Roger Ball, 1996

6.2.1b   ©TSM/John Maher, 1992

6.2.1c   ©TSM/George B. Diebold, 1997

6.2.2   Courtesy of Interlink Electronics

6.2.3   ©TSM/Lester Leftkowitz, 1997

6.2.4   PhotoDisc, Inc.

6.2.6   Courtesy of U.S. Robotics

6.2.7   Courtesy of U.S. Robotics

Voices from the Past art   Courtesy of the Computer Museum

Chapter 7

7.1.1   Copyright © 1997 MIDS, Austin, Texas

Surfer image   Uniphoto

Computers and mailboxes   Dennis Novak/The Image Bank

Man at computer   C.Vander Lendre/The Image Bank

Chapter 8

8.4.2   Courtesy of America Online

8.4.3   Courtesy of Microsoft Corporation

Courtesy of Netscape Communications Corporation

8.4.4   Courtesy of Netscape Communications Corporation

8.4.5   Wernher Krutin/PHOTOVAULT

Chapter 9

Chapter 10

10.4.9   Courtesy of Bagh Technologies

10.5.1   ©Walt Disney Company, photo supplied by Neal Peters Collection

10.6.3   Courtesy of M. Chu, University of Akron

10.6.4   Courtesy of National Climatic Data Center

10.7.1   Becky Cohen

10.7.2   Becky Cohen

10.7.3   Becky Cohen

10.7.4   Becky Cohen

10.7.5   Becky Cohen

3D Dinosaur   Courtesy of Viz Communications, Inc.

Ivan Sutherland   Courtesy of Evans and Sutherland, Inc.

Mona Lisa   Courtesy of Gryphon Software Corporation

Heart Blood Flow   Courtesy of Hewlett-Packard Corporation

Chapter 11

11.1.1   Courtesy of Prentice Hall, Inc.

11.3.2   © TSM/Tom Stewart, 1997

11.3.3   ©TSM/Chuck Savage, 1995

11.4.1   Courtesy R.L. Weide, Carnegie Mellon University

11.4.2   Courtesy R.L. Weide, Carnegie Mellon University

11.4.3   Courtesy R.L. Weide, Carnegie Mellon University

11.5.2   ©TSM/Pete Saloputos, 1995

11.5.3   ©TSM/Lightscapes, 1995

11.5.4   Courtesy of Motown Records

11.5.5   Peter Beyls, St. Lukas Art Institute, Gent, Belgium

11.5.6   Courtesy of Passport Designs, Inc.

11.7.1   Courtesy of William Barklow and the North American Loon Fund

11.7.2   Courtesy of Roger Payne

Chapter 12

Herbert Simon   Courtesy of The Massachusetts Institute of Technology

Oklahoma Bombing   Courtesy of Engineering Animation, Inc.

Aircraft Landing Simulation   Courtesy of Calspan Corporation

Virtual Surgery   Courtesy of Dr. Richard Satavaand Hich Techsplantation

12.1.1   Courtesy of Calspan Corporation

12.4.1   Courtesy of Maxis Software

12.4.2   Courtesy of Maxis Software

12.4.3   Courtesy of Maxis Software

12.4.4   Courtesy of Maxis Software

12.5.1   Courtesy Imagine That, Inc.

12.5.2   Courtesy Imagine That, Inc.

12.5.3   Courtesy Imagine That, Inc.

12.5.4   Courtesy Imagine That, Inc.

12.5.5   Courtesy Imagine That, Inc.

Index

Symbols

1-kilobyte memory chips, 2:4
3D graphics, 3:86
3D images, 3:83
100 LX calculator
    (Hewlett-Packard), 1:10

A

A-life, 4:31
AARON (Cohen, H.)
    adding color to drawings, 3:93
    description of, 3:92
    expert systems, examples of, 3:93, 4:23
    growth of, 3:93
abacus, 1:8
access
    time, storage devices, 2:25-2:26
    WWW (World Wide Web)
        ISPs (Internet Service Providers),
            3:26-3:27
        requirements for, 3:27
        Web browsers, 3:30-3:29
addresses, 2:24
    WWW (World Wide Web), 3:24-3:25
Advanced Research Projects Agency,
    2:141, 3:2, 3:6, 3:22
    Internet, purpose of, 2:147
advertising on the Web, 3:35-3:36
agents, 2:81

AI (artificial intelligence), 2:88
aircraft simulation, 3:136
algorithms
    definition of, 2:49
    finding, 2:49-2:51
    SimCity, 3:145-3:146
    Web site, 2:71
Akers, John F., 2:131
algorithms
    definition of, 2:115
    developing, 2:115
        flow charts, 2:115
        Nassi-Schneidermann charts, 2:115
        pseudocodes, 2:116
alpha testing, 2:117
Altair 8800 computer, 2:74
America Online, *see* AOL
American Heart Association,
    computer-assisted learning, 4:59
American National Standards
    Institute, *see* ANSI
analog computers, compared to
    digital, 1:13
analog signals, 2:136
    analyzing data
        correlation, 3:61-3:62
    percents, 3:59
    probability, 3:59, 3:60
    sampling technique, 3:61
    statistics, 3:59
animation and computers, 3:87-3:88

ANSI (American National Standards
    Institute), 2:14
antivirus, definition of, 4:82
AOL (America Online), 3:5
Apple Computer's LocalTalk Protocol,
    2:145
application generators languages, 2:106
Archie searches, 3:9-3:10
architecture
    Internet
        packaging information, 2:147
        protocols, 2:145
    network, 2:144
Argument field, 2:46
arithmetic
    instructions, 2:24
    units of CPUs, 2:53
ARPA (Advanced Research Projects
    Agency), 2:141, 3:2, 3:6, 3:22
    Internet, purpose of, 2:147
ARPAnet, 3:6-3:7
arrays, 2:110
art (visual), 3:92-3:93
artificial intelligence (AI), 2:88, 4:7
    common sense, 4:16
        artificial life, 4:31-4:32
        chaos, 4:30
        complex adaptive systems, 4:29-4:30
        genetic algorithms and
            programming, 4:31
    expert systems, 4:22-4:23
        rules of, 4:24
        structure of, 4:24

artificial intelligence (AI)

L

LambdaMOO, 3:11

Landsat 4 satellite communication, 3:55, 3:79

LANs (Local Area Network), 2:142

languages, 2:104

    HTML (Hypertext Markup Language), 3:32

        creating Web pages, 3:32, 3:34

        defined, 3:32

        tags, 3:32, 3:34

    robot (programmable) computers, 2:46, 2:48

    simulations, 3:147, 3:149

learning and computers

    advantages of, 4:48-4:49

    American Heart Association, 4:59

    CD-ROM technology, 4:55

    classical music, 4:53

    distance learning, 4:56

    goals of education, 4:52-4:53

    information age classrooms, 4:58

    Internet, 4:56

    local area networks, 4:55

    Papert, Seymour, 4:48

    presentation technology, 4:57

    skills taught, 4:49

        cognitive learning, 4:50

        psychomotor, 4:50

        social interaction, 4:51

    student-teacher relationship, 4:51

    systems, classification of, 4:15

Lehigh virus, 4:81

Lenat, Douglas, 4:16

letters (printed), recognizing, 4:17

Levy, David, 4:20

licensing (software), 4:76

line art, 3:80-3:83

links, 2:132

literacy and computer instruction, 4:52

loaders (program), 2:56

    fetch-and-execute cycle, 2:57-2:58

loading programs

    Paper and Pencil computer, 2:56

    robot computers, 2:47

local area networks (LANs), 2:142

    learning and, 4:55

logic bombs, 4:79

logic errors, testing programs for, 2:116

logical or comparison instructions, 2:24

loons, audio communication of, 3:122

loops

    description of, 2:113

    definition of, 2:50

    ending, 2:51-2:52

lossy compression, JPEG and, 3:78

low level language, robot computers, 2:48

M

machine language programs, 2:42, 2:104

machine-independent high-level languages, 2:105

Macintosh GUI (graphical user interface), 2:80

magnetic materials, storage, 2:29-2:30

Maillardet's Automaton, 4:4

mainframes, 2:61-2:62

malls on the Web, 3:37

MAN (Metropolitan Area Network), 2:143

management of files, 2:82

mark-sensor forms, 3:54

math skills and computer instruction, 4:53

matrix, 3:4-3:5

Mauchly, John W. , 2:60

McCarthy, John, 2:88

mechanical computers compared to electronic, 1:12

media, 4:71

medium, defined, 3:21

memex, 3:22

memory, 1:11, 2:53

    cache, 2:85

    definition of, 2:44

    RAM (random-access memory), 2:27, 2:85-2:86

    reading, 2:55

    ROM (read-only memory), 2:27, 2:75, 2:85

    storage, 2:29

    virtual, 2:86

menus, Gopher, 3:8-3:9

meter reading as data collection, 3:56

methods of transmission, network links, types of, 2:137

Metropolitan Area Network (MAN), 2:143

microcomputers

    CD-ROM technology and learning, 4:55

    cognitive learning, 4:50

    description of, 2:59

    diagram of, 2:61

    distance learning, 4:56

    educational system and, 4:44, 4:46

    goals of education using, 4:52-4:53

    history of, 2:71

    information age classrooms, 4:58

    Internet and learning, 4:56

    local area networks and learning, 4:55

    presentation technology and learning, 4:57

    psychomotor skills, 4:50

    skills taught, 4:49

    social interaction skills, 4:51

    student-teacher relationship and, 4:51

    teaching with, 4:48-4:49

    Web site, 2:71

microprocessors

    description of, 2:59

    evolution and use of, 2:61

    see also CPUs (central processing units)

Microwave (wireless) communication, 2:134

MIDI (Musical Instrument Digital Interface)

    description of, 3:120, 3:120

    instruments, using, 3:120

    sequencers, 3:121-3:122

Mil domain, 3:25

millennium crisis, 2:119

minicomputers

    description of, 2:61

    Web site, 2:71

Minsky, Marvin, 4:7

misrepresentation of data, 3:66

models

    advantages of, 3:133

    bank tellers, 3:149

    design and implementation, 3:146

    education and training, 3:135-3:136

    experimentation and testing, 3:134

    future prediction with, 3:132

    Monopoly game simulation, 3:137-3:138

        getting out of jail process, 3:139

        probabilities, 3:139-3:140

        return on investment, 3:141

        winning strategies, 3:141

    predator/prey problem, 3:147, 3:149

    programming languages, 3:147

    SimCity, 3:142

        long-range goals, 3:145-3:146

        overview of, 3:143-3:144

        planning details, 3:144-3:145

    simulation, 3:132

    systems

        description of, 3:137

        feedback, 3:137

technological familiarity and computer instruction, 4:53

teleconferences, 2:152

telephone conference bridges, definition of, 4:78

Telnet, 3:24

terabytes, 3:51

termite colonies in Australia, 4:30

testing
 models, 3:134
 programs, 2:116

Texas Instrument TI-108 calculator, 1:10

text
 files, 2:84
 searches, 3:30
 storage, 2:12-2:16

Texture of surfaces, 3:83, 3:85

TFTP (Trivial File Transport Protocol), 2:145

theft and computers, 4:73
 data diddling, 4:75
 piggybacking, 4:81
 salami-slicing, 4:74
 security measures, 4:75
 trojan horse, 4:74

theories, intelligence, 4:4-4:5

third generation high-level languages, 2:105

Thompson, Ken, 2:81

Thrifty ROman numerical BAckward looking Computer, see THROBAC

THROBAC (Thrifty ROman numerical BAckward looking Computer), 2:6

TI-108 calculator (Texas Instrument), 1:10

TIFF (Tagged Image File Format), 3:78

time
 bombs, definition of, 4:79
 compression, definition of, 3:132

Token-Ring Protocol, 2:145

top-level domains, 3:24-3:25

traffic density model, SimCity, 3:146

training
 education with models, 3:135-3:136
 neural networks, 4:28

transformation
 information, 2:5-2:12
 pictures, 2:14-2:17
 sound, 2:17-2:20
 text, 2:14

transistor chips, 2:2

translation
 definition of, 2:101
 programs
 assembled, 2:107
 compiled, 2:107
 interpreted, 2:107

transmission
 methods of on network links, 2:137
 single channel versus multichannel, 2:138

Transmission Control Protocol/Internet Protocol, *see* TCP/IP

tree networks, 2:140

Trojan horse, definition of, 4:74

Turings Imitation Game, 4:5

twisted pair links, 2:132

two-state characteristic of binary information, 2:7

U

UDP (User Datagram Protocol), 2:145

ultrasound imaging, 3:91

Uniform Resource Locators, *see* URLs

units of computers
 CPU (Central Processing Units)
 arithmetic unit, 2:53
 components of, 2:53
 control unit, 2:54
 instruction decoding unit, 2:54
 input/output, 2:52
 memory, 2:53

universities, Web sites, 3:10

UNIX, 3:8
 command line interface, 2:81
 GUI, 2:81
 UNCP, 3:5

uploading, 2:152, 3:30

URLs (Uniform Resource Locators), 3:24-3:25

Usenet, 3:4-3:5
 conferences, 3:4
 newsgroups, 3:2

user friendly, 2:80

user interfaces, 2:79-2:81
 command line, 2:79-2:80
 MS-DOS, 2:79
 UNIX, 2:81
 graphical user interfaces, *see* GUIs
 see also interfaces

UUCP, 3:5

V

validating models, 3:147

vector graphics, 3:82

vehicles
 computers, 1:7-1:8
 speedometers, 1:12

verifying models, 3:147

Verne, Jules, 3:7

Veronica, 3:9-3:10

virtual memory, 2:86

virtual reality
 definition of, 3:149
 hardware requirements, 3:150
 surgery, 3:151
 uses of, 3:150

viruses
 definition of, 4:81
 downloading software off the Web, 3:32
 preventing, 4:82

vision, importance of, 3:76

visual images
 animating, 3:87
 creating, 3:80-3:81
 3D graphics, 3:86
 hidden-line problem, 3:84
 line drawing, types of, 3:82-3:83
 perspective, 3:84
 shading of surfaces, 3:83, 3:85
 texture of surfaces, 3:83
 visual art, 3:92-3:93
 digitized, 3:77
 processing, 3:79-3:80
 satellite images, 3:78
 graphics formats, 3:77
 GIF, 3:77
 JPEG, 3:78
 TIFF, 3:78
 see also visualization of information

visual patterns, resonances, 4:17

visualization of information
 description of, 3:88
 false-coloring, 3:90
 population densities, 3:89
 sound made by knee, 3:90
 ultrasound imaging, 3:91

vocal communication, 3:104
 analysis and recognition of speech, 3:111
 continuous speech, 3:113-3:114
 disjointed speech, 3:112
 natural language communication, 3:114
 speech synthesis, 3:104
 digitized recordings of speech, 3:105, 3:107
 instructional language labs, 3:106

vocal communication

Oracle® Performance
Survival Guide

THE PRENTICE HALL PTR ORACLE SERIES
The Independent Voice on Oracle

ORACLE WEB APPLICATION PROGRAMMING FOR PL/SQL DEVELOPERS
Boardman/Caffrey/Morse/Rosenzweig

ORACLE SQL HIGH PERFORMANCE TUNING, SECOND EDITION
Harrison

ORACLE FORMS INTERACTIVE WORKBOOK
Motivala

ORACLE SQL BY EXAMPLE, THIRD EDITION
Rischert

ORACLE PL/SQL INTERACTIVE WORKBOOK, SECOND EDITION
Rosenzweig/Silvestrova

ORACLE PL/SQL BY EXAMPLE, THIRD EDITION
Rosenzweig/Silvestrova

ORACLE DBA INTERACTIVE WORKBOOK
Scherer/Caffrey